ISBN 978-0-266-53733-5
PIBN 10862643

This book is a reproduction of an important historical work. Forgotten Books uses
state-of-the-art technology to digitally reconstruct the work, preserving the original format
whilst repairing imperfections present in the aged copy. In rare cases, an imperfection in
the original, such as a blemish or missing page, may be replicated in our edition. We do,
however, repair the vast majority of imperfections successfully; any imperfections that
remain are intentionally left to preserve the state of such historical works.

THE

EDINBURGH REVIEW,

OR

CRITICAL JOURNAL:

FOR

JANUARY, 1885 . . . . APRIL, 1885.

TO BE CONTINUED QUARTERLY.

JUDEX DAMNATUR CUM NOCENS ABSOLVITUR.
PUBLIUS SYRUS.

VOL. CLXI.

LONGMANS, GREEN, READER, AND DYER, LONDON,
ADAM AND CHARLES BLACK,
EDINBURGH.

1885.

CONTENTS of No. 329.

CONTENTS of No. 330.

Page

THE

EDINBURGH REVIEW,

JANUARY, 1885.

N°· CCCXXIX.

ART. I.—*The Correspondence and Diaries of the late Right Honourable John Wilson Croker, LL.D., F.R.S., Secretary to the Admiralty from* 1809 *to* 1830. Edited by LOUIS J. JENNINGS. In 3 vols. London: 1884.

WE opened this book with curiosity. Mr. Croker held so high and so peculiar a position in both the political and the literary world, and filled it so long, that we expected to derive both entertainment and information from the perusal of his Diaries and his Correspondence. Nor have we been wholly disappointed by the book itself. Mr. Croker, indeed, can hardly be said to have kept a journal; and, if his articles had not been brighter than his letters, the animosity which he provoked in his lifetime would have been less intense. The true interest, however, of the work before us arises from the light which it throws on the times in which Mr. Croker lived, and on the characters of the men whom he knew. If the historian will not be compelled by its publication to restate many of his facts, he may possibly be tempted to repaint some of his portraits.

Before, however, we proceed to deal with Mr. Croker and his friends, we have a few words to say about the editor of these papers. Mr. Jennings's narrative is clear, full, and usually accurate. As a general rule, he has suppressed his own opinions, and he has certainly succeeded in throwing cold water on the heated caldron in which Mr. Croker's character has been boiling. He has had the good sense to add an index to the book, which we would recommend him to expand in some future edition; on several occasions we have found it useless as a guide to passages to which we wished to turn back. With a view also to their correction in some later edition, we may notice one or two errors which

have crept into Mr. Jennings's work. Lord Truro could
not have pledged himself to revise the Currency Laws in
1833. There was no Lord Truro for seventeen years afterwards. Mr. Littleton must have said 'Nolo,' not 'Volo
'Speakerari,' in the same year. It was not a Mr. Shearman,
but the late Sir Alexander Spearman, who was Mr. Herries's
confidential clerk in 1828. Sir Walter Scott did not say
that 'literature might do well enough for a staff, but was
'worthless as a crutch.' Unless our memory deceives us,
he said 'literature is a good staff, but a bad crutch.'
Louis XVIII. was not at Brussels on the day of Waterloo.
According to Lord Albemarle, who, we suspect, is right, it
was to some Austrian aristocrat, and not to the Empress of
Russia, that Sir R. Adair, whose father was a surgeon, was
introduced as 'le fils du plus grand seigneur (saigneur)
'd'Angleterre.' The arbitration of the King of Holland
on the Anglo-American frontier was not sought in 1833;
his award was given in 1831. It is unfair to say that the
King's award, 'as usual in foreign arbitrations, went much
'against England.' Lord Aberdeen himself called it 'an
'honest judgement.' It was in 1834, not in 1839, that Sir
Robert Peel was brought from Rome to form a Ministry.
Mr. Croker must have written '34,' not '45,' as the date
at which the union between Sir Robert Peel and the Duke
of Wellington took place. Mr. Phillips was not censured
for asserting Courvoisier's innocence after he had privately
admitted his guilt. The charge against him was, that,
'with a perfect knowledge where the guilt lay, he endea-
'voured to cast the suspicion of the guilt upon the inno-
'cent.' Mr. Sheil did not spell his name Shiel. When
Mr. Jennings says that Mr. Croker was seldom mistaken in
an age or a date, we suppose that he is thinking of
Lord Beaconsfield's description of Rigby, whom Lord Monmouth bought with all his dates, and that he has forgotten
the startling category of wrong ages and wrong dates which
Lord Macaulay detected in Mr. Croker's 'Boswell.' Perhaps
in some future edition Mr. Jennings will state accurately
when Mr. Croker's connexion with the 'Quarterly Review'
began and when it ceased. The 'Quarterly Review' itself
said, in July 1876, that his contributions to the 'Review'
extended over nearly half a century, from 1809 to 1854.
Mr. Croker himself wrote, in 1834, 'For twenty years I wrote
'in it, from 1809 to 1829, I never gave, I believe, one
'purely political article.' Mr. Jennings, however, writes
that 'from 1811 down to 1854, with the exception of an

' interval between 1826 and 1831, he seldom failed to supply
' an article for every number of the Review.' Mr.
Jennings may be right, but his statement is hardly consistent either with Mr. Croker's own account in 1834, or with
that of the ' Quarterly Review ' in 1876.

This point has some significance, because Mr. Jennings's
book fails to supply us with any list of Mr. Croker's contributions to the ' Quarterly.' We are occasionally told that
he wrote such and such articles. We are in some instances
informed that he did not write articles which were attributed to him. But we are nowhere given any exhaustive
account of what he did and what he did not write. No doubt
the conductors of the ' Quarterly Review ' may refuse to
attach a name to anonymous contributions. But, at the
same time, Mr. Jennings may rest assured that no defence
of Mr. Croker, however zealous it may be, can be complete
till the veil of the editor's ' we ' is stripped off his writings.
The most serious of the charges made against him as a
literary man is that his virulent and intemperate language
imparted a deplorable tone and temper to literary criticism.
This is what Lord John Russell meant when he wrote of Mr.
Croker's ' malignity; '* what Lord Macaulay meant when
he wrote of his rancour; and what Miss Martineau meant
when she declared that he had a ' malignant ulcer ' in his
mind. Some future writer may succeed in showing that Mr.
Croker was not the author of the many bitter articles which
were published in the ' Quarterly Review.' Recollecting
that Mr. Moore had said in his Diary, ' Poor Croker's name
' is made as free with as the devil's is with the lawyers—
' everything is laid to him ; '† remembering also Sir W.
Scott's description of Mr. Gifford, the earliest editor of the
' Quarterly Review,' that ' he flagellated with so little pity
' that people lost their sense of the criminal's guilt in dis-
' like of the savage pleasure which the executioner seemed
' to take in inflicting the punishment,' we expected Mr.
Jennings to show that, at any rate from 1809 to 1826, the
virulence of the Review was Mr. Gifford's and not Mr.
Croker's. But this is precisely what Mr. Jennings has
neither done nor attempted to do. In default, Mr. Croker
will still be held responsible for the harsh criticism for

---

* ' Malignity ' is the expression which another contemporary—Sir
Denis le Marchant—also applies to Mr. Croker. See the ' Memoirs of
' Earl Spencer,' p. 335.
† Russell's ' Life of Moore,' vol. iv. p. 254.

which the 'Quarterly Review' was notorious; and Mr.
Jennings's portrait of him will be regarded by well-informed
persons as both inaccurate and incomplete.

Incomplete portraiture in this book is not confined, indeed,
to Mr. Jennings's sketch of Mr. Croker. We were reminded
in reading it of the old story of an English traveller
painting an Australian savage. The friends of the savage
gathered round the artist, and when they saw that he had
drawn the portrait in profile, they assailed him for portray-
ing a man with only one side to his face. However convenient it may be for the artist to draw portraits in profile,
the biographer should avoid imitating his example. Yet
Mr. Jennings almost habitually produces only one side of
each man's character. We thought that reading had given
us some familiarity with such well-known personages as
George IV., the Duke of Cumberland, Lord Liverpool, and
Lord Hertford. Yet we are hardly able to recognise our old
acquaintances in Mr. Jennings's pages. He persists in constantly presenting to us those sides of their faces which were
the least commonly seen by their contemporaries, and which
are the least easily remembered by posterity. And what is
true of his sketches of these people is true to a still greater
extent of his portrait of Mr. Croker. Mr. Jennings introduces us to a rather dull personage—fond of his family, devoted to the memory of his only child—who for twenty years
occupied a laborious situation, who served his party both
with his speech and with his pen, but who could only on
rare occasions be credited with a witty saying, and who
could still more rarely be charged with a bitter one. Such
a man as Mr. Jennings describes is familiar enough to most
of us. The amiable old gentleman who thinks that Church
and Crown are being swept away by a violent flood of democracy, and who thrusts his own body into the breach in the
vain hope of checking the rising waters, has been seen in most
ages. We have all of us laughed at his unfulfilled predictions
and his genuine alarm. But was this Mr. Croker? or, if
this were Mr. Croker, had he no other side to his face? We
do not wish to say that when Mr. Thackeray sketched Mr.
Wenham, 'Lord Steyne's Vizier and chief confidential ser-
'vant (with a seat in Parliament and at the dinner-table),'
he drew a complete portrait of Mr. Croker. Nor do we desire
to imply that when Lord Beaconsfield drew Mr. Rigby's likeness as a man 'bold, acute, and voluble; with no thought,
'but a good deal of desultory information; and, though de-
'stitute of all imagination and noble sentiment, blessed with

' a vigorous mendacious fancy, fruitful in small expedients,
' and never happier than when devising shifts for great men's
' scrapes,' he succeeded in producing a perfect portrait. The
true Mr. Croker, it is plain, would never have advised Coningsby to make himself master of Mr. Wordy's 'History of
'the late War,' in twenty volumes.* But, just as Mr. Thackeray and Lord Beaconsfield only saw one side of Mr. Croker's
character, so Mr. Jennings has only given us the other side
of it. We must try to fuse the three characters into one if
we wish to know what Mr. Croker really was.

Before doing so, however, we must acknowledge our obligations to Mr. Jennings in another matter. Mr. Croker
occasionally preserved a good story; and some of the most
entertaining pages of this book are devoted to the reproduction of these anecdotes. Some of them curiously illustrate
the times. We were startled to learn that, so lately as
1820, ' some ladies and gentlemen of the county' of Cornwall came to an election ball at Bodmin,† 'in what they
' call a double-horse, i.e. a lady riding on a pillion behind
' a gentleman.' We were hardly less surprised to read that,
at the coronation of George IV., Lord Gwydir,

' *abused*, some say *struck* with his wand, one of the heralds for some
supposed breach of duty. The herald, with great good sense, took the
blow as a mere mistake, and said, " My Lord, you do not know our
" functions, characters, or duties; we are not servants—my family
" were gentlemen five hundred years before a Burrell was heard of."
Lord Gwydir was in fact in the wrong, and had treated the herald by
mistake as if he were one of the attendants.' (Vol. i. p. 196.)

Does Mr. Croker mean that Lord Gwydir would have done
right to strike an attendant? If so, we are thankful that
English gentlemen have reformed their manners as well as
their Parliament since the days of George IV. The other
anecdotes which are worth quoting are of a different character.

' When Archbishop Wake waited on King George II. to complain
of the famous blackguard song written by the Duke of Wharton on
the Archbishop, and the latter, to convince the King of the justice of

---

* Mr. Croker, it seems, was invited by Mr. Lockhart to review Sir
Archibald Alison's ' History of Europe.' But the review, which Mr.
Croker wrote or threatened to write, was so severe that Mr. Lockhart
declined to publish it. (Vol. iii. p. 12.)

† The electors of Bodmin in 1820 consisted of thirty-six corporators,
one-third in the rank of gentlemen, the rest tradespeople. Mr. Croker
was returned for Bodmin at the general election of 1820. (Vol. i. p. 165.)

his complaint, gravely began to read his verses, the old monarch in an ecstasy at one stanza cried out, "Bon! bon!" "How, Sir," said Wake, "do you call such execrable ribaldry good?" "Oh que non," replied George, correcting himself; "c'est mal, très mal, c'est exécrable; "mais il faut avouer que le drôle a de l'esprit."' (Vol i. p. 9.)

So much for George II. Here is a still better saying attributed to George IV. :—

'I must take a scrap of paper to tell you a joke attributed to the King, and I think a good one. You know William Peel married Lady *Jane* Moore, and his younger brother married Lady *Jane* Lennox. "The Peels," said H. M., "have still a hankering after the Jennies."' * (Vol. i. p. 265.)

Here is a very different story :—

'Captain Hall, of the "Lyra," who is just come home, and who is mad about certain simple islanders whom he fell in with in the China Seas, touched at St. Helena and saw Buonaparte, and told him the story of his interesting inhabitants of Loo-Choo, and happened to mention that such was the primitive innocence of the people that he could not discover that they had any offensive weapons. "Diable!" exclaimed Buonaparte, "et comment font-ils donc la guerre?" Hall dined some time ago at Vansittart's, and was relating this conversation, and everybody but Vansittart was greatly amused at the natural turn of Buonaparte's wonder. Vansittart, however, took no notice of it, but seemed absorbed in his own contemplations. Hall went on to say that he found Buonaparte quite incredulous upon this fact, and that, in order to persuade him of the extreme simplicity of the islanders, he added another circumstance, which was that he had not seen among them any kind of money. "No money!" cried Vansittart with the greatest vivacity; "good heavens! Captain Hall, how do they carry on the "government?"' (Vol. i. p. 111.)

Here is a witty saying of Madame de Staël:—

'Some one was laughing one day at the titles of the Haytian Empire, the Count de Limonade and the Duke de Marmalade. "This "would come," said Madame de Stael, "with a bad grace from us "French, who see nothing ridiculous in the titles of the Marquis de "*Bouillé* and the Duc de *Bouillon*. Nor ought the English to be "very facetious on that point, who see nothing absurd in Lord *Boyle* "and Mrs. *Fry*."' (Vol. i. p. 327.)

After dinner at the Pavilion, in 1818, the Prince Regent played a hand or two at patience, and Mr. Croker 'was rather ' amused to hear him exclaim loudly, when one of the kings

---

* Some of our readers, however, may not perhaps be aware that the spinning machine was called a 'Jenny' after Jenny Hargreaves, the inventor's industrious wife. But this version of the story has been denied by others, who state that the lady's name was Elizabeth.

' had turned up vexatiously, "Damn the king ! " ' But this story may be matched with one of the Regent's brother and successor. William IV., after his accession,

' startled those of his Council who did not know him by exclaiming in a familiar tone against the *badness of the pen* with which he was signing the oath administered to him by the Lord President, " Damn the " pen ! " ' (Vol. ii. p. 166.)*

These anecdotes may show our readers that they may find entertainment as well as interest in Mr. Jennings's pages; but we must now turn from light sayings to solid business. Mr. John Wilson Croker, the son of another John Croker, ' for many years Surveyor-General of Customs and Excise in Ireland, was born on December 20, 1780. He was educated first at Portarlington and afterwards at Cork, where he was under the care of ' one Knowles,' a gentleman who professed at that time to cure cacology— for young Croker stuttered—but who is now more likely to be recollected as the father of Mr. Sheridan Knowles. From Cork he proceeded in his sixteenth year to Trinity College, Dublin, where he formed an acquaintance with Moore the poet. In the first year of the present century he became a student of Lincoln's Inn; and in May 1807 he entered Parliament as member for Downpatrick. He had already succeeded in making some progress in his profession. He had concurrently acquired some little repute with his pen, and the ability which he had displayed introduced him to the notice of Mr. Perceval, who, at that time, led the House of Commons. In 1808, Sir Arthur Wellesley, who was ' the ' Chief Secretary for Ireland, requested him to take charge ' of the parliamentary business of his office during his ' absence in Portugal;' and in 1809 Mr. Perceval, on suc- ceeding to the chief place in the Ministry, nominated him to the Secretaryship of the Admiralty, an office which Mr. Croker filled under five Prime Ministers for more than twenty years.

In a short journal which he kept at the time, Mr. Croker recorded that he hesitated to throw up his profession for the purpose of accepting Mr. Perceval's offer. But

' when I arrived in London, on the morning of the 10th of Octo- ber, . . . Arbuthnot, Secretary of the Treasury, told me . . . I *must* accept, . . . for that I was bound in honour to obey Mr. Perceval's wishes, who had thought so kindly of me; that when he wrote to

---

* The story has already been told by Mr. Greville in a slightly different way. ('Greville Memoirs,' vol. ii. p. 3.)

desire the accession of Lords Grey and Grenville, he had determined, if they came in, to accept the seals of the Home Department, and had declared that he stipulated but for one appointment, which was that I should be his Under-Secretary.' (Vol. i. pp. 21, 22.)

We doubt this story, even though it is told on the high authority of Mr. Arbuthnot. It is very probable, indeed, that Mr. Perceval may have contemplated taking the Home Office in a Coalition Ministry. It was the department which he would naturally have preferred. But the prospect of a junction with Lord Grey and Lord Grenville was so vague, that we doubt whether Mr. Perceval had made any stipulation contingent on its taking place, and we are tolerably certain that in all the correspondence on the subject—and we have had access, we believe, at other times to the whole of the original documents—there is no mention of Mr. Croker's appointment as Under-Secretary. His nomination to the Admiralty was explained in a very different way by Lord Mulgrave, who told Lord Lonsdale that ' he had written to offer the Secretary of the Admiralty ' to Mr. Croker, who was active, quick, and intelligent, and ' who might go off to Mr. Canning if he was not attended ' to.'

Whichever of these two stories be correct, Mr. Croker's appointment testified to the respect in which his abilities were held. The Secretary to the Admiralty in 1809 enjoyed a salary which had been fixed at 4,000*l.* a year while the country was at war, and at 3,000*l.* when it was at peace. The office, therefore, was one of the most lucrative which the Minister had at his disposal. It is only just to add that Mr. Croker proved a highly efficient public servant, and that he remained loyal to Mr. Perceval throughout his lifetime. Soon after Mr. Croker received office, a very different man, Mr. Peel (as he was then), was appointed to an Under-Secretaryship in the same Ministry. Mr. Peel and Mr. Croker became warm friends; and perhaps the chief interest in Mr. Jennings's volumes is derived from the fresh light which they throw on Sir Robert Peel's character. We shall have much to say on this subject later on. For the present we wish to point out the opinion which both of them formed on the character and career of their patron. Writing from Ireland in October 1812, five months after Mr. Perceval's death, Mr. Peel says:—

' I hope we may fight out this battle as we have fought out many others; there was a time when I should have had less fears, and when perhaps, from every private and public feeling, I should have seen our little champion go forth with his sling and with his sword, and bring down the mightiest of his enemies, and felt prouder in his triumph.' (Vol. i. p. 46.)

Twenty years afterwards, during the Ministerial crisis of 1832, Mr. Croker addressed a long and powerful letter to Sir R. Peel, urging him to take office and save the Monarchy. The letter was dated May 11, the date on which Mr. Perceval was shot; and Mr. Croker added in a postscript—

'What an anniversary is this for such a letter! Was Mr. Perceval's task more difficult in 1809 than yours would be now? I think it was not, but I think also that he would not have declined it were he now in your position, and that no one else could be found to undertake it.' (Vol. ii. p. 180.)

To these two stories we may add this circumstance. Mr. Croker had only one child, a boy, who died at a very early age, and he named him after the Minister ' Spencer.'

Mr. Perceval's death and Lord Liverpool's accession to power did not deprive Mr. Croker of his office, but the general election which followed cost him his seat. Room, however, was found for him at Athlone, and Mr. Croker returned to Parliament. He represented Athlone till the general election of 1818. In 1819, by Lord Hertford's influence, he was returned for Yarmouth. We are not told by Mr. Jennings how Mr. Croker's intimacy with Lord Hertford, or rather with Lord Yarmouth, Lord Hertford's eldest son, began. All we learn is that Mr. Croker was dining with Lord Yarmouth in July 1818, and that in December 1818 ' Yarmouth, the most good-natured man ' alive, dragged' him down to Brighton ' for a few days' ' relaxation and exercise.' This visit was destined to be an important epoch in Mr. Croker's life. It evidently increased his intimacy with Lord Yarmouth, while it placed him in close communication with the Regent. Thenceforward he became Lord Yarmouth's vizier, while he was occasionally admitted to the confidence of George IV.

We do not wish in these pages to say much about Lord Yarmouth, who in 1822 became third Marquis of Hertford, or of Mr. Croker's relations with him. Mr. Jennings himself says that Lord Hertford's life was ' misguided and wasted,' and we see no object in attempting to delineate his repulsive character. We are willing to hope that Mr. Croker's apology for his patron is true, and that ' the lamentable doings of his ' latter years were neither more nor less than insanity.' Nor are we prepared to blame Mr. Croker for exercising ' a kind of

' practical superintendence ' over Lord Hertford's property.
Service of this kind, indeed, ought to be paid at the time,
and not remunerated by the repeated promises of large
legacies.   But we do blame Mr. Croker for the invariable
tone of his letters to Lord Hertford, and for meeting, without
remonstrance, at Lord Hertford's table company with which
he was ashamed to appear in public.   If Mr. Croker ever
addressed a single word of caution or advice to his most
intimate acquaintance, Mr. Jennings has not published it.
Instead of caution and advice, we find Mr. Croker feeding
Lord Hertford with flattery and gossip.   ' I admire your
' asking me to write for you—

> ' *You* who in one line can fix
> More sense than I can do in six.'

So the great Reviewer of the 'Quarterly' could condescend to write in 1839 to a friend whose excesses he was
excusing on the ground that he was insane.   Mr. Jennings
may take exception to Lord Beaconsfield's portrait of Rigby.
But his pages afford ample proof that one part of Rigby's
character was drawn from the life.   Rigby 'had become
' indispensable to his Lordship by more serious if not higher
' considerations.   And, what with auditing his accounts,
' guarding his boroughs, writing him when absent gossip
' by every post, and when in England deciding on every
' question, and arranging every matter which might other-
' wise have ruffled the sublime repose of his patron's exist-
' ence, Rigby might be excused if he shrank a little from
' the minor part of table wit.'   Such were some of the
functions which Rigby discharged for Lord Monmouth,
and such was the nature of Mr. Croker's service to Lord
Hertford.

Intimacy with Lord Hertford was originally the means
of bringing Mr. Croker into close communication with
George IV., and the acquaintance which Mr. Croker thus
formed with the King ripened into something very much
like friendship.   Mr. Croker emphatically stated that he
'loved' the King, and we have no desire to explain away
the expression.   The King, on his part, made Mr. Croker
the depositary of his confidence.   After the publication of
Moore's ' Life of Sheridan,' he actually dictated to him an
explanation of his conduct, which occupies twenty-four of
Mr. Jennings's pages, which was evidently ' intended to be
' made public at some future time ; ' but Mr. Jennings does
not seem to be aware that this conversation was partly used

by Mr. Croker as material for an article in the 'Quarterly
'Review.' This explanation deals with many circumstances
in his Majesty's career on which historians have usually
commented in strong language.

'On the subject of my supposed marriage with Mrs. Fitzherbert
(said the King), and the debate upon Mr. Rolle's observations,
some false statements have been made. When Fox mentioned it
to me, I contradicted the supposition at once with "pooh," "nonsense,"
"ridiculous," &c., upon which Fox, in the heat of debate, and piqued
by Rolle, was induced not merely to contradict the report, which was
right enough, but to go a little further, and to use some slighting
expressions which, when Mrs. Fitzherbert read them in the paper
next morning, deeply affected her, and made her furious against Fox.
Mr. Moore states that I applied to Mr. Grey to set the matter right,
and that when he refused I said, "Then we must bring Sheridan into
"play." There is not a word of truth in this. I had no kind of
communication with Mr. Grey on the subject.' (Vol. i. p. 292.)

The King in this passage, it will be seen, makes two
assertions. First, that Mr. Fox was right to contradict
his marriage; second, that he did not apply to Mr. (afterwards Lord) Grey. Without recalling the details of an un-
savoury story, we are able shortly to test both statements.
Mr. Croker himself says: 'The Prince certainly married
'Mrs. Fitzherbert with the left hand—the ceremony was
'performed by Parson Johns, who is still about town.'
In respect to the second point—' there exists, in Lord
'Grey's own handwriting, not only an account of his inter-
'view with the Prince, but also the unqualified assertion of
'that high-minded nobleman that the King actually con-
'fessed to him the fact of his secret marriage.' *

George IV.'s memory was notoriously untrustworthy.
He was under the delusion that he had been present at
Waterloo; and most people recollect the Duke of Wellington's reply to him when he was called upon by the King to
say whether he had not been at the battle: 'I have heard
'your Majesty say so a great many times.' Apparently the
King's memory in respect to his marriage was not more
trustworthy. We are afraid that his memory in other
matters was equally inaccurate. It is well known that the
delicate investigation into the conduct of the Princess of
Wales took place while the Whig Ministry of 1806 was in
office. According to George IV., after the fall of the Whigs,

* Jesse's 'Memoirs of the Life and Reign of George III.' (vol. ii.
p. 511), founded on Earl Russell's 'Memorials of Fox' (vol. ii. p. 289,
and note).

'Mr. Perceval saw the King (George III.), and received his commands for a new Ministry, but he made the reception of the Princess a *sine quâ non* of his undertaking the negotiations. He (the King) added, " I have seen that infamous woman (the Princess of Wales), "but what could I do? I consulted Lord Hawkesbury what I was to "do in the circumstances in which the Ministers had placed me. He "sent Mr. Perceval to me. Mr. Perceval said that the first steps must "be the reception of the Princess. . . . He told me plainly that with- "out this point there would be no Administration." ' (Vol. i. pp. 301, 302.)

Is it possible in a short paragraph to include a greater number of misstatements? Mr. Perceval in 1807 did not receive any command to form a new Ministry. He did not form a Ministry for two years and a half afterwards. The negotiations for the formation of the Portland Administration were conducted through Lord Eldon and Lord Hawkesbury; and the biographer of the latter goes so far as to assert that ' George III. saw no one but Lord Hawkesbury.' * The first message to the Princess from George III., informing her that it was no longer necessary to decline receiving her, was sent to her through the Whig Chancellor, Lord Erskine; † and it was afterwards expressly, though, as we believe, unjustly, insinuated by Lord Brougham that both Lord Eldon and Mr. Perceval deserted the Princess when political considerations induced them to reconcile themselves with her husband.

But the charge made by Mr. Moore in his ' Life of Sheridan,' which George IV. evidently felt most keenly, and which he was most anxious to explain, was his treatment of Mr. Sheridan in the closing years of his life. Moore says that Mr. John Taylor Vaughan, of Grafton Street, told him that he had been entrusted with the sum of 200*l.*, which he asked Moore to lay out in relieving Sheridan, who was lying, in miserable poverty, on his death-bed. Mr. Vaughan pointedly declared that he was only an agent in the matter, and the poet evidently understood that the money came from the Regent. Mr. Moore goes on to say that ' it would be ' safer perhaps to let the suspicion rest upon Mr. Vaughan's ' memory, of having indulged his own benevolent disposition ' in this disguise, than to suppose it possible that so scanty ' and reluctant a benefaction was the sole mark of attention ' by a gracious prince and master to the last death-bed

---

* ' Life of Liverpool,' vol. i. p. 228.
† Twiss's ' Life of Lord Eldon,' vol. ii. p. 28.

' wants of one of the most faithful and accomplished ser-
' vants that royalty ever yet raised or ruined by its smiles.' *

Such was the account which Mr. Moore thought proper to
publish in the lifetime of George IV. We are not surprised
that the King was seriously annoyed at it. But his own
version of the story does not materially differ from it. On
learning Mr. Sheridan's distress, he authorised his secretary,
Colonel MacMahon, to place a sum of 500*l*. in Mr. Vaughan's
hands for Mr. Sheridan's immediate relief. According to
George IV., a promise was given that, when the 500*l*. was
exhausted, more should be forthcoming. Mr. Vaughan,
'not without some pressing,' took 200*l*., and said that if
he found it insufficient he would return for more. 'He did
' come back, but not for more; for he told MacMahon that he
had spent only 130*l*. or 140*l*.'

There is nothing in this account which is inconsistent with
Mr. Moore's story, and there is nothing in it to justify the
harsh judgement which Mr. Moore pronounced. Having
regard to all the circumstances of the case, we do not know
that the Prince Regent could have found a better way of
relieving Mr. Sheridan's wants. We have no desire to imitate
Mr. Croker in condoning the faults of George IV., but we
are certainly not going to follow Mr. Moore's example, and
blame the King for a kindly and not injudicious action.

The intimate terms on which Mr. Croker stood with
George IV. gave him an opportunity of ascertaining the
King's views about public men. It is well known that George
IV. after his accession to the throne was dissatisfied with his
Ministry, and anxious to dismiss it. But we were hardly
before aware of the extreme tension in the relations between
the King and the Prime Minister. 'I saw his Majesty at
' two o'clock '—so Mr. Croker wrote on July 30, 1821—

'He was a *little warm*. Lord Liverpool had been just with him,
and . . . he began to complain of Lord Liverpool. He says that he
cannot go on with him, and that he will not. . . . Lord Liverpool was
captious, jealous, and impracticable; he objects to everything, and
even when he gives way, which is nine times in ten, he does it
with so bad a grace that it is worse than an absolute refusal. . . . But
he would bear it no longer; he is *rex Dei gratiâ*, and *Dei gratiâ rex*
he would be.' (Vol. i. p. 199.)

The King had hitherto been dissatisfied with the Civil
List arrangements, with the conduct of the Ministry respecting the Queen's trial, and with the Ministers' refusal

* Moore's ' Life of Sheridan,' vol. ii. p. 45 ?.

to appoint Mr. Sumner, Lord FitzCharles's tutor, to a canonry at Windsor.* But his displeasure was increased by the lamentable occurrences which took place in connexion with the Queen's funeral, and on August 17

'he renewed all his complaints against Lord Liverpool, and said roundly that he would not go on any longer with him.' (Ibid. p. 202.)

Mr. Croker seems to have mentioned the King's opinions to a friend, who carried the information to the Ministry, for on September 3

'I had a letter from Arbuthnot complaining that I had talked of the King's being dissatisfied, and the Government in danger.' (Ibid. p. 208.)

And on September 8

'I had a letter from Lord Liverpool, at Walmer, saying that he was very anxious to see the King as soon as possible, and begging me to inform him of his Majesty's movements.' (Ibid. p. 209.)

On September 11 'the whole Cabinet was summoned to ' meet the King,' and seemed to think that he was ' in-' clined to make an immediate change.' On September 16 the summons was obeyed. Lord Liverpool, with some of his colleagues, ' went to Carlton House, but the King ' would not see him. His Majesty saw the Chancellor and ' desired him to tell Lord Liverpool that if his lordship would ' abstain from speaking to him about *political arrangements*, ' he would receive him to-morrow.'

We confess we have read these passages with pain and surprise. They reflect, as it seems to us, much discredit on King and Minister. Here is the King declining to receive his first Minister, complaining of his conduct to a subordinate official in the Administration, and ultimately only seeing him on the express understanding that he would abstain from speaking about political arrangements. Here is the Minister, on the other hand, condescending to express to the very subordinate who had received the complaint his anxiety to see the King; submitting to be refused the audience to which he was entitled both as a peer and as

* Mr. Greville, writing on February 20, 1820, says: 'The Mi-' nisters had resigned last week because the King would not hear 'more on the subject of the Princess. It is said that he treated Lord 'Liverpool very coarsely, and ordered him out of the room. The 'King, they say, asked him 'if he knew to whom he was speaking.' 'He replied, "Sir, I know that I am speaking to my Sovereign, and I '"believe I am addressing him as it becomes a loyal subject."' 'Greville Memoirs,' vol. i. p. 25.

his sovereign's chief adviser, and at last accepting an audience on conditions which disabled him from offering the very advice which he was bound to give.   We are not surprised that Lord Liverpool's biographer, in narrating the history of 1821, should have suppressed these details, and left the public to learn, through Mr. Croker's posthumous journal, the arbitrary proceedings of the monarch, and the unworthy conduct of the Minister.

The difference, however, was ultimately healed; the Liverpool Administration was reconstructed and remained in power.   In February 1827 its chief was struck down by the fatal seizure which terminated his capacity for work.   On the evening after Lord Liverpool's stroke, Mr. Croker dined at the Speaker's, 'where there was not only ' no grief, but not even a decent pensiveness. . . .   No ' one seemed to think or care about poor Lord Liverpool,' struck down after fifteen years of power.   On the following morning Mr. Croker called on the Duke of Wellington, who assented to the suggestion which Mr. Croker made, that ' the best way—the only way—of keeping us together ' was to make Canning Minister, and to give Robinson the ' Foreign Office, with, if they wanted assistance in the ' Lords, a peerage.'   Some time after this Mr. Croker had some conversation with Mr. Peel, in which the two friends discussed ' in a light problematical way the course that different ' members of the Cabinet might take if Canning were placed ' at their head.   I mentioned Lord Westmorland as likely to ' resist.   Peel pooh-poohed that difficulty.   We were just then ' opposite to Lord Eldon's, and, pointing to his house, I said ' " Would *he* stay?" upon which Peel squeezed my arm tightly ' under his, and said " *He will if I do.*"   I had, and could ' have, no longer any doubt that Peel had no disinclination ' to such an arrangement—the squeeze of the arm seemed to ' say " I have settled all that."   I never heard, and Canning ' told me that he never knew, what had changed Peel's dis- ' position; for a change he, like me, thought it was.'

Yet the change seems to us perfectly explicable.   In the interval occurred the debate on Sir Francis Burdett's motion. The friends of what was then called the Protestant cause were elated by achieving in a new Parliament a narrow, but an unexpected, victory.   They, perhaps naturally, concluded that the division entitled them to a leader of their own way of thinking; and though Peel saw more clearly than they saw the impossibility of forming a purely 'Protestant' Ministry, he was not prepared to thwart the wishes both of the King and if his party by ... to form a 'Catholic' Administration. ... consequently declined to remain in office: and his ... was followed by the resignation of five other members of the Cabinet. Mr. Croker did not resign the subordinate situation which he held at the Admiralty, and we are inclined to think that he was perfectly justified in ... so. He had been the friend of Mr. Canning for more than twenty years: and he had always supported — on grounds peculiar to himself — the emancipation of the Roman Catholics. But having made up his mind to ... in his lot with Mr. Canning, he busied himself ... to add strength to the new Ministry. He exerted all his influence to induce Mr. Canning to conciliate great borough-owners like Lord Lonsdale, and to persuade the borough-owners to support the Ministry. He did not entirely succeed. Mr. Canning declined to be made the tool of the Tory aristocracy: and Lord Lowther, Lord Lonsdale's eldest son, retired from office. Mr. Peel not unnaturally resented the active course which Mr. Croker then took. Mr. Croker, who had been the depositary of his ' unreserved communications,' might, be thought, have abstained from direct or indirect interference. But Mr. Canning declared to more than one person that ' there was ' no one to whom he was so much indebted for suggestions ' as ' he was to Mr. Croker. Nobody likes to find the familiar friend in whom he trusts engaged in an intrigue against him; and Mr. Peel, who was not tolerant of hostile conduct, broke off his intercourse with Mr. Croker. This temporary misunderstanding was patched up six months afterwards; and the communications between the two friends were renewed. Yet we doubt whether they ever stood on exactly the same terms as before. The broken cup—to use Miss Kemble's illustration—may no doubt be mended, but mended cups can rarely be trusted to hold water.

Thus Mr. Croker, in 1827, parted from Mr. Peel and remained in office. He obtained as his new chief at the Admiralty no less a personage than the Duke of Clarence, the heir-presumptive to the throne. Mr. Croker regarded the Duke's appointment as Lord High Admiral as a triumph of policy. Convinced that the whole art of government lay in the manipulation of the chief pieces on the political chessboard, he hurried to communicate the tidings to discontented Tories. ' No true Tory '—so he wrote to Lord Lowther ' will like to commit himself in opposition for ' two generations ' (we presume that Mr. Croker meant two

reigns), ' and I hope and trust that most of them will con-
' sent to go on in the King's service.'   But the appointment proved a wretched one; and Mr. Croker himself had
ultimately to urge his Royal Highness's removal from office.
During his communications with the Duke, however, he
learnt one story which is worth preserving.   It seems that
in the previous reign

'His Royal Highness was advised to apply for an increased allowance, and Mr. Burke was selected to pen the demand.   While he was
writing the letter in the Duke's presence, he stopped, and, looking up at
his Royal Highness, said, in his Irish accent and quick manner, "I
" vow to God, Sir, I wish that, instead of writing letters of this kind,
" you would go every morning and breakfast with your father and
" mother.   It is not decent for any family, but above all for the Royal
" Family, to be at variance, as you all unhappily are." ' (Vol. i. p. 405.)

Mr. Croker retained under Lord Goderich and the Duke
of Wellington the secretaryship which he had held under
Mr. Perceval, Lord Liverpool, and Mr. Canning.   But, on
Mr. Huskisson's resignation in 1828, he evidently desired
promotion to the chief secretaryship of Ireland, vacant
through Lord F. Leveson's simultaneous retirement.   He
even took the trouble of going to Ireland and of seeing
Lord Anglesey, the Viceroy, who supported his appointment.   It is perhaps characteristic of the singular position
which Mr. Croker held that the Duke of Wellington at once
made up his mind that ' the appointment would not do,'
and Mr. Croker had to content himself with his old office
and promotion to the rank of privy councillor.

The crisis in the Ministry which had dazzled Mr. Croker
for a moment with the prospects of the Irish Office involved
Mr. Fitzgerald's appointment to the Board of Trade and an
election for the county of Clare, which Mr. Fitzgerald represented.   He was opposed by Mr. O'Connell, whose success
convinced the Duke of Wellington and Mr. Peel that the
emancipation of the Roman Catholics could no longer be
deferred.   Mr. Croker, it has already been remarked, had
supported the Roman Catholics for reasons which were almost
peculiar to himself, and which were eminently characteristic
of his opinions.   He did not care two straws about the
political enfranchisement of six millions of people; but
he thought that it would be easier to defend the position of
the Protestant minority if the grievance of the Roman
Catholics was removed.   But, though these reasons had as
much force in 1829 as when he first advanced them in 1819,
Mr. Croker oddly enough did not approve the great measure

of that year.   He was acute enough to see that, if the Tories
emancipated the Roman Catholics, the Whigs would be forced
to adopt some other policy; and, as Mr. Croker expressed it
in his old age, ' they were driven back upon Reform.'   Mr.
Jennings takes credit for the fact that Mr. Croker had
always been in favour of some reform; but he had only
advocated reform on the principle on which he had already
advocated Roman Catholic emancipation, or on the plan on
which the homœopathic doctor tries to heal his patient.
He thought that he could cure the patient of the disease by
administering the smallest possible dose of the poison which
caused it.   When reform really came, he regarded it with
an alarm which we are ready to believe was as genuine as
it was absurd, and he met it with an opposition which was
as resolute as it was mischievous.   Mr. Trevelyan has
pointed out in his ' Life of Fox ' that the Whigs in 1771 were
the first who showed what a minority could do by resolute
obstruction.   Mr. Croker, in 1831, improved on the example
of 1771.   He kept the House sitting through night after
night in Committee discussing small details for the sake of
delaying a great measure.   From uncompromising Tories
he received unbounded applause.   They, like Tadpole in
' Coningsby,' had an unwavering faith in ' Rigby's great
' speech on Aldborough.'   But even Mr. Croker could not
delay the inevitable end.   The Reform Bill was carried; *
and Mr. Croker shaking the dust off his feet retired from
Parliament.   In doing so, he took the trouble to explain his
reasons to the Duke of Wellington, in what no doubt seemed
to him an impressive and eloquent letter, and the Duke sent
him an answer, which will appear to most people excellent:

' My dear Croker,—I have received your letter.   I am very sorry
that you do not intend again to be elected to serve in Parliament.   I
cannot conceive for what reason.   Ever yours most sincerely,
                                            ' WELLINGTON.'

---

* Most people acquainted with the history of those times recollect
that Mr. Croker took credit for the circumstance that in the third
Reform Bill the Whig Ministry adopted many of his suggestions.   ' In
' its details,' he wrote to Lord Hertford, ' it is a great triumph for me
' and for our party, for there is not one of my points on which we
' divided in the Committee which is not conceded.'   But the triumph
only brought regret.   ' I am sorry to say that it was evident in the
' House that these alterations blind many foolish people to the deformity
' of the principle. . . .   If Peel and I cannot show the futility as to
' the great object of all these alterations, we shall, I fear, cut a poor
' figure in the division.'   (Vol. ii. p. 141.)   Did ever politician make a
more damning admission of the futility of his own conduct ?

Though he had retired from Parliament, Mr. Croker had no intention to abandon politics. Notwithstanding the 'great speech on Aldborough,' he probably sometimes doubted whether the House of Commons was the best arena for his abilities. He saw perhaps more clearly than greater men than himself the growing power of the press; and he thought that it was mere folly for statesmen to 'despise the 'journals or only treat them as inferior agents.' In 1829 he seriously suggested that some member of the Cabinet should be found with leisure to supervise or co-operate with the press.

'I have heretofore conveyed to the public articles written by Prime and Cabinet Ministers, and sometimes have composed such articles under their eye—they supplied the *fact*, and I supplied the *tact*, and between us we used to produce a considerable effect. . . . The success of that period, of which I was an humble though an active agent, was so complete that it turned the press—I mean the preponderating force of the press—right round; the Government had the voice of the journals, and the Opposition (what had, I believe, never before happened in the history of English parties)—the Opposition complained loudly of the *licentiousness* of the press; which only meant that they were no longer able to wield it exclusively to their own purposes.' (Vol. ii. pp. 22, 23.)

So wrote Mr. Croker in 1829. He does not satisfy our curiosity by defining the period at which the preponderating power of the press was turned right round by his influence. It could not have been from 1807 to 1813, for at that time Sir Vicary Gibbs was a law officer of the Crown, and Sir Vicary is said to have had one-half of the London newspapers under prosecution at the same time. It could not have been from 1813 to 1820, for that was the period of the Six Acts. It could not have been in the early years of the reign of George IV., for at that time Tory gentlemen formed themselves into an Association, which is still remembered as the Bridge Street Gang, for the purpose of publishing libellous and seditious periodicals. Whatever Mr. Croker may have meant by his statement, he deliberately thought in 1829 that the time had arrived for managing the journals; and in 1831 he reverted to his notion and decided on educating England in Tory principles through the medium of the 'Quarterly Review.' If Mr. Jennings be correct, Mr. Croker's connexion with our great contemporary had commenced in 1809 and terminated in 1826; it had, in other words, endured throughout the rule of Mr. Gifford, the 'Quarterly's' first editor. If Mr. Croker may be trusted, he had not himself

throughout that period contributed 'one purely political
' article, not one certainly in which party politics predo-
' minated.' In 1831 he resumed his connexion with the
' Review,' and commenced what Tadpole called in ' Coningsby'
his ' slashing' political articles. It is possible to infer, from
some isolated passages in Mr. Jennings's work, that neither
Mr. Murray, the publisher, nor Mr. Lockhart, the editor,
entirely approved the tone and the temper of some of Mr.
Croker's contributions. But they, at any rate, let him have
his way. And, no doubt, Mr. Croker enjoyed an advantage
from his position, which added value to his articles. ' Whis-
' pered as the productions of one behind the scenes '—to
quote ' Coningsby' again—' they were passed off as genuine
' coin.' The writer was in close communication with the
leaders of his party; after the formation of Sir Robert
Peel's second administration, he drew his information direct
from the Ministry; and both the Prime Minister and some
of his colleagues read some of the articles before they were
published, and suggested alterations in them. Mr. Croker's
ideal, therefore, respecting the press was again realised. The
Minister was supplying the fact, and he was supplying the
tact. Himself ' a wretched financier,' to use his own phrase,
he was easily induced to support the great financial measures
of 1842 and 1845; he never realised the obvious tendency of
the Budgets of these years; and though he was occasionally
alarmed at language attributed to Mr. Gladstone, who was
already proving himself the most capable of Sir Robert Peel's
lieutenants, and though he shared the fears which the country gentlemen displayed at the admission of Canadian corn
into the home market, he did his best to allay the growing
dissatisfaction of the Tories.

At the end of 1845, however, the terrible crisis occurred
which led to perhaps the most momentous measure of the
century, the repeal of the Corn Laws. Mr. Lockhart, as
editor of the ' Quarterly,' invited Mr. Croker to write upon
the subject; and Mr. Croker, adhering to the principles
which Sir Robert Peel had abandoned, severed himself from
the Minister. We shall have something to say later on as
to the manner in which Mr. Croker discharged his duty.
But, as the controversy cost him the Minister's friendship,
and as his own connexion with Sir Robert Peel was the most
important fact in his life, and his correspondence with Sir
Robert Peel forms the most interesting part of these volumes,
we are anxious before doing so to show how our knowledge of
that great man's career is increased by this publication. His-

tory, after all, will not concern itself much with Mr. Croker; but historians, for many generations to come, will take an increasing interest in the character of Sir Robert Peel. Everything which throws light on his career is matter for study; everything that increases his fame is, with us at any rate, matter for congratulation.

Mr. Croker probably made Mr. Peel's acquaintance soon after his entry into Parliament. Mr. Peel became Chief Secretary for Ireland in 1812, and thenceforward became Mr. Croker's correspondent. Mr. Peel had evidently little fancy for his Irish life.

'I have scarcely dined once at home since my arrival,' he wrote in 1812. 'I see no great prospect of it for some time to come, excepting with about twenty-five guests. I am just opening upon the campaign, and have visions of future feasts studded with Lord Mayors and Sheriffs-elect. I fancy I see some who think that the Government of England have a strange notion of Ireland when they put a man here who drinks port, and as little of that as he can.' (Vol. i. p. 47.)

But he had one quality which, we think, Mr. Froude has regarded as an indispensable qualification for the post of Chief Secretary. He was quite ready to fight a duel; and he actually proceeded to Ostend for the purpose of meeting Mr. O'Connell. It is well known that no hostile encounter took place. Mr. O'Connell and his second were arrested in London, and bound over to keep the peace. It is perhaps less well known that Mr. Peel subsequently challenged Mr. O'Connell's second, and proceeded again to the Continent for the purpose of encountering him. But, if Mr. Peel did not shrink from this part of the duties of an Irish Secretary, he hated his office. In the words of M. Guizot's excellent memoir of him, 'le séjour de l'Irlande lui était insuppor-'table;' and when, after his resignation of the Irish Office, Mr. Croker wrote, urging him to take Mr. Vansittart's office, with a view to his 'ultimate advancement to the highest 'office of all,' * he answered

'in the emphatic tone of a reverend pastor in the "Vicar of Wake-"field "—Fudge! I am thinking of anything but office, and am just as anxious to be emancipated from office as the Papists are to be

---

* Mr. Croker, in this letter, says: 'There was one voice that you 'were the person whom all the friends of good order would support. 'Some one had said that our *honest* friend wanted *eloquence,* and our 'eloquent friend *honesty,* but that you, uniting both, would unite the 'confidence of the whole party.' (Vol. i. p. 114.) Mr. Jennings, in two notes, indicates that our honest friend was probably Mr. Huskisson,

emancipated into it. I am for the abolition of slavery, and no men
have a right to condemn another to worse than Egyptian bondage, to
require him, not to make bricks without straw, which a man of straw
might have some chance of doing (as Lord Norbury would say), but
to raise money and abolish taxes in the same breath—"Night cometh
" when no man can work," said One who could not have foreseen the fate
of a man in office and the House of Commons. A fortnight hence I
shall be free as air—free from ten thousand engagements which I cannot fulfil; . . . free from Orangemen; free from Ribbonmen; free
from Dennis Browne; free from the Lord Mayor and Sheriffs; . . .
free from perpetual converse about the harbour of Howth and Dublin
Bay haddock; and lastly free of the Company of Carvers and Gilders
which I became this day (*sic*) in reward of my public services.'

It is a striking proof both of Mr. Peel's increasing reputation and of Mr. Croker's acuteness, that Mr. Croker, so early
as 1818, should have contemplated Mr. Peel becoming Prime
Minister. Nine years afterwards, when Lord Goderich was
forming his short-lived Administration, he again strongly
urged Mr. Peel's appointment to high office. Lord Goderich
met the suggestion with the remark: 'We have nothing to
' offer Peel but the Chancellor of the Exchequer, which I
' suppose he would not take.' Mr. Jennings would, we think,
have done wisely if he had added a note to explain why the
Chancellorship of the Exchequer was too small an office for
Mr. Peel's acceptance. The fact is that, up to 1831, the
Chancellorship of the Exchequer was one of the worst-paid
offices in the Cabinet. Each Secretary of State had, at that
time, 6,000*l.* a year; the Chancellor of the Exchequer only
about 3,000*l.* a year and a house. Pay implies rank; and,
in the first thirty years of this century, the Chancellorship
of the Exchequer, when it was not held by the Prime Minister,
or in conjunction with some other office, was usually either
conferred on young men like Lord H. Petty, or on inferior
men like Mr. Vansittart. It was the alteration of salaries by
the Whig Ministry of 1830 which first placed the office on a
level with that of Secretary of State.

We pass rapidly over the events of the succeeding years,
in order that we may consider Sir Robert Peel's conduct during
the Whig Administration. On leaving office in 1830 he announced to a meeting of forty official members of the House

---

and our eloquent friend Mr. Canning. The notes convinced us that
Mr. Jennings's knowledge of the period of which he is treating was
superficial and second-hand. No one with any acquaintance with the
state of politics in 1818 can doubt that Mr. Croker was referring to
Lord Castlereagh and Mr. Canning.

of Commons ' that he meant to retire to private life, to give
' no opposition, and not to lead the party.' But it was of
course no more practicable for him to carry out such a resolution than it proved possible for Mr. Gladstone to abandon
politics in 1874. His conduct, however, during the discussions on the Reform Bill was anything but satisfactory to Mr.
Croker. There was a true ring about Mr. Croker's utterances
which every Tory could understand. He, at least, never
doubted that Reform was ' a stepping-stone to a Republic.'
He did 'not feel, like Peel, that the fright goes off by habit.'
Mr. Croker, in fact, was in such genuine alarm that he could
think and write of nothing but of Reform and cholera, and
Sir Robert Peel answered his letter by telling him that he
had killed with his ' single gun thirty-six partridges the day
' before yesterday. Pretty well for the 8th of November.'
A man who in the days of muzzle-loaders could kill eighteen
brace of birds on a November day had obviously healthy
tendencies to counteract his fears. Very wisely, too, Sir
Robert Peel declined to have anything to do with the formation of a Tory Ministry in the crisis of 1832. It was in vain
that Mr. Croker pressed upon him 'the duty of saving the
' King, the country, and the world (!) from the obvious con-
' sequences of the re-establishment of the revolutionary
' government.' It was in vain that he wrote to him: 'If
' Lord Grey returns, see what must happen—the King en-
' slaved, the House of Lords degraded, the Bill passed, the
' revolution consummated.' Sir Robert Peel had probably
his own views upon all these matters, and he certainly preferred the partridges and leisure to office and humiliation.

In forming this decision we have no doubt that Sir Robert
Peel was right and that Mr. Croker was wrong. It was, in
fact, Sir Robert Peel's moderation in 1832 which increased
his influence in 1833 and led to his temporary accession to
office in 1834. Anyone who has studied the debates of the
first Reformed Parliament must have been struck with the
exceptional position which he occupied. Leader only of a
small and discontented minority, he became almost at once
the most considerable person in the House. The fact is that
the Reformed House was much better suited to Sir Robert
Peel than the unreformed Parliament. Sprung from the
middle classes himself, his success, his wealth, and his education had not estranged him from the people; and, though
he had resisted the enfranchisement of the 10*l.* householders,
he knew and represented their real opinions more accurately
than the Whig Ministers succeeded in doing. The new

House of Commons he declared at once ' to be a good one to
' speak to,' and we are not surprised at his statement after
reading what Mr. Croker said of it.

' For two nights and a half the vehemence and disorder were so
great that people began to think that the National Convention was
begun. Peel told me that it was "frightful," "appalling." This
induced him to rise late the third night, and read the House a most
able, eloquent, and authoritative lecture. While he arraigned the
foreign policy of Ministers, he expressed his determination to support
their conservative dispositions, and he deprecated those idle and violent
debates. The fate of the Government was, and he knew it, in his hands.
If he had chosen to listen only to passion and revenge, he could have
put them out. He wisely and honestly took the other line, and the
effect was instantaneous and prodigious. The storm moderated'—&c.
(Ibid. p. 202.)

The success which he had achieved perhaps taught Sir
Robert Peel his own power. A few days afterwards Mr.
Croker, to his great surprise, found his friend

' apparently resolved to accept office and make battle. He spoke
with great firmness and spirit, said he would do his duty, and,
if necessary, venture to form a Ministry, though he might think it
could not last a fortnight, but he said he would never give up his
principles to that House of Commons; he would be leader and not
led. He would try whether government could be carried on, and after
a fair experiment he at least would have done his part. . . . He
seemed to think there would be an entirely new combination, of
which the currency question would be the basis. On that he was firm,
but foresaw that Radicals and ultra-Tories would unite against him.'
(Ibid. p. 205.)

The opportunity did not come so rapidly as Sir Robert
Peel expected. It was not till the autumn of 1834 that the
death of Lord Spencer broke up the Melbourne Ministry, and
that Sir Robert Peel was summoned from Rome to form a
Government. In the few weeks during which his Administration lasted the Minister was engaged in a struggle which
was more difficult and more hopeless than that in which Mr.
Pitt had been involved half a century before. But, though
it afforded Sir Robert Peel opportunity for displaying large
views and statesmanlike capacity, it increased the distrust
which extreme Tories still felt of him. On his taking office
Mr. Croker wrote to Lord Hertford:—

' No power shall ever force me to serve under Peel. We are excellent friends, and shall remain so, which assuredly would not be the
case if we sat in the same Cabinet.' (Vol. ii. p. 245.)

In 1840 he wrote to the King of Hanover:—

' Peel's unhappy Administration five years ago did more serious injury to our Constitution in the three months it lasted than the Whigs have done since the Reform. Bill.' (Ibid. p. 366.)

But, though Mr. Croker expressed these opinions to his other correspondents, he does not seem to have carried them to Sir Robert Peel. The man whom no power on earth would force to serve under Peel was in his letter to the Minister ' Yours affectionately, J. W. Croker.' And when the victory at last came in 1841, and Sir Robert Peel found himself Minister, supported by a large majority, Mr. Croker became his vigorous apologist. In fact, at this period he so completely identified himself with the policy of his friend that, with an amusing vanity, he constantly wrote of the Ministry as ' we.' It seems strange indeed now that Mr. Croker should not have perceived the obvious tendency of Sir Robert Peel's measures. So far back as 1834 the Minister sent him a letter containing an account of a speech which he had just made defending Protection.

' I will show,' he wrote, ' that on the most approved principles of political economy there is no objection in principle to restraints on foreign corn, which does not apply equally to restraints on foreign manufactured goods. Therefore it follows that you are equally bound to repeal all duties not intended for revenue but protection; and the manufacturers, if they succeed in repealing the duty on foreign corn, must be at once prepared for the repeal of every protecting duty whatsoever.' (Vol. ii. p. 222.)

A forcible argument, no doubt, but painful reading for Mr. Croker, if he turned back to the old letter either in 1842 or in 1845. 'Between 1842 and 1846,' says Mr. A. J. Wilson, a well-informed writer, ' Sir Robert Peel repealed altogether ' the duties on between five and six hundred articles . . . and ' reduced the duties on a great number more. . . . It was ' not, however, from the importance as sources of revenue ' that the reduction or repeal of these taxes was significant, ' but because the fiscal policy of these four years was the ' beginning of a new era. Henceforth taxes were to be ' maintained for purposes of revenue alone.' It is plain enough, therefore, that Sir Robert Peel by his policy in office had gone far to destroy the argument on which he had resisted Free-trade in 1834. If, however, Mr. Croker had forgotten the letter which he had received in 1834, he ought to have perceived the obvious tendency of the Minister's language in 1842. Sir Robert Peel wrote to him on the 3rd of August in that year : —

'We must make this country a *cheap* country for living, and thus induce parties to remain and settle here. Enable them to consume more by having more to spend. . . . If you have to pay 64s. a quarter for 24,000,000 quarters of wheat, there is a dead loss of 12,000,000*l.* annually. Comparing the expenditure on one article with that which would be requisite were wheat at 54s., how will the 12,000,000*l.* be employed? In consuming more barley, more wheat, more articles of agricultural produce. It is a fallacy to urge that the loss falls on the agriculturists: they too are consumers; they lose almost as much in *increased poor rates* alone, the burden of which, as they contend, falls almost exclusively on them, as they gain by increased price. Lower the price of wheat—not only poor rates, but the cost of everything else, is lower.' (Vol. ii. p. 386.)

It is true that Sir Robert Peel went on to reassure his correspondent by adding: 'We do not push this argument to ' its logical consequences—namely, that wheat should be at ' 35s. instead of 54s.' Anybody who stopped to think must have seen that, if the argument were sound, it would sooner or later be driven home. If Sir Robert Peel was right that it was necessary to make the country cheap, and that the price of everything would be lowered if the price of wheat were lowered, there was no permanent stopping at 54s. a quarter. Mr. Cobden himself could not have put more strongly the case for cheap corn.

In writing thus, however, we are far from desiring to imply that Sir Robert Peel was insincere in proposing the sliding scale of 1842. We have no doubt that he would have clung to the compromise of that year if the potato had not failed. Mr. Croker, indeed, always persisted in saying that the failure of the potato was not the cause of Sir Robert Peel's policy.

'You remember,' he wrote to the Duke of Wellington, 'that I told you something that you did not know about *our friend's* (Peel's) conversion to Free-trade doctrines. I can now tell you . . . that it was nothing but the result of *fright* at the League. I always thought this, but I have had within these few days the most decided and authentic evidence of the fact. I could prove it in a court of justice by an indisputable witness, and yet he still goes on persisting in the humbug of the potato famine.' (Vol. iii. p. 65.)

It was in vain that the Duke of Wellington, writing from his own personal knowledge, assured Mr. Croker that he was mistaken.

'I cannot doubt that which passed under my own view and frequent observation day after day,' wrote the Duke. 'I mean the alarms of the consequences in Ireland of the potato disease. I never witnessed in any case such agony.'

The Duke, we presume, was not an ' indisputable witness,' whatever that may be ; for Mr. Croker immediately replied to him :—

' You were not deceived as to the *fact*, but only as to the *cause*. The agony was real and intense, but it was the agony of a man who was deluding and betraying his conscience and his colleagues.'

And, after this offensive reflection on his oldest personal friend, he proceeded to repeat his statement to Sir H. Hardinge, the Governor-General of India :—

' For all my affection for him (Peel) I cannot excuse this late tergiversation, and above all the deception of endeavouring to attribute it to the potato failure in Ireland. I can venture to assure you from my own knowledge that the Irish panic has had no more to do with it than the disturbances in the Punjaub. . . . The main and immediate cause was terror, cowardice. This I know, and I would not tell you if I did not—terror of the League, which he felt ought to be put down, but he had not nerve for doing that *de front*, and so he hit on the expedient of dissolving them by submitting to their dictation, as he will pacify O'Connell by repealing the Union.' (Ibid. p. 67.)

Such was the language which Mr. Croker held to his private friends. In the pages of the ' Quarterly Review' he used all his efforts to resist the Minister's policy. We agree with Mr. Jennings in thinking that the articles did not exceed the fair bounds of political discussion. They were offensive not in themselves, but because they came from Mr. Croker ; and accordingly when their author practically admitted the authorship, and suggested that, with the admission, the correspondence between himself and Sir Robert Peel should be closed,* Sir Robert Peel, in a letter of studied coldness, expressed ' an earnest wish that the same principle . . . may be extended to every other species of intercourse.' If Sir Robert Peel knew of nothing except the articles, we think that the terms of his letter were needlessly severe ; but if he had any knowledge of the language which Mr. Croker was addressing to the Duke of Wellington, Sir H. Hardinge, and other common friends, we are not surprised that he should

---

* Mr. Jennings does not mention one point about this letter. It is signed, ' Very sincerely and affectionately yours, *Up to the Altar*, J. W. Croker.' (Vol. ii. p. 94.) This singular termination is a paraphrase of a line in the article of September, 1846 : ' We who have been, ' *usque ad aras*, his humble followers and admirers.' The imputation in both cases seems to be the same. The faithful follower had been led up to the altar for sacrifice in blind confidence of his chief.

think that ' personal good-will cannot coexist with the spirit
' in which those articles are written.' *

With the separation from Sir Robert Peel the chief
interest in Mr. Croker's political career terminates. We
care very little for his subsequent correspondence with the
late Lord Derby, Lord G. Bentinck, Lord Lonsdale, and Lord
Hardwicke. With one great man, indeed, Mr. Croker retained
an intimate acquaintance to the very end. Mr. Croker's
friendship for the Duke of Wellington began in 1806; it
terminated only with the Duke's death in 1852; and, to
many readers, the most interesting passages in Mr. Jennings's volumes will be those which relate to the great Duke.

' When I first went to the Admiralty,' wrote Mr. Croker in 1826,
' Sir Roger Curtis . . . said to me " My dear friend, beware of *heroes*
' —the more you come to know them the less you will think of
' them;' and certainly he was right as far as my experience went with
many that set up for *heroes*. The grand exception was the *real hero*
—the Duke—who in mind and manners was the same, exactly the
same, when I first knew him in 1806, as he is now, and rose in my
admiration every hour that I saw him, always simple and always
great.' (Vol. i. p. 350.)

What the Duke was in 1808 Mr. Croker relates in a very
interesting anecdote. After talking of the business of the
Irish Office—

' He seemed to lapse in a kind of reverie, and remained silent so
long that I asked him what he was thinking of. He replied, " Why,
to say the truth, I am thinking of the French that I am going to
fight. I have not seen them since the campaign in Flanders, when
they were capital soldiers, and a dozen years of victory under Buonaparte must have made them better still. They have besides, it
seems, a new system of strategy, which has out-manœuvred and overwhelmed all the armies of Europe. 'Tis enough to make one
thoughtful ; but, no matter : my die is cast ; they may overwhelm me,
but I dont think they will out-manœuvre me. First, because I am

---

* We may add that the extracts which Mr. Jennings has given
from the September article to show that it is free from personal malice
do not contain any of the passages which were probably most offensive
to Sir Robert Peel. After quoting, for instance, Dr. Arnold's statement—' Peel has an idea about currency, and a distinct impression
' about it, and therefore on that point I would trust him for not
' yielding to clamour ; but about most matters, the Church especially,
' he seems to have no idea, and therefore I would not trust him for
' giving it all up to-morrow if *the clamour were loud enough* '—Mr.
Croker adds in a note : ' We confess that we think the " currency idea "
' would also fail if *the clamour were loud enough.*' Would anyone
tolerate such language from his closest political friend ?

not afraid of them, as everybody else seems to be; and, secondly, because, if what I hear of their system of manœuvres be true, I think it a false one as against steady troops.   I suspect all the Continental armies were more than beaten before the battle began.   I, at least, will not be frightened beforehand." ' (Vol. i. p. 13.)

It is thus evident that, before he sailed for the campaign of Vimiera, the Duke was meditating meeting the French attack in column with steady troops in line.   After the war was over, during the occupation of Paris, the Emperor of Russia and the King of Prussia

'insisted on the superiority of Buonaparte's system of an attack by *columns.*   The Duke took the other side, denied that it had ever been or could be successful against steady troops on a large scale, and he instanced Waterloo.   The two sovereigns, who had not quite got out of their *engouement* about Buonaparte, and who attributed their own successive defeats to the column system, persisted, though the Duke's reasoning was most clear and convincing; but at last he said he requested permission to show their Majesties his principle by the actual exhibition of the two systems by his whole army next day on the Plaine St. Denis.   This was the object of that great review.' (Vol. iii. p. 274.)

The Duke regarded 'Lord Beresford as the best officer we ' have for the command of an army,' Massena as the only one of Napoleon's marshals ' who had any pretensions to a com- ' parison with him.'   Buonaparte was ' with his prestige ' worth 40,000 men.'   But he placed the Archduke Charles, in knowledge of the art of war, above all other living generals.

'We are none of us worthy to fasten the latchets of his shoes, if I am to judge from his book and his plans of campaign.   But his mind or his health has, they tell me, a very peculiar defect.   He is admirable for five or six hours, and whatever can be done in that time will be done perfectly; but after that he falls into a kind of epileptic stupor, does not know what he is about, has no opinion of his own, and does whatever the man at his elbow tells him.' (Vol. i. p. 338.)

There is a pleasant story both of the Duke and of the soldiers of the opposite armies, told to Mr. Croker in 1828 :—

' The advance posts always gave notice to each other when they were in danger.   On one occasion, when the French army was advancing suddenly and in force, the French posts suddenly cried out to ours "Courez vite, courez vite ! on va vous attaquer."   I always encouraged this; the killing a poor fellow of a vedette or carrying off a post could not influence the battle, and I always, when I was going to attack, sent to tell them to get out of the way.' (Vol. i. p. 433.)

As for his officers—

' The Guards were the most troublesome people in the army when there was nothing to be done, and he had constant occasion to be vexed with them when in quarters and in the intervals of active operations; but when these recommenced, the Guards were the best soldiers in the army. None of them, he said, ever misbehaved when there was any duty to be done. *White's window would not permit it.* (N.B. *White's window* was .at that time the fashionable *tribunal* of the dandies.)'

As for the soldiers—

' I found the English soldiers always in the best humour when we were well supplied with beef; the Irish when we were in the wine countries; and the Scotch when the dollars for pay came up.' (Vol. i. p. 353.)

We may perhaps conclude these anecdotes of the Duke with a description which he gave on one occasion of a battle :—

' I told you that a battle was like a ball. One remembered one's own partner, but knew very little what other couples might be about; nor, if one did, might it be quite decorous to tell all he saw.'

The Duke paid Mr. Croker a last visit on September 2, 1852. Mr. Croker was staying at Dover, and the Duke went thither expressly to see his old friend, who was supposed to be seriously ill. Death came that month, but it was to the Duke and not to Mr. Croker; and with the Duke's death Mr. Jennings's labours might almost have closed.

Mr. Croker was a many-sided man, and consequently before ending this article we must add a few words on another aspect of his character. We have hitherto dealt with him mainly as a politician, but we do not forget that he was also a man of letters. He has not indeed left much permanent literature behind him. His articles have never been republished; his notes on Pope passed, after his death, into the hands of other persons; and he will probably be chiefly recollected hereafter as the editor of Boswell's ' Life of Johnson. It happens that this book was the cause of a great literary tempest. It was reviewed on its first appearance in these pages by Lord Macaulay, and Mr. Croker, husbanding his wrath for nearly eighteen years, retaliated by attacking the first two volumes of Lord Macaulay's ' History' in the ' Quarterly Review.' We have not much taste for discussing the quarrels of authors, but our task would be hardly complete if we did not make some reference to this portion of the subject.

In the debates on the Reform Bill Mr. Croker and Lord Macaulay had been brought into sharp political conflict. According to Mr. Roebuck, ' Mr. Croker was careful always ' to follow Mr. Macaulay in the debate, endeavouring to rival

' him in eloquence, and hoping to surpass him in the cogency
' of his reasoning.' * Lord Macaulay's temperament betrayed
him occasionally into taking a prejudiced view of his political opponents.   Slight personal intercourse in an Italian
tour—it may be recollected—at once removed the prejudice
which he had conceived against Mr. Goulburn, merely on
the ground of political difference.   A man who was not
tolerant of his most respectable political opponents was
likely to hate with a strong hatred the adversary who was
doing the work that Mr. Croker was doing; and in his
private letters to his sister he spoke of Mr. Croker with a
contempt and a loathing which he did not probably foresee
was ultimately to be made public.   Animated by these feelings, he promised to review Mr. Croker's chief literary work;
and he wrote the famous article which he himself claimed
had ' smashed ' the book.   ' See whether I do not dust this
' varlet's jacket for him in the next number of the " Blue
' " and Yellow; " ' I detest him more than cold boiled veal,'
so he wrote to Lady Trevelyan in July 1831.   The inference which Mr. Jennings draws from this passage, however, is so unwarrantable, that we trust he will see fit to
suppress or modify the whole of his criticism on it in a
future edition.

Mr. Jennings argues thus : In July Lord Macaulay threatened to dust the varlet's jacket.   ' From that time forth he
' waited impatiently for his opportunity to settle his account
' with Mr. Croker.'   Again: ' Macaulay has laid bare the
' entire process of flaying an author—first the threat to dust
' his jacket; then the urgent request to be allowed to review

---

* ' History of the Whig Ministry,' vol. ii. p. 200, *note.*   Mr. Roebuck
goes on to say : ' It was the " Quarterly," as Mr. Croker appeared to
think, against the " Edinburgh ; " and that which could not be said in
the House was given by way of supplement in the " Review."   The
" Quarterly," in March 1831, distinctly puts the two champions forward as literary and political rivals ; and anyone referring to its pages
would suppose that Sir Robert Peel and every other Conservative
played second to Mr. Croker, who is styled the *old flagellifer,* and
spoken of as
> ' *Alternis* aptum sermonibus, et populares
> Vincentem strepitus, et natum rebus agendis.'

Could it be that he was willing to comment in the Review upon
what he said in the House, and impartially give himself the palm of
victory ? '   Mr. Jennings has not noticed this passage.   But we could
fill our columns with charges against Mr. Croker which Mr. Jennings
has ignored.

' the book; lastly, the article itself.' But, in the first place, there was no urgent request to review the book. Lord Macaulay had merely promised in March, or four months before July, to review the book when it appeared. And, in the next place, the book had appeared, and Lord Macaulay's opinion of it had been fully given to his sister, in the month which preceded the threat to dust the varlet's jacket. The threat, therefore, was no threat; it was a mere statement of the shape which the review was already assuming. Instead of waiting impatiently to settle his account with Mr. Croker, the account was already in full process of settlement. Has Mr. Jennings mastered these dates? If so, does he still adhere to the charge?

As for the review itself, we agree with Lord Macaulay's main criticism. We think that Mr. Croker spoiled Boswell by incorporating Mrs. Thrale's anecdotes and much of Sir John Hawkins's lumbering book in the text. We think, too, that few authors would care to face the formidable assault which the reviewer made on Mr. Croker. Never before, and never since, to our knowledge at any rate, has reviewer detected so long and so serious a category of errors in any considerable work. If Mr. Croker's book survived the attack, it was not because it was a perfect edition of Boswell, but because many of its defects, when they were once pointed out, were capable of correction in later issues, and because, as Lord Macaulay himself admitted, ' there is much ' curious information in it.'

We have already shown that Mr. Jennings is inaccurate in stating that Lord Macaulay waited impatiently for his opportunity to settle his account with Mr. Croker. It would be much more true to say that Mr. Croker waited for nearly eighteen years to settle his account with Lord Macaulay. The opportunity seemed to come with the publication of the first two volumes of Lord Macaulay's 'History,' and Mr. Croker seized it to write an article which Mr. Trevelyan has described as ' so bitter, so foolish, and, above all, so tedious, that ' scarcely anybody could get through it, and nobody was ' convinced by it.' We are not going to refer to an article which is dead and buried, and which Mr. Jennings has refrained from disinterring. Mr. Croker was, in fact, incapable of writing a good review of the ' History.' No man can write a good review of any book who has not at least as much knowledge of the subject as the author whose labours he is reviewing. The common saying that a bad book makes a good review is based on this truth, that the reviewer is superior to the author. But Mr. Croker's knowledge was infinitely inferior to that of Lord Macaulay. Sir J. Macintosh's verdict on Gibbon and Burke, which is so strangely crude and untrue, might have been literally applied to him. Mr. Croker 'might have been taken from a ' corner' of Lord Macaulay's mind 'without even being ' missed.'

We rise, in fact, from Mr. Jennings's book with the conviction that Mr. Croker was neither a great politician nor a great writer. He had much information, but little knowledge ; much acuteness of vision, but no breadth of view. His articles were no doubt caustic enough, but his style was not good ; he was as fond of italics as a school-girl ; and the use of italics almost always implies an incapacity to emphasise argument by language.* He occasionally struck hard, but his blows were the blows of a shillelagh rather than of a rapier. He could knock down his adversary and trample upon him, but he had not the fencer's skill in parry and attack. If he had no lightness of touch, he was also destitute of the keener humour. We very much doubt whether Mr. Jennings has read the letters in which, under the pseudonym of 'Bradwardine Waverley,' Mr. Croker replied to the attack which Sir Walter Scott, writing as Malachi Malagrowther, made on the new Currency Law of 1826. We have ourselves read the letters through again since Mr. Jennings's work appeared, and we are surprised that so elaborate and tedious an attempt at humour should have found readers at the time.

Mr. Jennings tells us that 'the little controversy between ' Sir Walter Scott and Mr. Croker caused no interruption to ' their friendship,' but he omits to add that the credit of this circumstance is due exclusively to Sir Walter. This is the manner in which Mr. Croker could speak of a friend who had just sustained a grievous pecuniary embarrassment :—

'You are a cynical creature, Malachi, but your disposition to truth is stronger even than your bile, and forces itself through the melancholy mist in which a fit of ill-humour has shrouded your intellect.'

Is Mr. Jennings ignorant of this passage ? Will he, after reading it, still adhere to his statement that it is untrue to say that 'a quarrel was healed only by the magnanimity of

---

* The way in which Mr. Croker used italics may perhaps be inferred from some of the extracts in this article, where the italics are always Mr. Croker's.

' Scott ' ?   He proceeds to cite some letters from Sir Walter
.Scott in support of his own view, premising that a portion
of one of the letters, with a few variations in the text, was
published in Lockhart's ' Life of Scott.'   Few people who
have read that pathetic letter in Mr. Lockhart's book are
likely, we should imagine, to forget it; but we looked in vain
in Mr. Jennings's pages for the passages which had sunk
into our memory.   Mr. Jennings, we found, and not Mr. Lockhart, was the chief offender in suppression.   It was he, and
not Mr. Lockhart, who was giving a portion of the document.   Our author, we conclude, has been taking a lesson
in accuracy from his hero.

The passage which we have quoted from the Bradwardine
Waverley is a specimen of the language which Mr. Croker
could use to a friend.   Acerbity of this kind entered too frequently into his articles.   We do not, indeed, forget that
political controversy fifty years ago normally assumed a personal and aggressive tone, from which happily, with some
exceptions, it has lately been comparatively free; and that
Mr. Croker might fairly plead that he was not alone in his
sinning.   In an age, however, of rancour, Mr. Croker was
distinguished for the bitterness of his writings.   In 1854,
when Mr. Croker was seventy-four years old, Mr. Murray
and Mr. Elwin, much to their credit, frankly told him that
they would not publish an article displaying an acrimony of
feeling against the Buonapartes which would revolt the public
taste.   Nearly twenty years before the Duke of Wellington
had, in vain, remonstrated against the publication of an
offensive article on the battle of Toulouse, at the very time
when Marshal Soult was on an official visit to this country.
Mr. Croker could not see the indecency of attacking a
guest, just as he could not see the indecency of attacking
an ally.

We have already said, however, more of Mr. Croker than
we had intended to say.   It is hardly worth while discussing his
career: the true value of Mr. Jennings's book is the light
that it throws on the lives of other people.   But there is a
moral to be drawn from the book, which must be enforced.
Mr. Croker, in a political, not a personal, sense, was the
accurate representative of the old class of Tories who lived
in the days of the Reform Act. And what a picture does the
book afford us of their fears and of their follies!   Mr.
Croker, apparently quite seriously, wrote in 1831, ' I should
' like to know why a place like Dunwich, against which
' neither perjury nor bribery can be charged, should be dis-

' franchised, while Liverpool and Newcastle in the Potteries
' are to be preserved as samples of purity of election.' To
Mr. Croker it was a mere nothing that Liverpool contained
some 200,000 · people, and that Dunwich was submerged
beneath the North Sea. His was literally the creed which
a powerful, though forgotten, writer put into the mouth of
the Tories :—

> ' The dust of old Sarum is holy,
>   In our hearts live her ramparts and towers;
> No progress: improvement is folly,
>   The foes of green Gatton are ours.'

And we do not wonder at his creed when we read of
his alarms. He genuinely believed that Lord Hertford's
property and his own pension would be swept away by the .
Reform Act; 'and the Bill once passed, good night to the
' Monarchy, the Lords, and the Church.' Experience gave
a tolerably satisfactory answer to the prophecy, but it only
induced Mr. Croker to hazard another. The repeal of the
Corn Laws set him wondering how it was possible 'to
' maintain primogeniture, the Bishops, the House of Lords,
' and the Crown;' and years afterwards he apparently still
adhered to his old errors; for Lord Lonsdale wrote to him
in 1855, 'Your prediction in the end will be correct as to
' the effects of the Reform Bill, but it has been longer coming
' about than all of us thought.'

It is no doubt true that other and greater men, Sir
Robert Peel and the Duke of Wellington for example,
shared, in the first instance, the fears which were thus
expressed by Mr. Croker; and we do not deny that, in the
burning of Bristol, in the riots at Birmingham, in the
threat made by responsible persons to pay no taxes, and in
the attitude of the political unions, thoughtful men, the
friends of order, had ample reasons for anxiety and alarm.
But there was a wide distinction between the apprehensions
of Sir Robert Peel and those of Mr. Croker. The former was
concerned at the prevalence of disorder, the latter at the
transfer of political power from an oligarchy to the middle
classes. The one rapidly recovered his composure, and, like
Richard II. in the riots, became the people's leader; the
other could never even reconcile himself to the new system
or recover his political equanimity.

What was the veil which obscured Mr. Croker's vision,
and which prevented him from imitating Sir Robert Peel's
example in 1833? It was, we believe, that inherent dis-

trust of the people which has so often marred the fortunes of
the Tory party. The world which Mr. Croker saw and for
which he lived was the world to which Byron refers:—

> ‘ The twice two thousand people bred
> By no means to be very wise or witty.’

For the great mass of mankind he had not a generous
thought. They were hardly dreamed of in his philosophy.

With Sir Robert Peel the case was wholly different. He
habitually thought of the country, not of a class; and his
measures were uniformly directed to promote the national
good instead of the personal advantage of his acquaintances.
With Mr. Croker rank was regarded with a reverence which
was absurd.

‘ I dined on Saturday,’ he wrote to Lord Hertford in 1832, ‘at the
Duchess of Kent’s, with a large Conservative party—four dukes and
three duchesses, and the rest of thirty people in proportion. I was the
only untitled and almost the only undecorated guest.’ (Vol. ii. p. 176.)

If it were possible for Mr. Croker to forget his fears in
1832, we have no doubt that ‘ ce monsieur bien distingué ’
passed a very pleasant evening. Sir Robert Peel, on the
contrary, regarded rank almost with disfavour.

‘ I indulge myself in the satisfaction of answering a letter which not
only does not apply for a baronetage or a peerage, but absolutely
dissuades from the creation. The voracity for these things quite surprises me. I wonder people do not begin to feel the distinction of an
unadorned name.’ (Vol. ii. p. 410.)

Little traits of this kind reveal men’s real opinions more
accurately than more formal documents. The man who
regarded dukes and duchesses as a necessary element in a
good Conservative party was not likely to approve the extinction of the borough-owners. The man who lived and died
proud ‘ of an unadorned name ’ was certain to reconcile himself to the enfranchisement of the middle classes.

It can hardly be necessary to point out how false were
Mr. Croker’s predictions, and how right was Sir Robert
Peel’s policy. At the close of an article already too long
we cannot enter at any length into a new enquiry. Those
people, indeed, who have studied most closely the history of
the nineteenth century will not search for its chief events
in the Parliamentary history, or for its chief heroes in the
rolls of its statesmen. The inventors, the authors, and
the engineers have been the true benefactors of the age;
and their works may endure when the contents of the
Statute-book are forgotten. But, at the same time, there

are two great political achievements in the present century which stand out among all the rest. One of them was the first Reform Act, the second of them the repeal of the Corn Laws. The former gave to politics the impulse which the invention of the steam-engine gave to trade. The latter, by cheapening a nation's food, increased the comfort and multiplied the power of the people. To both Mr. Croker was opposed; and his opposition to both rested on the same mistaken views. He fancied that the Reform Act precipitated revolution. It is much more true to say that the Reform Act averted it. He imagined that free trade in corn would destroy the power of the aristocracy; and the aristocracy have never been so strong as during the last thirty-eight years. An aristocracy that is sustained by taxing the people's food may be swept away by a revolution. An aristocracy whose property depends on the same laws as the property of other people finds its position strengthened by every addition to the savings of the nation.

A few men, indeed, in our own time still talk of the virtues of Protection, and when bad years come, as they have always come at intervals, ascribe their advent to the existence of Free-trade. We presume that Mr. Jennings is one of those who are deluded by the specious name, Fair-trade. We sometimes doubt whether such men have ever thought out the consequences of their own arguments. Do they realise that, in 1882, the people of this country paid to foreign nations upwards of 63,000,000l. for grain and flour alone? Have they reflected on the many millions which would be added to this sum if the smallest possible protective tax were placed on foreign corn? Are they prepared, for the sake of securing a doubtful advantage to a few hundreds of landowners, to place this heavy tax on the people? Have they reflected that the burden of such a tax would be greater than the rental of all the land under wheat in the United Kingdom?

For Reform the British people are indebted to Lord Grey. They owe the boon of cheap food to Mr. Cobden and Sir Robert Peel. It was the mission of the old Tories, with whom Mr. Croker lived, to resist both these measures. In consequence of Reform Mr. Croker sacrificed his political career. In consequence of free trade in corn he sacrificed his chief friend. Whatever merit may be due to a man who lives and dies obstinately fighting for a wrong cause was his. We can give him neither as a man of letters nor as a man of affairs other praise.

ART. II.—1. *Forum Romanum, Via Sacra, and Aqueducts.* By JOHN HENRY PARKER, C.B., &c. Oxford and London: 1876–1883.

2. *Letters from Rome.* By RODOLFO LANCIANI. Athenæum, 1882-4.

3. *Rom und die Campagna.* Von Dr. TH. GSELL-FELS. Leipzig: 1883.

4. *Papers on Roman Topography in the Cambridge Journal of Philology, contributed by Rev. R. BURN, M.A., Trin. Coll., Cambridge.*

5. *Early and Imperial Rome ; or, Promenade Lectures on the Archæology of Rome.* By HODDER M. WESTROPP. London: 1883.

SINCE the establishment of the Constitutional Monarchy in Italy, a double problem has been working itself out —how to make Rome a modern capital, healthy, clean, and habitable, and how to preserve the margin of recovered ruins, and spread for the antiquary (that epicure of decay) his due table of the broken victuals of the past. Rome has been held in a double grasp of 'dead hands' for centuries. There was the dead hand of the Roman Pontiffs, and behind it the dead hand of time. The Rome of the Papacy has been disentangling itself from the modern and from the ancient city. The great barracks of monkery and the faded *palazzi*, with their shadowy sarcophagous courtyards and precincts, where gloom and uncleanliness strove for mastery, are rapidly vanishing from most quarters of the city. Modern taste and every-day needs have swept a large area into that straggling *rus in urbe* patched by tracts of arid desolation, the vineyard trailing over leprous-looking rubbish, the ilex nodding on the mouldered gatehouse, the scraggy tufts of plane and cypress clothing scantily the ruin-mounds of ages, and squalid cottages or deserted limekilns clustering fungus-like on the grey villa's walls. Through these the ædile of to-day breaks his way with plummet and trowel, and the faded remnants of shabby grandeur recede as he invades. Here and there, the pioneer of utilitarianism un-earths crumbled mosaics, scraps of painted wall-surface, decayed frescoes, fragmentary and chaotic glimpses of the golden age of empire. They peep from the chasm for a moment, catch the sunshine once again, and then return to earth and resume their thousand years of slumber. Yet surprises and discoveries come thick and fast; and, sifted from this refuse, the stock of monumental trophies which adorns the Capitoline Museum is said to have more than doubled in less than ten years. A policy of artistic reconstruction of the known haunts of classic interest wherever possible, and of careful preservation of fragments where impossible, has for some years prevailed; and the result is that the eye of the well-read *conoscente* may reclothe those spots with their ancient scenery, trace again the pavement of the Via Sacra, and reconstruct in imagination the temples and public offices which echoed the footsteps of Horace.

Rome, almost to the very year when the Gothic warshout shook her gates, went on being built and rebuilt; new piles were still added, old ones cleared away, sites thrown open or planted, then the avenues uprooted, and new designs displaced the old. Not so much the lavish prodigality of erection as the brief duration of the sumptuous result is the chief feature which impresses us in the monumental history of Rome. It was as though not only the reckless passions of a voluptuary were clothing themselves in the forms of architecture, but as though he could not enjoy unless he previously effaced, and took vengeance on his predecessor for having been first on the ground, with the certainty that the same retaliation would overtake himself. The reason was that the world was wide, and Rome after all was small. The wealth of plundered provinces lay in the despot's lap, to be squandered chiefly in that narrow area. Hence the fierce architectural emulation between Cæsar and Cæsar, and demolition as the condition of construction. Of this Augustus himself set the first example, rebuilding of marble the portico of Metellus, and naming it after his own wife and sister. This rivalry, however, was consistent with a widely different spirit animating the works which they reared. Some built as despots for purely selfish aggrandisement, some as epicures of art for lavish display, some as the foremost of public servants for munificent usefulness. But all found it politic to keep the lower orders employed, to break down the higher by the example of lavish expenditure, and beyond all to keep all orders alike amused. Thus the theatre and the circus, with the costly shows to which they were devoted, and on which neither blood nor money was spared, became a foremost care of state alongside of basilica and temple, palace and villa. More wild beasts

from further deserts, more barbarian gladiators from yet
remoter forests, all the fantastic savagery which the out-
posts of the empire yielded to contrast more effectively
with the sybaritic polish of the capital and the effeminate
ferocity of its demoralised masses, were a constant item in the
revenue of the Cæsars, and enabled the Roman populace to
live in a sense of perpetual triumph over the vanquished
world.

The gluttonous bloodthirstiness and the tawdry puerility
of the most popular exhibitions stamp the end achieved
with our abhorrence and contempt, while the physically
stupendous character of the means challenges our astonishment.   But the genius which wields at will the inert
weights of mass and wings them with a grand idea was
wanting, save in the periods of Augustus and Trajan.   The
lavish outlay of material, the servile splendour of extravagance, the fulsome repetition of pile added to pile, like
link to link of a chain or step to step of a ladder, they could
and did command ; and for this they embezzled the wealth of
East and West and turned on Rome the streams of provincial
taxation, including the blood-tax for the trained swordsmen
of the circus, like the converging aqueducts which sluiced
the Anio into the tunnels of the Campagna, to fill her baths
and flood her fountains.   Piled by mutual effacement thus
on one another's ruins, the successive stages of the Rome
of the Cæsars, ever changing its types and unfinished at the
last, and even to some extent the earlier republican city,
may now be studied somewhat as Dr. Schliemann studied
his six or seven historic or prehistoric cities on Hissarlik.
The spirit of research is awake among the successive deposits of wreck which choke the valleys of the famous Seven
Hills, and contemplates enclosing, in a single archæological *chef-d'œuvre*, the Forum, Via Sacra, Colosseum, the
Cæsars' Palace, Circus Maximus, and in part the Velabrum.
Rome is, or was till lately, silted up in her own ruin
wrought by her own sons ; and this domestic havoc furnishes
probably the larger portion of the 3,500,000 cubic mètres of
rubbish which the enthusiastic Signor Baccelli has removed
or is bent on removing.   There mingle, in kindred dust,
Jupiter Stator and Feretrius and Victor and Tonans, Venus
Victrix and Genetrix and Cloacina, Mars Ultor, Juno Moneta
and Sospita, Janus Bifrons and Quadrifrons, together with a
long list more.

But the period when demolition was most active was
that of the revival of letters and arts.   Previous destroyers

had assailed the surface only. The Cinquecentists hunted patiently below the stratum of wreckage and dug in order to spoil. Thus we are assured that

'in August 1546, the temple of Julius Cæsar was discovered in such a striking state of preservation that the marble slabs containing the *fasti consulares et triumphales* were still attached to the basement of the temple. In 1540 the beautiful flight of steps leading to Faustina's temple from the Sacra Via was still in perfect order, and so were the steps and the basement of the Aedes Castoris. Sallustio Peruzzi, son of Baldassare, could design the minutest details of the round shrine of Vesta, discovered for the second time in 1549. The shrine of Vertumnus, at the corner of the Vicus Tuscus * and the Nova Via, was likewise intact when discovered in the same year, 1549. And what remains now of this admirable set of monuments? Nothing except the rubble-work nucleus of their foundations and platforms. Pirro Ligorio, an eye-witness, asserts that as soon as a piece of marble was found, no matter how interesting and precious, it was sold on the spot, "come si "vendono i buoi a' macellarj," and either burnt into lime or cut into new shapes.'

Thus the descendants of the degenerate nobles who had made Rome a den of thieves in the earlier ages slightly modified their traditions, and, instead of levying black-mail on the present generation, plundered the past, looted their own Forum as eagerly as they would have sacked a Tuscan town, and gutted the very rubbish-heaps, which lay 'full 'fathom five' over Via Sacra and Palatine, till they reduced their city to that desert of ruin which the older parts of it have presented ever since.

. ' Suis et ipsa Roma viribus ruit.'

Profiting, however, by the spirit of zealous research and faithful conservation which have been guided and chronicled by Signori Baccelli and Lanciani, although sorely impeded by the extortionate prices demanded by private owners and the harpy-like propensities of the workmen whom they employ, we may now review the scene which of all others is supreme in interest, and endeavour to reconstruct descriptively the aspect of the Forum as it stood when Cicero declaimed from its Rostra, and before the great displacements made by Julius Cæsar to obtain an area for his famous basilica, greatly enlarged afterwards by Augustus. We will suppose the standpoint to be at the Lacus Curtius in the Forum,† a small depression within a railing, where

---

* This seems to be an error: it should be the Vicus Iugarius.
† The site is a little higher up the Forum, i.e. nearer the Capitol,

grew a solitary fig-tree, a seedling of the famous 'Ruminal' of the Comitium within sight. The railed-in space contained an altar without temple or other building, until, in a show of gladiators given by Cæsar in the Forum itself (and down to that period such exhibitions were common there), the altar was removed. It should be noticed that the ground-plan of the Forum is a longish wedge with the apex cut off, the long and short ends being about fifty and twenty yards respectively in length, while the sides of the wedge are each about two hundred.

Before, however, we dwell upon objects in detail, it may be well to notice the pavement of the area itself. Mr. Nichol says :—

'The surface of the open Forum, as we now find it, is paved where it was intended for the use of carriages, with large polygonal blocks of hard grey volcanic stone, called *silex* * by the ancient and *selce* by the modern Romans; and, where it is intended for foot passengers only, with rectangular slabs of travertine. The date of the first paving of the Forum is not preserved. The paving of the Clivus Capitolinus with *silex*, B.C. 174, is mentioned by Livy.'

The four angles of our truncated wedge nearly face the cardinal points. Turning, then, from the Lacus Curtius towards the northern angle, we should look straight at the Comitium, which lay in the extension of that angle, across the Duilian Column with its projecting galley-beak ornaments in triple tier, with the raised terrace of the Græcostasis † backed no doubt by a sheltering portico, open to the left of that column, while a little to the right of the same column, previous to the year 44 B.C., rose the platform of the Rostra in a position to command an audience at once in the Comitium to which it properly belonged and in the Forum; and immediately behind the Rostra rose the steps of the portico of the Curia Hostilia, down which in the early legend King Servius Tullius was hurled by his assassins. On these steps the statue of Attus Navius the Augur, the

---

than the ruined pedestal, supposed to be that of an equestrian statue of Domitian, familiar to all visitors.

  * Silex continued to be the favourite material for pavement to a much later period; or probably the word may have become conventional for pavement, whatever the precise materials, as *selce* among the Italians now. See Juv. Sat. iii. 272 and vi. 350. It may be safely assumed that when the Clivus Capitolinus was ordered to be paved, the Forum was already paved.

  † The waiting-place for embassies while attending the Senate, so called as first used by Greek convoys from Marseilles.

Merlin of Roman story, probably diminutive, would be visible, with an adjacent 'puteal,' under which his whetstone and razor were believed to be buried. All the principal buildings on the north-western or broader end of the Forum would present their angles obliquely to the eye. Thus to the left or west of the Græcostasis the eye would catch the façade of the Temple of Concord (a probably much less pretentious pile than that of which the ruin with marble pavement still crowns the Forum's upper end) with the Basilica Opimia emerging behind it, and a down-flight of steps towards the head of the Forum in front. The cella of this temple saw a crowded senate in its most famous period uneasy amidst the swords of M. Antonius. Here the first and third of his 'Philippics' were delivered by Cicero, this latter being perhaps repeated to the public from the very steps above named, as was also the third Catilinarian. Beyond the furthest projection of this temple we should glimpse the redoubted Tullianum or Well-house prison, and its infamous Gemonian Stairs rising against the Capitoline steep, but partly hidden by the sheltering portico of the Græcostasis. Over this latter area, slightly terraced above the Comitium, would rise the tall shaft of the Mænian Column, a sort of huge gnomon to which the Forum served as sundial, which, by its eastward shadow, as the sun declined towards the Tullianum, marked the 'hora suprema' proclaimed thereupon by the Prætor's official as closing the legal day. Between us and all these would stand the platform of the Rostra, of which we will further speak anon, between which and the Græcostasis, seen left and right respectively from the Curia Hostilia, the same officer noted the sun above their narrow interval, and straightway 'made ' it twelve o'clock, for all business purposes. But all these details are effaced by the Arch of Septimius Severus, which intrudes now its monopolising mass on every eye in this part of Rome.

Above the Græcostasis the Basilica Portia, built by Cato the Censor, probably in a severe and solid style, would form a more imposing mass than any building yet mentioned. Over the Basilica Opimia the ground crowded its sloping testudo of mutually overtopping roofs, upwards to the Temple of Juno Moneta and the Arx itself on the Capitoline, prominent on which would stand out the platform of augury, whence the State-magi of Rome, whose lore just now was depreciated, were believed to gather her future destinies by flight of fowl or other equally trustworthy signs. From the same Curtian centre next let the radius of view point due north-west; it traverses the line which bisects the Comitium, runs parallel to the south-western flank of the Temple of Concord, and impinges on the front of the Tabularium, standing one step above the level of that temple, even as this last above the Forum itself. The eye, in fact, ranges along the lower slope of the Capitoline, to which all the buildings lately named owe somewhat of their vantage, but are yet from their constant use and associations reckoned as members of the Forum. Where the several terraces and connecting steps of these different platforms began and ended is a question still open to excavation.

That ancient pile of time-blackened tufa in the (supposing it afternoon) shadowy corner to the left, stilted on a disproportionately tall base, is the venerable Temple of Saturn. The antiquarians of the republic could never quite agree how old it really was. Its elevation at once accommodates the sudden upthrow of the ground behind, and gives basement room for the ancient treasury of Rome in its vault below. It would present its eastern angle to the eye, showing on each containing side a rather crazy row of Tuscan columns with lumpy capitals, and no spark of Greek grace about it anywhere. But we must enlarge our angle to the left to get it into view. The remains now extant are those of the Septimian restoration, and between them and the picturesque bit of ugliness which we are reproducing there came another rebuilding by Munatius Plancus * in Augustus' time. The treasury crypts beneath are those which Cæsar plundered. Overtopping it in the rear the Tabularium impends with the Capitol at its back, the oldest record office in the world, carrying us back to the time of Sulla. Just above and behind Saturn the Capitoline ascent makes a sudden elbow to the left, doubling round the low and meagre portico of the Divi Consentes, with a statue of one of them in each of its openings, which, however, only give access to certain clerks' offices probably connected with the Tabularium on their flank. From the nearer angle of Saturn there runs a covered way, taking on its course the Senaculum or Senators' waiting-room, between the Comitium (front) and Concord (rear), and joining the angle of the Curia Hostilia, soon now to be pulled down by the Cæsarian party and rebuilt as the Curia Julia. We lose the traditional *locus asyli* behind the high square

---

* To him Horace addressed Ode I. vii., extolling the rural scenery about Tibur above the greatest civic and historic sites of Greece.

front of the Tabularium, which shrouds all but the two platform-brows of the Capitoline hill, and the asylum lies in the depression between them. That Capitoline, with its Tarpeian extremity in the south-west, forms the limit of the view towards the head of the Forum. Where its rise is steepest, the 'Hundred Stairs' catch a few of the westering sunbeams on some of their edges. The highest object of all crowning the plateau of the Capitol is the colossal statue of Jupiter Optimus Maximus, converted since its untoward salutation by lightning (*sua tela Tonanti!*) to face due east and look down upon the monuments of the Constitution about the Forum's head. If we continue enlarging the angle of vision somewhat to the south of west, we see over our left shoulder the Vicus Iugarius* opening into the Forum, and beyond its mouth the Temple of Ops, smaller than that of Saturn and hardly less antique, crouching as it were under his conjugal wing. Looking up the street as far as eye will travel, we see in the open the statue of Vertumnus,† marking the point where the god was believed to have stayed and turned the risen Tiber, foaming along the street in a flood which threatened the Forum itself. What meets the eye as still from the Lacus Curtius we face entirely round and reverse our frontage? The stately Basilica Julia at the period of which we were writing as yet was not. What occupies its area? Our converse view lights upon the close abutting fronts of the *veteres tabernæ*, rich with the memories of Virginius and the Decemvirs, and of the most beautiful of the 'Lays of Ancient Rome' which the genius of Macaulay has consecrated. A much smaller Basilica known as the Sempronia, of modest pretensions, with no vast marbled spaces, fronts the Forum immediately behind this line of open shop-fronts, for they are hardly more, and between it and the angle of the Tuscus Vicus the space is probably occupied by shops and private buildings.

No passage of history is so rich in massacres as the last age of the republic, no spot so deeply steeped in human butcheries as the Forum. It is as if all the scattered lightning of the proscription lists, wherever they might strike, converged hither at last. Thus the Lacus Servilius, near

---

* It nearly follows the line of the modern Via della Consolazione, which leads from the church of S. Nicola in Carcere to the column of Phocas.

† A marble plinth, supposed to be that of this statue, was exhumed near the spot indicated in the text in 1543 A.D.

the corner of the Tuscus Vicus just mentioned, became the morgue (*spoliarium*) of the victims of Sulla. They might be hunted down over an ever-widening field of opportunity, pounced upon in their villas, stabbed in their travelling carriages, seized in any hovel mean enough to escape notice, dragged from any shrine which might inspire the hope of sanctuary. Rome saw her consul struck down in his curule chair, her flamen of Jupiter sacrificed, the foremost of her orators pleading for his life in vain, the most venerable of her jurists bled to death in the most inviolable of her temples. But to the Forum, and mostly to its Rostra, in bitter irony of the weakness of persuasion against brute force, their heads were brought, if they were of sufficient importance to be deemed worthy so to adorn it. Mediæval vengeance stuck such trophies of a *coup d'état* on the gates. Roman policy deemed them most effective in the very central shrine of the city's life. The ghastly rites of political murder were incomplete unless consummated there. Cicero represents the blood-pools of a single riot as soaked up in sponges from the pavement, the Forum as piled with corpses, and the Cloaca choking with them. Allow what margin we please for the freedom of rhetorical description, there remains a fact sufficiently horrible to need no exaggeration. Meanwhile, in the intervals of respite, until the great theatre-building age of the early Cæsars gave them separate arenas, the Forum was the constant scene of gladiatorial exhibitions; and thus hecatombs of the meanest lives alternated there with those of the noblest. There is a curious anecdote of Mænius, whose house was purchased by Cato and Flaccus, the Censors, to make room for the Basilica Portia, that he reserved for himself the right of setting up a balcony over one column of the new structure, as a private-box from which he and his posterity might enjoy the gladiatorial spectacles in the Forum.* Thus it becomes the Aceldama of history.

If now from the Lacus Curtius we look right across the Forum to the north-west, the ' new shops,' somewhat similar and corresponding to the ' old ' ones, now at our back, meet

---

* Mr. Nichol, 'The Roman Forum,' p. 218, doubts the historical character of this anecdote, and treats it as a confusion arising probably from the Columna Mænia hard by and the 'Mæniana,' or galleries erected over the Tabernæ of the Forum; but it seems confirmed by Livy's statement, xxxix. 44 (which he himself cites), that an *Atrium Mænium* was actually purchased for the purpose named.

the eye. These are a continuous row of little dens behind fronts which are nearly all open, and each about ten feet square. All in both rows, but especially the 'new,' have more or less to do with the money market. Beyond these runs along the Forum's furthest edge the wall of the great Basilica, which shall be presently described. But in the margin between them are three curious fabrics: one, near where the arch of Septimius Severus afterwards rose, is unique in size, form, and material. It is a small, square bronze chapel, with bivalve doors, holding only the statue of its god Janus, famous omen of peace or war.* This venerable but stunted structure, like that dedicated to Saturn, a relic of the olden times, may be compared *qua* material to the shrine of Athenê Chalciæcus at Sparta.† The other two are detached archways, with probably chambers at the side and 'attics' over them, like our own Temple Bar of recent memory, and having each its image of the double-faced god. The more prominent of the two, the 'Medius Ianus,' would certainly have such appendages, forming as it did a money-lenders' den. Here sesterces clinked and parchments rustled, and here on any day of the month, always excepting the ka-lends—those *tristes kalendæ* which were the settling day—the sanguine speculator, or the needy spendthrift, or the young man of great expectations, might be seen founding slippery fortunes on borrowed capital, or discounting the hopes of a legacy. The last of these three is the 'Ianus imus,' of similar use but less notoriety than the 'medius.' This Janus monument (or series of monuments) has a topographical interest closely connected with its mythology and symbolism. It seems to mark the most important actual gate of an early civic area. With it corresponds its obverse diminutive, the 'Ianiculum,' on the further or river face of the city. This civic area was that of Rome before the trio of northern hills,

---

* It is believed to have continued down to the twelfth century. See 'Edinburgh Review,' October 1863, p. 360. This temple of Janus and the statue of Vertumnus (see above, p. 45) included between them the entire head of the Forum, the quintessence therefore of Roman publicity. Thus we see the force of Horace's playful remon-strance to his book on the eve of publication, 'Vertumnum Ianumque, 'liber, spectare videris,' Ep. I. xx. 1. The Janus, moreover, stood 'ad 'infimum Argiletum,' Liv. i. 19, where were, in Domitian's time and probably earlier, the booksellers' chief haunts, the 'Paternoster Row,' in fact, of Rome; albeit, beset also by cobblers' stalls, cf. 'Argique 'letum multus obsidet sutor,' Martial I. ii. 17; cf. iii. 1 *et al.*

† Cf. Thucyd. i. 134; Pausan. III. xvii. 2.

Quirinal, Esquiline, and Viminal, were included with the
southern group of four.   It was natural that the young city
of the Palatine and Capitoline should put forth its growth
first towards its river frontage and bring its shoulders, as it
were, up to the Tiber, thereby at once gaining a frontier of
defence and ensuring a water-way to the sea.   Taking those
older four hills as its earlier constituents, the need of a
nearly level space for meetings, markets, &c., would speedily
be felt, and would be met by immuring the Forum and the
Comitium.   This is, in fact, the growth as described by Livy.
The addition of the three northern summits is referred by
him to the large extension under the later kings.   The Servian agger and the Servian constitution of the civic fighting
force in centuries—the defences thus matching the citizens
who were to defend them—thus form one extension of power
and territory with that last-named addition.   But before
that addition was made which pushed forward the boundary,
this latter had already taken in the Comitium and the
Forum, and for perhaps a considerable interval rested there.
But that boundary must of course have had a wall, and that
wall a gate.   Thus Varro (De L. L. v. 34) mentions a 'Ianu-
'alis porta dicta a Iano, et ideo ibi positum Iani signum.'
And the gate on this front would be the principal gate leading, whether for war or peace, directly to the old Ager
Romanus, and communicating with the Latins, Sabines, and
other kindred tribes.   This is a reasonable account of the
apparent paradox of the gate, with its tutelar and his
shrine, being found near the middle of what, in the more
extended sense, was the civic area of Rome.   The 'medius'
and 'imus Ianus' may have been mere sallyports or secon-
daries in the boundary line.   But this gate was *the* Janus of
Rome, and its position explains its importance.   The Temple
of Janus and the archway adjoining thus represent the old
gatehouse and gate exactly on the further side of the Forum
where the line of needful defence, before the northern trio of
hills was included, ran along the valley lying at the north-
eastern foot of the Palatine.   Varro, *ubi supra* ,ascribes the
Janus erection to King Numa, on whom were fathered all
archaic details involving ritual; and in another passage a
little later connects the formal declaration, 'fari,' of the
boundary line with the erection of a temple, 'fanum,' to
mark it.   The etymological speculation need not trouble us,
but the fact of the two being connected may be accepted, and
the old shrine of Janus on the boundary and outlet of the
city taken as an instance of it.

Along the same margin of the Forum there are various pillars within sight, each with the well-known circular stall of the bookseller and his *capsæ*, containing the scrolls of popular authors, as Varro, Catullus, and Cicero himself. The rioters, who made the Curia their literal *chapelle ardente* over the body of their favourite Clodius when murdered by Milo, mobbed these stalls first and made their tinder out of the books. The highest Ianus, the actual temple, stood, as we have seen, at the head of the Forum; and the three seem to have been wholly detached from each other, and measure probably the whole space so named.* In the forenoon, Novius and Cicuta, with their slave-clerks, probably Greeks, about them, and other worthies of the same calling, would be seen sitting at the 'medius Ianus' like spiders in the coil of their web, to pounce upon their customers. If we time our imaginary outlook from the Curtius in the summer of 54 B.C., the scene beyond the Forum's edge will be thronged by a corps of builders with cranes, ladders, &c., reconstructing the finest Basilica of all those which narrow the sky above the Forum, that known as the Æmilia, or rather converting it into the newer Basilica Paulli. We will suppose it completed, as it stood ready for dedication, by another of the same great Æmilian house, with tall taper columns of Phrygian marble,

---

* It is controverted whether 'Ianus summus, medius, imus,' mean three distinct buildings, or, as Bentley has supposed (ad Hor. Ep. i. i. 54), a single street running the length of the Forum, and merely distinguished in respect of its two extremes and midpoint. From the circumstances that the Ianus Quadrifrons in the Forum Boarium consists of four arches built in the sides of a square; that the business of the money market, involving operations of weighing or counting, signing and sealing, and requiring secure repositories for the floating cash balances in case of a tumult, must needs require some adjuncts of buildings for these purposes; that the phrase '*ad* medium Ianum,' used by Cicero and Horace, is more suggestive of a building, even if only an isolated arch, than of that undefined area the middle of a street called the Ianus, which would rather be '*in* medio Iano,' also that this was the sunny side of the Forum, raked by the south-eastern sun during all the forenoon hours of business, the shadows of the *novæ tabernæ* being wholly insignificant; and that to think of men transacting the most lucrative business of the period in that unsheltered condition seems absurd; the older view impugned by Bentley and Mr. Nichol, but maintained by Becker and Mr. Burn, seems the most reasonable. The last-named writer mentions (p. 105) the foundation of an arch recorded by Labacco, as found in this part of the Forum, with a reference to Canina, 'Indicazione' (p. 245). It may have been the 'Ianus 'medius.'

its vast window spaces which span the entire intercolumnar breadths giving it an air of noble and stately lightness, in effect something like that of the Chapel of King's College, Cambridge; although the details and even the structural members wholly differ. It bears, for instance, medallion-shields each embossed with an Æmilian worthy's portrait. Its columns are Tuscan of the elongated type; the roof is gabled, and has a fancy pattern of bold device wrought in the tiles. If the day is warm, an awning, carried on ropes from the fronts of opposite basilicas with stout masts to assist in their intervals, will exclude the glare, but stunt the view down to the ground-floor masonry on either side. The patriotic statuary with which the Forum is crowded fall likewise into the shade. Heroes of the past, or even present, in bronze or marble, the more antique of a mannikin size, so throng the space all round the edges, that we are reminded of the head-borne board of a modern Italian image-vendor. Conspicuous among the collection is Venus Cloacina, with her fence of *cancelli* and subsidiary statues, at the Forum's head. A few paces in front of it is the famous Marsyas, with arm erected or nearly so, and head averted from the Janus on his left. But we miss him who once stood

> ' in the Comitium,
> Plain for all folk to see,
> Horatius in his harness,
> Halting upon one knee.'

Not far from him was his contemporary King Porsena, and Hermodorus of Ephesus, by whose aid the laws of the famous Twelve Tables were compiled; but those of other Greek worthies, Pythagoras and Alcibiades, were swept away by Sulla. The missing Horatius suffered by lightning, and was removed to a lower site by the direction, it was said, of Etruscan Augurs jealous of his fame. Their treachery, however, was discovered, and the statue again transferred to a higher but less central spot, to wit the Vulcanal; 'which arrangement ' turned out,' says Aulus Gellius, who narrates it, ' very much ' to the welfare of the republic.' Cicero remembered another group of diminutive heroes, the ambassadors whom the Fidenates put to death. Other twain killed by Queen Teuta the Illyrian,[*] C. Octavius similarly slain at Laodicea by Antiochus, and later still Servius Sulpicius the jurist, envoy

---

[*] According to the best authorities one only was actually put to death; see Polyb. ii. 8, and 'Dictionary of G. and R. Biography, &c.,' s. v. Teuta.

of the senate to M. Antonius in the last great civil war, who died on his errand, received the same honour. Camillus and his contemporary C. Mænius the dictator, Sulla (equestrian and gilded), Pompey 'the Great,' and later his great rival Julius, and his nephew the young Octavianus (also equestrian), swelled the throng of noble imagery. The Forum was becoming a mere Valhalla, where the dead crowded out the living, and could no longer hold the increasing collection. The *triumviri capitales*, whose tribunal was at the Mænian Column, the Prætor himself, who held court (both of them *sub Jove*) at the lower end of the Forum, were elbowed out of their chairs by the bronze and marble, and at last a sweep was made by authority of all save those erected by express decree of S.P.Q.R.

Those last-named tribunals were moveable and wooden through the whole republican period. The arrangements of the vice-chancellor's court in the lobby of the Convocation House at Oxford, with the raised magisterial seat and the *subsellia* for proctors, witnesses &c. below, save that the classic originals were unenclosed by walls, and accessible, therefore, by steps from behind, may give one a suggestion of what these latter were like. Besides their normal use, they served in political exigencies to express public opinion in an emphatic way; as when the mob-leading tribune Vatinius made a bridge of them by which to storm the platform of the Rostra, and seize the person of an obnoxious consul; or when the mob, without special leader, built of them, being doubtless seasoned timber, the funeral pyre of Clodius, and involved the Curia itself in the holocaust, or repeated in the same form their tribute to the memory of Julius Cæsar. As the successive great basilicas arose which were the glory of Roman architecture, and have bequeathed with the genius of Roman law their shell-model to the Christian Church, these tribunals were removed into their ample spaces, and no doubt when our Westminster Hall first received the Courts of Exchequer, King's Bench, and Common Pleas, the three all shared the same individual floor in a way not dissimilar to the Roman tribunals on the broad area of the basilica of Constantine.

Another antique group near where the Via Sacra led out of the Forum south-eastward was that of the Three Sibyls, called also the Three Fates.* They were the oldest of the

---

* The church of S. Adriano and that of SS. Cosmas and Damian are said by mediæval topographers to have stood 'in the Three Fates,'

bronze statuary of Rome, and seem to have stood near the edge of the Forum. Their name, when those of Forum and Via Sacra were lost, lingers late in Roman topography as a landmark. Probably some reminiscence of them, wafted over western seas, suggested the character and number of the witches in 'Macbeth,' whose entire connexion with the plot lies in unfolding glimpses of the future. At the extremity of the Forum, looking still across it, but down its narrowing length, as its truncate wedge tapers to the minimum width of sixty feet, the Arch of Fabius spanned the roadway, built from the spoils of the Allobroges, 121 B.C., and decorated with statues or medallions of the various Fabii who had won honour for Rome. Cicero speaks of ' descending from the Via Sacra,'* which commenced immediately beyond it 'into the Forum,' through it, and Horace must have passed and repassed it in his daily saunterings. If we now look over our right shoulder from the Curtius, we see in the south-east nearer corner the Regia,† at the time of our supposed survey the official residence of the Pontifex Maximus, with a small chapel behind it, in which were kept the sacred spears of Mars. It is believed to have been repeatedly burnt down; first, in the all-effacing Gallic conflagration, again in 210 B.C., and lastly, after being given up by Augustus, when he became chief Pontiff, to the use of the Vestals, in the great Neronian fire, 65 A.D., after which it was rebuilt no more. A few years, however, later than the time of our imaginary visit, a new pile blocked the view of its front from the standpoint supposed. On that site the first temple was raised in Rome to a deified man, ' Divus ' Julius,' the great dictator. This small but elegant monument, the subject of several poetic allusions, stood terraced on a lofty artificial platform, sixty feet long and half that depth, with ascending stair-flights on the sides, including in its massive plinth a semicircular space, believed to mark the spot where Cæsar's body was burnt, and ornamented with the beaks of the Antonian galleys taken at Actium. It was thus converted into a new Rostra. Its flank, seen in per-

---

meaning the portion of the area on the edge of the Forum which adjoined them.

* De Orat. ii. 66.

† Also called Atrium Vestæ. Horace's ' Ventum erat ad Vestæ,' Sat. 1. ix. 35, probably refers to it, as it fronted the Via Sacra, named in line 1, not to the *temple* of Vesta. The site of this Atrium is *not* that of the later ' House of the Vestals,' also called ' Atrium Vestæ : ' see the later part of this article.

spective, was a grove of thickly planted columns, in what Vitruvius calls the Pycnostyle fashion.

Hard by the Arch of Fabius, and near the front of the Regia, was a well-known landmark of the Forum, the ' Puteal of Libo,' a small erection in the form of a well-mouth, the conventional mode of covering a spot which, having been struck by lightning, was deemed *infaustum* or ' uncanny,' and which, though thus covered, might not be closed. Here was another haunt of the money market,* how differing from that of ' Ianus Medius ' we are not informed. In the adjacent area stood also a tribunal for legal business, perhaps that of the Prætor himself, although sadly disproportioned in space to the weight of business transacted there.

But the largest temple in the lower part of the Forum was that of Castor, built on a line with the Sempronian Basilica at our back, and separated from it by the width of the Tuscus Vicus of unwholesome fame, so that we must turn half face to the right to see it. It cherished the fond memory of the legend connecting its erection with the visit of the Divine Twins to the Forum, when, after watering their horses at the Fons or Lacus Iuturnæ, which stood at its eastern angle, they announced the victory of the Lake Regillus. It stood, like the Temple of Cæsar, on a high raised block of large area, outflanking the temple itself by a wide margin. From this massive table rose a colonnade with seven columns in front, and, reckoning the angle-column twice, seven on each flank, while an inside column at either end of the frontlet portico gave it further strength and beauty. To the Forum its wide stairs descended, and from their summit, thus preferred to the Rostra, various declamatory campaigns in the Forum were carried on by Cato, Cæsar, Octavianus, and others, often with a wild mixture of mob-law and violence. Earlier than any of these, the consuls, of whom Sulla was then one, were attacked while haranguing the populace from the same steps by a tribune

---

* 'Puteali et feneratorum gregibus inflatus atque perculsus'—Cic. pro Sextio, 8. ' Ante secundam Roscius orabat sibi adesses ad Puteal cras ' —Hor. Sat. ii. vi. 34 ; compare i. ix. 35 foll., ' Ventum erat ad Vestæ, quarta jam parte diei Præterita ; et casu tum respondere vadato Debebat ; quod ni fecisset, perdere litem.' Here ' ad Vestæ ' being the ' Atrium Vestæ,' or ' Regia,' the site has clearly a law court in its immediate neighbourhood. Festus gives the position as before the Atria. Festus, ed. Müller, p. 333 (Note 328), cited by Mr. Nichol.

with the opposition mob in the Marian interest at his heels. The one consul's son perished in the fray, and Sulla only escaped through taking refuge, by a strange irony of fortune, in the then empty house of his rival Marius, as the last place where he was likely to be looked for.   Like other temples— such was the Roman custom—it was repaired and kept up by contract, which gave occasion to the infamous Verres, then Prætor of the city, to swindle the representatives of the contractor—a minor and his guardians—out of over 17,000*l*. by means of a fictitious contract to a creature of his own. Some of the most telling passages in that famous unspoken oration, the Second Verrine, would draw their rhetorical sting from the temple, and its columns in particular, on which the question turned, standing in evidence before the eyes of the supposed hearers.   Its foundations, lately ex-humed, go back to the period of the kings; but the pillars which Cicero meant to have called as witnesses were then only about fifty years old when the whole was rebuilt.   The last rebuilding was in the time of Augustus, to which the extant three columns belong.   The mad emperor Caligula made it a mere vestibule to his own palace close behind at the foot of the Palatine, and would pose in the shrine as third deity to 'The Great Twin Brethren' standing 'bodkin' between their images to receive the adoration of his subjects.

In all these Forum buildings, save the modest rotunda of Vesta, just glimpsed through the majestic peristyle of Castor, the satiety of unbroken horizontal lines and flat surfaces would tend to weary the spectator accustomed to the sometimes heterogeneous but ever lively contrasts of northern or eastern towns.   Milton's descriptive line, attri-buting to even imperial Rome

'Turrets and terraces and glittering spires,'

is false in two out of the three elements which it thus associates.   There would be visible neither dome, minaret, cupola, dormer, nor bell-tower to give a piquant relief to the dull uniformity.   Beyond this, they would certainly suffer from the absence of any law of grouping being observed when each was placed upon the ground.   Its individual design might be a consummate study, but its surroundings were fortuitous.

Nearly contemporaneously with the erection of the noble Basilica Paulli, opposite to our imaginary spectator's eye, the Sempronian Basilica, together with its adjacent buildings at his back, was displaced by the Basilica Iulia.   Of this latter splendid monument the substructures are now revealed, and form the *pièce de résistance* in the rased surface of the Forum. It had, as we know from the Capitoline plan,* a triple row of Tuscan columns, eighteen by eight, and was a rectangle of 400 feet by 160 feet. We know from Pliny that the Centumviral Four Courts were held there, the building affording a large margin for the general public on its floor besides the ample gallery with further accommodation above. The din of business and the applause of sympathetic or interested listeners here went on for centuries where all is blank desolation now. The principles of that jurisprudence which has leavened the codes of all civilised nations formed the first school of their long-lived traditions here, where not one stone is left upon another to suggest the supremacy of law and the cession of arms to the gown.

The famous Rostra of the republic have already been spoken of. They consisted of a platform, probably of some three or four feet high, mounted by steps in the rear, and bristling with the traditional galley-beaks of the Antiates in front—wholly distinct, of course, therefore, from the similarly but more profusely decorated Duilian Column. In the year 44 B.C., the period in which Cæsarian policy changed so largely the face of the Forum, they were removed to a spot just in front of where the temple to Julius Cæsar, as mentioned above, was raised shortly after his death. These latter were called the Julian Rostra,† and, in the time of Constantine, on whose arch they are represented, were large enough to contain that emperor and his retinue in his address to the people from that level. They are fronted by a lattice-work screen, and have a statue at either flank, and a row of statues behind. Mr. Parker, in Plate XX. of his ' Forum,' shows what he claims to be the ruined base or nucleus of the base of the Rostra at the south-east corner of that space. Its ground-plan shows one curvilinear face, the other flat, the former almost touching the Temple of

---

. * A ground-plan of Rome traced on marble in the second century, and (Mr. Parker concludes from various indications) hung on the wall of a temple, now a ruin, at the back of the church of SS. Cosmas and Damian on the highest part of the Via Sacra. Mr. Burn and others suppose it to have been a pavement. If so, it could be only surveyed adequately by walking about on it, which would have tended to efface the lines. It seems to the present writer that Mr. Parker is right.

† Unless, as suggested by Mr. Nichol, this title indicates the lofty platform of Julius Cæsar's Temple itself, beaked, as we have seen, p. 52, with the spoils of Actium.

Julius in the rear of it, the latter being that which faced the audience, on which side a paved area extensive enough to hold it is said to be found. Mr. Nichol (p. 74) would place the site in the open area of the Forum opposite to the middle of the Basilica Iulia. But thus placed, the hearers would not be massed in dense column gradually widening in front, but would be a thin line extending widely right and left to outflank him. This seems fatal to the position; no one conversant with the first exigencies of public oratory would place a speaker at such disadvantage. But it was these later Rostra, wherever placed, that were garnished with the atrocious trophy of Cicero's head and hands.

The Rostra of the later empire are supposed to have reverted to the head of the Forum again, near the Arch of Septimius Severus and the ancient Græcostasis. Canina found reason for thinking that he had discovered their remains in a curved terrace near that arch. But there are no gaps such as the removal of the galley-beaks would have left in the front. The question, however, is void of interest, since, with the extinction of the republic, the whole *raison d'être* of the Rostra vanishes. Imperialism could find a pulpit anywhere.

As regards their form, the representations, none of them of an early date, show that the platform rested on arches, and was protected by a parapet, not unlike the piece of church furniture known as an *ambon*, or ancient desk for reading. One view of them even shows a desk, or something resembling it; but the execution is too rude, and the features too much conventionalised for us, to rely closely upon the details.[*]

Of the buildings above mentioned, the Temple of Vesta and the Regia perished in the Neronian great fire. The former was again destroyed in a conflagration in the reign of Commodus, together with the Temple of Apollo and its libraries on the Palatine, and most of the region (IVth) to which the Via Sacra belonged.

Close to where the southern angle of the Temple of Castor stands back from the Forum, stood the altar of Aius Locutius in the open at the edge of the Nova Via, really one of the oldest streets in Rome, and reminding us of the period when the Via Sacra, to which it found access behind the Atrium

---

[*] The Arch of Constantine has been already referred to. Two denarii are figured in Smith's ' Dictionary of Greek and Roman Antiquities' as bearing rude effigies of the Rostra early and late.

Vestæ, and the Forum itself were newly included in the boundary of the city. On the line of this Nova Via stands the lately discovered 'House of the Vestals,' between which and the Grove of Vesta on the slope of the Palatine it runs obliquely towards the south-west. With this previous more ancient boundary line are connected the ancient gates known as Romanula and Mugionis, both which Varro [*] connects with the Palatine and Nova Via, although their precise position seems not clearly ascertained.

The 'Column of Phocas,' which stands now as the king of the Forum, so called from the statue of that emperor in the early seventh century being placed there, is one detached from the façade of the Temple of Saturn, and turned into a tyrant's pedestal. In Byron's 'Childe Harold' it figures as the 'nameless column,' all marks of identification being buried below the surface. It stood like the mast of a wrecked and submerged vessel out of the water, while the dust of ruin went on rising like a tide around its base. Recent exploration has revealed the ignoble memory to which it was dedicated. The Miliarium Aureum and some other interesting monuments belong to the Augustan or later era, and thus find no place in our present survey.

We have seen that every face of the Forum was crowned with public buildings. There was, however, a single exception. A house in Nero's time stood 'circa forum,' belonging to Salvidienus Orfitus.[†] In the earlier Sullan period, a highly characteristic incident seems to show that this house was then a common tavern. It stood, perhaps, on the site occupied later by the Temple of Antoninus and Faustina, near the south-eastern corner, by the Arch of Fabius. There was a time—nay, various times—when the Roman Senate thought to put down usury by law, and the usurers took the following method of showing that usury was the stronger of the two. Some attempt was made to put the laws in force, and the Prætor, as in duty bound, entertained the suit, and fixed the day. Mr. Nichol adds :—

'Shortly afterwards, as he was sacrificing at the Temple of Castor, he was surrounded by a mob of usurers, and attacked at first with a stone. Throwing down his patera, he fled, and tried to take refuge in the Temple of Vesta; but his escape in this direction was cut off, and he was pursued into an inn or tavern, and assassinated. Though this crime was committed in the morning, and in the midst of the Forum, and rewards were offered by the Senate for information, with promise

* Varro, L. L., v. 34.   † Sueton., Nero, 37.

of impunity to accomplices, it was found impossible to detect the murderers, so powerful was the influence of the usurers over their own class and others.'

With this episode, illustrative of the 'optimi viri ad medium ' Ianum sedentes,' * we close the topography of the Forum.

The Pantheon, grand as it is, is a sort of architectural centaur. Others, Horace tells us, 'changed round to square' in their whims of building. Agrippa, 'for the third time ' Consul,' as the inscription testifies, united the two B.C. 27. Such, at least, has been the general belief which Mr. Fergusson, not without much probability, has lately impugned. He believes that the original *cella* was of the then usual square Etruscan form, and that the rotunda which has taken its place is due to one of the known restorations, or rather to one later still, but unrecorded. His opinion is founded on the vast scale of the vaulting, so greatly in excess of the Augustan standard, and on the 'constructive discharging ' arches,' which abound in the rotunda, with other features which point, he thinks, to the period of Constantine. Mr. Westropp adds to the above arguments, that the dome-vault of the *laconicum* of the Baths of Caracalla shows similar features which suggest contemporaneousness, and perhaps point to the same architect. One such token is the pumice-stone, largely used for its lightness in dome-vaults, and found in those Thermæ of Caracalla. Moreover, Vitruvius, who enumerates the round temples of Rome in the Augustan period, wholly omits mention of the Pantheon. Some would answer this last fact by ascribing to the Pantheon a totally different character, as being a supposed member of the Baths of Agrippa closely adjacent; in point of fact, no temple at all. This is flatly against the express statement of Dion Cassius, and all the traditions of the name; is moreover contradicted by the details of bas-relief on some of the walls, which are distinctly sacrificial; and merely shows that modern criticism can be at least as whimsical as ancient architecture. A third element of incongruity exists in the two modern campaniles on the top of dwarf balustraded towers interpolated between the portico and the rotunda. The ' Epigrammata Antiquæ Urbis ' shows that in 1517 they existed not.

On the Palatine itself the scars of ruin lie deeper in proportion as its pile of palaces was more dense. Byron wrote, in 1818, its description as—

---

* Cic. de Offic. ii. 25.

Cypress and ivy, weed and wallflower grown
Matted and mass'd together, hillocks heap'd
On what were chambers, arch crush'd, column strown
In fragments, choked-up vaults, and frescos steep'd
In subterranean damps, where the owl peep'd,
Deeming it midnight:—Temples, baths, or halls?
Pronounce who can; for all that learning reap'd
From her research hath been, that these are walls—
Behold the Imperial Mount! 'tis thus the mighty falls.

The researches of Cavaliere Rosa have, however, succeeded, since 1861, in disentangling a large part of the confusion thus powerfully painted. He penetrated down to a very ancient pavement of tufa blocks (*opus quadratum*), probably of the regal period, and representing the most ancient level. The most interesting remains were imbedded in ruin about eight feet higher, at which level has been laid bare what was probably the 'Area Palatina,' where Aulus Gellius attended the *levée* of the emperor, probably Hadrian or one of the Antonines.* Remains of two balconies overlooking this, and of a portico behind them, have also been found, with a spacious central apartment, probably the presence-room of Cæsar. A smaller apartment is supposed to have been the imperial *lararium.* Between the last two a large apartment, styled by the explorer the *tablinum,* but incorrectly, as Mr. Burn thinks, was entered from a court on the right, accessible from the above-named area. A magnificent cloistered court ran at the rear of these apartments. Its columns were all of Carian or Porta Santa marble. Their fragments, with parts of their bases of *giallo antico,* and of the richly inlaid floors, have been found *in situ;* but, having been previously excavated in 1720, nearly everything of value was stripped off. Earlier still, Pope Sixtus V. rifled the ruins, which rose once in massive reefs and boulders—the wreckage of architrave and peristyle—shivered shelves of marble, splintered crags of porphyry and serpentine. He carted away the nobler fragments, probably many wagon-loads, to build the Vatican. From that steep quadrangle of hill, the cradle of empire, the word 'palace' has gone the round of the Western world. Clothed with the *débris* of its own grandeur, it formed a noble quarry for Farnese, Aldobrandini, and Barberini to hew and hack. Similarly, the dismantling of Trajan's Forum is ascribed by some to

---

* As cited by Mr. Burn from 'Noct. Att.' xx. 1, 2, 'Journal of Philology,' ii. 3, p.-84, whence the above remarks are abridged.

Byzantine Cæsars of the seventh century, but no one quite knows how to assign *suum cuique* in this competition for loot. If the noble column had its statue dismounted at the same period, it stood so 'discrowned' for nine centuries, and is figured in that condition in the 'Epigrammata 'Antiquæ Urbis,' fol. x.   The same Sixtus remounted it with St. Peter, a neck of modern cylinder connecting the column with its new apex.   Mr. Burn adds that

'although the arrangement of the rooms is generally that of a Roman dwelling-house on a large scale, yet there is apparently no provision for domestic life, and all the parts of the building seem to have been public audience or banquetting rooms or their adjuncts.'

He quotes Statius's description of the 'emulous' foreign marbles from Libya, Chios, &c., and refers for illustration of it to the Museum attached to the Palatine excavations, where

' upwards of a hundred marble slabs of the most varied and beautiful colours and shades, all of which were collected in the ruins [of the Palatine] are there to be seen arranged and polished.   In the same museum a few exquisitely designed patterns in coloured stones polished and set in frames, which served as wall decorations, have been carefully restored, and show what costly magnificence and artistic taste the imperial apartments displayed.'

Amidst these artistic triumphs of combined grandeur and finish stalked in gloomy distrust of all beneath him, whether senator, freedman, or slave, the tyrant Domitian, along *ambulacra* veneered with the dazzling Cappadocian *phengitis*, whose mirror-like quality instantly revealed any presence beside his own.   The dagger he so much dreaded found him out at last.   The brick stamps point to his reign as the period of the building, the ground-plan of which alone can now be traced.

The greatest proof of the physical vigour of the Roman Government under the republic and empire is to be found in the aqueducts which fed the city, ministering at once to health, comfort, and luxury.

The excellence of the water-system, and its minute comprehensiveness of detail, is attested not only by the actual surviving aqueducts or their remains, but by the elaborate treatise of Frontinus, the chief ancient authority, whose report on the subject continued to be the service-directory for the water-system of Rome until the majority of the channels went to decay.   He was *curator aquarum* to Nerva and Trajan, and is believed to have died 107 A.D.   The aqueduct service included a staff of 700 men,* not only to supervise the distribution, but to cleanse and repair the conduits, cisterns, &c., when needed.   The nine 'ancient' aqueducts included in this report, to which seven of later date were added, cover about three and a half centuries in their period of construction: from 312 B.C., the date of the Appia, to 38 A.D., that of the Claudia and the Anio Novus.   The last was a diversion of the Anio bodily by clever engineering into Rome.   On the contrary, the bed of the small and shallow Almo, which dried up in summer, became merely a canal for the aqueducts of later date, the Aqua Crabra and Marrana.   To Rome the Anio, not the Tiber, was the ' Father of Waters,' for all purposes save the discharge of impurities.   Through the conduits of nearly all these aqueducts, turned upon her like the hose of so many fire-engines, Rome drank, bathed, and swam in the Anio.   Its main volume, as well as its adjacent and tributary springs, drawn from where the Lower Apennines approach most closely to the great Latin plain, flushed the Appia, Anio Vetus and Novus, Marcia, Claudia and Hadriana, as of course also the Marcia Pia and the Aqua Felice, the modern representatives of two of the former.   The source of the Anio proper is in the summit of the Monte Cantaro, about sixty-three miles from Rome, and some 2,200 feet above its level.   The spring, almost perennially snow-fed, never fails in the hottest and driest weather, and is always cool.   As regards purity, the Marcia † was highest in esteem,‡ and next to it the Claudia.   The Anio Novus had the largest supply, being, as said above, the river's residuary volume after being tapped by some other aqueducts. But it had the consequent variableness of quality with the river itself, and by carelessly infusing it when turbid after

* This probably refers mainly to the intramural service, and does not include the miles of tunnel, arcade, &c., which would have to be cared for independently.

† It was built in 145 B.C. by a Marcius Censorinus or Rex, perhaps the Consul of 149.   Shakespeare, ' Coriolanus,' ii. 3, mentions, with noteworthy anachronism, ' The Marcii Publius and Quintus, That our best water brought by conduits hither,' as the ancestors of the Coriolanus of the play, who lived, if at all, about three and a half centuries *earlier*.   Mr. Parker, who notices this, gives the date of the Censorinus, ' bis censor,' wrongly.   It was 265, not 294 B.C.

‡ Nero, in his outrageous contempt of rights human and divine, made the ' Fons Marciæ ' his bathing place, it being near his Simbruine villa mentioned below.   (Tacit. Ann. xiv. 22.)

rains, the *aquarii* sometimes spoilt the Claudian water. To
remedy this, the engineers of Nero (or perhaps Claudius) *
reconstructed in three vast successive dams the rocky gorge
of the headwaters of the Anio, each relieving the pressure
upon the others, the highest being at least 150 feet † above
the ordinary water-way. He thus gained, when the Pe-
lignian snows melting sent a flood into the river, three
terraces of lake and three precipices of foam. But the
useful rather than the picturesque was probably his object;
although the remains of his Simbruine Villa hard by mark
him as the only Cæsar who seems to have had a relish for
the wildness of nature, reveal the artist ‡ somewhere hidden
in the monster, and form a set-off against the gorgeous self-
idolatry of the Domus Aurea. The engineering object of all
this was to form a gigantic natural filter, so as to hold up
the stream and let its turbid charge settle in the bottom of
the basins, formed by breaking the rocky walls of the gorge,
and guiding the down-rolling fragments till they piled
themselves into three vast walls. Then the specus of the
aqueduct took its column of water from the topmost level of
the highest pool. In the river's normal state a lower specus
would be called into play. Nothing can give one a grander
notion of Roman engineering powers than the whole work,
with its attendant conduits and their locks and sluices,
tunnels and arcades, covering the fifty miles which lie between Subiaco and Rome. Signor Lanciani § ascribes the
destruction of this noblest of all the 'castles of water'
which the Romans raised to a great storm of 1303, which
swept the dams away, and strewed the gorge with their

---

* Mr. Parker, ' Aqueducts,' p. 58, speaks of ' the enormous reservoirs
' of Caligula and Claudius, commonly called of Nero,' and the ' lowest of
' the lakes of Claudius,' again p. 60. But throughout two previous
pages they are ascribed to Nero. Yet he certainly seems to be speaking
of the same waters.

† So Mr. Parker, who surveyed it minutely. Signor Lanciani seems
to put it (' Athenæum,' June 21, 1884) at 200 feet; whether they
measured from the same level is not clear. The latter adds its width
as 60 and thickness as 44 feet.

‡ ' Qualis artifex pereo ! ' are his last recorded words. The villa
and its surroundings, close to the modern Convent of S. Scholastica,
lay in a savage dell of the Lower Apennines. The higher dam sustained a bridge of seventy arches. The lake he fixed upon wound its
way for two miles under dense foliage and overhanging rocks into the·
heart of the mountain glen, with fishing and hunting lodges on its
shores. One of these is mentioned below in the text.

§ ' Athenæum,' June 21, 1884.

wrecks. Mr. Parker, writing with the aid of an expert, a native of the spot, and after studying the anonymous chronicle of the adjacent monastery,* tells the story more completely. The torrent in question flooded the uplands, including the lands of the monastery itself. ·To relieve it, two monks removed some of the blocks in the highest of the dams; but the water, gaining vantage, widened the aperture until it carried away the entire structure. The whole volume was then thrown upon the lower dams, which, it appears, were unable to bear the strain. They gave way, leaving their fragmentary boulders to clog the torrent which they could not stay. The gorge returned to nearly its natural state of a cataract, of volume variable with the season, wallowing in many foamy faces down a long declivity of rock. But, for the moment, the entire lowlands were inundated nearly to the gates of Rome. Thus, but for monastic ignorance of the simplest hydrodynamic principles, the work of the Neronian engineers might have been standing now.

These great life-arteries of Rome, converging in their tubular arcades of stone upon the heart which they nourished, must have presented, a few miles outside the southeastern gates, a truly imperial aspect to the provincial or foreigner; to St. Paul, for instance, and his company, during their last stage from 'Appii Forum and the Three ' Taverns.' Mr. Parker found in this subject of research a task which exactly suited him. The lines which, till they enter the city, suffer no entanglement, needed to be surveyed, measured, mapped, and photographed, their sources examined, and the qualities compared. He has done this with praiseworthy fidelity and unwearied toil; and while others may rival his labours, or dispute his conclusions as regards ' Roma Quadrata,' the Colosseum and the Forum, his volume on the Aqueducts will probably long continue to be the best modern authority on the subject. Not only the conduits, whether carried on arches or submerged in tunnels, but the 'piscinæ,' their filtration, the 'castella aqua-' rum,' or reservoirs, the locks, junctions, as well as sources and distribution, all come in for his notice. We have spoken of the grand figure which the ducts made outside the city. Among the more venerable of these was the Anio

---

* He says that there is evidence that the monkish chronicler was alive in 1390; thus the record comes very near the source of fact in its date.

Vetus, which recalls the memory of the war with Pyrrhus, having been built from its spoils, and of those sturdy champions of various hard-fought fields, M. Curius Dentatus and L. Papirius Cursor. It left the Via Latina at the fourth milestone, near the great junction and crossing of the aqueducts over which the Torre Fiscale has been built. Here six aqueducts meet and cross each other. The Marcian arcade (30 feet high), with three of these, makes one of its many angles, and the lofty Claudian arcade (50 feet high), with two more, was carried over it. Entering the city at this high level, the pressure requisite for effective distribution was retained. The traveller on his last mile into Rome must have had one of those noble conduits on either hand. Further from Rome they occasionally make rather long détours, eleven miles of aqueduct matching in one instance eight of road. The combined length of the nine referred to exceeded 285 Roman miles, of which 242 were subterranean and only 43 carried on structures, arched or not as need required, above the surface. The most perfect extant specimen of the arcaded conduit is that of the Claudia and Anio Novus combined (Parker, 'Aqueducts,' Plate XII.) The effect of the long and stately march of this royal road, superbly mounted on the same endless form of arch and pier, repeated as far as eye can reach in a vista of desolate grandeur, amidst the solitude of the Campagna, is wholly without parallel in the piteously picturesque. Its bold bluff cliff of sudden ruin looks you straight in the face across the enormous flat, like the petrified dorsal column of some extinct monster of the ancient world.

The highest reservoir of the Aqua Marcia is grandly nested among some of the finest and most artist-haunted scenery in Europe. It hangs on the edge of the hill below Tivoli, not far from where the kindred water of the Anio proper cascades down the steep—the 'præceps Anio' of Horace—while the *specus* or tunnel preserves its zigzag course to the same level or lower at the Villa of Hadrian in the valley. This reservoir had in the original construction of 145 B.C. two large chambers with an arcade connecting them, partly rock-hewn in the native travertine, partly built thereupon by art. Plate IX. gives a dead 'castellum' of the same Marcia. A forest fed by the centuries of moisture now withdrawn, has survived its drought and matured a growth of subsequent centuries above it. The Appia springs in an ancient stone-quarry on the same Anio's bank. Hence, perhaps, King Servius hewed the stones for his great wall,

floating them down the stream on rafts. What meets the
eye is a pool, apparently filled by drippings from roof of
cliff and earth above; but the unfailing water shows that
the spring is below. Hard by, two streams from a twin-
cavern meet at its mouth, and traversing the meadow in a
ditch-like specus, partly open, feed the Appia, which never
fails; but the soil is clayey, muddying the water after
rain. It has by its consequent deposit choked two-thirds
of the depth of its tunnel. In an attempt to restore it by
Pope Sixtus V. the clay was left hard, and the roof simply
raised the same number of feet. A part of it, thus partly
silted up and dismantled, reverted to its old use as a cart-
road in the quarry. The Virgo, 21 A.D., which now feeds
the Trevi fountain, and is known as the Acqua di Trevi,
draws soil similarly and needs periodical cleansing. It may
be traced from a reservoir near its source to the city by the
respirators at intervals of about 100 yards, mostly round
masses of concrete, but sometimes dwarf pyramids. Close
to its headwater there passes a strong and copious stream,
which has mineral properties, the river Herculeus, now
known as the Marrana. The notion was that the purer
stream, like the legendary Arethusa, resisted pollution from
this rival source; hence its name 'Virgo.' In ancient times
it supplied the baths of Alexander Severus and those of
Agrippa, and ended very near the Pantheon. After damage
by the Goths, it was restored by Pope Hadrian about 780
A.D., besides later repairs, and is still, as we have seen, of
service in modern Rome.

Frontinus computed the total water-supply at over 24,000
daily quinaries : of these 10,000 were distributed within and
over 3,000 without the walls ; but a balance of other nearly
11,000 was detected, being either wasted through want of
repair of works, or surreptitiously abstracted by private
persons. Mr. Parker computes this total as equal to a stream
20 feet wide by 6 feet deep constantly pouring into Rome,
with a full six times that of the Thames. A French
engineer has calculated this as equal to 332 gallons per
head of population, reckoned at a million total. Our own
most lavish rate, including that absorbed by manufactures,
is not above 40 gallons per head. This was the profusion of
water which astonished Procopius.* It is not easy to follow

---

* At the beginning of the ninth century, after the destructive
ravages of Totila, Vitiges, and the Saracens, the only aqueducts still
serviceable were the Appia and the Marcia. The former, eldest of

the calculation. By 'quinaries' Frontinus seems to mean pipes five quarter-inches in bore. But what length of such pipes formed the basis of his reckoning is less clear. If 24,000 quinaries contained 332,000,000 gallons, one may easily see that a quinary contained 13,833·3 gallons. The length of pipe taken may have been the average distance from the 'castellum aquæ,' placed where each aqueduct entered Rome (since there the distribution would needs begin), to the point of consumption. But how the 'French 'engineer' viewed it Mr. Parker does not say. It is obvious that such a volume of water, distributed everywhere about the city, would have sufficed to keep the surface of the seven hills ever moist. In the Esquiline * this was notoriously the case, as we know from Martial (Ep. v. xxii. 6): 'Et 'nunquam sicco sordida saxa gradu.' In fact, the result was probably to produce by evaporation an artificial climate.

In connexion with the banks of that upper Anio, where Horatian echoes still linger on the waterfalls, we may briefly notice one of the Neronian lodges lately rediscovered between Subiaco and Tenne, where a mountain stream under the monastery of St. Scholastica falls into the lake. Its walls are in the reticulated style, its pavements of the rarest breccias, and in it was found the figure of a sculptured archer, rather above life-size, nearly naked and kneeling upon one knee. Signor Lanciani in the 'Athenæum' of June 21, 1884, describes it artistically; but the scene appears to have been visited by Mr. Parker, doubtless under the guidance of Dr. Fabio Govi, a native, it seems, of Subiaco, and familiar with its local features.

A few remarks on the structural features of the Roman aqueduct may here be in place. Wherever a subdivision or a junction of streams took place, a *castellum aquæ* was erected, as also within the city where the stream was brought to a head for distribution. The *piscina* was a structure of

---

the whole system, would then have run, with slight interruptions of breakage and repairs, for eleven centuries. The fourteenth century was in every sense the low-water mark of mediæval Rome. During the Papal sojourn at Avignon her population, now shrunk to 17,000, reverted to drink their native Tiber, the aqueducts being choked or wrecked.

* 'Almost all the aqueducts of Rome entered the city on the Es- 'quiline Hill near the Porta Maggiore and the Porta S. Lorenzo,' says Mr. Burn, 'Journal of Philology,' x. 19, 2. Hence he gives a very natural interpretation of 'Esquilias . . . aquosas,' in Propert. 10 (v.) 8, 1.

more complex character, but easily represented by the following diagram. It had four chambers, the first of which, A, would be entered by the water at a high level, which then passed through a waste pipe into B below. Between B and C was a perforated wall enabling C to be filled from B. In the roof of C was a hole through which the water would then rise in D to the level of A. This arrangement conferred some of the benefits of a filter, since on each of the floors of A, B, and C successive deposits of any impurity would take place before the stream passed out of D on its further way. The *piscinæ* and *castella* were lined with a cement called *opus Signinum*, made of crockery shards, and when dry, so hard as to be broken with the utmost difficulty. This prevented leakage through joints in the masonry, and presented a surface which could at all times be easily cleansed. In waters strongly charged with chalky matter, small openings in the specus were left on the sides to let the chalky water escape. In the case of the Hadriana this has left a stalactitic deposit of lime against the side of each pier. Near Monte Cello, some piers have been removed for building materials, and the stalactitic masses remain, looking like concrete respirators of another aqueduct, but deceptively, as there is no pipe in any of them.

A	D
B	C

Mr. Parker noticed in the Colosseum a large chamber, at a level next above the podium, which he determined to be a reservoir for water by the termination of an aqueduct in it. Similarly, four arches of the Claudian conduit still remain close to the ruins of the Palace of the Cæsars, which it supplied; and Hadrian's Villa was served by branches from the Anio Novus, while the main stream, undisturbed, went on at high level on an arcade crossing the valley three miles below Tivoli. Fifteen of the vertical sections of the specus * of these aqueducts are given by Mr. Parker (Plate

---

* On this word Mr. Parker founded a conjectural emendation of certain passages in Frontinus, which speak of the ' Spes' or ' Spes 'Vetus' as a well-known landmark in approaching the city by the Esquiline gate. The epithet ' Vetus' distinguishes it from the 'Nova ' Spes' in the Forum Olitorium, there being two temples dedicated to Spes in Rome. Frontinus thus makes the ' Spes Vetus' a point where various conduits diverge, unite, or send off a branch. But if we are to read ' Specum veterem,' we must infer that every aqueduct so named had an old tunnel or channel, and, therefore, contradistinctively a new one also, which seems absurd. Even where in other passages ' Spem' stands without ' veterem,' the change to ' Specum' is unmean-

XXI.)   Some are angular, some square, but of the nine
ancient ones only two have rounded roofs, and none, ancient
or modern, a barrel-arch entire, all being square below.   A
curious letter of King Theodoric appears in Cassiodorus,
calling on the Roman Senate to assist in inquiring after
pilferers of the brass* and lead of the taps and pipes, or
divertors of water for furtive uses.   Within the last few
years, a large leaden pipe of great age, cased in ancient
brickwork, was found under the Via de Condotti, showing that the aquarian engineers distrusted the strength of
the lead without such support.†   But these are merely the
details of diffusion.   The principle and method of these
mighty pipes of masonry have furnished models which
modern cities have here and there copied on a scale suited to
their smaller bulk and scantier means.   Thus Milan completed the thirty-miles length of her Naviglio Grande in
1258, and the watershed of the Ligurian Alps was tapped by
Genoa for her own supply in 1295.

How much of ancient Rome lies still within reach of the
antiquary's adventurous spade is plain from the last notable
' find ' which has rewarded the efforts of Signor Baccelli,
the ' House of the Vestals,' and of which the patriotic show-
man, Signor Rodolfo Lanciani, blows the trumpet as follows
in the columns of the ' Athenæum : '—

' The cloisters of the Vestals offer the same sight which we have so
often witnessed and admired on the stage in Meyerbeer's *chef-d'œuvre*,
"Robert le Diable," when the magic power of the hero awakens from
their graves the souls of the deceased virgins.   Not less magical has
proved the power of Signor Baccelli, the Minister of Public Instruction, in recalling to life the souls of the Vestals.   People abroad cannot
conceive the faintest idea of the impression which everyone here felt in
stepping over the threshold of the Atrium Vestæ, in entering those
cloisters, the marble population of which is increasing in number and

---

ing; e.g. in ' Rectus vero ductus secundum Spem unicus intra portam
Exquelinam . . . diducitur,' i. 22.   Here ' secundum *specum* ' seems
to add a mere superfluity.   How else could it come than along its
specus or tunnel?   Besides all this, the mention of ' *Horti* Spei Veteris '
(Lampridius, Heliogab. xiii.) seems to show a tract or area taking its
name from the temple as well known.   Here, although Mr. Parker
cites the passage, ' Aqueducts,' p. 22, note t, he does not see that specus
is impossible.   In most of the passages we find spē is the exact reading,
which might just possibly represent ' specum,' but spei could not
represent ' specus.'

* Many such taps of brass or bronze may be seen at Pompeii.

† Comp. Hor. Epist. i. x. 20 : ' Purior in vicis aqua tendit rumpere
' plumbum.'

in importance every day. The noble, dignified portrait-statues of the *virgines vestales maximæ* are there standing in a long array, ready to welcome the visitors, and glad to have recovered possession of the house which, for eleven centuries, has been the witness of their joys and sorrows, the depository of their secrets, and from which they were brutally expelled in A.D. 394.' *

The same authority adds that the surface of the House excavated up to March last is 6,095 square mètres, with a maximum depth of 25 mètres. Marble pedestals have been found with inscriptions in number 28; inscribed marble slabs, 12; statues, 15; and important fragments, 11; busts or heads, 2. Perhaps the most remarkable item is a treasure of 835 silver coins with one golden Byzant (the Besant of heraldry), of which 828, or all but a very few, are from our country's ancient currency of the tenth century. We will briefly explain Signor Lanciani's account. The whole, with a bit of jewellery inscribed 'Domno Marino Papa,' were found in a terra-cotta jug, buried between the levels of the mediæval and the ancient pavements of the House. These silver pennies are believed to have been ' Peter's pence,' then newly set up by King Offa, the Mercian, and to have been used by the Pope (Marinus II.), 942-6 A.D., in paying an official salary. They range from Aelfred, his contemporaries and successors, downwards to 946 A.D., and recall the time when there existed between the Vatican and the Castle of St. Angelo a ' Burgus Saxonum,' or reception-place for pilgrims from our island ; and, further, when a large portion of the Palatine, including this corner, was the residence of the Popes from and after John VII., until the Frangipani assumed the rights of suzerains and took possession of the site. This curious piece of mediæval archæology comes down to us, as it were, sandwiched in between the upper and lower pavements of the House of the Vestals. The ' Byzant ' is of the age of Theophilus, 827–842, when, as for a long while before and after, this coin was current all over the West, and, according to some etymologers, accounts for the word ' sterling ' applied to all coin, as meaning to refer to

---

* See Milman, ' History of Christianity,' Book III. ch. viii., where the date given for the dissolution of the House and confiscation of its property is 382 A.D. But the House continued to be inhabited much longer ; as appears from the discovery of these silver coins, chiefly English, struck in the ninth century. Whilst these sheets are passing through the press, an admirable account of the ' Atrium Vestæ ' by Mr. Middleton has been read to the Society of Antiquaries (Nov. 25), which will doubtless be published in the ' Archæologia ' of that learned body.

the standard of the Eu-sterlings. A precisely similar collection is said by Commen. de Rossi to have been found in England in 1611. To the great disappointment of research, no Fasti or records of the Sisterhood, showing their successive members, has come to light. The inscribed pedestals of the *Vestales Maximæ*, or successive seniors of the order, to whom the headship of the House was entrusted, to some extent compensate for this deficiency.

Signor Lanciaui on these pedestals remarks :—

‘The Atrium Vestæ must have contained more than one hundred honorary pedestals, not because there were as many abbesses during the last four centuries of Vesta's worship, but because many statues represented and many pedestals named the same lady. The stonecutters and the limeburners of the middle ages have destroyed more than four-fifths of this magnificent series. We possess actually the originals or the copies of thirty-six inscriptions only bearing names of *vestales maximæ* ; of these twenty-eight were found in the Atrium itself, two on the Palatine, six in the various other quarters of the town.’

He gives, however, only the following fourteen names, with the dates or references, or both, as below: 1. Occia, Tacit. Ann. ii. 86, 38 B.C. to 19 A.D.   2. Junia Torquata, A.D. 19 to 48.   3. Vibidia, the generous protector of Messalina, Tacit. Ann. xi. 32.   4. Cornelia Maxima, murdered by Domitian, Plin. Ep. iv. 11.   5. Prætextata, whose mother was wife of a Sulpicius, Tacit. Hist. iv. 42.   6. Numisia Maximilla, A.D. 200.   7. Terentia Flavola, A.D. 215.   8. Campia Severina, A.D. 240.   9. Flavia Mamilia, A.D. 242.   10. Flavia Publicia, A.D. 247.   11. Cœlia Claudiana, A.D. 286.   12. Terentia Rufilla, A.D. 300.   13. A pedestal, name erased.   14. Cœlia Concordia, the last or last but one *Vestalis Maxima*.

Two or three of the later ones come in for special notice as follows :—

‘ No. 10. This lady was undoubtedly the most famous and venerable chief of the order. Her eulogies and her pedestals have been a plague to the discoverers of the Atrium. Not a week has elapsed since the beginning of our work without bringing to light some recollections of this priestess. Judging from the looks of the exquisite statue discovered, together with one of her pedestals, on December 20, Flavia Publicia was a lady of tall, queenly appearance, of noble demeanour, of a sweet and gentle, if not handsome face.’

Of the anonymous number 13 we have the following singular notice regarding the inscription, the erasure, and the probable cause :—

‘ “ Ob meritum castitatis pudicitiæ atque in sacris religionibusque

" doctrinæ mirabilis [name erased] . . . virgini vestali maximæ, ponti-
" fices viri clarissimi, pro Macrinio Sossiano viro clarissimo, pro meritis.
" Dedicata quinto idus Junias, divo Joviano et Varroniano consulibus."
Now, why should the name of this highly-praised priestess have been
erased?   Two reasons only can be given : either she happened to forget
the vows of chastity, or she was converted to Christianity.   The first
explanation does not seem satisfactory; not only because she was probably a mature, if not an old woman, when the crime and the *memoriæ
damnatio* took place, but also because the fall of a vestal would certainly
have been noticed and registered and proclaimed to the four winds by
contemporary Christian writers.   Conversion to the Gospel seems more
probable ; one of these conquests of the new faith in Vesta's Atrium is
actually mentioned by Prudentius, Peristeph., hymn 2.'

Of No. 14 we are told :—

' She was a great friend of the famous champion of polytheism,
Vettius Agorius Prætextatus. . . . Cœlia Concordia had raised a
statue in honour of Prætextatus in the Atrium itself; she received the
same distinction in the house of that nobleman.'

The House itself is described as a square oblong brick
building, having the Atrium for its most prominent feature,
which accordingly sometimes gives the denomination to the
whole.   Its architecture resembles that of mediæval and
Renaissance double-storied cloisters.   The ground-floor
counted forty-eight Corinthian columns of *cipollino* marble
with white marble bases, of which not a single piece is left
standing.   Those of the upper story were of *breccia corallina*,
and, as they were not convertible into lime, two entire
samples and many fragments have been found.   The lower
floor contained state apartments, with some perhaps used
for archives.   The living rooms were on the upper floor.
The whole area is 115 mètres by 53, of which the Atrium is
67 by 24.   A superb pavement of 12 mètres by 8, with
giallo, porfido, serpentino, and other marbles, in the style
of decoration fashionable under Septimius Severus, comes in
for notice.   The House receives a bad character for salubrity.
The ground-floor is 30 feet lower than the Nova Via, rests
against the cliff of the Palatine, and supports the street by
the back-walls of the state apartments.   Its bane was
naturally damp, which was combated by double walls, double
floors, ventilators, and hot-vapour currents in the inter-
spaces.   Some curiosities of hypocaustic construction are
here detailed.   But no ingenuity could increase the amount
of sunshine.   The ruins of the imperial palace suffice to
overshadow it even now at 9 A.M., and how much more when
it rose a hundred and fifty feet in the air.   Nothing could

compensate for this. And when sanitary rules began in the beginning of the fourth century to be better understood, a change in the regulations of the order is apparent, and an *archiater*, or officer of health, to the establishment occurs. These arrangements are presented to the eye in two Roman photographs of the Casa delle Vestali. One, numbered 3,358, shows the area on its longer axis from N.W. to S.E., looking towards the latter. Behind your standpoint lie the buildings at the south-eastern extremity of the Forum, and the Church of Sta. Maria Liberatrice at the northern angle of the Palatine stands over your right shoulder from behind, while a little further to the right rear is the Porta Romana. Prolong that longest axis along which you look, and you nearly thread the centre of the Arch of Titus standing at the higher level, with the Summa Sacra Via crowned by the church of Sta. Francesca Romana to your remote left centre, and in the interval between the church and the arch you glimpse the upper courses of the Colosseum in the depression beyond them. On your right the high ground of the Palatine rises crowned with the ruin of the Cæsars. The other photograph (3,093) shows the transverse of the former. You look now south-westward with the Sacra Via at your back, right at the broken lower courses of the Palace of Caligula. If the view were prolonged further to the left, it would show the northern angle of the Orti Farnesiani. The grove of broken statuary and stumps of columns ranged by the excavators along the south-western edge of the sunken area in the bottom—the ground-floor of the Domus—now faces you. It lies on your right in the previous view. Of the statuary, two figures of the *Vestales Maximæ* are in comparatively good preservation. They both wear a long stola drooping over the feet, but the one which should be the more important and interesting is an upper half-figure only, now mounted on an altar-shaped plinth. It is diminutively shown in the second plan in 3,358, the first being occupied by a similar plinth but empty. Both figures wear a loose hood, showing well the close-fitting cap with two or more filleted bands, which half covers the forehead or more, and drooping in easy folds on the shoulders. Each wears over her stola a large pallium, gathered over the left arm, and in the full-length wound rather closely about the figure, its upper folds being clustered round the waist. The projections of the arms are of course gone, and the full-length has suffered mutilation at the nose. She shows a rather pleasant though penetrating

expression. The half-length shows the noble massive head
and regular well-moulded features of a woman probably in
her fifth or sixth decade, who, in her youth, would have been
strikingly handsome. The superlative interest attaching to
these discoveries, especially the portrait statuary, although
of secondary artistic merit, is matter of just congratulation
to the Italian Government and its distinguished officers.
We hope they will forget a little soreness provoked by
certain officious volunteers of advice gratis as to how to
guide excavation and appreciate its results, which have
proceeded from certain amateurs in Western capitals; and
find their successful efforts appreciated by the long train of
pilgrim devotees which this recovery of the House of the
Vestals is sure to draw in the present winter.

The comprehensive guide-book of Dr. Gsell-Fels will be
invaluable to such of these sojourners as read German. Its
strong and weak point at once is that it is just what a
guide-book ought to be. The tourist will find exactly what he
wants to find, on a scale duly proportioned to its interest—
the great difficulty of such a work. But the book is not
always up to the mark of the latest discoveries. It knows
nothing of the new, and undoubtedly true, version of the
Cenci tragedy, given from the Roman archives by Signor
Bertolotti, and noticed in this Journal, April 1879; nothing
of the disproval of the famous portrait by Guido; nothing of
the fact of the supposed base of the Colossus of Nero hard
by the Colosseum being too small to have supported it, and
nowhere mentions that most interesting testimony to Roman
topography, the Capitoline Plan, found in the rubbish under
the wall of the Temple of Romulus, and throwing light
upon the Porticus Liviæ, Basilica Iulia, and other sites of
first-rate interest. Its maps, plans, indexes, and, in short,
the whole mechanism of the volume, are well executed. But
the monuments are sometimes incorrectly engraved—e.g. the
Arch of Titus has Ionic, not Corinthian columns. We
recommend the substitution of photo-engravings for these
in any future edition.

EXACTLY thirty years ago, in the pages of this Journal, attention was called to the abuses which then disfigured Private Bill Legislation. Much of what was thus exposed has been cured or mitigated, to the advantage alike of suitors and of the character of the Legislature. If we return to the subject now, it is chiefly because action in and out of Parliament has made the maintenance of the present system one of the topics of the hour. A bill has actually been introduced into the House of Commons, intituled ' A ' Bill to amend the System of Private Bill Legislation in the ' United Kingdom.' Its introducer is Mr. Sellar, the member for the Haddington Boroughs, and it is endorsed with the influential names of Mr. Horace Davey, Sir Lyon Playfair, and Mr. Raikes, each of the two latter having filled the office of Chairman of Committees of the House. It is obvious that by such a measure an essential change is intended in the present method, and it seems well that the occasion should be made use of to examine the facts as to the existing tribunal, the necessity for change, and the form that change should take if it is to be effected. It may be said at once that most of the comparatively limited number of persons outside Parliament who talk hostilely about the present system, talk with very little knowledge of the subject. They speak of it as of a gross, acknowledged, and somewhat ridiculous abuse; as if the tribunal had been established at haphazard; as if its decisions were commonly marked by folly, if not by something worse; and as if its expensiveness was at once unparalleled and gigantic. Shortly, they treat it as a blot, and not a small one, upon the page of English administration, which it is one of the first duties of modern purity and economy to erase. In all this there is a great deal both of misconception and exaggeration. In the first place the tribunal was not established at haphazard. It is an essential principle of social order that the State alone can deprive a man of his property, and that only for the public good, and after proper compensation. Such undertakings as are the subject-matter of private bill legislation—for example, railways, canals, docks, gas, and water works—are in England carried out either by private individuals or by local authorities, and a power to purchase lands and other property compulsorily is necessary to their prosecution; the State alone possesses, and can alone confer, that power; to the State, therefore, represented by Parliament, have the promoters of such undertakings naturally gone to obtain it. When there, they have advanced the only true plea for legislation, advantage to the public, and they have been met by the only possible counterplea, its negation.

Private bill legislation has therefore been the natural outcome of our method of national advancement by private enterprise, and so far there is nothing at all haphazard about it in theory. In practice its results might show, as some persons insist that they do show, a terrible account of recklessness, perversity, inconsistency, and incapacity, but that would be another matter. Upon investigation it is probable that all these charges would, in the main, resolve themselves into two, a waste of time and a waste of money. And the figures upon which these would be supported, startling as they are, may be laid to the account, not so much, after all, of the vices of the system itself, as of the enormous extent to which it has been applied. The patriarch who kept eighty animals for riding in his stables was, perhaps, not so much to be blamed for his extravagance as to be condoled with upon the largeness of his family. Parliament has similarly had presented to it no less than 3,700 private bills in the course of the last thirteen years. It must be admitted, however, that a goodly number of this multitudinous offspring were stillborn. The time undoubtedly was when it was scarcely possible to frame too strong an indictment against the Parliamentary committees by whom private bills were decided. But that time has long since passed away. We are far from holding up the modern committees of four members as a model tribunal. It may be admitted at once that there are to be found in them every now and then the elements of incapacity, of slovenliness, of narrow-mindedness, of self-conceit. We fear that the occasional inattention of individual members while highly important issues are being fought out before them has come to be accepted as a matter of course by suitors; and it would certainly be interesting to have a return of the number of letters consigned to the Post Office from the private bill committee rooms of both Houses. But the chairmen in Lords and Commons alike are almost invariably intelligent and painstaking, and, with one or two conspicuous exceptions, which it would be over-complaisant to ignore, and which, after all, may have their uses as a foil, they are as courteous as they are painstaking and intelligent. In the main they are fairly supported by their colleagues, and the excuse of the least assiduous of these would probably be that they trusted the chairman to listen to the arguments and to weigh the evidence, and were willing to make his decision their own. This apology would be the more noteworthy, inasmuch as it tends to show how often even now decisions which seem to be those of a group are, in effect, almost, if not altogether, those of a solitary mind.

It is right to insist upon what may be called the logical origin of private bill legislation—viz. the necessity that promoters are under of dealing with property, and the right of the individual to say, 'I will only part with my property at ' the bidding of the State itself for State purposes, and I ' appeal to the State itself in this particular instance.' It is to a very great extent because neither Parliament nor the public have felt the full force and bearing of this that a movement has arisen for the abolition of the system. The cry might well have been for reform rather than abolition. What has been wanted is a more direct recognition among members of both Houses that the work of select committees is a direct and important duty of the national representatives. A member of a select committee ought no more to think of writing letters while a case is going on before him than a Lord Justice during the transaction of business in the Court of Appeal. Apart from legal training, the want of which is, of course, an insuperable defect, good sense and industry are the two chief requirements in any body called upon to decide upon the merits of a railway, gas, water, or canal bill. There has been plenty of the first in both Houses, and, until lately, unemployed; the latter ought to have been forthcoming too. It may be stated without reservation that the natural tribunal to try such cases is Parliament, and that where there has been any unfitness apparent it has nearly always been resolvable into some form of disinclination. The immense difficulty found hitherto in the invention of any substitute affords no slight indication of the correctness of this view. How many able and enthusiastic reformers have come forward with scheme after scheme during the last fifteen years, only to have them rejected as inadequate and unworkable! The truth is, that a large portion of the public immediately concerned, promoters and opponents alike, still trust Parliament, with all its faults, in such matters as they will readily trust no other body; and if, in consequence of certain considerations, which we propose to mention, the necessity of some change is conceded, it may be stated positively that all parties interested desire that the change should be as limited as possible, and that, whatever is done, the inception and ultimate control of all such undertakings as are in question should still be reserved to Parliament.

Thus much for the character and origin of the tribunal itself, and the light in which it is regarded by those most interested in and conversant with the question of its maintenance or abolition. A separate word or two, however, about its expensiveness. The expenses are great; not out of proportion when the issues are vast and the litigants wealthy, but burdensome beyond endurance when the issues are trifling and the suitors poor. We have before us at this moment certain returns of expenses incurred by railway, canal, and tramway companies, gas and water companies, harbour and dock authorities, and town councils, local boards, and other similar bodies, in promoting and opposing bills in Parliament. These returns cover all classes of expenditure with the exception of that by landowners, and it may be suspected that if the expenses of promoting and opposing railway companies could be analysed, they would be found to cover the cost of many a landowner's opposition. The returns in question extend over eleven years, from 1872 to 1882 inclusive. They are as follows:—

		£
Municipal bodies, &c.	. . .	1,289,757
Railway, gas, and water companies	. .	4,664,874
Canal and tramway companies .	. .	416,043
Harbour and dock authorities .	. .	360,574
Total	.	6,731,248

Out of this total an aggregate sum of nearly 700,000*l.* is stated to refer to 'general legal and parliamentary expenses 'that cannot be divided.' Probably nearly all of this ought

to be deducted from private bill expenditure.   Of this item
615,087*l.* is returned by railway companies.   We may probably, without serious inaccuracy, set down the total expenses attributable to private bills under these returns at a
round sum of 6,000,000*l.*   This expenditure may be compared
either with the capital involved in the undertakings litigated,
or with the total annual expenditure of the various companies and public bodies undergoing it.   In either case it is
a very small percentage of the whole.   The railway companies figure for far the largest amount in it.   Excluding
the 615,000*l.* mentioned above, their expenditure before
Parliament was 3,309,625*l.* for the eleven years over which
the returns run.   Dismissing odd figures, we may therefore
say that they have spent some 300,000*l.* a year.   This is but
a fractional addition to an annual expenditure which must
considerably exceed 40,000,000*l.*   On the assumption that
the capital of the railway companies in the United Kingdom
is 800,000,000*l.*, the addition of this 300,000*l.* to their net
annual income would give ninepence extra per annum to
every holder of one hundred pounds of stock.   But it must
be remembered that the question is not whether this amount
can be expunged altogether from their accounts, but only
how much of it can be deemed excessive.   As to so much
of it as is incurred in the promotion of bills, it may be urged
that promotion cannot be expected to be cheap.   Full scope
ought to be given to those opponents of bills whose property
and interests are seen to be substantially attacked, and the
smallest opposition may launch any tribunal upon a long and
expensive enquiry.   The points of contact between a great
railway company and other interests, corporate and personal,
along its course, are so many and diverse, that the simplest
'Additional Powers Bill,' the objects of which to an inexperienced reader would seem altogether internal and
domestic, produces, and fairly produces, a score of opponents
who must be satisfied either by a settlement or a hearing.
For the costs involved in the opposition of railway companies
to new schemes they are themselves partly responsible.   The
older companies show a certain want of courage in refusing,
as they do, to allow a vast number of new schemes to pass
unchallenged.   How many a project has cost its thousands
of pounds in passing through Parliament for which the
public have subsequently never subscribed one shilling!
Would it have fallen any the less stillborn if the great companies had saved their money and let it alone?   To this
suggestion the companies might probably reply, 'If we thus

'contributed to the cheapness of promotion, we should be
'flooded with new schemes.' What, then, if the public did
not subsequently take them up? Admitting, however, that
the great bulk of opposition is unavoidable, we may still
urge that it must go on in lines parallel to the development
of the country, and that it must be expensive so long as the
tribunal before which it is conducted remains first-rate.
From second-rate tribunals to decide important issues may
the common sense of the country, recalled by the experiment
of the Railway Commissioners if by nothing else, for ever
shield promoters and opponents alike! These remarks as to
the expensiveness of the tribunal apply pretty much to all
other bodies contributing to the returns, except the smaller
municipal corporations. The system of provisional orders
shows how far the interjection of a local enquiry between
such bodies and Parliament can be expected to cheapen
legislation for them in the matter of gas, water, and tramways. There are those who think that the method might
be extended to other subjects of local administration and
improvement. If advisable, this could be done without any
radical change in the principle or practice of private bill
legislation. Whether or not it be advisable will appear
when we discuss the various substitutes that have been
suggested for the present tribunal.

Out of the 6,000,000*l.* paid by all classes during the last
eleven years, 380,160*l.* went in House fees paid to the House
of Commons alone. The corresponding amount for the
House of Lords is not given in the published return, but it
is generally supposed that the aggregate sum for the two
Houses reaches to 60,000*l.* a year at least. This to most
people wears the appearance of an indefensible item. It is
paid annually by some of the most energetic and wealth-
bringing sections of the population for the privilege of conferring benefits upon the nation at large. It looks like a
tax upon enterprise. It has been said that 'the whole ex-
'penses attending the fabric of St. Stephen's' are defrayed
out of it, whatever that vague phrase may mean. On the
whole, however, we are inclined to think that in this, as in
other points, the charge of expensiveness, though justified,
has been overstated. It must be remembered that this item,
even if it be exorbitant, does after all cover the provision of
a tribunal and all official expenses connected with it. If a
court were established there would be judges and a staff to
be paid; and if portions of the Palace of Westminster were
not utilised, special court buildings would have to be pro-

vided. For all these conveniences in the past suitors have rightly been expected to pay something. On the other hand, it is obvious that the character of the tribunal has added much, although the extravagance of promoters has added still more, to the expense of these investigations in one important particular, the production of witnesses. Shoals of perfectly useless people are brought like herrings up to London every session, only that unlike herrings they have to be expensively fed, instead of providing cheap food. It would have been interesting if some of the Parliamentary returns now before us could have been made to distinguish the amounts paid for the entertainment in London of deputations, of local witnesses, of Parliamentary committees, of town councils; for the hotel bills, and the sly dinners at Richmond, for the piles of plovers' eggs, the pails of turtle and of champagne. It is certain, also, that the evil conditions of the original railway mania have survived in the extravagant payments made to 'expert' witnesses, a vast deal of whose testimony is really valuable in inverse proportion to its skill. Counsels' fees were fixed at their present rate at a time when such rate was undoubtedly very high. As matters stand now, however, they fall below the standard of fees in equally important common law cases, and the incomes of the foremost leaders of the Parliamentary bar are not larger, perhaps not even as large, as they would be if those who earned them stood in an equally prominent position in either of the two other branches of the profession. One undoubted abuse is to be charged to the present system. It is in the nature of things that the best obtainable counsel should be retained by promoters and opponents as early as possible, in the hope that his services may be forthcoming at the moment of struggle. Committees are struck, and cases are brought on, without the slightest reference to the engagements of the bar, and with very little reference to the convenience of suitors; and the consequence is a great deal of wasted work on the part of counsel, and many lost fees on the part of clients. The easy *nonchalance* of Parliament upon this point would be amusing, if its effects were not so disastrous as they undoubtedly are. So long as a dozen committees are fixed for one week, suddenly, and none, it may be, for the weeks before or after, this abuse must continue. But, be the destined days of the tribunal many or few, surely some amendment might be made in this particular, and some regularity in the flow of business obtained, without loss to the dignity of members of Parliament.

There is no doubt, however, that the substitution of judges for select committees would do away with much of undue expense. A serious authoritative court would soon reduce local and ornamental witnesses to a small fraction of their present numbers. A trained judge would soon teach promoters and opponents alike to appraise at its real value, truth, when presented in the perplexing forms of fantastic intricacy which it now assumes in the mouths of too many skilled witnesses. The regular flow of work in two or three parallel and continuous streams would simplify the arrangements between counsel and client, to the comfort and advantage of both. A considerable sum, no doubt, in the aggregate would be saved out of the 500,000*l.* which, in round figures, the present annual expenses of private bill legislation may be said to reach. The saving would not be perceptible to shareholders in large companies; but by the promoters and shareholders of small undertakings, by the lesser municipal corporations, and by individual opponents of private bills, upon whom the burden of the present system most severely presses, the benefit of the change would be undoubtedly felt and cordially welcomed.

We have thought it right thus to point out, first, that the institution of the present tribunal was naturally evolved from the tacit determination of the country that such undertakings as railways, canals, waterworks, docks, and tramways, should be matters of private enterprise and not of State supply; and secondly, that the undoubted expensiveness of the tribunal has been denounced a little too loudly and without sufficient reference to the magnitude and diversity of the issues tried before it. One further note of apology may yet fairly be sounded: on the whole, its work has been a good deal better done than is commonly imagined. It is certain that the railway map of England might have been better drawn, but the mistakes in it are hardly to be called mistakes of the tribunal. The nation itself is responsible for its own railway map. Parliament has only had the power of dealing with the isolated schemes presented to it from time to time, and by sanctioning lines of which the actual merits were undoubted when regarded separately, has slowly pieced together the enormous aggregate of 18,000 miles. The result may be unsymmetrical, but this is a disqualification inherent in piecemeal conception and construction, and these are again inseparable from private enterprise. We need say nothing of earlier times: but since the new select committees were instituted Parliament has done the work that it has been set to do fairly well. Wrong-headedness, timidity, want of grasp, have of course been shown over and over again; but what tribunal, it may be asked, could have claimed absolute exemption from those qualities in the course of a quarter of a century?

But there are the strongest indications that, whether a change be or be not attributable to the demerits of the present court, a change is coming. There is, to begin with, an idea abroad, which is especially strong among those who are least conversant with the subject, that any change would be a reform. In the next place, the system has to contend with the growing weariness of Parliament. Those who administer it are growing tired of it. Men like less than they did formerly toilsome avocations which, though meritorious, bring no showy credit and no pay. Lastly, the institution of Grand Committees takes off the better men, of whom there is certainly not an increasing supply. The work of the Grand Committees, upon which no less than 130 members were employed last session, is more attractive, it savours more of the public business, and it may well be that many a good man finds there attention, consideration, and prominence, which he has failed to obtain in the House itself. The Grand Committee is, in fact, an unusually good Parliamentary audience. The personal composition of the private bill committee is consequently doomed to decline, and it will decline more rapidly as the formation and application of the Grand Committees become more general. It may even be that as the delegation of public business grows in extent, the furnishing of the private bill committees may become not inferior but impossible. Further, the issues involved in private bill legislation are in very many cases far more intricate and difficult of adjudication than they used to be. It was a comparatively simple question to decide in old days whether there should be the first railway communication between Liverpool, the Midlands, and London. The question of a second was not quite so easy; there are now at least four, and the advisability of others may soon have to be decided. There is also the question of a renewed and improved inland navigation, such as was inaugurated by the scheme for a ship canal to Manchester. The investigation of the various problems and statistics of traffic and transit involved in fresh railway and canal schemes nowadays calls for far greater labour and ability in the judge than was necessary five-and-twenty years ago. If this last consideration does not point to the incapacity of the ordinary Members of Parliament to transact private business, it at least in some measure accounts for their inclination to part with it. Apparently they do mean to part with it, and it is well therefore to be beforehand with legislation on the subject, and to do all that may be done to direct the channel of change before influential people are committed to any particular direction.

It must be borne in mind that whoever may assume the seats which Parliament is about to abdicate will be judges of expediency on a very great scale. Each promoter who approaches Parliament admits an absence of rights in his own case, by the very fact of praying for a bill to confer them. It is easy enough to find judges of rights; judges of expediency are not easy to find. Rights are definable; expediency is indefinable. To recognise what is definable you only want learning, acuteness, and care, which are comparatively common; to decide on what is vague and indefinable you want wisdom and nerve. These last are not easily found, when found they are not immediately recognised, and till they are recognised they are not trusted. It takes a long time for the public to dower an individual with a reputation for wisdom. Hitherto the public has in the main trusted what it has christened 'the wisdom of 'Parliament.' Though occasionally sorely tried by concrete exhibitors of the quality, it has not yet quite lost faith in the abstraction. It will take a long time before it becomes as confiding in the wisdom or as long-suffering over the shortcomings of any other tribunal, however composed. Nor will its hesitation be altogether unfounded. For if Parliamentary committees have been capricious, there is a great danger of the new court proving inelastic. The requisite combination will be rare in any one man, and the new judges will not be easy to find. It is obvious that they must be men of special experience, of decision of character, of legal training, of impartial position, and of first-class ability; if they are not all this, they will be no improvement whatever upon the present tribunal. The change would then simply involve the settlement of great matters by one commonplace man instead of by four. In anything that is arranged, the satisfaction of the suitors—we use the term in a somewhat technical sense, as it is understood in Westminster Hall—must be primarily considered.

The scheme most likely to commend itself from this point of view would be one which, while it set free the time, preserved the control of Parliament. The interference of the

court with private property and vested interest, inseparable
from the exercise of its functions, should be preceded and
confirmed by the direct action of Parliament; so that any
disability, discomfort, loss of privilege, property, or amenity,
which an individual might find himself called upon to suffer
for the public good, should be henceforth, as heretofore, the
direct act of the State.   This necessity—for it is nothing
short of necessity—disposes, if nothing else would, of a suggestion that has found favour with some persons, for handing
over all matters that are purely local, such as gas, water,
roads, sewage and drainage works, to the proposed county
boards.   It is impossible to predict how a non-existent body
may be constituted; but it is characteristic of the rashness
with which proposals are made on this subject, that those who
have advocated this particular expedient should not have
noticed that in almost every case to which it could be applied,
the county board would represent or contain one of the liti-
gating parties, so that the result would be to make a group
of men judges in their own case.   It is easy enough to
imagine the petty local tyrannies that would arise under
any such arrangement.   What chance, for example, would
A, a highly unpopular landowner, a portion of whose land
had been selected for a sewage farm, have, if he appeared to
oppose the scheme before one of the new boards, and to
suggest as an alternative that a plot belonging to B, his
highly popular neighbour, afforded a more convenient site?
A writer of the highest ability and eminence has lately made
some very valuable remarks upon the petty local and domestic
oppressions incidental to decentralised democracy. 'The
'world,' as he reminds us, quoting Machiavelli, 'is made up of
'the vulgar;' and undoubtedly, the will of the majority in a
rural district is too often the will of the meanest.   The
forms of such oppression would be almost infinite, but it is
perhaps worth while to suggest a few of them: a burial-
ground in full view of an important residence, or a sewage
farm, or the tall chimney of waterworks, or a huge gasholder,
in a similar situation; the enforcement upon a new local
railway company of useless stations; the refusal to sanction
some important undertaking because it interfered with some
trumpery local or personal interest.   Could a local tribunal,
made up perchance largely of traders, be safely trusted to
settle the price of gas or water for manufacturing and domestic purposes?   Could any county board be left to form an
area of supply for either gas or water, or to adjust the prices
per 1,000 gallons or per 1,000 cubic feet between the various

portions of such area ?   Would there be no danger of favouritism to portions of a district in arranging the completion of
one part of a scheme before another—were it the laying of
tramway rails, or gas or water mains—or in the allocation
of parts of a dock or harbour to particular trades or trading
firms ?   Could a local or county board be left to settle the
question of the uses of the lines or stations of an existing
railway by some little ' three-mile' company ?   It is obvious
that in the negative answers that must be given to every one
of these suggestions is contained a fatal string of objections
to entrusting any of the subject-matter of private bill legislation to county boards or any similar bodies.   It may be
said shortly of them, or of any other local authority, that
they could of course only act in matters purely local, and
that they would be precluded as to these by the self-interest
with which all or some of their constituent members must
inevitably be tainted.   They would, in fact, be saturated with
undue preference and reek of intrigue.

Objectionable, indeed impossible, for many reasons would
be any great extension of local enquiries by travelling commissioners appointed by the Board of Trade or some similar
department. To begin with, such commissioners could hardly
deal with railways at all. Except in a few instances, which are
scarcely worth notice, it might be said that there is no such
thing as a local railway.   Beyond a few insignificant branches,
such as are almost universally made without Parliamentary
opposition by or in agreement with the railway company out
of whose lines they are to run, and by whom they are to be
worked, there is scarcely a railway that can be projected
which either is not, or may not, become part of a new through
route, or which does not in some degree affect the interests
of one or more existing companies.   Such projects soon lose
upon close investigation a local aspect, which has probably
not been unconsciously worn.   A highly local railway is proposed between Piningbury and Starvington.   Nothing could
look at the first glance more natural, more local, more innocent.   Plenty of persons come from the district to say that
it is the one thing wanted to make their two towns merit a
change of appellation.   A little cross-examination soon discloses the fact, that the movement that has culminated in the
promotion of the bill did not commence in the neighbourhood ; that the engineer, the directors, the contractor who is
ready with his ' plant' and his money, are all strangers; and
that the flame of local excitement is entirely of their blowing.
The more serious evidence makes it clear that the construc-

tion of the line will or may revolutionise the transit of some vast mineral or goods traffic which has hitherto been carried by Company A, and that somehow or other Company B, which now carries none of 'the stuff' in question, and with whose lines the new one effects junctions over the dangers and difficulties of which the engineer of the former would almost weep to a committee under ordinary circumstances, is only opposing upon some trumpery matter of clause. It may turn out well to pass such a line; but is it a local affair? And where should the local enquiry be held? At Piningbury or Starvington, neither of which places has done more than help to christen the scheme, or at one of the great termini of the real traffic? and of these, at which? And by whom? It is obvious that the proper place for hearing such a case is London, and that the proper tribunal, if not Parliament, should be a delegate of the highest class whose services Parliament can command. Nor is this an extreme illustration. So wide indeed is the application of the dictum that few lines are local, that it might be altered, and the phrase ' few lines are provincial' would probably state a truth. The relations between the great railway companies are so intricate and so extensive, that one of two competing Scotch companies can hardly improve its routes in Aberdeenshire or Inverness-shire without affecting every English company whose lines start northward out of London. Even the domestic arrangements of Irish companies are becoming yearly a matter of increasing interest to English companies. The Irish Channel is bridged by lines of steamers which start from different English ports, to which different English companies practically monopolise the approaches. Intimate relations are proposed between one of the latter and an Irish company which deals with the traffic to or from Belfast or Dublin, Cork or Greenore. The other English companies immediately snuff danger, and demand either a share in the proposed arrangement, or its abrogation. Would an agreement of such a character be a local or even a provincial question? Why is it Irish more than English? Would a question involving the ' cross-channel business,' as it is termed, of the Midland, the North-Western, the Great Western, of England, not to mention the Great Northern of Ireland or other Irish companies, be likely to be unimportant, simple, or easily settled, by some second or third class official?

One argument against local enquiries must not be lost sight of, and that is their expensiveness. In that particular those who welcomed them as a substitute for Parliament, might find that they had got out of the frying pan into the fire. Counsel and witnesses may be costly and highly paid now that the enquiry is held in London. It may be a somewhat expensive bait that now tempts the local witness up to town. It may be that, as matters stand, a comfortable settlement of clauses with a deputation from a mayor and corporation is best achieved after the hearts of the good aldermen have been warmed with something choicer than ale. But the best counsel, and the most efficient engineers, and other experts, are still to be found in London, and their transportation into the country would be found expensive beyond all experience. It would prove far cheaper to keep bringing up the aldermen. If anyone doubts this, let him test the cost of moving a good engineer or other skilled witness fifty miles from Westminster; his hesitation will not long survive the experiment. And let no one think that these enquiries would be conducted by the cheap local practitioner, assisted by the cheap local engineer. Some energetic litigant would soon set the fashion of having his case presented in the best possible manner, and his example would before long be universally and properly followed. That it should be otherwise is contrary to all English experience.

Any person who has assisted either as counsel or judge at a local enquiry must acknowledge further, that some little advantage is obtained by a removal of the hearing to London in the mitigation of the heat of local passions. Contending factions are lukewarm before Parliamentary committees in comparison with their temperature at home. This is a minor consideration, but it is not without its value, although, of course, it would not avail without the greater reasons with which it is in harmony.

The evil of the double enquiry which now prevails has assumed such proportions in the eyes of many persons, that they have thought that any expedient which would get rid of it would do all that is needful in the way of reform. But there are other defects in the present system beside the double enquiry, which the achievement of a single hearing, taken by itself, would not remove. A single enquiry, if the tribunal were otherwise unaltered, would resolve itself manifestly into an enquiry before a joint committee of Lords and Commons. Neither House favours joint committees for this or any other purpose. They have seldom been successful. Their composition is calculated to provoke jealousies. If their numbers are uneven, one House must have a numerical preponderance, which is not after all avoided by making the numbers even, for in that case the chairman, to whichever House he belong, must have a casting vote. In neither House would the decisions of joint committees meet with the same unvarying consideration as do those of committees composed entirely of its own members; and an inclination towards repudiation would be intensified by every occasion upon which the Lords serving on a joint committee were known to have been of one opinion, and the Commons serving on it of another. Besides, the difficulty which would be experienced in manning respectably joint committees would be but slightly less than that which is at the bottom of the present movement; and it would never suit the dignity of the House of Commons to send a quota of second or third rate members to sit beside the peers.

To what then at last does the question of substitution narrow itself? Surely to that of the appointment of a few high-class judges to take the place of the select committees of both Houses. It is not given to the 'Edinburgh Review,' any more than to other authorities, personal or impersonal, to be consistent upon all matters and throughout all time. But we may own to a certain sense of satisfaction in being able to extract from our own pages in 1854 the following passage :—

'We hope to see the establishment of a judicial court within the walls of Parliament performing the same functions as committees on private bills. This court should be common to both Houses, to whom it should make its reports, and thus the double enquiry in Lords and Commons, now so vexatious and costly to the parties, would be avoided.'

These words were penned at a time when the proceedings of Parliament upon private bills had long been a scandal and a by-word, and when people had little hope that the reforms in progress would be sufficient to clear the legislative atmosphere. It could not readily be forgotten, among a sheaf of similar incidents, that the bill for a line of railway from London to Birmingham had been thrown out by the House of Lords in absolute scorn of the evidence, and that it had been subsequently passed—we believe in the very next year—upon the alteration of the land estimates from 250,000*l.* to 750,000*l.* But the reform proved to be substantial, the misdoings of the days of selfishness and corruption have passed below the horizon of this generation, and many persons will be found to express regret that a purer epoch should seem likely to close with a declaration on the part of

Parliament itself of the necessity for a delegation of part
of its natural work, upon the score of its own inability or
disinclination to perform it any longer. But the public will
insist upon retaining as much as may be retained of the protection and sanction of Parliament. It will insist that all
undertakings involving interference with property shall still
be embodied in bills; that all the formalities as to notices
and other compliances with the standing orders shall be preserved; that bills shall be read a first and second time in
each House as heretofore; and that the work of the court
of *locus standi* and of the select committees shall alone
be delegated to a judge. It will insist further that the
judge shall report to both Houses—it goes without speaking
that there shall only be one enquiry—but that his report
shall be considered final by neither; that is, that a vote
shall be taken upon the third reading as at present. It
would certainly be convenient, and it is probably feasible,
that one examination upon standing orders should suffice,
except in cases like those of additional provision; in fact,
the standing orders of the two Houses affecting private bills
ought to be consolidated, and to become standing orders of
Parliament.

The consolidation of the standing orders will afford an
opportunity for their general revision, and for their improvement in a few particulars. One ridiculous restriction
ought certainly to be swept away. We allude to the prohibition against the payment of interest during construction.
It arose during the days of the railway mania, and was probably intended to prevent the indefinite and fruitless occupation of territory, and the raising of capital for lines that
were never intended to be made, and its perversion to other
and sinister purposes. It is completely out of date now.
Nor is its unqualified repeal even now asked for; all that is
demanded is that the normal cost of the money raised to
construct a line of railway, calculated upon a reasonable
period to be allowed for construction, should be considered
as part of the cost of the works themselves, should be made
good to the subscribers, and that the amount should eventually be added to the capital of the company. This is perfectly rational and just. It is obvious that if a man hands
over 5,000*l.* in a lump sum to a contractor to build him a
house, and is not in a position to inhabit that house for three
years, it has cost him not 5,000*l.* but 5,000*l.* *plus* three
years' simple interest at least at the current rate of ordinary
investment. If he pay by instalments, he must charge him-

self interest on each instalment from the day of payment.
So with a railway. Each subscriber of 1,000*l.* towards an
undertaking that is to occupy a period of five years in
completion, subscribes not 1,000*l.* but 1,200*l.* if we calculate simple interest at 4 per cent., and if he pays his 1,000*l.*
on allotment; something less than 1,200*l.* but still considerably over 1,000*l.* if, as is usual, his subscription is spread
over several calls made at prescribed intervals. To refuse to
credit him in any shape or way with any portion of the
interest upon his 1,000*l.* during the period of five years, is
simply to force him to buy his shares at a premium. That
is the plain truth about the restriction; it forces all new
railway companies, who do not manage to evade it, to issue
their shares at a considerable premium. It should be remembered that generations of shareholders are short-lived,
that an enormous number of shares change hands during
the course of five years from causes altogether beyond the
control of their holders, and consequently that every sale of
such shares at par involves a compulsory gift at the bidding
of Parliament by the original holder to his transferee. Can
it be wondered at that capitalists decline to make such a
present to posterity? This hardship is aggravated by the
fact that the rule fails to reach the capital for new lines
raised by the old companies. These take care in many
instances in fixing the capital for a new line to have a
margin over the amount actually required for construction
large enough to cover the interest, and the capital, however
raised, bears interest at once as part of the general capital
of a revenue-bearing concern. Neither new nor old shareholders investigate the process by which this is achieved.
But this device is not always necessary; as a matter
of fact, the shares of most of the great companies are
at a premium, and the subscribers of new capital are
usually existing shareholders or their transferees. In such
cases, even if the interest upon the new capital be postponed,
it is issued at such a price below the current value of the
ordinary shares, that the difference represents to the allottee
the value of the interest lost in the postponement. But the
result, noticed or unnoticed, and however achieved, is that
the holders of new capital get interest from the date of
subscription, or the equivalent of such interest, and that
in one way or the other the money is raised without
difficulty. It is obvious that the result of this foolish, and
indeed iniquitous, because partial, restriction is to retard and
hamper the formation of new undertakings, and to prolong

within the reach of its operation the monopoly with which a new undertaking is intended to interfere. Indeed, it is notorious that 'the railway interest' in Parliament, working upon a certain amount of uneconomic perversity, alone maintains it. And its maintenance has the desired effect. Capitalists are beginning to see clearly enough what it means to 'stand out' of their interest for five years or more. They decline to advance their millions upon these terms; and the consequence is that schemes like the Regent's Canal Railway with a capital of 11,000,000*l.* languish and die, while the 50,000*l.* or 100,000*l.* which it may have cost to promote them is lost money; or else, in the manner of the Hull and Barnsley lines, they are made, but at the cost of the company throwing itself into the arms of contractors, with a result which the shareholders really do feel. No review of private bill legislation at this moment would be complete without an exposure of this matter. It is well known that the more enlightened authorities of the House of Commons were prepared last session, and even earlier, to agree to a resolution or to a standing order which would have cured the grievance, by allowing a reasonable rate of interest during a reasonable period; it is also well known from what quarter the opposition proceeded, and how the half-promised justice came to be withheld.

To return to the new procedure. It will be seen that if our view of minimisation of change be adopted, the proceedings upon private bills antecedent and subsequent to the judicial hearing will be exactly what they are now. We have already intimated that the judges should take cases of *locus standi,* in other words that the court which hears the case should determine, as select committees used formerly to do, what litigants had a right of appearance. The creation of a separate *locus standi* court in the House of Commons has been a failure, as everybody conversant with the business knew it would be from the first. It costs the country some 2,000*l.* to 3,000*l.* a year, and it adds, we believe, an appreciable percentage to the costs of suitors. In spite of the undoubted ability of many of its members, its decisions have never given satisfaction. It was instituted under the erroneous impression that it would save time and cost. It has wasted both. Under the old practice, when the select committees decided on the *locus standi* of an opponent to any bill before them, the question of a right to appear was postponed until the leading counsel for the promoters had made his opening statement, revealing his own case in all its bearings, and giving an outline of the evidence on which he intended to rely. He then read his opponent's petition, and stated his reasons for considering it irrelevant. He was followed by the counsel for the petitioner objected to, who made in his turn a preliminary statement of his own case, and of the class of evidence he intended to adduce. The committee were thus 'seised' of the merits of the case on both sides to an extent quite sufficient to enable them to dispose of the question of a *primâ facie* right to oppose. But the Court of Referees are not in that position. They know nothing of the merits of either promotion or opposition. They have the bill before them as originally printed, but they decline to consider any amendments that may have been made in it. They have also the contested petition before them, which, except for the sake of making an allegation verbally clearer, they decline also to amend. In vain, therefore, may a promoter urge that, although his bill did, as it stood in December, interfere with a petitioner's right, it leaves him untouched in its later form. The *locus standi* is granted. In vain, on the other hand, may a petitioner, whose petition fails in form, plead that a disclosure of the merits of the case, or the addition of fresh grounds of opposition which he has lately discovered, would procure him a hearing. He finds no place of repentance, though he seek it carefully with tears. Those who are responsible for the development of the practice of the *locus standi* court are not perhaps to be blamed overmuch for this want of handiness and elasticity. Both have probably arisen from a combined fear of lengthening the proceedings and of usurping the functions of the select committee. Not the less is the court a mistake, and it is obvious that its disappearance will be one of the features of the new order of things.

We have then no difficulty in stating with precision what in our judgement should be the constitution of the new tribunal. Judges should be appointed with the salaries, pensions, and rank in every respect of the judges of the High Court of Justice. Their precedence should be stated in the statute creating them. Their position cannot well be made too dignified, if they are to reflect Parliament to the nation. For reasons to be given presently we think they should be three in number. They might be called 'Judges ' of the High Court of Parliament,' ' Parliamentary Judges,' or ' Commissioners of the High Court of Parliament,' ' Par- ' liamentary Commissioners,' or by any equivalent name ; but we venture to suggest the first as by far the best official title. About their salaries and pensions there need be no difficulty. According to the returns already quoted, the suitors' fees have averaged more than 34,000*l.* a year for the last eleven years in the House of Commons alone, and these, not to mention the sums similarly paid to the House of Lords, obviously form a fund far more than sufficient to pay the new judges, their personal attendants, and the existing staff of the Private Bill Office. Although they would almost invariably sit singly, they should be empowered to sit together. They should be absolutely independent of the Supreme Court of Judicature, and this independence should be declared by statute. They should have full powers of subpœna, attachment, and committal for contempt, in fact all the necessary powers of a court of record. The respect in which they are ultimately held by the country will depend in a great measure upon the respect and reserve with which they are treated by Parliament. They will be as much the creation of Parliament as the Speaker in the House of Commons, or the Chairman of Committees in the House of Lords; and it will be for Parliament by respecting their decisions to enhance the national acceptance.

It is necessary to consider whether three judges will succeed in doing the work likely to be thrown upon them session by session. Upon this point an analysis of the proceedings upon private bills in both Houses for the years 1882, 1883, and 1884, seems pretty conclusive. These three years represent a high average of work to be done, and 1882 was the heaviest year by far that had been experienced over a long period, heavier even than 1873, which we believe, although the figures are not easily accessible, to have been in its turn heavier than any of its predecessors for some time previously. The number of days during which select committees were occupied in the consideration of private bills during the sessions mentioned were as follows: During the year 1882, committees of the Commons sat 522 days, and committees of the Lords 230 days; in all the two Houses sat 752 days. From this total must be deducted for the purpose of our calculation 146 days occupied by second enquiries, leaving a nett total of 606 days. In 1883 the consumption of time was, in the Commons 428 days, in the Lords 203 days, in all 631 days. In that year the second enquiries occupied 130 days, so that for it the nett total is 501 days. In 1884 the figures are, for the Commons 360 days, for the Lords 162 days, or a total of 522 days. The second enquiries occupied about 100 days, leaving a nett

total of 422 days. The three years show a descent in the
amount of work, but of this the depression in trade is probably in a great measure the cause, and it would be rash to
calculate that for many years the amount of business to
be done will be seriously diminished. The three nett totals
of 606, 501, and 422 days, give a yearly average of 510 days
nearly. To these must be added the time during which the
referees sat upon questions of *locus standi.* It is difficult,
indeed impossible, to state the exact number of days thus
occupied, for the court very often sits for a short time only,
in consequence of the settlement of its cases or of some
other accidental circumstance. It is safe to say that 20 days
for a session would be an ample figure to add under this
head. This addition would bring up the average of sessional
work from 510 days to 530 days. If three judges dealt
with this amount of work at the pace of select committees, it is clear that each would have to sit 176 days.
From March 1 to August 14 are 177 days, but of these 24
or thereabouts are Sundays. The total amount of working days, therefore, without allowing anything for holidays,
would only be 153 days for each judge, on the assumption
that they all worked equally. But a week at Easter must
be conceded for a holiday, and two or three days at Whit-
suntide as well. It would not, therefore, be right to assume
the working days of a session at more than 140 at the outside. But the working day of a judge would be actually
$5\frac{1}{2}$ hours against the nominal 4 hours of the House of
Commons, and the equally nominal 5 hours of the House
of Lords. The court would sit at ten o'clock, and would
not rise till four o'clock, with an interval of half an hour
for luncheon, and this difference, if worked out, will be
found to express a very substantial addition to its capacity.

The figures for the three years upon which we have been
calculating show that the average nominal working day of
Lords and Commons taken together was as near as possible
$4\frac{1}{2}$ hours. The average annual number of 530 days given
above, is therefore reducible into 2,290 hours. This would
give each judge 763 hours' work to do, and working at the
rate of $5\frac{1}{2}$ hours a day he would get through it in 138 to
139 days. But a very considerable reduction has to be
made here. The nominal working days of committees are
not the actual working days; what with unpunctuality—to
which we do not refer with any discourteous intention—
interruptions for divisions, and occasional adjournments to
suit the convenience of honourable members who have to be

in their places early, and other similar causes of curtailment, the real working day of Parliamentary committees is not what it seems. But further, he would be a very weak judge who did not cut the present proceedings short to a very considerable extent. Local evidence would be divided by four, the expatiations of skilled witnesses by two, and a very sensible abatement would be made in the display of over-ingenious or persistent counsel. One day in six would on a very moderate computation be saved in these several departments of waste of time, and the 139 days we have just assigned to the judge's labour would be reduced to 110 or 115 days in an average year. Taking as before the working session at 140 days, this would give a margin of 25 to 30 days to each judge. The combined court would thus have a margin of something between 70 and 90 days, which would be an ample reserve against the illness of a judge or other contingencies. In fact, it might be well to consider after a while, whether it might not be possible for the judges to relieve the business of the High Court of Justice from time to time by taking election petitions ; or whether some of the more important business now proposed to be given to the Railway Commissioners might not be handed over to the new judges. These are, however, suggestions for the future, and do not call for immediate settlement.

But it will be said, and rightly said, 'You must not take ' an average year ; you must so constitute your court that it ' may bear the strain of a very heavy one.' Let us then take the year 1882. For this year, it will be remembered, the nett total of Parliamentary working days was 606 days or 2,626 hours. This would give to each judge 875 hours or 159 working days of the court. If we deduct one-sixth as before for improved conduct of business, there will remain a nett total of 135 days, which would still enable him to complete his work within the session of 140 days. In short, the three judges would have a margin of 15 days, even with the business of 1882. But there is no reason whatever why the court should not sit during the period of prorogation to finish any 'remanets' with which it might be left at the end of a session. Engineers, solicitors, and Parliamentary agents may plead that they would like to have the autumn for the preparation of work for the coming spring sittings. Possibly ; they have always been accustomed to it, and very likely think that they could not do without it. If necessary, they will have to accommodate themselves to this inconvenience, if indeed it be one. The 'remanets' would not be numerous in any year; in most years there would be none at all. He would be a very unlucky or a very busy engineer who would often be obliged to leave a new survey to attend to the engineering evidence of a case in London. Nor need the attendance of a Parliamentary agent in court be so constant that he cannot keep things going at his office in Great George Street or its neighbourhood. But he would find at all events such autumnal distractions a rarity. A sessional or permanent resolution of the two Houses would readily provide for the taking up of bills in one session at the stage in which they were left at the close of its pre-decessor, but it would be best that a section in the Act of Parliament constituting the court should empower the judges to sit in or out of session.

A strong effort will be made to turn the tribunal into what has been called ' a travelling court.' We trust that there will be no clause in its constitution compelling a judge to hear a case out of London. To a discretionary power to sit elsewhere, if it be understood to be really discretionary, there can be no objection. But ninety-nine cases out of a hundred that deserve to be heard by a first-class judge at all will call for first-class counsel and witnesses, and would be, as we have already shown, better and more cheaply settled in London than out of it. In saying this, we take no account of the disturbance to business caused by moving the court. Simple gas, water, and tramway bills, and other easily arranged matters of purely local import, will be carried out as now by provisional orders. Whenever they involve issues important enough to warrant giving them a bill to themselves, or to induce opponents to be dissatisfied with the ordinary local enquiry and to appeal to Parliament, they come under the class of cases that are best dealt with by a metropolitan hearing. It has been suggested that the court should sit for one month in Edinburgh and another in Dublin. We cannot think that this injunction would be valuable. It would be highly inconvenient to move the court for a fixed period during the busy part of the year, between March and August, and to do so later would amount to making ' remanets' as a matter of course of all the Scotch and Irish business.

Upon this point of the stationary or movable character of the court, the classification of private bills inserted at the beginning of each volume of local and personal Acts is not uninstructive. These Acts are divided into nineteen classes, which are as follows :—

1. Bridges and ferries.
2. Canals, rivers, navigations, tunnels, and subways.
3. Charitable foundations and institutions.
4. Drainage and drainage embankments.
5. Ecclesiastical affairs, including tithes.
6. Estates.
7. Fisheries.
8. Gas-light companies.
9. Harbours, docks, ports, piers, quays.
10. Improvements in towns, municipal and county and local government matters, markets.
11. Inclosures of commons.
12. Parish affairs.
13. Personal affairs.
14. Railways.
15. Trading and other companies.
16. Tramways.
17. Turnpike and other roads.
18. Water companies.
19. Provisional orders confirmation.

In 1882 there were some 238 Acts passed of all classes; but out of these, classes 1, 3, 4, 5, 6, 7, 11, 15, and 17, which are eminently local and personal classes, only furnished fourteen bills, and of these scarcely any, if any at all, were opposed. Of the remainder, 117 were in classes 2, 9, and 14; that is, they referred to canals, rivers, navigations, harbours, docks, and railways, all of which it is obvious may afford subjects of extreme importance, not only to the localities immediately concerned, but also to the country at large. The rest were made up of the more important measures connected with town improvements, gas, water, and tramways, to which provisional orders, and consequently local enquiries, were either by their promoters or by public departments considered inapplicable. An analysis of the local and personal Acts for 1883 and 1884 would reveal the same state of things. It must further be borne in mind that every appeal to Parliament against the confirmation of a provisional order is an appeal from a local enquiry to a metropolitan hearing, from a subordinate to a supreme tribunal.

There is but little advantage in the suggestion that the judges should have power to appoint referees or deputies to try small disputes in purely local cases. Such disputes are generally settled now by the preliminary enquiry antecedent to the provisional order; whenever they are not so settled, it follows that they are not simple enough to warrant subdelegation. The point rather to be considered is whether there should not be a provision by which cases of a certain class should be capable of being reserved to Parliament; whether, that is, in cases that assume a national importance unusually direct and obvious—say, such a case as the Parks Railway or the Thirlmere water scheme—Parliament should not be able, without being supposed to discredit the new

court, to resolve that it should take the trial of the matter
into its own hands. It would not be easy to arrange this
because the two Houses might differ on any particular bill,
and it would not certainly be convenient that the House of
Commons should try a scheme by committee, and that the
House of Lords, refusing to do the same, should send it to a
judge who might differ from the House of Commons. Still,
that difficulty might be got over if the provision were thought
valuable; and it must be admitted that a declaration that a
particular case is unfitted for the ordinary procedure is not
unknown to the present system. The Parks Railway Bill,
the Thirlmere scheme, and the various competing schemes
for bridging the Thames below London, are all instances in
point. They were all referred to what are popularly known
as 'hybrid' committees, consisting of seven or ten members.
We see no objection to this, provided that such reservations
be not too frequent, and that powerful companies do not
abuse the operation of the rule. It ought never to be applied
to schemes merely on account of their magnitude. That
would be at once to discredit the judges and to restore to
Parliament the consideration of those very measures which
from the intricacy and difficulty of their issues committees
are least able to cope with. It should be confined to bills
which though private in form and inception have some
feature in them of direct national interest which takes them
out of the category of really private undertakings. For
instance, the question whether the country shall sacrifice the
beauty of Hyde Park and St. James's Park for any purpose,
however utilitarian, is national. The question whether
Thirlmere shall be made into a tank, even to slake the thirst
and wash the streets of Lancastrian towns, is national. So,
perhaps, is the question of the mode in which the metropolitan river shall be crossed in London itself. These are
all *cases in which the nation may be said to have a right to
appear.* But a proposal to make a new railway from London
to Brighton, or a ship canal to Manchester, or new docks
below Dagenham, or any other purely commercial speculation
that was merely eminent for size and importance among its
fellows, would not come under the excepted category. It
would be a mistake to express degree in terms of kind.

The one great danger of the tribunal has yet to be
pointed out. It is commonly expressed by those who feel it and
know what they mean, as well as by those who do not feel
it and would be puzzled to say what they do mean, but who,
being anxious to maintain the present state of things, adopt it

as a useful piece of cant, in the phrase ' a judge would be sure
' to run in a groove.'   ' The very uncertainty of the present
' tribunal is its excellence,' is another form of the same cry.
Here peeps out an old friend of college days whom many of
us knew then under the name of ' anceps medium.'   Turn
the cry into an argument, and express it syllogistically, and
it will be apparent at once that the terms ' groove ' and
' uncertainty ' are each used in two senses.   The persons
employing them may mean that a judge will be the possessor
of idiosyncrasies, which will grow with his own judicial
growth until he will always decide bills by hard and fast
rules of his own making, which he will not allow any special
circumstances in individual cases to modify.   Parliament, on
the contrary, has no idiosyncrasies, it does not act by rule,
it decides each case on its own merits, either as if there were
no precedents, or as if precedents were at least as much
honoured by supersession as by adherence.   If they mean
this they are not far wrong.   But a great many of them
have a very different meaning, which they would probably
decline to admit.   By ' uncertainty ' of Parliament they mean
that sort of uncertainty by which the very same bill, supported and opposed by the very same evidence and speeches of
counsel, may pass one House and be rejected by the other; or,
even if heard at the same time, were that possible, before two
committees of the same House in two adjoining rooms, might
be passed by one group of four gentlemen and rejected by
the other; that kind of ' uncertainty,' in fact, to which the
unlucky Manchester Canal Bill, to which we have already
referred, fell a victim.   That bill, which passed the Commons in 1883, but was thrown out in the Lords in that year,
was brought in in the House of Lords in 1884 and passed,
was then taken back to the Commons in triumph and there
thrown out, and this without the slightest essential alteration of scheme or circumstance !   This was of course a very
gross case.   It involved the anomaly of the rejection of a
measure which had passed both Houses.   The promoters of
it had a right to think that the Commons at all events were
pledged to it, and that when the Lords had passed it in 1884
it was safe.   There is something like cynicism in thus
encouraging promoters to spend money by the 100,000*l.* and
then, by reversal of a decision, making it all waste money
for them.   We do not say which of these conflicting decisions
was right or wrong, but it is obvious that this sort of
' uncertainty ' differs from the other, and that it is bad,
although many there be who tacitly favour it.   ' So long as

' it reigns,' they say in effect, ' you need never despair as to
' what you may pass, nor as to what you may upset.'   But
this sort of uncertainty is judgement by idiosyncrasy with a
vengeance.

Not the less will it be a vital necessity for the judges to
remember that expediency will be the great principle that
should guide them.   You cannot trim expediency into a
hedgerow.   For the new court you do not want a Notting-
ham or an Eldon.   Every case as it comes up will make
its own law.   We have already said that promoters have no
rights, that by coming to Parliament they acknowledge that
they have none.   This is very nearly, but not quite, true.
It would be almost as true to say that opponents had none.
Promoters have one main right, which is, that if their scheme
is of sufficient public advantage to outweigh its interference
with private interests it ought to pass.   The main rights of
opponents are two : first, that if the public advantage is insufficient the bill ought not to pass; and secondly, that if it
passes they ought to be compensated, but this last right is
not universal.   It is obvious that there is little scope here
for rule or precedent.   Expediency grows, dwindles, trans-
forms itself as social conditions vary.   A judge ought to be
able to play Aristæus or Hercules to its Proteus.   The weak
case of a few years ago may be the strong case of this year,
and the weak case again of a few years hence.   A judge
might be perfectly justified in 1890 in discarding the considerations on which he acted in 1885, and would be unequal
to his position if he were not ready so to do.   Certain social
principles, as these are understood in England, are involved
in the term ' expediency,' but that is all.

There is one particular in which judges accustomed to
the rigid practice of the law courts might fail at first, and
that is in the reception of evidence.   Parliamentary committees and the counsel who practise before them have often
been twitted with their laxity in this respect by those who
are unaccustomed to the particular procedure.   There is
some ground for the charge, and a certain amount of amendment would no doubt be insisted upon by a judge, even by a
judge taken from the ranks of the Parliamentary bar itself.
But it must not be forgotten that matters of expediency
must be to a considerable extent matters of opinion, and that
important facts and presumptions leading to opinion may be
incapable of strict proof.   The present practice as to evidence
before Parliament has grown out of the essential conditions
of the enquiries; it has accommodated itself to their neces-

sities. Every advocate of high position there has had his early training in courts of law or equity, and the Parliamentary method does not represent the progress of unscrupulous or careless practitioners imposing upon a weak tribunal—for it would be the interest of each one to keep the other in order—but it has arisen from a consensus of bar and tribunal to assimilate the procedure to the conditions of the business to be done. That is the principle underlying the practice; clumsiness on one side of the table and weakness on the other may and do sometimes obscure it, but in the main it is not overstrained, and certainly it ought not to be set aside. Any judge of high capacity would soon see this, and the court may fairly be left to build up its own rules and practice as to the form and quality of the evidence it will receive.

The establishment of the court will be facilitated by the existence of a competent staff. There will in the first instance be positively nothing else to do but to appoint the judges and their personal attendants. There will be nothing essential to alter, to begin with at all events, in the machinery of the Private Bill Office or elsewhere in connexion with the legislation. The only officials to be dispossessed or deposed will be the referees. All the immediate arrangements consequent upon the change could be made in a day. Opportunity should be given for the judges to confer from time to time with the chairmen of committees of both Houses with a view to the revision of standing orders when and where necessary, and to the framing of general orders for the conduct of business; but a long time would probably elapse before any such power was exercised upon anything beyond points of detail. In fact no change could well be less violent or more easily made. Not a man, except the referees, need lose his office, or indeed change his habits in any important particular; and as to Parliament itself, the House of Commons may find a precedent for its surrender of jurisdiction in the case of its own election petitions, and the House of Lords in the creation of the Divorce Court.

The only two classes of men who will feel the change are those members of the bar who habitually practise before Parliamentary committees, and the Parliamentary agents. The Parliamentary bar, as it has long come to be distinctively called, is, in its present condition, a growth of the last fifty years, and has contributed many great advocates to swell the illustrious roll of the profession. The presence of so many first-rate men in its ranks has probably been due, not to any unusual pecuniary temptation, which for the best men does not in fact exist, but to the charm and variety of the work, the pleasantness of the tribunal, and the autumn and winter leisure so dear to men of literary antecedents and tastes. These attractions have outweighed the sacrifice of judicial preferment, and of the excitements and ambitions of political life. Henceforth some of the peculiar features of their practice will be lost, but Parliament will now be obviously open to them, and there will be three judgeships at all events within their reach. While they were pleading before committees of Parliament there was at least ground for a disqualification based upon the idea that a member of Parliament might have undue influence with colleagues. But after the change there can be no better reason for excluding from the House of Commons a member of the bar who has pleaded for a railway company in the new court than there is now for excluding a railway director of the same company. As to the judgeships, it will be their own fault if they do not merit them, or some of them, from time to time. Little pity, then, need be wasted upon any change of status to be suffered by the Parliamentary bar.

As to the Parliamentary agents, it would be pleasant to feel that something could be done to secure their position. It is hardly out of place here to say that they form a group of gentlemen of whom everybody concerned with the private business of Parliament, from Lord Redesdale and Sir Arthur Otway down to the smallest official in the Private Bill Office, would speak with kindliness and respect. The business they carry on is highly technical, and yet the rules of its practice are almost entirely unwritten and traditional. It is clear, therefore, that the officials with whom they have to deal must rely very much upon their knowledge and candour, and that the lack of these must have contributed very materially to the quietude and smoothness with which transactions with and in respect to private bills are now carried. The utility of such a body is apparent and can be recovered, and it must be a long time before the private practitioner will be able to dispense with this sort of assistance. We believe that more than one attempt has been made by the more important members of that body, with the concurrence of the authorities of the House, to improve the conditions under which agency is conducted. At present any person, whatever his qualifications, may become a Parliamentary agent by going into the

Private Bill Office and signing a certain roll. Anyone may appear in person to plead his own cause before Parliament, as before a court of law. To gain audience on behalf of others he must constitute himself an agent, just as in some courts of law he must be a barrister, and in others a solicitor. An instance has been known of a woman tripping down stairs and signing the roll aforesaid, in order that she might appear upon a joint petition of herself and others; and a similar performance is said to have been executed by two or three Yarmouth fishermen upon another occasion. This, we think, shows that undue facilities are given for the assumption of an important function, and it is probable that in this, as in other respects, during the passage of the measure an opportunity will arise for the satisfactory settlement of the status of Parliamentary agents; at the same time, it is evident that the maintenance of this, as of all other orders of men, must depend upon its utility.

It is necessary to discuss the question of the selection of the judges. The notion of appointing lay 'experts' seems to us fatal to the scheme. To begin with: Who is an expert? Who could lay claim to the title in respect of all the eighteen classes of private bills? Would a railway manager necessarily have a faculty for judging between the merits of two sites for a cemetery, or for gas works, or for a sewage farm? Could he be supposed to be peculiarly fitted to settle some question of tithes between a rector and his parishioners, or the incidence of taxation over some drainage district in the fens? Or would an engineer necessarily be a safe person to adjudicate upon the thousand and one questions that arise amongst the different classes of inhabitants upon town improvement bills and similar measures, or upon the policy of sanctioning a new line to Brighton, or of introducing railway competition into Fife, or into certain of the districts occupied by the North-Eastern Railway Company? Engineering is but one element, not always by any means the most important element, in the merits even of those schemes that seem most largely to depend upon it. The truth is that an 'expert' usually means a man who knows one thing well, but that only. He is not, generally speaking, a man whose intellect has been trained by a wide and systematic education. Again, his quality of an expert is not long-lived; and what is he when he has lost it? It depends upon his day-to-day conversance with a business the conditions of which are constantly changing. If the greatest and most 'expert' of all railway managers were to leave his calling to-morrow,

what would he retain of all his craft in ten years' time?
How completely would his knowlege of to-day have become
obsolete by that time, even if it remained unimpaired! How
would the first manager of the London and Birmingham
Railway Company open his eyes if he could be suddenly
shown the ramifications and conditions of the business of
the London and North-Western Company, its gigantic offspring! Commerce upon a grand scale is an accomplishment
which, unless it is constantly exercised, must be re-learnt
every decade. Moreover, an expert, as long as he is an
expert, is a partisan. How could an ex-chairman or ex-
manager of a great and old-established railway company be
expected to overthrow all his sympathies and prejudices,
and give a fair chance to new companies, new systems of
trade, and grand experiments in transit? Imagine him set
to judge of a scheme that proposed to utilise on a great
scale the disused or half-disused inland navigations for the
conveyance of certain classes of goods and minerals! An
expert is useful in the witness-box; upon the judicial bench
he would be dangerous for a time, and effete afterwards.
He would be a little volcano, positively mischievous while
he was burning, and negatively mischievous when he was
burnt out. If the field of selection were left unlimited, it
is to be feared that jobbery would soon bring about the decadence of the tribunal. How convenient it would be every
now and then to offer some second or third rate politician,
who had grown into the dimensions of a party difficulty
without losing a reputation for 'common sense,' so pleasant
and so honourable a shelf! On the whole, the best training
known at present for these, as for other judgeships, happens
to be the business of the bar. Up to this time—and may
the fact long continue—the highest class of advocates have
usually been men who have begun life with a first-rate
education, and who have proved their intellectual metal and
moral fibre in the course of it. It is for this reason that
they come to the bar. They come because their antecedents
incite and their character nerves them to encounter the risks
and toils of a most uncertain and arduous profession. As
they proceed along its path, the range of their knowledge
widens, and their sympathies—for they are always changing
sides—extend. Their profession is a lifelong prolongation
of their education. In one sense they are experts, and experts of the best kind. They are experts who have no
predilections, and whose knowledge does not decay. If the
tribunal is to be permanent, and to be permanent it must

be trusted and respected by suitors and counsel alike, its seats should be filled by three of the foremost men obtainable from the ranks of that profession which forms the principal field at present for the production of judicial qualities.

In conclusion, then, we admit with something like reluctance that the time has come when Parliament will determine to part with this branch of its business. It would be unjust to say that in doing so it removes an abuse in consequence of pressure from without. In the main the work has not been so very ill done; and inasmuch as the causes of shortcoming are apparent and incidental, it is possible that a strong effort from within might have removed at least a great many of them. But the institution and probable increase in the number of Grand Committees has sounded a last and unmistakable note of change, and Mr. Sellar's bill, or some Government measure in place of it, will most assuredly become law. It is a change which should undoubtedly be taken up by the Government of the day, and though it should be in all points complete, it should be conducted with unusual caution and reserve. The country has a right to expect this. All the different classes of private bills involve an attack and a defence; every promoter is in some way an aggressor; some property, right, interest, liberty, immunity, franchise, or privilege is and must be menaced. Parliament has hitherto acted as the great national arbitrator between the parties; and it is about to delegate this most serious and difficult part of its functions. There is a risk attending this, and many who are ignorant of this risk hail the change without reservation; some, because they think it may be made to suit themselves in some minor particular; others, because minds which have a turn for small revolutions are always ready to brush away as an abuse institutions into the uses and origin of which they have not enquired. But the more sober and better instructed residue of those who have been brought into contact with the system, regard the step not without anxiety, and although they are content to see it made, desire also to have it safeguarded with all possible precautions.

ART. IV.—*Correspondance inédite de Mallet du Pan avec la Cour de Vienne* (1794–98), *publiée d'après les Manuscrits conservés aux Archives de Vienne.* Par ANDRÉ MICHEL; avec une Préface de M. TAINE. In 2 vols. Paris: 1884.

IN a hitherto unpublished letter, Mr. Thomas Carlyle speaks of the writer of this Correspondence in the following terms :

'At an early period of my studies on the French Revolution, I found the royalist side of that huge controversy to be an almost completely mad one, destined, on the whole, to die for ever; and thus, except where royalists had historical facts to teach me, had, after a short time, rather to shun than seek acquaintance with them, finding in their speculative notions nothing but distress and weariness for me, and generally, instead of illumination in my researches, mere darkness visible. It was in this way that I had as good as missed Mallet du Pan, confounding him with the general *cohue*, from whom I now find he was widely and peculiarly distinguished, very much to his honour indeed. Of all writers on the royalist side—indeed, I may say, on any side—Mallet seems to me to have taken incomparably the truest view of the enormous phenomena he was in the midst of.'

Later criticism has awarded to the enlightened royalists a high rank among the observers of the Revolution, and endorsed Carlyle's ample but tardy recognition of the merits of Mallet du Pan, as the best exponent of their sane and liberal views. The reputation of this writer has undergone strange varieties of fortune. At his death in 1800 he was one of the best known publicists in Europe. His pamphlets and articles had all through the Revolution been largely circulated in France, they had been read in England and translated in Germany. He had been consulted by all the leading statesmen and monarchs of the Continent, and his services to the cause of European freedom had obtained from Pitt the acknowledgement of a pension for his widow and a place for his son. Yet his name sank almost at once into comparative obscurity, and it was not until 1851 that the publication of his memoirs by M. Sayous,* which formed the subject of an article in this Journal, made known his life and opinions, and in some degree restored him to his proper place among the observers of the Revolution. Thirty years have increased his authority, without rendering his writings more accessible, and the present volumes, which to some extent

---

* Mémoires et Correspondance de Mallet du Pan, par A. Sayous, 1851; see 'Ed. Review,' vol. xcv., p. 481, April 1852.

supply this ·defect, are due to a suggestion of M. Taine, and to the school of critical enquiry of which that historian is the eminent representative.

The cause both of the long neglect of Mallet du Pan and of the reaction in his favour is to be found in a remark of that writer himself, that half a century at least must pass before an impartial account of the Revolution would be possible, and, whatever may be thought of Carlyle's qualifications for the task, his own confession proves that he made the attempt too soon. The fury of revolutionary and anti-revolutionary partisans, which in life isolated a man of the moderate opinions of Mallet, long continued to assail his memory and prevent an appreciation of his superiority. Forced to fight side by side with allies with whose objects and hopes he was not in sympathy, he was feared and distrusted alike by the royalists to whom the ' monarchien' was as odious as the Jacobin, and by the men of the Revolution who felt that he was the most dangerous because the most intelligent of their enemies.

Mallet du Pan is distinguished from the small band of French Liberals by the fact that he had before the Revolution borne his part in the practical politics of a free State. He brought to the study of that convulsion a great equipment of qualities natural and acquired, and the following summary of his early life, taken from M. Taine's striking preface, will best show how his previous training and experience fitted him for the work he had to do :—

'In 1789 Mallet du Pan, at the age of forty, had already passed twenty years in political education. He had, all his life, reflected on affairs of State. From his earliest youth he had deeply studied history, international law, and political economy, not as a mere student or amateur, but as an original thinker and independent critic. Manners, Governments, and Constitutions had been the subject of his close personal observation, for he had lived or travelled in Switzerland, France, Germany, England, and the Low Countries. A preparation still more fruitful had been his citizenship of Geneva. In that miniature State he had been able to gauge the conditions of liberty, its benefits and its dangers; he had witnessed the strife of classes, the defeat of old patrician families, and the triumph of a commercial middle class; the oppression and the demands of the ' natifs ; ' the troubles of 1777 and the revolution of 1782; he had seen a *coup d'état,* a proscription, and a provisional dictatorship succeeded by anarchy; he had seen in the streets a raging populace in arms, ready to plunge into madness and massacre ; he had beheld in anticipation, on a small stage, the drama which, ten years later, was to be played at Paris with the addition of a bloody fifth act. He had been, moreover, not merely a spectator, but an actor. At the outset, young Mallet had sided in a few pamphlets with the ——— in 1782 he was one of the "———" charged with the ——— of negotiating the ——— of Geneva. He became known in profession a publicist, and followed from day to day the events of contemporary politics. A guest and correspondent of ——— he exchanged letters with Samuel Romilly; he ——— it and ——— the work of ———; he edited the political portion of the 'Mercure de France' and at Geneva and Ferney. In London, Brussels and Paris he became acquainted with philosophers and politicians, with ministers and placemen, with ——— and ———. He canvassed and weighed the current theories on taxation, on commerce, on separation, on public law, and on the rights of men. He canvassed plans of revolution and suggestions of reform; he commented on the great events of the day—the revolt of the American Colonies, the trial of Warren Hastings, and the counter-revolution in Holland. In 1783 he knew, in short, not only France, but Europe.'

Established in Paris in 1784 as political editor of the
'Mercure de France.' Mallet's temper, education, and nation-
ality yet kept him singularly free from the ties and prejudices which so powerfully affect and embarrass the judgement of men in an epoch of convulsion. He was not a
Frenchman—he was born a republican—it was not therefore
by royalist sentiment that he was led now to support the
French monarchy. A Genevese Protestant of Huguenot
descent could not be influenced by religious passion in his
defence of the Catholic clergy and the old ecclesiastical
establishments of Europe. Official ties were not likely to
hamper a journalist whose connexion with the ministerial
system of France had been confined to transactions with the
censor of the Paris press; and the obligations of party can
hardly be said to have existed for one who was a centre of
attack from all the extreme factions to which France and
Europe were then a prey. His citizenship of a small neutral
State, his knowledge of the principal countries of Europe,
his open and liberal mind which had assimilated what was
best in the prevailing political philosophy of the time, its
cosmopolitan spirit, helped to make him a no less capable
and impartial observer of the other European States than
he was of France. In the letter quoted above, addressed to
the son of Mallet du Pan on the appearance of M. Sayous'
memoirs, Carlyle has testified to his possession of qualities
more important than any such external advantages, qualities
the want of which no experience and no training can supply.
He speaks of the

'rare sagacity with which Mallet judged the enormous phenomena
he was in the midst of. Almost from the first he sees, if not across

and through it, as I might say, yet steadily into the centre of it, and refuses to be bewildered, as others are, by what is of the superficies merely. This which, at fifty years' distance from the phenomena, were still a proof of some clearness of vision, amounted, in Mallet's case, to nearly the highest proof that can be given of that noble quality, and, we may say, of many other noble qualities which are indissolubly of kin to that.' ' On the whole,' he continues, ' I have learned very much to respect your brave father from this book. A fine, robust, clear, and manful intellect was in him, all directed towards practical solidities, and none of it playing truant in the air; a quiet valour that defies all fortune—and he had some rather ugly fortune to defy— everywhere integrity, simplicity, and in that wild element of journalism, too, with its sad etceteras, the "assurance of a man." What still more attracts me to him, I feel that his excellences are not such as appeal to the vulgar, but only to the wiser; his style, for example, is not what is called poetic, but it is full of rough idiomatic vigour, and conveys a true meaning to you, stamped coin; so of his conduct too, this is not drugged liquor, mock champagne, or other pleasant poisonous stuff, this is cool crystal water from the everlasting well : this will hurt nobody that drinks of it.'

Ten years' residence in Paris had given Mallet opportunities of personal acquaintance with many of the men who played a part in the Revolution. At Berne, from which place he dated the correspondence, he was in the very centre of intrigue and diplomacy, he was surrounded by *émigrés* and emissaries of every party. The correspondence which he kept up with a large circle of private friends of every shade of anti-revolutionary opinion formed one of the most important sources of his information, and, now that his journalistic work was for a time interrupted, one of his chief means of influencing public opinion. There was first of all the group of constitutional monarchists with whom Mallet had allied himself, in sympathy though not in hope, during the first months of the National Assembly. The Comte de Lally Tolendal was already known for his devotion to the memory of his father, the General Lally of Indian renown, executed under the old *régime.* His eloquence and his vigorous championship of the principles of liberty on the English pattern brought him early into prominence in the National Assembly, and early drove him from it into exile. He was a man of high and honourable character, and master of a literary style, forcible and rhetorical, which might perhaps have won him a free election to the seat in the Academy presented to him by Louis XVIII. at the Restoration. There was Mounier, the proposer of the oath of the tennis court, who like Lally Tollendal was driven from public life by the storming of Versailles by the Paris mob, and who remained faithful even under Napoleon to the principles whose triumph he did not live to see; and Malouet who, more fortunate, was able after 1815 to serve the monarchy as a minister and peer of France.

Mallet du Pan was later thrown into contact with many of the pure royalists, among whom were some who, though *émigrés* in fact, were as far as himself from sympathy with the incurable prejudices of their class. The Comte de Ste. Aldegonde,* the confidential friend and adviser of the Comte d'Artois, was one of his most frequent and sympathetic correspondents. The Maréchal de Castries, the burning of whose hotel, one of the first acts of violence of the Parisian mob, had drawn from Mallet a vigorous denunciation of the growing spirit of anarchy, was another noble of influence in the *entourage* of the princes, through whom Mallet was able constantly to give advice of a kind they were not accustomed to hear from those about them. There was Portalis, singularly untouched by the spirit of reaction, yet whose fame is chiefly connected with the restoration of order under the Consulate, with the Code and the Concordat, whose qualities have been described as ' good sense and good faith; ' and Montlosier, ' qui aimait la sagesse avec folie et la modéra- ' tion avec transport.' On a different level stand two very constant correspondents. The one is the Abbé de Pradt, the other the adventurer Montgaillard, whom Mallet has coupled with the royalist agent D'Entraigues, as the two most consummate liars to be found in France. Mallet's natural aversion to intrigue had been only confirmed by his experience in his attempt, in 1794, to unite the Constitutionalists and the other shades of royalism into a compact opposition through Th. de Lameth. It may be conceived that he formed no great hopes of a scheme, of which Montgaillard made him his chief confidant two years later, to

---

* Mallet's son has left a recollection of this interesting but little-known royalist: ' D'une grande famille des Pays-Bas il avait épousé Mlle. de Tourzel, gouvernante des Enfants de France. Il avait probablement été attaché au comte d'Artois avant la Révolution, et conserva toujours des relations de confiance avec ce prince, qui le chargea en 1795 d'une mission auprès de mon père; et je n'oublierai jamais les manières nobles, jolies, et cependant parfaitement simples du grand seigneur français. Mon père avait pour M. de Ste. Aldegonde une confiance et une amitié qui ne se démentirent jamais, et ce dernier sentit la mort de mon père comme il aurait senti celle d'un frère. La modération de son caractère et de ses opinions était au-dessus de tout éloge. Il fut placé par Louis XVIII. dans la chambre des Pairs après la Révolution.'

bring over Pichegru, then at the head of the army of the
Rhine, to the royalist side through the Prince de Condé, in
spite of the high opinion he had formed of the republican
general.   The Abbé de Pradt, a far abler man, whose remarkable pamphlet ' L'Antidote au Congrès de Rastadt,' was
even attributed to Joseph de Maistre, was one of those who
grew tired of exile when Bonaparte restored order to France,
and as Bishop of Poictiers, afterwards Archbishop of Malines,
Baron and Grand Cross of the Legion of Honour, the
confidant of Napoleon and his ambassador at Warsaw in
1812, and as pensioner of Louis XVIII., he was permitted
to gratify to the full the cravings of personal ambition.
A little group of friends had found an hospitable welcome
at the Court of the Duke of Brunswick, upon whom Mallet
du Pan once said that the dictatorship of Europe ought to
be conferred.   He maintained a close correspondence with his
fellow-countryman the Chevalier de Gallatin, who had there
obtained the post of privy councillor, and through whom
Mallet's views were regularly communicated to the Duke.
Others there were with whom from time to time he was
brought into contact—with Madame de Staël, for instance,
whom he may be considered to have judged with harshness,
and with Joseph de Maistre who submitted to him the
manuscript of his first political writings for judgement
and criticism—while with many of the statesmen by whom
he was consulted he carried on a private as well as a public
correspondence.

It is, however, his official correspondence which formed the
chief part of Mallet's work at this period.   He had left Paris
with a reputation and an authority altogether exceptional for
a mere man of letters.   As editor of the ' Mercure,' which he
had made the most important newspaper in France with
a circulation of 15,000, he had week by week ' treated of
' questions without dealing in personalities ; ' he had marked
with precision the nature and organisation of the growing
agitation; he is admitted to have given the only intelligent
and trustworthy account of the debates in the Constituent
and Legislative Assemblies.   His double mission in 1792 from
Louis XVI. to his brothers and the allied monarchs, and his
pamphlet on the nature of the Revolution—of which Burke
said that he might himself have been the author, and Pitt
that before reading it he had had no idea of the Revolution—
had made him widely known, and he was now consulted
by most of the leading statesmen among the allies.   He furnished notes and memoranda for the British Cabinet through

Lord Grenville, Lord Elgin, and Mr. Wickham, to Counts Colleredo and Mercy Argentau, to the Duke of Brunswick and the *émigré* Princes of France, to the Kings of Sardinia, Prussia, and Spain. But in the year 1794 these communications took a more regular shape, and Mallet was requested to undertake a political correspondence directly with the Emperor Francis. At the same time Baron Hardenberg and M. de Souza-Cotinho applied on behalf of their sovereigns for a similar correspondence. He gladly embraced these offers of employment. His previous experience had well fitted him for the post of ' Minister in partibus ' to the threatened monarchies. His means of information had always been exceptionally great. As editor of the 'Mercure' he had, as we have seen, personally attended the sittings of the assemblies. 'From 1789,' says M. Taine, 'hundreds of ' letters written on the spot, signed, dated, and verified, had ' brought him continual reports on the state of the pro- ' vinces. In 1791 and 1792 despatches of local administra- ' tions, reports of the meetings of the clubs, details, figures, ' and original papers of all kinds, which we now discover in ' the national archives, were communicated to him in the ' form of *résumés* or extracts.' The organisation of this intelligence department he had kept up on leaving France in 1792 ; he was now able to extend it by funds specially provided for the purpose. M. André Michel, the editor of this correspondence, has put together in a very useful introduction explaining the character of the work, proofs from internal evidence of the nature of his sources of information. Letters of the Baron de Staël, of Barthélemy, of other influential personages (the chief of the staff of Hoche, for instance), are put into his hands; he sends to Lyons a trustworthy person to verify his information upon the state of the town ; he receives textual accounts of the secret deliberations of Siéyès, Tallien, and Barras; his correspondents are drawn from the Committees of the Convention and the Councils of the Directory, the public offices and the armies of the republic and the Vendean rebels. His statements as to the condition of Paris have been verified in many cases by M. Taine's researches into the documentary sources of the history, which have led that writer to express the strongest opinion as to the general accuracy and fidelity of the information upon which Mallet du Pan relied.

The period embraced by this correspondence, from the end of 1794 to the beginning of 1798, is the dreariest and least known of the revolutionary epoch. Not a man concerned

in administration or in the active work of politics stands
forth from the picture, not an act either of destruction or of
reorganisation has left any permanent trace. The annals of
the Directory would be the meanest passage in French history
if they had not been relieved by the military triumphs of the
man who was to destroy it. The long-drawn analysis of
these barren years would indeed become wearisome from the
uniform baseness of men and events, were it not for the
answer which it supplies to the question how it was that a
Government so detestable and so detested, in administration
so weak, yet so tyrannical in the exercise of power, was able
not only to stand for four years, but to carry on with success
and glory a war against allied Europe. The character of the
whole period is one of internal conflict. The Government
welcomed after Thermidor as the liberators of France from
the tyranny of the Reign of Terror had lost its character of
strength and consistency at the same time as it threw off
the yoke of a savage dictatorship. The detestation of the
people for the men whom Mallet described as the ' valets
' qui ont pris le sceptre de leurs maîtres,' was brought to a
head by their inability, associated as they were in all the
crimes of their predecessors, to satisfy the popular demand
for ' peace and bread,' a demand which in the streets, in the
theatres, and in the cafés, with threats and curses, with
satire and with jest, was everywhere repeated with growing
intensity. The Directory which succeeded to this period of
anarchy no less faithfully adhered to revolutionary methods,
and was no less in opposition to the wishes of the mass of
the nation, but as the champions of France against the arms
of Europe they found in war their strength and safety.

The Jacobin conquest was the triumph of a minority. It
has been attempted to estimate the numerical strength of
the revolutionary mob in Paris, and the highest calculations
have put it at 16,000 out of a population of 600,000 souls.
Certain it is that at the election of Bailly's successor, as
Mayor of Paris, the Jacobin vote of 6,600 out of a total of
80,000 voters was sufficient to carry the day, and subsequent municipal elections gave the same result. The composition of the rank and file was even more insignificant
than their numerical strength, and the analyses of the police
have shown that the number of the *enragés* was swelled by
domestic servants, the lowest class of workmen, and the
residuum of the population, beggars living from hand to
mouth, and adventurers from all parts of France and Europe.
The abolition of the property qualification, on August 10,

1792, gave them complete mastery of the forty-eight sections of Paris, the assemblies which were the chief means of carrying out the orders issued by the clubs and committees of the Jacobin leaders. These assemblies were attended by the bravos of every quarter, the meetings were held at night to keep away respectable citizens, and those who attended were treated with personal violence, the Jacobins in default of other arms breaking up the furniture, and carrying their resolutions by force. The indifference of the middle classes, intensely conservative as they have always been, was even exceeded by their timidity. With the Reign of Terror the craven majority sank into a still deeper apathy.

'The patience with which the French have for fifteen months tolerated a system of imprisonment *en masse*, and the judicial assassination of hundreds by wholesale, convicts the nation of a moral turpitude which renders them fit subjects for any kind of oppression. In all that long period of murder, not a son dared to avenge the execution of his father, not a husband ventured to defend his wife, not a father to rescue his child, in a country where swords would once have leapt from their scabbards for the sake of a mistress or an epigram.'

The reaction of Thermidor gave rise to the one really popular movement of the Revolution. The organisation of the body known to history, though not to contemporary politics, as the 'jeunesse dorée,' served as a rallying point for the rising royalist feeling. Recruited from the middle classes, they were composed of students and lawyers' clerks, of the sons of bankers, officials and shopkeepers. With hats, cravats, and knee-breeches, to distinguish them from the sans-culottes or trousered Jacobins, with hair arranged in pigtail, or dressed *à la victime*, jagged and short behind and long at the sides, and armed with large knobbed sticks, they assembled in the cafés of the Palais Royal, organised a regular opposition to the Jacobins, attacked their clubs, hunted down the *buveurs de sang*, destroyed the busts of Marat, and attended the theatre to sing the 'Réveil du Peuple,' to hiss the 'Marseillaise,' or cheer ironically at the refrain, 'Tremblez, tyrants et vous perfides.' That but a small minority were the weak dandies portrayed by Thiers, and whose eccentricity earned for them from their enemies the names of 'Incroyables,' 'Elégants,' and 'Muscadins,' is proved by the heroic resistance they offered to the efforts of the rump of the Convention to perpetuate its power by the decrees of August 22. The cannon of Vendémiaire, which established the Directory and crushed the 'Jeunesse,' taught a lesson which for thirty years prevented any attempt at popular rising in the streets of Paris. Five years of baffled hopes of the restoration of order had produced a lasting impression upon the people; henceforth, when their will was being overruled by the Directory, when streets, bridges, and squares were bristling with troops and cannon, they went about their business or their pleasure with the same carelessness with which the 'Greeks of Constantinople ' in the last centuries of the Empire had seen every six ' months the dethronement or assassination of an emperor.' The Directory entered upon their rule with the immense advantage of a people to govern who placed their safety in a total abnegation of political sentiment, in so far as their opinion might commit them to any line of action; and the 30,000 troops encamped at the gates of Paris were necessary only to protect them against their own extreme partisans. Among the people only were heard the curses, threats, and epigrams against the Government with which Paris continued to resound. The well-to-do classes preferred to cringe to their tyrants, and indulge in the stupid and selfish optimism of the Constitutionalists of 1792. Observers have familiarised us with the picture of the manners of the Directory, and many passages in this correspondence bring out with new details and new illustrations the union of luxury and privation characteristic of the time. It was a state of things which was not confined to the capital. In Lyons—

' which is without bread or wood, where men live on rations of rice and burn their beds to warm themselves, where the pavement is still red with the blood of 7,000 citizens of every rank massacred and shot down last year (1794), there are two theatres and several public halls open and always full, and a brazen luxury flaunts in the spoils of its victims. The Revolution has completed the extinction of the moral sense. Ties of relationship are weakened, the most atrocious egotism reigns in all hearts, honour and sentiment, duty and self-respect are no longer to be found.'

The agricultural population was the one class which had gained in material prosperity. These advantages they were determined to maintain ; the *régime* of tithe and gabelle, of *parlements* and *intendants,* was gone for ever, but the departments were ill-disposed to a Government which either neglected the duties of administration or harassed them with requisitions in men, money, and kind, which persecuted the religion to which they still clung, and endeavoured to replace by republican usages the thousand social institutions of which the Church was the centre. Conservatism and dread

of change were then as now the leading characteristics of
the French peasantry, and it was even truer of them than
of the Parisians, 'that they would only turn upon the execu-
'tioner when his axe was at their neck.'   'No revolution
'will ever begin with the people,' is the profound reflection
suggested to Mallet by the spectacle he witnessed; it is a
reflection justified by the subsequent history of France, as
well as by that of other countries.   Princes and governments
have often played for the lives and fortunes of their subjects;
never before had the spectacle been afforded of a great
nation accepting its position as the stake in the game of
party strife.   It was a spectacle which might have aroused
the scorn even of a Frenchman, and may well explain the
passion with which Mallet, a foreigner, describes a nation

'at once cruel and frivolous, servile and licentious, impetuous at one
moment in its complaints, and forgetting them without motive in the
next, careless in suffering as in prosperity, incapable of foresight or of
reflection, selling in the morning like savages the bed on which they
are to lie at night; such in every age has been the character of the
people, such are they at the present hour, and such they will ever
remain until the end of time.'

'Les brigandages du Directoire sont des coups de poignard
'donnés à un cadavre.'   A double criticism is contained in these
words, and the character of the Government is treated in the
same detail as that of the demoralised nation which so long
supported its rule.   For the Directory soon showed itself to
be a mere continuation of the revolutionary *régime*, and maintained its power by availing itself of the division of opinion in
the country, and by holding the balance between disorganised
factions.   Dreaded by all, the new rulers of France feared
every party, and, relying in the last resort upon the Jacobins,
they were nervously sensitive to the secret disaffection of the
majority, whose opposition they had been obliged to crush
before they could establish their authority.   Their policy
thus continually betrayed a character of vacillation.   After
the *coup d'état* of Vendémiaire, they threw themselves upon
the party by whose aid they had triumphed, and the rule of
Terror started again into activity, until the Socialist conspiracy of Babœuf forced them to appeal to the support of
the moderate parties by turning out the Jacobins from the
places they had given them.   Obliged to follow rather than
direct the oscillations of public opinion, they alternately
punished and caressed their extreme supporters, or struck at
both parties by closing at the same time the anti-revolutionary cafés and the Jacobin club of the Panthéon, or by

proposing an amnesty for the members of the rebel sections and for the authors of the September massacres. The Directory, the ministers, and the Council were divided amongst themselves, and the Constitution, which, in accordance with the teaching of Rousseau, the example of America, and the experience taught by the rule of the Convention, had drawn a hard and fast line between the executive and the legislature, provided no means by which a deadlock between the functions of government could be avoided or overcome. 'The Directory cannot govern the Assemblies, it must ' therefore obey them, conspire, or perish.' The Councils, becoming at every election more moderate and anti-revolutionary, found themselves in two years in complete opposition to the Directory, and in the struggle of Fructidor 1797, in which the people stood neutral, the executive in command of the whole material power of the State was able once more to override the feeling of the nation expressed in their elected assemblies. Legislation, meanwhile, had been paralysed by this growing hostility and by the changing character of the Councils. The number of laws made from the beginning of the republic has been computed at 22,271, the majority of which it was impossible from their contradictory nature to execute. The instability of the laws destroyed all confidence; 'they were received like tempests, accepted ' with indifference, and forgotten as soon as made ;' and the Government superintended the execution of those only which aided them in the work of spoliation, or secured the ends of their party. Administration, indeed, had ceased to exist in the country ; the ministers and higher officials, grossly ignorant of the laws they had to administer, and of the wants of the people, were more occupied with the management of their army of constantly changing employés than with the duties proper to responsible government. Corruption was carried to its greatest excess by officials whose miserably inadequate pay was often two years in arrear, and such agents, naturally unable to exercise any real control, were universally ignored or disobeyed. Many provinces—the Vivarais, Cévennes, Rouergue, Haute-Auvergne, and Bas-Languedoc—were practically in a state of independence. The western departments were in open rebellion, and in all brigandage partaking of the nature of the ' chouan-' nerie ' was rife. ' Il n'y a aucune police dans toute l'éten-' due de la France,' and Paris, garrisoned by the troops of the Directory, alone afforded a semblance of government. The picture would seem overcharged had we not the avowal of the Directory themselves made to the Council of the Five Hundred in December 1796:—

'Every part of the administration is in decay, the pay of the troops is in arrear, the defenders of the country are in rags, and their disgust causes them to desert; the military and civil hospitals are destitute of all medical appliances, the State creditors and contractors can recover but small portions of the sums due to them, the high roads are destroyed and communications interrupted, the public officials are without salaries from one end of the Republic to the other; everywhere sedition is rife, assassination organised, and the police impotent.'

Such was the official account of the chaos into which administration had fallen. But for the purposes of maintaining its ascendency, and devoting the resources of the country to the revolutionary propaganda, the system of the Directory with its restless energy, its active and powerful will, supplied all mere deficiencies of administrative order. The very freedom from the ordinary restraints of morality and prudence was the great secret of its power. Burke insists upon the

' dreadful energy of a State in which property has nothing to do with the Government. The design is wicked, impious, aggressive, but it is spirited, it is daring, it is systematic. . . . In that country entirely to cut off a branch of commerce, to extinguish a manufacture, to destroy the circulation of money, to violate credit, to suspend the course of agriculture, even to burn a city or lay waste a province of their own, does not cost them a moment's anxiety. To them the will, the wish, the want, the liberty, the toil, the blood of individuals is as nothing.'

The record of the financial operations of the Directory amply justifies Burke's description. The issue of paper money was a resource which the Terror and the Convention had almost exhausted, and the country was experiencing the inevitable consequences of the abuse of an inconvertible currency. By the time the Directory came into office, assignats had been issued to the amount of twenty milliards of francs, and 100 francs in assignats was worth one and a half in coin. In two months the daily issue had risen from 100 to 600 millions, and the total had increased to forty milliards, while the value had fallen to ½ per cent. The Government plunged into a vortex of frantic speculation, and anything like an accurate record of its fabulous indebtedness soon became impossible. Since 1792 the Government had ceased to number the notes; each minister coined money to supply his public and private necessities; the country was flooded with false assignats, which it was impossible to distinguish

.from the real ones, and no kind of proportion had been kept between the alleged security and the gigantic superstructure of credit which had risen upon it. The official estimates give a pitiable idea of the incapacity and dishonesty of the republican financiers. Since the fall of Robespierre various computations had put the national property at from ten to seventeen milliards of francs in assignats, thus officially recognising the depreciation by reckoning at the speculative price which paper bore in the market. The Finance Committee in 1795 announced the national property as worth seven milliards of *écus.* The actual value of the national domains at the end of the Terror might have been put at from two to three milliards, but such confusion and corruption prevailed in their administration that a real estimate was perhaps impossible, and the nature of the security made it difficult to sell at all except at prices low enough to tempt speculators. Much, therefore, as the Government were able to profit by trading in their own paper issues, desperate measures were soon necessitated by the growing worthlessness of their paper. In a term of peace and prosperity Necker had never been able to raise in a single year a loan of more than 100 millions. The Directory now demanded from an impoverished nation a loan of six times that amount— a sum equal to a year's revenue was to be raised within six weeks from a people whose whole effective capital in money and paper did not amount to more than double the sum to be levied; and in spite of the most arbitrary and cruel methods of collection, in spite, in fact, of a general confiscation of money and goods, it may readily be conceived that not one-third of this loan was ultimately recovered by the Government. All taxation partook of the irregular nature of this loan, for regular means could never have supplied the immense necessities of the Directory. A large part was derived from the conquest and plunder of foreign countries, and the hope of foreign spoil was the principal inducement held out to the armies of France. At home the plunder of churches and of the 'Mobilier National' consisting of the confiscated plate, jewellery, and valuables of the *émigrés,* was soon exhausted. The national domains, almost unsaleable, were alienated with extraordinary recklessness. Indirect taxes, which had been in large part remitted by the first assemblies in an approach to free trade principles, were reimposed in all their severity, while of the direct taxes the most important and onerous was the land-tax, half of which was collected in kind—a system of wholesale plunder which

is one of the most distinctive marks of Jacobin rule.   Everything necessary for the support of the armies was obtained in
this manner ; grain of all kinds was collected in Government
granaries ; shirts, stockings, cloth, and linen were obtained in
the same way ; and at one time 30,000 horses, at another
100,000 pairs of shoes, were to be supplied by contractors who,
unpaid by the Government, enriched themselves by private
pillage.   Requisitions of men were not less fatal to the
prosperity of the country, nor less difficult to execute.   The
memory of the dragonnades was revived by the pursuit of the
young conscripts ; hussars and gendarmes carried on the
‘ guerre aux réquisitionnaires,’ who, at the least resistance,
were tied together in twos or fours, and in this fashion are
described as ‘ flying to the defence of liberty.’

In 1721 the scheme of Law had collapsed and shaken the very
foundation of credit, yet the issue of paper had not exceeded
one milliard and a half.   The destruction of thirty milliards
of paper at a time when half of the coin of the country had
left it, and the rest had been hoarded, might have been
expected to produce a catastrophe of incalculable dimensions.
The consequences of financial error and dishonesty, instead
of falling on the country in one crushing blow, extended
over a series of disastrous years.   The Revolution is distinguished by no one signal or special act of ruin, but almost
every financial operation was in itself an act of bankruptcy,
and every Government transaction a declaration of in-
solvency.

It would be a hopeless task to enumerate the cases in
which the Government suspended the payment of its creditors, sanctioned, by acknowledging, the depreciation of its
paper, or revoked the sales of State property.   It is enough
that repudiation began in 1792, when Clavière, the Girondist
minister of finance, announced that a new issue of paper
would be applied to defraying the expenses of the war instead
of paying the State creditors, and that it did not end till the
final act of bankruptcy by the Consulate.   If the holders
of the Government stock, whose condition was acknowledged
by the doles of bread and meat occasionally awarded to
them, were the worst sufferers by the Revolution, the officials
and pensioners were hardly better off, and the only classes
which profited by the general ruin were the speculators in
gold and silver coin and bullion.   The fortunes made by
these ‘ sangsues publiques,’ as they were called, whose
opulence was considered an insult to the general misery,
excited (however ignorantly) the bitterest feeling in the

popular mind, although the spirit of speculation had extended with the issue of assignats of small sums to every class of the population. Speculation was not confined to money, but prevailed with regard to the only other form of wealth which retained exchange value at a time when the state of the currency had necessitated a return to the primitive system of barter. Every shop was turned into a treasure house for the accumulation of commodities and provisions of the first necessity. The Government, with its hoards of grain and material for the support of the armies, joined in the struggle for existence. The average price of provisions rose to three times what it had been in 1791, while the average consumption was largely reduced. The farmers, except under extreme pressure from taxation and Government requisitions, could not be induced to part with their grain in exchange for assignats, and the Government had to come to the assistance of private traders. The sustenance of Paris thus fell upon the nation, and rations were throughout the Revolution served out to the citizens of the capital. Subventions to the bakers and butchers enabled them to buy provisions from without, and to sell at a price which, when 100 livres assignats were equal to two or three livres in coin, is represented by the statement that 100 livres in paper were worth from six to fourteen in coin in the operations of retail trade. This, when labourers were paid in paper worth from a quarter to half its nominal value, and officials and public creditors in paper at its full nominal value, meant a struggle for life of which Paris at this time presented a terrible picture. Crowds of people stood all night at the doors of the Treasury, of the shops, and of the places appointed for the doles of food; workmen diminished their hours of labour from want of strength to work longer, nor could strength be expected where life was constantly supported upon the most disgusting offal.

The decline of the population was both the cause and the sign of the diminished wealth and productiveness of the country. Mallet du Pan's estimates are doubtless in excess of the truth, but in the absence of adequate data for a calculation, the maintenance of armies beyond the frontier, the losses caused by emigration, war, and famine, and the utter neglect of the hospitals and charitable institutions, were all causes of the decrease of the adult male population which Lord Malmesbury noticed in his journey through the north of France. Mallet testifies to the 'vide immense' of men and the want of hands in the industrial pursuits, and the Government admitted the fact by the leave granted to the troops quartered in the interior to take part in the operations of the harvest.* The rate of interest which before the Revolution had stood at 4 or 6 per cent. per annum, rose during its course to 6 or 8, and never sank below 2 per cent. *per month*; credit was indeed destroyed, and no branch of industry escaped the general decay.

' No people were ever put to so cruel a test, none ever expiated their faults by greater sufferings; a capital of thirty milliards is becoming worthless in the very hands of its possessors; industry, commerce, and labour of every kind are destroyed at their source; the needs of the war have depopulated the empire, misery has no limits, famine again 'besieges Paris. . . . . Miserable skeletons daily fall dead of starvation in the streets, the distribution of bread presents the aspect of a siege, and the approaches to the bakers' shops resemble a field of battle.'

' Like the Louisiana savage who cuts down the tree in ' order to gather the fruit,' like a 'spendthrift dissipating his ' patrimony,' the Directory devoured the resources of the country with a profound indifference to any object but that of maintaining their own power. If peace for the allies meant a warrant of insurrection to their populations, much more for France would it have meant a revolt of the people and the armies against the authority of their rulers. ' Nous ' serions perdus si nous faisions la paix,' said Siéyès; the only hope of the Directory lay in the vigorous and unscrupulous prosecution of the war; and their system had all the force of a fundamental dogma, a policy of State, an object of fanaticism, and a result of necessity.

' This pretended Government treats France as Lord Clive treated the Hindus. They have accustomed the country to every kind of exaction and to the expectation of still worse things. . . . They fear the return of the generals and armies into the interior, they carry on a war of insolent proselytism into which they have imported every upstart passion, nor does it require much reasoning to perceive that a faction which is also a sect, which has founded a republic upon the hatred and destruction of kings, which has overturned an ancient

---

* M. Taine, in his latest volume, adduces some valuable evidence on this point. He estimates the probable deaths from privation at more than a million, and quotes the calculation of M. Léonce de Lavergne that another million perished in war from 1792 to 1800. Bordeaux lost a tenth of its population, Reims an eighth, and Lyons, after the siege, was reduced from 130,000 to 80,000 inhabitants. Against these losses must be set the very noticeable increase in the infantile population resulting from early marriages.

monarchy, massacred a royal house, and founded its policy as well as its security upon the extension of its destroying principles, will only lay down its arms when it has no longer the strength to carry them.'

'The destiny of France,' said Mallet du Pan (he might have added that of Europe), hangs on these two words 'peace 'and war.' The course of the Revolution had already been decided by the outbreak of the war in 1792. Two years before this, Mirabeau, in a note to the Court, had stated his belief that peace was the greatest of interests to all who had anything to lose, and that in view of the disposition of foreign powers it would not be difficult to maintain it. But whatever might be their interests, the inclinations of all parties were gradually becoming more warlike, and Gouverneur Morris observed a unanimity of opinion in favour of war. In view of his later policy it is important to observe Mallet's attitude on this question. He was not less positive than Mirabeau as to the supreme necessity of peace:—

'It is impossible,' these are his words, 'for a true friend of the monarchy to consider the approach of war without terror.' 'War will only strengthen the Revolution and render it more atrocious.' 'I venture to predict that it will not be for the preservation of the throne, nor for the friends of monarchical government in France that our armies will triumph, while if they are defeated our royalty, our laws, and our liberty will fall under the dominion of force.'

Mirabeau had believed in the possibility of preserving peace; it is at least certain that the motives which urged the powers to war were feeble compared with reasons which made combination against a common enemy difficult, and an honest alliance impossible.

The territorial ambition and mutual jealousies of the three great Eastern powers now centred round the struggle for the possession of Poland. Catherine, fresh from Turkish conquests, was intent upon securing Poland for herself; Dantzig and Thorn seemed indispensable to round off the frontier of Prussia, isolated in Europe and living on the reputation of her past greatness; while Austria was already busy with schemes for the exchange of Belgium for Bavaria. The Congress of Pillnitz, as Mallet thought, had given evidence of the desire of the powers for peace, but its language to France was to the last degree arrogant and hostile, and it only inflamed the patriotism of the French nation, which Brissot and his colleagues desired to turn to actual war. The insulted patriotism of the French exclaimed that the allies had treated with the *émigrés*, and had threatened interference in the internal affairs of France. It is unnecessary to trace the course of the negotiations, or to attempt to apportion the responsibility for a war on which either side embarked with little thought of consequences. Mallet du Pan foreshadowed these when he spoke of the complexity of the interests of modern States, of the ramifications of international policy, of the impossibility of inspiring thirty sovereigns, each afraid of the other, with anything like an idea of common interest; and observed, that there never perhaps existed in Europe a condition of society which offered greater hopes to the authors of a social convulsion.

The three years which elapsed from the declaration of war entirely altered the aspect of affairs, and the condition of Europe at the beginning of the year 1795, when the correspondence opens, already justified the darkest apprehensions. Not only were the French delivered from all danger of foreign invasion, but Holland and Belgium had fallen into the hands of France; Sweden, Tuscany, and Sardinia had already treated with the Republic; Spain and Prussia were about to be added to the list of neutral powers, and the most important German State after Austria had already betrayed the empire and agreed to the cession of the left bank of the Rhine at the general peace. To this result the jealousy and disunion of the allies had contributed at least as much as the thoroughly aroused patriotism of the French people, or the revolutionary ardour of her generals. The whole course of the French war, up to the final partition of Poland, had been governed by the vicissitudes of intrigue in the East, and the result had been to leave the field clear for the machinations of the only great potentates of Europe, Catherine of Russia and the Jacobin Government of France. Well might Burke exclaim, in criticising the selfish policy of the allies, that there could be no honour in a society for pillage. As Prussia had sought her interests in peace, so Austria found that the only chance of recovering her losses or of indemnifying herself by fresh conquests lay in carrying on the war. There is a peculiar appropriateness in the choice of the present correspondence for publication, rather than of that with the Court of Prussia, written as it was for the only Continental power which remained at war with the Revolution, although the address to the Emperor with which it opens may seem a bitter satire upon his motives :—' Your ' Majesty is at this moment the pillar of social order, and ' every eye is turned towards your throne, the most solid ' support at this crisis of religious as of civil authority, and ' of the common weal.'

From the very beginning the party attacked in the Brunswick Manifesto had retaliated by a propaganda of their principles in the camp and country of the enemy, and the Girondists, the principal authors of the war, were the first to formulate this policy. The realisation of the scheme of ' philosophic conquests' had been interrupted for a moment by the Jacobin rule, and by the death struggle of factions within the Convention, and Danton, the most nearly allied of the Jacobins to the Gironde, alone seems to have had a definite conception of foreign policy. The revolution of Thermidor brought to the front the remains of the Gironde. Of this party Mallet observes, that

'neither the horrors of that sanguinary *régime* nor the oppression under which they groaned during the dictatorship of the Committee of Public Safety, neither their misfortunes nor the death of so many of their number upon the scaffold, neither experience nor reason, nor the duty of closing the bleeding wounds of their country and of giving her peace, had touched these theorists. They would sooner see the universe in ashes than abandon their design of submitting it to their doctrines. "On peut tenter, on peut espérer la conversion d'un scélérat, "jamais celle d'un philosophe."'

The foreign policy of the Directory was characterised by the philosophic insolence, the spirit of proselytism, and the desire of universal revolution which animated that sect. The Decree of Fraternisation of 1792 was followed with literal exactness by the Directory in every country into which their armies could penetrate. All the authorities—so ran that famous document—the nobles and priestly classes, as well as every privilege contrary to equality, were to be suppressed. All taxes and former sources of revenue were to be remitted, property was to be placed under the administration of the invaders to guarantee the expenses of the war, while to aid them in regaining their liberty the republican coinage was to be placed at their disposal. The people were then to be summoned to primary assemblies, to elect their civil and military magistrates under the surveillance of Conventional commissioners. No plan was too gigantic for the dreams of the Directory, none too extravagantly immoral to be proclaimed to their intended victims. They aimed at nothing short of a peace which should overturn the rights of nations; but they hoped to arrive at such a peace by effecting partial pacifications, and endeavouring in this way to split up the coalition opposed to them. Powers thus neutralised were treated rather as vassals and satellites of the Great Republic than as independent States, and the Directory is found protesting, on the one hand, that the Swedish *people* may always count on their feelings of affection, and, on the other, insisting on the expulsion of French *émigrés* from Savoy or of the British minister from Switzerland. The arms of the Directory did not constitute half the danger which their enemies had to fear. The rule of the French envoys in the smaller neutral States was compared to that of the Pashas in Turkish provinces. Their mission was to stir up by every means dissatisfaction among the people against their rulers, and so prepare the ground for the entry of the troops who were to complete the work. Every country which had the misfortune to be in diplomatic relations with France received in its midst trained Jacobins, who, using their official character as a cloak, turned their legation or consulate into a meeting-place for traitors and conspirators. Mallet du Pan, ' Citoyen de Genève et combourgeois de ' Berne,' has traced with the pen of a patriot the history of the destruction of Switzerland, which he had happily not been permitted to witness. In 1797 he was illegally driven from Berne on the demand of Bonaparte, whose vengeance he had incurred by three letters published in a newspaper in, Paris on the subject of the Italian campaigns. On the annexation of Geneva to France he had the honour of being excluded by name from ever becoming a French citizen, for his revelations on the ' affreuses histoires ' of Venice and Geneva had struck a powerful blow at the Directory, and furnished the leaders of the Council of the Five Hundred with the arms necessary for their attack. Dumolard's speech on the foreign policy of the Government was based upon these letters, and sounded the first note of the struggle of Fructidor.

The allied Powers were little fitted for a contest with such enemies. ' When Europe was invaded by 200,000 barba-' rians, it was not nearly so incapable of offering a resist-' ance as it has now become by its own act.' The balance of power had been overthrown by the Revolution. During the preceding century it had been possible for either of the German powers to stand single-handed against France, for Austria in the war of succession and Prussia in the seven years' struggle had held their own against their German rival and France combined. The immense accession of territory to the French State now exposed Germany to the full force of attack from the north and west, for the intervening bulwarks of Belgium, Holland, and the German provinces west of the Rhine no longer existed. The double position of Austria as a German State and as head of the empire was another source of weakness, and the correspondence of Mallet was intended to strengthen Colleredo as against Thugut, to inspire an imperial as opposed to a narrowly selfish national policy. The enthusiasm of the French found no counterpart in the policy of the allies. Defence is usually weaker than attack, and the championship of the principles of social and political order, although a task which appealed to the sympathies of a Gentz or a Burke, could not be expected to awaken a response among princes who displayed heroic insensibility to the general interests, or among populations whose condition was in many cases worse than that of the French before the Revolution. The leaders of Germany were unable even to appeal with effect to the sentiment which in the long run was to prove fatal to French ascendency— the national patriotism of Germany; they persisted in their stupid and selfish schemes of aggrandisement, and of the annihilation of France as a political power, at a time when Europe was being devoured ' bit by bit like the leaves of an ' artichoke ' by the Great Republic. Amid conditions which both for France and Europe had totally changed, they continued to fight as they had fought all through the century, and to make war upon a nation 'frénétique et désocialisée,' on the basis which they had employed in the struggle against Louis XIV.

The correspondence is full of the boldest criticism of the ambiguity of conduct, the uncertainty of principle, ' the ' effeminate presumption without measure in its terror or its ' confidence ' which constituted the policy of the allies. Of all the errors of that policy none were more fatal than the connexion with the *émigrés*, whom Burke has described as ' a well-informed, sensible, ingenious, high-principled, and ' spirited body of cavaliers,' and in whose restoration, together with that of the *ancien régime*, he placed his chief hopes of a counter-revolution in France. Mallet estimated very differently their capacity and judgement. An expedition like that of Quiberon could have been undertaken only by men totally ignorant of the feeling of France, and he has no words strong enough to blame their wrongheadedness, their egotism, their folly, their want of character and good sense.

' As absurd as on the first day of the Revolution, they have learnt only how to march to the prison or the scaffold, a contemptible and servile virtue which will never embarrass their tyrants.' ' We look in France for a leader of force and wisdom. We find a king buried at

Verona, passing his days in retirement and self-effacement, the first prince of the blood established at Holyrood, a military command in the hands of a third who is far too feeble to inspire any feeling of terror or confidence, and whose absolute spirit and plan of counter-revolution by force of arms repel three-fourths of the partisans of the throne. We find obscure and imbecile agents employed without discernment. . . The obstinate idea,' he continues, ' of recovering France by miserable attacks in detail, by theatrical plots, by means of the " chouans " who are permitted to attack all who have not assumed the livery of Coblentz, the absence of all object, of all leadership, of any principle of concentration, the absurd idea that the nation will rise against its representatives to set up the old *régime*, the total ignorance of what is to be hoped or feared from the war, the constant neglect of all means of persuasion or of policy, the contrast so often apparent between operations from the exterior and events in the interior : '—

such are the faults which Mallet signalises as those which will lead, if anything can, to the establishment of the republic in France. In these lines we have more than a criticism, we have an indication of a policy which Mallet never ceased to press upon the powers. He had endeavoured to measure with accuracy the real sentiments of the French, and to reveal to the Emperor, in his careful analyses, the actual strength of the anti-Jacobin elements in France. The conclusion he had arrived at was that the vast majority was unfavourable to the Revolutionary Government, that their only articulate motives were a desire for the return of peace, of plenty, and of prosperity, a hatred of foreigners, and a dread of the restoration of the old *régime*. The former government was, he said, as much ' effaced in public opinion ' as that of Clovis.' ' It is the same with feudalism, with ' the power and popularity of the Church, and with a thou- ' sand usages as totally buried as though they had never ' existed.' Mallet was in absolute disagreement with Burke, as little acquainted at this time with the public opinion of France as he had been blind to its condition before the Revolution, in his estimate of the necessity or possibility of a restoration of the old order in France. He attached no superstitious importance to any one form of government. A born republican would hardly, like Burke, found an argument upon the danger of a republic as a neighbour, and we find him declaring that whether the Government were monarchical or republican mattered little : it was the Revolution with which it was impossible to treat. Mallet, however, had, like Mirabeau, come to the conclusion that in France the monarchy was ' the only anchor of safety ; ' and he saw among the people no such prejudice against a modified and constitutional form of monarchical government as existed against the *ancien régime.* The Constitution of 1791 had been accepted with immense enthusiasm in France, and in spite of the persecution from which its adherents had suffered even more than the pure royalists, it still harmonised with the sentiments of the majority of the bourgeois and country proprietors. It was a return to this Constitution that Mallet du Pan had hoped for before the death of the Dauphin. It offered the advantage of a system already known and consecrated by law and usage. Its fatal weakness, the powerlessness to which it had reduced the executive in the person of the king, might, he thought, be remedied, so as to give some hope of stability for a constitutional government. But if the people would accept, they would and could do nothing of themselves to bring about such a counter-revolution. ' Jamais un pareil peuple ne s'arrachera de lui-même au joug ' qu'il s'est donné.' The necessary impulse might, Mallet hoped, be given by the action either of the allies or of the ' chouans,' by means of the foreign or of the civil war. All hope from the royalist insurgents had, however, been lost from the moment when they took up arms without waiting for the time when they could have acted as the auxiliaries of a party in the legislative body, in Paris, or in the country. Disconnected risings in pursuance of plans dictated from abroad, brigandage practised by the rebels upon all who had not totally abjured the Revolution, upon constitutional priests and royalists, upon peasants and townsmen, had led to a system of bloody reprisals, to the discredit of the royalist cause, and finally to the destruction of the rebels themselves. A combined and well-supported movement and some rapid successes might have placed the Vendeans in a position to avail themselves of the moral resources offered by the state of France. By a formal proclamation to the people, and to the Assembly, they should have demanded a free convocation of the primary assemblies, and laid before them for decision the question between monarchy and the Revolution. Some such policy as this would more seriously have embarrassed the Government than any number of battles, and given a *point d'appui* to the reactionary feeling of the country.

Whatever criticism applied to the conduct of the civil war applied with even greater force to the conduct of the foreign war. The allies should have appeared not as principals but as auxiliaries of a party in France, not as enemies of the nation but as enemies of a faction. The ' folle manie de ' batailler ' should have had no place in their councils. Not

a step should have been taken without full consideration of
its effects in France, without concert with the counter-revolu-
tionary leaders in the country.   ' Never will the people re-
' cognise a king given them by their enemies.'   They should
have relied upon moral means rather than upon arms.   Again
and again Mallet counsels the issuing of proclamations which
should reassure the French as to the intention of the allies,
and dispel their prejudice that the allies would pretend to
dictate the laws or government under which they were to live,
or that they were armed for the restoration of the *ancien
régime.*   He insisted that it would be all over with the republic
if the Powers could reduce the question to the solemn and
definite alternative of peace and monarchy, or war and re-
publicanism; and that such a declaration, supported by
strong defensive measures on the Rhine, and a succession
of short and sympathetic exhortations, would reveal to the
people a possibility of ending their miseries, and encourage
the royalists to organise a combined movement.

It was the same policy which Mallet du Pan had recommended at the beginning of the war on the only occasion on
which he played an official part in the theatre of the great
events of the Revolution.   The history of the issue of the
Brunswick Manifesto is now sufficiently known, but it is
interesting to note the differences between the proclamation
which appeared and the Memorial in which Mallet set forth the
views of Louis XVI.   The Manifesto was most inflammatory
in its tone.   The threats indiscriminately levelled at all who
had acquiesced in the Revolution were but poorly counterbalanced by a paragraph which extended the protection of
the allies to those who should instantly concur in the re-
establishment of order.   In the Memorial which Mallet presented to the allied monarchs, but which was not adopted, he
insisted on the necessity of inspiring both terror and confidence; he would have used extreme threats only against the
extreme leaders of the Revolution, whom he carefully distinguished from the people, while he spoke of the danger and
injustice of confounding the less extreme factions with the
Jacobins.   The differences between the two documents,
serious as they are, are, however, chiefly differences of detail
and of manner: they agree in their pretensions of interference in the affairs of a foreign State, in their appeal to one
party against another, in their object—a restoration of the
power of the King by means of a counter-revolution, to be
effected, if necessary, by force.   The effect of the issue of the
Manifesto was disastrous; it is to be feared that the result

would hardly have been different had Mallet's Memorial been adopted as the basis of a proclamation, and it is difficult to understand how he could have persuaded himself that the foreign war conducted as he had recommended would have been preferable in its results to a civil war, or would have averted its horrors.   Criticism has attacked his conception of the possibility of a counter-revolution in the constitutional sense, and his estimate of the strength of the anti-revolutionary feeling in the country.   It is indeed impossible to read the correspondence without being struck by the general hopefulness of the tone—a hopefulness derived rather from his knowledge of the internal condition of France than from any real confidence in the action of the allies.

The biographer of Rivarol, while placing Mallet du Pan in the front rank of political philosophers, has described him as inferior to the subject of his memoir in practical sagacity, in the prognostication of coming events.   Rivarol, he says, saw that the Revolution, begun by excess of liberty, would end in excess of tyranny.   Mallet du Pan and Joseph de Maistre both believed that the Revolution would end in a restoration—a restoration, according to the Savoyard prophet, to be in some way an open manifestation of the will of God ; according 'to the Genevese philosopher, the fruit of a ' war without selfish ambition or too crushing defeats, the ' disinterested triumph of a European police coinciding with ' a reaction of disillusion and repentance of a whole people.' It is precisely, perhaps, as a practical policy that Mallet's action can be defended, and on this ground it compares not unfavourably with the paradoxical and illusory expedients recommended by Rivarol, or the advice he gave in 1792 : ' S'il veut régner, il est temps qu'il fasse le roi.'   Theoretically nothing could be more unsound than the policy of foreign interference, for no maxim in politics seems more indisputable than that one nation should not interfere in the domestic disputes of another.   Nothing could have been more imprudent than for the King to traffic with foreign powers. But the war was none of the King's making, nor, as we have seen, of Mallet's counselling.   It must be borne in mind that Mallet did not go to Frankfort until Louis XVI. had made every effort to prevent the war, and he himself had done all that was possible to point out its dangers.   The allies were approaching as enemies whether the King interfered or not, the revolutionary parties in the capital were pressing forward to destroy him, and his only chance lay in attempting to play the part of a mediator.   The same line of argument applies with equal force to the policy which Mallet continued to urge upon the allies. Peace being out of the question, it only remained for one who, unlike Rivarol, refused to stand aside, to counsel the conduct of the war upon reasonable and intelligible principles. Mallet du Pan, it must be admitted, deceived himself as to the effect the war would have in uniting public opinion in France against the foreign enemy. He was wrong in thinking that the timid and long-suffering majority would revolt against the Jacobin rule. He was mistaken in his view of the objects of the allies. But the correspondence fully proves that he did not long retain these illusions. ' L'Europe est finie,' he had exclaimed on hearing of the Peace of Bâle. The Italian campaigns, he confesses, first led him to abandon all hope that the powers would ever unite in good faith against a common enemy. It is true that he believed that the Revolution would end in a restoration, and time showed that he was right; it is not true that he believed it to be imminent.

' It is in vain,' he said, ' to count on the fall of the Republic. These who consider that the imperishable Republic will perish in time are certainly right; but if they mean that its fall in the more or less remote future will save Europe, if they fancy that everything will suddenly change from black to white, they are mistaken, for the Republic of to-day may be succeeded by a monarchical or dictatorial Republic. Who can tell? In twenty years a nation in ferment may give a hundred different forms to such a revolution.'

Political foresight is a higher gift than the guesswork which so often goes by the name of political prophecy. Yet a just appreciation of the possibilities of the future is a quality to which posterity at any rate attaches great importance, and Sainte-Beuve observed that Mallet in his previsions was ' as rarely as possible in such a *mêlée* wrong.' With Burke he had been the first to see that the Revolution would run its course through anarchy to despotism. It would not be difficult to show from his writings that he foretold every form which the Revolution would take; he even, as Sainte-Beuve says, foresaw the Monarchy of July. His clearness of vision had nothing in common with the sublime and prophetic spirit of Joseph de Maistre, a spirit modified in Burke by an English training and a practical experience of liberty. Eloquence in him was the outcome of a revolted moral sense, the follies and crimes of the Revolution stirred the fiery indignation with which he lashed them. Reflection, liberty, and conviction gave the tone of manly reason, of strong intelligence, which appear in every line he wrote. His power of observation has been compared to that of the physician, his work was a 'monograph of the revolutionary fever,' his analysis of public opinion was a 'moral dissection.' His judgement upon nobles, *émigrés*, and clergy, 'royalists in ' France and royalists in emigration, Parisians or provincials, ' administrators of the Constituent Assembly, proconsuls of ' the Convention, functionaries of the Directory, men of the ' Terror, of Thermidor, of Vendémiaire, *feuillants*, Girondists, ' and Jacobins,' are, says M. Taine, exact and penetrating. No one except Burke, he continues, has so perfectly comprehended the Jacobins, 'their fanaticism, their sectarian in- ' stincts and methods, the logic of their dogmas, their ascend- ' ency over the illiterate or half-educated, the might and ' maleficence of their dreams, their aptitude for destruction, ' their incapacity for construction, and their appeal to the ' passions of murder and dissolution.' Mallet du Pan was perhaps less successful in realising and painting the characters of individual men. The Revolution had so far failed to bring to the front one commanding spirit, and the evident mediocrity of all the actors he was called upon to criticise confirmed him in the conviction that the course of history was little influenced by the characters of individuals. 'Il n'y a plus ' d'hommes, il n'y a que des événements.' It was impossible, indeed, to attribute the course of events to any profoundly combined plan of any individual or party. 'Their very ' crimes were impromptu.' They were all alike the victims of a movement which they could not stop, whose incendiary force they were obliged to use. 'It is not Bonaparte, nor ' Siéyès, nor Merlin who reigns, it is the irresistible movement ' which the Revolution impresses upon men and affairs.'

There was, however, one figure which, for all after history, gives the keynote of this chaotic period, and Mallet's failure to recognise Bonaparte has been made the object of the severest criticism. He does not even mention Bonaparte in connexion with the *coup d'état* of Vendémiaire, and his later remarks read strangely indeed in the light of after history : ' Ce petit bamboche à cheveux éparpillés, ce bâtard de man- ' drin que les rhéteurs des Conseils appellent jeune héros et ' vainqueur d'Italie, expiera promptement sa gloire de tré- ' teau, son inconduite. ses vols, ses fusillades, ses insolentes ' pasquinades.' Such was the criticism of the campaign of 1796. Next year he is the 'instrument of the Directory ' and the Jacobins to intimidate the country;' and many observations of this kind show how little Mallet at this time anticipated the *rôle* which the young republican general was to play. History throws a halo of romance and mystery over the beginnings of heroes, and contemporaries may well be pardoned for not seeing in the early life of such men all the signs of future eminence which posterity delights to emphasise. It is to be remembered that of the foremost writers of the Revolution, Mallet du Pan and Rivarol alone share the disadvantage, which is the gain of history, of having given their ideas to the world in works which, once printed, it was impossible for them to recall or retouch; they alone wrote of the future without the assistance which actual experience of it gave to so many of the authors of the most famous memoirs and 'recollections' of the time. Even in such works we may look in vain for signs of earlier appreciation, and among a people busy enough with the immediate future, but caring or thinking of nothing beyond it, it may be doubted whether there were many who took a juster view of the fortune in store for Bonaparte. Barras, who first employed him, had certainly no idea of abdicating in his favour. The Directory indeed feared him, but only as they feared all their armies and generals, as they feared Hoche and Pichegru. Mallet du Pan saw at any rate that the Directorial *coup de main* of Fructidor 1797 had destroyed the illusion of republican constitutionalism, and paved the way for the rule of a single man, that the 'first general, the first accredited chieftain ' who could raise the standard of revolt might carry half the ' country with him.' Bonaparte was not yet strong enough, and Mallet might be excused in thinking that unless some new theatre of war presented itself, his chances were gone, at a time when none but his own *entourage* of military adventurers believed in his destiny, when he himself, fearing his ' grande nation ' much more than the princes and generals of Europe, was obliged to undertake the Egyptian expedition because his position was untenable at home.

It is worth while to follow Mallet in his speculations upon the future of Bonaparte beyond the pages of this correspondence. In an article in the 'Mercure Britannique' he states his views upon the revolution of November 10, 1799, which destroyed the Directory and established the Consulate. That revolution seemed to him of a new order, and in its way as fundamental as that of 1789. ' The materials, means, results, ' and authors are all different; it is the first time the ' military element has triumphed over the civil power.' The ascendency of the genius of Bonaparte is clear to him; he treats with the respect it deserves the idea of these ' poor ' innocent *émigrés*, who fancy that Bonaparte was about to

' play the part of Monk.' Neither did he share the illusion of those who thought that the new reign would be short or fleeting. 'Bonaparte is king. I see an immense power ' placed in the hands of a man who knows how to use it, ' who has on his side both the army and the public.' Mallet, who saw but the beginning of his career, understood perhaps no better than others the character of Napoleon, but he would have had no occasion to modify the judgement contained in the following words written during the Egyptian campaign :—

' Never were valour and contempt for humanity, capacity and false greatness, intelligence and ignorant jugglery, insolent immodesty and splendid qualities, united to the same degree as in this man, extraordinary rather than great. His head is in the clouds, his career is a poem, his imagination a storehouse of heroic romance, and his stage is large enough for all the excesses of his will or his ambition. Who can say where he will stop? Is he sufficiently master of events and of time, of his own sentiments, of his own future to decide for himself? '

In the face of such comprehension of Bonaparte's past, and of the possibilities of his future, criticism like that of M. de Lescure refutes itself, when he says :—' A political ' tactician of the old school, Mallet du Pan understood ' Bonaparte as a statesman no better than Würmser or ' Beaulieu understood him as a general.'

Other portraits there are which give interest to the correspondence : Cambacérès, for instance, the second consul, whose amiable and honest, but feeble character is admirably hit off; Carnot, 'fort et fin;' 'ce pauvre petit philoso-' phailleur La Reveillère-Lepaux;' Talleyrand—'the least ' scrupulous, the most immoral of men, whose ambition ' would be boundless were not his indolence even greater ' than his ambition;' the young Maret, the future Duke of Bassano, 'without experience, but without other perversity ' than that of his ideas full of ambition, much too clever for ' his age, and versed in the Machiavelism of the revolutionary ' policy, with the manners and exterior of a gentleman;' Barras, 'qui joue le roi et le Genghis Khan,' not unmindful of his birth, and having much at heart to be considered and treated as a person of quality; a man of limited ability, without morality, honour, or education, 'having the tone and ' courage of a soldier, and bearing himself in politics with the ' same audacity as in his debauchery.' But the most powerful and elaborate of Mallet's portraits is that of the silent coadjutor of Bonaparte in the *coup d'état* of Brumaire, the Abbé Siéyès. A man so superior to the mob of agitators could not

see France a prey to their intrigues without endeavouring
to become their master. The political metaphysician had
qualities which eminently fitted him for the task he set himself. Fertile in resource, he could wait in silence without
conceiving chimerical plans; he united dexterity and constancy, and no one, when a great occasion demanded it,
' could better preserve control over himself, or obtain it over
' others.' Siéyès was the author of the general plan, and of
the preparatory steps of the *coup d'état.* But the time had
come when the necessary impulsion for another change
could only be found in military force. 'Il me faut une
' épée,' he exclaimed in an epigram which ended, as another
had begun, the Revolution. When Bonaparte adopted his
scheme the civil arm sank into insignificance; the famous
Constitution, the most impracticable but the most ingenious
system of checks and balances ever devised, was adopted,
shorn of all its distinctive features, and the philosopher who
had been the oracle and epitome of the revolutionary epoch
ended his days as a count and a pensioner. It has been
said that, while his position was one of opposition to the
historical school of Montesquieu, he was not more in harmony
with the logical school of Rousseau. His favourite studies
had always been of an abstract character; this taste was in
him intensified by a positive aversion for the study of history,
and to judge of the present by the past was with him to
judge of the known by the unknown. In his incapacity for
any but *à priori* methods in politics he belonged to the
revolutionary tribe; he differed from them, and this it was
that gave him his strength, in his conception of the possibilities of democratic society. He believed in the possibility
of representative government. The elaborate constitutional
schemes to which Siéyès clung all through the Revolution
were an attempt to escape from the logical conclusion of the
doctrines of Rousseau as exemplified in the Jacobin experiment
of government. The Directorial system, in so far as it drew
a line between the different functions of government, was
the fruit of his genius; in so far as it lacked the 'jury con-
' stitutionnaire,' a plan for the further division and balance
of powers, he repudiated it. He refused a seat in the
Directory, but remained their political adviser—a step in
accordance with his dislike of open responsibility, his talent
of ' doing evil as Providence does good without being per-
' ceived.' The whole passage in which Mallet has described
this ' Catalina en petit collet' is a masterpiece of satiric
portraiture :—

'L'Abbé Siéyès est l'homme le plus dangereux qu'ait fait connaître la révolution. Dès le premier jour il l'a mesurée théoriquement, mais sans en prévoir les horribles conséquences. Républicain avant les états-généraux de 1789, il n'a pas perdu un jour de vue le renversement du trône, de l'Eglise, de la religion catholique et de la noblesse. Heureusement cet opiniâtre et pénétrant novateur est le plus lâche des mortels : aussitôt qu'il a vu le danger, il s'est enseveli dans l'obscurité. Quiconque lui fera peur le maîtrisera toujours. Misanthrope atrabiliaire, de l'orgueil le plus exclusif, impatient et concentré, charlatan impérieux et jaloux, ennemi de tout mérite supérieur au sien, personne n'a plus que lui l'art de s'emparer des esprits en affectant le seul langage de la raison, de couvrir d'apparences plus froides ses passions, son maintien, son style. Dans un pays où tout le monde se mêle de raisonner et où les prestiges de la philosophie ont séduit tous les rangs, l'abbé Siéyès est un homme important. Cependant, jamais il n'obtint ni dans la première assemblée constituante, ni dans la convention actuelle, dont il est membre, de crédit permanent. Mirabeau, qui le connaissait, le méprisait et le haïssait, l'avait réduit au silence. . . . Il est capable d'ordonner les plus grands crimes pour faire adopter ses théories. Nul ne prémédita plus longtemps, plus froidement, avec plus de réflexion, l'abolition de la Royauté. Ennemi de tout pouvoir dont il ne sera pas le directeur spirituel, il a anéanti la noblesse parce qu'il n'était pas noble, son ordre parce qu'il n'était pas archevêque, les grands propriétaires parce qu'il n'était pas riche, et il renverserait tous les trônes parce que la nature ne l'a pas fait roi.'

Mallet, as we have seen, had no illusion as to the significance of the revolution effected by Bonaparte. He recognised with satisfaction that new prospects of order were opening for France, and saw the advantage of the exercise of a firm and tutelary government by a man in whose talents the people had confidence. But there is nothing to show that he would have become reconciled to a system which was faithfully to carry out the revolutionary traditions in its contempt for the rights of nations, or that a man who had so retained his faith in free government that at the end of the century he could pen an elaborate panegyric upon the career of Washington, would have acquiesced in a government, beneficial indeed compared with anarchy from which it sprang, but directly opposed to that liberal political system which had been the distinction of Switzerland, and whose traditions now lingered only in America and England. Even had he been able to overcome the personal animosity of Bonaparte, the ties which bound him to England, which had become, after the destruction of his own country, the home of his adoption, were stronger than any which might have called him to France. From the first the English Constitution had exercised over him the same fascination as

over many of his contemporaries. English history and
English literature had been his favourite studies.   He
had visited England before the Revolution, and placed his
son with a tutor at Walthamstow. In the 'Mercure de
'France' his most valuable articles had been those which
treated of English affairs, and they possess an exactitude,
an animation, and an appreciation of the significance of
passing events which it would be hard indeed to parallel in
modern contemporary journalism. He had awakened, and
kept alive in Europe, the interest excited in England by
the trial of Warren Hastings.   Before the assembly of the
States-General he had sought to instruct the French in lessons
of liberty, and warn them of the dangers of hasty innova-
tion, by a series of articles upon De Lolme's history of the
English Constitution.   Of his opinion on the part played
by England in the war we gather little from the correspondence, and that little is unfavourable. The extreme
unpopularity of England in France made her the worst
possible instrument in the policy of counter-revolution.   The
general opinion that her objects were entirely selfish had
gained much colour from her action in confining herself to
operations against the French colonies; and the brutal
conduct of the British troops under the Duke of York had
drawn from Mallet a remark, which the presence of the
Cossacks in Italy in 1799 confirmed, that any army which revolted the population would only serve the Revolution.   For
the same reason he had blamed the Comte d'Artois for following the British flag, and stated his belief that the reputed
connexion of the Vendeans with England would complete the
unpopularity of their cause. Although he had drawn up
memorials for the British Cabinet, and formed connexions
with the British ministers at Brussels, Turin, and Berne,
who had, as usual, received his suggestions with sympathy, he
does not seem to have entertained from the action of England
any hope of a result in the sense of his own recommendations, and it is curious to notice how small a part the
English alliance occupies in the pages of the correspondence.
It was not until May 1798, when the character of the war
was somewhat changed by the fact that England alone continued it, and by impending changes in France, which were
to result in placing England in the forefront of the champions
of national independence, that Mallet du Pan sought a
home in the only country which afforded any chance of
security—in which it was still possible for an ' honest man to
' think, speak, and act.' The enthusiasm called forth by

Bonaparte's threatened invasion had in some measure prepared him for the spirit he found, and he had already remarked upon the fact that a direct opposition of principles and conduct was only to be found between the free countries of England and America and the pretended apostles of liberty. The reality surpassed his expectations. ' I fancy ' myself in another world, in another century.' In spite of crushing taxation and constant alarms, calmness, order, and enthusiasm are everywhere displayed. But with all this ' superb display ' he saw that the real question at issue was hardly understood at all. Voltaire, sixty years before, had remarked that in no country were the sources of information so rare as in England, that in none was there greater indifference to matters of external interest; and Mallet asked himself how all this enthusiasm and energy would prevent France from devouring Europe bit by bit, and carrying on the work of universal dissolution.

The first thing for an exile who had lost his income, his savings, his library, and all his worldly possessions in the Revolution, was to assure for himself and his family a means of livelihood. Mallet's reputation and his friends enabled him to start without Government assistance a journal, called the 'Mercure Britannique,' a newspaper appearing every fortnight, which was to direct the efforts of Europe against the French, and enforce the lessons of ten years of revolution. Five hundred subscribers it had been calculated would be sufficient to support the author; the number soon rose to eight hundred—a large circulation for a foreign newspaper published in England; it was much read on the Continent, and several times republished after his death. These few volumes —for the work lasted only two years—contain the maturest fruit of his genius and experience, and in turning to it, after the diplomatic correspondence in which the last few years had been passed, one cannot but feel that his own instinct was right in telling him that he was at his best as a journalist. ' J'aime mieux avoir à faire au public qu'aux négociateurs.' The correspondence indeed is distinguished, as we have seen, for its just and powerful analyses of public opinion in France and of the spirit of parties, for its outspoken criticism of the conduct of the allies, and above all for an intelligible view of policy urged with spirit and consistency, and enforced by appeals to experience. But it would be in the highest degree unfair to base a judgement of the author upon these volumes alone. Written for a special purpose, they deal with a restricted portion of the subject, and their faults are perhaps inseparable from such a species of composition. A certain optimism was both prudent and politic in writing to the parties upon whom success or failure depended: it depended, for instance, on the allies, it depended, Mallet might flatter himself, upon the advice he gave them, what use Bonaparte might make of the unexampled opportunity presented to him. Some exaggeration and violence of tone, some repetition of ideas, are certain to be found in a series of secret memoranda presented to a Cabinet, and published, as historical criticism now demands, in the exact form in which they were written. It is to the works in which he appealed to Europe and to posterity that we must turn for broader views; it is in the pages of the 'Mercure' that we must look for the philosophic statesman, rather than in the pleadings of an advocate and diplomatist. If we are wearied, for instance, by the iteration of gloomy forebodings of the fate of Europe, of the irresistible might of the Revolutionary movement, of the impending dissolution of social order, we may turn to a passage, one among many, to words which seem rather those of an historian than of one who had suffered from the convulsion every misfortune but the guillotine :—

'The annals of the world have preserved the memory of many such climacteric eras, in which the intoxication of unreason working upon human passions has seized upon society to destroy its harmony and punish generations of its members. We hear it said that the Revolution is unparalleled in its horror. Nothing, not even the wonder of fools, is unparalleled in this world. As for horror, was it, alas! less grievous to be a loyal royalist in Paris when Charles the Bad assassinated the Marshal de Champagne in the very arms of his sovereign? Was it less grievous to be the Admiral de Coligny in 1572 than the Prince de Condé in 1793? Was it less grievous to be the descendant of Aurungzebe, or of Michael Palæologus, than of Louis XIV.? For contemporary witnesses every event is unique, and yet history offers us a succession of perpetual but dissimilar horrors. It is the honourable task of the historian to discriminate between them; the learning of a pedant can discover their resemblances.'

The passage which follows is so characteristic of the author at his best, both in style and matter, that we may be excused for quoting it in the original :—

'Ce qui sert à faire de la Révolution de France un tableau sans exemple, ce ne sont ni ses doctrines, ni ses crimes, ni ses origines, ni ses malheurs: c'est le caractère particulier de ses auteurs et de ses victimes; c'est ce mélange de méchanceté usurpatrice et de fanatisme scolastique enté sur la vanité nationale; c'est cet enchaînement de crimes rendus nécessaires par d'autres crimes, dans ces transitions graduelles de l'esprit d'indépendance au besoin d'un despotisme régulier;

c'est cette inconstance des opinions après la fièvre de l'enthousiasme ; c'est cette union du génie des sectes à celui des conquérants, qui attaque à la fois les territoires et les institutions, les religions, les usages, les mœurs, les propriétés et les sentiments publics ; c'est ce concours de l'hypocrisie avec la férocité, du langage des lumières avec la bassesse de l'ignorance, des sophismes avec les forfaits, et d'une corruption perfectionnée avec la brutalité des temps de barbarie : c'est, enfin, ce contraste éternel entre les principes et les actions, entre l'empire des idées et celui des intérêts, entre la force des hommes et celle des événements : contraste qui, après avoir enfanté une suite de vicissitudes, les a perpétuées, et qu'on n'explique ni par des déclamations, ni par des fables apocalyptiques sur les causes secrètes.'

Mallet distrusted, as we have seen, the power of contemporaries to judge of passing events. He was no less modest as to the utility of writing on them at all. ' L'écrivaillerie,' he often said, quoting Montesquieu, ' est le symptôme d'un ' siècle débordé.' It was with the words, ' It is idle to fight ' a revolution with sheets of paper,' that he had abandoned his editorship of the ' Mercure de France.' As a duty he entered upon the editorship of a new journal; with growing disgust at the exigencies of ' his detestable scribbling ' he carried on the work until it brought him to the grave. But the necessity of speaking what was in him was strong to the end, and he has acknowledged in touching words his gratitude to the nation which gave him the power to do so :—

' J'ai perdu, avec la Suisse, patrie, parents, amis : il ne m'en reste que des souvenirs déchirants. Je serais peut-être sans asyle si le ciel ne m'eût réservé un port où je puis accuser, sans les craindre, des tyrans en démence, dont l'orgueilleuse impuissance menace vainement ce dernier boulevard de la vieille Europe. C'est sous la protection d'une nation inébranlable que je dépose ici et mes récits et mes douleurs. Sans sa magnanimité j'éprouverais encore le tourment du silence. Jamais trop de reconnaissance ne payera le bienfait de cet affranchissement.'

ART. V.—*The Works of Edmund Spenser.* Edited by the
Rev. Dr. GROSART. In 8 vols. London : 1883.

IT often happens that some eminent characteristic of a
great poet has almost escaped observation owing to the
degree in which other characteristics, not higher but more
attractive to the many, have also belonged to him. Spenser
is an instance of this. If it were asked what chiefly constitutes the merit of his poetry, the answer would commonly
be, its descriptive power, or its chivalrous sentiment, or its
exquisite sense of beauty ; yet the quality which he himself
desiderated most for his chief work was one not often found
in union with these, viz. sound and true philosophic thought.
This is the characteristic which we propose to illustrate at
present. It was the characteristic which chiefly won for
him the praise of Shakespeare :—

> ‘ Spenser to me, whose *deep conceit* is such
> As, passing all conceit, needs no defence ; ’

and it was doubtless the merit to which he owed the influence which Milton acknowledged that Spenser’s poetry
had exercised over his own. There is more of philosophy
in one book of the ‘ Faery Queen ’ than in all the cantos of
his Italian models. In Italy the thinkers were generally
astute politicians or recluse theologians ; and her later poets,
excepting of course Tasso, cared more to amuse a brilliant
court with song and light tale than to follow the steps of
Dante along the summits of serious song. England, on the
other hand, uniting both the practical and the meditative
mind with the imaginative instincts of southern lands, had
thereby strengthened both that mind and those instincts,
and thus occupied a position neither above nor beneath the
region of thoughtful poetry. In the latter part of the
sixteenth and earlier part of the seventeenth century, she
possessed a considerable number of poets who selected, apparently without offence, very grave themes for their poetry.
It will suffice to name such writers as Samuel Daniel, John
Davies, George Herbert, Dr. Donne, Giles Fletcher, Habing-
ton, and, not much later, Dr. Henry More, the Platonist.
These poets, however, came later than Spenser, and were
not a little indebted to him, while yet they were, in some
respects, unlike him. Some of them selected themes so
abstract and metaphysical as to be almost beyond the limits
of true poetic art. The difficulty was itself an attraction to

them, and their ambition was more to instruct than to delight. Spenser loved philosophy as well as they, but was too truly a poet to allow of his following her when she strayed into 'a barren and dry land,' or of his adopting the didactic method when he illustrated philosophic themes. Truth and beauty are things correlative; and very profound truths can be elucidated in verse without the aid of such technical reasoning processes as those with which Dryden conducted his argument in the 'Hind and Panther,' and Pope in his 'Essays.' Spenser's imagination never forsook the region of the sympathies; but it had the special gift of drawing within their charmed circle themes which for another poet must have ever remained outside it, and of suffusing them at once with the glow of passion and with the white light of high intelligence. It is true that he dealt much in allegory; but though allegory is commonly a cold thing—always, indeed, if it be mere allegory—yet whenever Spenser's genius is true to itself, his allegory catches fire and raises to the heights of song themes which would otherwise have descended to the level of ordinary prose. Had Spenser's poetry not included this philosophic vein, it would not have been in sympathy with a time which produced a Bacon, whose prose is often the noblest poetry, as well as a Sidney, whose life was a poem. At the Merchant Taylors' Grammar School, Bishop Andrews and, as is believed, Richard Hooker, were among his companions; and when he entered Cambridge, Pembroke Hall was at least as much occupied with theological and metaphysical discussion as with classical literature.

We may go further. It was in a large measure the strength of his human sympathies, which at once forced Spenser to include philosophy among the subjects of his poetry, and prevented that philosophy from becoming unfit for poetry. As he was eminently a poet of the humanities, so his philosophy was a philosophy of the humanities; he could no more have taken up a physiological theme for a poem, like Phineas Fletcher's 'Purple Island,' than a geographical one, like Drayton's 'Polyolbion.' The philosophy which interested him was that which 'comes home to the business 'and bosoms of men.' It was philosophy allied to life—philosophy moral, social, and political. Such philosophy is latent in all great poetry, though it is in some ages only that it becomes patent. It is with his political and social philosophy that we shall begin, proceeding afterwards to his philosophy of man.

We know from Spenser's letter to Sir Walter Raleigh
that to embody a great scheme of philosophy was the end
which he proposed to himself in writing the 'Faery Queen.'
That poem was to consist of twelve books; and the hero of
each was to impersonate one of the twelve moral virtues
enumerated by Aristotle. This poem he proposed to follow
up by a second, the hero of which was to have been King
Arthur after he had acceded to the throne, and which was
to have illustrated the political virtues. We learn from
Todd's ' Life of Spenser' that at a party of friends held
near Dublin, in the house of Ludowick Bryskett, the poet
gave the same account of his poem, then unpublished, but
of which a considerable part had been written. Bryskett,
on that occasion, spoke of him as 'not only perfect in the
' Greek tongue, but also very well read in philosophy, both
' moral and natural.'

Unhappily, only half of the earlier romance was written,
or at least has reached us, and no part of the second; but
much which belongs to the subject of the second poem may
be found in fragments scattered over the six books of the
' Faery Queen.' One of these political fragments vindicates
the old claim of poets to be prophets; for the great revolutionary dogma expounded in it is one which, though its
earlier mutterings may have been heard at the time of the
German Anabaptists, did not ' open its mouth' and ' speak
' great things ' for two centuries after Spenser had denounced
the approaching imposture. That imposture is the one, now
but too well known, which, in the name of justice, substitutes for it the fiction of a universal equality in the interests of which all human society hitherto known is to be
levelled down and remodelled. Artegal, Spenser's emblem
of Justice, rides forth on his mission accompanied by his
squire Talus, the iron man, with the iron flail. On the
seaside they descry ' many nations' gathered together:—

'There they beheld a mighty gyant stand
    Upon a rocke, and holding forth on hie
An huge great paire of ballaunce in his hand,
    With which he boasted in his surquedrie *
That all the world he would weigh equallie,
    If aught he had the same to counterpoize;
For want whereof he weighed vanity,
    And filled his ballaunce full of idle toys;
And was admired much of fools, women, and boys.

* Pride.

He sayd that he would all the earth uptake
And all the sea, divided each from either;
So would he of the fire one ballaunce make,
And of the ayre without or wind or weather:
Then would he ballaunce heaven and hell together,
And all that did within them all containe;
Of all whose weight he would not misse a fether;
And looke what surplus did of each remaine,
He would to his own part restore the same againe.

. . . . . .

Therefore the vulgar did about him flocke,
And cluster thicke unto his leasings vaine,
Like foolish flies about a hony-crocke
In hope by him great benefit to gain.'*

The Knight of Justice here breaks in, and affirms that the giant ought, before restoring everything to its original condition, to ascertain exactly ' What was the poyse of every ' part of yore.' The giant knows that the best mode to meet an unanswerable reply is by reiteration:—

' Therefore I will throw downe these mountains hie,
And make them levell with the lowly plaine,
These towring rocks which reach unto the skie,
I will thrust down into the deepest maine,
And as they were them equalize againe.
Tyrants, that make men subject to their law,
I will suppresse that they no more may raine,
And lordlings curbe that commons overaw,
And all the wealth of rich men to the poore will draw.'

Artegal retorts that what the sea devours of the land in one region it surrenders in another, and that if the field did not augment its stores by drawing decayed matter into its bosom, it could not send up the living harvest the next year. In all this interchange Nature but obeys the great Creator.

' They live, they die, like as He doth ordaine,
Ne ever any asketh reason why;
The hils doe not the lowly dales disdaine;
The dales do not the lofty hils envy.
He maketh kings to sit in sovereinty;
He maketh subjects to their powre obey;
He pulleth downe; He setteth up on hie;
He gives to this; from that He takes away:
For all we have is His: what He list doe He may.'

---

* Faery Queen, Book V., canto ii., stanza 30.

He takes the giant at his word, and bids him test his boasted power.

> ' For take thy ballaunce, if thou be so wise,
> And weigh the winde that under heaven doth blow ;
> Or weigh the light that in the east doth rise ;
> Or weigh the thought that from man's mind doth flow.
> But if the weight of these thou canst not show,
> Weight but one word which from thy lips doth fall ;
> For how canst thou those greater secrets know,
> That doest not know the least thing of them all ?
> Ne can he rule the great that cannot reach the small.'

We have all heard of the English socialist whose triumphant appeal, ' Tell me, is not one man as good as another ? ' was unwittingly confuted by the answer of his Irish boon-companion, ' To be sure he is, *and better !* ' So far as equality exists at all, it exists not by nature, but through man's law, so bitterly inveighed against by the advocates of equality ; for Nature, while she is rich in compensations, makes no two things equal. Notwithstanding, the giant accepts Artegal's challenge. He places the True and the False in the opposed scales of his balance, but can get no further :—

> ' For by no means the False will with the Truth be wayd.'

He next puts Right and Wrong into his scales, but fails once more :—

> ' Yet all the wrongs could not a litle right downe-way.'

The prophet thus turning out an impostor, Talus scales the rock, scourges him with his iron flail, flings him into the sea, and disperses the multitude.

Spenser, however, does not take one-sided views of things. He sees a connexion between the madness of revolutionary idealisms and that tyranny which ' maketh a wise man ' mad.' Before we make acquaintance with the giant Equality, we are brought to the castle of a bandit chief, Pollente, who has grown to wealth through extortion.

> ' And daily he his wrongs encreaseth more ;
> For never wight he lets to pass that way,
> Over his bridge, albee he rich or poore,
> But he him makes his passage-penny pay ;
> Else he doth hold him backe, or beat away.
> Thereto he hath a groome of evill guize,
> Whose scalp is bare, that bondage doth bewray,
> Which pols and pils the poore in piteous wize,
> But he himself upon the rich doth tyrannize.' *

---

* Book V., canto ii., stanza 6.

Pollente has a daughter, Munera; to her he brings his ill-gotten spoils, and with them she has purchased all the country round. Eventually Artegal slays the giant, and Talus, rejecting the bribes of Munera, drags her from under a heap of gold, her hiding-place, cuts off her hands, which are made of gold, and her feet, which are silver, and casts her into the flood.

Another ethical craze of our later time seems to have been anticipated by Spenser—that which claims for women all the civil and political privileges and functions which belong to men, and denounces, as the 'subjection of woman,' even that domestic obedience of the wife to the husband which is the noblest example of willing submission. That a wife's obedience is based neither on servile fear nor abject self-interest, but on that principle of love which is the characteristic crown of womanhood, is witnessed to in the expression, ' Thy desire shall be to thy husband, and he shall ' have the rule over thee.' The root of that claim to domestic equality which would revolutionise the whole domestic life is patent. Those who sustain it assume that obedience is, even when necessary, still essentially a degradation. This is a ' vulgar error.' Obedience to a spurious authority, and obedience extorted by mere force, in each of these there exists degradation; but where the obedience is paid willingly, and paid where it is due, there obedience and authority are but two converse forms of excellence, mutually supplemental. This principle of correlative though contrasted forms of excellence was appreciated by the ages of chivalry; children knelt to their parents, and the 'faithful servant,' who inscribed that name alone on the title-page of his story of the 'knight without fear and without reproach,' regarded the title 'servant' as an honourable one, not less than the title master.

The 'Amazon Republic' was a Greek conception, and evinced that clearness which belonged to the Greek intelligence alike in its serious and in its sportive moods. The Greek insight perceived at once that, while the equality of the sexes may substantially exist in the way of compensatory advantages and disadvantages, it could not exist in the material form of identical rights and functions. In that form, woman must have either less than equality, or more. The lady who remarked, ' I do not want women to take their stand with men ' on the great stage of life, because unless we sat behind the ' scenes we could not pull the wires,' understood that women possess at present a very real power of their own; and the

Athenians said of old, that if Pericles governed Athens, so
did his wife, since she governed him, and so did their child,
since he governed her. Here is the indirect equality produced by compensation. It is in its complete Amazonian,
not its incomplete, form that Spenser deals with this quaint
moral problem; and there is a deep sagacity in his mode
of solving it. The Knight of Justice hears that a certain
Amazon Queen, Radigund, by way of righting the wrongs
of her sex, has established herself in a castle, and that she
defies all knights to combat, first binding them to submit
to her terms. The Amazon is not actuated by zeal for her
sex; next to the inspiration of pride comes that of spite; and
an idle fancy has been followed up by an envenomed grudge.
Neither is Artegal's resolve to do battle with the Amazon
grounded merely on his sympathy with the knights thus
degraded;

> ' " Now sure," said he, " and by the faith that I
> To maidenhead and noble knighthood owe,
> I will not rest till I her might do try ! " '

Her masculine claims he regards as an insult to all that is
best in maidenhood and womanhood—a virtual denial of their
true powers and dignities.

Artegal is victorious at first, and his enemy falls; the
knight throws away his sword; the Amazon revives and
resumes the fight; Artegal can only step backwards, protecting himself with his shield; she redoubles her blows;
and he, by the terms of their battle, becomes her slave. But
the battle has not really been fought with equal weapons;
and it is owing to her beauty and his weakness that he sits
ere long ranged with her other vassals, distaff in hand, and in
woman's garb.

The conqueror is punished for her pride. She loses her
heart to her captive in spite of her self-scorn, and she fails
in her attempt to win his love. Her charm is for him gone.
She has lost the power of woman by claiming that which
belongs to man; she has snatched at the shadow, and dropped
the substance. It is woman that avenges the wrong done to
womanhood. Britomart hears that her lover is in distress,
and flies to his aid, though she believes that he had forgotten
her. The virgin warrioress assails the castle of the Amazon,
vanquishes her in single fight, and liberates the captives.
Britomart is the loftiest of Spenser's heroines. Another
poet would have made her turn in scorn from Artegal when
she saw him among the knights plying the distaff. She does

not do this. She is not woman unsexed, but woman raised above woman, and therefore woman still. The sacred obedience of love binds her to the better part. When she first saw him amid the servile crew,

> ' She turned her head aside as nothing glad.'

But she looks on him again, and sees, not what is before her, but what she remembers. She makes him lord of the conquered city ; and to it she restores peace and gladness.

Let us turn next to Spenser's philosophy considered with reference to the joys and duties of life, personal and domestic. That philosophy was a comprehensive one, and regarded human life in at least three aspects. The first is the ordinary life of men lived wisely; the second is the life spiritual founded on faith in worlds unseen; the third is life lived unwisely, and dominated either by sensual passion or by pride.

Let us begin with his philosophy of ordinary life when wisely led. It is set forth chiefly in the Second Book, or the Legend of Temperance. The first canto tells us of the husband under a witch's spell, of the self-slain wife, and the deserted babe—all three the victims of lawless passion in the form of corrupt pleasure. In the second canto the destructive passion is anger : two knights strive in fratricidal fury aggravated by the arts of their two lady-loves. These sirens allegorise the ' Two Extremes,' and are contrasted with a third sister, Medina, or the ' Golden Mean,' who endeavours to bring the warring knights to concord. It is not from war that she dissuades them, but from unworthy war. According to Spenser's philosophy, man's condition is by necessity ' militant here on earth;' but the wars like the loves of men should have in them little in common with those of the inferior kinds ; it was thus that Sidney wrote of ' that sweet ' enemy, France.' Rancour in the form of slander and detraction is yet more severely judged than the most relentless war. It is the first offence punished in the temple of justice.

The secret of human happiness, according to Spenser, is self-control, especially in the use of lawful things. It is that dignity in which man was created, and that belongs not to his spirit alone, but to its earthly tabernacle also, which, far more than any servile fear, binds him over to resist all to which that dignity is opposed. The mandates of conscience constitute the true glory and beauty of the world we inhabit. They are ' exceedingly broad;' and only in proportion as he rejoices in them while he obeys them, does man possess the ' freedom of the city ' in which he dwells.

Lives ruled by these radiant and benignant laws advance through boundless spaces in security as well as swiftness, like the planets which move without collision through the heavenly regions because they are faithful to their prescribed orbits; while lawless lives break themselves against unseen obstacles, and fall helpless. This is the doctrine illustrated by the ninth canto of the second legend which describes the House of Temperance. When Guyon and Prince Arthur reach its gates, they find them barred against the attacks of a barbarous foe. Here we have one of Spenser's Irish experiences :—

> ' As when a swarme of gnats at eventide
>   Out of the fennes of Allan doe arise,
>   Their murmuring small trompetts sownden wide,
>   Whiles in the aire their clustring army flies,
>   That as a cloud doth seeme to dim the skies,
>   Ne man, nor beast may rest or take repast
>   For their sharp wounds and noyous iniuries,
>   Till the fierce northern wind with blustring blast
> Doth blow them quite away, and in the ocean cast.' *

The foes at last dispersed—the emblems of the passions that besiege the soul—the gates of the castle are thrown open, and admittance is given to the knights by the princess who keeps state within.

> ' Alma she called was, a virgin bright,
>   That had not yet felt Cupides wanton rage;
>   Yet was she woo'd of many a gentle knight,
>   And many a lord of noble parentage,
>   That sought with her to lincke in marriage;
>   For shee was faire, as faire mote ever bee,
>   And in the flowre now of her freshest age;
>   Yet full of grace and goodly modestee,
> That even heven rejoicéd her sweete face to see.
>
>   In robe of lilly white she was arayd,
>   That from her shoulder to her heele downe raught,
>   The traine whereof loose far behind her strayd,
>   Branchéd with gold and perle, most richly wrought,
>   And borne of two fair damsels which were taught
>   That service well; her yellow golden heare
>   Was trimly woven and in tresses wrought;
>   No other tire she on head did weere,
> But crowned with a garland of sweet rosiere.' †

Alma entertains her deliverers ' with gentle court and

---

* Book II., canto ix., stanza 16.
† Book II., canto ix., stanzas 18–19.

'gracious delight,' and, after they have rested, leads them all round her castle walls. Next she shows them the stately hall set with 'tables faire,' where all is bounty without excess, and the 'goodly parlour' in which sit many beautiful ladies and knights who 'them did in modest sort amate,' and where even the son of Venus behaves with an approach to discretion :—

> 'And eke amongst them little Cupid playd
> His wanton sportes, being retourned late
> From his fierce warres, and having from him layd
> His cruel bow, wherewith he thousands hath dismayd.'

Not all of Alma's pupils are yet perfect in her lore. One of these is called 'Praise-desire;' she sits 'in a long purple 'pall' with a branch of tremulous poplar in her hand, and to Prince Arthur's demand as to the cause of her sadness she replies that it has come to her from 'her great desire of 'glory and of fame.' Another maiden has an opposite fault —an undue fear of human dispraise.

The princess leads the warriors next to a tower which commands a view of far realms. Therein three stately chambers rise one above another, each the cell of a sage. These three sages are emblems of the Future, the Present, and the Past. The walls of one chamber are painted with 'infinite 'shapes of things dispersed there,' shadows that flit through idle fantasy to charm or to scare it; devices, visions, wild opinions, and soothsayings. Here abides the sad prophet whose kingdom is the Future—a sick imagination.

> 'Amongst them all he sate which wonnèd there,
> That hight Phantastes by his nature true;
> A man of yeares, yet fresh as mote appere,
> Of swarth complexion, and of crabbed hew,
> That him full of meláncholy did shew;
> Bent hollow beetle brows, sharp, staring eyes,
> That mad or foolish seemed; one by his vew
> Might deeme him borne with ill-disposed skies,
> When oblique Saturne sate in th' House of Agonies.'

The second chamber is painted over with the types of all that imparts dignity to state; magistracies, the tribunals of justice, the triumphs of sciences and arts. This is the kingdom of the Present; and the sage who sits in it, a strong man of 'ripe and perfect age,' though his wisdom has all come 'through continual practise and usage,' represents practical judgement, and has for his kingdom the Present. The third sage symbolises memory, and the Past is his domain.

These three sages are, we are told, severally imperfect, because they dwell apart, each in a world of his own. Each makes too much of what occupies his special field of vision. The fault is that of disproportion, one closely allied to defective self-control. Neither imagination, judgement, nor memory, is fit to rule. These are but Alma's counsellors, each ministering a knowledge which becomes wisdom only when blent with the knowledge of the other two.

Next to a temperate will, the secret of a happy life, according to Spenser's philosophy, is a contented temper and that humility from which content springs. Such is the lesson taught to Calidore, the Knight of Courtsey, by the old shepherd Melibee. Happiness, he maintains, is from within, not from without:—

> ' It is the mind that maketh good or ill,
>   That maketh wretch or happie, rich or poore ; '

and for this reason he affirms, that those who earn their ' daily bread ' are the most fortunate. That the lowly condition, when at its best, does not exclude genuine refinement, is a lesson which Calidore learns from Pastorell, the supposed daughter of old Melibee, though in reality a maiden of high degree.

It is while Calidore, a great knight of the Faery Queen's court, dwells with the shepherds, that there is vouchsafed to him that exquisite vision, the emblem of human life, a maiden in maiden attire, and with rosy crown, standing on the summit of a sunny slope environed by the Three Graces and a hundred mountain nymphs, who dance around her, and pelt her with roses. That soft and serious human creature in the midst, we are told,

> ' Seemed all the rest in beauty to excell.'

Hers is the twofold human dower of spiritual greatness and of earthly infirmity ; the dancing choir that encircle her are the blameless gifts of ' boon nature,' and the graces that beautify life. Those elemental powers need no apparel, and wear none. She needs none, and yet she wears one ; for the order to which she belongs is bright, not with innocence only, but with modesty, and she is herself a mystery both of sanctity and of gladness. The mortal creature to whom those graces minister has inherited a higher gift than theirs.

> ' Divine resemblaunce, beauty soveraine rare.'

The quotations we have made express Spenser's estimate of human life when, with its twofold capacities, it has neither risen above ordinary humanity nor fallen below it. It is an estimate in some degree founded on the ancient philosophy, with its 'mens sana in corpore sano,' and yet more on that spiritual teaching which regards man's estate as at once peaceful within and militant without : peaceful, because protected from the storms of passion and lawless ambition; militant, because a ceaseless war with evil is an essential part of our earthly probation. With those two conditions of human well-being Spenser blended another; viz. the constant presence of that high beauty which haunted him wherever he went, alike amid the splendour of courts and in lonely vales, and which he regarded as one of God's chief gifts to man. The spirit of beauty is ever accompanied in Spenser's poetry with the kindred spirits of gladness and of love—a gladness which has nothing in common with mere pleasure, and a love which rises far above its counterfeits. With him man's nobler affections are not mere genial impulses; they are themselves virtues girdling in an outer circle those Christian virtues that stand around humanity, as, in Calidore's vision, the mountain nymphs encompassed those Three Graces who ministered to the rose-crowned maiden. The mode in which Spenser associated the virtues as well as the graces with his special idea of womanhood—an idea very remote from that common in our days—is nowhere more beautifully illustrated than in Book IV. c. x., where Scudamour describes the temple of Venus and the recovery of his lost Amoret.

> ' Into the inmost temple thus I came,
> Which fuming all with frankinsence I found,
> And odours rising from the altars flame ;
> Upon a hundred marble pillars round
> The roof up high was reerèd from the ground,
> All deck'd with crownes and chaynes and girlonds gay,
> And thousand precious gifts worth many a pound,
> The which sad lovers for their vows did pay ;
> And all the ground was strewd with flowers as fresh as May.'

In the midst stands on the chief altar the statue of the goddess to whom they sing a hymn. Round the steps of the altar sit many fair forms :—

> ' The first of them did seeme of riper yeares
> And graver countenance than all the rest ;
> Yet all the rest were eke her equall peares,
> And unto her obayed all the best.
> Her name was Womanhood; that she exprest
> By her sad semblant, and demeanure wyse ;

> For stedfast still her eyes did fixèd rest,
> Ne roved at random after gazers guyse,
> Whose luring baytes oftimes doe heedless harts entyse.
>
> And next to her sate goodly Shamefastness,
> Ne ever durst her eyes from ground upreare,
> Ne ever once did looke from her dais,
> As if some blame of evil she did feare,
> That in her cheek made roses oft appeare;
> And her against sweet Cherefulnesse was placed,
> Whose eyes, like twinkling stars in evening cleare,
> Were deckt with smyles that all sad humours chased,
> And darted forth delights, the which her goodly graced.
>
> And next to her sate sober Modestie,
> Holding her hand upon her gentle hart;
> And her against sate comely Curtesie,
> That unto every person knew her part;
> And her before was seated overthwart
> Soft Silence, and submisse Obedience,
> Both linckt together never to dispart;
> Both gifts of God not gotten but from thence,
> Both girlonds of his saints against their foes offence.
>
> Thus sate they all around in seemly rate;
> And in the midst of them a goodly mayd,
> Even in the lap of Womanhood there sate,
> The which was all in lilly white arrayd,
> With silver streames amongst the linnen strey'd;
> Like to the Morne when first her shining face
> Hath to the gloomy world itself bewray'd,
> That same was fairest Amoret in place,
> Shyning with beauties light, and heavenly vertues grace.'*

Scudamour stands in doubt—

> ' For sacrilege me seemed the church to rob.'

Observing, however, a smile on the countenance of the goddess, he persists :—

> ' She often prayd, and often me besought
> Sometimes with tender tears to let her goe,
> Sometimes with witching smyles; but yet for nought
> That ever she to me could say or doe
> Could she her wishèd freedom fro me move,
> But forth I led her through the temple gate.'

It is easy to trace the same benignant philosophy in all these descriptions. The wisely led life is a life of truth,

---

* Book IV., canto x., stanza 52.

of simplicity, of justice, of human sympathy and mutual kindness, of reverence for humanity in all its relations, and of reverence for God. The unwise life is the opposite of these things.

But the ordinary human life, even when wisely led, constitutes in part only Spenser's ideal of human life. It includes an extraordinary portion, a mountain land ascending high above the limit of perpetual snow. This is the life which seriously aims at perfection, the life lived 'from above,' and of which faith and truth are not the regulative only, but the constitutive principles. It is set forth in the 1st Book and 10th Canto of the 'Faery Queen.' Una has discovered that the Red-Cross Knight, though zealous for the good, is as yet but scantly qualified by knowledge or strength for that enterprise on which he was missioned from the Faery Court. That he may learn goodly lore and goodly discipline, she brings him to the 'House of Holiness.' It is presided over by one who represents heavenly wisdom.

> 'Dame Cœlia men did her call, as thought
> From heaven to come, or thither to arise;
> The mother of three daughters, well up-brought
> In goodly thews and godly exercise;
> The eldest two most sober, chast, and wise,
> Fidelia and Speranza, virgins were,
> Though spoused, yet wanting wedlock's solemnize;
> But faire Clarissa to a lovely fere
> Was linkèd, and by him had many pledges dere.' *

At the gateway sits a porter, 'Humiltà.' Entering, Una and her knight find themselves in a spacious palace court, whence 'a francklin faire and free,' by name Zeal, ushers them to a stately hall. There they are welcomed by 'a ' gentle squire, hight Reverence.'

We are next introduced to Cœlia's daughters, Faith and Hope. Spenser describes them as Raphael would have done, had he painted in words :—

> 'Thus as they gan of sondrie thinges devise,
> Loe, two most goodly virgins came in place,
> Ylinked arme in arme in lovely wise;
> With countenance demure, and modest grace,
> They numbred even steps and equall pace;
> Of which the eldest, that Fidelia hight,
> Like sunny beams threw from her christall face,
> That could have dazed the rash beholder's sight,
> And round about her head did shine like heaven's light.

---

* Book I., canto x., stanza 4.

She was arayèd all in lilly white,
And in her right hand bore a cup of gold,
With wine and water fild up to the hight,
In which a serpent did himselfe enfold,
That horrour made to all that did behold;
But she no whitt did change her constant mood :
And in her other hand she fast did hold
A booke, that was both signd and seald with blood ;
    Wherein darke things were writt, hard to be understood.

Her younger sister, that Speranza hight,
Was clad in blew that her beseemèd well ;
Not all so chearful seemèd she of sight,
As was her sister ; whether dread did dwell
Or anguish in her hart, is herd to tell :
Upon her arme a silver anchor lay,
Whereon she leanèd ever as befell ;
And ever up to heven, as she did pray,
    Her stedfast eyes were bent, ne swervèd other way.' *

A groom, Obedience, leads the youthful knight to the
guest-house ; and the next day Fidelia begins to instruct
him in her sacred book ' with blood ywritt :'—

' For she was able with her wordes to kill,
And raize againe to life the hart that she did thrill.

And when she list poure out her larger spright,
She would command the hasty sun to stay,
Or backward turne his course from heven's hight.'

The knight waxes daily as in knowledge so proportionately
in repentance ; but Speranza teaches him to take hold of
her silver anchor ; and Patience, a kindly physician, pours
balms into the wounds inflicted on him by Penance.   He is
next consigned to a holy matron, Mercy, that he may have a
share in all her holy works.   Mercy leads him into her
great hospital—

' In which seven bead-men that had vowed all
Their life to service of high heaven's king '

initiate him, each into the duties which belong to his several
function, the office of the first being to provide a home
for the homeless, of the second to feed the hungry, of the
third to provide raiment for ' the images of God in earthly
' clay,' of the fourth to release captives, of the fifth to tend
the sick, of the sixth to inter the dead, of the seventh to
take charge of the widow and the orphan.   With all these

---

* Book I., canto x., stanza 12.

sacred ministrations the knight is successively made acquainted, and thus fitted for a glimpse into the more exalted region of contemplation and the interior life.

> ' Thence forward by that painful way they pass
> Forth to a hill that was both steepe and hy,
> On top whereof a sacred chapel was,
> And eke a little hermitage thereby,
> Wherein an agèd holy man did lie,
> That day and night said his devotion,
> Ne other worldly business did apply ;
> His name was hevenly Contemplation ;
> Of God and goodnes was his meditation.
>
> Great grace that old man to him given had ;
> For God he often saw from heven's hight ;
> All were his earthly eyen both blunt and bad,
> And through great age had lost their kindly sight,
> Yet wondrous quick and persaunt was his spright,
> As eagle's eye that can behold the sunne.' *

Hearing that the youth has been sent to him by Fidelia to learn ' what every living wight should make his marke,' the aged man shows him the celestial city descending from heaven.

> ' As he thereon stood gazing, he might see
> The blessed angels to and fro descend
> From highest heaven in gladsome companee,
> And with great joy into that citty wend,
> As commonly as friend does with his friend.' †

The knight exclaims in ecstasy, ' What need of arms since ' peace doth ay remain ?' He is answered that his task must be accomplished before he is fit to enter into his rest; but that notwithstanding, whilst labouring on earth, he is to be a citizen of the Heavenly City as well as of God's city on earth.

Such is that supernatural life, at once active and contemplative, which, according to Spenser's philosophy, admits of being realised even upon earth by its choicer spirits. Between the two lives there is much in common as well as much diversity. In each life man's course is a warfare : in the ordinary life man has to fight against his own passions, and against all who would injure his fellow-man; in the extraordinary life the combat becomes one for the establishment of a divine kingdom. In each the joy of life

---

* Book I., canto x., stanza 47.
† Book I, canto x., stanza 56.

comes largely from beauty and from love; but in the sublimer life both of these are spiritual things. In both lives fame is won, but only in the higher is it the direct voice of God. In both there is commonly suffering, but in the higher that suffering is purification. The higher life has for its patrons Fidelia, Speranza, and Charissa, with whom are conjoined that other triad, Humility, Patience, and Purity; but those twelve virtues known of old are also ministering spirits to both lives, and belong to a cognate race; while that great mother Virtue, Reverence, the mystic Cybele of the House of Virtues, is the connecting link between the two classes of virtues. The higher life is as superior to the lower as the statue is to the pedestal; but that pedestal is yet hewn out of the same Parian marble. The ordinary human life, when wisely led, is thus the memorial of a more heroic life, once man's portion, and destined to be his again, and not the mere culmination of the life which belongs to the inferior kinds, as Epicurus esteemed it.

The contemplative sage tells the Red-Cross Knight that, though he knows it not, he is himself sprung from the race of England's ancient kings:—

> ' From thence a faery thee unweeting reft,
>   There as thou slep'st in tender swadling band,
>   And her base elfin brood there for thee left :
>   Such men do chaungelings call, so chaunged by faeries' theft.'

According to Spenser's estimate, humanity itself is such a changeling, and perpetually betrays its lofty origin. Spenser's philosophy, both of the humbler and the more exalted human life, will be best understood when contrasted with the two chief forms of life depraved, as illustrated by him. A large part, perhaps too large a part, of his poem is given to this subject; but it will suffice here briefly to sketch his general scheme of thought. Moral evil he contemplates in two aspects, that of the body insurgent against the soul, and that of the soul insurgent against its Maker, or passion on the one side and pride on the other. The former vice is rebuked chiefly in Book II., the Legend of Temperance, and the latter in the Legend of Holiness, or Book I. In the Legend of Temperance passion is exhibited in its two predominant forms of sensuality and ambition. The perils and degradations of an animalised life are shown under the allegory of Sir Guyon's sea voyage with its successive storms and whirlpools, its ' rock of Reproach ' strewn with wrecks and dead men's bones, its ' wandering islands,' its ' quick-

'sands of Unthriftihead,' its 'whirlepoole of Decay,' its sea monsters, and lastly its 'bower of Bliss,' and the doom which overtakes it, together with the deliverance of Acrasia's victims, transformed by that witch's spells into beasts. Still more powerful is the allegory of worldly ambition, illustrated under the name of 'the cave of Mammon.' The Legend of Holiness delineates with not less insight those enemies which wage war upon the spiritual life. As the aims of that life are the highest man proposes to himself, so its foes are the most insidious. Una, the heroine of this legend, means Truth; and the first enemy with whom her knight has to contend is Error, a serpent woman, with her monstrous brood. A craftier foe assails him soon, the magician Archimago or Hypocrisy. Separated by him from Truth, the knight becomes subjected to Falsehood and Delusion, emblemed in Duessa, by whom he is lured to the House of Pride, the great metropolis of Sin in its most exasperated form, that of a spiritual revolt. He next becomes the thrall of Orgoglio, the giant son of Earth, or Pride in its vulgarer form of vainglorious and animal strength.

In the latter legend the vices which make up the life of Pride, in the former those which make up the life of Lawless Sense, are exhibited with a keen insight and deep moral logic. In those two forms of evil life the three pagan champions, Sans-foy, Sans-loy, and Sans-joy, have a part corresponding with that which the Christian virtues, Fidelia, Speranza, and Charissa, sustain in the spiritual life. A certain symmetry, perhaps undesigned, always makes its way into Spenser's poetry. The philosophic Poet's mind is, indeed, by nothing more marked than by this unintended and often unconscious congruity in its conceptions, and the entire coherency of part with part in its descriptions. Thence proceeds the harmony constantly found in Spenser's poetry, as long as he resists his unhappy tendency to allude covertly to the persons and events of his day, and deals in simplicity with the great ethical theme with which his genius had deliberately measured itself. Such harmony is the most conclusive proof that a poet does not write at random, but has 'a vision of his own,' and a vocation to set it forth.

We have hitherto confined our remarks to Spenser's philosophy of human life, first in its social and political relations, and secondly in those of a domestic or individual character. Occasionally however, his philosophy made excursions into regions more remote, and dealt with subjects more recondite than these his favourite themes. To do justice to his genius we must note the two most remarkable of these excursions. Ten years after Spenser's death the first six books of the 'Faery Queen' were republished with a fragment of the lost second part, consisting of 'two cantos ' of Mutabilitie.' In this fragment there is a simple large-ness of conception, and a stern grandeur of expression, which suggests the thought that the later half of his work would probably have surpassed the earlier in mature great-ness. It belongs essentially to Spenser's philosophic vein, and embodies a train of dark and minatory thoughts, though they issue gradually into light, on the instability of all things human—thoughts such as might naturally have presented themselves to a philosopher in an age when much which had lasted a thousand years was passing away. In the re-motest parts of Europe omens of change were heard, like those vague murmurs in the polar regions which announce the breaking up of the ice; and in Ireland unfriendly echoes of those voices muttered near and nearer around that ruined mansion, one of old Desmond's hundred castles, within whose halls some strange fortune had harboured the gentlest of England's singers. The 'temple-haunting' bird had in-deed selected a 'coigne of vantage,' and hung there his 'pendent bed and procreant cradle;' but he had been no 'guest of summer,' nor at any time had 'heaven's breath ' smelt wooingly by his loved mansionry.' It was from a securer abode, in the heart of the Rydalian laurels, that musings as solemn, though less sad, prompted the dirge of the modern poet as he looked upon England's ruined abbeys :—

> ' From low to high doth dissolution climb,
> And sinks from high to low, along a scale
> Of awful notes whose concord shall not fail.' *

The poet of Faery Land sees a prophets' vision ascending out of the cloud that rests on the pagan days. A portent, not a god, but more powerful than the gods, and boasting a lineage more ancient, a child of Titan race, one more warlike than Bellona and more terrible than Hecate, both of them her sisters, claims a throne higher than that of those later Olympians who had cast down an earlier hierarchy of gods. Her name is Mutability. She had witnessed their victory; she had given it to them; why should they not acknowledge her as their suzeraine? On earth she had established her reign in completeness, and not over men alone. The seas

---

* Wordsworth, 'Ecclesiastical Sketches,' Part III.

had left dry their beds at her command, continents had sunk
beneath the waves, mountains had fleeted like clouds, rivers
had filled their mouths with desert sands, kingdoms had
risen and fallen, and the languages which recorded their
triumphs had died:—

> ' That all which Nature had establisht first
> In good estate, and in meet order ranged,
> She did pervert, and all their statutes burst.
>
> .   .   .   .
>
> Nor she the laws of Nature onely brake,
> But eke of justice and of policie,
> And wrong of right, and bad of good did make,
> And death for life:'

It remains for her but to reign in heaven as on earth—not
in the majesty of a divine law, but in lawlessness become
omnipotent. This portent scales the heavens, making way
at once to the most changeful of its luminaries, Cynthia's
sphere.

> ' Her sitting on an ivory throne she found,
> Drawn of two steeds, th' one black, the other white,
> Environed with tenne thousand starres around,
> That duly her attended day and night;
> And by her side there ran her page, that hight
> Vesper, whom we the evening starre intend;
> That with his torche, still twinkling like twylight,
> Her lightened all the way where she would wend,
> And joy to weary wandring travailers did lend.
>
> Boldly she bid the goddesse down descend,
> And let herself into that ivory throne;
> For she herself more worthy thereof weend,
> And better able it to guide alone;
> Whether to men, whose fall she did bemone,
> Or unto gods, whose state she did maligne,
> Or to the infernal powers.' *

Cynthia scorns the intruder, and 'bending her hornèd brows
'did put her back.'

The Titaness raises her hand to drag the radiant and
inviolate divinity from her seat. The result is narrated in
a passage of marvellous sublimity. Dimness falls at once on
that glittering throne and the ' fire-breathing stars ' that surround it; and, at the same moment, the eclipse reaches the
earth, perplexing its inhabitants with fear of change, and

---

* Two Cantos of Mutability, canto vi., stanzas 5, 6, and 9.

ascends to the seat of the gods.   They rush simultaneously
to the palace of Jove,

> 'Fearing least Chaos broken had his chaine.'

The Father of the Gods reminds them that long since the
giant-brood of earth had piled mountain upon mountain in
vain hope to storm ' heaven's eternal towers,' and tells them
that this anarch is but the last offspring of that evil blood.
While the gods are still in council, the strange Visitant is
in among them.   For a moment she is awed by that great
presence ; the next, she advances her claim.   Jove had de-
throned his father, Saturn ; her own father, Titan, was
Saturn's elder brother.   On earth she has hitherto abode an
exile, yet there she has conquered all things to herself.   She
demands at last her birthright—the throne of heaven.   An
inferior poet would have made this portent hideous as well
as terrible.   Spenser knew better.   He knew that revolution
and destruction wear often on their countenances a baleful
loveliness of their own, for which many a victim, disinterested
in madness, has willingly died.   The following lines are in
Homer's grandest vein :—

> 'Whil'st she thus spake, the gods that gave good ear
>   To her bold words, and markèd well her grace,
>   Beeing of stature tall as any there
>   Of all the gods, and beautiful of face
>   As any of the goddesses in place,
>   Stood all astonied ; like a sort of steeres,
>   'Mongst whom some beest of strange and forraine race
>   Unwares is chaunced, far straying from his peeres ;
> So did their ghastly gaze bewray their hidden feares.'

For Jove alone the portent has no terrors :—

> ' Whom what should hinder but that we likewise
>   Should handle as the rest of her allies,
>   And thunder-drive to hell ? With that he shooke
>   His nectar-deawèd locks, with which the skyes
>   And all the world beneath for terror quooke
> And eft his burning levin-brond in hand he tooke.
>
>   But when he lookèd on her lovely face,
>   In which fair beams of beauty did appeare,
>   That could the greatest wrath soon turn to grace
>   (Such sway doth beauty, even in heaven, beare),
>   He staide his hand ; and having changed his cheere,
>   He thus againe in milder wyse began :
>   " But ah ! if gods should strive with flesh yfere,
>   Then shortly should the progeny of man
> Be rooted out ; if Jove should do still what he can." '

He bids her submit.' The Titaness summons Jove to meet
her before the tribunal of an impartial arbiter; and by nothing does the poet more subtly impress us with the magic
power of this strange claimant, than by the Thunderer's
consent to leave his Olympian throne, and stand her co-
suitor before an alien potentate. That potentate is one
whom our age challenges more often than Spenser's did.
Her appeal is to the 'God of Nature.' The place of judgement is

> 'Upon the highest heights
> Of Arlo-Hill (who knows not Arlo-Hill?)
> That is the highest head in all men's sights
> Of my old father, Mole, whom shepherd's quill
> Renounèd hath with hymnes fit for a rural skill.'

'Old Mountain Mole,' a name as familiar as that of the
river 'Mulla,' his daughter, to the readers of Spenser,
designates the Galtee range which rises to nearly the height
of 3,000 feet at the north-east of Kilcoleman. Arlo-hill
is Galtymore, and overhangs the glen of Arlo, now spelt
Aherlo. This mountain-range is here constituted by him
a Parnassus of the north, and he tells us how that glen was
long frequented by the gods, and especially by Cynthia, and
how it was forsaken by the latter because she had there
been betrayed by one of her nymphs, Molanna, while
bathing in her favourite brook, to the gaze of 'foolish god
'Faunus:'—

> 'Since which, those woods and all that goodly chase
> Doth to this day with wolves and thieves abound;
> Which too, too true that land's indwellers since have found.'

Those 'thieves' were the original dwellers on Desmond's
confiscated lands, who had taken refuge in the forests surrounding the Galtees. There is a profound pathos in the
last line quoted, one which may possibly have been written
but the day before those wild bands issued from the woods
of Arlo, and wrapped in flame the castle of its poet, thus
grimly closing the four wedded and peaceful years of his Irish
life.

On the appointed day the gods assemble on Arlo Hill—
the gods of heaven, of the sea, and of the land (for the in-
fernal powers, we are told, might not appear in that sacred
precinct), and not the gods alone but all other creatures.
In the midst 'great dame Nature' makes herself manifest.
She is invested with attributes so mysterious, and tending
so much towards the infinite, as to suggest the thought that
Spenser, in some of his lonely musings, had occasionally

advanced to the borders of a philosophy little guessed of in
his own time.   Some such philosophy has sometimes set up
a claim like that of Spenser's Titaness, and striven to push
religion from her throne.   According to Spenser's teaching,
those pretensions derive no countenance from Nature.   Nor
was the cause of Mutability that of political revolution alone;
it was also that of unbelief, of lawlessness against law, and
of endless restlessness against endless peace.

> ' Then forth issued (great goddess) great dame Nature,
> With goodly port and gracious majesty,
> Being far greater and more tall of stature
> Than any of the gods or powers on hie;
> Yet certes by her face and physnomy,
> Whether she man or woman inly were,
> That could not any creature well descry,
> For with a veile that wimpled every where
> Her head and face was hid, that mote to none appeare.' *

Nature, we are told, is terrible, because she devours whatever exists; and yet beautiful, for she is ever teeming with
all things fair.   So far she resembles the Titaness, but only
so far.   The glory of her face is such that the face itself is
never seen by mortal eye.   To each man she is but as a
semblance descried in a mirror.   The soul of each man is
that mirror, and according to what that soul *is* she *seems.*
Her veil is never withdrawn.

> ' That, some doe say, was so by skill devised,
> To hide the terror of her uncouth hew
> From mortall eyes that should be sore agrized,
> For that her face did like a lion shew,
> That eye of wight could not indure to view;
> But others tell that it so beauteous was,
> And round about such beams of splendour threw,
> That it the sunne a thousand times did pass,
> Ne could be seen but like an image in a glass.'

She sits enthroned upon the level summit of the hill, and
the earth instantaneously sends up a pavilion of mighty
trees that wave above her in adoration their branches laden
with bloom and blossom; while the sod bursts into flower at
her feet, and old Mole exults

> ' As if the love of some new nymph late scene
> Had in him kindled youthful fresh desire.'

The Titaness draws near to this venerable being,

> ' This great grandmother of all creatures bred,
> Great Nature, ever young, yet full of eld,

---

* Canto vii., stanza 5.

> Still moving, yet unmoved from her sted;
> Unseen of any, yet of all beheld ; '

and appeals to her against the king of the gods,

> ' Since heaven and earth are both alike to thee ;
> And gods no more than men thou dost esteem :
> For even the gods to thee as men to gods do seeme.' *

The Titaness impeaches, not Jove only, but all the gods, for having arrogated to themselves, as divinities supernatural, what belongs to Nature only, and to herself as Nature's vicegerent. She insists that she has conquered to herself all the elements, not the land and the sea only; for the fire does not belong to holy Vesta, nor the air to the queen of the gods, but both alike to her. She summons witnesses, and at the command of Nature her herald, Order, causes them to circle in long procession around the throne. First come the four Seasons, next the twelve Months. Here is one of the pictures :—

> ' Next came fresh April, full of lustihead,
> And wanton as a kid whose horne new buds ;
> Upon a bull he rode, the same which led
> Europa floting through the Argolick fluds ;
> His hornes were gilden all with golden studs,
> And garnishèd with girlonds goodly dight
> Of all the fairest flowers and freshest buds
> Which th' earth brings forth ; and wet he seemed in sight
> With waves through which he waded for his love's delight.' †

The Hours follow, and the pageant is closed by Life and Death.

The Titaness next turns to Nature, and makes, in the name of all who have passed before her, their common confession; it is that all alike live but by change, and are vassals of Mutability. The Father of Gods and Men replies. His answer consists less in the denial of aught that is affirmative in her statement than in the supplying of what that statement had ignored :—

> ' Then thus 'gan Jove : " Right true it is that these
> And all things else that under heaven dwell
> Are chaunged of Time, who them doth all disseize
> Of being, but who is it (to me tell)
> That Time himselfe doth move and still compell
> To keepe his course ? Is not that namely Wee
> Which pour that virtue from our heavenly cell,
> That moves them all and makes them changèd be ?
> So then we gods do rule, and in them also thee.'

---

* Canto vii., stanza 6.   † Canto vii., stanza 33.

The reply of Mutability is simply an appeal from reason, interpreting objects of sense, to the mere senses when they have discarded reason :—

> ' But what we *see* not, who shall us persuade?'

Again she enumerates her triumphs, and demands a verdict in terms which surreptitiously remove the cause from the higher courts of Nature's judicature, and confine it to one created by herself.   But Nature takes counsel not with eye and ear only, but with mind and spirit also :—

> ' So having ended, silence long ensued ;
> Ne Nature to or fro spake for a space,
> But with firm eyes affixed the ground still view'd.
> Meanwhile all creatures looking in her face,
> Expecting the end of this so doubtful case,
> Did hang in long suspense what would ensue,
> To whether side should fall the sovereign place ;
> At length she, looking up with cheerful view,
> The silence brake, and gave her doom in speeches few.
>
> I well consider all that ye have sayd,
> And find that all things stedfastness doe hate
> And changed be : yet being rightly wayed,
> They are not changèd from their first estate ;
> *But by their change their being do dilate ;*
> And turning to themselves at length againe
> Doe worke their own perfection so by fate ;
> Then over them Change doth not rule and raigne,
> But they raigne over Change, and do their states maintaine.
>
> Cease therefore, daughter, further to aspire,
> And thee content thus to be ruled by me ;
> For thy decay thou seek'st by thy desire ;
> But time shall come that all shall changèd bee,
> *And from thenceforth none no more change shall see.*
> So was the Titanesse put downe and whist,
> And Jove confirmed in his imperial See.
> Then was that whole assembly quite dismist,
> And Nature's selfe did vanish, whither no man wist.' *

According to the philosophy of Spenser it was impossible that Mutability should enjoy a final triumph, because her true function is to minister through change to that which . knows no change.   Revolution is but a subordinate element in a system which includes a recuperative principle, and tends ever to the stable.   To the undiscerning eye things seem to pass away ; to the half-discerning they seem to

---

* Canto vii. of Mutability, stanza 59.

revolve merely in a circle; but the motion is in reality upward as well as circular; as it advances, it ascends in a spiral line; and as it ascends it ever widens. When the creation has reached the utmost amplitude of which it was originally made capable, it must then stand face to face with the Creator, and in that high solstice it must enter into the sabbath of His endless rest. Thus only could it reflect the Divine Perfection after which it was created. To understand this teaching, we must bear in mind its complement in another part of Spenser's philosophy. He held with Plato that all things great and abiding, whether in the material or the moral world, were created after the pattern of certain great ideas existing eternally in the mind of the Creator, inseparable from His essence, and in it alone perfectly realised. Creation is thus a picture of the uncreated; and the cyclical revolutions of time present an image of eternity, notwithstanding that the 'opposition of matter' renders it impossible that that picture should ever be wholly faithful to its great original. Turning our eyes downward, we trace the same law in the descending grades of being. It is thus that man, himself the mirror of the Divine, is mirrored, though with a corresponding inferiority, by the inferior animals, which, not only in their chief affections, but in their intellectual processes, and often even in their social polities, rehearse, on a lower stage, parts which man is permitted to enact more nobly on a higher one. But between the creatures thus ranged on the lower and the higher stages of creation there exists one great difference: those only that occupy the highest platform possess the gift of secure progress. That progress is made through striving and pain :— the whole life of man here below, whether his individual or his social life, was regarded by Spenser as a noble warfare destined to end in victory and peace. Through such probation it becomes from age to age a vaster and a purer thing; and its mutations, notwithstanding the confusions and the sufferings they entail, are but the means through which virtue ascends, and knowledge grows wider.

Among the chief ministering spirits through whom this final development of humanity is to be effected, are the twelve great virtues of the ancient philosophy, the illustration of which he had selected as the theme of his song. That change completed, Humanity is, as Spenser's philosophy teaches, to gaze open-eyed on Divinity, to be changed into its likeness, and to enter into its rest. Wordsworth, in his 'Vernal Ode,' recognises also in the cyclical revolutions of time an image of eternity; but he does not in that poem, though he does in his 'Stanzas on the Power of Sound,' affirm that, their work accomplished, there remains for man an endless Sabbath.   Spenser ends his legend with an aspiration :—

> ' O that great Sabaoth God grant me that Sabbath's sight ! '

This is the voice of a spirit wearied with the storms of our lower sphere, but not daunted or weakened by them.   No one can read the last verse without joining in the gentle poet's prayer.

We cannot close our remarks on Spenser's philosophy without a reference to a very remarkable canto of his ' Faery ' Queen,' in which he blends his musings on humanity with others on nature, and on what is higher than nature, and thus crosses the path of the old-world philosophic poet Lucretius, who also discoursed of nature and man's life—leaving in his philosophy a very little corner for the 'im-' mortal gods,' who seem, indeed, to have had little business there, and indeed to have been admitted but by courtesy. Spenser's philosophic reverie will be found in his ' Garden ' of Adonis ' (Book III., Canto vi.).   Human life as there described has nothing in common either with that higher, that ordinary, or that depraved form of life illustrated by him elsewhere.   It is not an actual but a potential life, the conception of an existence neither fallen nor restored, and of an earth with neither benediction nor malediction resting upon it; an earth with one sorrow only—the transience of all things.   The Garden is the domain of an endless productiveness, decay, and renewal.   In it abide perpetually the archetypal forms of living things :—

> 'There is the first seminary
> Of all things that are born to live and dye,
> According to their kinds.'

The ever-teeming soil is encircled by two walls, one of iron and one of gold :—

> ' And double gates it had which opened wide,
> By which both in and out men moten pas ;
> Th' one faire and fresh, th' other old and dried ;
> Old Genius the porter of them was,
> Old Genius the which a double nature has.
>
> He letteth in, he letteth out to wend
> All that to come into the world desire ;
> A thousand thousand naked babes attend

> About him day and night, which doe require
> That he with fleshly weeds will them attire;
> Such as him list, such as eternal fate
> Ordained hath, he clothes with sinful mire,
> And sendeth forth to live in mortall state,
> Till they agayn returne, back by the hinder gate.' *

Their condition is an endless alternation of glad life and painless decay.

> 'After that they againe retourned beene
> They in that garden planted bee agayne,
> And grow afresh, as they had never seene
> Fleshly corruption, nor mortall payne:
> Some thousand yeeres so doen they there remayne,
> And then of him are clad with other hew,
> Or sent into the chaungeful world agayne,
> Till thether they return, where first they grew;
> So like a wheele arowned they ronne from old to new.'

Countless swarms perish successively, yet the stock is never lessened:—

> 'For in the wide wombe of the world there lyes
> In hateful darkness, and in deepe horrore
> An huge eternal Chaos, which supplies
> The substaunces of Nature's fruitful progenyes.'

The substance is immortal; the successive forms 'are 'variable and decay,' for though they have but one foe, with him they cannot contend. That enemy is 'wicked Time,' who mows down all things with his scythe.

> 'Yet pitty often did the gods relent
> To see so faire things mard and spoilèd quight:
> And their great mother Venus did lament
> The losse of her deere brood, her deere delight.'

Her realm has this sorrow alone. It is unshaken by jealousy or pain, doubt or shame. Over this central seıt of her rolling sphere there rests 'the stillness of the sleeping 'poles.' Here the spring-tide and the harvest-tide blend, and the autumnal vine overhangs the vernal elm. Here grows

> 'every sort of flowre
> To which sad lovers were transform'd of yore.'

Here Venus finds at will her lost Adonis where she laid him dead—

> 'And sooth it seems, they say; for he may not
> For ever dye, and ever buried bee

---

* Garden of Adonis, Book III., canto vi., stanza 32.

In baleful night, where all things are forgot;
All be he subject to mortalitie,
Yet is eterne in mutabilitie,
And by succession made perpetual,
Transformed off, and chaunged diverslie;
For him the father of all formes they call;
Therefore needs mote he live that living gives to all.'

There are passages in this poem, as we have said, which
remind us of Lucretius, but the contrast is greater than the
resemblance.   What in the Latin poet is a cynical, though
imaginative, materialism becomes transfigured in the verse
of one whose touch changes matter itself into spirit.   The
lower side of the philosophy receives its interpretation from
the higher, and becomes, though not the whole truth, yet a
portion of it.   If the seeds of all bodies spring up sponta-
neously from the fruitful soil, yet souls innumerable throng
the air above them, and it is their breath that imparts life to
their 'fleshly weeds.'   If no gardener is needed there 'to
'sett or sow,' yet Nature only thus exercises a sacred might
bestowed on her by one who is above Nature, and has commanded her to increase.   Whatever she may be in Cythera
or Paphos, the goddess of love is here a true 'Venus Gene-
'trix,' a Power, compassionate and benign, more the mother
than the wife, bringing forth, not in sorrow but in gladness.
A healing influence works on through creation; Nature is no
more suffered to prey on her own offspring; the wild boar
of the forest which slew Adonis, and ever wars on youth
and strength, is 'imprisoned in a strong rocky cave.'   In
this earlier 'Island Valley of Avilion,' humanity heals its
ancient wound, and awaits the better day.   The spirit of
hope here triumphs over the Lucretian spirit of despair.

The teaching of the pessimist philosopher of antiquity,
whose ambition was to draw the most original of poems
out of the wildest system of physics—like sunbeams extracted from cucumbers—was the opposite of this, except in
points of detail.   Not our world only but all worlds were
fated to perish utterly, leaving behind them nothing but a
whirl of atoms to fill their place; that is, they were to end
like his own poem, which closes significantly with the plague
at Athens.   A few remarks will not here be out of place comparing the great Latin philosophical poet, as he is commonly
regarded, with the English philosophic poet of the Elizabethan period.   Each of them found his country passing
through a momentous crisis; each must have largely affected
its growing intelligence for good or for evil; each had great

poetic gifts, and in some respects similar gifts, for Lucretius, like Spenser, had an ardent imagination, a descriptive power till his time unrivalled, vivid imagery, impassioned eloquence, and remarkable gifts of style, diction, and metre; and each united the courage with the perseverance needful for success in a high enterprise of song. A poet is best understood when compared with another, at once like him and unlike.

The great difference between the two philosophic poets lay in those moral and spiritual constituents of man's being by which the action of his imagination as well as of his understanding is secretly directed. In Spenser there lived an abiding spirit of reverence; and therefore for him all phenomena received their interpretation from above: for Lucretius it came from below; and his delight was to show how all great things are but small things making the most of themselves. The intellect of Spenser was a far-reaching one; it descried the remote analogy; it discerned what is lost alike upon the sensual heart and the merely logical intelligence; it accepted high thoughts as authentic if at once recommended by venerable authorities and in harmony with universal aspirations, whether or not their nature rendered them susceptible of dialectic proof. It could retain a serene faith when shrewdness winked and grimaced; and it could no less abstain from credulity when challenged by philosophic theories recommended chiefly by their strangeness and their confidence. Lucretius, on the other hand, had a vigorous but an animal intellect. He saw the wonderfulness of matter not more keenly than Spenser, who understood its witcheries perhaps but too well; but he was so dazzled by it that he could see nothing besides, and for him spirit did not exist. To him Nature was all in all; and for that reason he did not realise her highest greatness, viz. her power of leading to something higher than herself. To the Greek mythologists who had laid the basis of Greek poetry, Nature had been a divinity; to the Christian poet and philosopher she reflected a divine radiance; to Lucretius she was a Titaness slinging firebrands through the universe she had shaped, and shaping all things with no final aim but that of slaying them, and slaying herself on their pyre. For his guide he followed exclusively a single teacher of his own selection, and one even in the pagan world ill-famed—Epicurus—passing by with contempt all the heads of the Greek schools during six centuries, and worshipping that one with an idolatrous but not disinterested devotion.

Seeing all things from below, Lucretius never grasps the

nobler idea essentially included in each; he sees but the accidents that obscure it. In religion he sees nothing but fear; in authority but imposture; in man but animal instincts intellectualised. In woman he sees no touch of womanhood. He advises his disciples . never to meddle with so noxious a toy as love; but his mode of preaching self-restraint is worthless, since it provides no substitute for troublesome pleasures, either in lofty duties or in nobler joys, for which, on his principles, there remains no place. It is not merely that the Lucretian philosophy does not encourage moral or spiritual aspirations. It is militant against them. It commands us imperiously to tread down the very desire of immortality; and yet its denial of immortality is a wholly illogical assumption, based on another assumption wholly arbitrary : viz., that 'mind' and 'soul' are but material things, not less than the body, and must therefore share the body's doom. Such a philosophy, in recommending 'moderation,' recommends but apathy; and men not dyspeptic or exhausted do not become apathetic to please philosophers.

There is nothing positive in Lucretius's vivid appreciation of matter which does not find place equally in Spenser's philosophy. What the latter abjures is the negative part of it. In Spenser's poetry the creation is ever regarded as 'the 'resplendent miracle,' and material joys as, in their degree, objects well worthy of pursuit and gratitude; but in that poetry under material enjoyment there ever lurk the humanities, and under these something greater still. It was but the narrowness of the Lucretian philosophy which made it identify a belief in matter with a disbelief in spirit—that narrowness which so often explodes into fanaticism, with its combined characteristics of audacity and of intolerance. The Lucretian philosophy is an abject one, not because it failed to anticipate Truth then unrevealed, but because it denied and denounced truths which had been retained with more or less clearness by most of the early religions and by many philosophies, such as the spirituality of man's being, a Divine sanction to conscience, and the immortality and responsibility of the soul—beliefs which had, during sequent ages, created civilised societies with all that was best in their arts, poetry, and literature. Pagan antiquity had also retained the belief in a Providence that shaped man's life to gracious ends; and its Prometheus, a Titan, though not a god, had endured as well as laboured for man. The Lucretian gods are material beings made, like the rest of the universe, by the 'concurrence' of material atoms; and, like all besides, they are destined to perish. In the meantime they sit apart in festal rest, seeing in man's life, its joys, its agonies, its trials, and in all besides external to themselves, nothing worthy of their interest. This is to make the gods not only after the image of men, but of the meanest among men. Spenser insists on a God who helps man, not because He is Himself man only, but for an opposite reason:—on a God for whom, *since He is infinite* in all the dimensions of infinitude, it follows that as nothing is too great, so nothing is too small. There are those by whom that sublime idea is stigmatised as 'anthropomorphism,' while the Lucretian conception is applauded as sublime. This is not sincere thinking. It cannot be justified by the excuse 'sublime *as poetry.*' Low sentiment and incoherent thought are not changed into great poetry because they are expressed in dignified language.

That physical philosophy on the exposition of which the poetry of Lucretius was wrecked made a large boast. In that aspect it has an important relation with our theme; for true poetry does great things, but does not make a great boast. It was to illuminate mankind, to break down all moral and intellectual thraldom, and to kill all religion, as the easiest way of curing its corruptions—a design as philosophic as though all government were to be destroyed because it includes administrative abuses; all art, because it sometimes ministers to depraved tastes; and all science, because its professors often make mistakes. How was this wonderful work to be effected? Not by experimental demonstrations—they are seldom appealed to by Lucretius, except in the way of demolishing counter theories—but by hardy scientific dogma, and the *pecca fortiter* of fearless assumptions. Atoms could neither be seen, felt, nor brought within the ken of scientific analysis; but it was easy to assume not only that they existed in incalculable number, but that they are of various shapes, solid, indestructible, possess weight, and even that their 'uncertain sideway movement' is 'the only possible origin of the free-will of living beings.' So again of *Films.* These are slender veils cast, as Lucretius affirms, from the surface of all objects incessantly and into all the regions of space—a valiant assumption, but one wholly fabulous. It is amusing to observe how the same philosophic credulity which accepts all assumptions condones all incoherences. The emancipating discovery asserts that 'nothing comes from nothing;' yet it asserts also that, without any creative cause, there existed a perpetual

downward rain of atoms; it believes that no Divine mind
gives law to matter; yet it maintains also that Nature's
course is uniform—nay, that a 'concurrence of atoms'
driven against each other in perpetual storm, eventually
combined into all the wondrous forms on the earth—the
structure of hand and eye, and brain! All that this
philosophy regards as needed to justify its imperious claim
on our acceptance is that its dogmas, however fantastic,
should be *conceivable,* that they should be capable of being
expressed in association with distinct *images,* or brain-pic-
tures—things confounded by feeble thinkers with distinct
thoughts—and that they should derive some plausible support
from analogies. Its chief weapon is reiteration. It multi-
plies instances, takes for granted its inferences from them—
inferences which are but the preconceptions of a confident
fancy—and thus eludes those troublesome questions on which
the true issue of the argument depends. Drawn aside as if
by an 'elective affinity' towards the most materialistic views
on all subjects, this philosophy hardily rejected even the
material truths asserted, some five hundred years before, by
Pythagoras, such as that the earth moves round the sun,
as well as its sphericity and gravitation—truths probably
maintained by many in the days of Lucretius, though subsequently denied by the Ptolemaic system. It affirmed, moreover, that the universe is always dropping downward, and that
the real size of the heavenly bodies is little more than their
apparent size to the eye. Amidst these strange aberrations
of a false philosophy, the 'purple patches' of real poetry
survive, to vex us with the thought of the poetry Lucretius
might have given to us had Plato, not Epicurus, been his
master, and to remind us that high genius is seldom extinguished wholly by any abuse of the gift.

It was fortunate for England that a philosophy in essentials the opposite of Lucretius's, inspired the poetry of that
great man who opened the literature of the Elizabethan
age, and into whose grave the younger poets of that age
flung their pens, acknowledging him as their master, as he
had acknowledged Chaucer to be his. His genius might
otherwise have exercised that influence, stimulating indeed,
but both sensualising and narrowing, on English letters which
Boccaccio certainly exercised on Italy, and for which no
compensation could have been adequate. Spenser's philosophy was ideal at once and traditional. It made no small
points; but great ideas brooded over it. He did not boast
himself as the great expositor of one self-chosen master.

His humble pride was that his long-laboured work embodied the best moral teaching of the chief masters both of antiquity and of Christian times. It was not a weapon of war. It derived no stimulus from hatred. It included within itself an unpretentious yet a coherent logic; but it passed far beyond her narrow pale in its genial strength, extending itself as widely as human sympathies, and soaring as high as man's noblest aspirations. That a poet so manifold in interest, and so profound in thought, should to so many readers, though not to the best, appear simply dull; and, again, that an ancient poet the greater part of whose poetry was devoted, like that of Dr. Darwin in the last century, to the versifying of Natural Philosophy, and whose Natural Philosophy was a chimera, should yet, with many readers, take the place often claimed for Lucretius, are phenomena hard to be explained. It is true that the adage 'first come, first ' served,' applies to books, and that many an old one retains a reputation which, if new, it could never acquire. It is true also that a compliment to a classic is often a compliment to one's own scholarship; and that with, not a few, the lesser qualities of poetry, possessed in eminence, are more impressive than its highest qualities less energetically exerted. We may also, perhaps, in our attempt to solve the problem, find help in one of Spenser's best known allegories —best known because it illustrates so many a strange passage in human life—the allegory of Illusion or the witch ' Duessa.' She represents an idea constantly in the mind of Spenser. No poet ever fixed a more reverent gaze on philosophic truth, or one more faithful to follow her ' whitherso- ' ever she goeth,' through the tangled labyrinths of thought or action. Yet no one felt so strongly how close beside her there treads an opposite spirit; a spirit potent alike to make the true seem false, and the false seem true, the fair seem foul, and the foul seem fair. Such is the magic power with which Duessa now re-invests her faded form with the loveliness of a youth long vanished, and now raises a mist and binds a mask of decrepitude on some beautiful rival.

It was no doubt the profound sincerity of Spenser's genius which made him muse with such a haunting sadness on that spirit of Illusion. He had had personal experience of its power. He had his own illusions, religious, political, and personal, several of which he had detected and repudiated. He had replaced the Puritanism of his early training with a form of Christianity half-Patristic and half-Platonic; although in his politics it still stretched itself,

like a 'bar sinister,' across a shield glowing with loyalist
' gules' and chivalrous devices. He had seen some of his
nearest friends changeful in principle, but ever persistent in
worshipping as divinities the idols of a fancy at once proud
and servile. He had doubtless observed that there often exists
a strange and cruel resemblance between opposites, and that
the illusion is often the more complete the more absolutely
they stand opposed to each other. It is thus that hypocrisy
resembles virtue, and that, as a consequence, virtue may be
easily mistaken for hypocrisy; that the visionary is like the
' man whose eyes are open,' and *vice versâ*; that bashfulness
may be like guilt, and callous insensibility like innocence;
that silence may betoken alike the fulness of content or an
absolute despair; that, to the superficial, communism may
seem the political realisation of the early Christian ethics
of alms; that indifference to truth may claim to be the
perfection of charity. The most fatal errors have ever been
those which include in them high truths, though misapplied.
Without that element they would not have proved attractive
to elevated minds; and for an analogous reason the most
exalted truths may long wear a form the most repulsive
even to the good.

The dreadful power of illusion is a thought naturally
brought home the most to minds at once reflective and imaginative. It was familiar to Shelley as well as to Spenser,
unlike as were those two poets, and it is remarkably illustrated by him in the ' Revolt of Islam,' canto i. stanzas 25–27.
In the beginning of things, as we are there told, ' a blood-
' red comet and the morning star' hung in fight on the
verge of Chaos. These two militant shapes are the rival
powers of Evil and Good. Evil triumphs, and changes the
morning star into a snake, which is sentenced to creep over
the earth in that false semblance, abhorred by all, so long
as the conqueror's reign endures. Transformations not less
startling take place every day in the moral world. What is
despicable when contrasted with that which is above it, may
yet well appear admirable to one who can measure it only
with what is below it. Shelley, who had in him much of
Lucretius's poetic audacity, was himself, for a short time,
the prisoner of a materialistic philosophy as wild. When
he became a translator of Plato, that grim skeleton, if it
ever revisited his dreams, may perhaps have reminded him
of Spenser's Duessa, stripped of her glittering apparel.

ART. VI.—*The Army Estimates for* 1884-85.

THE usual excuse alleged for indifference to the numbers and efficiency of the army is, that England being an island, it is the naval, not the land forces which call for most attention; that the navy constitutes our first line of defence, and that we may safely trust to it to prevent an invasion. Our greatness, our prosperity, our safety, and our very food, undoubtedly depend in large measure on our maritime strength. As to an invasion, that is a calamity which is extremely improbable. Still we must bear in mind that the most eminent British and foreign authorities on the art of war consider that it is by no means impossible in spite of our fleet. As therefore a prudent commander always guards against even the most unlikely peril, provided it is within the limits of possibility, so a far-seeing Minister would provide against even so improbable a contingency as an invasion of England. For this reason alone it is necessary to maintain an efficient standing army. But there are other arguments in support of such a policy. One is, that our colonial dependencies must be guarded; the other, that our fleet requires harbours and coaling depôts all over the world, and these if not strongly garrisoned would be liable to fall into an enemy's hands. It is evident that we cannot rely solely on our navy for the protection of our honour and interests, but that our maritime armaments must be supported by land forces.

This much being conceded, it is obvious that an army insufficient in numbers or inferior in efficiency would be a delusion as inducing a false confidence, and indirectly a mischievous source of wasteful expenditure. We have, as reasonable people, the choice between no standing army at all, and one adequate for the purposes for which it is maintained. It is a subject of regret that our military policy has in some respects always been of a hand-to-mouth nature, especially as regards numbers. Instead of considering carefully what are our military needs, and adjusting the strength of our army to them, we have reversed the process, and acted as if our requirements were to be met only as far as the strength of our army at the moment admitted. Let us assume, however, as far as regards mere numbers on paper, that our army is sufficient for any work likely to be imposed upon it, and confine ourselves solely to the question of efficiency.

Is our army efficient? It ought to be so considering the amount of talking, writing, time, and money spent upon it during the last fifteen years. Some say it is so: that, of course, it is not yet perfection; that there is always room for improvement; but that, considering the special circumstances of the country, there is little really to be complained of. Those who entertain this view are, with few exceptions, civilians, who hold or have held office in connexion with the War Department. There is also a handful of able soldiers, mostly of staff experience, and the followers of Lord Wolseley, who endorse this opinion. On the other hand, the pessimists include the bulk of present and past regimental officers, who declare emphatically that the service is not going, but has gone, to the Devil, and that practically we do not possess an army worthy of the name. Midway between the optimists and the pessimists stand a small but experienced and thoughtful body of officers—among the most eminent of whom may be reckoned Sir Frederick Roberts and Sir Lintorn Simmons, who, while frankly admitting that some of the recent changes have been wise and beneficial, assert that in certain respects our military reformers have proceeded on faulty lines, and express an opinion that in the matter of military expenditure we do not get our money's worth, and that the army as a fighting machine is at the present moment very far from being efficient.

It is our object in this paper to examine the statements of the moderate men; to ascertain what are the most glaring defects in our military system; and to suggest remedies for their removal. The optimists base their statements and arguments almost entirely on official returns. These, however, are so framed, that without the key of practical knowledge they fail to give full information. Hence the public can be easily induced to believe what they are officially told, more especially as they do not wish to be convinced that the taxpayers' money has been spent to no purpose. From the labyrinth of dry statistics and vague official utterances, we will endeavour to extract the real facts of the case.

The first topic to be dealt with is the numerical strength of the army. We need not here give precise figures: indeed absolute accuracy with regard to the present moment is not within our power. For our purpose it will suffice to quote the annual return of the British army on January 1, 1884, by which it appears that it was then 7,842 below the authorised establishment; and Lord Hartington's speech at the Lord Mayor's banquet on November 10, when he said that during

the past twelve months the effective strength of the army
had been increased by 'something between 4,000 and 5,000
' men, while the strength of the reserve has also been in-
' creased by between 5,000 and 6,000.' As, however, the
establishment fixed by the estimate for 1884 is 140,314·
as against 137,632 in the previous year, and the deficiency
on December 1, 1883, was 7,842 for the whole army, includ.
ing India, there seems to us very little ground for satisfaction. It is true that the deficiency has been diminished,
while at the same time the establishment has been increased;
still it may be estimated to amount at the present time to
at least 5,000 men, or the equivalent of five strong battalions.
During the last eighteen months recruiting has certainly
been far more successful than it had previously been; but
how has this result been achieved? 1st, by diminishing the
minimum age from 19 to 18; 2nd, by reducing the minimum
chest-girth and height to 33 inches and 5 feet 3 inches respectively. In addition, *all* men have lately been allowed
to complete twelve years' service with the colours, with the
privilege of re-engaging at the expiration of that time to
complete service for pensions. Not only has it been found
necessary to allow men to prolong their service, but they
have actually been bribed to do so, by bounties of 2*l.* in
England and 12*l.* in India. Hence the drain by men passing
to the reserve has been largely checked. Under these circumstances it is not a matter of surprise that the numbers
'wanting to complete' have substantially diminished. It
would indeed be strange if they had not. We will go further
and say that it is a powerful proof of the unpopularity of
the army that our ranks are not even yet full.

As regards efficiency, it is difficult in face of conflicting
statements to arrive at a correct decision. Lord Wolseley
declares that the army was never in so efficient a condition,
and the official statistics in some respects support this view.
On the other hand, day by day, particular instances of
individual regiments are brought forward which justify a
completely opposite conviction, and the almost universal consensus of regimental officers is the reverse of Lord Wolseley's
assurances. In addition to written and spoken testimony
there is the evidence of the eyes of all who look carefully
at any body of soldiers; and this testimony is to the effect
that there is far too large a proportion of young soldiers in
regiments at home, and that an alarming number of them
are wanting in physique.

What is the minimum age and physique suitable for a

soldier in the field? for that evidently is the only true test of efficiency. On the Continent it is universally accepted that, as to age, 20 is the lowest age at which a man is fitted for a soldier's life; and, as a matter of fact, by the time a man is dismissed from recruit drill in foreign armies, the average is 21. The principal military medical authorities in England also fix the minimum military age at 20, the constitution not being developed, and gristle largely taking the place of bone even at that age. Of course there are exceptions, but as a rule it is admitted that a man at the earliest is not sufficiently developed to be able to withstand the strain of a campaign before he attains his legal majority. As to height there is a difference of opinion. Regimental officers, influenced by the old traditions of the service, and looking much to appearances, object to short men—i.e. men under 5 ft. 6 in. Experience, however, shows us, that though perhaps the ideal height for a soldier is between 5 ft. 7 in. and 5 ft. 10 in., many men below even 5 ft. 5 in. are sturdy, active fellows, and if possessed of more than the proportional chest-measurement and muscular strength, are quite capable of performing all the functions of a soldier. The point is, however, that with only proportional chest-measurement and muscular strength a man under 5 ft. 6 in. is not suited for the army; and we may add that, whatever his height, he ought to have a chest-measurement of 35 inches. If he has a height of less than 5 ft. 5 in. he finds it hard to keep up on the march with his taller comrades, or to handle his rifle with efficiency, owing to the shortness of his legs and arms; while deficient chest-measurement means in many cases a weak chest, small powers of endurance, and a want of vigour in the organs generally and the muscles. If the men below 5 ft. 6 in. in height were organised in separate corps we should not much object to a reduction in the standard even to as low a point as 5 ft. 4 in.; but a lowering of the chest-measurement below 34 in. at the lowest we consider most objectionable. Having thus premised, let us turn to the annual return for 1884. It will suffice if we concern ourselves solely with the infantry of the line and the Royal Artillery, who numbered roundly 140,000 out of the 173,000 non-commissioned officers and men in the whole army.

In the artillery there were on January 1, 1884:— 591 under 18; between 18 and 19, 450; and between 19 and 20, 1,244: i.e. a total of 2,285, out of 30,000 men, below the military age. In the infantry of the line there were, below

18 years of age, 2,088; between 18 and 19, 5,177; and between 19 and 20, 7,935: making a total of 15,200, out of 110,000 men, below the military age. The above figures are, though official, by no means accurate, for there are no means of checking recruits' statements as to their age, and it is matter of notoriety that they frequently assert that they are older than they really are. Large additions must, therefore, be made to the totals above arrived at; in fact, we shall not be far wrong if we estimate the proportion of infantry of the line and artillerymen under the military age as 1 in 7. It is also worthy of note that the proportion of men under the military age is much smaller in regiments abroad than in those at home; the exact numbers on January 1, 1884, being according to the annual report as follows:—Artillery—home, 1,969 out of 14,382; colonies, 147 out of 4,402; India, 169 out of 11,483. Infantry of the line—home, 12,846 out of 48,642; colonies, 1,424 out of 20,573; India, 882 out of 40,793.

With the question of age is closely connected that of length of service, for it is evident that even if a soldier is above 20, he is useless until he has ceased to be a recruit. Technically he ceases to be a recruit about six months after enlistment; practically, he cannot be considered, even in the infantry, a finished soldier under a year. On January 1, 1884, there were in the Royal Artillery, at home 2,476, in the colonies 177, and in India 276 men who had less than one year's service. In the infantry of the line the numbers were, respectively, 16,933, 1,388, and 2,313. Owing to the briskness of recruiting in the course of 1884 the proportion of men of less than twelve months' service is of course now much greater.

Turning to height, we find that on January 1, 1884, there were in the artillery 3,612, and in the infantry of the line 10,845 men under 5 ft. 5 in. in height; and 3,840 and 19,567 respectively between 5 ft. 5 in. and 5 ft. 6 in. The report is significantly silent as to how many men are 5 ft. 3 in. to 5 ft. 4 in.

As to chest-measurement, in the artillery, on the date above mentioned, there were 481 under 33 in., 520 between 33 in. and 34 in., and 2,530 between 34 in. and 35 in.; while in the infantry of the line, 2,449 were under 33 in., 6,486 between 33 in. and 34 in., and 15,765 between 34 in. and 35 in.

By including the Foot Guards, the Household Cavalry, and the Royal Engineers, the authorities are able to make a fair average of height and chest-measurement for the whole army; but the facts which we have given speak for themselves, and will scarcely, we think, be considered as justifying the assertion that the army is in a satisfactory state as regards age, height, and physique. From the returns before us it is impossible to ascertain with accuracy how many men fail to fulfil the requirements of active service, for some of the disqualifications overlap each other. For instance, a man may be over 20 years of age, have a chest-measurement of 35 in. and a stature of 5 ft. 6 in.; but, on the other hand, he may have only three months' service. Again, another man may have the proper height, chest-measurement, and service, and yet be only 18 years of age. Lastly, a third man may be of proper height, age, and service, but may be deficient in chest-measurement. Still the figures which we have quoted above are sufficient to prove that, as regards either age, service, or physical requirements, a large proportion of the men, costing as much as efficient soldiers, are unfit for soldiers' work.

The inference from all this is that the army is so unpopular that we cannot get a sufficient number of men possessed of military qualifications. If further proof of the unpopularity of the army be needed, it can be afforded by the subjoined figures. During 1883, 3,707 men deserted; 1,505 were discharged as of right on payment of 10*l.* within three months after enlistment; while by indulgence 2,108 men obtained their discharge by purchase, and 818 free. This makes a total of 8,138 men sick of the service.

The fact of the unpopularity of the army being clearly established, the question arises, What are the causes of such unpopularity, and how can they be removed or modified?

There is, undoubtedly, in this country a prejudice against military service, arising from the active competition of the labour market, and partly because during the stress of great wars it was of old the practice to fill up the ranks with the sweepings of the gaols and workhouses. Such a method of recruiting naturally lowered the social status of the soldier, and the feeling of contempt for him was increased by his frequently being addicted to dissolute conduct and foul language. Hence the most respectable classes of society combined to ostracise the man who had taken the King's shilling. This feeling is becoming weaker, we are happy to say, owing in some measure to the fact that all classes are represented in the volunteers, who have acted as a connecting link between the civil population and the regular army. Another cause was the notion—false for the last thirty years at least—that for the smallest offence a soldier was liable to be tied up and flogged almost to death. The truth is that, for some years before the total abolition of corporal punishment, a soldier had to take a great deal of trouble to get flogged. The memory, however, of the cruel and indiscriminate punishments inflicted during the early part of the century has not yet quite died out. Probably, however, the most active of existing causes is the growing impatience of the present generation of any sort of discipline or subordination, an impatience noticeable in all classes, ages, and occupations. Many a man has expressed to an officer his dislike to enlisting, or letting his son enlist, in the following words:—'I,' or 'he, would 'have too many masters.' Another objection, which weighs strongly with all below the lower middle classes, is that by enlisting the freedom to be unwashed, unshorn, untidy, and unpunctual, would be lost.

The undoubted discontent in the army itself and the army reserve reacts on the civil population. Civilians will ask with surprise why is the army discontented, seeing how much has been done for it since the Crimean war? It is quite true that in many respects the soldier of to-day is infinitely better off than his predecessor of the time of Wellington. He is more comfortable in barracks, his clothing is superior, his pay is better, when sick he is more skilfully treated, more carefully looked after, he is provided with ample means of spending his leisure time in a pleasant and harmless manner, and the discipline is infinitely milder. On the other hand, the regulations are so frequently changed that he lives in a constant state of doubt and apprehension. Formerly the regiment was selected by himself, and became his home till, his period of engagement over, he retired on a substantial pension. He knew his officers and comrades, they knew him, and a strong feeling of brotherhood and *esprit de corps* grew up. Now, he cannot select his regiment, for the two battalions are practically two regiments; and as soon as he is beginning to feel at home and know the ways of one battalion, he is transferred to another, where the majority are strangers to him, and where he has to learn a fresh system of interior economy. Till lately, too, he felt that he had no sooner become acquainted with his duties and accustomed to his life, than he was discharged, to recommence his old occupation, having lost much of his skill and aptitude for labour, and seeing his former fellow-workmen far ahead of him. It is true that he

took with him deferred pay to the amount of 18*l.*, but that
was generally either wasted in dissipation or consumed while
waiting for an occupation.   As to the 6*d.* a day reserve pay,
that was evidently insufficient for his maintenance, so employment of some sort was a necessity; but employers naturally
objected to engage a man who, judging from recent experience, might any day be called away to rejoin the colours on
mobilisation.   We have used the past tense so far because
now a man is not obliged to quit the active army till he has
earned a pension.   Though, however, the evil cause is dead,
the effect remains, and the country is still full of discontented reserve men, who, often half-starved, are never tired
of abusing the service, and act as so many zealous anti-
recruiting missionaries.   There are several other causes of the
unpopularity of the army, which, though they only indirectly
affect recruiting, help to increase the discontent of those
actually serving and to prevent enlistment.   These causes
we will deal with in the course of our suggestions for making
the military career more attractive and the army more
efficient.

On this subject Sir Frederick Roberts, in an able article
which appeared a few months ago in the 'Nineteenth Cen-
' tury,' let in a flood of light.   Stated briefly, Sir Frederick's suggestion is that the authorities should adopt ' free
' trade in the army;' which means, that if a soldier, after a
short probation, finds the service distasteful, he should be
allowed to pass into the reserve.   But before examining his
scheme, let us consider the preliminary observations and arguments which lead up to it.   He says that both short and long
service have failed to produce the necessary number of recruits.   He, therefore, naturally arrives at the conclusion
that there is some other cause for the deficiency.   If the
army is not attractive, recruits will not come; and ' if we
' are to have a voluntary army, we must have a contented
' one.   To get recruits, in the first place, we must make
' military service popular; and to keep a sufficient number
' of men in the ranks, we must deal fairly and honestly with
' our soldiers.'   The large annual demand for recruits is not
needed merely to fill up the vacancies caused by death, a
reasonable amount of invaliding, a small percentage of discharges for misconduct, and ordinary discharge or transfer
to the reserve.   These all represent what may be termed
legitimate expenditure of men; but, unfortunately, there is
in addition much avoidable waste.   This waste proceeds from
an excessive number of deaths and invaliding, caused slightly

by carelessness about the sanitary condition of certain barracks—for example, the case of one of the barracks at Cairo; but mainly proceeding from invaliding and death, the inevitable result of enlisting unfit men and working them too early; from desertion; the purchase of, and the claim by indulgence to, free discharges; and a discreditable proportion of expulsion from misconduct. The figures are striking. We have shown above that in 1883 no fewer than 8,138 took, or purchased, their discharge prematurely, or deserted. To these must be added 1,059 men discharged for misconduct, and an indefinite number of men who died or were invalided because they were unfit for the service from the beginning, and a few who were the victims of unsanitary barracks. We probably shall not be far wrong if we estimate the total avoidable waste during 1883 at 10,000 men. A similar view is taken by Captain White in his able pamphlet called 'The Truth about the ' Army.' He thus expresses himself:—

'For the years 1876–8, nearly 27,000 men left the ranks within three years of their enlistment, and all the money spent upon them was wasted. This sum amounted to over 1,500,000*l*. The waste of nearly one-third of the entire number of recruits enlisted was due to death, invaliding, desertion, purchase of discharges, and discharge of bad characters. Of these 27,000 men not one was added to the reserves, for which everything else was sacrificed; and in a Blue Book, to which I shall refer again presently, it is stated that the total cost of these men, " which represents an actual expenditure of more than " 500,000*l*. yearly, has not only been absolutely useless, but it would " have been far better for the service had it never been incurred."'

These men had not in any way repaid the expense they had entailed on the taxpayers.

In addition to the large preventible waste which renders it necessary to enlist a number of recruits in excess of that required to fill the inevitable vacancies, there is another cause for the great demand for recruits. We refer to the excess over a reasonable ratio of men in hospital, which is the result of enlisting immature and weakly youths, and to the number of men in prison. The general return shows that during 1883 no fewer than 10,614 suffered imprisonment by courts-martial. What was the precise number of men undergoing imprisonment at any one time we are unable to say, but we may fairly estimate it at 2,000, or the number of rank and file of two battalions on a war footing. If the army was without these 2,000 men strong enough for its duties, they were a superfluous expense, and 2,000 recruits less annually would have been required. If the army, on the other hand, needed those men, it suffered a loss in efficiency.

The question of avoidable waste is evidently closely connected with that of the popularity of the army and the number of recruits annually needed. If the army were as popular as employment in the police and in the service of the great railway companies, in which there is always an excess of the supply of eligible candidates over the demand, men of physical fitness and good character would compete for permission to enlist and would regard discharge as a serious evil. How then can we make the army popular? We believe it can be done, provided we modify the principles of engagement and the details of treatment.

Sir Frederick Roberts advocates what he calls ' free trade ' in the army, his explanation of which is briefly as follows:—

' 1. That soldiers should be made to understand exactly the terms under which they enlist, and, once they have accepted those terms, no change should be made in them without their consent.

' 2. That army service generally should be made easier and freer; the status of the soldier raised; and, so far as may be practicable, more consideration paid to his wants and feelings.

' There must, in fact, be free trade and reciprocity in the army ; by which I mean the sweeping away of many hard-and-fast rules which now unnecessarily hamper the soldier's life from the hour of his enlistment until the day of his leaving the army. Men ought not, and, indeed, in these days of enlightenment, will not be forced to submit to this, that, or the other irksome condition to which, when enlisting, they had no sort of idea they would be subjected.

' What we want is, that the contract to be made between the State and the soldier should be advantageous to the former and satisfactory to the latter.'

In other words, we should offer the soldier clear and fixed terms, and should make the recruit seek for the army instead of being sought for. Not only this, but we must have no more privilege of extension or shortening of service 'till ' further notice.' It is true that in all great matters the terms under which the recruit is enlisted are, and always have been, adhered to. But in little matters—such as the disposal of old clothing, for instance—changes are frequent. Besides, concessions are made, such as those lately granted with regard to extension of service—avowedly as an experiment—but the withdrawal of them leaves the soldier with the feeling that he has been unfairly dealt with ; and there are alterations in practice which, though legal and not a breach of faith, create irritation. Again, the spirit of the law, if not its letter, was broken by calling up the reserve for the

Egyptian war of 1882, which certainly was neither an invasion nor a great emergency. The fear of a repetition of such a measure has greatly increased the difficulty experienced by the reserve men in obtaining employment. How real this hardship is, and what are its consequences, may be seen from the following extract from Sir Frederick Roberts's article:—

'The prejudice against employing a reservist (liable to be called away for active service) is so strong, that the mere fact of a man being one often interferes with his chance of getting permanent employment. Indeed, to obtain this he may have to deny the fact of his belonging to the reserve, and even to forego the advantage of drawing reserve pay. This accounts for the otherwise unintelligible fact of so many reservists of good character failing to apply for their pay. When the reserve has been called out we have heard much of the large percentage of those enrolled who have answered to the call, but we have heard nothing of the numbers who are quarterly struck off the rolls of the reserve—they are not included in the total against which the percentage is struck.'

With regard to the main terms of engagement, such as should *primâ facie* make the army attractive, we may be permitted to observe that it is not a mere question of money. The Duke of Cambridge and others have said that to get men you must pay the market price. Of course, if the pay were doubled, there would be a greater flow of recruits of good character and physique, and against the large increase of expense there would be a saving in the cost of deserters, invalids, deaths, premature discharges, men in prison, &c.; but the addition to the estimates would nevertheless be substantial, and we doubt whether our difficulties would be overcome solely by an addition to daily pay. Taking into consideration the incidental advantages and emoluments of the soldier, he is not, as it is, so badly off while serving as many people imagine. On the other hand, he has to incur dangers which fall to the lot of few others save sailors and miners, he surrenders his independence, he is bound, whether he likes it or not, to complete a lengthened period of service, and he is practically condemned to celibacy.

Sir Frederick Roberts thinks that in the first place the terms of enlistment should be altered, and that the line should be placed on the same footing as the guards—viz. that a recruit should have the option of enlisting either for three years' army service, to be followed by nine years in the reserve, with the privilege of converting the latter into service with the colours; or for twelve years' army service. The reserve would,

according to this scheme, be mainly composed of the three
years' men ; but to render the terms more elastic, Sir Frederick
Roberts proposes that, as an indulgence, a man should, under
ordinary circumstances, be allowed to pass from the army to
the reserve at any time—in very exceptional cases free ; in
others by purchase according to a gradually falling scale.
Thus we should have a home army chiefly consisting of three
years' men, and a colonial and Indian army of twelve years'
men.   Sir Frederick Roberts combats the idea that many of
the three years' men might refuse to extend their service
when wanted to go abroad, by saying that the conditions
should be made so attractive that re-engagement would be
looked on as a privilege.   We quite agree with the able
Commander-in-Chief of the Madras army in principle, but
would suggest some slight modification.   We would enlist
all recruits for the infantry for one year, and for the artillery
and cavalry for two years.   At the end of that time they
should be allowed, *and tempted* if good men, to re-engage
successively for five years at a time until twenty-one years in
infantry and artillery, and twenty years in the cavalry had
been completed, with power to the authorities to refuse to
allow the last re-engagement if the man showed signs of
failing physical activity, or to limit the engagement during
the last four or five years to shorter periods than four or five
years.   A pension should be given after sixteen years' service,
and an addition should be made to the rate for every additional year.   Passage to the reserve at any time should be
allowed, as Sir Frederick Roberts proposes ; but in addition
we suggest that infantry men who, at the end of eleven
years, and cavalry and artillery men who, after twelve years'
colour-service, did not re-engage for pension, should be permitted to enter the reserve, renewing their engagement in
the latter every four years, a proportion of their reserve
service counting with their army service for pension.   An
infantry man, who originally enlisted at the age of nineteen,
served eleven years with the colours, and subsequently twelve
years with the reserve, would be only forty-two when he
definitively reverted to civil life, and would be, in the majority
of cases, a valuable man up to that age.   If he became, during
the last two or three years of his service, somewhat corpulent
and inactive, he might be passed into a veteran reserve, and
destined simply for the defence of our large garrison towns,
such as Dover, Portsmouth, or Plymouth, or, in case of a
war, he might be employed at the base of operations.

Even after completing twenty-one years with the colours,

a man, if physically fit and not more than forty-two years of age, might, with advantage, be allowed to spend two or three years in a veteran reserve with a view to increasing his pension. It is true that few soldiers, after eighteen years' service, are worth much physically; but every officer of experience will bear us out in saying that many a soldier who, on his discharge, appeared to be a thoroughly worn-out old man, seems, if visiting his old corps after an absence of a year, to have got back two or three years of his youth. It is the guard duty (he frequently has only three nights out of four in bed); the sudden changes from the fœtid hot air of the guard-room to the cold, raw winter atmosphere; the closeness of the barrack-rooms with the draughts of the passages; and the hurried manner in which meals are devoured—that do more than anything else to wear out a soldier. It may be contended that in the event of a reserve man who has only served one year with the colours, he would require constant rubbing up in his drill and musketry if he is to remain effective. This might easily be managed by arranging that every three years, but at any time he might select, he should be required to join a regiment or depôt for one month, and that every year he should do, in his immediate neighbourhood, some six drills and rifle-shooting of two hours each. These drills should take place close to his residence, and on days and at hours most convenient to himself.

As to the passage from the active army into the reserve at any time, either free or on a small payment, it would greatly diminish desertion, and extinguish the irksome feeling of being tied down for a certain period to an irksome occupation. Even if a man likes soldiering fairly well, he is irritated at the thought that should he at any time become weary of it, or see a good opening in civil life, he cannot quit the colours before a certain fixed date. The permission recently accorded to a limited number of reserve men to rejoin the colours should be extended to all. Hitherto, many reserve men, unable to obtain employment, have presented themselves as recruits, and have not unfrequently incurred the penalties due to fraudulent enlistment. The reason why we suggest one year in the case of infantry, and two years in that of cavalry and artillery, for the length of short service instead of three years, as suggested by Sir Frederick Roberts, is, that in one year an infantry, and in two years a cavalry or artillery soldier can thoroughly master his drill. Three years is either too long or too short a time. It is longer than is required for drill, and shorter than is needed for training. For the benefit of our non-military readers we will point out that there is a wide distinction between drill and training, though the two are often confounded. A soldier may be said to be thoroughly drilled when he has mastered the mechanical part of his work, can use his weapon properly, and can manœuvre with precision. He is trained when completely imbued with the spirit of discipline, and when he instinctively obeys the word of command, and does the right thing promptly under the most disturbing circumstances. Training is therefore a work of some time, and we have no hesitation in saying that the soldier who, after seven years with the colours, passes into the reserve, has not long begun to be animated by the military instinct. Indeed, in many cases it may be said not to have arrived at its full development. By fixing the length of short service at one and two years, a large flow into the reserve would be secured, bad men would be discovered and got rid of, and desertions, the largest proportion of which takes place during the first year's service, would be reduced to a minimum; for the most discontented soldier would prefer waiting a few months to incurring the risks attendant on an illegal violation of his engagement.

Again, it is not till the recruit period has been completed that a soldier begins to find his life tolerable, and contemplates with satisfaction the idea of making the army his career. In short, we are of opinion that by adopting a preliminary probationary period, both the service and the recruit can be best suited. To induce a man to extend his service after the probation and the various periods above mentioned, some recognition of the principle that the journeyman is worth more than the apprentice, should be recognised. Apart from good-conduct pay, which is dependent on behaviour, not on proficiency, the private of one month's standing receives, under present regulations, precisely the same pay as the veteran of twenty years' service. This is neither reasonable nor just, and is felt by soldiers as a grievance. We do not think it would be advisable, or even possible, to reduce the pay of recruits. In the infantry a soldier averages about sixpence a day clearance after paying for necessaries, clothing materials, and the various stoppages. That seems a large sum for pocket-money; but, after all, it does not go very far if we consider that out of this sixpence a day the soldier has to pay for his beer and tobacco, postage and stationery, and a bloater or bit of butter with which to eke out his breakfast or tea of dry bread and tea or coffee. We would not, therefore, reduce the pay of the recruits, but we would add one penny a day at each re-engagement. This would make a graduated distinction between the younger and the older soldier, and enable the latter either to accumulate a sum in the savings bank, give him a comparatively handsome amount for his furlough, or enable him to indulge in little additional luxuries while with the regiment. These extra pennies should, moreover, be as inviolate as his present pay as regards forfeiture. The addition to the estimates would not be so alarming as might be thought, for the total regimental pay for officers and men is only four and a half millions this financial year, and against the increase would be set off the saving in prison, law, hospital charges, &c. Besides, it is worth while paying a little more to obtain a contented and efficient army.

But this is not the only reform needed. When Lord Cardwell announced that the soldier would in future obtain a clear shilling, there was great rejoicing, which was converted into the strongest indignation when it was found that what was really meant was that the soldier was to be only partially clothed and fed, and that from the shilling all deficiencies had to be made up. The feeling that they had been deceived has ever since been rankling in soldiers' breasts; most of all, recruits, when they find that the clear shilling really means only a clear sixpence, consider that they have been swindled. The argument that the soldiers serving at the date of Lord Cardwell's announcement, and those who have since enlisted, deceived themselves, and could easily, on looking into the matter, have ascertained what they really were to receive, is foolish. In dealing with the illiterate class from which we draw most of our recruits, there should be no ambiguity about the terms, no possibility of misunderstanding, for the lower orders are naturally suspicious, and soldiers are proverbially sensitive about their pay. Besides, we have, as practical men, to deal, not with that which ought to be, but with that which is. Under the existing system a soldier is provided by the State with a uniform, including boots, renewed periodically, but he is often required to pay out of his own pocket for a new pair of trousers, serge frock, or forage cap, while it is evident that his two pairs of boots annually are not sufficient, and the cost of additional boots and repairs to those which he possesses is defrayed by the man himself. He also, on enlistment, is furnished with a free kit of necessaries, comprising under-clothing, knife, fork, and spoon, brushes, blacking, braces, razor, towels, soap, &c. This kit he has to keep up at his own expense. It is plain, from the above, that the soldier is *not* clothed by the State. The result of this arrangement is constantly recurring stoppages, which often leave the soldier with only one penny a day pocket-money, cause great irritation and discontent, and are fruitful causes of desertion. Neither is he fed by the State; for all he obtains in the shape of rations is 1 lb. bread and ¾ lb. meat daily. The balance, in the shape of groceries, vegetables, milk, &c., is defrayed out of the messing fund, for which 4*d.* a day is stopped from his pay. In addition he is charged with washing at ½*d.* a day, hair-cutting 1*d.* a month, and barrack damages, for which he is lucky if he gets off with 1*d.* a month. If he belongs to the library, the subscription is 3*d.* a month. We endorse Sir Frederick Roberts's recommendation that whatever sum is called pay should be free of stoppages, so that the soldier may know exactly how he stands, and the captain and colour-sergeant be relieved of much clerical work and time-consuming accounts. As the most careful infantry soldiers, under fairly favourable circumstances, clear 7*d.* a day, it would be desirable to fix his pay at that sum, and for the State to defray all charges connected with the items above mentioned, unless, of course, in cases of carelessness and waste.

While on this topic we may, with propriety, be allowed to call attention to the question of food. Doctors and regimental officers are agreed in saying that the present ration is insufficient. Considering the amount of bone, skin, and waste in ¾ lb. meat, that a large proportion of our soldiers are growing lads, and that all soldiers pass much of their time in the open air, 1 lb. of meat should be issued. We are convinced that were the rations increased, there would be a great improvement in both the sobriety and health of the army. The soldier has now nothing between 4.30 or 5 P.M. one day and 8 A.M. the next day, with an early morning drill intervening. In fact, the only solid meal he has in the twenty-four hours is his dinner. The result is that he seeks to allay the pangs of hunger, which, in a growing lad, are severe, by indulging in drink and chewing or smoking strong tobacco. The complaints of insufficiency of food have become louder of late years for this simple reason: formerly a large proportion of soldiers consisted of men who had finished growing, including many who, from long service in hot climates, had but little appetite. Hence the comparatively few recruits profited by the surplus of their older comrades. Now the growing and consequently ravenous lads are in the large majority, and a 'wolf in the 'stomach' is a general characteristic.

In addition to an increased ration some improvement in the arrangements for meals is highly desirable. All regimental officers have experience of the fact, that if they do not, within a very few minutes, visit all the rooms of a regiment at meal times, they find in the last rooms that the meal is over and the table deserted. Indeed, the rapidity with which their food is bolted by soldiers is almost incredible, and it stands to reason that meals thus scrambled through not only afford insufficient nourishment, but actually sow the seeds of indigestion, dyspepsia, and other complaints. What are the causes of this objectionable hurry? In our opinion an explanation can be easily given. A great improvement has taken place of late years in the preparation and variety of soldiers' dinners, but the latter might with advantage be increased. The appearance of the table is not attractive. If it looked more inviting, the food would be more enjoyed. Finally, were beer allowed to be taken with food instead of afterwards at the canteen, the soldier would be tempted to linger over his meals. In truth a barrack-room is a very uninviting apartment, owing partly to traditional martinet rules, partly to the draconic regulations of the barrack department, and the thirst for barrack damages. In some regiments, commanding and company officers encourage any attempt to make the barrack-room look more cheerful by suspending against the walls photographs, coloured illustrations from the weekly papers, &c. In others the object seems to be to produce as close a resemblance as possible to a prison cell. Again, just before and just after the recognised official winter period, the allowance of coals is too small. We contend that the object of the authorities should be to make the barrack-room homelike and as comfortable as possible compatible with cleanliness and neatness. In fact, the less like the typical barracks the soldier's abode is made the better.

Great complaints are made by the 'unco guid' of the idle dissipated habits of the British soldier. These statements would be less general were the conditions of his life better understood, his natural requirements more carefully considered. He indulges in drink and dissipation, not from any inherent love of them, but from want of reasonable means of recreation. It is true that there are the reading-room

and library, with books, games, and newspapers, and in most
barrack-yards opportunities of indulging in athletic sports.
But the precincts of the barracks are associated in the soldier's mind with officialdom, drill, and countless restrictions.
The shadow of the sergeant is as it were over everything.
Besides, men cannot be reading or playing draughts for ever,
and they love to indulge in a stroll about the town or the
neighbourhood. As an object for their walk, or in order to
quench the thirst arising from it, they look in at some public-
house, by no means particular as to its reputation or the
class of people they meet there. To counteract this tendency it would be an excellent thing if in every large
garrison town there were a soldiers' club—not too near the
barracks, so as to give an object for a walk—conducted with
as few restraints as possible. There are many ' soldiers'
' homes,' but they are less useful and attractive than they
might be. It would be better to establish genuine clubs,
managed by a committee of soldiers of all ranks, senior
officers only exercising a general supervision over them.
The fullest freedom should be the rule; but excess in any
sort of liquor, or foul language, or quarrelling, should be
sternly suppressed. The authorities might feel certain, that
the members themselves would watch jealously over good
order, and non-admittance or expulsion would be regarded
as a serious punishment. Male civilian friends should be
also eligible for introduction by members, either as visitors
or honorary members. The funds for current expenses
would be found by the men with a little help from the
canteen funds, the officers, and the well-wishers of the
army generally, in the first place. Any War Office interference, or even more than a benevolent and judicious
supervision on the part of the officers, would however be
fatal to success.

It may be urged by military conservatives in proof that a
soldiers' club would do no good, that the public-houses most
frequented are those pot-houses which cluster round each
barracks on a radius of a quarter of a mile from the
barrack-gate. That is true; and these public-houses are
especially mischievous, not so much from the quantity as the
quality of the liquor consumed, and women of the worst
class congregate in them. Our proposal is to provide a
decent house of call for the soldier who wishes for an object
for a walk, and to induce men who do not wish or have not
time for a long walk to take their pleasure in the precincts
of the barracks. But then the barracks must be made a

real home, and occupations suited to all sorts of tastes provided. Many soldiers are very fond of gardening, and a more healthy occupation they could not indulge in. Besides, flowers would help to beautify the barracks, and the vegetables would be a welcome addition to the mess. It is not, however, in human nature for a man to sow when it is uncertain that he will ever reap. Again, workshops would be invaluable, both as a means of keeping up a soldier's skill in the trade he followed before enlistment, or for enabling him to earn a living on discharge. Here, however, as in the case of gardening, the constant change of quarters at uncertain intervals is a serious obstacle. Had we a military system, it would be possible to keep a regiment for two or three years at each station, to the great saving of expense alike to officers, married soldiers, the officers' and sergeants' mess, and to the public; and soldiers' clubs, gardens, and workshops might be established. From the latter could then be turned out much that is now provided either by Government factories or contractors, and the regiment would become an independent little colony as well as a comfortable home. To carry out localisation and territorial connexion to its full extent, the home battalion as well as the depôt should be stationed in its own district. This would be practically impossible, owing to the demands of Ireland, and the necessity of assembling a certain number of troops at Aldershot. Moreover, it is urged by persons whose opinions are entitled to respect, that men do not care to enlist in a regiment likely to be stationed near their own home. They say that, on the contrary, many men enlist in order to get away from their friends and surroundings; that some of them have got into a scrape, and wish to disappear for a time. Others fear the reproaches of their relations, the contempt of their friends for having assumed that badge of social inferiority—among certain classes—the Queen's uniform. To this we make answer, all these objections, if well founded, are opposed to localisation; that more or less they are inseparable from localisation of even the present imperfect character. But we think their strength is somewhat overrated. If the steps we advocate were adopted we should induce a good class of men to deliberately adopt the army as a profession, in which case there would soon be an end to the present social inferiority of the soldier, and the red or blue coat would become a title to respect. At all events, whether a perfect localisation be adopted or not, there is no earthly reason why a battalion should not be kept for two or three years in one station, and know within a month or two when, under ordinary circumstances, it would be transferred to another garrison.

Among the causes which tend to make the army unpopular are, to quote Sir Frederick Roberts's words, 'the many ' petty troubles and inconveniences soldiers are subjected to, ' without apparently any reason or necessity: objectless ' repetitions of purely parade movements; constant guard-' mounting with its accompaniment of impaired health from ' " sentry-go; " being associated with bad characters; the ' constant and distasteful work required from recruits.' There is, we are sorry to say, too much truth in this statement. Some of the annoyances of which soldiers are the victims are due to a desire on the part of officers and sergeant-majors to bring the men up to an artificial standard of smartness and barrack-room neatness. Within certain limits smartness and neatness are conducive alike to efficiency and discipline. Beyond a certain point they cease to accomplish that object, and only harass the men. That such is the case is proved by the fact, that in some regiments the men, though less worried than in a martinet corps, are just as efficient and soldierlike. As to drill, there can be no question that half the movements and exercises practised are utterly useless for fighting purposes. The late Sir Charles Napier used to say, that only a few movements, and those of the simplest nature, were ever practised on the field of battle; yet notwithstanding our short service, and the many military accomplishments, as they may be called, which the soldier has now to acquire, we cram him with drills, useless in themselves, and which tax his memory, weary his muscles, and try his temper. Take for example the bayonet exercise, a very pretty performance when smartly executed before an inspecting general, but never by any chance turned to account in war, and difficult to master. Again, much time is spent on battalion movements; yet a battalion now-a-days never fights in close order with lines of mathematical straightness and a perfect touch. At least half the battalion movements might be struck out of the 'Field Exercise' with advantage. Many of the movements now taught have always been recognised as of no practical utility; but it was formerly thought necessary to occupy the soldier in order to keep him out of mischief. In these days he has plenty of useful occupation without taking up his time with that which does not render him more efficient as a fighting man; yet the traditional practice has survived its excuse. The men take great interest in tactics or any other rehearsal of the duties which devolve on them in time of war; constant drill, however, they detest. We should endeavour to convince the soldier of the necessity of the instruction which he undergoes and interest him in it. Any instruction which makes a demand on his wits, not only interests him but improves his intelligence and increases his efficiency. Field bridging and engineering is a pleasing variety after the monotony of barrack-yard drill, and calls forth intelligence. Signalling, provided too many men are not taken from their more immediate occupation, fitting themselves for fighting, is another good employment, and we have seen soldiers listening with the most earnest attention to the instruction of a commanding officer who, being supposed to occupy a farmhouse with his battalion, explained on the spot what steps should be taken to place that building in a state of defence. Among useless and irksome duties may be reckoned some of the fatigues. We have known large numbers of men taken from a battalion which in 1878 was expecting every day to take the field, to roll a lawn-tennis ground. The commanding officer, knowing that it was his first duty to train his men for war, chafed inwardly at this misappropriation of his men's time, but was obliged to yield to superior orders. On guard there are in some garrisons far too many men employed. A certain number are indispensable, but in many cases they might without detriment to the service be diminished. Indeed, in a large number of instances a military policeman, or an occasional patrol, would be far more useful than sentries. The filling of beds with straw is a work which is by no means pleasant, and consumes some valuable hours every three months. A palliasse thus filled is most uncomfortable to lie on for the first few days, and it is a question whether hair mattresses could not be supplied as cheaply, while the soldier would be saved much unpleasant and unprofitable work.

Statistics prove that in 1883, out of 3,717 men who deserted, 977 had less than three months', 536 less than six months', 301 less than nine months' service, thus showing that the recruit period is exceptionally irksome. It cannot well be otherwise. Many of the recruits are so awkward, we may almost say misshapen, that their framework has, as it were, to be completely rearranged. The loafing ex-mechanic too is greatly given to spitting, chattering, and looking about; while the ex-ploughboy has probably never before in his life stood upright without moving, for a second. Thus the muscles and mind are alike wearied, and the drill instructor, who has forgotten his recruit griefs, frequently fails to sympathise with those whom he is anxious as quickly as possible to transform from careless louts into smart intelligent soldiers. They too often also omit to make allowance for stupidity, set it down as obstinacy, and adopt a bullying tone under the misconception that they are showing off their own smartness. Nor are non-commissioned officers the only offenders. In the riding-school it seems to be a tradition, that the timid or awkward recruit should be jeered at by the riding-master and made the butt of stupid jokes, which have been handed down from generation to generation. Sometimes indeed the horse is purposely so startled by a sudden crack of the whip that a fall is almost inevitable. In short, the object of the riding-master in many cases would seem to be to test, rather than to gradually strengthen, the recruit's nerve. Of course what we have said with regard to rough and inconsiderate treatment of recruits is by no means universally applicable, but it is sufficiently so to justify us in calling for increased supervision by commanding officers of the instruction of young soldiers. Supposing, however, that there were nothing to complain of in this respect, the manner in which the recruit's time is spent is evidence of want of judgement on the part of the authorities. Taking the infantry, it stands to reason that the recruit has enough to do in learning to clean his arms and accoutrements, to put on the latter, to pack his valise, to fold his great-coat, to arrange his bed and belongings according to regulation, and to learn his drill, and how to use and handle his rifle, without being required in addition to attend school and the gymnasium. Too much is evidently crowded into the twenty-four hours. Besides, drill, gymnastics, and school do not go well together, unless the day is begun with the latter. To expect a recruit with fingers frozen by a cold drill, or with muscles wearied in the gymnasium, to have a steady hand for writing, is unreasonable. We would suggest that school should be limited to one hour after breakfast till after the recruit has been dismissed drill, and that gymnastics should be altogether postponed till that period.

The importance of raising the soldier's status we have already dealt with. This must be to a certain extent a work of time, and its accomplishment depends, first, on improving the condition of the soldier, and thus enabling the authorities to reject all but respectable men; secondly, on the education of public opinion, and the growth of an enlightened patriotism in the country. The police are respected because they are, and always have been, with few exceptions, worthy of respect. If soldiers were for the most part worthy of respect, they too would obtain it after the prejudice arising from obsolete traditions had worn off. Nothing would accelerate the advent of that good time so much as the disappearance of the loafing, unemployed ex-soldier. At present not only is the country overrun by reserve men eking out their sixpence a-day with odd jobs, and telling all who will listen what a fatal mistake they made in enlisting, and by men who having finished their reserve service have not even that pittance, and are still more bitter, but, there are not a few old soldiers possessing medals for the Crimea and the Indian Mutiny, who are in the receipt of parish relief; and this fact shocks the moral sense of the community and renders soldiering unpopular among the classes from which our recruits are drawn.

It is quite as important that a soldier should be as contented after leaving the army as while actually serving. Much could be done to bring about this desirable state of feeling if it were established as a principle that, qualifications being considered, the best avenue to certain appointments in the lower division of the Civil Service was through the army and navy. We can conceive no man with a greater claim on the patronage of the Government than one who has endured banishment and risked not only his health but his life for the country. To many a commission is neither a boon nor an object of desire; whereas all soldiers would look forward with eagerness to obtaining a post under Government on the expiration of their military engagement. The appearance in the ' Gazette ' from time to time of a list of ex-soldiers appointed to Government situations would do more to stimulate recruiting, both as to quality and quantity, than any measure we can devise. The adoption of such a system would also tend indirectly to raise the social status of the private soldier. Foreign Governments have set the example with great success: why should not the plan succeed in this country? The question has been nibbled at for some years past, and is still, we believe, under consideration, but has never been boldly and frankly approached. It is asserted that the wholesale admission of soldiers would lower the social status of the public offices. As, however, it is only proposed that the lower appointments should be reserved for ex-soldiers, we do not see how that argument applies. We go farther indeed, and maintain that if non-commissioned officers are often found qualified to receive commissions and to associate with officers, the clerks of the lower division need not shrink from being called upon to work with the former. It is also pretended that ex-soldiers are not qualified to perform the duties of Civil Service clerks. This pretext for exclusion is simply ridiculous, and without a shadow of foundation. Soldiers are trained to habits of discipline, punctuality, and method, and the daily occupations of colour and staff sergeants admirably fit them for the more mechanical work of a Government office. This is especially the case with orderly-room clerks, paymaster-sergeants, and quartermaster-sergeants; and taking them as a body, the sergeants of the British army are solidly educated, not a few indeed possess a superior education. On January 1, 1884, five per cent. of the non-commissioned officers and men held first-class certificates. In addition to clerkships there are a vast number of miscellaneous appointments, such as messengerships, park-keeperships, caretakers' posts, &c., which only need steadiness, intelligence, and a plain education. The customs and excise abound with these. There are also a large number of messengers in the Law Courts and the Houses of Parliament. The messengerships in the latter are seldom conferred on retired soldiers, yet ex-sergeants of the officers' mess are perfectly qualified for them. Certainly they are as well qualified as bloated butlers and decayed valets. To make use of subordinate Government appointments, however, as a means of stimulating recruiting and rendering the army more popular, it would be necessary, first, to expressly reserve for ex-soldiers and sailors a certain number of these posts; second, to ignore, both with regard to Civil Service pay and Civil Service pension, any military or naval pension. We have often heard soldiers say that any military pension which they might possess should be regarded as payment for past services, and protest against the practice of merging it in civil pay or pension. As to any examination, it should be merely qualifying, and only sufficient to test the candidate's qualifications for his actual work.

Among incidental causes of the unpopularity of the army may be reckoned—(1) the heavy blows recently dealt at *esprit de corps*; (2) the present organisation of the infantry of the line. The two are, in fact, closely connected with each other. Formerly, a man could enlist in the regiment for which he had a fancy. This fancy depended on various considerations. The intending recruit might have had a father or brother in the regiment; or some of his friends might be serving in it

—and it is notorious that as regards enlistment one man in a village often would set the example to half a dozen of his acquaintances; or the squire's son might hold a commission in the corps; or there might be something attractive in the uniform or history. Now *esprit de corps* has little or no influence on recruiting; and the substitute, which may be termed *esprit de département*, is very inefficient. Many a man has said, 'I will enlist in the 93rd or the 43rd if I can be sure ' of remaining in those corps, but I know nothing of the Priu- ' cess Louise's Argyll and Sutherland Highlanders or the Ox- ' fordshire Light Infantry. If I cannot soldier in the regiment ' of my choice, I will not soldier at all.' Thus a recruit of the very best description is lost. On joining his regiment formerly, the recruit soon began to regard it as his home, and to devour with avidity all the famous traditions of the corps as related by the old soldiers round the guard-room fire. He was proud to belong to such an historical regiment, and rapidly acquired a conviction that there was not its equal in the army. His officers stimulated this feeling, and all ranks felt that no sacrifice, not even that of life itself, was too great to keep up the renown of the corps. Officers and men too, from serving for years together, the places of both being often, in time, taken by their respective sons, acquired a spirit of union and mutual affection which will never be seen under the present system. We have heard a commanding officer say, 'One of my sergeants is the son of a private in ' the company which I commanded when a captain, and at the ' depôt the sergeant-major is the son of my old servant.' Such circumstances, by no means uncommon in the past, naturally gave rise to a strong hereditary feeling of mutual attachment between officers and men, and, combined with other things, raised *esprit de corps* to the level of a religion.

Certain of the, so-called, advanced military reformers pretend either to ignore *esprit de corps* or maintain that the old *esprit de corps* will, in time, be succeeded by one of a wider nature. As to the value of *esprit de corps*, it has been proved on hundreds of occasions. When all goes well its importance is not, perhaps, very apparent; but when a desperate effort has to be made to turn the tide of victory, or when a retreat, always depressing, is being carried out under the most demoralising privations and perils, when the bonds of discipline become weakened by the imminence of disaster, the fear of death, and exceptional bodily sufferings, then *esprit de corps* steps in, acting, as it were, as a soul to mere machine-like discipline. Had *esprit de corps* nothing

to do with the gallant soldiers who went down in the ' Birken-
' head ' as steady in their ranks on deck as if on parade, sacrificing themselves for the sake of the women and children?
Were the 42nd not stimulated by *esprit de corps* when, to
obtain a superhuman effort, Sir John Moore called out to
them in Egypt, ' Highlanders, remember your fathers ; ' and
at Corunna, ' Highlanders, remember Egypt' ? When Captain
Stanley, at the crisis of the struggle at Inkerman, shouted
to the 57th, ' Die-hards, remember Albuera,' was it not *esprit
de corps* which secured him a noble response? Finally, when
Sir Colin Campbell, at Balaclava, addressing the isolated
and unsupported 93rd, told them it was necessary they must
die at their post, and his brave Highlanders gave back the
laconic answer, ' Aye, Sir Colin, we'll do that,' was not *esprit
de corps* a motive power of surpassing strength ? But now
where is *esprit de corps* ? It has been enfeebled, if not
destroyed, by the existing system and organisation, and
though in time a broader, yet, in consequence, diluted *esprit
de corps* may come to be associated with the territorial regiment, for many years we shall have, in its place, a soulless
discipline. There will be, it is true, eventually a crop of
glorious traditions relating to the new regiment, and as the
latter consists of two battalions, there will be a double
chance of corporate renown, but the fame of each individual
battalion will be but a history of the past.

Civilians, deluded by well-rounded periods, scarcely realise
the existing conditions of service in the infantry. As regards
regular soldiers, a regiment is divided into a home battalion,
a foreign battalion, and a depôt, which are, for all practical
purposes, three distinct corps. The officers are interchange-
able, and this fact, combined with short service, renders it
impossible for them to acquire that knowledge of, and interest in, their men as under the old single battalion system.
As to the men, they enlist either for a particular territorial
regiment or for general service. If the latter, they are liable
to be transferred to any other corps within three months
of enlistment. A recruit first goes to the depôt, where he
remains a few weeks, receiving little but the roughest and
most elementary instruction. On being sent to the home
battalion he recommences his drill *ab initio*, and finds that
he is to unlearn certain little details of system. A year
later, just as he is beginning to feel at home and to know
the officers and non-commissioned officers of his company,
and to make friends, he may be sent out to the foreign
battalion. He again finds himself surrounded by strangers,

and compelled, in trifling matters, to adopt a different system; for no two battalions are precisely alike as regards interior economy. After serving with the foreign battalion for three or four years that battalion is ordered home, and he is liable to be transferred to another corps to complete his period of engagement. In addition, he may be tempted by a bounty and the prospect of active service to volunteer to a regiment about to enter on a campaign. He is also liable to be transferred without his own consent if invalided from abroad, if his corps being ordered abroad his health renders him unfit for foreign service, or if his corps being ordered abroad he is within two years of the termination of his army service. From the above it is apparent that the soldier is in a constant state of transfer, and that everything militates against the union of a battalion.

How this system works may be gathered from the following extract from a pamphlet called 'Fifteen Years of Army ' Reform, by an Officer:'—

' In February 1879, in consequence of the Isandlana disaster, five battalions were required to embark for the Cape. And what happened? They had to leave at home, for physical causes, youth &c. 1,045 men, or 209 per battalion on an average, and to obtain from other regiments, by volunteering, 1,414, or 283 on an average. The 91st Highlanders embarked 893 strong, of whom no fewer than 374 were volunteers from eleven different regiments who joined the day before embarkation. In this regiment 260, and in the 21st Regiment 305 out of 888 men were under twelve months' service. And one point ought to be very specially noted in view of what has since occurred. The 21st was a regiment of two battalions, and the authors of the Localisation Scheme, as far back as in 1870, had declared that their plan, in its perfection, can be at once worked in all regiments possessing two battalions; yet in 1879 the state of affairs in the 2nd battalion of the 21st was no better (it was actually worse) than in the 58th, 91st, and 94th, which were linked battalion regiments.'

Coming down to a later period, viz. 1884, and quoting Captain White's pamphlet, ' The Truth about the Army,' what do we find?

' That when, in March last, three regiments first for foreign service —i.e. in the First Army Corps for active service—embarked for the Mediterranean, out of a strength of 1,700 privates, 960 men of less than two years' service, over 500 *had never fired a shot or had any instruction in musketry*, and it was estimated that 700 of them were under twenty years of age—boys, in fact, who, on active service, would simply have died like rotten sheep if subjected to privation or over-exertion. In another corps on the home establishment, the average height about the same time was 5 feet 4½ inches, and the average chest-measurement 34½ inches.'

... ... the Army Estimates, in
... ... attalions, or nearly one-
... ... battalions at home, must
... ... circumstances.' Considering
... ... moment be ordered off to
... ... recurring little colonial
... ... a satisfactory statement.
... ... went compelled to obtain
... ... reserve cannot, without
... ... less than a serious cam-
... ... assimilate more than a cer-
... ... whatever source obtained,
... ... volunteering the battalions
... ... inefficient.

... ... refrain from giving the
... ... service paper, the 'United
... ... in question appeared about
... ... real change in our army

... ... thirds of the infantry men paid,
... ... able to do soldiers' work—i.e. take
... ... of the twelve line battalions
... ... 650 of all ranks, after deducting
... ... than a year's service, and men
... ... the battalions lower on the roster,
... ... service would be found to be

... a few weeks ago, General Sir
... that each home battalion re-
... and supply drafts for the
... recruits a year, and that conse-
... more than a year and a half's
... only show that our army is
... be, but that it is also un-
... impopular we should not suffer
... and could get a better stamp

... that there is great difficulty.
... under the present system, we
... under 19 years, we cannot get
... the limit of age natu-
... but there are other objec-
... of 20 has generally settled
... artisan, especially in our
... probably married by that

time. If he has settled down, the only chance of inducing him to enlist lies in the fact of his being unable to find work. In such a case either his character or his skill is probably of an inferior description, and he becomes, to use the words of one of the most able of our military essayists, ' a conscript ' of hunger.' Often, indeed, such a man enlists only to obtain temporary means of subsistence, and with the intention of deserting as soon as he has tided over the bad time. Many more adult men would, however, be procurable if the army were rendered an attractive profession instead of being as it is at present a *pis aller* for those who are failures in civil life. It is surely within the limits of possibility that the army might be made, for young men at all events, as popular as the police or service under a railway company. If such a result were attained, we could reject all those unfit for a soldier's real work and unable to bring proof of good character. There must, however, be always a difficulty in obtaining a sufficient number of recruits let us diminish the annual waste as much as we may. To supply the deficiency, it has often been suggested that the army should imitate the navy, and train boys for the service. There are thousands of unconvicted lads sent to industrial schools, as a preservative against crime. There is no reason why such lads should not turn out very efficient soldiers, for their military training might commence at the industrial schools themselves. They would not come with the taint of actual crime; they would be superior to ordinary recruits, in that the previous history of the former could be accurately ascertained. The objection to such a method of feeding our army is, that at 16 they are generally discharged from either industrial or other charitable schools, and according to our contention they would not be physically fit for actual service for another four years. Even those who approve of taking lads who promise to make good soldiers as early as 17 would hardly venture to recommend a further reduction of the age standard. The army of the future, in which too many of our young soldiers ought to be classed, may be very useful in the future, but for present wants it is useless. In the navy the nature of the service is such that suitable work can always be found for a certain number of boys; it is not so in the army, if we except drummers and musicians. The Duke of Cambridge once observed that he should be very glad to see battalions of boys if they were 'in addition to the establishment.' That is the point. It is not to be expected that any War Minister or Commander-in-Chief would consent to boys being substituted for men, seeing that while the boys would be useless, they would cost nearly as much as men.

The obstacle is not, however, insuperable. Boy-battalions to the number of, say, seven of 1,000 each might be formed, consisting of youths between 16 and 19. Allowing for deaths, invaliding, &c., these battalions would give about 2,000 recruits of 19 to the active army annually. While in the boy-battalions a boy would be educated, drilled, and taught a trade; at 19 he would be an accomplished soldier, and having been carefully and properly fed during two or three years, would be in a good physical condition. Their army engagement should not commence till 19, and while in the boy-battalions they should only receive two-thirds of the ordinary daily pay, with a slight addition if promoted to the rank of lance-corporal or corporal. The sergeants should be picked men from the line. The boy-battalions should be stationed in barracks by themselves, but should be available for general duty at home in the event of an invasion. They would be quite efficient as a portion of the garrison of a fortress. By posting them to line battalions low down on the roster, it would be almost certain that they would not serve abroad till they had attained the age of 20. A lad from the boy-battalions, having been well fed and cared for during two or three years, would be more capable of enduring hardships and fatigue than the ordinary recruit of 20. Probably few of our readers are aware that there is a precedent for boy-battalions. During the first few years of the present century there was at least one such corps, some of the members of which were as young as ten or twelve.

It will be objected to the various suggestions which we have made, that if adopted, the army estimates would be largely increased. We do not think that such would be the case. We have a firm conviction that we do not get full value for the money spent on the army. Economy is practicable in several particulars. We will try to show how it may be effected. A saving would inevitably be produced if we enlisted none but physically efficient men of good character, and made soldiering attractive; for there would be a considerable reduction in the number of deaths, deserters, men in prison, men prematurely discharged, and men in hospital. There is also room for changes of organisation and system, by which large sums could be saved. The organisation of the British army is founded on no principles, but is either a mere relic of the past or the result of piece-

meal military alterations. Take for instance the organisation of infantry regiments, beginning with the battalion.
The size and number of companies were originally regulated
as to their maximum by the limit of the power of direct
control by respectively the captain and colonel. It was
found that according to this rule the strength of a company
should not exceed a hundred men, and the number of companies eight to ten. But there are powerful arguments in
favour of reducing the number and increasing the strength
of companies—of adopting, in short, the continental organisation. Obviously four large are more likely to work
together for a common end than are eight small companies.
It is easier to find four than eight good company leaders. A
strong company can provide its own supports and immediate
reserves; a small company cannot. Lastly, by reducing the
number of companies from eight to four, a substantial economy would be effected, because they would be commanded,
in time of peace, by a smaller number of officers. There
might also be a slight reduction in the cost of non-commissioned officers. Were four companies suppressed, the pay
and allowances of four colour-sergeants would be saved. A
similar economy might be effected in the cavalry by, in
imitation of all continental armies, abolishing troops, and
making the squadron the administrative as well as the tactical sub-unit.

In certain continental armies the field battery consists of
eight guns instead of six as with us. For manœuvring
purposes a six-gun battery may be handier than an eight-
gun battery; but that is all that can be said in favour of the
former. An eight-gun battery is a more powerful tactical
unit than a six-gun battery. It can be more conveniently
subdivided, and the action of three eight-gun batteries can be
more effectively combined than that of four six-gun batteries.
In regard to economy, there is no question, as may be seen
by a comparison between the establishment of twenty-four
guns organised in four batteries, and the same number of
guns organised in three batteries. The subalterns—viz. one
to each division of two guns—would be the same, as also
the subdivision, or the men and horses of each gun. The
difference would be, as it were, outside the divisions and
subdivisions. There would thus be a saving on the home
establishment of the pay, allowances, horses, &c. of one
major, one captain, one battery sergeant-major, one battery
quartermaster-sergeant, one farrier-sergeant, and two trum-
peters. In the field there would be the additional saving

of one medical officer and one veterinary surgeon. The
artillery is, in the matter of lieutenant-colonels and colonels,
a most extravagant corps. Not unfrequently there are to
be found in a garrison as many, or nearly as many, officers
of this rank as batteries. As a rule they are of no more
use than the fifth wheel of a coach, and like it add much
to friction. Half of them might be abolished with great
advantage to the State.

It may be argued that in the above suggestions for economy are involved a considerable diminution in the number
of senior officers, and that the result would be a stagnation
of promotion. That objection can easily be disposed of. If
the proportion of senior officers be reduced, it will be easier
to find good men for the higher ranks, while a system of
promotion which depends for success on the compulsory
retirement of efficient officers because they have attained a
certain age, by no means the average age of inefficiency, and
on having more officers than are needed for the higher grade,
stands self-condemned. By a combination of elimination
in the rank of subaltern, and selection in the ranks above,
promotion will regulate itself, and the best men will, in
the army as in other professions, come to the top at a
comparatively early age. Nor are our objections confined
to the unnecessarily large number of field officers; they also
extend to the superabundance of generals. These have been
reduced of late, and the diminishing process is not even yet
at an end. But the number decided on has been determined
on no principle. According to the estimates for the current
year, there are ninety-five general officers on the active list
unemployed. Abroad, rank and employment go together,
and this is clearly the proper rule, with the exception that,
considering the numerous little expeditions which are constantly despatched from England, we ought to have a small
margin—say, five generals, ten lieutenant-generals, and thirty
major-generals; or, including field-marshals, about half the
present number. This margin would enable the authorities
to give general officers a little rest between quitting one
appointment and taking up another, and would suffice for
ordinary cases. In the event of a great European war, some
of the youngest and most capable of the generals on a reserve list might be temporarily recalled to active duty and
be employed at home, and in addition a few colonels might
be promoted.

The staff of our army is another item in which a saving
might be effected, especially as regards the staff of expedi-

tions, which are largely in excess of that considered necessary in the German and other foreign armies. The rate of
staff pay likewise needs recasting. A captain on the staff
draws a penny a day more pay than his own colonel, and a
lieutenant employed as A.D.C. is better remunerated than a
junior regimental major. The only excuse for this scale is
that a staff officer has to supply himself with horses, horse-
trappings, and expensive staff uniform. Were the distinctive uniform of a staff officer to consist of a scarf and special
head-dress, and his horse found him by the State, the staff
pay might be reduced.

We have already alluded to the enormous sums annually
spent on the frequent changes of quarters. We shall therefore only observe here that the amount is close on 300,000*l.*
for the current year, and that much of it might be saved,
with great advantage alike to the State and individuals.

A very serious item in our military expenditure is the cost
of the regimental depôts. The establishment of these involved an expenditure of about four millions, and the annual
cost is, for the infantry alone, some 250,000*l.* in pay and
allowances, omitting the lieutenant-colonel as commanding
the sub-district rather than the depôt itself. As regards the
regular army, these depôts are nothing better than costly
recruiting offices. Were they swept away to-morrow, the
service would not in the slightest degree suffer. The real
depôts are the home battalions, and these, owing to their
weakness, the large periodical drafts which they have to
send to the foreign battalions, and the constant presence of
a large number of recruits, are little more than drill squads.
Tactical instruction is impracticable save in the sixteen
battalions on the higher establishment, and the pressure of
duty on the few men available has much to do with rendering the service unpopular.

There is the additional disadvantage of this system—the
idea of having one battalion at home to feed one abroad cannot always be carried out. What then can be substituted?
That an attempt should be made to provide a remedy is
clear, for experience proves that not only does the existing
system fail to fulfil the expectations of those who founded
it, but also that it is most unpopular and has inflicted a
deadly wound on *esprit de corps.* Surely, given a certain
number of men, it ought not to tax ingenuity much to
arrange that from the depôts alone should be furnished the
men needed by the foreign battalions; especially as, owing
to the recent practical restoration of long service, the

strength of the periodical drafts will soon be diminished.
The strength of each battalion depôt should be at least, on
an average throughout the year, 200 rank and file, and no
man should quit the depôt till he had been thoroughly
drilled, and was fit, as regards age and physique, to go on a
campaign. Some twenty-two years ago the Duke of Cambridge publicly stated that it was his opinion that the
service companies of a regiment should be composed exclusively of men fit, at a moment's notice, to embark. We
thoroughly agree with his Royal Highness. The adoption
of such a system would greatly facilitate mobilisation; for
commanding officers, when ordered to take the field, would
no longer have to transfer their unfit men to the depôt;
at most, they would have to eliminate perhaps a dozen
sick or physically unfit men. The home battalions being
composed entirely of drilled soldiers of the military age,
might, without disadvantage, be somewhat reduced in
numbers.

Were the scheme above sketched out adopted, not only
would economy be secured and efficiency increased, but also
it would be in the power of the War Office to add largely to
the popularity of the army by restoring the autonomy of regiments and thereby reviving *esprit de corps*. We have pointed
out many causes for the unpopularity of the army and the inefficiency and extravagance of our military system. Nor have
we been content with merely indicating defects, but have
suggested remedies. Some of these would, however, be only
partially effective, and certainly there would remain much
avoidable expenditure, unless the whole spirit of our military
administration were changed. Our army costs, in round
numbers, sixteen millions a year, of which only about four
and a half millions are spent on the regimental pay and
charges of the fighting men, including the auxiliary forces.
The remainder is swallowed up in feeding, clothing, doctor-
ing, housing, moving, punishing, and administering these
fighting men, and in pensions, half-pay, &c. The salaries
and miscellaneous charges of the War Office alone amount to
245,257*l*., being an increase over last year of 34,000*l*. In
addition there are many administrative and clerical expenses, which cannot easily be disentangled from that confused mass of figures called the Army Estimates. A considerable proportion of this cost could be saved, and much
friction and delay avoided, were the centralisation in which
we revel exchanged for the decentralisation which it is the
constant object of those practical people the Germans to

bring to perfection.   Colonel Charles Brackenbury is well
known as one of the members of what is called 'the advanced
' school,' yet in his preface to Major J. W. Buxton's ' The
' Elements of Military Administration,' he roundly stigma-
tises our system of military administration as 'faulty from
' the root.'   He goes on to say :

'Well-founded complaints will never cease till we can dig up by the
roots that system of centralisation, the faults of which we recognise in
other countries, but cannot perceive in our own. . . . In every campaign, however small, there comes a breakdown in administration
somewhere.   Then arise throughout the country cries of disappointment and of wrath against those who administer the system.   Some
unfortunate official is gibbeted because he has not accepted responsibility and acted for himself.   That is to say, he has not, at perhaps
fifty years of age, suddenly cast behind him every tradition of his
department, every habit to which he has been carefully trained, and,
in the midst of new and arduous tasks, constructed for himself a new
theory of duty and a new set of regulations, at the risk of censure for
his rashness.   Is this fair ?   We tie up in tight folds, during peace,
the limbs of our minor officials, heedless of their cries and the absurdity of our doings.   When war comes, the bands are suddenly cast off,
and we say, " Go and administer before the enemy." '

There can be no doubt in the minds of those who have
looked into the matter that there is an immense amount
of clerical work, costing much time and money, which, if
not positively mischievous, is perfectly useless.   This work
falls on regiments as well as on departments, and absorbs
much time which the exigencies of the service require to be
spent on other things.   An efficient reform of the army must
begin with a reform of the War Office itself.

In conclusion we would only make the following remarks.
The large armies of the continental States are, in time of
peace, usually resident in fixed quarters and employed on
garrison duty or military instruction.   A large portion of
the British army is, on the contrary, engaged in active
service in all parts of the world.   With 60,000 men in India,
with 16,000 men on the Nile, with 30,000 men in Ireland,
with an expedition on its way to South Africa of about 5,000
men, and with the Mediterranean garrisons, a mere fraction
of the army remains in Britain, barely sufficient to supply
the necessary reliefs to the forces abroad.   We are, in fact,
attempting to carry on extensive military operations with
a very small peace establishment.   It is apparent to every
one who will honestly consider the subject that the present
military establishment is not adequate to so great and various
a task, and that our system of military administration is

grievously in fault. An addition of 20,000 or 25,000 to the army is not at all more than is urgently required. Nor would the increased expense be as large as might be supposed, because the regimental pay and allowances do not amount to one-third of the army estimates, and we have an excess of officers unemployed. The army is weak because Ministers have not the courage to make the necessary demand on the House of Commons. But if the people of England are resolved to maintain their position in the world —to defend the possessions of the Empire in many parts of the globe, to provide for the security and peace of the United Kingdom, and to place the country in a position to defy insult and aggression—they must be content to pay for it. They pay not only for their greatness and for the protection of their interests abroad and at home, but for their exemption from the heaviest of all taxes, the conscription, the tax of blood, which is levied indiscriminately and universally by all the other States of Europe on their subjects. It is impossible to rate too highly that inestimable blessing of personal liberty which every Englishman enjoys, and an efficient voluntary army is the alternative we adopt in preference to the system which weighs so heavily on every male citizen of the Continent. The magnitude of those enormous continental armies is not without effect upon ourselves. They compel us to spend more than we desire on naval and military armaments; but the state of the world being what it is, England has no choice but to be prepared for any emergency that may arise.

ART. VII.—1. *A History of the Birds of Europe, including all the Species inhabiting the Western Palæarctic Region.* By HENRY E. DRESSER, F.L.S., F.Z.S., &c. London: 1871–1881.

2. *A History of British Birds.* By the late W. YARRELL. Fourth Edition, revised to the end of Part 26 by Professor NEWTON, F.R.S., and HOWARD SAUNDERS, F.L.S. London: 1884.

3. *Bird Life.* Being a History of the Bird, its Structure and Habits. By Dr. A. E. BREHM. Translated from the German by H. M. LABOUCHERE, F.Z.S., and W. JESSE, C.M.Z.S. London: 1874.

4. *Siberia in Europe.* A Visit to the Valley of Petchora, in North-East Russia; with Descriptions of the Natural History, Migration of Birds, &c. By HENRY SEEBOHM. London: 1880.

5. *Our Summer Migrants.* An Account of the Migratory Birds which pass the Summer in the British Islands. By J. E. HARTING, F.L.S., F.Z.S. London: 1875.

THE prominence which is given to the natural history of birds in such publications as the 'Field' and 'Land 'and Water,' and the frequent correspondence on all the incidents of bird life, prove the wide-spread interest which is felt in the feathered races. A few years since the 'Field' published some interesting statistics relating to migration which had been collected by the numerous correspondents of that journal, and these were afterwards abridged by Mr. J. E. Harting in his volume on 'Our 'Summer Migrants.' But an observer of migrants should himself be stationary, like Gilbert White, and the majority of country people who are interested in this branch of natural history are in these days almost as migratory as the wandering birds.

A similar attempt to that of the journal just mentioned has since been made under the auspices of the British Association. A committee was appointed to arrange the details of the proposed enquiry, and a very happily conceived method of collecting the necessary data having been resolved upon, printed forms and letters of instruction were distributed, by permission, among the keepers of the lightships and lighthouses on our coast. A more stationary, and, we may add, a more attentive and competent, set of observers could not have been selected for the task of watching the migrants and their landing or departure; and four annual reports, based on the replies of about two hundred observers, have since been prepared by such able ornithologists as Messrs. J. A. Harvie Brown, John Cordeaux, Philip M. C. Kermode, R. M. Barrington, and A. G. More, each gentleman dealing with a particular portion of the coast. Other observers, in other parts of the world, such as Mr. Gätke, of Heligoland, and Colonel Irby, of Gibraltar, have devoted themselves to the same work of general observation at various salient points, while a numerous staff of explorers, of whom Mr. Seebohm and Mr. Russell Wallace are admirable examples, have conducted their observations and collected the facts of bird life in all its aspects in every continent and country of the world. India is a little beyond the scope of our subject, but in speaking of the birds of Europe we may glance even at India, a country not too distant for the visits of the faster fliers in the season. India had been well explored some years since, as the appearance of the ' Birds ' of India,' by Mr. Jerdon, testified, but the congenial task of observation in a land so varied and extensive has been continued, there as elsewhere, by relays of naturalists from England who have found themselves stationed in that country, and a new edition of Mr. Jerdon's work, reprinted under the supervision of Lieut.-Colonel Godwin-Austen, F.R.S., shows both the method and extent of recent explorations and discoveries in ornithology in India. In all countries, in fact, the facilities, and we might say the rage, for travel in this age in which we live have borne fruit in connexion with our subject. The habits of birds have been everywhere observed, their regions marked out, and the range of their migrations defined.

In any attempt to explain phenomena so remarkable as some of the periodic movements of birds a knowledge of the facts relating to them is absolutely indispensable, and some progress has undoubtedly been made since the period, not very long ago, when naturalists gravely debated the pros and cons of the hybernation of swallows in pools and ponds, or since that more ancient time when the augurs watched the flight of birds and found an omen of good or evil according as the eagle might take its flight from left to right or the contrary. But the longer migrations of the feathered races, especially when they cross the sea, and not always by the nearest and easiest route, are still sufficiently puzzling. It will be well, therefore, in the course of our remarks on migration, if we advance gradually, considering first the simpler cases, which present no difficulty. It is obvious that some birds are always resident in this country, such as the sparrow, which supplies its wants the whole year round in the neighbourhood of our homesteads. Some of these residents are wanderers—in fact, every bird is a wanderer more or less when it shifts its quarters during the year in seeking its food. Some years since an expedition of rooks took their flight from the north coast of Scotland, crossed the Pentland Firth, and landed in the Orkney Islands, where a land proprietor near Kirkwall had been trying for years to raise plantations such as rooks might build in. But the brine blasts of the Atlantic drifting over the cliffs of Hoy had prevented his success, and the rooks, baffled in their object and finding only stunted shrubs instead of trees to build in, recrossed the straits after a short and fruitless visit. The experimental flights of birds for the sake of discovering nesting places, food, or some other object, must not be regarded as either vagrant or mysterious; for whatever name may attach to such excursions, they belong to a kind of migration which is constantly occurring. They may be compared, perhaps, to the rambles of gipsies, who set up their tents wherever they can find a vacant spot by the roadside, or perhaps they may be more accurately likened to the extension of a fir forest, which literally marches up the slopes of a Scotch hill and occupies new ground by the scattering of its seeds. By such 'accidents,' by wandering and migration in the case of man and other animals, and by an analogous seizure of new sites in the case of vegetables, the world has been peopled and planted.

In his work on the 'Distribution of Plants and Animals' Mr. Wallace remarks that migration in its simple form may be best studied in North America, where it takes place over a continuous land surface with changes of climate north and south. We have there every grade of migration, from that of species which merely shift the northern and southern limits of their range a few hundred miles, to that of some other species which move over 1,000 miles of latitude and are birds of passage in all the intervening districts. Some have extended their range under conditions favourable to them and induced by human agency, such as the rice bird and the Mexican swallow, and we may be sure that in all parts of the world the range of birds has always extended under favouring conditions of one kind or another. The cultivation of fresh tracts of land will bring such birds as follow the plough into new districts, and the pressure of an advancing bird population will carry the individuals composing it into all parts where life can be sustained. As the birds increase in any district they naturally wander farther, for the same reason that man himself emigrates from an overcrowded country. There is of course a distinction between migration and distribution, but when migrating birds become more widely distributed from any cause the range of their migration must necessarily be extended. So far as the initial motive is concerned all migrations are similar, though they differ widely in their extent and in the circumstances that attend them. The golden-crested wren, having exhausted its means of subsistence in a particular spot, travels perhaps a mile to the sunny side of the hill and finds there the desired aspect and its necessary food. This is an example of the simplest form of migration and of its shortest distance. The habit of wandering is well represented by the movements of the common starling. Starlings, we are told in 'Bird Life,' conduct themselves in a very singular manner, 'vanishing' with their young after the nesting time, 'associating rest- 'lessly with rooks,' 'flying from one part of the country to 'another, still congregating in larger masses, and then depart- 'ing.' This is a romantic rather than a scientific view of the 'conduct' of the starling, for no bird can be more regular and reasonable in its habits. It associates with rooks in England ; it is seen sitting on the backs of buffaloes in Egypt, and it is a matter of no small interest in connexion with its general motives that Charles Waterton induced the starlings of Walton Hall to alter their habits of breaking up into small families in spring. He provided the birds with convenient nesting places, and they became at once congregating builders like the rooks. Mr. Yarrell and his editors have written a full account of this bird, but even these competent authorities seem a little uncertain as to its migrations. 'About midsummer,' says Mr. Yarrell, ' some begin to cross 'the sea, and it would seem to be the ordinary habit of this 'species to move westwards as autumn approaches.' In fact, the starlings have travelled farther west in the United Kingdom than they were formerly accustomed to do. Mr. Rodd, author of 'The Birds of Cornwall and the Scilly Islands,' observed in 1873 that starlings reached farther west every year; he added that they were formerly unknown in the western counties, except as winter visitors, and that they had reached Truro and had bred for some years past at Trebartha, where they may now be seen throughout the whole of the spring and summer months. A correspondent in a journal of natural history recently remarked upon the scarcity of starlings in a district of Cardiganshire, and another correspondent took up the story and told of the unusual flight of starlings at that time in his part of Devonshire. The same western movement has included Ireland. Mr. R. L. Patterson, in 'The Birds, Fishes, ' and Cetacea frequenting Belfast Lough,' reported the circumstance of the starling having lately gone farther west than he had been in the habit of going in recent years, though not farther than it had reached seventy or eighty years ago. Mr. Patterson tells us starlings were quite rare in the neighbourhood of Belfast about thirty years since, where early in the century they had been abundant. About forty years ago they almost entirely disappeared from the neighbourhood, and after reappearing in small numbers they have gone on increasing, till at the present time flocks of 10,000 and 12,000 or more are not uncommon.

All these fluctuating movements, which occasion so much surprise and interest in the districts they affect, are dictated by the stomach. As a general rule starlings in early autumn quit dry arable districts, and seek those which are moist and pastoral. In hot dry years their food in the eastern counties fails them early, and in severe winters they are locked out of the same East Anglia by frost. They are missed in some parts of the country soon after midsummer and lost to others by October. They begin to move westwards then. In some localities the instinct of flocking is developed in September, when they begin to roost in company, forming what appears to be a 'fortuitous association,' first of thousands, then of tens of thousands. Their favourite roosting place is among the reeds at the shallow end of a large pond, whither towards sunset they hasten in little flocks and parties from all quarters, flying high and first alighting on some convenient fir trees for the purpose of holding a confabulation before descending among the reeds. Most birds confabulate at meeting; even the unsocial heron utters an unearthly quawk on spying a companion; but few birds chatter like starlings when collected in large flocks at their evening meeting before going to roost. The strong flying powers of this most robust and cheerful bird have been well described by Yarrell, and all who have seen them rendezvous according to their habit as autumn approaches must have observed their surprising power of wing displayed in rapid aerial evolutions, which they appear to engage in from excess of joy and for the sole purpose of displaying their wanton strength.

Some birds of inert constitution or slight strength of wing fly only from necessity. The feeble landrail, rising unwillingly with dependent legs, the type of unwilling effort and incertitude, would not be expected to indulge in aerial evolutions; the rook, on the contrary, often sports and plays aloft, while the swift is incomparable in its frolic flight; but a flock of starlings is unique in the number of the performers and the character of their flight. The whole aerial array seems to obey the signs or orders of a leader. Its formations—for they seem nothing less—are continually changing. Whether by command or by an effort of mutual sympathy, they wheel, close, open out, reform, rise higher from the ground, or again descend towards it, with wonderful precision notwithstanding their very rapid flight. Sometimes, as in other evolutions conducted before an enemy, they extend in a long thin line, which presently is seen to undulate, then to spread out like a sheet in the air; and then, at the will of a commander, as one might well believe, the exercising mass takes the form of a spiral figure, becomes pear-shaped, assumes the likeness of a smoke-like cloud, and the next moment becomes a dense and almost perfect globe. The easy motions of these birds in flight were well described by Gilbert White when he said 'starlings as it were swim along.' They are always active, whether racing along the grass in pursuit of food or amusing themselves in the air, whether streaming softly, as they sometimes do, close to the ground, dropping like a shower of falling stones into their roosting covert, alighting on the grass, or mounting and circling aloft. Their manœuvring is magnificent.

Naturalists have drawn distinctions between different kinds of migration, which they have classified as those of spring, when our summer migrants arrive, departing again after breeding, and those of autumn, by birds that winter here and depart from our shores in spring. The 'birds of passage,' as they are called, which pass through a country without remaining long, are bent on exactly the same business as the true migrants. They are simply passing to their quarters. A fieldfare prefers England to the Arctic circle in winter, and comes here accordingly, and, if he rests on Heligoland, he is there a bird of passage. In spring he returns perhaps. A bird of passage may breed in the north or south; he may pass the particular spot where he is observed as a bird of passage in autumn or in spring; his migration may be long or short; but he is at each end of his two journeys a true migrant, like the swallow, or like those sweet warblers in our groves and hedges which disappear entirely at their season, while the partial migrants—pied wagtails, woodcocks, snipes, and others—do not entirely leave us. The song thrush and robin are among the birds which as species remain always with us, but the number of individuals of all these kinds is increased by migration in spring and autumn more extensively than casual observers might imagine. The redbreasts, though they do not flock at the end of summer, pass constantly southwards, prompted by their migratory instincts, and do not stop at the Channel. Another movement of a migratory character on the part of the same familiar birds is that which brings them to our homesteads on the approach of severe weather. This is not migration in the ordinary sense, and it offers no problem hard to solve, but the short journeys are undertaken with the same object as the long ones, and they may serve as illustrations of the first promptings of the instinct of migration. The flight from wood and field offers no difficulty; it is guided evidently by sight and memory of former flittings; or perhaps some of the inexperienced birds may wander hither and thither for a while seeking the shelter and food they need, finding it haphazard, or failing to do so and perishing in their search. The long flights of cranes and other strong-winged birds have formed the subject of theories still wilder than the flights perhaps, and arising from the insufficiency of the facts relating to them. The argument should be inductive. The short flittings perhaps will be found to explain the longer, and thus the mystery may be found to rest on simple causes after all.

We have shown the frequency with which several supposed residents wander, and Professor Newton tells us in his able article in the new edition of the ' Encyclopædia Britan- ' nica ' that ' there is scarcely a bird of either the palæarctic ' or nearctic region whose habits are at all well known of ' which much the same may not be said ; and hence we are ' led to the conclusion that every bird of the northern hemi- ' sphere is, to a greater or less degree, migratory in some ' part or other of its range.' Even the staid rook wanders, reaching Dunvegan Wood in the Isle of Skye, and increasing with the timber in Argyleshire. We have not met with it in Shetland, and it has not yet reached Greenland. It occasionally visits such scattered islands as the Faroes, and in some countries it is a regular migrant. In Norway it is as a rule a migrant, arriving in February, March, or April, and leaving in October and November, but sometimes it remains through the winter both in the coast districts and in the

interior. Occasionally, as in 1842 and 1843, it comes in large
flocks in all parts of Norway below the fells. It is common
in South Sweden, rare in the north. In the south of Finland
it is 'tolerably rare;' common in Central Russia, where it
nests in large colonies. It breeds sometimes as far north as
Archangel. It winters frequently in the birch woods of the
Ural; and Mr. Jacovleff speaks of it as being numerous at
Astrachan, whence it migrates for a short time only, and
therefore cannot go far. It is met with in the Baltic provinces and in Poland, and is said to be a migrant throughout
North Germany everywhere but in the mountains. There is
a large rookery in the Nassau territory. In Denmark it is
a migrant, taking up its residence in the country during
summer and leaving for the south in large flocks in October
and November. The rook builds in large colonies in Belgium,
and would perhaps be as numerous in Holland as in England
but for the common practice of destroying the nests everywhere except in the province of Guelderland, where it is
allowed to remain unmolested in the woods and parks of
the Dutch nobility. In France the rook is a winter visitant
only in the south, while it breeds in the north and is generally common. It winters in Spain from November till
March, and frequents Southern Europe at the same season,
appearing in Sicily and Sardinia, but never remaining in
those islands to breed. A writer to the 'Ibis,' in 1864,
records its presence as a bird of passage at Malta in the
months of October and November and December, associating
during its visit with the starlings and jackdaws, as it does
here. Lord Lilford, to whom, as president of the British
Ornithologists' Union, Mr. Dresser dedicates his volumes, has
seen the rook in Corfu and Epirus, where it winters in large
numbers. Captain R. M. Sperling has observed many young
birds of the year in Greece in the winter, from which he infers
that only the young migrate to that country. They never
remain to breed in the northern provinces. In Belgium,
Southern Russia, and Bessarabia it is common, especially
along the great rivers. In the Crimea it only leaves in the
most rigorous winters, and returns to its nesting places in
February. It is numerous in the Caucasus, and Canon
Tristram, who met with it in Palestine, wrote as follows
to the 'Ibis:'—

'We were riding across the plain from Nablous on the road to
Jerusalem, when for the first time we noticed the rooks fearlessly following Arab ploughmen at their work. They seemed to smell powder
as promptly as their fellows in England; but we obtained two, which

although December was far advanced had no denudation of the basal portion of the mandible. We occasionally met with small flocks in the cultivated districts of Central Palestine, but did not come across any rookeries, unless the gathering at the Mosque of Omar at Jerusalem may be so termed. Jerusalem and Nablous seem the head-quarters of the race; indeed, in a country so bare of wood the rook must be as hard put to for a home as in Central France after the Revolution had stripped the *châteaux* of their ancestral timber. At Jerusalem we found the species very abundant in winter, congregating in the central inclosure of the Mosque every evening along with jackdaws, a few hooded crows, and the two species of ravens as familiarly as it does with the first of these in England. The different species appeared to go out to feed together, and returned in consort to roost every evening.'

In Egypt the rook is described in Captain Shelley's 'Birds 'of Egypt' as being common in the Delta, except during its absence in the breeding season. It is rarely seen south of Cairo, its favourite food of snails and slugs being entirely absent from Upper Egypt. It is rare in Algeria. We learn from Dr. Jerdon's 'Birds of India' that the rook is found in the Punjaub and in Cashmere in the cold weather, as well as in Afghanistan, feeding chiefly in the ploughed fields. It frequents the steppes and wooded districts of Turkestan, migrating southwards in winter. In China and Japan this familiar bird is replaced by the closely allied form *Corvus pastinator,* which differs in having the head and neck glossed with purple and not with green.

Among the numerous recent books on ornithology, Mr. Dresser's 'History of the Birds of Europe' is the first general work in the English language since the publication of Gould's 'Birds of Europe' and of Dr. C. R. Bree's book bearing the same title. The investigations of travellers and naturalists have added considerably to our knowledge of the feathered races, and Mr. Dresser accordingly is able to include 175 species which had not been previously described in any English work on ornithology. Mr. Gould's list included 449 species; Temminck's, in his first edition of the 'Manuel d'Ornithologie,' 324 species, and in his second edition, after deducting bad species and those which are extra-limital, 462 species. Mr. Dresser is able to enumerate 624 species, including 10 which are restricted to the Atlantic islands and 27 to North Africa; and with the advance of ornithological researches, especially in the less explored districts of the Caucasus and Asia Minor, the number of European, or more correctly of western palæarctic, species will probably be still further increased.

In settling the limits of the great bird region embraced by his work, Mr. Dresser very properly adopted natural instead of political boundaries. Few barriers, not even the Atlantic or the deserts of Africa, are quite impracticable for the passage of wings. The wonderful movements of migration, occurring at a height sometimes of four miles above the earth, at a speed of forty geographical miles an hour in some cases, frequently defy all boundaries. The red-spotted bluethroat passes from North Africa to Heligoland in a single night, and other specimens of birds have passed at a stretch from the Old World to the New. According to Mr. Gätke, whose observations in Heligoland have extended over forty years, they have passed in a direct line from Newfoundland to Ireland, and although Mr. Dresser excludes American birds from the European fauna he mentions six species obtained and preserved by Mr. Gätke in Heligoland after crossing the Atlantic.

The western palæarctic region may be taken as including all Europe to the Urals, the British Isles, Ireland, the Faroes, the Azores, Madeira, the Canary Islands, the strip of North Africa bounded by the Desert, the Caucasus, and Asia Minor, with the exception of the Jordan valley. As our migrants do not cross the Atlantic even so far as the Azores, America is not included in this Greater Britain, and in that direction the ocean may be looked upon as the effective barrier of their wanderings. The boundaries of the bird region in the east and south can only be fixed approximately. Mr. Dresser, however, has placed the Ural range and the Ural River as boundaries in that direction, drawing a line thence along the western shores of the Caspian to the frontiers of Persia, and thence across the Euphrates southward along the borders of the Arabian Desert to the Red Sea. In Africa the tropic of Cancer forms his boundary, extending the domain of the European birds to the first cataract of the Nile in Eastern Africa, and about as far as the Ouro River on its western side. In mapping out the bird districts rigid and undeviating lines must be discarded, as being inappropriate in the case of creatures endowed with such wonderful powers of moving from one part of the world to another. We may divide the palæarctic region broadly into a warmer and colder region, these islands and Central Europe, with the countries extending to the Urals and the Caucasus, belonging to the latter.

It is obvious that various sub-regions must be included within these wide boundaries. Both the distribution and the migration of birds are liable to occasional modification, and are sometimes restricted within a somewhat narrow range, while in other cases they extend over the widest limits. At first sight it would appear that the only barriers capable of limiting the range of birds must be the widest seas or the loftiest mountains, and that their unique powers would render them the most ubiquitous of creatures. But in spite of the restless gulls and petrels, sandpipers and plovers, which are respectively the greatest wanderers by sea and land, there are numerous birds whose travels are by no means so extensive as their powers of volition. They never travel without a purpose, and many groups of birds exist, as in the case of other animals and of plants, which are strictly confined within narrow limits.

Seeking our examples of isolated species outside the boundaries laid down by Mr. Dresser, there are several western perching birds—pigeons and parrots—whose farthest wanderings are limited within the confines of a few small islands or of particular valleys and mountains. The blue macaw and other birds of South America keep to their respective sides of the Amazon, and never venture upon crossing that river; while some of the monkeys of the same region observe at present the same rule, and keep to their own particular forests, though adjoining districts similar to their own, but on the wrong side of some petty stream, might seem to invite them. Distribution in both these cases is influenced by the supply of food; and scarcity, arising from an increase of the population or from some other cause, would occasion immediate emigration, as it has done everywhere in all ages among all sorts of animals, winged or otherwise. The same conditions which influence distribution affect migration. There are birds of the plains and of the woods. In Scotland capercailzie frequent the large fir forests of Taymouth and Dunkeld; grouse prefer the moors, ptarmigan the snow-capped crest of Ben Nevis, while at the base of that mountain, below the belt where grouse are found, the partridge breeds on the cultivated land and seeks its food in the fields. All these phenomena connected with the distribution, the permanent residence of birds, and their migration, or occasional shifting of residence, are determined by food, climate, the prevalence of destructive enemies, and the convenience of nesting, as in the case of the numerous sea birds which quit the level shores around the English coasts and resort to Shetland in the breeding season for the sake of its cliffs and sea-bird cradles, as well as for the small fry that swarm among its *voes* and creeks.

'In South America,' says Mr. Wallace, 'the same birds are comparatively scarce in the forest plains, where monkeys are very abundant, while they are plentiful on the open plains and campos, and on the mountain plateaux, where these nest-hunting quadrupeds are rarely found.'

The character of the soil and site also influences bird life, and therefore migration. There are birds of the swamps and streams, of the mountains, the deserts, and the grassy plains. Speaking generally the migrants that resort to our shores in winter come from the northern sub-region already indicated. Our summer migrants, the swallow, cuckoo, nightingale, and others more or less familiar, come from the southern sub-region, from the Mediterranean basin, from the Nile as far as the first cataract, the Pyrenees, Alps, Balkans, Caucasus, and other districts belonging to the second of the two great divisions of what Mr. Dresser has designated the European bird region. It is interesting to observe at what a leisurely pace migration proceeds in some districts, how rapid it becomes under a pressing emergency, how thorough and complete the removal of the birds is in localities where the food supply absolutely fails, while in others it is only partial, a limited bird population always remaining. The migrants quit the burning plains of Central Africa on the same principle that they leave the inclement north. In each district the animal and vegetable food which abounds in one case in winter, in the other in summer, entirely fails them, and their banishment is complete. But the manner of leaving differs, since there is rarely any urgency in the exit from the warmer countries, where the period of migration frequently extends over several weeks. In autumn, on the contrary, the climate of the north sometimes closes up all food resources suddenly, and at such times a continual stream of birds arrives on our shores, showing how great the pressure in the rear must be. Naturalists have observed the same phenomena, both in other countries and other times. Homer, for example, described the autumnal flocking of waterfowl to the rivers of Inner Asia, and Dr. Brehm, writing the other day of what he had seen in Eastern Soudan in September, observed that the migrating storks 'literally covered the broad level lands by 'river sides, and when they rose filled the whole horizon.'

It must not be imagined that migratory travels are free from danger. On the contrary, stray birds which have lost their way from the effects of storms driving them from their course, or from ignorance of their route, or the failure of an instinct which is not unerring in their case, are common. A curious example of the occasional adventures of migrants occurs in the case of American birds, especially the shore birds from North America, which sometimes pay us visits, that our naturalists appreciate, though the birds themselves had no intention of crossing the Atlantic. It is curious too that these birds usually appear on our eastern coasts, and not on the shores nearest their homes. It is true that there are very few ornithologists in Ireland, where rare birds are particularly scarce, and where, from that cause perhaps, the number of bird observers is very few; but the numerous gunners of Ireland are alive to the commercial value of rare birds, and American visitants, if there were any, would soon find their way to the market.

The majority of the stragglers from across the Atlantic reach the east coast by the same route which has carried several Transatlantic birds to Heligoland, an island 100 acres in extent and the most wonderful bird land in the world, where 15,000 migrant larks have been caught in one night, and where several species of American birds have been captured which have never been taken elsewhere in Europe. The wind is the agent of these ocean trips. The victims are species which breed in the high northern latitudes, and on their way to their winter quarters they are driven out to sea by violent western gales, stormy winds of the North Atlantic which strike the coast of Norway. Having reached Norway, the wanderers cross with allied species to our east coast, and thence they follow the shore line to the Land's End, a spot where Transatlantic stragglers have been found in greater numbers than elsewhere in the United Kingdom except in Norfolk and Suffolk.

Probably no portion of the correspondence in journals devoted to natural history is more eagerly scanned than that which reports both the regular and the unwonted arrivals of birds which either come in due course or are driven into new neighbourhoods by hunger. Such facts are observed perhaps with greater interest owing to our consciousness that we cannot wing our own way up wind, or down, by means of any mechanical contrivance, with all our scientific skill. In this respect we cannot rival

' The happy birds that change their sky
To build and brood, that live their lives
From land to land.'

The birds, therefore, are watched with universal interest. Everybody misses the shriek of the swift at its departure; everyone mourns that assemblage of swallows which betokens the end of summer, the close of a season of life and production and the approaching advent of winter. Our position in Europe is favourable to the observation both of the spring and autumn migrants—of those which arrive from the north to winter here, and of those which come from the south, breed at the period when food is most abundant, and then depart to avoid the season of scarcity.

Our southern downs and eastern coasts are good positions for observation; but most of our southern migrants and many others converge at Gibraltar, one of the three points where the birds from beyond the Mediterranean cross that sea for Europe, and again on their return. Colonel Irby, author of the 'Ornithology of the Straits of Gibraltar,' observes that 'the best site for watching the departure of ' the vernal migration is at Tangier, where, just outside the ' town, the well-known plain called the Marsham, a high ' piece of ground that in England would be called a common, ' seems to be the starting point for half the small birds that ' visit Europe.' During a Levanter, or easterly wind, which they prefer for their passage, he has watched them all from this point—raptores such as kites, honey buzzards, and the other predatory species, songsters, and the rest.

Mr. A. E. Knox, author of 'Ornithological Rambles in ' Sussex' and an original observer of the habits of the several migrants, has watched them to the coast and witnessed their return. Following their autumn movement from the interior of the country, the various detachments may be observed arriving and departing one after the other. Early in September the departing wagtails reach the coast, passing on so steadfastly that even the Downs are a well-known rendezvous for migrants at this period, and here the vast flocks alight for rest, and then resuming their journey westwards, they reach the shores of Kent, and cross the Channel at its narrowest part. At the return of the wagtails about the middle of March, Mr. Knox has seen them on fine days approaching the coast aided by a gentle breeze from the south, their well-known call note being often distinctly audible from a considerable distance at sea and long before they came in sight. In favourable weather small parties may be noticed continually dropping on the beach. At this time their sudden appearance may often be observed when, after a few days' lingering on the coast to regain their strength, they commence their dispersal over the inland parts of the country, and in a few days the fields, where hardly a wagtail could previously be seen, abound with them. Every parish in England may be said to reflect these movements. Speaking of several migratory birds, Mr. Harting says ' there is something almost mysterious in the way in which ' numbers of these small and delicately formed birds are ' found scattered one day over a parish where on the pre- ' vious day not one was to be seen.'

The pied wagtail may be taken as a representative among those small birds that gather on our coasts in great flocks at their departure, and disperse on their return to enliven the country and restore the bird population of the interior. It is both a resident species and a partial migrant, leaving us at the approach of winter. The white wagtail is altogether a migrant, local in its distribution and remaining with us through the summer only, though abroad it ranges through- out the whole of Europe and farther south into the heart of Africa. The grey wagtail, on the contrary, does not go far north in Europe—not farther, Mr. Harting thinks, than Northern Germany. It may be regarded as one of the birds of mystery, since we read in Professor Newton's edition of Yarrell's ' British Birds ' that its movements vary un- accountably as regards places even within a short distance of each other. It is a winter visitant in the southern counties and a summer visitant in the north of England. Except the dipper it is the most aquatic of all the passeres, placing its nest near water in the bank of a stream or the crevice of an overhanging rock, concealing it so skilfully that Mr. Harting waited long before he found the opportunity of watching it in the act of building its nest.

So far as the United Kingdom is concerned, Professor Newton marks off the habitual breeding places of this very interesting, restless, graceful little bird by a line drawn from the Start Point to the Tees, curving southwards so as to include the Derbyshire hills. Nests are occasionally found, however, even in the southern counties, and towards the end of summer the bird makes its appearance even in Shet- land. Its southern migrations sometimes end this side of the Channel, but they extend as a rule to the countries of the Mediterranean, North Africa, the central highlands of Abyssinia, the Azores, and perhaps to India, China, and Japan; but this is one of the several birds whose range has not been ascertained, for although travellers are numerous, naturalists possessing exact knowledge, enabling them to distinguish between closely allied species, are not so, and those observers who have reported the grey wagtail in the far east are believed by some ornithologists to have confounded it with the wagtail *Motacilla melanope*, an allied form with a shorter tail. As a species, therefore, it is a permanent resident like the pied wagtail; as an individual it is a migrant. The habits of this bird are solitary. It is usually found in pairs or in small family parties on the stony margins of brook sides, where it seeks water beetles, wading in the shallows or running rapidly along the banks, springing into the air occasionally in pursuit of insects. It is the shiest of the wagtails, except during migration, when an overpowering instinct emboldens it and it does not scruple to approach dwelling-houses, and even to enter large towns, where it chases the flies over the roofs of the houses. It is, in fact, tamed and made friendly by hunger, just as that other shy bird the wood pigeon becomes familiar under compulsion of another kind, when it suddenly throws off its timidity and builds, and sits, and rears its young in our gardens.

The arrivals of migrants are influenced by the strength and direction of the wind. They seldom fly dead to windward, but generally within three or four points of the wind. A strong wind checks their progress. They cross the sea at all hours of the day and night, flying on fine starlight nights at a great height, so that numbers must pass over unobserved, or only detected by those weird sounds the noise of wings and cries described by Tennyson in the 'Passing of Arthur'—

> ' And fainter onward, like wild birds that change
>   Their season in the night, and wail their way
>   From cloud to cloud.'

The direction taken by the flocks of passerine birds in spring is from east to west along the entire east coast of England and Scotland, with a noticeable inclination from the S.E. and S. In 1879 the main body of immigrants crossed over at the southernmost stations, where the North Sea is narrowest; in 1880 they arrived upon the midland and south-eastern portions of the coast. The direction of the migrants passing southwards in autumn was along the coast line from north to south. The period occupied in migrating by any given species varies, and often extends over several weeks, or even months. Migrants, in fact, seem to be crossing the North Sea all the year round, and no sooner does the ebb of the autumn migration cease than the flood sets in and birds begin to pass northwards again.

We learn from these reports, and from other statements,

that there are rules of the road, which the feathered tribes obey ; some travel by night, some by day, and the latter as a rule are said to seek safety in their numbers and the rapidity of their flight. Preserving strict order during their journey, some of the migrants maintain a wedge-shaped disposition of their masses with a leader in front, as geese, ducks, and cranes. Rooks and jackdaws have a curious habit of varying the height at which they fly. They generally press forward on their journey at a great elevation, till suddenly some among the number drop down several hundred feet with closed wings, when others follow suit, till presently the whole company has changed its level and is pressing on at only a hundred feet from the ground. The flocks of migrating birds are usually irregular in shape, with open spaces between several batches. Swallows catch insects as they go, and a pilot bird usually precedes them. Among all the migrants the flight of storks, if we may pass for a moment beyond our own boundaries, affords the most beautiful spectacle, owing to their extraordinary powers of wing and to the gambols and aerial *ballets* which they practise while still advancing rapidly with each successive sweep of their strong wings. All birds of prey in large bands display the same sportive disposition on the wing.

Dr. Brehm says that the hours of travelling vary both by habit and from other causes. As a rule the birds that travel by day rest in the afternoon, unless when anxious to get on, when they make an evening journey and start again before daybreak. The anticipation of bad weather turns skylarks and several other day fliers into nocturnal migrants for the nonce. Cranes in a hurry travel by night, or when they have been disturbed in their roosting places. The true nocturnal migrants which 'fly by night,' like the witches in 'Macbeth,' include several bad fliers, and some which are not so. Among them are the owls, goatsuckers, kingfishers, buntings (poor fliers), quails, moorhens (weak on the wing), bitterns, night herons, ducks, dippers or water ousels, missel thrushes, blackbirds, nightingales, robins (feeble in body, strong at heart).

An advantage of the night passage is that the birds pass untroubled by the enemies that at other times molest them. All migrants alike are hindered by adverse weather, but not by a moderate head wind, which is advantageous to them, whereas a stern wind disturbs their steering process. Whatever leaders they may follow, the majority are invariably well led. Some birds find it more convenient to take the journey alone. They do not all travel on the wing—grebes, cormorants, and divers using rivers, lakes, and even seas, in the course of their passage, gathering their usual aquatic food on the way. There are also land as well as water migrants, such as the landrail, who may be met with during migration both in Spain and Egypt, and from the interior of Africa as far as 12° north latitude, passing through our corn fields by obscure routes, craking in the next field to the village and the county town, but always safe, for few dogs can flush him and the nearest land grip hides him.

As to the height at which migrants make their passage, they are probably guided by the same considerations as balloonists, and are anxious to catch a favourable current of wind wherever they may find it. The higher flights are safest, and the curlews and other strong fliers may ' wail ' their way' too high for the ear to detect them; while many small birds may be seen, as the light-keepers have reported, feebly struggling against adverse winds at low levels and beaten in the contest. On dark nights thousands succumb from another cause when, tired and puzzled by the bright light, they strike against the lanterns of the lighthouses. The flocks of birds that arrive with a favourable wind, we are told, often show no signs of fatigue, and pass at once to the interior without alighting on the coast for rest.

The gathering of flocks of migrants at their departure commences in the neighbourhood of Brighton, Shoreham, and Worthing early in September, and the meadow pipits are the birds that first put in an appearance. With the pipits came, till lately, the bird catchers, and it is on record that one of these men caught with a clap net twenty-four dozen meadow pipits near Brighton in a single morning. Tree pipits and pied and yellow wagtails also arrive early. Many of these birds are bred in the northern and western counties, and having reached the Downs, they probably do not cross the Channel unless under compulsion of unusually severe weather later in the year. Many of them certainly remain with us through the winter. After these come the finches—goldfinches, greenfinches, and chaffinches.

In the cage-bird business the staple trade for October used to be in linnets, goldfinches, and larks, whose ' autumn ' flight' commences the last week in September and continues through October. The late-hatched birds take their flight last. They stay near their natal places in the midland counties or elsewhere till they are in full feather, and then set out for the sea, mustering as they go.

The flight of the various tribes of birds ends between the first and the middle of November, when those occasional migrants, including always some of the goldfinches which remain on this side of the Channel, retire to various secluded spots among the Downs. The home-keeping migrants were known among bird catchers as 'harbour birds,' because they harboured in Sussex while others emigrated; and in April the ' harbour bird ' was recognised by its dull, indifferent plumage and shyness, while the flight birds were known by their advanced plumage, acquired in a warmer climate, and by their tame and unsuspicious manners. In spring countless larks, linnets, and finches arrive during March and April, and after resting for a while pass on to the various counties which last year gave them birth.

Wheatears have been seen in Sussex at an earlier date, but these perhaps were not migrants; for this bird, like the stonechat, sometimes winters with us, and the individuals that do so are less shy than the strangers and more tolerant of a near approach. The wheatear is a night traveller, and is rarely seen to land on our shores later than early dawn. Though short-winged its geographical range is very extensive, extending over the whole of Great Britain, the colder regions farther north, the Faroe Islands, Iceland, Greenland, Lapland, Norway, Sweden, Denmark, throughout Europe to the Mediterranean, and farther east to Egypt, Arabia, Asia Minor, and Armenia. Its name is most probably derived from the *white ear* which is conspicuous in its spring plumage; or from the time of wheat harvest, which corresponds to its best season for the table. Hundreds of dozens of wheatears were formerly trapped upon the South Downs during wheat harvest, as Gilbert White and others have observed, but among the changes since the 'Natural ' History of Selborne ' was compiled we have to notice a general diminution in the numbers of some kinds of birds and a great increase in others. The practice among South Down shepherds of snaring wheatears in autumn has declined, and wheatear pie is no longer the boast of Eastbourne. The landrail has become much more plentiful, since Gilbert White rarely saw more than one or two specimens of this ' rare ' bird in a season, while at present three or four are often bagged in a single day's partridge shooting. The common bunting was also a rare bird in 1768 in White's district. It is now a very common one.

The whinchat, a bird very unequally distributed in different parts of England, and in Scotland as far as Caithness and

the Hebrides, where it arrives a fortnight later than in
Sussex, lands on the south coast at the end of the first week
in April precisely. It never winters here like the stonechat,
and is very numerous in the southern counties, and comparatively scarce in Ireland, exactly the reverse of this being
the case with regard to the stonechat. Mr. Harting has
noticed extraordinary numbers of the bird in some seasons,
while in others he could scarcely count two or three in a
parish. They alter their plans, he says, in cold wet springs,
which check the migration by inducing them to spend the
summer at some place north or north-west of their winter
quarters and nearer to them. These quarters may be the
coasts of Africa from Senegal or Gambia to Egypt, or in
Nubia, Abyssinia, Arabia, and possibly Persia, and as far
eastward as the north-west provinces of India.

The whinchat arrives a little later than the other chats,
and is the greatest traveller of their class, its migrations extending to Japan. Those whose tastes lead them to visit often
the wilder spots and more retired furze fields and wastes of the
Downs or other localities, are well aware how suddenly the
handsome little male stonechat, in his wedding dress— head
of jet black, white collar, ferruginous breast—enlivens such
spots by his sprightly presence. The furze is in full blossom
of yellow and gold early in May, soon after his arrival, and
at that particular time he mounts his thorny perch and
does his very best in the way of impassioned song—hoarse-
throated, harsh-voiced little monster as he is—jerking his
tail all the time. On May 1 the grasshopper warbler commences chirping like a cricket; and about this time all the
summer warblers and migratory choristers are in tune.

Five species of the warblers, grouped under the generic
term Sylvia, or fruit-eaters, are common in gardens, and are
all fine songsters, much esteemed as cage birds. The blackcap, garden warbler, and, to a less extent, the whitethroat
and lesser whitethroat are all favourites with the bird
catchers, and are all common to the neighbourhood of the
metropolis and its fruit gardens of Kent, Surrey, and Middlesex, and to the south-eastern counties generally. As
might be expected, these species follow cultivation, and they
are now dispersed over portions of Great Britain where they
were formerly unknown or rare, showing by one more illustration the dependence of the distribution of birds on the
food supply. Like the nightingale, the blackcap migrates
almost due north and south, ranging from Lapland to the
Cape. It is resident in Madeira, the Azores, and the

Canaries, and is also found in Northern Africa and Southern Italy at all seasons, while in Spain and Portugal it is a bird of passage only, found only during the periods of migration in spring and autumn.

Among all the migrants the swallow has, perhaps, attracted most attention in all ages and countries. It arrives in Sussex villages with remarkable punctuality; none of the migrants perform their journeys more rapidly than the swallows and their congeners. A swift with young ones, or during migration, covers from 1,500 to 2,000 miles a day. It begins business feeding its young about 3 o'clock A.M. and continues it till 9 P.M. At that season, therefore, the swift spends nearly eighteen hours upon the wing, and it has been computed that at the ordinary rate of travelling of this very fast bird it would circumnavigate the globe in about fourteen days. At a push, if it were making forced flights, the swift would probably keep on the wing, with very brief intervals of rest, during fourteen days. The speed of the whole tribe is marvellous, and seems the more so when compared with that of the swiftest of animals that depend for their progressive powers on legs, however many legs they may be furnished with. The hare is swift, yet in Turner's well-known picture of rain, steam, and speed, the hare's fate is sealed; she will be run over and crushed by the engine rushing in her wake. The swiftest animals would soon break down at forty miles an hour, which the swallow unconsciously accomplishes, merrily twittering all the while. All the swallow tribe are found in every part of Great Britain, including Shetland, except the swift, which is not found in those islands. Dr. Saxby, author of ' Birds of ' Shetland,' says that one day a poor fellow, a cripple, who happened at the time to be exceedingly ill off and in want of food, came to him with a swallow in his hand. The Doctor ordered the man some dinner. It seems he had opened his door, restless and half famished, when in flew the swallow and brought him, so to speak, a dinner. ' After this,' said the poor fellow, ' folk need na tell me that the Lord does na answer prayer.' The swallow can hardly be inelegant. When it walks, however, it does so with particularly short steps, assisted by the wings, and in accomplishing any journey longer than a few inches it spreads its wings and takes flight. It twitters both on the wing and on the nest, and a more incessant, cheerful, amiable, happy little song no other musician has ever executed.

So far as migration is concerned, our predecessors believed, before and since the time of Gilbert White, that swallows wintered in deep pools. Modern naturalists are not keener-sighted than Gilbert White, but they travel more, and the ocean telegraph can be used to report retreating birds as well as approaching storms. The swallows disappear suddenly; they are followed across the Channel, watched at Gibraltar, reported coasting along the shores of North Africa, and then duly cabled as catching flies and twittering at Cairo or Jerusalem. The swift remains in England about three months, coming the first week in May and leaving early in August. During their brief but welcome visit you may count this familiar bird of our villages in packs of fifty or sixty coursing and screeching round the church tower or amusing the village as they cross and recross the street by their wild and headlong flight and mad exuberance. And so familiar, so home-like is that wild screeching, that one would not willingly diminish the number of swifts. In some cases this has been done by stopping up their nesting holes in repairing the roofs of old buildings which used formerly to harbour them. Every church tower should accommodate a hundred pairs.

Much has been said of that ' inexplicable longing ' and ' incomprehensible presentiment of coming events ' which occasion birds to migrate from certain districts before the food supplies begin to fail. Quails, woodcocks, snipes, and many other birds, it is said, are in the finest condition at the time of commencing their migration, while none of them are emaciated at that season, so that the pinch of hunger, it is argued, cannot have yet affected them. But it should be remembered that fat as well as lean birds may feel that pinch, and that birds are very fast-living creatures, full of life, movement, and alertness, quick to observe, to feel, and to act. In the rapid digestion of their food they are assisted by a special organ which grinds down such items as grain, gravel, nails, or needles, swallowed in mistake or from caprice or curiosity, with astonishing facility. They prefer feeding nearly all day, and when well crammed they sometimes become as plump as ortolans, or as well-fed quails, whose skin bursts when they fall to the gun. But when the appetite is urgent, obesity does not by any means preclude hunger. Twelve hours' fast and snow and a change of wind are very urgent facts in the lives of these quick creatures in the autumn of the year, and then begins that sudden migration which the lighthouse keepers have observed.

It is impossible to imagine creatures more practical and full of action and freer from ' presentiments ' than birds, engaged as they are from day to day snatching their food at Nature's board. Perhaps we may compare them to the guests of Macbeth, since all goes well so long as the ghost abstains from making his appearance; but very suddenly sometimes, in the case of the northern birds, the spectre of hunger puts them to flight. Fat or lean, they must go on the instant, and that is why they arrive pell-mell upon our coast; but, as the country to be cleared of its birds of summer is extensive and the distances of the journeys various, they naturally arrive at intervals.

Those parts of Africa and Siberia which are rendered absolutely sterile at certain periods of the year by heat and cold lose their bird population entirely during the winter months. Seebohm, writing from the valley of the Petchora, north of latitude 50°, where the country is alternately desolate and teeming with life, says that although birds resort to the Arctic regions to breed by millions, the number of species to be found within the Arctic circle is comparatively small. These regions are frost-bound during eight months out of the twelve, and the ground covered with snow from three to six feet deep. The few birds that remain within the Arctic circle forsake the tundra where they breed to find food in the pine forests, 'a few only remaining where the shelter of ' a deep valley or watercourse gives cover to a few stunted ' willows, birches, and hazel bushes. Practically it may be ' said that there is no spring or autumn in the Arctic regions. ' Summer follows suddenly upon winter, and the tundra as ' suddenly swarm with bird life.' Food most lavishly supplied forms the attraction of the migrants. 'Seed- or fruit-' eating birds find an immediate and abundant supply of ' cranberries, crowberries, and other ground fruit, which have ' remained frozen during the long winter and are accessible ' the moment the snow has melted; whilst insect-eating ' birds have only to open their mouths to fill them with ' mosquitoes.'

It is evident that the more uniformly adverse the climate may be at particular seasons, and the larger the extent of surface affected by its influence, the more complete must be the migration of the birds. Long-continued frost is their implacable enemy, and inclement weather of any kind is hostile to them. During that series of wet summers and severe winters which occurred throughout Europe early in this century the bird population became seriously reduced by the failure of their usual food supply, and in much more recent years the warblers and insect-finding birds have been known to suffer severely from the effects of unwonted cold or deep snow. Occasional calamities of this kind have over-taken both hemispheres, and north and south have each suffered in turn.

The migrations of birds are world-wide. The birds of North America make corresponding movements to those of Northern Europe, travelling in a north-easterly and south-westerly direction and at the same seasons. The countries of the Gulf of Mexico form the chief retreat of the North American migrants, especially Mexico itself with its three zones and great variety of climate. But some of them go as far as the West Indies and New Granada. A great number winter in the Southern States. Their method of migration is the same as that which has been described elsewhere. They follow the routes marked out by Nature. The kinds of birds are in many cases the same, or they are at least American representatives of the same families that form the migrants of the Old World. They travel southwards in the autumn and return again in spring.

The migrants of the southern hemisphere are constrained by their situation to reverse the direction of their periodic movements, flying northwards to escape the rigour of winter and returning south in spring. From March to September some of the most inhospitable regions of the south are quite deserted; even the wingless penguins quit their native shores of Tierra del Fuego and the Falkland Islands after the breed-ing season and swim to milder regions, while many of the birds which have bred in Patagonia and Southern Chili depart on the approach of winter. The same rules, according to Gould, govern the movements of birds in Australia, where several species migrate in summer to the southern portion of the continent and to Tasmania to breed.

The most persistent of our migrants are the soft-billed feeders upon insects, such, for example, as the swallow, which usually defers its departure till late in September, when one of the last insects it feeds on—the daddy longlegs, the parent of the mischievous tipula, which leaves its chrysalis during that month—rises from the pastures by millions. The tits, which supplement insects with a vegetable diet, are less easily inconvenienced and are only partial migrants. In some locali-ties they remain, in others they ramble, and in others they find it necessary to migrate in earnest to a distance. The permanent resident, as already said, developes into a local race or distinct species, of which we have already given examples. Another case in point is that of our English coal titmouse, which is only slightly different from its *alter ego* the coal tit of the Continent, *Parus ater*, while the blue titmouse of North Africa, *Parus teneriffe*, is a divergent form from the blue tit, *Parus cœruleus*. The insectivorous dipper can obtain its food by merely flitting from stream to stream without undertaking long travels or migrating to southern climes, and, owing to its isolation, it has developed into three forms in Europe only. Our familiar chaffinch is a rather far-reaching migrant; but the chaffinch of the Azores has become distinct, being non-migratory and specifically separable. The same may be said of the resident turtle dove of the north-east of Africa, which has sprung from the same stock as our own.

Mr. Wallace has some excellent remarks on migration in his 'Distribution of Plants and Animals.' After describing it as an exaggeration of the habit of moving about in search of food, and varying with circumstances, he takes the nightingale as an example. The nightingale inhabits almost all North Africa, Asia Minor, and the Jordan valley. Early in April it passes into Europe by the three bird routes over the Mediterranean, and spreads over France, part of England, Denmark, and the south of Sweden, which it reaches early in May. It does not enter Brittany, the Channel Islands, or Wales, except the south of Glamorganshire, and rarely visits any English county north of Yorkshire. It spreads over Central Europe, through Austria and Hungary, to Southern Russia and the warmer parts of Siberia; 'but it nevertheless 'breeds in the Jordan valley,' says Mr. Wallace, 'so that in 'some places it is only the surplus population that migrates. 'In August and September all who can return to their 'winter quarters.' Some writers have divided the movements of animals, mammals as well as birds, into annual or periodic, regular and irregular. Monkeys, imitating men, ascend the Himalayas in summer to a height of 10,000 or 12,000 feet, and in winter descend again. Wolves everywhere seek the lowlands in severe weather, and antelopes in dry seasons move southwards in great herds, nearer our South African settlements than their usual range. The lemming, the Alpine hare, the Arctic fox, and the reindeer yield to the same motive, in some cases regularly, under the pressure of hunger, in others only when favourable seasons and great increase of numbers have occasioned a subsequent period of unusual scarcity. Perhaps the movement which then takes place may be rather called an incursion than a true migration; but we prefer not to overburden our pages with terms and nice distinctions of this kind, since we must regard all removals from one locality to another as lesser or greater migrations. Some of the most marked examples of this instinct are the true migrations of fishes, when the salmon enters the rivers to breed and the herrings and mackerel approach the coast with the same object, their movement being as marked as that of our coast birds when they gather to their accustomed breeding places among the rocky fastnesses of Shetland and other islands of North Britain.

It may be said of migrations generally that they are induced by the necessities and restrained by the limited powers of some birds. In studying the habits of our most familiar birds we find that some of them merely wander from place to place in the land where they were bred, while others, like the thrush, ramble over three continents. All birds, however, travel more or less, and they flit that they may feed. The ostrich and other birds devoid of the powers of flight are in much the same position as the mammals as regards the means of migration; the wrens, being short-winged, are indifferent migrants. According to Mr. Seebohm it is easy to determine the geographical range of some genera from an examination of the shape of the wing. In the genus *Acrocephalus,* or reed warblers, for example, he says, ' *A. turdoides* has a very pointed wing; its migrations ' extend from South Sweden to the Transvaal. *A. orientalis* ' has a wing only a little less pointed, and its migrations are ' almost as extensive, reaching from Japan to Borneo. But ' *A. stentorius* has a decidedly more rounded wing, and the ' limits of its migrations are from Turkestan to India; whilst ' *A. syrinx* has the roundest wing of all, and appears to have ' become a resident in the island of Pouape.' According to Mr. Seebohm, therefore, the wings grow shorter as the distance lessens; and, on the other hand, as the migrations extend the wings lengthen. We have already noticed certain bird stations where particular species are restrained within narrow limits. In this respect birds resemble plants, and in each case there are tropical and Arctic species, besides those of lesser range, such as Alpine, Iberian, or Scandinavian species. It is evident that in the peopling of the world with its present forms of life plants must have been the pioneers of birds, and that the geography of plants must bear some relation to the distribution of birds. No stronger evidence has yet been offered of the division of continents, and the consequent changes in the distribution of land and sea, than that which is presented in the close relationship of the groups of plants which are stationed now on opposite coasts, and which were formerly united. But in considering that branch of natural history which Humboldt, M. de Candolle, Mr. Wallace, and other enquirers have explored, it is evident that birds, as well as plants, have been cast into separate groups by those changes in the distribution of sea and land to which we have just referred. If this fact be borne in mind, it will be found to assist in explaining both the routes which some birds follow in migration and the separation of allied species. Beyond the limits of particular kinds of birds closely related species are generally found. Our rook, for example, exists as an unaltered rook with denuded bill, as in England, as far east as the river Obb; but in China and Japan, which it has not colonised, a closely allied form replaces it. The American golden plover is scarcely separate from *Charadrius fulvus*; and our oyster catcher is unknown in North America, but it has its representative in *Hæmatopus palliatus*. Islands having hard boundaries are the frequent homes of local forms. Spitzbergen has its peculiar ptarmigan; the Faroe Islands and Iceland have their own wren, and the starling of the former islands, having a larger bill than the English starling, has only just escaped being ranked as specifically different from that well-known bird. We have two species of birds which do not occur elsewhere, the *Parus britannicus* and *Lagopus scoticus*, while our *Acredula rosea* has only a very restricted range beyond the borders of this country. Bird life, therefore, offers the same examples of what the older naturalists called 'centres of creation of particular species' as the vegetable kingdom; but there is this difference between plants and birds: they both migrate, but the former have done so chiefly under the direct guidance of gods or men, as when Bacchus distributed grapes, or Minerva created the olive, as Neptune did the horse, or when the generals of Rome brought the bay and a score of other plants into Britain; while the latter migrate voluntarily, in pursuit of their own interests entirely.

We have birds, such as the robin, blackbird, and song thrush, which are resident with us and migratory in Germany; and, with regard to the formation of species, Mr. Seebohm observes that those which have just been mentioned probably have only ceased to migrate within comparatively recent times, 'and we may fairly conjecture that should the English ' climate remain long enough favourable to the residence of ' these birds, they will develope into local races, which will

' eventually have rounder and shorter wings than their
' continental allies.'

We have already shown why birds migrate; the question
how they migrate has still to be dealt with. Are they
directed in their course by some special instinct peculiar to
their race? We hear the flocks of the birds of passage
making their flight high in the air almost with awe. As
Longfellow says—

> ' And above in the light
> Of the star-lit night
> Swift birds of passage wing their flight
> Through the dewy atmosphere.

> ' I hear the beat
> Of their pinions fleet
> As from the land of snow and sleet
> They seek a southern lea.

> ' I hear the cry
> Of their voices high,
> Falling dreamily through the sky,
> But their forms I cannot see.'

The act of migration is assisted by the powers which
birds possess, in common with some other animals, of finding
their way—powers which are no doubt derived from habits
of close observation. A partiality for former haunts and an
affection for old breeding places bring the sand martin back
to the same hole in the sand pit, the swallow to her chimney,
and the starling to her crevice in the wall. The powers
which admit of this return to the old nesting place must
greatly assist migrants in determining their route. In a
very able paper on this subject Dr. Weissmann remarks [*]
that the young Indian does not possess intuitively an
exact acquaintance with the features of the forest, but his
keen faculties of observation are readily trained till he
becomes an expert. The young bird needs the same kind
of training. He possesses from the shell, Dr. Weissmann
thinks, a talent for geography, so that he learns his lessons
with ease and rapidity. The same authority remarks that
the young birds need discipline at first, that the older and
more experienced migrants lead the way, and that when the
younger ones refuse to follow the mother birds make ceaseless efforts to urge them forward. Dr. Weissmann has no

---

[*] On the Migration of Birds, '.The Contemporary Review,' February
1879.

doubt laid down a rule which is pretty general. The rare birds which sometimes reach our shores are usually stragglers and young birds; but Mr. Seebohm assures us that in the valley of the Petchora the young, and therefore the least experienced, birds of North Europe are, in the autumn of the year, the first to commence the great annual migration to the south. They may perhaps be less patient of adversity and bad weather than the older birds, and if they know not whither they go in taking the passage of the sea they certainly know, on reaching our western coast, whither they ought not to go, and they do not attempt the Atlantic. Birds in migration often cross both sea and land at great heights. Mr. Gätke, of Heligoland, admirable observer as he is, says correctly, so far at least as some birds are concerned, that the contour of the countries they pass over, their river valleys and their mountain ranges, do not influence the choice of route. How many great rivers, for example, Richards's pipit must cross, almost at right angles, during its autumnal flight from Dauria to France and Spain! On the other hand Dr. A. E. Brehm, in his attractive volume entitled ' Bird Life,' describes the migrants as travelling generally by such natural routes as the Mississippi, which opens a way for the birds of passage of North America, as several of the great European rivers do in our own hemisphere. Probably the methods differ according to the routes and circumstances. Mr. Tennant, in taking observations of the sun, saw some black specks moving across the spectrum of his telescope, and these were birds flying at an estimated height of ' several miles.' At this distance above the earth, land and sea, valley and mountain, would lie spread out as a map below, and it is not easy to conceive by what means these far-sighted creatures find their way under such circumstances. They can only fly high in clear weather, and are baffled, brought to the level of the ground, and stopped in their passage by anything which obscures the view, such as clouds, mist, or darkness.

There is another method of migration, and in particular cases birds appear to be guided by the natural highways of the countries they traverse. A river or valley is followed until its course deviates considerably from the true line, when it is forsaken for the direct path. If a range of mountains lies directly across the line of flight, its passes are used in crossing it, whatever direction they take. In Switzerland, as in the Pyrenees, the roads in the deepest

passes are always used by the birds of passage. In Germany
the Rhine is a European Mississippi as a main track for
birds; the Danube, Elbe, and Oder are subsidiary routes;
and numerous other rivers assist the autumnal exodus.   In
France the valleys of the Rhone and the Garonne are
the main thoroughfares; in Spain, the Guadalquivir and
Guadiana; in Russia, the Vistula, Dnieper, and Don, and
chief of all the Volga.   In North-Eastern Africa the Nile
proves a waterway which directly affects the bird population
of England; and assuming that the Euphrates and the
Tigris do not lie within our proper limits in treating of our
birds of passage, we may still mention, for the sake of illustration, that every river of Asia which runs north and south
assists the birds, just as in another hemisphere the Connec-
ticut, Hudson, Delaware, Susquehannah, and Mississippi
help on their road the starved-out vagiants of the north.
Aquatic birds follow the great rivers and lakes by routes
which various observers have traced.   In making their way,
for example, one great body reaches Central Europe from
the Black Sea by way of the Danube, another ascends the
Rhone from the Gulf of Lyons.

Probably none of the marvels of migration are more surprising than the instinct of a well-bred young pointer, without experience, who is taken into the field for the first time,
and at the scent of game stands staunch, stiffens his tail,
crouches on his belly, slobbers at the mouth, and can scarcely
be persuaded to move towards the covey.   It has often been
asserted that birds are moved by a similarly imperative
instinct on commencing their migration, and that cage-birds
share at that period the agitation of their wild congeners.
There is reason to believe, however, that this is merely a
social excitement occasioned by the anxious cries of the
migrants, and in support of this view Marcel de Serres states
that the black swan of Australia, when domesticated in
Europe, has been known to join the wild swans in their
northward movement, migrating with them in the wrong
direction.   It may be that birds do not experience the instinctive enthusiasm which has been attributed to them;
still we may believe that they take their course under the
influence of the same hereditary impressions as the pointer.
In crossing the Mediterranean, for example, they keep the
old track, even under altered circumstances, by the exercise
of what may be described as hereditary memory, the result
of 'accumulated tendencies' which have left their stamp
upon the brain.   Almost all the migratory birds of Europe

go southward to the Mediterranean in autumn, move along its coasts east and west, and cross over in three places only —either from the south of Spain in the neighbourhood of Gibraltar, from Sicily over Malta, or to the east by Greece and Cyprus.

The apparent difficulties of these routes are greatly minimised by the fact that the migrants are always, or almost always, in sight of land, making the passage when the wind is favourable and only attempting it in clear weather. Mr. Seebohm's observation in regard to the young birds preceding the others in the northern region explored by him does not apply here, since the old birds go first—the males often leaving before the females—and the young migrants follow later and alone, seldom going so far as the old ones. Many of the young birds in fact do not cross, but remain in the south of Europe. The same rule applies to the migration northwards in spring, many young birds stopping short of the extreme Arctic regions, which the old ones reach, and the old taking the lead. It is hardly necessary to discuss these passages of the Mediterranean exhaustively. It is enough to say that they date from a period of time which cannot be measured. The islands of Malta and Cyprus, which are now useful, and indeed essential, to the weaker birds as resting-places, formed in the diluvial period—as the fossil elephants in their caverns prove—parts of strips of land which divided the Mediterranean into two great salt-water lakes, while a similar strip from the African coast to Gibraltar cut off the western lake from the ocean. At three points, therefore, the passage of the existing sea was made on dry land, just as in recent geological times, probably before the glacial epoch, the passage from the Continent to Britain was made by a similar highway. The forests in which these prehistoric migrants built their nests still lie buried in the shallow waters of the North Sea, and similar evidence of the sinking of the land exists in the shallow waters surrounding the islands of the Mediterranean, which is elsewhere of ocean profundity. A submergence of land, slow perhaps as the gradual elevation of Scandinavia, which is now proceeding at the rate of two and a half feet in a century, would not bar the passage of the birds. Guided by hereditary instinct, generation after generation they would reach the shore and follow the old routes. The sea-passage is, however, dangerous and sometimes disastrous, and a further division of the continents would entirely bar the migration of such birds as the quail, which are now common to either continent, and would then become separate in locality and probably distinct in species.

We shall not carry this subject further. Some writers have reached the conclusion that the present bird routes are identical with the old ways by which the earliest distribution northwards took place. The different species, they say, move to and fro in directions which they must necessarily have taken in their earliest diffusion. The common white wagtail, for instance, winters in Africa and reaches Greenland in the spring by England, the Faroe Islands, and Iceland, taking the same ancient and inconvenient track as the barnacle goose, in accordance with the same pre-glacial custom. But being in Greenland, the absurd bird, we are told, might readily find winter quarters much nearer than Africa on the east coast of America, where it is nevertheless never seen. Knowledge and science should certainly surpass instinct; but when Lord Cockburn, sitting on the hillside with his excellent shepherd, complained of the folly of the sheep, declaring that if he had been a sheep he would have kept under shelter, the man replied, 'My Lord, if ye had been a 'sheep ye'd have had mair sense!' and he may have been right. It is evident that numerous habits are formed and instincts implanted at the bidding of some persuasive teacher or under the influence of some strong inducement. Performing dogs and circus horses are all bribed by food, and tricks and habits, learned with pains, sometimes become instincts like those of pointers or hounds, who assist sportsmen by their artificial and hereditary endowments, standing stock still or following the particular kind of quarry they have been trained for generations to pursue. Avoiding further analysis of an abstruse question, we must be content with conclusions which may thus be briefly summarised :—
In districts where the supply of food never fails, the instinct of migration could never have been developed. We may look for it in its lowest form in those home-keeping birds whose flittings in search of food are least extended; and in its highest state of development in such travellers as the swallow or the nightingale, the wild swan or the stork. These birds have learned by compulsion the art of travelling, as Shakespeare puts it, 'farther than from home,' and as the distances were increased the instinct was strengthened. Their land routes, as we have seen, became sea passages, but the migrants were still prompted and guided in their distant journeys by the irresistible force of an hereditary impulse, and by those remarkable faculties of observation and recol-

lection which birds, dogs, and horses all possess, as well as by their marvellous powers of vision.

But when all is said, science has done but little to explain the extraordinary faculties which impel and enable the bird creation to encircle the globe, to seek for food and warmth in unknown lands, to steer their course with unerring precision across the depths of air and tracts of ocean, and to return in season to their wonted nests.

> ' Who bid the stork, Columbus like, explore
> Heavens not his own, and worlds unknown before ?
> Who calls the council, states the certain day,
> Who forms the phalanx and who points the way ? '

These are not the results of acquired knowledge or experience, but of creative intelligence and design which has implanted in every living thing the peculiar conditions and powers necessary to its existence.

ART. VIII.—*Papiers et Correspondance de la Famille Impériale.* Paris : 1870.

BY a decree published in the 'Journal Officiel' of the French Republic on September 7, 1870, the Minister of the Interior appointed a Commission charged with the collection, classification, and publication of the papers and correspondence of the Imperial family which had been seized at the Tuileries on the overthrow of the Empire, three days before. The President of this Commission was M. André Lavertujon, who, on October 12, addressed a report to M. Jules Favre, then *interim* Minister of the Interior, indicating the progress made up to that date by the Commission, and suggesting the appointment of M. Taxile Delord, Laurent-Pichat, and Ludovic Lalanne, to replace MM. de Kératry, Estancelin, and André Cochut, who had been called to the exercise of other functions, the first-named of the three being made Prefect of Police. This report, approved and countersigned by M. Jules Favre, states that on September 24, the first fasciculus of the papers in question had been published; that fasciculi, composed each of two octavo leaves, had succeeded nearly every other day; and that the contents of a volume of 500 pages had been already passed through the press. Copies of each number, as they appeared, had been sent to the public prints; and not only had most of the documents been republished by

them in entirety, but counterfeits had been circulated among
the public, with which the Commission had not regarded it
as any part of their duty to interfere. The Commission
insist, in a brief preface, that the publication of these
papers has an absolutely official and impersonal character,
the work having been undertaken in the sole interest of
truth. The Commission, according to the preface, did not
judge—it simply drew up an inventory; it attempted no
polemical work, but impartially prepared the materials of
history. The documents, copied under the responsibility of
the secretaries to the Commission, were examined by the
President, and submitted to the control of the Government
of the National Defence. After publication the original
documents, carefully catalogued, were deposited in the
national archives.

Such is the account, given with all the dry precision of
an official report, of a publication of a more startling nature
than often comes within the purview of the historian. Amid
the portentous echoes of the time, when the ears of men
were stunned by such tidings as those of the capitulation
of Sedan, the collapse of the Empire, the siege of Paris,
and the death-struggle of France, it might well be the case
that items of what might almost be called personal gossip,
which in less tempestuous times would have rung through
Europe, would appear dwarfed to undue proportions by the
terrible news of each day. We are not prepared to say
that any effort was made by those who were most compro-
mised by the papers in question to collect and to destroy the
published copies. But the rarity of the volume—only one
other copy than the one before us having met our eyes, and
that on the table of an ambassador—certainly tends to
confirm that not unnatural supposition. At all events it
will be, as the Commission has said, 'in the interest of
'truth' to adduce a few of the proofs thus unexpectedly
furnished of what the Second Empire cost France.

It is difficult to approach an enquiry of the kind without
a strong sense of the grim humour of the event. The
ink will hardly run from the pen without leaving traces of
a certain amount of malice, using the word in its French,
and not in its English, sense. That those very documents
which, by reason of their intimately private nature, should
be entrusted to no minister, secretary, or archivist, but kept
in the personal custody of the Sovereign himself, should be
thus collected, kept, and at last made public for the special
service and delectation of King Mob, is a new incident of

the drama of *La République dans les carrosses du Roi.** The
scene in fiction—if it be fiction—which the event most
closely resembles, is that of the hurried destruction of the
most private papers of the Duc de Mora in the terrible
eighteenth chapter of Alphonse Daudet's tale, ' Le Nabab.'
No more characteristic instance of the mutability ' of fate,
' and chance, and change in human life ' has been inscribed
on the pages of history since ' the lofty grave tragedians '
of Greece first showed how powerful a charm the tale of
the reverses met by the most conspicuous actors on the
world's stage exercises on the human mind.   The rapacity
of the solicitors that begirt the temporary throne; the more
than questionable titles by which in many cases the imperial
charity was drained; the mystery hanging over some en-
tries; the broad, fierce, garish light in which others stand
revealed; the magnitude of the sums derived by the Bonaparte family, its dependants, its tools, and its flatterers,
from the taxpayers of France, during a term of eighteen
years; the base servility of the applicants; the utter naked-
ness to which France was stripped by a horde of plunderers,
as was shown in the time of her need—these things are well
adapted to overcome us with special wonder.   It was in the
Court of Louis XIV. that the creed of the courtier was thus
briefly formulated:—

> ' Toujours prendre,
> Jamais rendre,
> Et encore prétendre.'

The advice was followed by the ravenous pack of place-
hunters under the Empire—from the mock disinterested-
ness of those who vaunted that they only sought to serve
the Emperor or to save France, to the most barefaced and
unblushing mendicancy—that surrounded the throne of the
Emperor Napoleon III.

The papers and correspondence of the Imperial family
form two volumes, one of 480, and the other of 288 pages.
They commence with the brief announcement, as an excuse

---

* A similar incident had, however, twice before occurred in the
course of the French Revolution, when the mob broke into the
Tuileries, and pillaged the private papers of the Sovereign. The
documents found in the celebrated *coffre de fer* of Louis XVI.
were used against him on his trial, though in fact they contained
nothing to support a capital accusation; and the documents found in
the cabinet of Louis-Philippe were published in the ' Revue Retro-
spective ' in 1848. But these papers contained absolutely nothing
which was not creditable to the family of the fugitive king.

for failing to come to dinner with Barras: 'Bonaparte est
'arrivé cette nuit,' written by Josephine, who signs herself
Lapagerie Bonaparte, to Botot, secretary to Barras, then
Director, at the Luxembourg, on December 5, 1797. Of this
curious letter, containing the words, 'Vous connaissez
'mieux que personne, mon cher Botot, ma position,' a facsimile is given in the volume. The last entry is a despairing telegram, headed '*Maire à Guerre*, Paris' ('*Guerre*' being
the Minister for War), dated Sainte-Marie, September 3, 1870,
4.30 P.M., to the following effect: 'In a few days Strasburg
'will be nothing but a heap of ruins. Schlestadt, which
'has just been invested, will doubtless share the same fate.
'Have we no one to come to the succour of our unhappy
'Alsace?' Later in actual time, though earlier in the book,
comes a despatch from the director of the telegraph at
Lyons to the director-general at Paris, dated 1.50 P.M. on
September 4:—

'I am compelled to transmit the following despatch:—" French
"Republic, Commune of Lyons. The Provisional Committee of Public
"Safety of Lyons to the Municipal Council of Marseilles: Republic
"proclaimed at Lyons. Immediate organisation of a Republican
"Government, and of necessary measures for the defence of the
"country." A commissary of the Provisional Committee is in per
manence in my cabinet. Armed men guard the entry of the post.
What are your orders?'

In 1815 events marched almost as rapidly, though revolution
then lacked the magic aid of the electric telegraph. But
we now turn to the papers which relate more especially to
the Second Empire.

The third document printed is a facsimile receipt, dated
Elysée National, April 26, 1851, and signed 'Louis-Napoléon
'Bonaparte,' acknowledging a loan of 500,000 francs from
Marshal Narvaez, then chief of the Spanish Ministry; a
loan repaid on June 2, 1852. This is followed by a series
of notes, without either signature or date, but appearing
from internal evidence to have been written between the
months of July and August, 1852, on the characters of the
prefects of the Republic after the *coup d'état* of December
1851. These functionaries are divided into 'prefects to
'dismiss' (those of whom the dismissal is urgent and indispensable being distinguished by an asterisk); 'prefects
'to change;' 'prefects whose situation does not for the
'moment require either dismissal or change, but with
'whom one or other measure will soon become proper,' and
'prefects who can be, for the present, maintained at their

'posts, some of them being advanced.' The first quality which appears to be regarded by the reporter is that of ' devotion,' a word the use of which is enough to show that the speedy proclamation of the Empire was in contemplation in July, 1852. The notes do not err either by circumlocution or by excess of courtesy. Thus of Ponsard (Loire) it is written : ' Neither brilliant qualities nor pro-' minent defects; has recently committed faults in his de-' partment which prove a want of political tact that com-' promises his situation in the Loire.' First for character (such as it is) comes Foy (Ardennes). ' Absolute devotion ; ' character frank and loyal; good sense ; active and laborious ; ' thoroughly knows his department, where he is loved and ' esteemed.' Another runs thus : ' Féart (Gers). Sincere ' devotion, intelligent and active administrator ; offends by ' excess of ardour, and by too much care of his personality.' At the head of the prefects whom it is urgent to change comes ' De Saulxure (Ardèche). Nature mediocre and ' vulgar ; has created, by his maladresse and want of tact, ' a situation which it will be inconvenient for the Govern-' ment to prolong in the Ardèche.' Intended, no doubt, for few eyes but those of the Prince President, this cynical and measured document bears the heading ' Ministry of ' General Police.' The Minister must have required perfect command of his features when politely receiving public officers whose fates were thus indicated, and whose characters were thus dissected and weighed, in a report that may have lain on his desk during the interview.

With unusual gallantry the Commission have suppressed the name of a great lady who adopts the coaxing style of mendicancy.

' Sire,—It is I again, but I come all in a tremble ; for this time I am very frightened. Your Majesty will perhaps weary of his bounty, and send me roughly away. I beg him not to be angry, and to pardon me if I am really tiresome.

' I have learned that there are several places of chamberlain vacant at this moment; and as this position was occupied by my grandfather, the Count de ——, under the Emperor Napoleon I., I have always hoped to obtain one day of your Majesty this great favour for my husband, who is so ardent in his desire and ambition to obtain it. Sire, pray grant me this favour ! My husband is not too young ; he is thirty-three, and the livery of your *servants* would become him so, Sire. It is so easy for you, Sire, to make people happy, and you know how a charge of this kind flatters a whole family. Sire, do not refuse me—at once, at all events I have such an ardent desire to succeed. Pardon me, I conjure you, and give your poor little subject a pretty word of consent. I lay at the feet of your Majesty my tender and respectful homage.'

It is not only from poor little subjects of the gentler sex that the cry, 'Give, give,' echoes through the Imperial correspondence. Not that the ladies had by any means less than their fair share of the bounty. A 'note of the sums 'paid by the Emperor to Miss Howard' (created Comtesse de Beauregard), between March 24, 1853, and January 1, 1855, amounts to 5,449,000 francs. On July 24 following, however, we find a letter from this lady to an unnamed friend (probably Mocquard), which she begs him to burn, complaining of the non-fulfilment of engagements towards her, and apparently wanting 2,500,000 francs more. 'You ' know,' she says, 'my position. I pray God that there ' may be no more question of money between me and him ' who has quite another kind of interest in my heart.' A brief *note sans date* runs: 'There has been sent into Spain ' to Madame the Comtesse de Montijo, by the means of ' MM. de Rothschild, (1) on February 4, 600,000 francs; ' (2) on April 2, 89,739 francs; (3) on May 27 (Mocquard), ' 668,421 francs. The Empress had regularly 100,000 francs ' per month.'

' After official figures which the Civil List Commission has furnished us,' say the Commission for the publication of the correspondence, ' the balance-sheet of the Imperial munificence may be thus stated for the whole reign :—

	fr.	c.
Allocations, subventions, and pensions .	19,857,374	72
Gifts, succours, and indemnities . .	28,881,895	55
Encouragement to art, science, literature	2,566,941	53 '

To this total of a little over two millions sterling have to be added

'various allocations on the privy purse, a special fund which the Emperor reserved for his personal use. Under this head was annually distributed about a million of francs by the hands of M. Ch. Thélin, keeper of the privy purse. Account should also be taken of certain expenses met, at least in 1863, under the Minister Persigny, by the Department of the Interior, of which we have found some traces in the papers submitted to our examination, under the title of " Political " Fund." At 300,000 francs a year for this, we obtain a total of about three millions, and adding the different items together we arrive at a general total of 74,306,211 francs 80 centimes, or, remaining within the limits of the Civil List, seventy or seventy-one millions; a sum equal to that which we have previously attributed, on vouchers, to the Imperial family.'

As to this we are told in a 'note on the expenses of the 'Civil List of Napoleon III. from 1853 to 1870 : '—

'It is easy to form a rough estimate of the money pocketed, since 1852, by the Bonaparte family. It is enough to add to the dotations paid for some of its members the regular allocations of which the Commission has already published the table, of which the annual total varies from 1,200,000 to 1,400,000 francs. This subvention commenced on December 25, 1852, and only closed with the Empire. Account must also be taken of a capital of 5,200,000 francs, distributed, by decree of April 1, 1852, to a certain number of favoured relatives. Without speaking of gratifications, debts paid, and other liberalities, of which the detail will follow, the general account of the Imperial family is as follows, according to the official tables of the Civil List :—

		fr.
Dotations (1860-1870) . . .		16,849,999
Dotations of the Palais Royal and of Meudon (1857–1870) . . .		4,953,639
Allocations (1853–1870) . . .		30,033,531
Divers expenses		1,758,116
General total		53,595,285

If we add to this sum the capital given, 5,200,000 fr., we find more than fifty-eight millions absorbed, without any utility for the country, by the family of those who have led us to Leipzig, to Waterloo, and to Sedan.'

Fifty-eight millions of francs, however, respectable an item as it may be considered, is far from exhausting the debit side of the account opened with France for the 'Imperial family' on December 2, 1852. The fixed and regular resources of which the head of that family disposed, from that date to September 4, 1870, comprised (1) the dotations of the Civil List, 25,000,000 francs; (2) the dotations of the Imperial family, 1,500,000 francs; (3) dotations of the Palais Royal and of Meudon, 350,000 francs ; (4) dotations, moveable and fixed, of the Crown, from 4,000,000 to 8,000,000 francs. On the average the receipts of the Civil List constantly exceeded the sum of 32,000,000 francs *annually*, which hardly covered the expenses of the Court and of the great officers of the Crown.

The final 'recapitulation' arrived at by the Commission runs thus :—

'So, without keeping count of certain hundreds of thousands of francs annually pocketed for an unknown number of years, the balance-sheet of the Bonaparte family is as follows:

	fr.
Jérôme Bonaparte (4 persons)	37,078,364
Baciocchi family (1 person)	6,244,626
Lucien Bonaparte (22 persons)	12,762,500 ·
Murat family (12 persons)	13,577,933
Mmes B. Centamori and Bartholini (2 persons) .	524,375
General total	70,187,796 '

This sum, amounting to upwards of two millions eight hundred thousand pounds sterling, was paid by the French nation to the Bonaparte family, without any utility to France, on the ground of relationship to the Chief of the State.

Compared with the mendicants and flatterers by whom he was surrounded, the irresponsible distributor of this golden shower looks almost respectable by force of contrast. We have touched on the delicate question of bounty to feminine claimants. The volume before us gives proof that the number of these was by no means very restricted, although particulars of the payments are rarely on record. Two letters signed Marguerite Bellanger indicate a *lacuna* of this kind of no inconsiderable extent. And if the statement be correct that certain portions of the landed estates of the Crown were alienated in the direction indicated, it is obvious that large donations may have escaped the notice of the Commission. An alphabetical list, filling sixty octavo pages of small print, is printed by the Commission ' as the ' fruit of long and minute study.'

' It is not,' the authors add, ' a complete list of the pensioners of the Empire. Who could hope to draw up such a list ? We find in it by no means all the high dignitaries and great officers—the public knows them well enough—nor the multitude of small suppliants whom the necessities of life have brought under the Caudine Forks of the Imperial charity. We have only been able to present specimens of each category to which the liberalities of the Civil List have applied : avowed complicities ; services rendered to the person, the ideas, the relatives, or the friends of the prince ; solicitations supported by military, clerical, or domestic influences ; lastly, aid to merit or to misfortune. It is rémarkable how small are the last, without, however, being few. Among so many benefactions there are few which do not hide, or rather betray, some *arrière-pensée*. This will be readily seen by a glance at the biographical and anecdotic remarks which accompany most of the names cited in these pages.

' We hope to be pardoned for having transgressed the bounds of the Civil List in order to trace the secrets of the Presidency and the vicissitudes of that adventurous life which led Louis-Napoleon from Strasburg and Boulogne to the Tuileries and to Wilhelmshöhe. Only thus can we show the origin of certain fortunes and of certain devotions. By the way, too, we have perhaps illuminated some obscure points, so much the more interesting to those who wish to know thoroughly the man, as to his habits, his friends, and his family, avowed or clandestine. We have thought it right to profit by the vouchers which fell into our hands, and have thus brought under contribution the private accounts of Louis-Napoleon from 1844 to 1848, following the variations of his private fortune before and during his captivity, and finding even the price of the workman's clothes in which he escaped from Ham.'

These were not costly—a blouse, a shirt, a pair of pantaloons, a cap, an apron, a necktie, and a handkerchief, costing all together exactly a sovereign.

The services rendered to the adventurer in the early part of his career seem to have been paid for with no niggard hand. The first receipt from Miss Howard for 1,000,000 francs on March 25, 1853, is in discharge of all her rights and interest in the domain of Cività Nuova in the March of Ancona. On this property, in 1850, a sum 'of 324,000 francs was lent to Louis-Napoleon by the Marquis Palla-vicino, which was repaid in 1852, with interest, through the hands of the Duke of Galliera. This million, however, is only one out of nearly six given to the same individual. The Comtesse Emilie Campana accepted on July 29, 1851, a bill drawn by the President of the French Republic for 33,000 francs. By 1870 she had received 'approximately ' 400,000 francs.' Miss Mary Gwynne received between 1846 and 1868 at least 132,000 francs by way of pension, besides 25,000 francs as an 'establishment ' on her marriage in 1852, and 12,500 francs by way of 'succour' in 1868. An unknown lady, under the initial T., received in 1857 the sums of 90,000 francs, 30,000 francs, and 80,000 francs. Alexandrine Vergeot figures as recipient of numerous sums of varying amount, finishing with 25,000 francs in August 1852. These are only some of the most salient figures on the face of the alphabetical abstract. The list is of enor-mous length, and contains some names we are surprised to find there, with singular details as to the nature of the claims on the Imperial purse. In 1866 the Emperor appears to have had nearly a million sterling in money and secu-rities deposited with Messrs. Baring. This, however, was the nominal value of the securities which was contested by M. Piétri. At page 152 we find Messrs. Baring's list of the investments.

The demands on the bounty thus freely distributed can be compared to nothing so aptly as to the consentaneous howl

with which the great array of professional beggars, at Pozzuoli,
at Pisa, or at any great centre of continental mendicancy, are
wont to set off in pursuit of a newly arrived visitor. ' I
' drown, at this moment, for want of four bank-notes of
' 1,000 francs,' writes Albéric Second to M. Conti. ' Ah !
' if you could only make my cry of anguish reach the ear of
' the Emperor ! ' However, the result is highly gratifying
from the point of view of *messieurs les mendiants.* This is the
acknowledgement of the Imperial munificence :—

> ' Dear Sir,—The Emperor has deigned to hear and to attend to my
> cry of distress. Make, I beg you, my cry of joy and gratitude reach
> his Majesty, and believe in the sentiments of high consideration of your
> devoted servant, Albéric Second.'

From the cry of distress, pure and simple, we pass to the
cry of importunity. M. Pierre Bonaparte, as M. Conti calls
him—' the Prince Pierre-Napoléon Bonaparte, as he styles
himself—received from the bounty of his cousin, between
April 1, 1852, and the close of 1863, the respectable sum of
2,273,000 francs. From the commencement of 1864 his
monthly allowance was reduced from 2,500 to 2,000 francs.
In 1867 it appears that the Emperor expressed his disapproval
of the intention of Pierre Bonaparte to legitimatise certain
natural children by marrying their mother. Having failed
at the same time to become a representative for Corsica,
M. Pierre Bonaparte writes thus :—

> ' Deprived of all credit, of all participation in affairs, of all chance of
> improving my condition, I hope for the assistance of your Majesty. If,
> Sire, you would buy my property in Corsica, I could complete my modest
> establishment in the Ardennes. This Corsican estate would be admi-
> rably situated for the establishment of a model farm, a police barrack,
> or any other administrative foundation. I must sell it, and I do not
> expect to get much for it, unless your Majesty agrees to my proposal.
> It would be a benefit that I should never forget. Of your Majesty,
> Sire, the devoted cousin, Pierre-Napoléon Bonaparte.'

The reply, drafted by M. Conti, states that it is impossible
to grant M. Pierre Bonaparte's new demands, that the
Corsican property would be useless to the Emperor and only
an expense, and that the budget is too heavily charged to
allow of such a sacrifice. On this the claimant invokes the
aid of the Church, and begs the Emperor to receive the
Archbishop of Paris, whom he has acquainted with 'his
' situation.'

Later in publication, although earlier in point of time,
are three letters from this same irrepressible member of the
Lucien-Bonaparte branch of the Imperial family, who,

besides an annual subvention of 100,000 francs, is credited with a monthly allowance of 5,000 francs from 1856 to 1859. In the latter year, doubtless for reasons, this monthly allowance is reduced to 2,500 francs. In June 1861, Pierre Bonaparte writes to the Emperor :—

'Your Majesty having left Paris without granting me the audience which I solicited, I take the respectful liberty of writing in all confidence. Your Majesty has kindly allowed me 2,500 francs more per month as long as I stay in Corsica. This addition, half of that which your Majesty granted me at first, does not allow me to live on the footing which I have adopted. I am not now again asking your Majesty to give me 5,000 francs per month. I have suffered too much from the malignant fevers of Corsica to think of returning there during the *malaria*, that is to say, before the end of October. But the need of activity, which is an imperious law of my nature, will call me next month into the Ardennes, where I have rented some hunting-grounds. I must house myself there, well or ill, to avoid expense; but if your Majesty will kindly give me, in the Ardennes, the 2,500 francs additional which you gave me in Corsica, it will allow me a different kind of establishment.

' I shall be very grateful to your Majesty; and I do not hesitate, Sire, to present this request to you, because you ought to be persuaded that, if you please to put an end to my inaction, I shall be happy to consecrate to your glorious enterprises all that remains to me of aptitude and energy.'

It is mournful to find that this seducing appeal—the writer was then in his forty-sixth year—only elicited the reply, written in pencil on the margin: ' Mocquard, refuse *politely.*'

'The Prince Achille Murat' received by gift of April 1, 1852, the sum of 200,000 francs, payable by instalments of 10,000 francs each, with interest at 5 per cent. He also received an annual subvention of 24,000 francs. In 1864 his debts, amounting to upwards of 83,000 francs, were paid for him, and Madame Achille Murat received in 1852 a *don* of 200,000 francs. In September 1869, this personage, who, at the same date in the following year, had received in all the sum of 936,870 francs out of the 5¼ millions of francs 'absorbed by the Lucien-Murat family,' thus represents his hard case :—

' After eight months spent in the Caucasus, Sire, I have returned to join in Africa the new regiment in which, at my brother's request, your Majesty has deigned to place me, persuaded that the arrangements made during my absence would permit me to resume my service, and thus to efface by my conduct, in the opinion of your Majesty, my past faults. Sire, nothing or almost nothing is changed in my sad situation.

To the present time the funds employed have hardly been enough to extinguish the debts contracted on promises to pay, in which the honour of my name was engaged, so that all the annoyance, all the scandal, with which I was menaced before my departure, menace me still. In Africa, as at Paris, my presence will awaken the animosity of my creditors. I shall be followed, hunted, arrested, exposed to daily claims, incessant and threatening, which ill-will will not fail to stir up; and your Majesty is too just to wish that, under such conditions, I should rejoin my regiment, in which the disrepute by which I should be surrounded would deprive me of the esteem of my comrades, and render my existence and my service in the midst of them completely impossible.'

Monsieur Achille concludes by asking for an audience to submit to his Majesty his *véritable* condition. It is painful to find a pencil note, in the handwriting of the Emperor, traced on the margin of this appeal: ' Refuse. The ' Emperor will not mix himself up with his affairs.'

A munificence (however vicarious) that descended so freely on the somewhat numerous objects of a tender, if a discursive, affection, and that was so readily awakened by the claims of relationship, however distant, was naturally extended to a large class of friends, whom the Commissioners for the arrangement of the Imperial correspondence call by the rude name of accomplices. As to this, however, it is obvious that the papers collected indicate but a very small part of the benefits reaped by this special category of claimants. Morny, Magnan, Maupas, Fialin, and Fleury, as M. de Kisselef informed Lord Malmesbury,* were the confidants of the *coup d'état* in 1851. Of the first, whose influence and great wealth became notorious, few traces are found in the papers of the Tuileries. There is, however, a letter from M. Jecker to M. Conti, chief of the Emperor's Cabinet, dated December 8, 1869, which throws some light on M. de Morny's command and use of a more rapid road to wealth than by the solicitation of ' gratifications ' or of pensions.

'You are no doubt ignorant,' writes the banker, 'that I had as partner in this affair' (the claims on the Mexican Government, 'mon affaire des bons') 'M. le Duc de Morny, who engaged, in consideration of 30 per cent. of the profits of the affair, to compel acknowledgement and payment by the Mexican Government, as at first. There is a voluminous correspondence on the subject with his agent, M. de Marpon. . . . As soon as this arrangement was concluded, I was perfectly supported by the French Government and its legation in Mexico. . . . Under the empire of Maximilian, and at the instance of

* Memoirs, vol. i. p. 394.

the French Government, the settlement of my business was taken in hand. . . . At the same time M. le Duc de Morny died, so that the dazzling protection which the French Government had granted me ceased completely.'

M. Conti, indeed, wrote to the Commission to say that on the receipt of this letter he had ordered M. Jecker out of his room; but the Commissioners reply that, as the banker had then lost his chief support, not to say his most powerful accomplice, it does not follow that the facts averred by M. Jecker are imaginary. We related the fate of poor Jecker, who was shot by the Commune, in a recent number of this Journal.

Of Magnan we do not find in the papers before us traces at all proportionate to the part he played in the conspiracy. But the bâton of a Marshal of France is no trifling guerdon, and neither military nor diplomatic appointments are included in the analysis given in the 'note on the expenses of 'the Civil List of Napoleon III.' A remarkable note, signed L. Magnan, informs M. Piétri that on the death of the Marshal his debts amounted to 835,000 francs, towards which funds were forthcoming, from specified sources, to the amount of 685,000 francs, while, 'as you see, we remain in face of a 'difference of 150,000 francs, for which we do not fear to 'solicit the intervention of his Majesty.' As a testimony to the military claims of Magnan on his country, we find, in a 'private report,' the uncomplimentary note: 'Some of the 'marshals are abhorred by the soldiers: Castellane, Pélissier, 'Magnan.'

The name of Maupas we have only found in this part of the correspondence in a report of M. Rouher, in which the former is qualified as an ex-minister, not worthy of the attention of the Emperor in a contemplated creation of senators. The memoirs of this person are before us, showing how wise, good, and disinterested he always was. They form an admirable pendant to the memoirs of M. Claude, chief of the private police, the weak point of each (beyond their mutual contradictions) being our hesitation as to accepting, on any point, the unconfirmed word of either writer.

Of Fialin, afterwards dignified by the style of Comte, and later of Duc, de Persigny, the notices are many. It is equally certain that they are not exhaustive. There is no reference to his Ministerial appointments, with a palace in Paris and a large salary, or as ambassador to England. In the alphabetical list contained in the note on the Civil List, the payments made directly to this active Bonapartist amount

to only 442,500 francs. But 'we find among the papers of
' M. Bure a pencil note, which is suggestive. It runs·thus :
' " Secret offer to Persigny of 100,000 francs, for the au-
' " thorisation by the prince of the enterprise of the docks
' " for the Rouen Railway." ' The word ' prince' shows that
this kind of traffic, of which M. Jecker gives so flagrant an
instance in 1869, was in full operation under the Presidency
of Louis Bonaparte. And it throws a sudden and fitful
gleam of light on a remarkable anomaly, namely, that while
only from 10,000 francs to 15,000 francs per month is
allowed in the accounts of the *Cassette particulière de
l'Empereur* for current expenses, of which the items are
not otherwise specified, evidence is given further on that, in
about fourteen years of imperial rule, Louis-Napoleon had
been able to invest in diamonds and in various specified
stocks no less a sum than 933,000*l.*, a sum which, in this
instance alone, is noted in English currency. It must be
said, however, for M. de Persigny, that with all his faults
he was the most faithful and devoted friend of the Emperor,
and that he died poor.

To pursue the fortunes of the select band of friends most
devoted to the Empire :—

'Fleury,' says the note on the expenses of the Civil List, ' (commandant, then general), orderly officer of the President, first equerry,
then grand equerry, and director of the stud, finally ambassador to Russia,
has disposed of enormous sums. The minimum of his regular budget
may be valued at the sum of 1,200,000 francs. In July 1850 Baring is
ordered to pay him, in London, 45,000 francs. On April 9, 1852, Fleury
received 48,000 francs for the establishment of the stables. This sum
and many others do not form part of an allocation of 400,000 francs
for the same object.'

In 1869 it appears that the supervision of the press is in the
hands of Fleury. His attaché, M. de Verdière, writes on
January 21, 1870 : 'Our poor Emperor gives hardly a sign
' of life. Perhaps he fears to displease his new ministers, or
' else he is simply the cold man whom we ought to know.'

A perennial munificence, which no avowed sources of
income are at all adequate to maintain, did not exclude the
exercise of special displays of bounty on certain occasions.
The twenty-fifth of the papers published by the Commission, under the title ' Cost of a Christening,' gives an
account of the expenditure on the occasion of the birth
and baptism of the Prince Imperial. Medals in diamonds
head the list, at a cost of 25,000 francs. Doctors and *sages-
femmes* received 68,000 francs. The *layette* cost 100,000

francs.   The several societies of dramatic authors and composers, men of letters, dramatic artists, musicians, painters and sculptors, industrial inventors, and medical men of the department of the Seine, received 10,000 francs each. Ninety-three thousand francs were given to the benevolent ' bureaux ' of the department of the Seine, and of the communes in which lay the estates of the Crown.   The ' agents ' of the interior service ' of the Empress received gratifications equal to four months' wages, amounting to 11,000 francs.   Forty-four thousand francs were allotted to giving *gratis* performances at the theatres on March 18, 1856.   The parents of children born on the 16th of that month shared among them 50,000 francs.   For medals to be given to authors and composers of verses and *cantate* addressed to their Majesties, and to the pupils at the Lycées, 85,000 francs were allowed.   The relatives of the godchildren of their Majesties received 20,000 francs.   The service of the stables, for the baptismal cortège, is set down at 172,000 francs; and 160,000 francs were distributed in gratifications to the hired servants of their Majesties' household.   The total comes to the modest sum of 898,000 francs.

To support a *régime* so beneficent to those who had introduced it into France, an organisation existed as to which, apart from any reference to morality or to permanent policy, it would be hard to speak too highly.   We catch, indeed, but one or two glimpses of this system, but they are enough to reveal the magnitude, as well as the symmetry, of certain distinct departments of the organic whole.   There can be little doubt that the method was inherited from the First Napoleon, who to his almost unrivalled military genius is known to have added the talent of wide-reaching and yet detailed organisation.   The portions of the Imperial method which come most fully into relief, from the important documents printed by the Commission, are those which regard the application of systematic pressure to the formation, or at all events to the expression, of public opinion. Under this head rank two distinct agencies, the intimate relation of each of which to the other and to the whole Imperial *régime* becomes most apparent when regarded in this light.   Of these one is the *cabinet noir*, or organised bureau for extracting the secrets of private correspondence. The existence of any such machinery was always denied by the Imperial Government.   It is a remarkable instance of that genius for plot which may be regarded as one of the chief characteristics of the *régime*, that this infamous service was so organised as to be unknown to the directors of the Post Office. The evidence now adduced consists of a note from M. de Persigny to the Emperor, enclosing a detailed report, both without date, but containing annotations in the Emperor's writing. Five letter-carriers and four *concierges*, who are all named, were bribed by M. Saintomer, the director of the secret police of the Ministry of the Interior. The letter-carriers entering, in the ordinary discharge of their duties, into the lodges of the porters, either received letters committed to their charge, or delivered those sent to their address after examination. The letters received from the *concierges* were usually sent by carriages to M. Saintomer, 18, Rue Las Cases, where they were opened, copied, and reclosed for ordinary delivery. The operations were rarely suspected. The extent and audacity of the surveillance thus effected were such that 'during the sojourn of the ' Emperor at Plombières and at Biarritz the correspondence ' received by Madame de Castiglione was opened and read by ' the agents of the Minister of the Interior,' as well as that of M. Hyrvoix, of M. Fould, and of Madame de Montebello. Agent spied agent, and the reports of all were centralised in the hands of the Emperor.

The other agency referred to is what is termed, in so many words, 'the organisation of the press.' Of this we have, as is not unnatural, much fuller information than of the *cabinet noir*. The Minister of the Interior was provided with an 'Etat de la Situation de la Presse,' which recalls, by its order and detail, those *états* of the state of the army which formed so constant a study for Napoleon I. In March 1868 a 'note sur le rôle de la presse dans les ' élections ' was drawn up by M. F. Girardeau. It points out that down to that time the Ministry of the Interior had been in the habit of treating as enemies of the Empire all candidates who were not patronised by the administration. This tactical error had led to the formation of a 'liberal ' union,' which gradually attracted the support of all equivocal candidates, of whom many would have accepted, and some had even solicited, official support. The error committed by the Government lay here. The attention of the Government ought to be specially directed to these equivocal candidates, since it is by them that the 'second ' turn ' is arrived at, and it is by this second vote that the elections are actually determined. To meet this condition, M. Girardeau suggests the formation by the press, without the intervention of the Government, of a 'dynastic union.'

The administration would present, as usual, a list of official candidates, who would be openly supported by the five avowed government journals. Eleven other Parisian journals, forming the 'dynastic union,' are each to bring forward a candidate whose election would be regarded as a personal success, and who would each sign a declaration of 'dynastic 'faith.' That one essential point assured, the whole gamut of constitutional opposition would be harmonised, and a friendly centre would be formed in the Chamber. Thus, instead of consolidating an opposition out of all those who were not devoted servants of the Empire, there would be assured a general body of supporters of the Government, including all who were not radically hostile to its existence. For the mass of the public, for the provinces, for foreign countries, the single fact would be evident: 'the avowed enemies of 'the dynasty are beaten—the friends of the dynasty are 'elected.'

As to the mode in which the organisation of the press was effected, we find a remarkable note, drawn up by one of the *chefs du bureau* of the Ministry of the Interior, *division de la presse*, under date April 5, 1869. It includes a report from the *chef du bureau* of the departmental press, in which, department by department, the reports of the Prefects on the newspapers are summarised, and the sums demanded for subsidising the indicated journals are set down. The total general demanded is only 100,000 francs. But this sum is without prejudice to the secret-service money dispensed by the Prefecture of Police, in which, out of a sum of 2,000,000 francs, 297,540 francs is allotted to the 'service of the press.' It is also exclusive of the large sums paid, from the *cassette particulière* of the Emperor, and from other sources, for the support of particular journals. Thus we find a list of receipts from 'le journal, le Peuple Français,' from March 1, 1869, to July 30, 1870, amounting to 14,721 francs. In May 1870 M. Granier de Cassagnac (whom we find, in another note addressed to M. Conti, asking for 750 francs per month during the session for 'Le Pays') received 16,000 francs as a second payment on account of a sum of 160,000 francs. Besides 'Le Peuple,' 'Le dix Décembre' and 'L'Epoque' appear to have been supported, in part or altogether, by the Emperor. Thus of the cost really incurred in the manufacture of public opinion we obtain only imperfect and tantalising glances. We are struck, in some cases, with the modesty of the sums required. Thus, in the department Puy-de-Dôme, 'the prefect requires for the organisation of 'the press in the arrondissement of Thiers 500 francs.' In the Hérault 'the prefect requires 500 francs for a cheap 'editor.' But in the Bas-Rhin we find mention of 'the 'supplementary subvention of 30,000 francs.' 'We are 'assured,' says the note cited, of 'the reorganisation in the 'departments of twenty-seven journals, and of the addition 'to their staffs of thirty-three writers sent from Paris.' 'Four orders of measures, varying according to circum- 'stances,' have been adopted by the *bureau de la presse*.

'(1) Subventions destined to assure either the existence or the devotion of journals; (2) subventions destined to increase their publicity, that is to say, by sending gratuitous numbers during the course of the elections to counterbalance the same system which the Opposition has adopted in a large proportion; (3) subventions destined to strengthen the editing by means of the addition of new writers; (4) choice and despatch of writers, whether at the expense of the candidates or at that of the proprietors of the journals. This system, which meets the exigencies of the situation as intimated by the prefects, has already received a commencement of application proportionate to the resources of which the service can dispose.'

The action of the administration, however, would be incomplete if limited only to the 'devoted' journals. It was regarded as necessary to assure an indirect influence on the opposition papers. The means of attaining this end are of two kinds. One is to make sure of a practical proportion of aid among the correspondents of the papers; the other is to make use of the species of monopoly which the Havas establishment has acquired for telegraphic despatch, which it conducts in all the departments, and for the journals of every shade of opinion.

'On the first point, besides the Pharaon Correspondence, an arrangement has been concluded with the Cahot Correspondence, which serves twenty-seven journals, for the most part of the *tiers-parti*. M. Cahot will come daily, during the period of the elections, to take instructions at the Ministry. He has undertaken to introduce into his articles for the journals as much as is compatible with their political line, without discovering his relations with the Government.

'The Havas Correspondence has always been in daily relations with the Ministry. Whenever a contradiction, or a rectification, or a useful bit of news ought to be put in circulation without loss of time, this agency condenses it into telegraphic form and spreads it throughout France. We have agreed that this service shall be rendered more active, and that it shall be the medium of all communications which it is not fit to make directly. The primary importance of this mode of rapid publicity may be judged of from the fact that M. Havas serves 307 journals.

'Lastly, whenever it is judged necessary, notes or correspondence will appear in the Belgian journal " Le Nord." It is unnecessary here to mention the other relations established with the German and the English journals, whose interest during the period about to arrive is of a pecuniary nature. These relations comprehend twenty journals, most of them of the first importance.'

In a report on the *cabinet noir,* to which we have before referred, it is incidentally stated that the Paris correspondence of the ' Times ' is inspired by the Minister of the Interior, and that, in consequence of the refusal of M. Péreire to give to M. Collet-Meygret, then ' Director of Public Safety,' 500 shares in the new Paris Gas Company at par, at a time when they were quoted at 611 francs premium on the Bourse, the latter had caused the banker to be attacked violently in the foreign journals which he influenced. Of course, statements of this nature are not to be accepted as undeniable. It is well known that the ' Times ' newspaper was one of the energetic opponents of the Imperial *régime,* and was certainly not under any foreign influence. But it will be noted that these details are given in a report of the most private nature, addressed to the Emperor, found in his possession, and annotated in his own handwriting.

In spite of the ability of the authors and supporters of the Imperial *régime,* and of the organisation of the administration of the Post-Office, of the press, of the army, even of the moderate opposition, on the one central principle of devotion to the dynasty, the correspondence affords unmistakeable proofs that the Second Empire came into being with the germ of its dissolution. Already, in October 1868, the shadow of coming disaster was cast from the German frontier. In that month General Ducrot writes from Strasburg to General Frossard, the governor of the Prince Imperial, alarming news. Madame de Pourtalès, up to that time a Prussian in her sentiments, and a passionate admirer of King William and of M. de Bismarck, had just returned from Berlin ' with death in her soul,' owing to ' the ' conviction that war is inevitable, that it may burst out at any ' moment, and that the Prussians are so well prepared, and so ' ably led, that they are certain to succeed.' In the November following, Lieutenant-Colonel Stoffel wrote from Berlin, where he was military attaché to the Embassy, to M. Piétri, Prefect of Police :—

' We are suspected by all the Prussian nation ; certain parties detest us, others distrust us, and the least prejudiced regard us as at all events tiresome ; they feel towards us as one man does to another who is always in his way. Thence the general state of opinion, which I sum up in these words—animosity, mistrust, or irritation against France. Such is the fatal consequence of the events of 1866. Nothing can be done so long as the general situation remains the same ; and the state of affairs which I have indicated is growing worse and worse.'

In May 1867 M. de la Valette, Minister of Foreign Affairs, telegraphed to M. Benedetti, Ambassador at Berlin, that the Prussian Government was making large purchases of horses in Hungary, in Poland, and in Ireland. In the previous month an agent of the Minister of War, put on the track of M. de Moltke, Major-General of the Prussian army, reported that that officer had been visiting the French frontier and studying the positions—Mayence, Birkenfeld, Sarrebrück, Sarrelouis, Trèves, and the valley of the Moselle. To the request for further instructions the brief order ' Follow ' him ' is the reply. The elections of 1869, in expectation of which so much was done for the manipulation of the press, were disconcerting for the Government. 'We await ' the result of the elections,' telegraphs the Emperor, on November 17, 1869, to the Empress, then on her journey to the opening of the Suez Canal, 'which will all be bad.' ' I have only to-night,' he telegraphs again to Ismailia on the 22nd, ' the result of the elections, but no one attaches im- ' portance to it. Whether it be Peter or Paul, the candi- ' dates are all bad.' Then come letters illustrating the ministerial crisis of the close of 1869. M. Emile Ollivier starts by night, with his head in a muffler, and without his spectacles, so as to be ' quite unrecognisable,' to an inter- view with the Emperor, and on January 2, 1870, becomes Minister of Justice. Soon we see the pressure of his hand on the magistrates in expectation of the *plébiscite.* ' (*Justice* ' *to all the Procureurs Généraux.*) Tell all the Judges of the ' Peace that I shall see them with pleasure in the plebiscitary ' committees.' (' *Justice to the Procureur Général, Lyons.*) ' Arrest immediately all the individuals who direct the Inter- ' national. We prosecute it at Paris. The situation becomes ' grave.' ' Have you seized the International? It is at ' Toulouse.' ' I am informed that the meetings at Marseilles ' are intolerable for their violence. Do not hesitate to make an ' example; and above all, strike at the head. Catch the ' advocates, the gentlemen, rather than the poor devils of ' the people.' Thirty-two telegrams, between April 23 and May 6, 1870, contain orders for repression or for arrest. And then on May 9 comes a despairing letter to the Emperor from General Lorencez, commanding at Toulouse: ' It is with a broken heart, Sire, that I express to-day to 'your Majesty my sorrowful deception as to the vote of the 'garrison at Toulouse.'

Such was the ruined and tottering state of that Imperial edifice from which a relief was sought by a leap into the Prussian war. How little the French army was prepared to meet the strain, we shall presently see. The interest of the great drama now becomes more intense. It is hardly too much to say that nowhere, either in history or in fiction, can we find a parallel to the tale of the fall of the Second Empire, as ciphered by the fiery signals of the electric telegraph. It is not only the magnitude of the events, the shock of the opposing forces, the rapidity with which disaster eclipses disaster, the total reversal of the insolent hopes with which war was wantonly commenced, the unexampled scale of military defeat. All these exist. But the mode in which, by the aid furnished to the soldier by the inventions of Wheatstone and of Stephenson, bodies of men were moved and provisioned by the German strategists with the certainty of the chess-board and with the speed of the swallow; and even more the brief, hurried, nervous announcement, at the centres of government, of the blows sustained by the nation—announcements almost contemporaneous with the blows themselves, and often as significant by silence as by speech—are utterly without precedent. No such instance of ' turning the accomplishment of many years into an hour-'glass' was possible, in the region of history, before the lightning had been subdued to bear the messages of man. This official correspondence is marked by even more breathless rapidity of incident than can be indicated by the shifting scenes of the theatre.

To the reader who, furnished with a good map of the seat of war and with a note of the dates of the chief events in the months of July and August, studies the despatches now brought before the public, the dramatic presentation of this fierce but short contest is fully intelligible. At the same time the despatches are, on many points, signally and perhaps purposely silent or misleading. For the general reader some aid like that which Shakespeare derives from the introduction of the chorus in ' Henry V.' is desirable. The great tragedy of the Franco-Prussian War consisted of five acts, three only of which are sketched out in the documents before us. Of these the first extends from the declaration made by M. de Gramont before the Corps Législatif on July 6, to the battle of Wörth on August 6. The second contains the series of unvaried military disasters and disgraces from that turning-point of the martial tide to the capitulation of Sedan on September 2. The third act is the Revolution, the fear of which was the *raison d'être* of the war. The fourth and fifth acts, comprising respectively the fall of Strasburg and Metz and that of Paris, we have to read elsewhere. The contrast between the utter want of preparation of the French, their insane boasting, their divided councils, the absolute want of strategic provision and order, the fear of the republicans rather than of the invaders, on the one hand; and the steady, well-planned, well-ordered march of that mighty host which, almost at the same moment, seized with an irresistible grip Strasburg, Metz, and the French Emperor and army at Sedan, is a lesson in war and in policy which England would do well to lay to heart.

The rapid drama of the Prussian war, as sketched by the captured telegrams, occupies a space of sixty-two days. At 3.10 p.m. on July 6, 1870, M. Conti telegraphs from Paris to the Emperor at St. Cloud : 'The declaration of the 'Minister of Foreign Affairs, very able, very definite, and 'very firm, has excited the most lively enthusiasm in the 'Legislative Body.' ' Receive,' telegraphs M. de Persigny on the same day to his master, 'my most ardent congratula- 'tions. All France will follow you. The enthusiasm is 'unanimous.' On July 14 the Emperor telegraphs from the Tuileries to General Frossard, commanding the camp at Châlons : 'If there is war, I should like you to have the 'command-in-chief of the Engineers.' On the 16th the Minister of War directs that the despatch of the troops from Metz and the continuation of the works of the fortifications, are to be under the orders of General de Failly until the arrival of Marshal Bazaine. On the 18th General de Failly telegraphs to ' War, Paris : ' ' I am at Bitche with seventeen 'battalions of infantry. Send me money to feed the troops. ' Bank-notes refused. No silver in the public treasuries of ' the neighbourhood. No silver in the military chest.' Two days later comes the despatch from the intendant-general at Metz to the War Office : 'There is at Metz neither sugar, ' nor coffee, nor rice, nor brandy, nor salt, but little pork ' or biscuit. Send in all haste at least a million of rations ' towards Thionville.' On the same day General Ducrot telegraphs from Strasburg to ' War, Paris ' : ' To-morrow ' there will be hardly fifty men to guard the fort of Neuf- ' Brisach ; and Fort Mortier, Schlestadt, La Petite-Pierre, ' and Lichtenberg are equally unprovided. It is in conse- ' quence of the orders which we carry out. It would be easy

' to find resources in the National Guard, but I do not feel
' authorised to do anything until empowered by your Ex-
' cellency. It seems certain that the Prussians are already
' master of all the passes of the Black Forest.' On the 21st
the general commanding the 2nd Corps telegraphs from St.
Avold to ' War :' ' The depôt sends enormous packets of maps '
(no doubt of Germany) ' useless for the moment. We have
' not one map of the frontier of France. It would be better
' to send more of what would be useful, and of which we are
' completely in want.' ' I have arrived at Belfort,' telegraphs
General Michel on the same day; ' have not joined my
' brigade, have not found general of division. What must
' I do? I don't know where my regiments are.' ' There is
' silver at Strasburg,' replies ' War' to General de Failly's
despatch from Bitche, three days after its date, ' and you have
' a railway to that place. No revolvers in the arsenals ; we
' have given officers sixty francs to procure them from the
' trade. You must wait for the Emperor, and act according
' to circumstances.'

On July 24 the general commanding the 4th Corps
telegraphs from Thionville to the major-general at Paris:
' The 4th Corps has neither cantines, nor ambulances, nor
' vehicles. Everything is completely wanting.' ' The 3rd
' Corps,' says the intendant of that body on the same day,
' leaves Metz to-morrow. I have neither overseers of in-
' firmaries, nor workmen, nor ambulance wagons, nor ovens
' for the campaign, nor train, nor instruments for weighing ;
' and for the 4th Division and the division of cavalry I
' have not a single functionary. I pray your Excellency to
' relieve me from the embarrassment in which I am; the
' Quartier Général not being able to help me, though there
' are there more than ten functionaries.' ' To-day,' telegraphs the sub-intendant at Mézières to ' War' on July 25,
' there are neither biscuits nor salt meat in the fortresses of
' Mézières or of Sedan.' Thus along the whole line of
frontier, from Mézières to Belfort, there is an almost total
want of men, of provisions, and of the munitions of war.
At the great fortress of Metz, on August 9, besides the arms
destined for the *garde mobile* of the department, only 30,000
breech-loading ' fusils' and 18,000 of the model of 1866
are found by General Soleille. On August 8 the intendant
of the 6th Corps has ' not a ration of biscuit, nor of pro-
' visions for the field,' at the same time that the intendant
of the army of the Rhine is applying to him for 400,000
rations. Forty-five telegrams, from July 18 to August 21,

tell the same infamous story. From Bitche, Metz, Thionville, Mézières, Sedan, Strasburg, Belfort, Verdun, Perpignan, the arsenal of St. Omer, Epinal, Langres, Besançon, Nîmes, come demands for bread, biscuits, ammunition, cartridges, tents, cooking vessels, wine, brandy, sugar, coffee, bacon, dry vegetables, fresh meat, bedding, shirts, shoes, small arms, bayonets, harness, and money. In every instance the want is urgent. The replies of Marshal Montauban to this torrent of complaint and of requisition are not forthcoming.

With France in a condition which can only be understood on the assumption of the long-continued pillage of her resources by functionaries of every grade, there is a grim and terrible humour in some of the earlier despatches from the Emperor, who, in spite of all denials, is now shown to have commanded in chief down to August 31. 'Louis is 'very well,' telegraphs his father to the Emperor from Metz on July 30; 'he has slept for sixteen hours straight 'on.' 'Send me a bracelet for the wife of the prefect,' says another telegram of the same date. 'Little Malakoff has 'found two more trefoils with four leaves. I will send them to you,' telegraphs the Empress to the Prince Imperial on July 31. 'I have no news of MacMahon,' telegraphs the Emperor, still at Metz, on August 6, to the Empress, at 3 P.M. At that moment was raging the crucial battle of Wörth, where, in about equal numbers, 120,000 French and Germans, under the command of a marshal of France and of the Crown Prince of Prussia, were engaged in a hand-to-hand struggle, which extended over nine miles of country, and which left 14,000 corpses for interment in the field. At what hour the news reached Paris does not appear. At 2.25 P.M. of August 7 the Empress telegraphs to her husband : 'I am highly satisfied with the resolutions taken at the 'council of ministers, and I am persuaded that we shall 'hunt the Prussians to the frontier at the point of the 'sword.' But at 12.35 of the same day she had telegraphed to the Princess Mathilde at St. Gratien : 'I have bad 'news of the Emperor. The army is in retreat. I return to 'Paris, where I convoke the council of ministers.' The battles of Wörth and of Forbach were being fought at the same time. 'The state of public opinion is excellent,' telegraphs Emile Ollivier to the Emperor at 9.45 P.M. on the same day; 'to stupefaction, to immense grief, have succeeded con-'fidence and enthusiasm.' Englishmen, passing through Paris at the time, bear witness to the general display of the former emotions, but saw nothing of the latter.

Twelve days later than the battle of Wörth came the decisive action at Gravelotte, which proved the success of the Prussian strategy in the effectual masking of Metz, under which fortress they penned up Bazaine and his force, to be taken at leisure when they had destroyed the wandering army of the Emperor. On the 16th the Emperor arrives at Etain on his way to Verdun. The object of the movement is not stated. In point of fact it was a hasty flight in order not to be shut up in Metz. 'My dear mama,' the Prince Imperial telegraphs the same day, 'I am quite well, ' so is papa; everything is going on better and better.' But on the following day, from his quartier général—where is not stated—the Emperor enquires of the mayor of Etain, ' Have you any news of the army?' The two regiments which escorted the Emperor to Etain seem to have been intended as the *avant-garde* of the retreat of all available forces on the camp at Chalons, or indeed on Paris itself, as announced in a letter to the Empress, of which we have only a telegraphic acknowledgement from the Minister of War. ' I implore the Emperor,' signals 'War,' 'to renounce this ' idea, which looks like the abandonment of the army of ' Metz, which cannot, at this moment, effect a junction at ' Verdun. The army of Chalons will be 85,000 men within ' three days, without counting the corps of Douay, which is ' 18,000 men, and which will rejoin in three days. Can you ' not make a powerful diversion on the Prussians, already ' weakened by several combats? The Empress shares my ' opinion.' 'I yield to your opinion,' replies the *César manqué*; 'do not delay the movement of the cavalry. Bazaine ' urgently demands munitions.' This is dated at 9.4 (not said whether A.M. or P.M) on August 18, the day of the battle of Gravelotte. 'If, as I believe,' telegraphs MacMahon on the following day to Bazaine, ' you are shortly obliged to ' retreat, I do not know, at the distance at which I am ' (Chalons is some eighty-five miles from Metz as the crow flies), 'how to come to help you without uncovering Paris. ' If you think otherwise, let me know.' It is probable that this telegram reached a Prussian address. Bazaine's inadequate grasp of the situation is indicated by a telegram to the Emperor, at Chalons, on the 18th: 'I do not know what ' is the provisioning of Verdun.'

The movement of the army of Chalons, under the nominal command of Marshal MacMahon, but really under the personal command of the Emperor, is intelligible on no hypothesis but that of the terrified flight of a ruined, helpless, and

utterly incompetent commander before a master of the art
of war.   Headquarters were at the Chalons camp from
August 17 to 21; at Rheims on the 22nd and 23rd; at
Réthel on the 24th; at Le Chêne Populeux on the 27th;
at Carignan on the 30th; at Sedan on the 31st. A despatch
from Marshal MacMahon to 'War,' at Paris, on the 27th,
reveals the key to this unprecedented aberration.

'The first and second armies,' says the Marshal, meaning German
armies of more than 200,000 men, 'block Metz, principally on the left
bank [of the Moselle]; a force estimated at 50,000 men would be
established on the right bank of the Meuse to hinder my march on
Metz.   Information reaches me that the army of the Prince Royal of
Prussia is marching on the Ardennes with 50,000 men.   It must be
already at Ardeuil.   I am at Le Chesne with a little more than 100,000
men.   Since the 9th I have no news of Bazaine.   If I advance to meet
him, I shall be attacked in front by part of the first and second armies,
which, favoured by the wood, may bring up a force superior to mine;
at the same time attacked by the army of the Prince Royal of Prussia,
cutting off my retreat.   To-morrow I shall reach Mézières, whence I
shall continue my retreat, according to circumstances, towards the west.'

Two other telegrams have a terrible significance. One is
from MacMahon to the Minister of War on August 24: 'I
'fear to meet again in the Ardennes great difficulties in
'supporting the army from the country—difficulties which
'will become insurmountable if we manage to join Bazaine.
'I require that considerable convoys of biscuit should be
'sent towards Mézières, say 2,000,000 rations.' On the day
preceding the Emperor had telegraphed to the Minister of
War that it was essential to send to Rheims a force considerable enough to protect the communication, which each
day's retreat rendered it more easy to cut off.   Still more
damnatory is a despatch from 'War' to Marshal MacMahon,
so far back as August 19: 'I learn from certain sources that
'the corps are not guarded, that no serious reconnaissance
'has been organised to the present moment.   I make an
'exception for the cavalry division of General Fénelon,
'which has given us useful information.   I know that the
'corps of Failly, at Chaumont and at Blennes, has neither
'scouts nor sentries.   This want of vigilance has allowed
'small parties of the enemy to cut the railways.   Be good
'enough to give orders that vigilance should be redoubled
'on the moment.'   Such was the result of playing at
soldiers, at the cost of France, under the shadow of a great
military name, by a man who was neither a statesman nor a
soldier.   The Ministry at Paris had to complain of the

absence of all proper vigilance in the army on which all
depended, and which was under the personal command of
the Emperor!

Of the great catastrophe at Sedan we learn little from
the papers under notice, except how inevitable it had become from the moment that, repulsed from Paris by the
Empress and the Minister of War, the Emperor allowed
the mighty wedge of the Prussian army to be driven between his army and the capital. 'Have you reflected,'
telegraphed the Empress, in a despatch which, found torn
into fragments, was pieced together by the Commission,
'on all the consequences which will follow your return to
'Paris under the blow of two defeats?' 'You have only
'before you a part of the forces which block Metz,' telegraphs 'War' to the Emperor on August 27. 'In the
'name of the Council of Ministers and of the private
'council,' telegraphs the same Minister to MacMahon on
the 28th, 'I demand that you carry succour to Bazaine,
'profiting by the thirty hours' advance that you have on the
'Prince of Prussia.' Short and decisive is the reply: 'Sedan,
'August 31, 1870, 1.15 A.M.—MacMahon informs the Minister
'of War that he is forced to move on Sedan.' And then
on September 4 comes the news, from the Empress to her
mother, the Countess de Montijo at Madrid: 'General
'Wimpfen, who took the command after the wound of
'MacMahon, has capitulated, and the Emperor has been
'taken prisoner. Alone, without forces, he has yielded to
'what he could not help. All the day he was under fire.
'Courage, dear mother; if France will defend herself, she
'can. I will do my duty.—Your unhappy daughter, Eugénie.'
It is impossible not to uncover the head in presence of so
much constancy displayed, at the supreme moment, by a
lady who had just lost all. But the inability to see the
situation in its true colours, that is betrayed by the first
jubilant despatches of Conti and of Persigny, is no less
apparent in this last utterance from the Tuileries.

The third act of the drama was brief: 'The agitation is
'great in Paris,' telegraphs the Prefect of Police at 9.40 of
September 3, 'to the Empress. War, Interior, Governor of
'Paris, General Soumain.' 'Bands promenade the Boule-
'vards and the principal streets, uttering seditious cries.
'At 9 P.M. several hundred individuals attacked the
'police station on the Boulevard Bonne-Nouvelle.' 'While
'the Chamber,' says a telegram signed 'Hubaine,' addressed
to 'Prince Napoleon, Palace Pitti, Florence,' 'assembled in

'its bureaux, deliberated, the mob invaded the tribunes.
'The National Guard proclaimed the Republic. It is a fact
'peaceably consummated thus far.' Then follows the last
despatch sent from the Tuileries on September 4. It is
signed by M. Filon, the preceptor of the Prince, who sent
most of the despatches of the Empress, and is addressed to
M. Duperré, who on the preceding day had been desired to
await new orders at Landrecies. 'Paris, 1.50. Duperré, à
'Maubeuge. Filons sur Belgique. Filon.'

So fell the Second Empire. It had called down the
thunder of war on undefended France in order to stifle the
yell of the Revolution. It fell by two blows, either of
which would have been mortal, received on the field of
Sedan on September 2, and in the streets of Paris on September 4; and of all the miseries and humiliations which
the German invasion, self-defensive as it was on the part of
the invaders, brought upon France, none were more severe
than, if any approached the violence of, those inflicted on
Paris by the furies of the Red Republic.

ART. IX.—*A Bill for the Redistribution of Seats at Parliamentary Elections, and for other purposes relative thereto.*
Ordered by the House of Commons to be printed on the
1st December, 1884.

A CALM has succeeded the storm of last autumn. No
    sooner had the two great parties in the State ceased
their contest for victory, than the tumult dropped, and
on either side the object, for which this fierce conflict had
been raised, appeared to be regarded with an amount of
apathy which might be mistaken for indifference. This fact
suffices to prove how artificial and unsubstantial was the
struggle, with its popular demonstrations, its interminable
harangues, its mountebank exhibitions, and its preposterous
menaces. If it was ever intended to transfer the seat of
legislation from the Senate to the street, and to inaugurate
that form of government—*Public-Meeting Government*—which
the late Mr. Bagehot denounced as the worst in the world,
the reaction has been complete, the needle has gone round
to the opposite pole. Legislation has been transferred from
the Senate, not to the street, but to the closet; and a complete measure has been introduced to Parliament which it
would have been impossible to pass without the pre-arranged
concurrence of the leaders of parties. Those leaders un-

doubtedly derive their power and their commission from the strength which they represent respectively in the two Houses of Parliament. Their authority rests on the discipline of their respective parties, and as such it is complete; all the clamour of electoral or non-electoral bodies out of doors had but little to do with the matter. A difficult and complicated scheme of legislation, involving a total subversion of the old forms of representation in England, and touching many highly sensitive interests, could only be brought to maturity by an honourable and straightforward negotiation between the leaders of parties, and it is creditable to English public life that, the basis of agreement being once established and accepted, the negotiation was carried on with a promptitude, a practical acuteness, and a fairness which were as conspicuous on one side as on the other. Fortunately, with us, such transactions are placed in the hands of men of high personal honour, who are united by the ties of social intercourse and many common interests and opinions, even when they are most divided upon the politics of the day. The object on both sides was, and is, to remove the anomalies of the old system of representation, and to establish in place of it a fair, equitable method of ascertaining and recording the opinions of the nation. What the effect of these changes may be it is beyond the power of man to foresee. They depend on the opinions which may prevail amongst generations yet unborn. It would have been a contemptible and nugatory attempt to manipulate for any temporary object, or in view of any present party advantage, the vast constituencies of the United Kingdom. On the true principles of popular government, the will of the majority must prevail and will prevail; but, on the other hand, due liberty and power ought to be secured to the opinions of the minority, which, in the never-ceasing changes of the world, will perhaps be the majority of to-morrow. We utterly repudiate the devices and artifices by which scheming politicians may snatch an apparent victory or disguise a defeat. The triumph of truth is the only cause worth fighting for. As long as the conflict of parties lasted, we observed with regret that there was on both sides a disposition to view the conduct of the opposite party with excessive suspicion, and to impute to opponents dishonest motives and intentions. These, we suppose, were the tricks and artifices of war; but on the restoration of peace it was discovered that practical business could be honourably performed by honourable men,

and that their differences could be reconciled by a plain
understanding.

Some years ago the present Earl Grey suggested (if our
memory does not deceive us) that on certain questions of
national interest, requiring the intervention of the Legislature, and rising above the level of party politics, it would be
highly advantageous that they should be considered and
prepared, before they are presented to Parliament, by a
Committee of Council, composed (as such committees frequently are) of statesmen of various political opinions. That
is, or was, the practice in France, where legislative measures
were frequently discussed and prepared by the members of
the Conseil d'État before they were laid before the Chambers. The discussions of five or six men of experience round
the Council Board are conducted in a very different spirit
from the debates in Parliament, stimulated by party feeling
and publicity. These may, with propriety, come afterwards.
Practically this is what has been done on the present
occasion, though with somewhat less of a formal character.
Had a similar course been adopted two years ago to settle
the new rules of Parliamentary procedure, in which both
parties were equally interested, since the object was to
facilitate the transaction of business by the House of Commons, a vast deal of time and labour might have been saved.
So, too, measures of the nature of the Criminal Code might
be prepared for the acceptance of Parliament—measures
which it is impossible for the House of Commons to examine
in detail or to pass; and the fatal obstruction which often
paralyses the action of the Legislature would be defeated.

It would be ungrateful in ourselves not to acknowledge,
with undisguised satisfaction, that the result of this great controversy up to the present time corresponds as nearly as possible with the views we expressed, and the hopes we scarcely
ventured to entertain, in the last number of this Journal.
We pleaded to the best of our ability for a rational compromise of the dispute. We pointed out the dubious and
mischievous effects of a protracted resistance, which would
probably have led to the resignation of the Ministry, followed by a stormy general election. And although we attached but little importance to the intemperate language of
popular meetings, and the desperate attacks on the House
of Lords for having retarded the passage of an incomplete
measure for a few weeks, we are well aware that no good
result could be anticipated from measures carried with great
heat and violence. The good sense of the nation, in men of

all parties, except the avowed enemies of the Constitution, was manifestly in favour of some such pacific arrangement. All the leading organs of the press urged it. The cry of 'No 'surrender' met with no response except from the most foolish or mischievous of politicians. Happily more moderate views prevailed, and this, although neither party scored a triumph or sustained a defeat. That some hesitation subsisted before the leading champions could be prevailed upon to lay down their arms is not improbable. But in this emergency the Constitution provided a remedy in the moderating power of the Crown.

A few days after the accession of her present Majesty, on July 5, 1837, Sir Robert Peel addressed to Mr. Croker a letter on the functions of the Sovereign, some parts of which we are not sorry to quote in this place, for it appears to us to be a model of sound monarchical and constitutional principles, suggested, as was natural, by the recent demise of the King and the accession of so youthful and inexperienced a Princess.

' The theory of the Constitution is, that the king has no will except in the choice of his ministers, that he acts by their advice, that they are responsible, &c. But this, like a thousand other theories, is at variance with the fact. The personal character of the sovereign, in this and all other governments, has an immense practical effect. . . . Respect for personal character will operate in some cases ; in others the king will have all the authority which greater and more widely extended experience than that of any single Minister will naturally give. A king, after a reign of ten years, ought to know much more of the working of the machine of government than any other man in the country. He is the centre towards which all business gravitates. . . . The personal character of a really constitutional king of mature age, of experience in public affairs and knowledge of men, manners, and customs, is, practically, so much ballast keeping the vessel of the State steady in her course, counteracting the levity of popular Ministers, of orators forced by oratory into public councils, the blasts of democratic passions, the ground-swell of discontent, and the ignorant impatience for the relaxation of taxation.'

' " Luctantes ventos tempestatesque sonoras
Imperio premit."

This is the proper function of a king—a function important in other times. . . . But at this crisis of our fate we are deprived of this aid.' (*Croker Papers*, vol. ii. p. 316.)

This last exclamation may have been true, or supposed to be true, when Victoria had been but a few days on the throne, although events showed not long afterwards that the personal will of the Queen was not without influence on public affairs. But it is unquestionably not true at the present day. The experience of a reign extending over nearly half a century, an assiduous attention to the business of State and the duties of her great office, a scrupulous adherence to the fundamental principles of the Constitution, and the respect invariably shown to the estates of the realm in their respective functions, have invested the Queen with a degree of authority the more exalted and effective, as it has been very rarely exercised and never abused. It could not be exercised more opportunely or with better effect than when the two branches of the Legislature had reached a point which threatened a collision; and if we are not misinformed, the royal influence was interposed on this occasion with so much tact, energy, and reason, that it powerfully contributed to solve the difficulty. It was precisely a case in which a power, standing above parties and untouched by their contentions, might reconcile differences which were, as the result has proved, more imaginary than real. The leaders of the Tory party boast of their loyalty to the Crown. The Ministers of the Queen owe deference to the Sovereign they serve. None of them can be supposed to be hostile to the Monarchy. Something might on both sides be yielded to patriotism and to reason, urged with the authority of a Queen; and, in point of fact, if this transaction was assisted by the means to which we believe that it may be attributed, no incident of Her Majesty's reign reflects greater honour on her political sagacity, or displays in a more signal manner the just constitutional influence of the Crown. Perhaps the arrangement which has restored peace to our councils, and which holds out a prospect of the settlement of a great controversy, could not have been accomplished without it.

No doubt there are those who, whilst they approve the dish, are not satisfied with the cookery or the cooks; they accept the result, but they are dissatisfied with the means employed to arrive at it. These are sentiments we do not share. We are not prepared to admit that party ascendency is the necessary or sole basis of legislation, or that a measure loses anything of its value because it is the result of a combination between the leaders of the Government and the Opposition. On the contrary, if the object is not to obtain a party triumph, but to arrive at a just and equitable adjustment of a great national system of representation, the chances of success are largely increased by such an arrangement. Does any one suppose that so large and comprehensive a scheme could have been evolved from the inner consciousness of the House of Commons, and especially of such a House of Commons as we have at present? Or that it could have been hammered into shape by the tedious process of debate? *Tot homines quot sententiæ.* The number of proposals and amendments to proposals would have been infinite, and most of them would have borne the stamp of party passion or personal interest. The experiment was tried in 1867, when a crude Reform Bill, or rather several Reform Bills, were flung on the table of the House of Commons by a feeble Ministry, and were at last transformed and moulded into an Act more by the Opposition than by the Treasury Bench.

A Reform Bill can only be framed by the councillors of the Crown—by men capable of looking beyond the minor motives and objects which influence the members of a popular assembly; and we see no reason to regret that such a measure has been framed by a more enlarged body than a committee of the Cabinet. We believe that on neither side have any unworthy sacrifices of principle been made, and the result bears every mark of honest practical workmanship. And after all the House of Commons is deprived of none of its undoubted rights of discussing and modifying in debate the details of the measure. Some parts of it are undoubtedly open to criticism. The main principles of the bill have been adopted by the House on the second reading; but when the bill is in committee, after the vacation, we are prepared for a fuller examination of its peculiar provisions. But the House of Commons will not be disposed, by a rejection of any fundamental part of it, to defeat the bill. The consequences of such a triumph of opposition by a coalition of malcontents would be the immediate resignation of the Ministry, a dissolution of Parliament, followed by an election under the existing franchise, and the transfer to the Tories of the duty of presenting a measure for the redistribution of seats to another House of Commons. We presume that such a contingency is not what any member of the Liberal party desires, and we dismiss from our minds the possibility of such a catastrophe.

The English people, partly from the antiquity of their institutions and partly from their habitual respect for tradition, live in a world of anomalies, of which they are unconscious until some unwonted agitation or emergency drags them to the light of day. The House of Commons of the Ante-Reform period was believed by men as wise as Burke and as liberal as Canning to represent the people of England in spite of its hundred and fifty nomination boroughs and all the marvellous incongruities of a restricted franchise. The bare idea of touching the sanctuary of the Constitution drove Mr. Croker into hysterics, and wrung a cry of alarm from the Duke of Wellington. The Reform Bill of 1831 reminded the country, as it were on a sudden, that after all the right of sending representatives to Parliament is not as immoveable as the hills, but that it must naturally follow the movement of population and industry, and must be extended with the growing numbers and intelligence of the people. In the last half-century, we believe, about three hundred and fifty seats have been changed or modified in their occupation. There is nothing immutable in the writs which convoke the representatives of the people. But, although large steps have from time to time been taken in the path of Reform, the representation of the people of the United Kingdom is still full of strange anomalies, and we will endeavour briefly to point them out.

1. The inequality of the franchise in counties and in boroughs, which will be abolished on January 1, 1886, by the Act that has now received the Royal assent, was accepted as a principle of the Reform Bills of 1832 and 1867. It was held as a constitutional doctrine of those times that the county and borough constituencies were of a different nature, and that the knights of the shire in some manner counterbalanced the burgesses of the towns. This led to the singular and anomalous result that whereas the population of the counties and of the boroughs is 13,688,902 for the counties and 12,285,557 for the boroughs in England and Wales, the number of electors for the counties is only 966,721, whilst the number of electors for the boroughs is 1,651,732. And the disparity in the number of members returned is still more striking—the numbers being in England and Wales 297 for the boroughs and 187 in the counties. If the number of inhabited houses is taken as a test of the number of householders, in the counties it is 2,733,043 and in the boroughs 2,098,476 ; in the boroughs the householders have the franchise, in the counties a 12*l.* tenancy was required. It is obvious, therefore, that the boroughs have a large excess of voting power and of representatives in direct contradiction to the actual distribution of the population. But, in point of fact, this distribution between town and country is, in the present state of England, more imaginary than real. The towns not represented by borough members form part of the counties. In many counties, espe-

cially in the north, the population is more urban than rural. There the principal industries of the people are not agricultural, but mechanical. It is impossible to draw the line of distinction between the classes, and it approaches to absurdity that a householder living within the limits of a borough should have a vote, and that the small tenant living outside those limits should have none. There are rural voters in boroughs, and there are urban voters in counties; the mere accident of residence gave or withheld the franchise. This anomaly is swept away by the bill which has now become law. So far a positive advance has been made.

2. But the moment the franchise is equalised in boroughs and counties the anomaly of their respective representation becomes more enormous. It is said that two millions of voters will be added to the electoral body, and, judging from the number of inhabited houses, that may be about the number. But all these newly enfranchised electors belong to the counties; the number of borough electors remains unaltered. The consequence is that the county electors would amount to upwards of three millions, and the borough electors to not much more than half that number. Yet the boroughs return 110 more members than the counties.

3. A superficial examination of the existing state of the representation, without entering into statistics, suffices to show that the south of England enjoys a disproportionate number of seats as compared with the north; and it is notorious that whilst the population of the southern boroughs tends to decrease or to increase slowly, that of the northern towns augments with astonishing rapidity. We regret the change. We regret the tendency to the accumulation of the population in enormous masses in the metropolis and its suburbs, and in the centres of manufacture, to which the people are attracted by the hope of higher wages and more constant employment, and by the depression of agriculture and the less productive industries of the south. But the fact exists, and can no more be checked, resisted, or denied than the phenomena of nature; and it is equally certain that, whatever may be the consequences, political power must follow the movement of population, industry, wealth, and intelligence. The greater cannot be governed by the lesser element, nor the stronger by the weaker. Doubts indeed may be entertained as to the ultimate effect of the change on the future welfare of the nation, and on its physical, moral, and even industrial condition; but it is not within the power of laws to control it, or to defend the anomaly arising

out of it. And here it may be added that no part of the
United Kingdom has made so vast a progress in population,
wealth, and intelligence in the present century as Scotland.
The representation of Scotland was fixed at the Union and
by former Reform Bills, under a different state of the country,
and it is universally admitted that Scotland has not her fair
share of Parliamentary representation in the number of her
members and the peculiar distribution of their seats.

4. Nothing is more striking than the extreme inequality of
the number of electors represented by the same number of
members in the existing constituencies. In the counties this
is less sensible, for, with the exception of Rutland and Hunt-
ingdon, few of the county members represent less than 6,000
or 7,000 constituents; some, however, rising to six or seven
times that number. But in the cities and boroughs the
contrast is preposterous. We have counted twenty-seven
boroughs in England and Wales in which the electors are
below one thousand, and this by the side of the enormous
constituencies of Liverpool 61,000, of Leeds 51,000, of
Glasow 68,025, of Marylebone 41,000, and many more. In
Ireland the anomaly is still more patent. The electors of
all the boroughs and cities of Ireland put together amount
to only 59,687, or less than the electorate of the single
cities of Liverpool or Glasgow. There are but eight Irish
boroughs that can be said to have a constituency at all. The
twenty-two remaining seats are mere rotten boroughs—such
as New Ross with 225 electors, or Portarlington with 140.
It is incredible that such a state of the representation should
have lasted so long. Yet the member of Parliament who
represents one of these pitiful hamlets has the same amount
of power as a member for the largest county or city in the
kingdom.

5. Another element of inequality results from the fact that
the City of London returns four members; seven of the
county divisions or boroughs return three members each,
subject to the minority clause; one hundred and eighty
of the electoral bodies in the United Kingdom return
two members each, and the remainder one member only.
The Scotch counties and boroughs return one member only,
with three or four exceptions recently made. Hence it
follows that a citizen of London is represented in the House
of Commons by four times the voting power of an elector
north of the Tweed, and every elector returning two members
has twice the voting power in the House that is enjoyed
by the elector for a single seat. We shall have occasion to

consider the question of double and single seats hereafter; at present we simply point out the fact that this inequality exists, and that an elector who returns one member has half the power of the elector who returns two.

Many more anomalies in the existing representation might be detected by a closer examination; for our present purpose these points suffice. They may be reduced to these five heads:—

1. The unequal franchise in counties and boroughs.

2. The unequal representation of counties and boroughs in proportion to the population respectively.

3. The unequal representation of the south and the north of England, and also of Scotland and Ireland, in relation to their population.

4. The extremely unequal number of electors in the respective constituencies.

5. The inequality arising from the representation of constituencies by varying numbers of members, one by four, some by three, many by two, and the remainder by one only.

These are the anomalies, inequalities, and consequent injustices which the bills brought before the Legislature in the present session, one of which is passed, are intended to remove. We shall now proceed to consider by what means they are calculated to attain that object. The answer is briefly this. The principles of the Redistribution Bill consist in the subdivision of large constituencies, and in the adoption of single representatives, as far as practicable, for each electoral division.

The bill for the extension of the franchise to county resident householders having now become law, though its operation is suspended for a year, it is needless to revert to that branch of the subject, and we shall dismiss it with one remark. If the extension of the franchise to the county householders were to come into operation unaccompanied by a redistribution of seats, the anomalies and injustices which we have pointed out in the preceding pages would be increased to an intolerable extent; for whilst two millions of electors would be added to the counties, they would be represented by the same inadequate number of members as before. In round numbers, the electorate for the counties would be twice as numerous as that for the boroughs, but this vast electorate would return to Parliament about three-fifths of the number of representatives. In other words, the representatives of the borough electors, being the minority of the electorate, would largely outnumber in the House of Commons the representatives of the county electors, who are the majority.

We now proceed to investigate the two main principles of the Bill, namely—(1) the subdivision of large constituencies; (2) the preference given to single seats. It is not too much to say that the country has been taken by surprise by the magnitude of the change contemplated by this measure, and was not prepared for so wide a departure from the traditional forms of Parliamentary representation established for ages amongst us. Public opinion is still unformed, and will be gradually moulded by discussion, to which we would endeavour in all humility to contribute a share; and we shall proceed to lay before our readers some of the reasons which lead us cordially to adopt both these principles, and to show that if this great change in the representation was to be made at all, it could not be made with safety and justice in any other manner.

Short as the time is since the production of the Bill, the defence of it is rendered easy, if not superfluous, by the astonishing alacrity and agreement with which its provisions have been accepted by the country. Men are everywhere dealing with it as if it were already the law of the land. The whole effect of the measure has been discounted alike by the electors and by the candidates of the future. Even the subdivision of the large borough constituencies is accepted without serious opposition. The ill-judged but self-sacrificing efforts of Mr. Courtney and his friends to assail the first principles of the measure by their theory of proportional representation have produced no effect at all. Never did a change of such magnitude and importance meet with so general an approval.

The first point that strikes the eye is the disfranchisement, as it is termed, of 79 boroughs returning 88 members, and the withdrawal of the second member from 36 others. Schedule A and Schedule B, in 1831, were less formidable, and no doubt a large number of honourable gentlemen are shaken in seats to which they cling with affection. But probably their fears, and certainly the grievance of the boroughs in Schedule I, are exaggerated. These boroughs are not in reality disfranchised at all; they are united to electoral divisions of the vicinity, which will increase their importance, and receive from the principal towns a local name. They will lose something of their local and parochial character—what the French call 'l'esprit de clocher'—to embrace larger interests. At the same time the divisions to which they will belong are not so large as to submerge and swallow up the boroughs each division may contain. When identity of franchise is established between boroughs and counties, the line of distinction between them, for Parliamentary purposes, is effaced. It is impossible to define it. This is the very distinction which the promoters of the Franchise Bill sought to remove. The electorate and the character of the representation are both enlarged. One effect of the subdivision of counties is, therefore, to give a different, and a broader, character to the electorate of the boroughs contained in them. They lose the nominal distinction of returning a purely local representative, but they acquire a share in the county representation of increased power.

But to effect this object it is essential that the electoral divisions should be as nearly as possible equal and not too large. Nothing is more deserving of consideration than the evil effects and injustice of very large undivided constituencies returning a plurality of members. In the first place, there can be but few of them, and these are in the great centres of population. They stand, therefore, on a different footing from the average constituencies of the country. An elector in a vast constituency like that of Liverpool, returning a plurality of members to the House of Commons, has a far smaller share of political power and influence than a voter in Portarlington. But, on the other hand, he has a larger share of representation in the House of Commons. He has less personal and more vicarious power.

In very large constituencies it is obvious that the independence and importance of each individual elector is diminished and sometimes lost. It is impossible for candidates to be personally known or appreciated by fifty thousand electors. Hence the management of these elections falls entirely under the control of a committee of wire-pullers and managers. The larger the constituency the less the liberty of choice. That is the real strength of the modern organisation known by the American name of Caucus. In the United States, where the number of voters is enormous, there is probably less real liberty of election than in any other country. The elections are carried by party management, against which the convictions and the will of the individual elector are powerless. And here we may quote a witness of undeniable authority, Mr. Arthur Forwood, the honest and well-known manager of the Liberal party in Liverpool. These are his words in a letter to the 'Times' of December 6:—' *Practi-* ' *cally*,' he says, ' *in the larger constituencies the independent*

' action of the electors diminishes in proportion to the growth of
' their number. I state this from experience gained in a
' highly responsible position in the largest electorate of the
' kingdom.'

If then we wish to establish a just equality between the
constituencies and the representatives of the kingdom—if we
desire to encourage and raise the independent action of the
electors, which is the essence of freedom—if we seek to
paralyse the action of the Caucus which is employed to
enslave them by converting these bodies into the instruments of a single will directing their combined movements
—the remedy is that which is proposed by this Bill, namely,
to reduce the numbers of each constituency to a moderate
average by subdivision. If it were possible to divide the
whole electorate of four millions and a half equally amongst
the members of the House of Commons, the result would
give between six and seven thousand electors to each seat;
and as the constituencies in the metropolitan boroughs must
for special reasons be considerably larger, the average for the
rest of the kingdom would be somewhat lower. Liverpool
with its 61,500 electors, subdivided into nine constituencies,
would have about 6,800 in each of them. The general principle of the Bill is to assign from five to seven thousand
electors to each division. In the metropolis and the largest
boroughs their number is unavoidably exceeded; yet it will
seldom extend to more than seven thousand voters—in a few
cases to nine thousand.*

If the representation of the people is to be based on the
principle of numbers, and if equality of representation is
aimed at, it becomes inevitable that the boroughs of the
metropolis and its suburbs, and the huge industrial boroughs

---

* If we compare the number of electors under the existing household suffrage in the principal towns with the population of those towns,
it appears that the electorate varies from one-seventh to one-ninth of
the population. Thus—

Birmingham has a population of 437,000, with 63,000 electors—
rather more than one-seventh.

Liverpool has a population of 596,000, with 61,500 electors—rather
more than one-ninth.

Edinburgh has a population of 228,000, with 28,000 electors—about
one-eighth.

Aberdeen has 105,000 population and 16,000 electors—about one-
seventh.

It may be assumed that on an average a constituency of 50,000 will
give 7,000 electors.

of the north, should receive a large increase of members. We place in a table the largest of them, with the proposed number of seats.* In the new metropolitan divisions the number of electors can only be calculated by approximation, and we therefore omit them. And for the same reason we omit the county divisions which are taken on the basis of a population of 50,000. But the argument applies alike to all. Nothing, we contend, could be more dangerous and unjust than to devolve the choice of five, six, or even nine members on a single constituency; for it must be done by an organised list of candidates framed by the directors of each party. All independence of choice is extinguished; and the victorious list proscribes in its totality the representatives of the opposition. The experiment has been tried in France with consequences fatal to true freedom, and abandoned; though M. Gambetta sought to revive it as an instrument of despotic power. The *scrutin de liste* is the most baneful invention of democratic despotism. The only security for the independence of large constituencies is subdivision.

We yield to none in the desire that the minority of a populous constituency should have some share in the representation, and that the opinion of one party should not be silenced and unrepresented because it happens in an election for a plurality of members to have polled a few votes less than its victorious rival. It is just that the adverse party should, in the measure of its strength or its weakness, have some voice in the affairs of the country. The minority clauses of the Act of 1867 were intended as a

* The following is the table referred to:—

	Registered Electors	Seats		Registered Electors	Seats
Birmingham .	63,485	Seven	Nottingham. .	20,013	Three
Bradford. . .	27,689	Three	Salford . . .	22,876	Three
Bristol . . .	26,502	Four	Wolverhampton	23,422	Three
Hull	29,102	Three	Glasgow . . .	68,025	Seven
Leeds. . . .	51,228	Five	Edinburgh . .	28,876	Four
Liverpool . .	61,525	Nine	Dublin . . .	14,928	Four
Manchester .	51,153	Six	Belfast . . .	21,492	Four

Several anomalies are apparent on the face of this list. Thus Bristol and Belfast have each *four* seats, though several more populous boroughs have but *three*. Liverpool has *nine* seats, but Glasgow, with a larger constituency, has *seven*. A part of Glasgow, however, will fall into a division of the county of Lanark.

recognition of this principle ; but their application has been limited, and their beneficial effect much contested. They are swept away by the present Bill. The scheme of what is termed 'proportional representation' is no doubt suggested by the desire to do justice to the minority of the electorate, and to prevent superfluous votes being thrown away, by diverting them to a second candidate. But, in spite of the mathematical skill and ingenuity with which this and some similar proposals have been worked out by men of great scientific ability, we are utterly unable to conceive that they are practically applicable to the capacity of four millions and a half of British voters. We are not convinced that the principle is sound, and we believe that the application of it would be ridiculous and unintelligible. It would require a singular amount of progress in education, not to be expected for two or three centuries, before our voting-papers could be adjusted by a mathematical theorem—the *Pons Asinorum*, as Mr. Gladstone called it, of the British electorate. Moreover, this form of proportional representation or double voting is exclusively applicable to constituencies returning more than one member. It does not touch the election of single members or elections caused by the vacancy of a single seat. It does not touch the very large number of single seats already existing in all parts of the kingdom, and especially in Scotland. Least of all could it be reconciled and applied to representation under the new system, which largely increases the number of single seats, and leaves but a scanty margin of double ones.

The true method to arrive at a fair representation of minorities in large constituencies is to subdivide them. The accident of residence determines, to a considerable extent, the character and the political opinions of the inhabitants. If all are united in a common mass, the most numerous class of the population must outvote all the others. But if the quarters of a great city or a large county are enabled to return their respective representative, each of them may hope to send to Parliament a man of their own opinions and interests. It has been objected to this redistribution that it does not provide for the representation of minorities. In our humble opinion it does meet that want in the only fair and straightforward manner in which it can be approached.

Amongst the collateral advantages to be derived from a subdivision of constituencies, two deserve notice: a much larger proportion of the electorate can be brought to the poll, and the expenses of each single candidate are notably

diminished.   At the contested elections of 1880, out of the
68,000 electors of Glasgow only 31,000 voted; out of the
48,000 electors of Hackney 28,000 voted.   We merely quote ·
these cases as examples of a prevalent fact.   It is impossible
to bring very large masses of electors to record their votes,
partly from indifference to so small a fraction of power, and
partly from the size of the electoral area, which places the
candidate out of reach of many of his constituents, though
it imposes on him an excessive amount of labour.   By the
same rule, the expenses of an election for a very large constituency are unavoidably great, and will be considerably
reduced when an election can be conducted by one local
committee on each side acting within an area easily accessible to the candidates in person.   These are not small
advantages.

It is urged in opposition to this part of the measure by
some critics who speculate on the ulterior results of it, which
are necessarily uncertain and obscure, that the subdivision
of large cities into wards will place the election at the mercy
of parochial authorities, and that the members returned will
be men of contracted local influence, less qualified to deal
with the national interests in Parliament; and that this
result will lower the character and composition of the House
of Commons.   We do not share this opinion.   Men elected
to fill municipal and parochial offices are not of a high stamp,
because their duties are comparatively humble.   These are
not the duties, and they do not require the qualifications, of
statesmen.   Municipal and parochial offices are not sought
for by the most cultivated and intelligent classes of society.
But if the wards of a great city are enabled to send members
to Parliament, their suffrages will be courted by men of a
higher class.   It is probable that a generous emulation will
arise between them to secure the services of men of eminence
and ability.   The choice of a member of Parliament will not
be governed by the same considerations as the choice of an
alderman.   Nor, after all, are we much alarmed by the cry
of excessive local influence.   There are abundant examples
in the existing House of Commons of men who represent
nothing but local influence and local importance.   And it
ought to be so.   A man of great local influence, well known
to his fellow-citizens or his neighbours by the public services
he has rendered to them, is far preferable to a stranger sent
down to contest a seat by the Reform or the Carlton Clubs,
or imposed on the electors by an irresponsible caucus.   There
is no merit in the election of a casual politician, because he

happens to be the son of a celebrated statesman or of a grandee, having no previous connexion with the place. It is more reasonable that the choice of the electors should fall on a man they know, whose interests and manner of life are identified with their own.

A more plausible objection appears to be, that the sub-division of seats may in some instances favour the return of what are called 'faddists'—of those mischievous persons who from false notions of humanity, or some other crotchet, devote their energy to the injury of the human species. But has not the existing House of Commons its full proportion of bores, bullies, and buffoons? Does it not contain a certain number of strenuous promoters of contagious diseases—a pack of anti-liquorists and anti-vivisectionists? And have we not seen men of undoubted intellectual capacity stoop to accept these degrading pledges in order to catch the votes of fanatical sectaries? It is an evil that such whimsical notions should affect a single seat; but it is a greater evil that they should turn the balance of parties in a large constituency. Nothing can be more humiliating and discreditable to the representative of a large and enlightened constituency than that he should condescend to owe his seat to a reluctant acquiescence in terms which he knows to be ridiculous and contemptible, if they are not positively wicked.

In the year 1265, the forty-ninth of Henry III., says Mr. Hallam, when the King was a captive in the hands of Simon de Montfort, Earl of Leicester, writs were issued to all the sheriffs of England, directing them to return *two* knights for the body of every county, with *two* citizens or burgesses for every city or borough contained within it. This is the epoch at which the representation of the Commons was indisputably established; and all the writs issued for England in succeeding reigns bore the same peculiar provision. At the accession of Henry VIII. two hundred and twenty-four citizens and burgesses were sent to Parliament from one hundred and eleven towns, London alone sending four. This traditional usage that two members should represent each constituency was therefore deeply rooted in the Constitution, and it was rarely departed from until Schedule B of the Reform Act of 1832 reduced the representation of a considerable number of boroughs to a single member. It does not appear that any provision was thought of as to the relative efficiency of the representation. The highborn and opulent gentry were vastly outnumbered, says Hallam, by peddling traders; and the same number of *two* was deemed sufficient for the counties of York and Rutland, for Bristol and for Gatton—facts more easy to wonder at than to explain.* We are not aware that any satisfactory explanation has been given of the motives which caused this uniform number of *two* to be adhered to from all constituencies, whether large or small. The notion that it was intended to provide for the personal safety of the members is scarcely tenable; perhaps it was intended to preserve them from oppression or corruption. But the fact was so, and it is a peculiar provision, we believe, of English representation.† There were, however, even before the first Reform Bill, a few boroughs returning single members, such as Abingdon, Banbury, Bewdley, Chipping Wycombe, Higham Ferrers, and Monmouth. Monmouth and Wales were first enfranchised by Henry VIII., who gave *one* member to most of the Welsh counties and to all the Welsh boroughs. The Irish Parliament, before the Union, consisted of 300 members— 64 for the shires, 14 for seven cities, 2 for the University, 220 for one hundred and ten boroughs, all being double seats. The Act of Union retained all the knights of the shire (64) and University seats, but reduced the cities and boroughs to single seats, in number 34. So that the number of Irish members who entered the Parliament of the United Kingdom was 100.

In Scotland it was otherwise, and the forty-five members added to the House of Commons at the Union were each elected for single seats, thirty being allotted to the counties and fifteen to the boroughs and groups of boroughs. This subject was much debated by the Commissioners appointed to negotiate the Union. The existing share of taxes and the number of the people (in 1707) were taken as the basis, and the number forty-five was agreed to, being somewhat in excess of what Scotland was then entitled to. Oliver Cromwell, in his temporary union of the two kingdoms or commonwealths, had estimated Scotland at *one-thirteenth* of England.

---

* Hallam's 'Constitutional History' (ed. 1846), vol. ii. p. 202.

† The chapter on Parliamentary Antiquities in the 'Constitutional History of England,' by the present Bishop of Chester (chapter xx. vol. iii. p. 405), is one of the most learned and interesting portions of that work. But he does not clear up this point of the double representation, though he shows that the representation of the people of England has for certain undergone numerous changes, and been governed by no uniform principle. Every borough had a history and a franchise of its own. In the reign of Edward IV. Much Wenlock was the only English borough that had only one representative.

But under Queen Anne the grouping and settlement of the boroughs were rearranged by the Commissioners, and *one* member was assigned to each group on January 29, 1707. This arrangement remains but slightly altered to this day, but ten members have been added by more recent Reform Bills to the representation of Scotland. It does not appear to have struck the Commissioners of 1707 that there was any unfairness in assigning one member to the Scottish groups of boroughs, whilst the English boroughs had two members each.*

We have then a clear precedent of single seats established by the Union in Scotland, and much earlier in some English boroughs and in Wales; to which must be added the representation of the boroughs in Schedule B in 1832, which lost one member, and similar reductions which have been carried further by later Reform Bills, when several more boroughs were reduced to one member. There are now in the United Kingdom 189 boroughs returning one member only. These members for single seats certainly do not suffer the slightest diminution of rank or consideration from that circumstance. But their constituents, returning one member only, are unquestionably placed in a position of inequality to those boroughs which return two. We believe the principle of single seats to be so just that we wish it could be extended to all of the constituencies. But it seems that a class of boroughs between 50,000 and 165,000 inhabitants are to retain their double seats; we presume because they are not

---

* Single seats were introduced for the first time by Cromwell in the Parliament of 1653. He left only eighty-six seats to the cities and boroughs, each sending one representative, except London, which had four, and Bristol two, the residue being left to the counties in proportion to their population, varying from fourteen for Yorkshire (in three Ridings), and eleven for Devon and Kent, to two for the smaller counties. Wales had twenty-five members, Scotland and Ireland thirty each. It does not appear, however, that the electorate of the counties, returning a plurality of members, was subdivided. Clarendon says, ' Cromwell did not observe the old course of sending writs ' out to all the little boroughs throughout England which used to send ' burgesses (by which method some single counties send more members ' to the Parliament than six other counties do); he thought to take a ' more equal way by appointing more knights for every shire to be ' chosen and fewer burgesses, whereby the number of the whole was ' much lessened; and yet the people being left to their own election, it ' was not by him thought an ill temperament, and was then generally ' looked upon as an alteration fit to be more warrantably made and at ' a better time' (Clarendon's *History*, vol. vii. p. 35).

large enough to be divided. They are, however, only twenty-four in number, an inconsiderable amount which impairs the uniformity of the measure. This anomaly might be avoided by enlarging the area of such boroughs as require it to raise the number of electors on the register to a divisible number.

The effect of the double seat is this : if two candidates of the same party are returned, the elector is doubly represented by two members; if opposite candidates are returned, their voting power on party divisions is annulled altogether, and the elector is not represented at all. That alone is a considerable argument in favour of the single seat. A single member, or two candidates for one seat, are better known to a limited constituency than a plurality of members and candidates can be to a large one; and the juggling which often takes place by the transfer of the second vote, which falsifies the true result of an election, becomes impossible.

On all these grounds we contend that a single vote for a single seat in each constituency is the fairest and most direct mode of ascertaining the true opinion of the electors. But when an electorate is large, the admission of a plurality of votes becomes peculiarly vicious, and leads to false and perplexing combinations. To empower the electors of Liverpool to vote at once for nine members, with perhaps eighteen or twenty candidates in the field, would give rise to endless confusion and all the evils of the *scrutin de liste*. When that system prevailed in France, all the representatives of each department being classed in one or the other list, there were upwards of eighty members and twice as many candidates for the department of the Seine. The consequence was that the electors barely knew the names of their representatives. A similar result has recently occurred at the elections in Belgium. All the members for the city of Brussels, we believe eighteen in number, were carried on one ticket and of one colour. The Catholic party took every seat, and the Liberal party was virtually disfranchised. That result would have been impossible if the electorate had been divided into wards.

Reference has been made in the House of Commons to the recent elections of the Canton of Geneva as illustrating the subject, but the facts have not been accurately stated. They are as follows :—The Grand Council of Geneva consists of one hundred members. The City and the Canton are divided into three *arrondissements* : the City returns thirty-eight deputies, the left side of the Rhone and Lake forty-one deputies, the right side twenty-one deputies. *Each elector votes for the totality of the deputies in his division by the scrutin de liste.* Hence, if a small Conservative majority is returned in the City and on the *rive droite*, and a very large Radical majority on the *rive gauche*, the latter will prevail over the two former divisions, although they represent · three-fifths of the electorate. This [is what has recently happened. On the totality of the electorate the Conservatives have 600 or 700 majority, but the Radicals are returned to the Council in a majority of 51 to 49. The case is of interest because it affords a complete example of the manner in which a minority may defeat a majority when the elector votes for a plurality of representatives by the *scrutin de liste.*

But if subdivision is necessary or expedient in large boroughs and county divisions, much more is it the case in the vast constituencies of the metropolis and the suburban districts. And here we arrive at the most difficult part of the scheme of redistribution. It is impossible to apply to the vast population of the metropolis, approaching five millions, the same arithmetical proportions which have been applied to other parts of the country; for at that rate London and its suburbs would return about one hundred members, and the capital would exercise an amount of power over the great Council of the Empire which it has never possessed, and which we trust it never will acquire, for the predominance of a great capital is fatal to the freedom of a nation. The metropolis is therefore at present subdivided into nine constituencies, the cities of London and Westminster and seven boroughs returning twenty-two members; the number of electors in some of these boroughs being amongst the largest in the kingdom, as Lambeth 55,000, and Hackney and Finsbury above 47,000. The number of representatives is inadequate, and the number of electors, respectively, excessive. By the new Bill the number of metropolitan members will be raised to fifty-nine, each member representing a single district or constituency. The object of this large increase is to represent as fairly as possible the multifarious classes and interests of this vast and populous region. It would be unjust and absurd that the small householders of Lambeth or Hackney should overpower by mere numbers the culture, the political experience, and the property of the City or the West End. And the more the electorate is divided, the more chance there will be that each class may make its just influence felt in the elections. In this Bill the principal London parishes are taken as the most convenient and appropriate limit of the new districts. The boroughs which now return more than one member will be subdivided into wards, corresponding to the number of members to be returned, and the principle of single representation will be carried out in the divisions of the metropolis as in the large towns, with the exception of the City, which is to retain two members. We are entirely convinced that this is the only mode by which a strictly equitable distribution of electoral power in so vast a body can be arrived at, and the subdivision of seats is the only principle which can reconcile the allotment of so many members to the metropolis with the principles of freedom. We have heard it said that the Irish of this or that district of the metropolis will carry a Parnellite member, or that the sugar-bakers may return a saccharine member for a portion of the Tower Hamlets. Be it so, if they are the most numerous householders of the division. It is far better that they should return one member of their own choice and colour, instead of influencing the election of a plurality of members by coalescing with the party supposed to be most favourable to their views and objects.

But in the distribution of seats among the districts of the metropolis in the present Bill we observe a very great disparity between the population of the respective districts and the representatives allotted to them. Thus Fulham has a population of 42,000 and one member; Hampstead, 47,000 and one member; St. George's-in-the-East, 47,000 and one member. These are the smallest constituencies. But St. George's, Hanover Square, with a population of 89,000, has but one member; Marylebone, with a population of 154,000, two members, or 77,000 to each division: Holborn, with a population of 82,000, one member; Lambeth, with a population of 253,000, four members, or about 63,000 to each division: by which it would seem that the outlying districts first named are to be more powerfully represented than the most active, wealthy, and intelligent parts of the metropolis.

Thus, although we are entirely satisfied with the principles of this great measure, which appear to be framed with no oblique object of party advantage, but on broad and just views of popular representation and national freedom, yet we find in it some anomalies in matters of detail which will perhaps be modified when it passes through the crucible of Parliamentary debate. To attack the principles of subdivision and single seats would clearly be to reject the measure altogether and lead to disastrous consequences, and we attach but small importance to the feeble opposition which may be got up against it. The chief merit of the Bill is that it makes purely local objects and intrigues subordinate to national interests. But the strictest rules are open to exceptions, and in some instances the rules have been departed from rather than enforced. We think the City of London should retain the four members it has returned to Parliament from time immemorial, considering that although it has fewer resident householders than some of the suburbs, it comprises the greatest commercial interests in the Empire and the world. It is strange to refuse to the City of London the four members who are given to Edinburgh and Dublin as the capitals of the sister kingdoms. The number of electors for Dublin is only 12,000; for the City of London 22,000. They might vote in four divisions of 5,500 each.

Some of the seats appear to be singularly allotted. Thus Bristol has four members to 25,000 electors, and Bradford three members to 28,000. Liverpool is to have nine members, and Glasgow only seven. In Ireland, it remains to be seen what the number of electors will be when the small boroughs are abolished and the franchise extended in the counties; but it is obvious that Ireland has been treated with extraordinary favour. We believe it to be wise as well as just to place Ireland on a footing of perfect equality with the other portions of the United Kingdom, but it is Quixotic to go beyond that line. On every principle of population and wealth it is demonstrable that the present number of the representatives of Ireland is too large and ought to be diminished by ten seats at least—the more so as five seats have been added to the Irish representation since the Act of Union was passed.*

Of all the provisions of the Bill, that which has excited the greatest amount of surprise and dissatisfaction is the proposed increase of the number of members of the House of Commons to 670, and we have no doubt it will be strenuously resisted. The seats required to make up the addition to the Scotch representation could easily be obtained by slightly diminishing the large number of seats allotted to some of the great towns, and by reducing the Irish representation to its true limits, in accordance with the general principles of the Bill. We do not scruple to say that we should prefer to reduce the number of seats both for England

---

* Two of these seats have, however, been lost by the disfranchisement of Sligo and Cashel.

and Wales and Ireland, in order to provide the twelve additional seats which Scotland justly demands, rather than submit to the evil of an addition to the House of Commons.

It is not unnatural that politicians who refer exclusively to their party interests, should speculate upon the effects this great measure may produce on their relative party strength. If we believe some of the speakers and writers of advanced Liberal opinions, it would appear that England never before enjoyed a liberal government or possessed a democratic electorate. They forget that the main strength of the democratic party lies in the large cities and small boroughs, in which household suffrage was introduced by the Tory Reform Bill of 1867; no addition at all is now made to this urban electorate, but rather the reverse, for the large towns are to be divided and the small boroughs abolished. But the main strength of the Conservative party lies in the English counties; the number of their representatives is notably increased; county divisions absorb a multitude of small boroughs; and we see no reason to suppose that the addition of a large number of labouring men in the agricultural districts of England will materially alter the political character of their representatives. These men share to a great extent the opinions, and even the prejudices, of their employers. It appears to us absurd to suppose that the votes of the peasantry will change the aspect and the procedure of the House of Commons. Yet some of the enthusiastic promoters of the extension of the franchise to the rural districts persuade themselves that a new era is about to dawn on Britain—that we are to witness no more obstruction, no more rash wars, no more discontent, but a period of wise and active legislation and peace, under the indisputable ascendency of a Liberal majority. On the other side, it is hoped by the Tories that the country vote will oppose a considerable check to the democracy of the great towns, and that the Conservative party will be strengthened by the change. In our judgement these anticipations are alike unfounded. We applaud this Bill because we believe it to be *just*, and because the mechanism of election is improved by it. But nothing certain can be known of its party results, and the probability is that the conditions of party strength will not be materially changed by it. They will remain, as they ever have been and now are, variable, fluctuating with the questions and emotions of the day, with the influence of rival statesmen, with the services they may render or the errors they may commit. The permanent and uncontested ascendency of one party is not to be expected or desired in the interests of freedom itself: it is of the essence of the British Constitution that political power is checked and disputed by the action and counter-action of two leading schools of opinion. It were well if any change could restore to the House of Commons the dignity and the consideration it once enjoyed. The strength of the electorate and the power of that House may be increased, but the respect of the nation is paid not to its power, but to the wisdom with which that power is used. Political wisdom comes from above, not from below. It is a product of experience, of education, of thought, of a disinterested regard for the interests of all classes in the State. These are the qualities which raise the noble science of government above the miserable intrigues of 'rings,' and 'caucuses,' and selfish factions. These are the gifts which entitle men to be the chosen rulers of a free people. There is always some danger that the masses of the electorate may be misled by false views of economical interests, or by impulses of religious intole-rance, or by the revival of national panics or enmities, for their ears are as open to false prophets as they are to their truest advisers. But the larger the constituency of the nation is, and the more divided its interests and opinions, the less are error and passion likely to triumph over truth and reason. The broad basis on which the Constitution rests is its best protection against faction and the best security for its duration.

NOTE.

The Marquis of Montcalm and the Post-boy.

In an article on the 'Memorials of the Merivale Family,' in the last number of this Journal (vol. clx. p. 545), we quoted from a letter of old Mr. Samuel Merivale a rumour or conjectural anecdote stating that the Marquis of Montcalm, who had recently fallen at Quebec, was the same individual who 'had shot the poor boy who was driving him from Tavistock to Plymouth at the beginning of the War.' This is clearly a case of mistaken identity, and if anyone shot a postboy at that time it was certainly not the Marquis of Montcalm, the hero of Quebec. For the publication of this anecdote has not escaped the attention of the representatives of that illustrious person, and we have received from the present Marquis of Montcalm the following letter, which will be read with considerable interest. As far as we are our-selves concerned, we regret that we should have caused any annoyance to the family of the Marquis of Montcalm by borrowing an erroneous statement from Mr. Merivale's letter. But the details we are now enabled to produce from the most authentic source are a complete answer to the charge, and we are indebted to the Marquis of Montcalm for his permission to publish them.

Paris, 6 rue Casimir-Périer, November 24, 1884.

' Sir,—In the October number of the " Edinburgh Review" there is a bibliographic notice of a work, recently published in England, entitled " Memorials of the Merivale Family." In reviewing this book mention is made of a curious and, most assuredly, a very unlooked-for revelation—that of a murder committed on the person of a postboy by my great-grandfather, the General, Marquis de Montcalm, whom the lad was conducting from Tavistock to Plymouth.

' It is affirmed that the high rank alone of the general saved him from the punishment he so justly deserved. The reviewer, who seems to give credence to the adventure, is, however, very naturally surprised at such impunity, the supposed murderer being in the service of a power at the time at war with England.

' The respect I owe to the name I bear, which honoured name unfortunately ends with me, enjoins me here to give a most decided denial to the accusation ; and I now apply to your well-known esteem for historic truth and to your courtesy to make that positive denial as public as has been this most extraordinary affirmation. The General de Montcalm, my great-grandfather, never set a foot in England, and I can prove it ; but the accuser himself renders my task easy by precising the date. According to Samuel Merivale, the murder was committed at the commencement of the Seven Years' War, which was declared on May 18, 1756. My great-grandfather was in his family in Languedoc, where he had passed the winter of 1755–1756, when he received in the month of February 1756 a letter from the Comte d'Argenson, Minister of War, informing him that the king had named him to command the royal troops then in North America. Before the end of the month the general was at Versailles, where he had hastened to thank the king for his appointment ; and, after a delay of five weeks, scarcely sufficient to make the necessary preparations for such an expedition, he sailed for Quebec, where he landed on May 21. England knows well that he never returned.

' It suffices to compare these dates to prove Montcalm's innocence. Nothing is to be added by his grandson, and I will not even inquire after the origin of such a suspicion arisen against the vanquished warrior whose memory has been so nobly honoured by England.

' I remain, Sir, your most obedient servant,
'MARQUIS DE MONTCALM.'

No. CCCXXX. *will be published in April.*

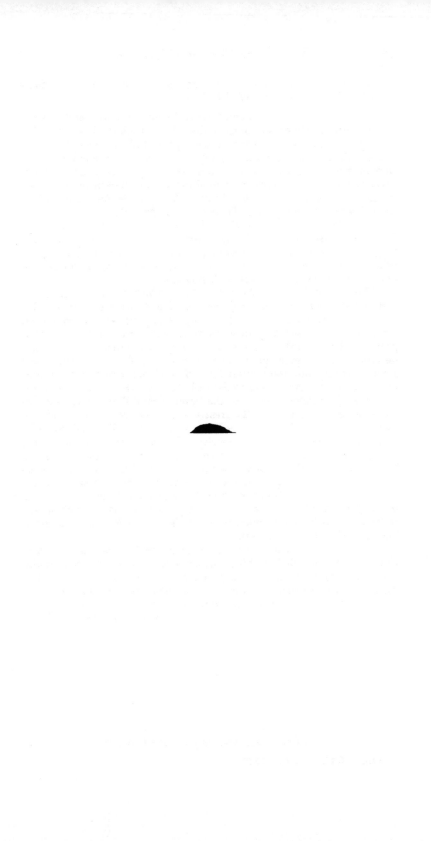

THE

EDINBURGH REVIEW,

APRIL, 1885.

№ CCCXXX.

ART. I.—1. *Celtic Scotland.* A History of Ancient Alban. By W. F. SKENE. Edinburgh: 1876.

2. *Historical Tracts.* By Sir JOHN DAVIES, Attorney-General and Speaker of the House of Commons in Ireland. Dublin: 1787.

3. *Report of the Royal Commission on the Crofters in the High-lands of Scotland.* Presented to Parliament 1884.

THE full and fast river of our time has many curious eddies in its course, and none are more curious than those which carry the looks and the longings of men back to primitive conditions of society. The causes are clear enough. The battle of life is sore on many, and it is only natural that they should envy a time when, as they imagine, there was no such battle, or when victory was equally easy to all the combatants. Yet nothing can be more certain than there never has been such a time since the gates of Eden closed. Of the condition of Man in the days which were really primeval we are absolutely ignorant. But as we see him in the light of the very earliest traditions, we see him, as he is now, a Being bound to labour, and a Being fitted for it with great varieties of faculty and with deep-seated inequalities of power. We see men already divided into tillers of the ground and into keepers of herds and flocks. Both of these established avocations presuppose a long course of effort, and of all the needs under which effort is evoked. Moreover, when individual Person-alities are dimly seen, we see them divided, as they are divided now, not only according to inequalities of mental aptitude, but according to inequalities, cutting deeper still, between the good and the bad, between the virtuous and the vicious.

Moral qualities, even more than intellectual gifts, have been the great secret of individual success. From the beginning the sacrifices of some men have been not accepted, because of ' sin lying at the door.' And when real history begins it is always the figures of great men that first appear upon the stage. They are the centre of every group. They are the reason and the cause of every movement. The qualities which had secured to the family of Abraham his great pastoral wealth in Ur of the Chaldees, were the same qualities on account of which the exclusive possession of a whole country was promised to him and to his children. That was the earliest Land Charter of which we have any knowledge. But it was a Charter which could not be, and was not fulfilled, except by battle. Without the sword of Joshua, neither the faith of Abraham nor the lawgiving of Moses would have placed the chosen people in possession of the Promised Land. And so it has been ever since. In all the early movements of Mankind the great qualities of individual men have been the cause of every success, the foundation of all authority, and the indispensable condition of all secure enjoyment. With the single exception of the glimpse presented to us of the condition of Palestine between the arrival of the great Patriarch at Mamre, and the migration of his children into Egypt, we have no knowledge of any ancient people who were able to occupy a land so comparatively empty that they could live in it without fighting. The beautiful story of the parting of Abraham and of Lot* is the earliest account we have of a dispute about the possession of land, and contains within itself almost the whole philosophy of the dispersion of Mankind. But it was a case of dispersion under conditions which were not and could not be lasting—conditions, namely, under which vast tracts of country were as yet unappropriated. Even then, strange to say, we are told that there were many native tribes already established in the land, and that famines were occasionally sore among them. It can only have been an occupation on sufferance that was then enjoyed by the Hebrew brethren when they had as yet nothing of their own—'no, not so much to set their foot ' on.' This is clearly expressed in the speech of Abimelech to the Patriarch: ' Behold my land is before thee, dwell ' where it pleaseth thee.' † But this was not ' possessing ' the land,' as they hoped to possess it, and as the promise was that they should possess it. Exclusive ownership was

---

* Gen. xiii. 5-9.   † Gen. xx. 15.

the promise, and without exclusive ownership there could be no freedom and no security. God, indeed, had made that land of Canaan in the same sense in which He has made all the corners of the earth. But He had not made it for all men, but for that particular family of men whom He made strong to take it, and to hold it until by unfaith they lost it, and its sceptre departed from them. No other conquering Tribe has ever been charged with the same mission, or has brought the same gifts to men. But it may be said with truth that, generally speaking, every conquering Tribe has had some mission, and has added something above its fellows, and above its enemies, to the progress of the world. And although we know little—curiously little—of those great migrations westward from Central Asia which, during several centuries, covered the ground of Europe with fresh and ever fresher deposits of human character, this at least we do know, that they were from the first fighting races, continually reducing to bondage those whom they overcame, and themselves passing under service to the leaders whom inborn inequalities of mind had raised to positions of command.

The famous and powerful sketch which has been left by Tacitus of the German Tribes, as they were known by him, does indeed present a picture of social equality, in which personal pre-eminence found only a personal and temporary recognition. And, no doubt, so long as they remained in their own woods and marshes, fighting with none but inferior races, living only on cattle and on the chase, neither having nor desiring a settled life, or peaceful and agricultural pursuits, the polity described by Tacitus might be strong enough. But we know what followed. During the dim centuries when the Barbarian nations were gathering behind the forests of Germany and the marshes of the Danube, coming, as Tacitus ignorantly supposed that no migratory nations could come—not by sea, but overland from distant centres of origin and overflow— during those dim centuries the Germans and all the swarms above them to the north, and behind them to the east, were closing their ranks, and consolidating their strength under one great Polity of military subordination, and of power regulated and transmitted through hereditary succession. There is no greater mistake than to suppose that this Polity, which culminated in the code of law and usages since grouped under the name of the Feudal System, was founded on any unnatural usurpation, or that the authority which

came to be vested under it in Chiefs and Kings was anything
more than an embodiment of the facts of nature, and an
expression of the insuperable necessities of the case. Under
such conditions of fierce competition, determined always by
the arbitrament of arms—conditions of perpetual and chronic
war—it was not possible that success could be attained, or
civilisation could be established, except by resting upon
those through whom, and by whom, Power could be wielded
best. Thus, for example, the feudal principle that every
holder of land must hold it under tenure from some Superior
in whom the dominion lay—this principle did not grow out
of any theory, but was the simple recognition of the facts of
life. It had come to be true as one of the necessities of the
age, long before it was formally recognised as one of the
doctrines of the law. There is no value in land except
when it can be held in peace. But in times when there
was a universal scramble for the possession of it by rival
Tribes, it never could be held in peace except under the protection of those who were strong enough to defend it. And
no man could have this strength except by leaning on the
existing organisation of society, and on the personal authority
of those who were at its head. Nor is there any truth in the
idea which has been sedulously spread that those northern
races, who were the last to accept the Feudal System in its
final form, were races who lost by that acceptance any
individual freedom or any social equality which they had
enjoyed before. The truth is all the other way. Amongst
these races the same general causes had not only established the same dependence of the body of the people on
the authority of Kings and Chiefs, but had made this dependence much more arbitrary and oppressive than under
the perfected forms of feudalism.

The usages which spring up in a rude condition of society
are subject to developement, like other things, in two very
different directions. When the conditions are favourable
to the establishment of a settled government and of an
advancing civilisation, these usages become more and more
subject to reason and to judicial definition; whatever elements there were in them of mere despotism and injustice are
dropped out or softened down; and, finally, all the elements
which remain become built up into a well-ordered system of
government and of law. When, on the contrary, the conditions of society are not favourable—among tribes which are
never destined to grow into great nations—such usages
become subject to a developement very different indeed. It

is the developement of corruption. The grosser elements assert themselves more and more; they become not only stereotyped, but enlarged and strengthened. What was due to mere violence becomes still more violent, what was undefined becomes more and more purely arbitrary. What was due originally to natural power and to just authority becomes yielded up to the purest tyranny, until the whole system may grow into one of chronic rapine—fatal to any progress in wealth, or in government, or in law.

Of all these processes there never has been a more conspicuous example than in the customs and usages of that branch of the Celtic race which, pushing farthest west, possessed itself of Ireland. There—in that remotest region of Europe—it became secluded from the movements and the life of the continental world. The elaborate, learned, and conscientious work of Mr. Skene, which we have placed at the head of this article, gives us probably as much as we shall ever know of the earliest organisation of society—if organisation it can be called—among the Scoto-Irish Celts. It began with all the elements of inequality which we find at the foundations of every society. In the first place, it began with the conquest of some so-called aboriginal race which was reduced to bondage. In the second place, it began in the leadership of Chiefs, who from the first seem to have enjoyed greater ascendency than among the Teutonic Tribes. In the third place, among the men who were nominally equal in respect to freedom, there was a very early developement of those differences in wealth which spring directly from the ineradicable distinctions of personal gifts. We are accustomed to think of the word 'capital' as denoting a form or condition of wealth which belongs to later stages of human society. But this is a complete mistake. Both the word and the thing come down to us from archaic times. When flocks and herds were almost the only embodiments of wealth, all the power which riches can ever give was vested in the man who by strength or skill had become possessed of more sheep and oxen than his neighbours. When tillage hardly existed, and when land had all its value from the cattle it would feed, no man could possess land except by having stock to eat its grass. These were the 'capital'— the Heads or Capita—which alone constituted wealth, and he who had none of these could only hire them from the stronger and the abler men who had them. Then, as money was hardly known, the hire must consist mainly in services of some kind. This, therefore, was another

door, besides Tribal allegiance or military subordination,
through which the ranks of bondsmen were recruited, and
the authority of Chiefs became more and more firmly established. It is not a little remarkable that the earliest
title in Celtic society which practically corresponds to the
modern idea of 'landlord' was a word signifying 'cattle-
'lord.' This was the Bo-aire—the Cowlord. It was by
paying service to him that poorer men could alone secure
the enjoyment of that which was then the prime necessity of
life.*

Nor was this direct form of hire the only form in which the
weaker members of a Tribe came to owe and to render service
to its Chiefs. When wars of conquest ceased, intertribal wars
began. They were continual and fierce. The earliest records
of Irish Celtic society show it to have been a society vexed by
continual contests, and every victory was followed by plunder
and devastation. The one great necessity, therefore, of even
the beginnings of peaceful and agricultural life was the
necessity of protection. And this protection could only be
secured from those who wielded the authority of arms. To
get this protection service would be rendered as its price.
And besides the services rendered always, even in the intervals
of peace, special and extraordinary services would be willingly rendered in times of actual danger, or under any
circumstances demanding the special action of the chiefs.
Thus on a multitude of occasions, and under a great variety
of circumstances, customs and usages would establish a corresponding variety of dues and of services from the ordinary
members of the Tribe towards those who ruled it and defended
it. No less than seven different causes have been enumerated
on account of which free men willingly came under terms of
servitude to Chiefs. And then when servitude had once been
accepted, it became permanent. Bondage was even more
hereditary than freedom. Then, again, as the earliest Tribal
organisation broke up into the later organisation of Septs or
Clans, every step of the change involved some increase to the
natural and necessary pre-eminence of those who led. Their
power of inviting and accepting the adoption and amalgamation of 'broken men' from other Tribes—men who necessarily
became direct dependents on themselves—was a power which,
in being necessary to the strength of the Clan as a whole,
was at the same time specially conducive to the concentration
of that power in the hands of its Chief.

* Skene's 'Celtic Scotland,' vol. iii. pp. 143, 144–171.

During more than 600 years from the time when Tacitus described the German Tribes, these changes were working themselves out among the Celts in the profound obscurity of Ireland. The first distinct glimpse we have of them is in the strange way in which they affected even the organisation of the early Christian Church, which to a very large extent was shaped in Ireland after the habits and ideas of the Celtic Tribes and Septs. Its great Monastic Institutions were essentially Clans, and its Abbots were rulers in virtue of their birth, after the manner of succession which prevailed among their Chief and Kings. But Christianity supplied rules and imposed restraints to which there was nothing comparable outside the Church. And so the old Irish Celtic customs, in contact with no higher civilisation, became more and more arbitrary and oppressive, and culminated in a system of tenure, of dues, and of exactions, which was the most barbarous in the world, and was utterly incompatible with any progress in the arts of peace. And all this was of purely native and purely Celtic growth. There is no grosser misrepresentation of history than to pretend that the miseries of the Irish people in respect to the tenure of their land were due to the English conquest, or to the subsequent introduction of foreign laws overriding the native liberties and customs of the country. They were due, on the contrary, to the refusal of the English invaders to impart to the people they conquered the benefit of the higher and better laws which had been built up in England under legal modifications and interpretations of the Feudal System. It was the great shame of England and the great curse of Ireland that for many centuries the benefits of English law were rigidly confined to a few districts of the country; that beyond those districts the native laws were considered good enough for the people, and that even the English settlers were often eager to adopt the barbarous customs which liberated them from the restraints of law, and left them free to turn the arbitrary character of native customs to their own account. 'Hibernicis ipsis ' Hiberniores ' was the boast of some of the Anglo-Saxon settlers; and if this meant, as in some cases it did, that they conceived a warm sympathy and affection for the Irish people, it was a worthy boast. But if it meant, as in fact it did really mean in a great majority of cases during many centuries, that strangers who brought with them a higher code of laws gave up these laws and adopted, and even aggravated, all that was rude and uncivilised in native customs—then it hid, under a plausible phrase, one of the greatest evils which afflicted Ireland, and one of the greatest derelictions of duty with which the English settlers can be charged.

In the most interesting and instructive 'Historical Tracts' of Sir John Davies, who was Attorney-General and Speaker of the Irish House of Commons in the reign of James I., we find conclusive evidence of the barbarous and oppressive nature of the old Celtic customs, and of the desire of the people to escape from them. Whenever they had the knowledge requisite to enable them to understand the difference, 'they were ' humble suitors to have the benefit and protection of the ' English Laws.'* It was through the use of purely native and old Celtic customs that the great Anglo-Irish Chiefs exercised their greatest oppression. 'The English lords,' says Davies, 'finding the Irish exactions to be more pro-' fitable than the English rents and services, and loving the ' Irish tyranny, which was tied to no rules of law or honour, ' better than a just and lawful superiority, did reject and ' cast off the English law and government, received the Irish ' laws and customs, took Irish surnames, &c. &c.'† Nor does Davies speak without a definite meaning in all this denunciation of the old Celtic customs. He had too vivid a picture before him of the results of these to be deceived by words which have a popular sound, and by usages which look as if they had a popular origin and effect. He saw around him the inevitable effects of so-called Tribal rights in the ownership of the soil. He knew that the individual appropriation of land was the first step from barbarism to civilisation, from widespread waste to cultivation and adequate production. He, therefore, specially denounces these usages, which made the individual appropriation of land difficult or impossible—usages which were not unsuitable to a primitive and semi-barbarous condition, but were also specially suited to keep men down to that level and to prevent them from ever emerging from it. He had before him their ruinous effects.

'Again,' he says, 'in England, and all well-ordered commonwealths, men have certain estates in their lands and possessions, and their inheritances descend from father to son, which doth give them encouragement to plant and build and to improve their lands, and to make them better for their posterities. But by the Irish custom of Tanistry, the chieftains of every country, and the chief of every Sept, had no longer estate than for life in their chiefries, the inheritance whereof did rest in no man. And these chiefries, though they had

---

* Davies' Tracts, p. 89.   † Ibid. p. 116.

some portions of land allotted unto them, did consist chiefly in " cuttings " and " cosheries," and other Irish exactions whereby they did spoil and impoverish the people at their pleasure. And when their chieftains were dead, their sons or next heirs did not succeed them, but their Tanistres, who were elective, and purchased their election by strong hand; and by the Irish custom of gavelkind, the inferior tenantries were partable amongst all the males of the Sept, both bastards and legitimate, and after partition made, if any one of the Sept had died, his portion was not divided amongst his sons, but the chief of the Sept made a new partition of all the lands belonging to that Sept, and gave every one his part according to his antiquity.

'These two Irish customs made all their possessions uncertain, being shuffled and changed, and removed so often from one to another, by new elections and partitions, which uncertainty of estates hath been the true cause of such desolation and barbarism in this land as the like was never seen in any country that professed the name of Christ; for, though the Irish be a nation of great antiquity, and wanted neither wit nor valour, and though they had received the Christian faith above 1,200 years since; and were lovers of music, poetry, and all kind of learning ; and possessed a land abounding with all things necessary for the civil life of man ; yet (which is strange to be related) they never did build any houses of brick or stone, some few religious houses excepted before the reign of King Henry II , though they were lords of this island for many hundred years before and since the conquest attempted by the English: albeit, when they saw us build castles upon their borders, they have only, in imitation of us, erected some few piles for the captains of the country : yet, I dare boldly say, that never any particular person, either before or since, did build any stone or brick house for his private habitation, but such as have lately obtained estates, according to the course of the law of England. Neither did any of them in all this time plant any gardens or orchards, inclose or improve their lands, live together in settled villages or towns: nor make any provision for posterity : which being against all common sense and reason must be needs imputed to those unreasonable customs which made their estates so uncertain and transitory in their possession.

For who would plant, or improve, or build upon that land which a stranger whom he knew not should possess after his death ? for that (as Solomon noteth) is one of the strangest vanities under the sun. And this is the true reason why Ulster and all the Irish counties are found so waste and desolate at this day, and so would they continue to the world's end if those customs were not abolished by the law of England.'

If now we turn from the Celts of Ireland to the Celts of Scotland, we find evidences, as abundant as a much more obscure history can afford, of a social condition which began in substantially the same system. The Chiefs seem always to have had, from the earliest times, a much more arbitrary power than among the Teutonic Tribes, as described by

Tacitus.　In war they did not consult their followers;[*] and, as in the earliest authentic accounts we have of the Highlands, the Tribal stage had long passed into the stage of Clanship, we find fully developed all those powers of adoption, of leadership, and of hereditary authority which constituted practically unlimited rule.　But all the developements of time in Scotland were in the direction of modification, of amelioration, of wise and temperate legislation, in direct proportion as the Provinces became united under one Crown, and subject to one Parliament.　In this civilising process, beyond all question, the introduction and establishment of the Feudal System played a most important part.　Historians speak of the silence, of the comparative rapidity, and of the completeness of this great legal conquest as if it were a profound mystery.　But, in truth, there is no mystery at all. The Feudal System spread because it was the best possible embodiment and expression of ideas which had been long familiar, and of facts which had long come to be of universal prevalence.　All ranks and conditions of men found their personal interest in accepting it—because it gave legal definition to customs which had previously been undefined, and held out to a growing civilisation that which is its first condition, and which has always an irresistible attraction to the minds of men—a logical and reasonable system of defined rights and duties, under which all classes knew what they might and what they might not do.　This was the real strength of the Feudal System, although it was greatly helped by the actual spread of a Teutonic population over a large part of Scotland—by the marriage of a Saxon princess to Malcolm Canmore, a contemporary of the Conqueror—and by the subsequent close alliances of the Celtic Chiefs with the Norman and Anglo-Saxon aristocracy.　These were indeed adventitious advantages, and causes of diffusion, which were of inestimable value; but nothing marks more strikingly the real adaptation and fittingness of the Feudal System into pre-existing conditions than the fact that the old Celtic titles, derived originally from the language of Tribes and Clans, became universally translated, without any sense of break or change, into the titles which were known and established over the rest of feudal Europe.　The Celtic 'Mormaers' took their natural place as Saxon Earls holding under the King; whilst under the Earls again the Celtic

---

[*] Sir Walter Scott, quoted in Skene's 'Celtic Scotland,' vol. iii. App. p. 457.

' Toisechs ' took their corresponding place as Chiefs of Clans.
Thus, in the organisation of the Celtic parts of Scotland,
'we find,' as Mr. Skene has said, 'a gradation of persons
" possessing territorial rights within them, consisting of the
' Ardri, or supreme King, the Mormaer, and the Toisech,
" and the latter of these as not only possessing rights in
" connexion with the land, but also standing ·in a relation
" to the Tribe or Clan which occupied them as leader.'*
All this was essentially allied to the Feudal ·System, and
so when that System came into contact with the vaguer,
less definite, but fundamentally analogous customs which
had arisen out of the necessities of life among the Celtic as
well as among the Teutonic Tribes, it naturally absorbed
these customs into itself, and gave to them a legal and well-
regulated definition. Among the Celtic population, indeed,
in exact proportion as the remoteness of the country withheld them longer from the benefits of this System, we find
their own more ancient usages tending not to greater freedom among the mass of the people, but to more absolute and
arbitrary power in the hands of those who were their Chiefs
and rulers. Accordingly, the civilisation of Scotland began
in the Lowlands, where the Feudal System was earliest established, and along the whole eastern districts which were
outside the Highland barrier. Just in proportion as they
were outside that barrier of rough hills and mountains, they
were inside the advancing line of mixed races, and of laws
becoming more just and settled through all those processes
of natural selection which mark the history of an advancing
people.

There is no more striking illustration of the perfect continuity between things new and old in the establishment of
the Feudal System than is to be found in the earliest extant
feudal Charters conferring grants of land. In Scotland
they begin with the Eleventh Century. For brevity and
conciseness they have been always the wonder and admiration of modern lawyers. If they had purported to give or
to secure anything which had not been well known before,
this striking brevity would have been impossible. If they
had conveyed new rights and imposed new duties, it would
have been necessary to describe these, and to explain them.
But as they neither did nor professed to do anything of the
sort—as they were nothing more than a new form of acknowledgement and security for ancient rights which had been

* ' Celtic Scotland,' vol. iii. pp. 57-8.

familiar in the actual transactions of life for centuries
before—it was not necessary to explain anything.   Dominion
over and absolute property in land, with all its incidents,
had been vested in Kings and Chiefs, and in others under
them, in Scotland, as in all other countries, time out of mind.
Hence, the earliest feudal Charters could be, and were, actually
confined to a few lines on parchment, expressing nothing
but the promise and the faith of those who had the
actual power to grant, and the name and designation of
those who were in a position to accept, all the well-known
powers and obligations of ownership in land.   The earliest
extant Charter of lands in Scotland is by King Duncan,
son of Malcolm Canmore, and of the Saxon Queen Margaret
(1094–7).   It is a grant to a Religious House, the Monks
of St. Cuthbert.   It simply specifies the lands by name, and
refers to the 'service' due therefrom as the essence of
their value, and that service as previously possessed by a
certain Bishop Fordan.   All rents and dues at that time
necessarily took principally the form of 'service,' and it was
the right of receiving 'service' from any given lands that
alone in that age constituted its value.   There was no attempt
or need to specify what they were, further than by reference
to the continuity of enjoyment from a former owner.   It is
this definite reference to well-known pre-existing rights that
is one of the most striking features of the early Charters, and
which made it possible for them to be so concise.   The same
general character belongs to all the Charters given by the
Scottish Sovereigns during the eleventh, twelfth, and thirteenth centuries—that is, from the death of Malcolm
Canmore, in 1092, to the death of Alexander III., in 1285.
Almost the same brevity appears in the Charters which were
granted after the War of Independence, and as rewards for
the services rendered in it.   Bits of parchment one inch in
breadth, and a very few inches in length, were enough to
convey great Earldoms and Baronies in the days of David I.
The whole valley of Douglas, sixteen miles in length, from
Tinto to Cairntable, was conveyed to the good and brave Sir
James Douglas by King Robert the Bruce, in a Charter of not
much larger dimensions.   Eleven lines on a small parchment
had been enough to convey the whole of Annandale to an ancestor of King Robert the Bruce himself by King David I.
And when, at a period somewhat later, Charters became more
extended in form, and purported to specify a little more
expressly that which they conveyed, it seems as if all the
resources of language were exhausted to enumerate and in-

clude complete rights of possession of every kind and degree over every kind and description of land embraced within the ancient and well-known boundaries of the estate. In one Charter by King Robert the Bruce, which is now before us, a free Barony is given in 'fee and heritage' over extensive lands in the heart of the Western Highlands, under the following almost poetic words descriptive of its surface and belongings, 'by all its righteous metes and marches, in wood and plain, 'meadows and pastures, muirs and marshes, petaries, ways, 'paths, and waters, stanks, fish-ponds and mills, and with the 'patronage of the churches, in huntings and hawkings, and 'in all its other liberties, privileges, and just pertinents, as 'well named, as not named;' then follow the words which are really the essence of every Charter, being the words which convey an assurance of secure and peaceable possession, such as only the feudal Lord, the King, could give, and in return for which the fealty of the Vassal was to be yielded. The estate was to be held 'as freely and quietly, fully and 'honorably, as our other Barons hold or possess their baronies 'of us.' In a Charter granted by David II., son and successor of Robert the Bruce, to an ancestor of the Argyll family, we have a curious illustration of the fact that these feudal Charters were frequently a mere confirmation of rights and powers which were really of much more ancient date—rights which had been acquired by the Celtic Chiefs, under their own system, and by their own pre-eminence among their own people: for the Charter to which we refer confirms and secures to Gillespie (Archibald) Cambel 'all the liberties 'and customs' which had belonged to a progenitor, who is designated by his Celtic patronymic of Mac Duine. Here we are carried back to times when this patronymic of Mac Duine had arisen among the Dalriadic Celts (who were a conquering and colonising colony from the 'Scots' of Ireland) in the period between the fifth and the seventh centuries.

Such examples as these—and there are many more—are an excellent illustration of what Charters of land really were. They were nothing more than the sign and seal of a new authority set upon a long continuity of leadership, and upon a long continuity of possession of which that leadership had been the real origin, and of which it had always been the real title and guarantee. During centuries of a growing civilisation, that leadership had supplied whatever elements there were of authority, of security, and of acknowledged obligation, in the nascent organisation of the State. Those who held that leadership had originally won it by superior qualities of head and hand; and through many rough and troublous generations they never could have kept it except by a continuity of powers as hereditary as the continuity of names. Nor at any time during the five or six hundred years between the dawn of Celtic history in Scotland and the date of these new Charters had these leaders of the Clans and of the people rendered a better or a nobler service to the country than in that which secured to them those new confirmations of old rights from King Robert the Bruce and from his descendants. The contest in which that Sovereign won the independence of his native country against all the chivalry of one of the greatest military Powers then existing in Europe, was a contest memorable for all time. Perhaps we can hardly realise fully now all the qualities of courage, tenacity, and patriotism which were exhibited by those Chiefs and Barons who stood by the Bruce during all the vicissitudes, discouragements, and almost despairs of that deadly struggle. And when at last the fate of Scotland came to be decided on that famous field in the valley of the Forth, we can hardly realise how stout the hearts must have been which clustered round the standard of the ' Bored ' Stone.' * It is said that the English cavalry alone exceeded in number the whole army of the Bruce. Their furious charges had to be met by a manœuvre of the infantry with pikes, that seems to have anticipated the formation of squares with the front rank kneeling, against which the French cavalry ' stormed themselves away ' at Waterloo. It is imposible, even now, after the lapse of more than 570 years, to read any account of that battle without emotion. For we must remember all the political and social questions which depended on it. For good or for evil, tremendous issues follow on the gain or on the loss of national independence. Where there is an inferior people it may often be well that they should be conquered. The mixture of a stronger race, and the bringing in of better laws, may be the best of all results. But where the seeds of a strong national civilisation, of a strong national character, and of intellectual wealth have been deeply sown in any human soil, the preservation of it from conquest, and from invasion, and from foreign rule, is the essential condition of its yielding its due contribution to the progress of the world. If the English conquest of Scotland had been completed in the fourteenth century, it is not im-

---

* A stone which remains to this day on the Field of Bannockburn, upon which the Standard of the Bruce was planted in the battle.

possible, it is indeed highly probable, that the later history
of Scotland might have been like the later history of Ireland.
Who, then, can compute or reckon up the debt which Scotland
owes to the few and gallant men who, inspired by a splendid
courage and a noble faith, stood by the Bruce in the War
of Independence, and on June 24, 1314, saw the armies of
the invader flying down the Carse of Stirling? Some of
these men were the descendants of ancestors who had held
the same relative place, and had rendered the' same relative service in all the older contests which had built up the
Kingdom and the Nation—which had united under one Crown
the divided dominions of the Picts and Scots—which had
secured the Lothians for Scotland, and established the boundaries of the Kingdom at the Tweed. Never, perhaps, has
there been a more honourable origin for the tenure of land,
and for dominion over it, than that which was consecrated
by the Charters of the feudal centuries in the hands of those
Chiefs in Scotland who had already won and held them for
many generations. In some cases the same lands are to
this day owned by lineal descendants of the men who fought
with Bruce. In others, derivative tenures coming from those
Charters as their legal source have been the subject of inheritance, of exchange, and of sale during the course of five
hundred years. And during all these centuries it can be
shown that the successive holders have continued to be the
leaders of the nation in the ever opening and widening fields
of action on which all the triumphs of an advancing civilisation
have been won. In their hands was vested the only power
which in those rough ages could maintain any civil peace
or political organisation. It was they who introduced the
Norman culture and the Norman law, and it was, as we shall
see, through their wise and gradual legislation that agricultural husbandry was raised to the dignity of a profession,
and was provided with that legal security which could alone
enable it to become an art.

And this brings us to that other great branch of historical
inquiry which concerns not the ownership but the cultivating
occupation of the land. The earliest glimpses which we get
of agriculture in Scotland are connected with the landed
possessions of the Church. And one of the very first of
these glimpses is in some ways the most interesting of them
all. In the narrative of the life led by St. Columba on
the island of Iona, 1300 years ago, left us by the monk
Adamnan, we see a quiet picture of all the operations of a
farm hardly differing at all from those which constitute the

ordinary operations of a modern farm, except that they were more complete and embraced a more varied provision for the comforts of life. There was a mill in which the monks ground their own corn into meal. There were cows and a cowhouse or byre. There were milk-pails carried from the pastures to the monastery on horseback. There was a barn for the storage of grain. There was a kiln for drying it, and a bakery for bread. There was the sowing and the reaping, and there were wheeled carts or carriages for the conveyance of heavy articles.* But these early ecclesiastical communities worked the land themselves, or with the help of servants or bondmen. In Iona, at all events, their land was too small in extent to induce them to let out any part of it on hire. But in this, as in all other cases, a different practice arose naturally out of different conditions. The Church acquired in the Middle Ages more and more extensive grants. That which conferred the island of Iona on Columba, the great Missionary of the sixth century, was before the age of formal Charters, and it seems doubtful whether it emanated from a King of the Picts or of the Scots. But it is curious that the most ancient notice of it which has come down to us lays special emphasis on the feature of it which was novel at the time. That feature was the substitution of 'definiteness' for 'indefiniteness' in the tenure which was asked and given.† The Monks were wise enough to require something better than the vague Tribal tenures which we have seen denounced by Sir J. Davies as common among the Irish Celts. And so throughout the Middle Ages the Church was in this as in many other matters the great civilizing agency in establishing security of tenure in the ownership of land. Ecclesiastics became the largest landowners in the kingdom. The lands so granted could not be wholly cultivated by their own servants and bondmen as the few fields could be cultivated in the little island of Iona. But in principle there is no difference, and in practice there is a natural and inevitable transition between cultivators paid by food or wages and cultivators paid by being allowed to retain a certain portion of the produce. Nor, again, is the transition less easy or less inevitable from this condition of things to that in which the cultivators undertake their work for a definite term of years, and on definite conditions as to the amount they are to pay in produce, or in the price of produce, or in

---

* Adamnan's Life of St. Columba, pp. 361-2.
† Celtic Scotland, vol. ii. p. 88.

services, or (as was often the case) in all three forms of rent. In all cases the essence of the transaction is the same. The tenant gets from the lord or owner of the soil that one thing which he himself has not, and could not otherwise get—namely, the assurance of a right of possession and of cultivation, which was to exclude all others, and in which exclusive possession he was to be protected and defended by the owner whose alone it was, and who alone could lend it and assure it to another. Very often the owner gave or lent other things besides this. But this exclusive enjoyment—this peaceful possession, even when it stood alone —was that for which the tenant or holder was always too thankful to pay a portion of the produce as its price or rent. Very often—generally, indeed, in very early times —when the actual cultivators were very poor, the owner of the land gave or lent something more than the mere possession of the soil. He lent also the instruments of husbandry, and the cattle, sheep, or goats, or other stock, which yielded perhaps the greater part of the whole produce of the land. This is still the footing on which land is let in no small part of Europe under what is now called the metayer system, and which in Scotland was at one time very common, under the name of 'steelbow.' But with the progress of wealth, and of the population of free men, it became more and more possible to let land on definite leases to a class of cultivators having sufficient capital of their own to furnish the necessary stock. The transition here, as in other cases, was natural and easy, since leases had been common under the Roman law, and the ecclesiastics, who first made such covenants, must have been more or less familiar with the customs of their brethren in the south of Europe.

During the five hundred years which elapsed between the death of Kenneth Macalpine and the beginning of the War of Independence, Scotland had made great progress in wealth and civilisation. The Church Dignitaries and the Monastic Bodies had acquired great landed possessions, in the management of which they had been the leaders in agricultural improvement. Accordingly it is in connexion with one of these estates that we have the earliest extant copy of a Scotch lease. It is an agreement or contract between the Abbot of Scone and two gentlemen, father and son, whose name was de Hay del Leys, for the lease of certain lands near Perth. It is dated 1312—two years before the battle of Bannockburn. In many ways this document is remarkable. In the first place, its business-like and definite legal form indicates clearly enough that, although it happens to be the first of these contracts which survives, it must have been drawn out on principles and on practices, if not in a form, which had been long familiar. There could not be a better example of the full powers then involved in the ownership of land, and of the perfect freedom which governed the relations between those who desired to let, and those who desired to hire, the exclusive right of cultivation. Moreover, it is remarkable in this—that the terms of the contract are in their nature those which have come to be designated as an ' Improvement Lease '—that is to say, a lease under the terms of which the lessee was only too glad to execute certain improvements upon the land, and to pay for, and out of, the increasing produce a moderate share of that increase in the form of rent. The term was for thirty years. The rent was to begin at two merks for two years ; to rise to three merks the third year, and so on, one merk more for each year till the sixth. Then for the six following years it was to remain at six merks—that is, until the end of the twelfth year. Then for the eight following years to the end of the twentieth year the rent was to be eight merks ; and then for the ten remaining years of the term it was to be ten merks. Besides this rent they were to grind their corn at the mill of the Convent, and to pay the usual dues on this necessary service. They were to be at liberty to cut fuel (peat) on the farm ; but for their own use only, and were strictly prohibited from selling it. The Convent retained its right to pasture its cattle on the common grazing, and to cut fuel on ' the moors and marshes ' when they shall have need. The tenants were further bound to build on the farm competent buildings for themselves and their husbandmen, which they were to leave so built at the end of their term ; and, finally, in case of the Convent losing the land by any revocation of the royal gift under which alone they held it, the tenants were held bound to leave the farm along with their husbandmen, and with no other compensation than the abatement of one year's rent for the year in which they might be so dispossessed.

This lease exhibits all the essential features of the contracts between free men for the hire of land which, down to our own time, have for the long period of about 550 years prevailed in Scotland, and which, the moment domestic peace and security returned, resulted in an extent and a rapidity of agricultural improvement which has never been surpassed in any country. The secret of its success lies in its definiteness, and with its definiteness, in its justice. The particular stipulations might vary infinitely according to the nature of the subject let. The term of years might vary from five to nineteen, or thirty, or the term might be for a life, or lives. There might or there might not be a bargain about improvements. It depended obviously on the cheapness or dearness of the rent whether improvements would or would not be remunerative, without any other compensation than that secured by the increased production arising out of them. This, too, was generally a matter of express stipulation. In the lease now referred to, the houses built were to be left without any compensation. Probably the houses of that time were made of turf and wattles. But in many other cases the leases provided for the payment of what were called ' meliorations '—that is, for the value of improvements of a special kind. Sometimes they provided for an optional 'break' in the lease at seven years, or some other period short of the full term, and specified that the 'meliorations' should be due to the tenant only if his enjoyment ended at the shorter term, and should be extinguished if it lasted to the end. He could thus calculate securely how far his outlay would be returned. Again, as regards another great source of value in the Middle Ages— namely, dues in the form of labour—there might or there might not be an exaction of services in labour, besides a rent in money or in produce. But the one essential feature in all such lettings by lease was that every stipulation was definite, limited, and precise. Both parties knew exactly what they were agreeing to. If services were included, the amount and nature of the work to be done were generally specifically mentioned. Already, in the previous century, the thirteenth, we find from the rental of the great Abbacy of Kelso, that the Monks had introduced the same principle of definiteness and precision into their arrangements, even with their husbandmen, who had no leases, but who were only tenants at will. The stipulations with these husbandmen as to the services they were to render were so precise that they fixed the occasions on which they were to have their food from the Abbey and when they were to feed themselves.* And more than this—it is observable that at the time of this rental the whole of these services were in process of being gradually commuted into money. As Churchmen were the great lawyers and conveyancers of these early centuries, as well

---

* Burton's ' History of Scotland,' vol. ii. p. 195.

as the greatest landlords and agriculturists, we can understand the influence they had in establishing throughout
Scotland the inestimable blessing of clear and definite covenants in the letting of land. It is to be observed, however, that
these covenants were strictly confined to the relations between
the owner and the tenant, or, as the lease-holding tenant came
to be called in Scotland, the 'Tacksman,'—'tack' being the
name for a lease. No notice whatever was taken in most of
these leases of any class of men subordinate to the lease-
holder or Tacksman. The full powers of exclusive possession
which the owner enjoyed, and in which ownership consisted,
were lent or granted, on the stipulated conditions and for a
given time, to the lessee who hired them. He had full
powe over all inferior or subordinate tenures, if any such
existed. In the case of this earliest extant lease, given by the
Abbo of Scone, there is an express condition that the actual
husbandmen or cultivators were to remove from the land
along with the tenant himself at the termination of the lease.
They might or they might not be mere servants or bondmen.
They were the 'agricolæ' of the old Chroniclers, the 'bondi'
and 'nativi' of the earliest Feudal Charters. They were
regarded as yearly tenants, and in the eastern districts of
Scotland they were often the remains of the old Celtic population.* But, whatever their status was, whether bond or
free, it is clear that they were not recognised as then having,
either by law or custom, any right of occupancy in restriction
or limitation of the full right of ownership. If they cultivated any land at all for their own use, it must have been
only as sub-tenants at will of the 'Tacksman' or lessee, and
as he could not give any possession longer than his own,
they were to leave the farm when he left it. The power of
sub-letting was itself generally a matter of express stipulation. Sometimes it was specially allowed. Sometimes it
was specially prohibited. When there was no stipulation it
seems to have been considered as allowed.

At this time, it is to be observed, the principles embodied
in the lease rested on no special legislation, but on the much
stronger foundation of the acknowledged rights involved in
ownership, as these had come to be developed through the
course of many centuries. All Charters, as we have seen,
had taken them for granted, and they had grown up so
naturally and so reasonably, and so much as a matter of
necessity, that they required neither definition nor support.

---

* Skene, vol. iii. p. 85.

But we have one most extraordinary indication of the fundamental value attached to the full rights of ownership in land, and of the insuperable objections which were then entertained against any division of those rights or any limitation of them except such as might flow from perfect freedom of contract between free men.   This indication is afforded by an entry in the proceedings of one of the early Parliaments of James I. held at Perth in the year 1429— an entry of a most anomalous kind.   It appears that the system of letting land on lease to 'Tacksmen' had become so prevalent that attention had been much called to the consequent sudden removal of the actual cultivators or husbandmen who had previously occupied the lands so let. James I. did not ask his Parliament to remedy this inconvenience by giving to such cultivators any 'fixity of tenure' which would be obviously incompatible with undivided ownership and with the progress of agricultural improvement.   He did not even ask therefore for any positive statute on the subject.   But he proposed to, and obtained from the Barons and Prelates who were the great landowners present at Perth, a promise or engagement that for the future they would give one year's notice to all cultivators or husbandmen whose removal might be involved in any new leases they might grant.*   At a time when there was much uncultivated land, and no difficulty in obtaining the occupation of it, this promise was probably quite effectual to prevent any serious hardship to the cultivating class.   It is not, however, till twenty years later that we find the earliest legislative landmark in the history of tenures.   The first Act of Parliament on the subject arose out of the necessity of deciding whether the owner of land could make agreements binding on his successors by purchase or on other 'singular successors.'   Each new owner, in buying land, bought or succeeded to all the full rights of ownership. Could he be deprived of them by the act of those who had preceded him?   To admit that he could was in one sense an immense extension of the powers of ownership, because it extended those powers even beyond the grave, and made the 'dead hand' prevail over the living.   Yet, in another sense, it would be a great limitation on the powers of ownership, in the hands of the living, because it made them subject to promises and engagements to which the living owner had never been a party.   Whether were the

* Acts of the Parliament of Scotland, vol. ii. p. 17.

dead or the living to prevail? Were all existing and living owners to be deprived of their freedom over their own estates because their predecessors had chosen to limit their own freedom during their own lives? This was one aspect of the question, and it was the aspect in which the question might most naturally be regarded by an Assembly of rough Chiefs and Barons, who were themselves also the greatest landowners in the kingdom. But there was another aspect of the question—namely, this : What was just to those who had taken leases from one owner and found themselves suddenly in the hands of another? Again: What was the best principle to adopt in the permanent interests of agriculture and of all the classes who had interests in land subordinate to the interests of ownership? This was the question which had to be decided by the Parliament of Scotland in 1444, and the manner in which they did decide it is an excellent answer to the ignorant claptrap which assumes that all ancient legislation, having been enacted by the classes connected with the ownership of land, was necessarily guided by a purely selfish spirit. It would be more true and philosophical to admit that, on the whole, in every advancing country, each generation has had at least as much conscience and as much sense of justice as our own. So it was certainly in the fifteenth century in Scotland; and, although in that case, as in all other similar cases, the decision which was just was also, in the long run, the decision most conducive to the interests of those who might have been tempted to think otherwise, yet the reasons which influenced that decision were reasons of conscience dictating a wise and reasonable policy.

It is, indeed, remarkable that these considerations, and not what we should now call reasons of political economy, are especially set forth in this statute, as the determining considerations in the case. The wording is curious:—

'It is ordained for the safety and favour of the poor people that labour the ground that they, and all others, that have taken or shall take lands in time to come from Lords, and have times and years thereof, that suppose the Lords sell or alienate these lands, the Takers shall remain with their tacks on to the ische (expiry) of their times, into whosoever hands these lands come (pass), for such like male (rent) as they took them for before.'

This is indeed sound, wise, and civilised legislation—directed to the encouragement of deliberate contracts by insisting on their binding force against the party which was then the strongest—and on their binding force, too, especially in the case of a change of ownership, so that leases should be valid against all comers. It has been supposed that the words 'poor people that labour the ground' indicate some very specially low condition of the agricultural classes. But this is by no means a necessary implication. It does, indeed, imply that leases were given to tenants who were poor. But the protection which the statute gives is not confined to this class, but is expressly extended to ' others '— to all who, whether poor or comparatively rich, should make bargains for the hire of land for definiteytimes and for fixed rents. The historian is right when he describes this law as ' a wise and memorable act in its future consequences on the ' security of property, the liberty of the great body of the ' people, and the improvement of the country.'*

It will be observed that this legislation not only places no restriction on absolute property in land, but that it implies and assumes as belonging to that property the most complete and unrestricted rights. As between the owner and the lessee it implies that the lessee could have no other rights than those he might stipulate for in his lease. He could enforce these, and beyond these he had none to enforce. He was in no way protected against himself. He might agree to render services of any extent, but they must be sufficiently definite to be capable of legal enforcement. Neither in this way nor in the way of rent in money or in produce could the owner add anything during the stipulated term. On the other hand, at the end of that term all the lessee's rights ceased, because this was part of the contract. Thus both parties could have confidence— that one essential element in all the transactions of business. Then, again, as between the lessee and those under him there was no interference of the law. The lessee could exercise all the absolute rights of ownership which his lease conveyed to him. If his lease allowed him to sublet, he might do so under whatever conditions he could obtain from others. If his lease did not allow him to sublet, the prohibition would be enforced. If the lease was given to the 'poor people that laboured the ground,' the same rights and obligations applied to them that applied to the wealthier 'tacksmen.' Those who held the land under the lease could deal with all others of their own class precisely as richer lessees could deal with them. The one great characteristic feature of this system, and its one immense superiority over

* Tytler's 'Hist. of Scotland,' vol. iv. p. 66.

Celtic and all other mere local customs, was in the substitution of certainty for uncertainty, of definiteness for indefiniteness, of known and settled law for mere vague usages and tradition.

Very nearly 300 years passed from the date of this enactment to the date of the last of the Civil Wars of Scotland. They were centuries of almost perpetual trouble, during which many of the Scottish Sovereigns died a violent death, and the nation hardly ever enjoyed for a single generation, throughout its entire territory, anything like a settled peace. Yet some steady progress, on the whole, was made in the cultivation of the country under the application of this system of definite tenures and of legal rights conveyed by instruments capable of exact judicial interpretation—a system which gradually made its way by dint of its inherent merits even into the heart of the Highlands. We have now before us a lease of lands in Skye, granted on the Dunvegan Estate in 1754, which in respect to the sub-tenants is almost an exact counterpart of the lease granted by the Abbot of Scone in the twelfth century. The lease is granted to the Tacksman with his sub-tenants. But it is specially declared that their tenure must be of no longer duration than his own, and he expressly covenants to remove them along with himself and servants at the termination of the lease.

There is no idea more absolutely unfounded than that which supposes that in the Highlands the poorer classes had some ancient rights of occupancy which their brethren in the low country did not enjoy. It rests on the same delusion as that which we have seen so effectively exposed by Sir J. Davies in the corresponding case of the Celts of Ireland. In the Scottish Highlands even more than in Ireland the Chiefs were absolute. The mass of the people were 'hands,' and nothing more. As Mr. Burton says in his 'History of 'Scotland,' their one great craving was for immediate leaders to guide and command them.* Personal fidelity was their one great merit, and in the last civil war it shone with immortal lustre in the protection they afforded, against every temptation of wealth and of reward, to their defeated and fugitive Prince. The idea of rebelling against their King because of his tendency to despotism or of his aversion to constitutional liberty, was an idea quite foreign to the Highlander. It is true that some powerful Clans, such as the Sutherlands in the north and the Campbells in the south,

* Vol. iii. p. 95.

espoused the cause of the Constitution. But this was entirely the doing of the Chiefs. The people followed their Chiefs and not any political aspiration. Of political liberty they had no conception, nor had they any knowledge or experience of the local institutions which among other races had been the germ of that desire. It is a grotesque misinterpretation of historical facts to confound primitive and semi-barbarous modes of cultivating land in wild and undivided pastures, or village customs for dividing cattle and plots of land, with any ideas of true communal institutions or communal independence. Such institutions and such ideas are often, indeed, a natural growth among primitive populations, which are purely or mainly agricultural, and which are blessed with quiet possession during long intervals of time. Great waves of foreign conquest have passed over such institutions in the East, and have left them as they were. In India the conquerors have used them, have taxed them, without suppressing or destroying them. But the Highlands of Scotland during the Middle Ages were afflicted with continual wars between Clan and Clan, and the occupation of the people was habitually predatory. In such conditions of society the dependence of the people upon Chiefs who could alone lead them with success, and who could alone protect them from being plundered and massacred by their neighbours, became more and more absolute. Poetry and fiction have cast a glamour over the history of the Highland Clans which is rudely dispersed when we come to look into that history in detail and to read it in naked prose. The sumptuous volumes of Family History which have been edited by Mr. William Fraser are full of interest in the vivid glimpses they afford us of life in the Highlands as it was led in the three centuries to which we have referred. One of these histories which has been already reviewed in this journal, the 'Chiefs of Grant,' is especially rich and instructive in this respect. We see there that as one of the consequences of internecine and barbarous contests between the different Clans it very often came to pass that the very existence of these Clans and of the population of extensive areas, depended on the action of the Chiefs in recruiting the people from other districts, and in planting them in the country of which these Chiefs were at once the rulers and the owners.

There is a hideous story which illustrates this condition of things told in the 'Chiefs of Grant.'[*] In revenge for

***

* Vol. i. p. 113, note.

the murder of a kinsman somewhere in the valley of the Dee, the Chief of Grant had incited and joined the Earl of Huntly in slaying all the men in the country of the Dee where the murder had taken place. Some time after, on visiting Huntly at his castle of Strathbogie, he was shown between sixty and eighty orphan children who had been carried off when their fathers were slain, and were now fed at one long trough, as pigs are fed, one row of children eating at each side. This sight is said to have caused such remorse to the Chief of Grant that he carried off the whole of these children from one side of the trough and took them to his own estate on Strathspey, where they were settled, *taking the name of Grant,* whilst those on the other side of the trough were in like manner kept by Huntly and *took the name of Gordon.* This is only an extreme case of a process which on a more or less extensive scale was going on perpetually all over the Highlands, the Clans being recruited by the Chiefs from 'broken men' of all kinds who were attracted to them either by the desire to share in adventure and in plunder, or else by the desire of living under powerful leaders who could protect them in the possession and enjoyment of the lands granted by the Chiefs. How impossible it was in such a condition of society for the 'poor people that 'laboured the ground' to have or to dream of having any rights or hold over the land independent of the Chiefs! Even the most powerful of these could not always defend their people from the utter devastation of their lands. The raids made upon each other by the Clans were often on the scale of a civil war. We have a notable example of this in the 'Chiefs of Grant,' being a detailed account of the ravages effected on the estates of the same Chief of Grant in Glen Urquhart by the Macdonalds, Camerons, and others in the year 1544. The whole crops of oats and bear, with several hundreds of head of cattle of all ages, with sheep and horses, and every kind of goods and stock, were swept away.[*] If even the great Chief of Grant could not defend his territories and dependents from such calamities, we can well understand what must have been the condition of tenants under weaker Chiefs. They could only defend their people by leagues and alliances, or by accepting practical or formal vassalage under bigger men. Accordingly, we find that so early as the fourteenth century in the reign of David the Second, the Lord of the Isles, who was then virtually an

* Vol. i. p. 112.

independent Sovereign over the Western Isles and western coasts of the Highlands, had begun to grant regular feudal Charters to the Clans who were subordinate to him; whilst these Chiefs again began almost as soon to grant subordinate tenures to their clansmen and tenants.

Thus, in the Highlands as well as in the Lowlands, only more gradually, the arbitrary customs and usages which are apt to grow up, and to become more and more oppressive in such barbarous conditions of society, were brought under legal definition and control through the steady progress of the Feudal System with its written Charters and its written leases. The essence of these documents lay in the pledge given of protection on the one side, and of definite rents or services on the other. To this very day in all leases of land in Scotland there is one stereotyped phrase which carries us back to the stormy times when they began to be given. In that phrase the proprietor engages to secure the tenant in his exclusive possession of his farm 'at all hands and ' against all mortals'—or, as in a still older form of words, ' against all deadlie,' which means against all violence. It is needless to say that this pledge has its full and correspond- ing meaning in peaceful times. It implies and expresses the fact that the right which a tenant enjoys to exclude all other men from the land he hires is a right which he derives from the owner, and from him alone, and that this consti- tuted the principal obligation for which his rent was due, quite irrespective of any aid or help which he might also get in the way of 'permanent improvements' made at the owner's cost. This last and quite separate source and cause of rent took in those early times generally the form of ' steelbow'—a system under which the whole stock of cattle and of sheep was supplied by the owner of the land. In later times, that is, since the Civil Wars and since scientific agri- culture began, this secondary source of rent, namely, inte- rest on the immense outlays necessary for drainage, which was unknown in the Middle Ages, as well as for buildings and inclosures, became larger and larger in proportion, until now it would be very difficult indeed to estimate how much of rent represents only the guarantee of exclusive possession, and how much represents the accumulated outlays of many generations. Both are inseparably united and combined.

The Parliament of Scotland did once again interfere with the tenure of land during the seventeenth century, and its interference was in the same wise and beneficent direction —the direction namely of checking or putting an end to arbitrary exactions founded on ancient Celtic usages and customs. In 1617 an Act was passed abolishing the customary and irregular fines which went under the name of ' Caulpes,' which were fines on the death of a vassal or tenant—fines consisting of the most valuable possession of the deceased, such as horses, mares, cows, or oxen for the plough. The statute declares that in the Highlands this exaction was often made by more than one Chief and Chieftain in succession, ' to the utter impoverishment of the ' lieges and tenants of the Crown, so that they were pauper- ' ised and rendered unable to pay any settled rents and dues.'

It will be observed, however, that although the tendency of legislation and of the Feudal System was in the direction of fixed rents and dues as against indefinite and arbitrary exactions, yet this process had been applied only to vassals or proprietors holding under Charters, and to ' tacksmen ' holding under written leases. It did not interfere with the relations between these leaseholding tenants and their sub-tenants, and who must have constituted the greater part of the population. Accordingly, it is in this relation that we find that in the Highlands as elsewhere vague and indefinite obligations had an inevitable tendency to abuse. It may be well to give some idea of the nature of these services which were founded on and derived from genuine old Celtic usages. We find an excellent account of them in the very interesting sketch of the northern counties by the well-known Sir John Sinclair, given in a paper he contributed to the Board of Agriculture in 1795. He says:—

' A proprietor formerly let a certain small extent of land to his tenants, for which he received a trifling acknowledgment in money (specie being then very rare in the country) the rent being paid in grain or *victual*, that is bear and oatmeal. In addition to the rent, the tenants of that description were bound to pay the following services, namely, tilling, dunging, sowing, and harrowing a part of an extensive farm in the proprietor's possession, providing a certain quantity of peats for his fuel, thatching a part of his houses, furnishing *simmons* or ropes of straw or heath, for that purpose, and for securing his corn in the barn-yard, weeding the land, leading a certain quantity of turf from the common, for manuring the farm, mowing, making, and ingathering the hay, the spontaneous produce of the meadows and marshy grounds, cutting down, harvesting, threshing out, manufacturing, and carrying to the market or seaport a part of the produce of the farm. Besides these services the tenants paid in kind the following articles, under the name of customs, namely, *straw cazzies* (a sort of bag made of straw, used as sacks for carrying grain or meal), ropes made of hair for drawing the plough, *floss* or reeds, used for these and similar purposes, *tethers,* or ropes made of hair, which being fixed in the ground by a peg or small stake, and the cattle tied to them, prevented them from wandering over the open country; straw for thatching, &c. The tenants, also, according to the extent of their possessions, kept a certain number of cattle during the winter season; paid vicarage, or the smaller tythes, as of lamb, wool, &c., a certain number of fowls and eggs; in the Highlands, veal, kid, butter, and cheese; and on the sea-coast, the tithe of their fish and oil, besides assisting in carrying sea-ware for manuring the proprietor's farm. In some parts of the country the tenth sheaf of the produce or tythe was exacted by the proprietor in kind. Sometimes also a certain quantity of lint was spun for the lady of the house, and a certain quantity of woollen yarn annually exacted. Such were the various sorts of payments which almost universally prevailed in the county of Caithness about thirty or forty years ago; but of late they have been converted by the generality of landlords either into grain or money, or have fallen into disuse.'

We have a striking picture of the extent to which abuses from this cause did actually prevail, and the height to which they grew, in a very remarkable paper published in the Appendix to the Report of the Crofter Commission. It is a letter addressed by Duncan Forbes of Culloden to John, Duke of Argyll and Greenwich,* dated 1737, on the Duke's Island estates, of which Forbes had accepted the charge during the Duke's frequent absence in the public service. It appears from this letter that the lessees or Tacksmen of farms on those estates had imposed upon their sub-tenants such heavy dues and exactions of an uncertain and arbitrary nature that the people thereby, coupled with their own ' ridi-' culous processes of husbandry,' were reduced to the greatest poverty, and Culloden seriously declares that the islands were threatened with total ruin and depopulation. It is not less instructive to observe as characteristic of the Highlanders that their prejudices in favour of old ancestral usages and their suspicion of all novelties was so intense that they could not be brought even to understand the advantage of regular leases and of fixed rents which Culloden offered to them, and it was only by direct compulsion that they were brought to come under the new conditions, although these were eminently favourable to themselves. We have now before us a Report on the same estates dated five years before the letter of Culloden, which throws still further light upon the condition of

* The Dukedom of Greenwich was conferred on the Second Duke of Argyll, in 1719, for his military services in the Wars of Marlborough and for his political services to the reigning Family. It is now extinct.

the sub-tenants all over the Highlands. It shows by the whole tenor of its narrative and of its recommendations that these sub-tenants neither had nor supposed themselves to have any rights of occupancy, except such as they derived from the proprietors, or from those to whom the proprietor had granted leases. It is to be recollected that in 1732 the Highlands were still under the constant fear of civil war. It was the time between the two great Jacobite risings of 1715 and 1745, and it appears from the Report to which we have referred that the tacksmen were very often directed to get rid of all the people who were suspected of disaffection to the reigning Sovereign and to replant the country with faithful and loyal men. The statesman who had taken so prominent a part in the Council Chamber at Kensington in securing the Protestant succession,* was not likely to neglect this great interest on his own estates. The Macleans and the Camerons seem to have been special objects of suspicion. Accordingly, in the Report we speak of from the Sheriff of the county to the Duke of Argyll in 1732, we find that on three large farms in the Island of Mull, the Tacksmen, being Campbells, 'had gone a good length to plant ' their several districts with people of the same name or ' their friends '—and it is added that the new tenants, besides being more loyal men, were better farmers, and had begun to manage their lands better than the rest of the country. Here we have an example, far on in the eighteenth century, of precisely the same powers of ownership over land, and the same right and practice of introducing or planting new men, which we have seen exercised in the sixteenth century by the Chief of Grant, and of which we have abundant evidence in every document during the previous five hundred years. No 'clearances' of modern times are to be compared in sweep with those which were common in the Middle Ages. There is one other most significant fact connected with this Report, and that is that it disproves the idea that the yearly tenants, sub-tenants, or 'crofters' paid only rents fixed by any custom or usage. The Sheriff informs the Duke that until these poor people could be assured of protection against the exactions of the Tacksmen, they naturally were shy of 'offering with any 'frankness' for the lands they had occupied, and that without such offers 'no tolerable information could be 'obtained of the value of the country, since it was by the

* Mahon's 'History of England,' vol. i. p. 133.

' competition of tenants that the value of land can be known.'
This sentence was written forty-four years before the publication of the 'Wealth of Nations.' The worthy Sheriff
was not talking political economy. He was talking simply
common sense, and giving emphatic although unconscious
testimony as to the basis on which ultimately rent had
always been arrived at in the Highlands.

It may be well here to give the precise terms on which
new leases were granted on the Argyll estates in pursuance
of the new system of abolishing all uncertain or arbitrary
dues and services. These terms are to be found in numerous
new leases given in 1739 and in following years as the old
leases expired. The rent was specified in Scots or sterling
money, as the case might be, and thereupon followed these
words :—' And that (sum) in full satisfaction of all herezelds
' (fines), casualties, and other prestations (obligations) and
' services whatsoever, which are hereby discharged, except
' the services of tenants for repairing harbours, mending
' highways, or making or repairing mill-leads for the general
' benefit of the island.' This exception was just and reasonable, because the works for which these special services
were retained were all for the benefit of the farms and town-
ships held by the tenants. It is to be recollected that as
regards roads these were not at that time provided for by
public rates. Special services for special purposes of a similar
kind, such as for the upkeep of local roads—still called ' ser-
' vice-roads '—which are not supported by rates but are used
by tenants, are in some cases retained to this day, the number
of days' work being generally specified or fixed. Such services
as these are perfectly reasonable, and have as precise and
definite a value as the rent itself, and they must not be confounded with the old services founded on Celtic usages, the
vice of which lay in their vague and indefinite character and
extent. Many of the new leases given at this time contained
other important stipulations in the interests of agricultural
improvement—such as for the erection of houses built of
stone instead of houses built of turf and wattles—for the
erection of fences, for the taking of corn to a regular mill
instead of the barbarous practice of burning the straw in
order to get at the grain, and for putting a stop to various
other practices which were equally barbarous, but which
had been equally universal in the Highlands.

Such is the system of tenure which has prevailed in
Scotland ever since her civilisation began, and of which it
is hardly too much to say, that her civilisation is in no small

degree a direct result. Agricultural improvement is at once the foundation and the sign of every other kind of progress. The substitution of ' Definiteness for Indefiniteness ' in contracts for the hire of land, which as we have seen attracted the attention of early Chroniclers in connexion with the monks of Iona, is a substitution which means nothing less than the substitution of law and order for violence or fraud. Under the growing spread and the final establishment of written contracts all over Scotland, both in the Lowlands and in the Highlands, the surface of the country was during five hundred years very slowly and gradually reclaimed from moor and marsh and ' shaggy wood,' in spite of all the waste and devastation of continual civil wars. And when at last those civil wars were closed in 1745, the nation started forward in the path of agricultural improvement at a rate and with results which we believe to be unparalleled in any other country in the world. In the Reports of skilful men employed by the Board of Agriculture * towards the close of the last century to examine into the condition of things in every county of Scotland, we have a striking picture and record of skill and of enterprise in outlay which was the result of confidence in the law,—and especially of confidence in clear, precise, and definite contracts. The Reporter for the county of Aberdeen remarks on the ' careless languor ' and indolence ' of agriculture in England at that time, as compared with the energy and activity of the same industry in Scotland, and he ascribes the difference to the ' indefinite ' claims' for poor-rates, tithes, &c., and especially to the uncertainty attending a yearly tenure which affected the English farmer. In Scotland the tenants almost universally sought for and received the security of a long lease. But everywhere the proprietors of land were the great improvers. Within half a century they had changed the whole face of the country. The names of the most prominent are given in these Reports. But their name was legion. Probably no body of men so limited in number has ever effected in so short a time so great an economic revolution—such an immense development of industry,—such a bounteous increase of production. They provided not only the capital, but what was even more important, they provided the knowledge and the enterprise which reformed and transformed the

---

* This Body was founded in pursuance of an address to the Crown voted by Parliament on the motion of Sir John Sinclair. It was incorporated by Royal Charter in 1793. It was dissolved in 1816.

ignorant and wasteful husbandry of the Middle Ages. The conditions which they inserted in their leases were all directed to extinguish practices which were injurious, and to insist on methods of cultivation which were beneficial for the tenants themselves as much as for the proprietors.

It would indeed be a matter for deep regret if under the discouragements of an agricultural depression which at present is nearly universal in Europe, and seems to affect equally every form of ownership and of occupancy, the tenantry of Scotland should be tempted to doubt of the fundamental soundness of the system under which, until a very few years ago, they undoubtedly prospered greatly. It is obvious, however, that men who have entered into contracts for the long period of nineteen years on the assumption of an average scale of prices for various kinds of produce, may be placed in a most disadvantageous position if that scale of prices suffers any very great and very lasting fall. This is an evil which can only be met by concessions and readjustments where these are equitably called for. On the other hand, all farmers who enter upon farms at the present time, and who secure the lease usual in Scotland, will derive all the benefit of rents calculated probably on an abnormal fall in values. But of this we may be sure : that every legislative interference with perfect freedom between man and man in matters of business will simply be a backward step from 'Definiteness to Indefiniteness,' — which must be the greatest of all discouragements to enterprise, because it is the heaviest of all blows to confidence in the investment of capital.

ART. II.—1. *Our Chancellor.* Sketches for an Historical
Picture. By MORITZ BUSCH. Translated from the German
by WILLIAM BEATTY KINGSTON. 2 vols. London: 1884.

2. *Souvenirs Diplomatiques: L'Affaire du Luxembourg le Pré-
lude de la Guerre de* 1870. Par G. ROTHAN. Paris: 1883.

3. *Souvenirs Diplomatiques: L'Allemagne et l'Italie,* 1870-
1871. Par G. ROTHAN. Vol. I. Paris: 1884.

BY the translation of Dr. Busch's last volumes on the great
German Chancellor, the English reader is enabled to
get a more complete view than has hitherto been possible of
the political and domestic life and opinions of Prince Bismarck, and such an one, we presume, as he would wish Europe
to entertain. The relations of Dr. Busch with the Chancellor have been long and intimate, and his connexion
with him as Under-Secretary of State and in private life
has given him exceptional advantages for composing these
volumes. Where the Chancellor does not speak himself in
these pages—and great part of them are taken up with passages from his speeches, despatches, letters, and conversation—the work must be mainly an echo of his opinions
and statements, except, indeed, when Dr. Busch adopts the
language of eulogy to an extent which the Chancellor's
modesty would prevent him from using. Dr. Busch is a
thorough partisan of the principle that might is right; and
he finds nothing but what is laudable in any part of the life
and policy of the Prince.

The publication of this book, however, is calculated to
alleviate the severity of former judgements concerning the
Chancellor and his public career, and in domestic and social
life it presents him in an amiable light. There is much in
the volumes which is of high interest, although there is
great repetition—to which, indeed, the scheme of the author
lends itself—for, as he assures us, the work is no complete
biography or history, but a collection of studies and sketches
to supply materials for a characteristic portrait, to be executed
hereafter by some more skilful hand.

In studying the life of any illustrious man, we feel interest
in knowing what were his convictions in the highest spiritual
matters; what was his theory of life here and hereafter, and
of the relations between man and God; and this is especially
so in the case of Bismarck, who has not only been an instrument in the hands of Providence in re-forming the map
of Europe and moulding anew the destinies of nations, but

has been in conflict for many years with the greatest ecclesiastical power in the world.   It must be owned, however,
that after reading the chapter called by Dr. Busch ' His
Religious Views,' we get no very definite notion of what
really is the Chancellor's religion.   A belief in God, in a
divine order of the world, and in a personal existence in a
future state and, to a certain extent, in revelation, seems
to form for him a sort of rude basis of religious belief,
with which he has remained satisfied without raising on it
the superstructure of any definite creed.   In religion, as in
politics, he confesses that he has arrived at successive stages
of developement.   In the days when he was known as the
tolle Junker, he was first a rationalist and, apparently for
some time, an unbeliever.   Then for several years he went
through severe physical, moral, and even pecuniary trials,
and felt a desire to seclude himself from society, and even
at one time had a design of emigrating and retiring to the
Polish forests with his last few thousand thalers in his
pocket and commencing life anew as a farmer and a sports-
man.   As he approached his thirtieth year a psychical change
came upon him, which was probably due in part to the influence of the young lady who became his wife in 1847.   This
lady, Johanna von Puttkamer, was the daughter of a Nether-
Pomeranian landowner, and both her father and mother,
being people of a fervent Moravian spirit of piety, opposed
themselves to the betrothal of their daughter with one so
noted for his wild habits as the ' Mad Squireen.'   Goethe
has shown in the ' Story of a Fair Soul ' how he could be
affected by the simple piety of a Quakeress ; and Bismarck
was, it is probable, more deeply influenced.   After the accession, too, of Frederic William IV., there was a great increase
of piety, or at least of pietism, in the higher circles of Prussian nobility.   The spiritualism of Schleiermacher had displaced the rationalistic influence of Voltaire and Rousseau.
Rationalism came in polite circles to be considered somewhat vulgar, and was associated with revolution; and even
philosophy in the crabbed phraseology of Hegelianism not
only was made an instrument for undermining all existing
institutions, but appeared to be pre-eminently unæsthetic.
A religious and unctuous phraseology was the fashionable
protest against New Hegelianism and revolution.   Bunsen,
Stahl and Gerlach were in vogue, and the doctrine of
original sin · and of the corruption of human nature was
employed to exorcise the spectre of anarchy.

In a letter written to his wife in 1851, four years after his marriage, Bismarck shows the change which had come upon him, and the sense of the inanity of this world's existence finds expression frequently in his correspondence in phrases recalling the musings of Hamlet in the churchyard.

'The will of God be done! Everything here is only a question of time—races and individuals, folly and wisdom, war and peace, come and go like waves, but the sea remains still.' 'There is nothing upon this earth but hypocrisy and juggling; and whether this mask of flesh be torn from us by fever or grapeshot, fall it must, sooner or later. When it does, a resemblance will make itself manifest between a Prussian and an Austrian (if they happen to be of the same height) which will render it difficult to distinguish the one from the other; the skeletons of fools and wise men present pretty much the same appearance.' (Vol. i. pp. 112, 113.)

Nor have the prodigious successes of his later life altogether removed these gloomy impressions, as appears from the following anecdote:—

'It was twilight at Varzin, and he was sitting—as was his wont after dinner—by the stove in the large back drawing-room, where Rauch's statue of "Victory casting Wreaths" is set up. After having sat silent for a while, gazing straight before him and feeding the fire now and anon with fircones, he suddenly began to complain that his political activity had brought him but little satisfaction and few friends. Nobody loved him for what he had done. He had never made anybody happy thereby, he said; not himself, nor his family, nor any one else. Some of those present would not admit this, and suggested "that he had made a great nation happy." "But," he continued, "how many have I made unhappy! But for me, three great wars would not have been fought; eighty thousand men would not have perished; parents, brothers, sisters, and widows would not be bereaved and plunged into mourning. . . . That matter, however, I have settled with God. But I have had little or no joy from all my achievements—nothing but vexation, care, and trouble." He continued for some time in the same strain. His guests kept silence; and those amongst them who had never before heard him say anything of the kind were somewhat astonished. It reminded one of Achilles speaking to King Priam in his tent before Ilion.

'Wir schaffen ja nichts mit unserer starrenden Schwermuth :
Also bestimmten der Sterblichen Loos, der Armen, die Götter,
Trübe in Gram zu leben, allein sie selber sind sorglos.'

(Vol. i. p. 114.)

After acquaintance with his peculiar religious views, we are not much surprised to learn that the Chancellor is superstitious. He apparently believes in ghosts, because he thought he heard a door open and footsteps in a room adjoining that in which he slept, but arose and found nobody.

He is firmly convinced that Friday is an unlucky day, and that he has had various misfortunes and mishaps for beginning business on Friday. He refuses to do business on the 14th of October, because this day is the anniversary both of Hoch-kirch and Jena; he objects to dining thirteen at table, and believes that people should have their hair cut, and that woodmen should only fell trees, in the last quarter of the moon.

Dr. Busch has a chapter called 'The Junker Legend,' in which he shows through what changes the Junkerdom of Bismarck's early youth has passed. Although the term 'Junker' has been applied by the Chancellor's enemies to him as a term of reproach, he has never rejected it, and, indeed, rather glories in it. The word '*junker*' in early German, and indeed in late German, as Uhland's ballads testify, had no worse signification than that of a young lord or squire, and there is nothing opprobrious in the terms *Kammerjunker* and *Jagdjunker*. Towards the end of the last century, however, the terms *Junker, Junkerei,* and *junkeriren* began to have a contemptuous meaning, and were applied to signify a provincial squireen, a petty village tyrant who maltreated his vassals, and was passionate, overbearing, and devoid of reason—a sort of German Squire Western. After the revolution year of 1848, the word "Junker" acquired a worse signification, and was applied by the party of Pro-gress to the extreme Conservative party.

That in the days of his wild and stormy youth Bismarck should have had the appellation of *der tolle Junker* applied to him is no marvel, nor that it should have clung to him during the early years of his parliamentary career, especially since he was capable at that time of smashing a beer-glass on the head of a political opponent in a Berlin beerhouse, and then asking what there was to pay for the damage; but what is really extraordinary is that he should have claimed the title as a badge of honour, and made it the harbinger of such astounding success. Of the exuberance of the Chancellor's early life the world has heard much, and, if we credit Dr. Busch, the accounts of its wildness have not been over-stated.

'This was the continuation of his "Sturm und Drang" period—the transformation of a collegian's frivolity into that of a provincial Junker. It was then that the young ladies of neighbouring mansions, their mammas and aunts, shuddered whilst their papas and uncles, shaking their worthy heads and prophesying dread calamities, told tales of furious carouses, during which floods of champagne and porter were ingurgitated; of breakneck rides across country, worthy of the Wild Huntsman; of pistol-shots with which visitors at country houses were aroused from their slumbers in the dead of night; of audacious defiances to all that was respectable and conventional, carried out with infinite mischievousness and insolence. The prophecies of evil to which these excesses gave rise have, at least, remained unfulfilled; for the fermenting must, after throwing up its exuberant scum, became clear at the right moment; what sort of liquor it ultimately turned out everybody knows.' (Vol. i. p. 170.)

When the first wild fury of youth had exhausted itself a little, and Bismarck began to turn his attention to politics, he became one of the original founders of the famous ' Kreuz Zeitung,' and, as soon as he got into Parliament, made himself notorious as the representative of the politics of Junkerdom. He even astonished the Left on one occasion by rising in his seat in the Lower House to claim the appellation for himself with the assurance that he could convert ' Jun- ' kerdom' into a title of honour and distinction. After the March days of 1848 and the excesses of the Berlin mob and the storming of the arsenal, he made himself still more remarkable by his opposition to the introduction of any further popular elements into the State, and even opposed the vote of thanks to the King for the grant of a Constitution. It was at this juncture that he made the famous speech, ' If great cities, headquarters of revolution as they are, con- ' tinue to disturb the peace of the country, they must be ' swept from the face of the earth.' In another speech he said he gloried in the reproaches of obscurantist and medieval tendencies, and at the revision of the Constitution he spoke very strongly against the right of the Diet to regulate taxation. Although he became in time more reconciled to the principles of constitutionalism, he would not hear of parliamentary supremacy, nor of such expressions as the will of the people, and in one of his speeches on that matter he produced one of his finest images—' No decision upon ' these principles can be arrived at by parliamentary debates, ' or by majorities; but sooner or later the God of battles ' will settle the matter with one cast of his iron dice.' Later he gained for his royal master, with the help of the iron dice of the God of battles, the imperial crown which he disclaimed for him as the recipient of a popular assembly.

It is remarkable, in returning to these early speeches of his, to find how strongly he was opposed at that time to two of the great national movements in Germany—the one to get possession of Schleswig Holstein, and the other which ·

aimed at the unity of Germany. He hesitated not to declare that the first Prussian war in the Duchies was 'an in-'iquitous, disastrous, and revolutionary undertaking,' and it was to his single-handed defence of the Manteuffel Ministry for accepting what was called, at that time, the humiliation of Olmütz, that Bismarck owed his first official appointment. He was not long in getting the reward for this speech, for he was speedily—though not without some misgivings on the part of the King and his ministers—appointed Prussian pleni-potentiary at the restored Federal Bund, and thus it was as an uncompromising supporter of Austria and the Con-federation that the future victor of Sadowa made his entry into public life.

Bismarck represented Prussia for eight years at Frank-fort. He afterwards styled them eight years of grief and vexation without respite, and attributed to them a serious illness; but it was here that his theory of statesmanship became completely transformed, and that he renounced his allegiance to Austria and conceived the idea of a united Germany under the supremacy of Prussia. The change was not long in coming. He became disgusted with his mission to Frankfort, and wrote in May, 1851, soon after his arrival, to his wife: 'Frankfort is hideously tiresome. No one—' not even the most malignant sceptic of a Democrat—could ' conceive what an amount of quackery and humbug there ' is in this diplomacy.' It was not surprising that the impatient and ambitious Junker should be displeased with his business and his intercourse with his fellow members of the Bundestag. The Bundestag was, in fact, a peace con-gress sitting under the presidency of Austria, and its object was defensive and not offensive. Its great aim was to pre-serve the map of Europe as it was; and if Europe enjoyed so many years of peace after the Congress of Vienna, no small share of praise is due to the smaller States of Germany. Bismarck, however, commenced by following the instruc-tions which had been given to his predecessor, General von Rochow, adhering to the same line of policy as had obtained in the days of Hardenberg, Ancillon, and Metternich—that is, to come to an understanding with Austria on all grave measures before they were submitted to the other Federal States.

The supremacy of Austria in Germany at that date was so paramount that it takes now an effort to recall it. Frederic William IV. had replied to a deputation of the German States that he would consider it the happiest day of his life to hold the washing-ewer at the coronation of an Emperor of Germany; and in a letter to Prince Metternich in 1848 he wrote : ' A Cæsar, as special elective chief of the ' special German realm, appears unavoidable. But I will not ' be that Cæsar. It is my ambition to become Arch-General-' issimo of the Empire;' and Bismarck himself, in 1850, spoke of Austria ' as the representative and heir of a German ' power which had often and gloriously wielded the sword of ' Germany.'

The reports which Bismarck addressed from Frankfort to Manteuffel had given such an impression of his ability, both to Manteuffel and the King, that he may be said henceforward to have had complete control over the policy of Prussia, and her relations to Austria in the Bund ; and his antagonism to Austria increased year by year until he succeeded not only in ousting her from the German hegemony, but finally, at Sadowa, gave her a death-blow as a German power. The King frequently summoned Bismarck from Frankfort to consult with him, and in the course of one year he made no less than thirteen journeys by royal command from Frankfort to Berlin.

It so happened that at this time Russia was represented at Frankfort, when Bismarck arrived there, by a young Russian—Prince Gortschakoff—who divided his time for four years after Bismarck's arrival between his duties as Russian envoy to the Diet and those of Russian minister at Würtemberg in attendance on the Grand-Duchess Olga, who had espoused through his negotiation the heir presumptive of the crown of Würtemberg. The mutual good understanding which was established at that time between these two politicians, which Bismarck cultivated most assiduously as long as he had any need of the good offices of Russia, had a portentous influence on the history of Europe, and without such an understanding there would, in all probability, have been no Sadowa, no dismemberment of Denmark and France, and the formation of the German Empire would have been indefinitely delayed.

Of the successive gradations through which the present Chancellor's estrangement from Austria passed until he arrived at the conclusion that the defects of the federal relations of Prussia with Austria could only be cured *ferro et igne*, these volumes offer abundant evidence. When the Sultan declared war against Russia, in October, 1853, and the Western Powers followed his example in the following year, Austria and Prussia restricted themselves to summoning Russia to evacuate the principalities, and declaring that they would regard the incorporation of these provinces by Russia as a *casus belli*. But even this proceeding was not to the taste of the German Central States, and least of all to that of Bismarck, who declared that Prussia had discredited herself by this co-operation with Austria. In fact, at Hanover, Dresden, Munich, Stuttgart, and Cassel sympathies were wholly with Russia, and the interference of the Western Powers was qualified as a usurpation. The general desire was for an alliance with Russia.

Bismarck's letters and despatches written at this time are full of anxiety to stand well with Russia; at the same time, the political foresight which they disclose is quite astonishing, and when Austria, on December 2, did enter into a treaty with the Western Powers, Prussia refused to join, but stood independent and aloof.

'It has rejoiced my heart,' he wrote on Dec. 19, ' that your Excellency should have answered the questions about our accession to the Treaty (Austria and the Western Powers) and our so-called isolation with cold dignity and without *empressement*. As long as we shall continue to manifest unaffected fearlessness, people will respect us and be careful not to menace us. If it were only possible to let Austria know that our patience and brotherly love are not inexhaustible, and that we have not forgotten the road to Moravia, I feel convinced that her fear of us would do more to further the cause of peace than her reliance upon our support actually does.' (Vol. i. p. 313.)

According to outward and superficial appearances, Prussia, with her policy of keeping her hand free (' die freie Hand '), had descended to the rank of a third-rate power. It was even a question whether she should be admitted to the Congress of Paris, and Manteuffel had to wait in the ante-room while the plenipotentiaries of Europe were in deliberation. Neither England, nor Austria, nor Turkey showed any readiness to admit her to the honours of the Congress, and, strange to say, she was only at last received at the instance of the Emperor Napoleon III. It was the French Emperor who was urgent that the Power who was subsequently to dethrone him should resume her place in the councils of Europe.

Bismarck's political foresight divined at once that as soon as the war was over there would be a *rapprochement* between Russia and France, and what he thus foresaw was almost immediately realised. The Russian representative, Count Orloff, was treated with exceptional politeness and cordiality in all the difficulties which arose in the interpretation of the Treaty of Paris. The arguments of the

... plenipotentiary were supported by the plenipo-
... of France; and in all the conferences which ...
... institution of votes was almost ... England
... on one side—France, Russia, and Prussia on
...

... despatch from which the ... ...
... ... his conviction that ... ...
... ... Austria for our ... ...
... ... on the war in the ... ...
... pretensions of Austria ... ...
... despatches, reports, and ... ...
... ... One volume ... ...
... Foreign Office ... ...
... as his political ... ...
... in the ... ...
... ...

... at this time was ... ...
... were forwarded ... ...
... no way ... ...
... affairs at the ... ...
... Denmark ... ...
... frequent visits ... ...
... have to ... ...
... ... and he ... ...
... Count ... ...
... recall ... ...
vexed at ... ...
... government ... ...
... on his ... ...
politischen ... ...
... the post ... ...
... cons... ...
skin and ...
it has ...
... could c... ...
the ...
...endship ...
the post...
...peror at ...
...burg ...
on May ...
Schleinitz ...
... ...

The new Prussian ambassador arrived at St. Petersburg three months after the famous speech of the French Emperor to Baron Hübner, on New Year's Day. He found his former colleague, the Russian Chancellor, still full of resentful feeling, and using all his influence to push Austria into a declaration of war. The two ministers were inseparable and made no secret of their mutual ill-will to Austria in the *salons* of St. Petersburg. Bismarck on his side, however, fretted and fumed at the difficulties which he found at Berlin in getting his views adopted as to the advisability of a Franco-Russo-Prussian alliance; for when war broke out in Italy, the king and the ministers at Berlin were still discussing as to whether Prussia should not go to the assistance of Austria, and whether she was not bound to do so by Federal obligations. So far was he as yet from getting the policy *ferro et igne* accepted there.

After the battle of Magenta there was some talk of an armed Prussian intervention, and of a mobilisation of the Federal troops, which would probably have taken place if Napoleon had crossed the Adige. At this news Bismarck, we learn from his letters, became dangerously ill. The doctors, he wrote, covered his body with cupping-glasses as large as saucers, with mustard plasters and enormous blisters. 'I was already half way on the road to a better world when I convinced my doctors that my nerves were disordered by eight years of incessant worry and vexation, and that in continuing to weaken me they would bring me to typhus fever or imbecility. My good constitution carried me through, thanks chiefly to some **dozen bottles of good wine.**'

The dozen bottles of good wine and occasional jibes at the 'Philistines of the Spree' and the 'bigwigs of Potsdam' enabled him to go on with his Russian mission. At the news, however, of the note of remonstrance addressed by the Cabinet of Berlin to Count Cavour, after Castel Fidardo and the conquest of the kingdom of Naples, he again thought of resigning his post and going into the political arena, to use again his own expression, ' in political bathing-drawers.' It is from this period that the baldness of the Chancellor and the reduction of the abundant hair of his youth to the three hairs of the Berlin comic papers is said to date.

Bismarck achieved not only political but marked social success at the Russian Court and in upper Russian society. The Prussian Minister, owing to the ties of relationship

Russian plenipotentiary were supported by the plenipotentiary of France; and in all the conferences which ensued, the distribution of votes was almost invariably England
and Austria on one side—France, Russia, and Prussia on
the other.

In the same despatch from which the last extract is taken
Bismarck declared his conviction that 'ere long we shall
' have to fight Austria for our very existence,' and he continued to carry on the war in the interior of the Frankfort
Diet against the pretensions of Austria, and to write to Berlin
masses of despatches, reports, and private letters all to the
same purpose. One voluminous report of his is known in
the Prussian Foreign Office as "The Little Book," and may
be regarded as his political testament, recapitulating his
experiences in the Diet for the use of his successor, Von
Usedom.

His life at this time was one of incessant agitation. Great
projects were fermenting in his brain, but for the present he
could see no way of bringing them to maturity. He varied
his labours at the Diet with rapid journeys across Germany,
France, Denmark, Sweden, Courland, and North Italy. In
his frequent visits to Paris he became assured that Austria
would have to fight for the possession of Lombardy and
Venice, and he returned in a still more aggressive mood to
worry Count Rechberg. At one time it was considered that
his recall would be necessary to preserve peace, and he was
so vexed at the want of recognition of his views by his own
government that he designed quitting the service, and carrying on his political action in 'political bathing-drawers'
(*politischen Schwimmhosen*) when an offer was made to him
of the post of Prussian ambassador at St. Petersburg. So
he consented to carrying on his political career 'in a bear's
' skin and with caviare,' as he expressed it. Perhaps,
too, it had been hoped at Berlin that the snows of Russia
would cool his political ardour; but at all events his views
of the value of a Russian alliance and his well-known
friendship with Prince Gortschakoff qualified him especially
for the post, for which he presented his credentials to the
Emperor at St. Petersburg on April 1, 1859, the forty-
fourth anniversary of his birthday. Acquaintance with St.
Petersburg only strengthened him in his anti-Austrian views,
for on May 12 he addressed his famous letter to the Minister
Von Schleinitz, which he concluded by saying that the only
radical cure for the infirmities of the Bund was to be made
ferro et igne.

The new Prussian ambassador arrived at St. Petersburg three months after the famous speech of the French Emperor to Baron Hübner, on New Year's Day. He found his former colleague, the Russian Chancellor, still full of resentful feeling, and using all his influence to push Austria into a declaration of war. The two ministers were inseparable and made no secret of their mutual ill-will to Austria in the *salons* of St. Petersburg. Bismarck on his side, however, fretted and fumed at the difficulties which he found at Berlin in getting his views adopted as to the advisability of a Franco-Russo-Prussian alliance; for when war broke out in Italy, the king and the ministers at Berlin were still discussing as to whether Prussia should not go to the assistance of Austria, and whether she was not bound to do so by Federal obligations. So far was he as yet from getting the policy *ferro et igne* accepted there.

After the battle of Magenta there was some talk of an armed Prussian intervention, and of a mobilisation of the Federal troops, which would probably have taken place if Napoleon had crossed the Adige. At this news Bismarck, we learn from his letters, became dangerously ill. The doctors, he wrote, covered his body with cupping-glasses as large as saucers, with mustard plasters and enormous blisters. ' I was ' already half way on the road to a better world when I ' convinced my doctors that my nerves were disordered by ' eight years of incessant worry and vexation, and that in ' continuing to weaken me they would bring me to typhus ' fever or imbecility. My good constitution carried me ' through, thanks chiefly to some dozen bottles of good ' wine.'

The dozen bottles of good wine and occasional jibes at the ' Philistines of the Spree' and the 'bigwigs of Pots- ' dam ' enabled him to go on with his Russian mission. At the news, however, of the note of remonstrance addressed by the Cabinet of Berlin to Count Cavour, after Castel Fidardo and the conquest of the kingdom of Naples, he again thought of resigning his post and going into the political arena, to use again his own expression, ' in political ' bathing-drawers.' It is from this period that the baldness of the Chancellor and the reduction of the abundant hair of his youth to the three hairs of the Berlin comic papers is said to date.

Bismarck achieved not only political but marked social success at the Russian Court and in upper Russian society. The Prussian Minister, owing to the ties of relationship which existed between the courts of Berlin and St. Petersburg, had always enjoyed exceptional favour among the diplomatists accredited to the Czar, and been allowed admission to the family circle. Bismarck, as an admirer of Nicholas, as an adversary of anti-Russian liberalism at Berlin and of Austria, was admitted to such terms of familiarity as no Prussian minister had ever enjoyed before. The Czar never failed to invite him to his bear hunts, and always took him with him in his suite in his interviews with the Prince Regent at Warsaw and Breslau. He acquired no less popularity among the influential classes of the Russian capital, and he omitted no opportunity to improve it. He adopted Russian ways, wore a Russian hunting-dress at hunting and shooting parties, which he never failed to attend ; he harnessed his horses in the Russian style, kept four young bear-cubs in his house, who amused his guests with their antics and scratched his footmen's calves. He even had a professor of Russian in his house, and surprised the Emperor one day by speaking in the Russian tongue.

When Bismarck quitted Russia after three years' residence there, no one doubted that he was destined to play a great part in the history of Germany ; and in fact, after filling for a few months the post of Prussian ambassador at Paris, he assumed, in October, 1862, the presidency of the Prussian Ministry.

The most surprising political evolutions and revolutions have combined always at the critical moment of Bismarck's career to fill his hand with trumps ; but then he knew how to play them. Such a surprising conjuncture was created by the last insurrection of Poland and the encouragement it received from the Western Powers. However much Bismarck had ingratiated himself with the Court and upper circles at St. Petersburg, there would have been small chance, as matters stood, of Russia being so false to her traditional conservative principles as to stand quietly by while Bismarck tore up the map of Europe for the profit of Prussia. The encouragement given to this abortive insurrection by Austria, France, and England, and their subsequent abandonment of the Poles, form humiliating pages in their diplomatic history. They aggravated the sufferings and swelled the torrents of blood and tears of the unfortunate Poles, incurred the resentment of the Czar and all Russians, and enabled Bismarck, by the adoption of an entirely opposite policy, to ingratiate himself still more with Russia, and to render Russian policy subservient to his own. It was

Bismarck who, by a quiet hint about Schleswig Holstein at Berlin, stopped all further intervention of England in behalf of the Poles, and caused the Queen's messenger to be recalled by telegraph while on his way with an admonitory despatch to St. Petersburg.   Nor was his service confined to diplomacy; he made the frontier convention of February 1863, and, by the strict guard which he kept on the western frontier of Russian Poland, relieved the Czar's forces of half their work in suppressing the insurrection.   Russia, in the belief that she had escaped from an immense danger, placed Bismarck next to Prince Gortschakoff as a creditor on her gratitude.

The time was now ripe for what Bismarck still considers his *coup de maître* on the Schleswig Holstein question. Those who place any confidence in the Chancellor's protests of indifference as to the Oriental question will do well to mark the different phases of expression through which he passed until he secured the duchies for Prussia.   At first he condemned the Schleswig Holstein movement in indignant terms as revolutionary, and, as long as he wanted to keep England in good humour at the time of the Polish insurrection, affected to speak of it as a *marotte* of Austria's and the little German States.   He even offered to prevent the Federal execution in the Duchies, if Denmark would accept the mediation of England, and so get England to separate from France and decline the Congress proposed by Napoleon III.   He thus killed two birds with one stone, created a coldness between France and England, and got England to keep quiet on the Polish question.   After this Bismarck had no objection to the Federal execution, and then occurred another of his astonishing strokes of good luck, the sudden death of Frederic VII. of Denmark on November 15, 1860, which gave a fresh impetus to the German longings for the Duchies.   This event roused the Prussian Chancellor to incredible activity; he became all things to all men; he cajoled England and France; made use of the Bund as a catspaw, and then set it coolly aside; overawed the smaller States, and suppressed the candidate of their choice; got Austria to join him in a work of spoliation, and then framed a pretext for quarrelling about the division of the spoil and despoiling the spoiler.   This was his first step towards enlarging the frontiers of Prussia.

Dr. Busch himself lets us know what Bismarck thinks of this diplomatic campaign of his, and he has reason to be proud; for if Macchiavelli and Frederic II. were both to return to life, they would declare that no statesman ever profited so much by their teaching and example :—

'He said to us at Varzin in 1877 : "That is the diplomatic campaign of which I am proudest." Baron von Holstein asked, "You wanted the Duchies from the very beginning?" "Yes," replied the Prince, "certainly I did, immediately after the King of Denmark's death. But it was a difficult job. Everybody was against me—several coteries at Court, Austria, the petty German States, and the English who grudged us the harbour of Kiel. Crowds of the Liberals were opposed to it who all of a sudden discovered that the rights of princes were matters of importance—in reality, it was only their hatred and envy of me—and even the Schleswig-Holsteiners themselves did not want it. I had to contend with all these and I know not whom besides." ' (Vol. i. p. 367.)

One of the most characteristic touches in his handling of this question was an argument he held with Sir A. Buchanan, our ambassador, that this spoliation of Denmark was an indirect recognition of the rights of Christian IX. as Duke of Holstein. This truly Bismarckian piece of logic was, as we all know, adopted by the judges of Berlin, who, when the claims of all the pretenders to the Duchies were laid before them, ousted them all, and declared that the King of Denmark alone had a rightful title, and therefore Bismarck concluded that since he was dispossessed of this title by Austria and Prussia, they alone had acquired it. The next step naturally of this logic was to oust Austria and so give Prussia the sole possession of the province.

The diplomatic skill which Bismarck displayed in preparing for war with Austria; the formation of the secret alliance with Italy; his intrigues to obtain the benevolent neutrality of France; the difficulties which he had to overcome the aversion which the immense majority not only of Germans but of Prussians, beginning with the King himself, felt for this war; the adroit use of the Russian Chancellor,— surpass, in our opinion, the diplomatic achievements of his Schleswig Holstein campaign, notwithstanding his own predilection for the former transaction.

'It is well that we have won,' said Moltke to Bismarck after Sadowa, 'or the old women of Berlin would have 'beaten you to death with wet dusters.' 'Der eiserne Graf,' in fact, felt immense disquietude about the possibility of a reverse. Just before the commencement of hostilities he made use of the strange expression that 'God Almighty was 'capricious;' and at Paris he said that after all he might be going on his way to a second Olmütz, and hinted that there were worse ways of death than the scaffold; and when he started for the seat of war said, ' I will come back by ' Vienna or Munich, or I will charge with the last squadron, ' and one that will not return.'

It may be imagined, indeed, that the ' Iron Count ' had still his misgivings, for we read with unutterable astonishment that, only a fortnight before the commencement of hostilities, Bismarck made overtures of peace to Austria, and proposed that they should unite their vast armies, already on a war footing, and both fall upon France. Dr. Busch makes this statement on the authority of the Saxon Minister, Von Friesen, who stated to Dr. Busch on January 28, 1883, that he had the account from Bismarck himself. If there is anything more astonishing than the disclosure itself, it is the satisfaction which Dr. Busch apparently finds in revealing it.

The statement of Count von Friesen is as follows :—

' About a fortnight before the commencement of active hostilities Bismarck sent the Austrian General von Gablenz's brother, a Saxon then living at Berlin, to the Emperor in Vienna, with offers of peace on the basis of Dualism and common action against France. Gablenz was to tell His Majesty that we had six to seven hundred thousand men in the field, whilst the Austrian forces were also very numerous; we had therefore better come to terms, execute a change of front westwards (Prussia in the North, Austria in the South) against France, reconquer Elsass, and make Strassburg a Federal fortress. There was no just cause on hand for a war with France: but our excuse would be that the French had also done us a great wrong by seizing Elsass and Strassburg in time of peace.' (Vol. i. p. 382.)

Thus, although Bismarck could find no just cause of war against France, he deliberately proposed to make war upon her to get out of his difficulty with Austria. And yet the Prussian minister had left nothing undone to secure the good will of France without, however, having entered into or extracted from the Emperor any positive engagements—and doubtless, as long as he could feel a reasonable assurance that France would not interfere with his projects, he did not want any. However, he succeeded in creating a strong party among the leading advisers of the Emperor, known as the *parti de l'action,* in favour of a Prussian alliance. Of this party the Prince Napoleon was the chief. What was wisdom in Bismarck was consummate folly and infatuation in Napoleon III. Prince Rudolph Metternich, on finding Napoleon so sage and so moderate at the Congress of Paris, said—' C'est la raison cristalisée ; ' but later, when he found

him in league with Cavour, said, ' The Emperor has yet some
' fine cards in his hands, but the revolutionary Empire will
' go to wreck on the Italian reef.'

The unity of Germany was, in fact, a logical sequence of
the unity of Italy. Nevertheless there is this excuse for the
French Emperor, that no one at that time believed that Prussia
was able to cope with Austria; for, in fact, the present military strength of Prussia is quite of recent date, and is due
to the reforms of the present Emperor when Prince Regent,
assisted by Moltke and Roon, since the humiliation of
Olmütz, when the Prussian ministers avowed they had not
50,000 men to place in the field.

The news of the astounding victory of Sadowa, the utter
defeat of Austria, and the superiority of the needle-gun,
came upon the Cabinet of Paris like a thunderclap. Nothing
but abortive diplomatic tentatives had taken place on the
part of France to prepare her for so great an event. She
had really no available army. The blood and treasure of
the nation had been squandered away in the foolish expedi-
dition to Mexico, and no measures taken to repair her losses,
so that Prussia became as rapidly as in a transformation
scene the mistress of Europe, and the diplomatic and military
incapacity of France was revealed to all.

It is true the French Emperor by a telegraphic despatch
was able to stop the Prussian army on its march to Vienna
and to save Saxony from the fate of Hanover; but this was
but a temporary advantage, and in spite of the acceptance
by the two belligerents of the Emperor's mediation and
of the preliminaries of Nikolsburg, Austria and Prussia
shortly made peace behind his back, and the smaller states
of Germany followed suit in making secret conventions by
which virtually they placed their military forces at the disposal of Prussia.

The catastrophe of Sadowa was more fatal in its final
results to France than to Austria; it gave a shock to France
which shook the Empire to its centre and filled its ministers,
in the words of M. Rouher, with ' patriotic anguish.' This
tremendous event, too, brought an almost immediate change
in the direction of foreign affairs, notwithstanding the
unarmed state of France, since she could not then have
placed 80,000 men in the field. Drouyn de Lhuys, who had
opposed all along the counsels of the *parti de l'action*, and
represented in the French Cabinet the principle of balance
of power in opposition to that of nationalities, counselled an
armed demonstration on the frontier, and the French Emperor

at first had resolved to follow his counsels. The most passionate appeals had been made from without to the Emperor not to let the opportunity go by, and one of the most eminent ministers of the German Confederation warned Napoleon that if he did not do so, ' in four years you will be forced to ' make war against Prussia, and you will then have all ' Germany against you.'

But the most remarkable utterance on this occasion was that of the Queen of Holland, whose majestic beauty and charm of manner and superior intelligence, which she inherited from the wisest and most accomplished sovereign of Germany, were equally admired at Paris and the Hague. She had been much at the Imperial Court, and was sincerely attached to the personal qualities of the French Emperor, whom the Queen Hortense used to call *le doux entêté*. When she heard of the vacillating counsels of the Imperial Cabinet, she wrote, exactly a fortnight after Sadowa, a letter to the Baron d'André at the Hague, which was found among the papers in the Tuileries in 1870. It contains the following passages, and their vehemence is explicable by the fact that she was pleading *pro domo sua*.

' Vous vous faites d'étranges illusions. Votre prestige a plus diminué dans cette dernière quinzaine qu'il n'a diminué pendant toute la durée du règne. Vous permettez de détruire les faibles; vous laissez grandir outre mesure l'insolence et la brutalité de votre plus proche voisin; vous acceptez un cadeau [Venice], et vous ne savez même pas adresser une bonne parole à celui qui vous le fait. Je regrette que vous me croyiez intéressée à la question, et que vous ne voyiez pas le danger d'une puissante Allemagne et d'une puissante Italie. C'est la *dynastie* qui est menacée, et c'est elle qui en subira les suites. Je le dis, parce que telle est la vérité, que vous reconnaîtrez trop tard. Ne croyez pas que le malheur qui m'accable dans le désastre de ma patrie [Würtemberg] me rende injuste et méfiante.

' La Vénétie cédée, il fallait secourir l'Autriche, marcher sur le Rhin, imposer vos conditions ! Laisser égorger l'Autriche, c'est plus qu'un crime: c'est une faute. Cependant je croirais manquer à une ancienne et sérieuse amitié si je ne disais une dernière fois toute la vérité.'

Whether in the then disarmed state of France, and with the terrible experience of 1870 behind us, such measures would have been efficacious, may of course be doubted, but it must be remembered that Austria had still a victorious army in Italy of 120,000 men, and Prussia was already showing signs of exhaustion. It must be added, too, that at that time all South Germany was wild with indignation at Prussia for her 'fratricidal war,' and at the exactions of her generals, Vogel von Falkenstein and Manteuffel, at Frankfort and on the Rhine. At any rate the Chancellor of Germany, in a remarkable speech made on January 10, 1879, in the Reichstag, allowed that an armed demonstration of France at that time would have had the most serious results for Prussia. ' Although France,' he said, ' had then but few troops at her ' disposition, nevertheless no very great number of French ' troops would have been sufficient, united with the numerous ' corps of Southern Germany, to make a respectable force. ' Such an army would have laid us under the necessity of ' covering Berlin and of abandoning all our successes in ' Austria.'

. However, before the passionate appeal of the Queen of Holland reached the Tuileries, the momentous decision had been already taken. After a crisis of great intensity in the Cabinet, and after a debate of most dramatic interest presided over by the Emperor, who was then in a state of great physical suffering from his cruel malady, Prince Metternich telegraphed to Vienna that France would only interfere in the Austro-Prussian conflict diplomatically. It is to the pages of M. Rothan that we owe the revelation of the interior agitations of which the Emperor's Cabinet was the scene at this crisis. However, even after this emotional scene the Emperor did not decide wholly on abandoning the policy of Drouyn de Lhuys; it was the Prince Napoleon and M. Rouher aided by M. Nigra and the Prussian Minister, Von Goltz, who gave the death-blow to the policy of intervention.

Then commenced that series of imbecile negotiations with victorious Prussia which Bismarck rightly termed the *politique des pourboires*. The Emperor, still deluded by his romantic dream of being regarded as the champion of the principle of nationalities, and urged on by Prince Napoleon and the *parti de l'action*, and also by those necessities of the inner politics of France which Metternich had touched upon in describing the Empire as a revolutionary empire, persisted in the delusion that Prussia, lately so humble and so prodigal of offers, was now, in the hour of her triumph, still desirous of coming to a private understanding with France, and of making such concessions as she had been ready to make before her hour of triumph. Upon this the French minister Benedetti, who had fostered the Prusso-Italian alliance, had orders to proceed to the headquarters of the Prussian army to confer with Count Bismarck.

Drouyn de Lhuys shortly after gave in his resignation, and then on the 16th of September appeared the famous circular of M. de Lavalette, who took the office of French Foreign Minister *ad interim* until M. de Moustier could arrive from Constantinople to fill it permanently. This astonishing circular, read by the light of subsequent events, proves that the French Emperor had succeeded in throwing himself into a complete state of hallucination. It was a song of praise of the Treaty of Prague, with the assurance that the aggrandisement of Prussia was another guarantee for the security of France.

Bismarck on his side left nothing undone to maintain the French Emperor and his ministers in their excellent dispositions, and to instil into them a belief that he desired nothing so much as a firm alliance with France, and that the two nations could in that case settle their frontiers as they pleased, and set at defiance all interference and control from the rest of Europe. Bismarck himself, in a speech in the Reichstag in 1879, spoke of his eagerness to be on good terms with France, and of the benefits which Prussia had derived from her friendly behaviour.

'I had every reason for keeping up this good understanding, by means of which I succeeded—not only whilst I was Envoy in Paris, but throughout the difficulties of the Polish 1863 crisis, when France was opposed to us—in maintaining such a favourable disposition towards us, that, in the Danish question, France's friendly behaviour cut the ground from under the feet of other powers which had a fancy not to allow us to fight out our quarrel with Denmark single-handed. Still more, during our heavier struggle with Austria in 1866, France's self-restraint would certainly not have been carried so far as (fortunately for us) it was, had I not bestowed every possible care upon our relations with her, thereby bringing about a "benevolent" connexion with the Emperor Napoleon, who, for his part, liked to have treaties with us better than with others; but who undoubtedly did not foresee that the 1866 war would terminate in our favour. He reckoned upon our being beaten, and upon then according us his protection—benevolently, but not gratuitously. Politically speaking, however, it was lucky for us, in my opinion, that he remained amicably disposed towards us, and particularly towards me, up to the battle of Sadowa.' (Vol. ii. p. 8.)

As to what proposals really were made for compensation to be given to France for Prussian victories, whether in Belgium, or in the Palatinate or the Rhenish provinces, and who first made them, there is a direct conflict of evidence; and we have to place on one side the testimony of Benedetti, General Govone, and General La Marmora, and on the other that of Prince Bismarck. The Chancellor declares that he merely ' let the French statesmen revel in their extra-' ordinary illusions as long as might be without promising ' them the least thing even verbally.' The Chancellor, with great violence in a speech in the Lower House, denied that he had ever held out a prospect to anybody of ' ceding a ' single German village or even as much as a clover-field.' However, there are the despatches of Benedetti, written immediately after interviews with Bismarck, and those of General Govone, similarly written, and published by La Marmora in his pamphlet ' Un po' più di luce,' which assert the direct contrary. Dr. Busch says ' future historians will ' not hesitate a moment as to whether they shall believe ' the Chancellor or the Frenchman who passed through the ' Oriental school of lying and intriguing in Egypt, the ' member of the Italian Consorteria, and those whom both ' appealed to as witnesses '—which is simply an appeal to character.

The disaster of Sadowa was not only a surprise for France, it was one for all Europe ; in fact, not only was the axis of European politics displaced, but Europe itself was eclipsed and the Treaty of Prague gave a final blow to the treaties of 1815, which the French Emperor had so unwisely just before denounced in violent terms at Auxerre. Even after this stupendous victory, however, the situation of Count Bismarck and of Prussia was critical. The health of the ' iron Count' had given way under the terrible strain which had been put on all his faculties ; his digestion, his legs, and his nervous system, were all disordered ; and he was in a state of such prostration that it seemed he would not be able to carry out the great work he had commenced with such astonishing success. He was absent from Berlin from the beginning of September to the end of November, and during his absence everything went wrong in the Government of Berlin ; the carrying out the new annexations in the presence of the hostility of the population, and the establishment of the Confederation of the North seemed beset with invincible difficulties. Throughout all Germany there was nothing but indignation and recrimination at this new order of things, and in Prussia itself the opinion was largely current that her minister had undertaken a task beyond her strength, and he became for the moment very unpopular ; while the king, who had been with such difficulty dragged into the war, was beset with rival influences, and Herr von Savigny and Herr von Goltz disputed the succession of the great minister.

All at once, however, he reappeared upon the scene, and this reappearance was a new triumph.

The author of Sadowa began again with renewed energy the work of carrying out the policy of Frederic the Great, in organising the Prussian State with her annexations, trusting to diplomacy and to future wars to settle those relations with the German States south of the Main which had been left in so unsatisfactory and undefined a state by the Treaty of Prague.

'He knew,' says M. Rothan, 'that it is not by subordinating State policy to sentiment, nor by fighting for generous ideas, that empires are founded or preserve their preponderance. Therefore he pursued his aim with implacable obstinacy, persuaded that if violent and arbitrary proceedings excite momentarily and justly the public conscience, future generations only regard the grandeur of the work without troubling themselves about the means exercised to accomplish it, nor about the sacrifices and bloodshed which it has cost.'

Count Bismarck had, however, another motive besides a sanitary one for retreating to Varzin. He wished to put an end to his negotiations with the French minister Benedetti as to the *politique des pourboires,* which the French Government, without any due regard for its dignity or security, still continued to follow. But the Government of Napoleon III. found itself in a very difficult position. In spite of the flaming circular of M. Lavalette glorifying the new doctrines of the agglomeration of nationalities, the French nation had a sense of their having been outjockeyed in their position as the mediating power of Europe. In the *salons*, in the clubs, and in the *cafés* there was a current expression at this time 'Vous avez Bismarqué,' 'Il a Bismarqué,' used in playing games of skill or chance to denote taking an unfair advantage; and M. Piétri, the Préfet de police, in his reports made known to the Emperor that discontent pervaded all classes of society. The time was gone by when it could be said 'Quand la France est satisfaite, l'Europe est contente.' Benedetti therefore received instructions to make fresh endeavours to bring the Berlin Cabinet to some territorial arrangement in accordance with former Prussian assurances, which might restore somewhat in the eyes of the French nation the prestige of the French Government; and Benedetti, who was conscious of having, to the detriment of France, encouraged the *connubio* between Prussia and Italy, set to work energetically to meet the wishes of the Imperial Cabinet. The negotiations which took place with this view were carried on partly *vivâ voce*, and partly in cipher, and so secretly that M. de Moustier, the French minister, took no one into his confidence, but ciphered and deciphered the despatches which passed between Paris and Berlin and the Hague himself. But, in spite of these precautions, M. Benedetti, who in other respects showed himself a competent diplomatist, committed an act of incredible simplicity by leaving a draft project for an offensive and defensive alliance with Prussia in his own handwriting, written, as he* represents, ' en quelque sorte sous la dictée' of Count Bismarck, in the hands of the latter ; and in this draft treaty provision was made for the cession of the Duchy of Luxemburg, and finally of Belgium, to France.

The famous question of Herr von Bennigsen, addressed to the Prussian Government in the Reichstag, which there is little doubt was made by arrangement, put a stop to this negotiation about Luxemburg, and announced to astonished Europe that we were on the eve of another great war. A war would have infallibly ensued had the French Government been prepared for it; and the war party at Berlin, aware of the weakness of France at this time, used all their efforts to precipitate the crisis. At the time of the interpellation of Herr Bennigsen, the treaty which was to have conveyed Luxemburg to France was on the point of being signed by the King of Holland, with the concurrence of Prussia. The reply of the Chancellor, the manifestations of the Reichstag, the violent declamations of the Prussian press brought the negotiations to a standstill, and the French Government saw the possession of the duchy whisked away from them just as they were about to lay hands upon it. Conscious of its military weakness, in spite of the efforts which were being made to reorganise the army by Marshal Niel, the French Government had determined to yield to no provocation whatever, and restricted its demands to the evacuation by Prussian troops of the fortress of Luxemburg.

M. Rothan, who has, with the aid of documents not before made public, traced the story of these negotiations with a masterly hand, gives the credit of averting war at that time from France to Lord Derby, then Lord Stanley, and the Queen. After the countless delusive offers and ' négociations ' dilatoires' with which they had been mocked by Count Bismarck, they could not reduce their demands to less than the evacuation of the fortress of Luxemburg. The internal situation of the French Government, and the excited state of public opinion as to the failure of these negotiations, could not permit them to reduce their demands below this. The French Government, in their extremity, had applied to Russia and to England to use their influence at the Prussian Court to procure the evacuation of the fortress of Luxemburg. Of the good will of Austria they were already assured, for Count Beust had in noble language refused a roundabout tentative of the Count von Tauffkirchen, an emissary of Bavaria, to get Austria to join Prussia in an offensive and defensive league against France. Russia, however, through Prince Gortschakoff, replied in a derisory way to the advances of the French. The *entente cordiale* between Bismarck and the Russian Chancellor had been strengthened by the mission of General Manteuffel immediately after Sadowa, in which Russia was offered *carte blanche* as to Eastern affairs if she would leave Prussia undisturbed in the West. Prince Gortschakoff would not admit to the French Ambassador that the internal affairs of a country were any argument in diplomacy, and, when mention was made of Luxemburg, talked glibly of Crete, and the urgent necessity of coming to an understanding about the state of the Christians in Turkey.

The English Government, however, could not remain indifferent to the danger of a fresh European war, and to the appeal of a neighbour power—what fresh changes in the map of Europe might not a war between France and Prussia produce!

'Therefore,' we quote from M. Rothan, 'Lord Stanley and his colleagues, contrary to the traditions of English policy, after exchanging some frank explanations with the Cabinet of the Tuileries, requested the Queen Victoria to come out from her mourning and make herself a decided advocate of peace with the King of Prussia. " I know what " has passed," said the Queen to the Prince de la Tour d'Auvergne. " Herr von Bismarck, although he denies it now, has encouraged you to " lay claim to Luxemburg. I know, too, that the Emperor restricts " himself to demanding the evacuation of the fortress, and I have given " the King William my opinion on the matter." The Queen was convinced that if all the Powers came to an understanding to tell Herr von Bismarck that he was in the wrong, he would yield. She recalled the language that was held at Baden on the eve of the German war, and she was uneasy at hearing that the Prussian minister was always talking of the military preparations of France. " That makes one reflect," she said, " and allows one to suspect the intentions of Prussia."

'Lord Stanley by a special Queen's messenger sent together with the letter of the Queen urgent instructions to Lord Augustus Loftus, then ambassador.

Meanwhile, however, Count Bismarck had taken himself off to Varzin, where he remained five days.

'After five days he returned to Berlin, and was present with M. Benedetti at a concert given in honour of the marriage of the Prince of Flanders with the Princess of Hohenzollern.

'The French ambassador and the Prussian minister looked at each other from a distance without endeavouring to come together. They had, indeed, nothing but mutual reproaches to exchange.

'Lord Augustus Loftus, who was present, had an unpleasant part to play, but he did it in a resolute way. He had his instructions in his pocket for five days, but the flight of Count Bismarck had prevented all action, and he waited with impatience for the king to speak to him, and as soon as he did so informed his Majesty forthwith of the wishes of his Government for peace and the evacuation of the fortress of Luxemburg, and, in reply to an observation of the king about the state of public opinion in Germany, said that the public opinion of Europe was to be considered in preference to that of Germany.'

The king did not appear to receive these observations with much favour. However, on the morrow M. d'Oubril, the Russian Minister at Berlin, paid a visit to the president, and to him the Chancellor admitted that Prussia would accept a conference respecting Luxemburg on a basis which implied the evacuation of the fortress.

The remark with which Bismarck wound up this affair is characteristic of the man. A few days after he met M. Benedetti at dinner at the Russian minister's, and, after touching glasses with M. Benedetti at dinner, on leaving the table drew him aside, and congratulated him on the change of feeling at Berlin, and added: 'On a fait ceci, et ' l'on voudrait faire encore bien des bêtises.'

The tension of the situation, however, was only relieved for the moment; it was still difficult to get Prussia to retire from the menacing and suspicious position which she had taken up, and in which war seemed possible at any moment. The semi-official newspapers continued to accuse France of excessive armaments, and of inventing pretexts for war; and if war was prevented at that time, the merit is chiefly due to the tact and ability which the present Lord Derby displayed in managing the conference at London, though the final formula as to the 'collective guarantee' for the neutrality of Luxemburg was due to the inventive genius of Baron Brunnow.

Neither France nor Europe knew the great peril from which the former had been delivered by the Conference of London just before the opening of the 'Exposition Univer- ' selle,' when Paris had decked herself out in all her splendour, and the Imperial Court was preparing to receive a succession of kings and emperors with splendid hospitality. Of all the visitors assuredly none excited greater curiosity than King William of Prussia with Bismarck and Moltke who came in attendance upon him, and the Emperor Alexander. Strangely enough, it was the King of Prussia who, by his frank and gallant bearing, succeeded in captivating the good graces of the Emperor and the Imperial Court, and was the most popular. To the outward eye, France and the Second Empire were then in the very zenith of power and prosperity. There were those, however, who knew how meretricious was all this external display, and from what imminent peril France had just escaped; and perhaps, as the Emperor Alexander was one of these, it was this knowledge, and the knowledge also how much France had just been indebted to Russian diplomacy, which induced him to treat his imperial hosts and their pageants with cavalier reserve.

Bismarck, however, had not gone to Paris without hesitation. Some of the newspapers, especially that of Granier de Cassagnac, 'Le Pays,' expressed themselves in terms of violent indignation at his proposed visit. 'We hope,' wrote the Imperial publicist, 'that the Prussian minister ' will not push his audacity to the point of afflicting us ' with his presence and braving our legitimate resentments.' However, a hint from the king that a refusal to go to Paris might be construed into fear of assassination overcame all hesitation, and he went and was well received. How much akin his talk in Paris was to that which he formerly held there, and how little real indignation he felt at the idea of France taking Belgium—an idea which Napoleon III. had at first scouted as an act of brigandage—may be seen by the following reference to a conversation which he had with the Duke de Bauffremont in the garden of the Tuileries, the substance of which he repeated at Versailles in 1870, and in which he really spoke with contempt of Napoleon III. for not having seized Belgium in 1866 :—

'The Versailles commentary ran thus:—"In the summer of 1866 " Napoleon had not the pluck to do what was the right thing from his " point of view. He ought—well, he ought to have taken possession " of the subject of Benedetti's proposal, when we were marching " against the Austrians, and have held it in pawn for whatever might " happen. At that time we could not stop him, and it was not likely " that England would attack him—at least he might have waited to " see. If we proved victorious, he ought to have tried to work with " us, back to back, and to encourage us to commit excesses. But he " is a Tiefenbacher, and always will be." ' (Vol. ii. pp. 39, 40.)

The predominance of Count Bismarck in the councils of Prussia was even now far from being so absolute as it became later. He had still rivals in the king's favour, although death speedily removed one, Count Goltz, and the other, Count Harry Arnim, fell through his own vanity and presumption. Even after the Conference of London, Bismarck's policy was much decried and suspected both inside and outside Prussia. As for the Confederation of the North, it was still in a chaotic unsettled state, and the constitution he had given it was not considered capable of being carried out. He was considered the foe of internal liberty in Prussia, and it was even hinted that he was capable of wading through blood and slaughter to a throne. His overwhelming assertion of his own superiority, his impatience of opposition, and his irritable temperament created him many enemies.

It is of course vain to speculate on what would have been the fate of Bismarck had he met with any antagonists in the area of European politics who were his equals. But his wonderful success is more than half explained by the absence of anyone in the circle of European politics able to cope with him. Count Rechberg, Napoleon III. and his ministers, Prince Gortschakoff, became, one after the other, his accomplices and his dupes, and it is really astounding that not one of them learnt anything either from their own faults or the faults of their predecessor, or were put on their guard by Bismarck's own reckless avowals of the policy he meant to pursue.

As for Napoleon III. and his ministers, even after Sadowa and their perilous escape from the difficulty of Luxemburg, they set at defiance all past experience and allowed the Chancellor to goad them into a declaration of war which doubled the stakes of Sadowa. The Franco-Prussian war of 1870 was but a counterpart, and a consequence, of the war of 1866; and with the utmost candour Dr. Busch avows that Bismarck did contrive to provoke that war which was to be the crowning success of his ambition, and at the same time to throw in the eyes of Europe all responsibility for it on the French. He repeats in Bismarck's own words his reflections in Paris in 1867, as to what might have been the result of a war with France about Luxemburg, and that he had scruples about the sufficient strength of Germany at that time. In 1870 this scruple was effaced.

Of the undue vehemence of the language of the Duc de Gramont, and of the temerity with which the Cabinet of the French Emperor seized upon the sudden revelation of the candidateship of the Prince Hohenzollern to Spain, no censure is sufficiently strong.   Never was Europe so taken by surprise.   On June 30, 1870, M. Emile Ollivier had said, ' Never was the peace of Europe so secure ;' and on July 6, after the violent declaration of the Duc de Gramont, war was imminent.   The only excuse for the Cabinet of Paris is that it was still smarting under the sense of having been completely duped by the wily diplomacy of the Prussian minister in the Austro-Prussian war, that the menacing attitude of Prussia during the negotiations about Luxemburg had left behind feelings of lively indignation; and that, on the very eve of starting to receive French hospitality at the time of the ' Exposition Universelle,' Bismarck had again defied France, and indeed Europe, by the organisation of the German Customs Union, an insidious way of undermining the Treaty of Prague, which restricted Prussia to the north of the Main.

However, admitting that all that can be said of the folly of the French Imperial Cabinet, and of the demand for the renunciation of the Hohenzollern candidateship, and the impolicy of the pressure which was put on the King of Prussia to give a guarantee against a recurrence of the Hohenzollern candidateship, peace would have been secured had it not been for the memorable telegram despatched by Bismarck to the Prussian legations abroad and sent to the journals for publication.   Futile and ill-advised as we may think at the present day the raising of this Hohenzollern question was on the part of France, it is certain that at the commencement of the diplomatic struggle the sympathies of Southern Germany were with France, and that if the question of the *casus fœderis* had been raised at that time for war purposes at Stuttgart and Munich, Prussia would have met with a direct refusal—a refusal which would have given one hundred and fifty thousand combatants fewer to Prussia, and left communication open with Austria.   Even in the interior of Prussia, the adversaries of the Minister became loud in their protests against his aggressive policy, and after the deceptions which France had encountered, and the immense increase of Prussian power, the indignant declaration of the French Minister of Foreign Affairs that France would not permit the Empire of Charles V. to be built up again did not seem too vehement.   Bismarck had never found himself in a more difficult position, and it needed all his coolness and audacity, aided by his habitual good fortune and the extreme folly of his adversaries to come without detriment out of the situation. How he managed not only to escape without damage from this difficulty, but to turn the tables on France and to outwit and beat them overwhelmingly in the diplomatic struggle before the war began, and to throw upon the French Cabinet all the odium of a causeless war, is one of the most curious chapters of his history. As usual, retirement to Varzin, waiting for events and speculating on the faults of his adversaries, formed no small part of his system of action.

The good sense and moderation of the King of Prussia had contrived, without his appearing personally on the scene, that Prince Anthony of Hohenzollern should notify to the Spanish Government that his son withdrew his candidateship, and the monarch had promised Benedetti that he would approve of the renunciation. This was an immense success for France—honourable to the King of Prussia and honourable to France. The adversaries of Bismarck were enchanted, and Stuttgard illuminated. All seemed settled ; but, unfortunately, it did not suit the views of the Extreme Right, nor even of the adversaries of the Empire. The telegram of the ' père Antoine' was treated in a derisory manner by the extreme parties, and it was declared that nothing less than the direct participation of the King of Prussia in the renunciation, with guarantees for the future, could be accepted. The French ministers, who imagined they had achieved a great diplomatic victory, found themselves mocked and derided on all sides ; and the Duc de Gramont, excited by the conflict of passions and intrigues by which the Court and the Chambers were agitated, proceeded in the fatal path of asking for further guarantees against a resumption of the candidateship.

King William had certainly done all that his dignity as a king could permit him to do, and the blame of the war henceforward rests between Bismarck and the French Cabinet. To avoid all appearance of complicity in the conciliatory action of the king, Bismarck retired to Varzin. As soon, however, as the atmosphere became again troubled, he appeared in the field of action. Having come to Berlin and there learnt the fresh demands of the Duc de Gramont, he telegraphed to Baron Werther, in Paris, that if the French Government had any such communications to make he could not lay them before the King for official consideration, but that they must be made through the French Embassy at Berlin. By this means he threw all the blame of failure of future negotiations on the luckless Benedetti, who, with all his goodwill and undoubted diplomatic ability, had the *main malheureuse* in his negotiations with Bismarck. It may well be said that to the incessant use of the telegraph is largely due the miscarriage of these negotiations. Had it not been for the daily, or almost hourly, use of this instantaneous means of communication, and had negotiations been carried on in the old style, when passions had time to cool, and reflection to come in, a peaceful issue might have been the result; but war was virtually decided on in a week.

The Duc de Gramont, by telegraph, again urged Benedetti to make one more attempt to get the king to say that he would forbid the Prince of Hohenzollern to revoke his renunciation. Benedetti, as is well known, made a last attempt to move the king further at the railway station at Ems; but the king declined to say any more, and informed M. Benedetti in the most courteous terms through an aide-de-camp that he could say no more after having given his entire approbation without reserve to the renunciation.

It was the report of this interview as made by Bismarck to the Prussian embassies in Europe by telegraph, and as communicated by him to the newspapers, which was the immediate cause of the war. This report announced to the world that the King of Prussia had refused to see the French ambassador, and sent him word by an aide-de-camp that he had nothing more to say. It was this report, taken for granted as being true, which the Duc de Gramont described to M. Emile Ollivier 'as a slap in the face given to France,' adding that he would rather resign his portfolio than submit to a similar outrage. Dr. Busch describes the fabrication of this telegram thus :—

'With respect to the occurrences at Ems, the Chancellor received a full report by wire from Privy Councillor Abeken, then in the King's suite, with the Royal permission to publish its text. When this telegram arrived, Counts von Moltke and von Roon were dining with Bismarck, who read Abeken's report aloud to them. Both generals regarded the situation as still peaceful. The Chancellor observed, that would depend a good deal upon the tone and contents of the publication he had just been authorised to make. In the presence of his two guests he then put together some extracts from the telegram, which were forthwith despatched to all the Prussian Legations abroad, and to the Berlin newspapers in the following form :—

'"Telegram from Ems, July 13, 1870. When the intelligence of the "Hereditary Prince of Hohenzollern's renunciation was communicated "by the Spanish to the French Government, the French Ambassador

" demanded of His Majesty the King, at Ems, that the latter should
" authorise him to telegraph to Paris that His Majesty would pledge
" himself for all time to come never again to give his consent, should
" the Hohenzollerns hark back to their candidature. Upon this His
" Majesty refused to receive the French Ambassador again, and sent
" the aide-de-camp in attendance to tell him that His Majesty had
" nothing further to communicate to the Ambassador." ' (Vol. ii.
pp. 54, 55.)

This despatch was sent on the night of the 13th–14th to
all the Prussian diplomatic agents, and it was also published in an extra sheet in the ' Nord Deutsche Allgemeine
' Zeitung.' The effect of it in Paris was exasperating, and on
July 18 war was declared.

It was believed both in Paris and Vienna that the princes
and peoples of South Germany would remain neutral at first,
and then after a great victory—deemed as inevitable as the
Austrian triumphs had been in 1866—would become the
allies of France. This belief, however, was quickly annihilated. Three days after the declaration of war, the King
of Bavaria placed his army under the command of the King
of Prussia, and Würtemberg and the rest of Southern
Germany followed suit. The folly with which the French
Government themselves established the *casus fœderis* and
threw all South Germany into the arms of Prussia, is unsurpassed in the history of nations.

It was at Stuttgard that the aversion to Prussia's policy
of aggrandisement was the deepest; yet four days before
the declaration of war, the Comte de Saint Vallier transmitted by telegraph the indignant protest of the Baron von
Vahrenbühler against French presumption, a protest which
reads like articles of impeachment against the Paris Cabinet.
One of the most striking passages of this despatch ran as
follows :—

'The acts of the King of Prussia had for four years sown in our
hearts deep feelings of indignation, but your imperious demands have
forced us to remember that he is one of the chiefs of the German nation,
and that if he submitted to insults on the part of a foreign government
it would fall on all the German States. You make our cause a common one with his, you throw us into the arms of Prussia, you cement
our alliance. Yesterday I declined Prussian overtures ; now I shall be
obliged to accept them. I know that it is the same at Munich.
Prussia now can count on the alliance of the South.'

So infatuated, however, was the Duc de Gramont with his
confidence in the military strength of France, as reported
by Marshal Lebœuf and other generals, that he replied to

the Comte de Saint-Vallier 'that he was mistaken if he imagined that France desired the neutrality of the German Southern States. 'We do not want it,' he said; 'it would 'embarrass our military operations. We must have the 'plains of the Palatinate for the extension of armies.' When M. Rothan saw him on July 23, he found him so secure of French victories that he disdained all alliance, and beheld in his mind's eye the new weapon, the 'mitrailleuse,' sweeping the Prussian armies off the face of the earth.

Such overweening presumption could not fail to meet with its reward. The successes of Prussia were so sudden and so overwhelming that they took all Europe again by surprise; and as in 1866 France was in such a state of military un-readiness as not to be able to exercise any mediating in-fluence between Austria and Prussia, such was the case in 1870 with respect to the other European Powers. England, after the revelation of the intrigues with respect to Belgium and of Benedetti's draught treaty, although written 'en 'quelque sorte sous la dictée' of Count Bismarck, and in the presence of the general condemnation of the declar-ation of war, could not, in spite of the friendly feeling which existed towards France, be expected to take any active part in coming to her assistance; the more than benevolent neutrality of Russia had been secured by the secret under-standing of many years' date between Gortschakoff and Bismarck; and the offensive and defensive alliance with Austria, Italy, and France, which Count Beust had been labouring to bring about since 1869, had been wrecked on the question of the temporal sovereignty of the Pope, which with strange pertinacity the French Cabinet insisted on up-holding to the very last moment; and it may be truly said that to the inflexible resolve of the French Cabinet to uphold the Papal temporal power were really due the loss of Alsace and Lorraine and the payment of five milliards.

The French Emperor, indeed, made up his mind at last to abandon the temporal power of the Pope, but only after the Prussian successes had declared themselves, and after Austria had received an intimation from Russia that any hostile movement on her part against Prussia would be treated as a cause of war. Even Russia, however, in the presence of the tremendous successes of Prussia, began to have doubts of her policy in emancipating that State from all European control. Nevertheless Russia was able to obtain a com-pensation by the abolition of the provisions of the Treaty of Paris concerning the Black Sea, and after the signature of

the preliminaries of peace at Versailles the new Emperor
of Germany telegraphed the expression of his lifelong gratitude to the Emperor of Russia for his attitude during the
war.

It must be allowed that, whatever may be said of the
policy by which Bismarck raised Prussia to the height of the
great military power of Europe, he has used his power for
the maintenance of peace and for the maintaining the map
of Europe in the state in which it was left at the Treaty of
Frankfort. His attitude during the whole of the Russo-
Turkish war was irreproachable, his presiding influence at
the Congress of Berlin was exercised with consummate tact
and judgement, and he used his authority to reconcile the
opposing claims of England and Russia in a most masterly
way. It is well to read in his own words his notion of the
way in which a peace mediator should fulfil his functions.

Very shortly after the Congress violent and abusive articles
appeared in the Russian press, and especially in the 'Golos,'
said to be the confidential organ of Prince Gortschakoff,
attacking Prince Bismarck's domestic and foreign policy, and
accusing Prussia of the same ingratitude with which it accused
Austria at the time of the Crimean war. It is impossible,
of course, to know what verbal engagements did exist between the Russian and Prussian Chancellors; but at any
rate it is clear that Gortschakoff did not consider they had
been observed, for the relations of the two statesmen were
never so cordial as before, and Bismarck let slip few occasions
for speaking disdainfully of his former colleague.

Dr. Busch sums up their relations in these words, which
no doubt represent the Chancellor's views:—

'As a matter of fact, Prince Gortschakoff had not been able to make
Germany as dependent upon Russia as he had hoped to do; he had
not, at the Congress, obtained the support from Prince Bismarck to
which he considered himself entitled; he had always cherished a sneak-
ing kindness for France; finally, the contrast between his own mediocre
achievements and the greatness of the statesman who had guided
Germany's policy with such splendid success, angered and annoyed
him.' (Vol. ii. p. 138.)

The chapter in these volumes relating to Bismarck's relations with Austria has excited much attention in that country,
for Dr. Busch asserts in it that a defensive treaty has been
drawn between the German Empire and Austria. The present foreign minister, Count Kalnoki, and the last, Count
Andrassy, have both given explanations to the Austrian and
Hungarian delegations, but it cannot be said that they have

thrown much light on what are the specific obligations undertaken by either party to the treaty, but that a treaty of some sort exists there is no doubt. We know that Bismarck's early sympathies were with Austria, and it appears that these sympathies have never wholly died out, but that his aim is still to establish some such sort of union as existed before 1866 between New Germany, only with a Prussian hegemony instead of an Austrian.

Dr. Busch reports that the Chancellor's way of looking at the situation was as follows:—

' " Matters standing thus "—in this strain will have run the German Chancellor's thoughts in the presence of these phenomena—" we must look out for an ally ; for, although France appears quite peacefully disposed just at present, we cannot be sure that she will not attack us should a favourable opportunity present itself for so doing. England is of but small account for a war on terra firma ; it therefore is obvious whose alliance we must seek. Every intelligent and unprejudiced person of the forty-two millions inhabiting the German Empire would wish that we should be on good terms with both Russia and Austria at the same time. If, however, we are, as now, compelled to choose between our two neighbours, there can be no hesitation about our choice. Not alone national motives point unmistakably to Austria-Hungary, amongst whose populations may be reckoned ten millions of Germans ; for the Magyars are also on our side, and have been so for years past, the Poles of Galicia have not the least desire to be Russianised, nor have the Czechs, if we except a dozen or so of *Intransigeants*, who make a great deal of noise signifying nothing. And even were Austria altogether Slav, we should have to give her the preference. Russia is strong enough to take care of herself, and we cannot be of much use to her as Allies. On the other hand it is essentially Austria's interest to have us for friends. *Per contra*, she can materially aid us in carrying out a policy the main object of which is the maintenance of universal peace. If Austria-Hungary and Germany unite with this object in view, and stand back to back with their two millions of soldiers, like a gigantic square in the centre of the Continent, before the eyes of those who desire to break the peace, the more exalted Nihilistic politicians in Muscovy will scarcely venture to attempt the fulfilment of their projects." ' (Vol. i. pp. 400, 401.)

The secret treaty with Austria was at last concluded at Gastein in September 1879. In a preliminary discussion with Count Andrassy, who had succeeded Count Beust in the office of Austrian Foreign Minister, he succeeded in converting that statesman to his views, after which he proceeded to Vienna, where he was received by the emperor with especial honour. Francis Joseph, at a diplomatic dinner given in the Chancellor's honour at Schönbrunn, advanced to the

threshold of the drawing-room to receive his guest. The
two following days were passed by Andrassy and Haymerle,
Andrassy's destined successor, in discussing and settling the
details of the treaty with Bismarck.

> 'Its text,' says Dr. Busch, 'is not yet known to the public, but
> we are aware that it is a defensive alliance between Germany and
> Austro-Hungary, stipulating that in case one of those States shall be
> attacked by two or more Powers, the other contracting party shall come
> to its assistance *vi et armis.*'

Whatever, however, may be the stipulations of this alliance,
we are told they were such that the Chancellor had great
difficulty in getting it accepted by the Emperor William,
since it seemed to indicate a distrust of the personal friendship which the Czar Alexander II. had also shown to his
uncle. Since its formation, however, Alexander II. has
fallen a victim to the dynamite of Nihilistic assassins.
Skobeleff, who was one of the leaders of the anti-German
party in Russia, is also dead. Gortschakoff has disappeared
from the scene; and though Ignatieff, another of the leaders
of the same party, was Minister of the Interior for a time,
he was only a short time in office, and the successor of
Gortschakoff, M. de Giers, by his visits to the Chancellor at
Varzin and at Friedrichsruhe, has shown his wish to be on
terms of good understanding with his powerful neighbour,
and, according to all outward appearances, the Triple Alliance was re-formed again last autumn at Skiernivice.

In the discursive chapter headed ' Diplomatic Indiscre-
tions,' Dr. Busch gives us some of the Chancellor's utterances respecting diplomacy in general, and of some of the
diplomatists in particular with whom he has been brought
in contact. The greater part of these speeches are extremely disparaging. It was not to be expected that the
Chancellor should show much admiration for his colleagues
of the Frankfort Diet, or that he should take too favourable a view of the merits of his adversaries, M. Thiers and
M. Jules Favre. But Prince Gortschakoff, to whose support during a long political career he owes so much, comes
in for a good share of 'the rough side of his tongue,' and
there is hardly a single Prussian statesman or diplomatist
of whom he does not in these pages speak in terms of depreciation. Is the explanation that in his overweening sense of
supremacy he can bear no brother near the throne? Dr.
Busch, in his condemnation of what he is pleased to style
Pathotechnics, or the introduction of sentimentalism into
diplomacy, cites with admiration the Chancellor's account

of Jules Favre—it is difficult, however, to believe the Chancellor was right in his conjecture that Jules Favre really 'made up' and painted his cheeks for the occasion.

'After the conferences at Haute-Maison and Ferrières the Chancellor, speaking of Favre, said: " It is quite true that he looked as if he had " been crying, and I made some endeavour to console him.   But, after " inspecting him carefully, I came to the conclusion that he had not " squeezed out a single tear.   Probably he hoped to work upon me " and move me by play-acting, as the Paris lawyers are wont to do with " their audiences.   I am firmly convinced that he was painted as well " —white on his cheeks and green round his eyes and nostrils—cer- " tainly he was the second time, here in Rothschild's château, upon " which occasion he had ' made up' much more grey and infirm, to " play the part of one deeply afflicted and utterly broken down.   His " object was to excite my compassion, and thereby induce me to mode- " rate my demands and make concessions.   But he ought to have " known that feelings have nothing to do with politics." '   (Vol. i. p. 263.)

His account of M. Thiers is more favourable, though still disparaging enough.

'Thiers suited the Chancellor better than Favre, although he once remarked of the former, " There is scarely a trace of the diplomatist " about him; he is far too sentimental for that trade.   He is not fit " to be a negotiator—scarcely even to be a horse-couper.   He allows " himself to be ' bluffed ' too easily ; he betrays his feelings and lets " himself be pumped." (Vol. i. p. 264.)

One can hardly wonder at his disdain for the Duc de Gramont and Emile Ollivier.

'In certain Bismarckian utterances pronounced shortly before and during the war, Gramont repeatedly figured as a combination of wrongheadedness and dullness.   The Chancellor also spoke of Ollivier with undisguised scorn.   Of these persons he once remarked, " Gramont " and Ollivier are pretty fellows ! Were I in their place, having brought " about such a catastrophe, I would at least enlist in some regiment, " or even become a franc-tireur, if I had to be hanged for it.   That " great strapping fellow, Gramont, would do well enough for a soldier." ' (Vol. i. p. 266.)

The English diplomatists come in for the largest share of the Chancellor's approving judgements.

'Upon the same occasion he spoke in praise of Russell's compatriot, Lord Napier, formerly British Envoy in Berlin, as a man with whom it was very easy to get on; also of Buchanan, whom he described " as dry but trustworthy." " And now we have got Loftus," he continued.   " The position of an English Minister in Berlin is one " of special responsibility and difficulty, on account of the family

" connexions existing between the English and Prussian Courts. It
" exacts the greatest possible tact and attention from its occupant."
He then became silent; but his silence spoke. Subsequently, however (no Englishman being present), he expressed, and in very forcible
terms, his opinion that Loftus in no way fulfilled the above-mentioned
requirements.' (Vol. i. pp. 226, 267.)

Lord Augustus Loftus was succeeded by Lord Odo Russell,
who filled for fourteen years with consummate ability this
important post. No Minister of Great Britain ever displayed
greater tact in dealing with an overbearing Power, and one
of the results of his much-lamented and premature death
has been the outbreak of direct personal aversion and hostility between the chiefs of the British and German Cabinets,
to which Prince Bismarck has mainly contributed by his
discourteous and undignified language.

We may ascribe the Chancellor's unfavourable opinion of
Prince Gortschakoff to the incident of the year 1875, when it
was publicly reported that the Prussian Government had only
been again prevented by the efforts of the Czar of Russia
and Prince Gortschakoff from declaring war against France,
and when the Russian Chancellor took occasion to address a
circular despatch to his envoys abroad, beginning ' Main-
' tenant la paix est assurée.' Bismarck denies that there
was any truth in the statement that Prussia was then meditating another war, and declares that the whole alarm was
got up between Gortschakoff and Gontaut, the French ambassador at St. Petersburg, in order that the former might
be gratified with the praises of French newspapers and be
styled the saviour of France, and speaks of the Russian
Chancellor with what little verisimilitude his own relations
with him for thirty years testify, as being governed in his
policy by a feeling of favouritism for France.

' Upon Gortschakoff the Chancellor pronounced judgement to me as
follows, in March, 1879 :—" Without the least reason, many people
" take him for a particularly clever and skilful diplomatist. He never
" has any really great object in view, and therefore cannot point to
" any remarkable success. His policy is not that of Czar Alexander,
" nor is it a Russian policy, but one dictated and guided in the first
" place by considerations personal to himself, and in the second by his
" predilection for France, which his master does not share. His chief
" characteristic is a highly developed egotism; his chief aim the grati-
" fication of his yearning to be esteemed a politician of the first class,
" which is just what he is not. Hence his chronic disposition to invent
" scenes in which he can play a part likely to elicit applause from
" public opinion. The Russian Chancellor has only exhibited any
" personal activity during the past four years ; and no expert will

" venture to say that his operations have revealed either adroitness or
" perspicuity." ' (Vol. i. p. 267.)

As to Prussian ' Excellencies,' Dr. Busch says he can only
quote such of his remarks as apply to persons no longer
living.   And these remarks deal chiefly with Von der Goltz,
the Prussian ambassador at Paris, who so successfully
succeeded in hoodwinking the French Emperor and his
minister both before and after the Prusso-Austrian war ;
Count Harry von Arnim and Von Savigny—all of whom
he suspected of wishing to replace him in the direction of
Prussian affairs—and Count Bernstorff.   M. de Savigny was
of French origin, and descended—like Brassier de Saint
Simon and so many others who have distinguished themselves in the Prussian service—from a French family which
had emigrated to Prussia after the revocation of the Edict
of Nantes.   M. de Savigny was a Catholic.   He was the
brother-in-law of Count Harry von Arnim.   He was a man
of considerable ability, and had considerable credit at court.
He worked harmoniously with Bismarck, and was on cordial
terms with him until Bismarck suspected he was aiming at
the presidency during a ministerial crisis.   The Chancellor
contrived to exasperate Savigny to such a degree that the
latter gave in his resignation, and the king sacrificed him to
Bismarck, as he afterwards (and with more reason) sacrificed
Von Arnim.   Bismarck was reinstated more firmly than
ever in the presidency, and on being congratulated he replied, ' You can offer me twofold congratulations, for not
' only do I remain Chancellor, but I have besides the good
' luck to have got rid of Savigny.'

As the Chancellor disdains the graces of eloquence, it is
only natural that he should be no real orator ; nevertheless,
his speeches possess a rude knotted strength, and the frequent
occurrence of tortuous, rugged, and involved sentences has
caused him to be compared as a speaker to Cromwell.   He
hits frequently on striking images and on condensed forms
of expression, some of which have startled Europe.   He is
not above using French words and phrases and proverbs
when they suit his turn.   His use of French words, indeed,
is sometimes made in a way which we should not consider
good taste in England, as when he says, ' Such compliments
' obtain a wide retentissement.'   However, he has struggled
hard to prevent the importation of French Liberal doctrines
into Germany, and said on one occasion, ' I fail to perceive in
' France's present condition any temptation to us to clothe
' our healthy body in the Nessus mantle of French theories

' of government.' On one occasion he said, 'A war made by
' Prussia to establish the Union would remind me of the
' Englishman who fought and overcame a sentry in order to
' hang himself in the sentry-box.' He exclaimed to the Opposition in the Diet, 'You are like Archimedes with his circle,
' who did not notice that the city had been captured.' After
Sadowa he exclaimed, ' The game is not won yet; we have
' only doubled the stakes.' Another of his expressions is,
' We cannot hasten the ripening of fruit by holding a lamp
' under it.' He observed of an aggressive motion in the
Chamber, ' When I first read Deputy Lasker's motion, it
' struck me that its author must have felt something like
' Hotspur, as described by Shakespeare, when complaining of
' the tiresomeness of his life just after he had slaughtered
' half a dozen Scots. Nothing was going on; a little variety
' had to be imported into the situation.' During the debate of October 1878 upon the Repression Bill, he said,
' Speaking from an agricultural point of view, progression
' is capital manure wherewith to prepare the soil for a crop
' of Socialism.'

The following comparison is very humorous. He was replying to the long-winded speech of the leader of the Pro-
gressists, which filled twenty columns of the Parliamentary
Reports:—

' I have often had the pleasure of listening to specimens of his
eloquence, which have always impressed me as resembling a performance
of the "Maid of Orleans," the interminable triumphal procession in
which at first surprises you. When it goes by for the third time,
however, you exclaim Good God! why, there are the same people in
the same dresses as before marching across the stage again !'

In his letters to his sister and to his wife there are many
passages of quaint description. Holland he describes as
a vast meadow, always flat and always green, upon which
bushes grow, cattle feed, and towns cut out of old picture-
books stand. Of Russia he writes from Moscow to his
wife :—

' Green has every right to be the Russian national colour, as it is.
I slept through forty of the hundred (German) miles hither, but the
remaining sixty were all shades of green. Bushy brakes dotted with
beeches cover the swamps and hills—luxuriant grass, long green
meadows—such is the country for ten, twenty, forty miles at a stretch.
Moscow, viewed from the heights, resembles a pasturage. The zinc of
the roof is green, the cupolas are green, the soldiers are green, and I
have no doubt the eggs now before me were laid by green hens.'

Among his reminiscences of Court life we find the

following amusing account of one of Humboldt's famous readings at the Royal Palace :—

'The old gentleman used to be horribly annoyed when he could not have all the talking to himself. I remember that once there was some body at the King's who took up the conversation, and quite naturally— for he could talk in an agreeable manner about things that interested every one present. Humboldt was beside himself. Growling, he filled his plate with a pile of goose-liver pie, fat eels, lobster-tails, and other indigestible substances—a real mountain ! It was quite astounding what the old man could put away. When he could positively eat no more, he could no longer keep quiet, and so made an attempt to get the conversation into his own hands. "Upon the peak of Popo- " catepetl," he began—but it was no use ; the narrator would not be cut short in his story. "Upon the peak of Popocatepetl, seven " thousand yards above " . . he resumed, after coughing and raking up his throat to attract attention ; but again he failed to get his oar in, and the narrator calmly went on. "Upon the peak of Popocatepetl, " seven thousand yards above the level of the Pacific Ocean," . . . he exclaimed in a loud agitated voice, shaken by grief and indignation ; but all to no purpose, the other man talked away as steadily as before, and the company listened to him and to him only. Such a thing had never been heard of ! Humboldt sat down in a fury and plunged into profound meditations upon the ingratitude of courtiers.' (Vol. ii. p. 261.)

The Chancellor appears in his most amiable light in his family relations, his home life, and his love of the country and country scenes. His marriage has already been mentioned as having wrought a great change in his existence. He addresses his wife as 'my heart,' 'my beloved heart,' and when absent on political missions sends her sprigs of geranium from Peterhof, heatherbells from Bordeaux, and edelweiss from Gastein. On the sixteenth anniversary of their marriage he declares to her that 'she brought sunshine 'into his bachelor life.' Writing from Biarritz he says: 'My conscience smites me for seeing so much that is beau- ' tiful without you. If you could be suddenly carried hither ' through the air, I would straightway take you off to St. ' Sebastian.' From the pavilion of Stanislaus Augustus, near Warsaw, he wrote : 'The wind blows recklessly over ' the Vistula, and works such havoc on the chestnut and lime ' trees surrounding me that their yellow leaves hurtle ' against the panes ; but sitting here with double windows, ' tea, and thoughts of you and the children, I can smoke my ' cigar comfortably.' The Princess, we find, is of a quick, lively disposition, with a good share of mother wit, intelli- gence, and good taste ; she is a careful and prudent housewife, and when she accompanied her husband to St. Petersburg the little dinners and evening receptions at the Prussian Legation in the Stenbock Palace were especially appreciated by society in the Russian capital, although the Prussian minister could not vie with his French, English, and Austrian colleagues in splendour and display. We have seen that the lady inherited from her parents a spirit of evangelical piety, which seems to have hardened her especially towards the infidel French nation, as we are told she urged the Chancellor on to effect their extermination.

'Two days after the fall of Sedan the Chancellor read aloud to us an extract from one of her letters praying, in Scriptural language, that the French might be destroyed. "May I ask how the Countess "is?" enquired Prince Albrecht (Oct. 29, 1870) whilst dining with the Chancellor at Versailles. "Oh," replied the latter, "she is all "right, now that her son is getting better; but she is still suffering "from her grim hatred of the Gauls, whom she would like to see shot "and bayoneted, every man jack of them, even the tiny children, *who* "*really cannot help having been born of such abominable parents.*" A few days later he imparted to us a remark made by her conceived in a not much milder spirit than the above—"I fear that you "will not find any Bibles in France, and therefore shall send you the "Psalm-book, so that you may read the prophecy against the French : "I say to you the godless shall be exterminated."' (Vol. ii. p. 278.)

The Prince has three children, a daughter and two sons. The daughter, the Countess, was born in 1848, and married to Count Rantzau, who has three children. Of his two sons, Counts Herbert and Wilhelm, the former has taken to diplomacy, and is well known in our capital; the latter studied law and has been to Parliament. Both served in the French war as dragoons, and Count Herbert was wounded at Mars la Tour. From his letters and his habits it is apparent that the Prince's love of the country is no affectation. In many of his letters there are passages of descriptions of natural scenery which could have been written by no one who was not a lover and minute observer of nature; some are quite landscapes in print.

When residing on his estates in Pomerania, or in the heart of the Sachsenwald, not a day passes in which he does not make excursions among the neighbouring beech woods and pine forests. 'What I like best,' he remarked to Dr. Busch, 'is to be in well-greased boots far away from 'civilisation.' Talking at Versailles about his old cowherd Brand, 'one of those old pieces of furniture with which the 'memories of my youth are indissolubly bound up,' he ob-

served, 'whenever I think of him I am reminded of heather
' bloom and buttercups.'

Up to the age of sixty the Prince was famed for dexterity
in all sorts of manly exercises.   In his youth he was a bold
and untiring horseman.   At Königgrätz he was twelve
hours in the saddle, and the day after the fall of Sedan he
rode from six in the morning to midnight; by his own confession, however, he has been thrown some fifty times, and
once fell badly at Varzin and broke three ribs.   He was also
a good swimmer, and a letter written in 1851 shows us the
strange figure of the Prussian Chancellor swimming by moon-
light in the Rhine.   He is, too, an excellent shot with all
kinds of firearms, and was noted for being able to decapitate
duck after duck with a pistol as they swam in the ponds at
Kniephof.   The walls and floors of his house at Varzin
exhibit an accumulation of trophies in the form of antlers
and skins and stuffed creatures and heads of creatures, spoils
brought home from the mountains and forests of various
parts of Europe.

The Chancellor speaks French, English, and Russian with
facility, and reads Italian and Polish.   Goethe and Shakespeare are his favourite authors, he has small fancy for
Schiller, and is addicted to the reading of French and also
English novels.   One could hardly expect to find Bismarck's
name associated with Petrarch and Laura, yet he prepared a
humorous surprise for a leading member of the Progressist
party by presenting him from his pocket-book with a little
bit of olive which he said he brought him as a peace-offering
from Vaucluse.   The Chancellor does not appear to take
much interest in art or the theatre, but he is partial to
music.   Writing to his wife in 1851, he describes his condition as 'sound and hearty, but tinged with melancholy
' home-sickness, yearnings for forest, ocean, desert, you and
' the children all mixed up with sunset and Beethoven.'

The Chancellor's health, which affords so many opportunities for a retreat to Varzin, is, we are told, really not
good, so that he who was formerly an incessant smoker
has now abandoned the habit altogether.   Nervous irritability, periodical sleeplessness, a stomach out of order, a
varicose vein, and neuralgic pains, form a respectable total
of maladies.   He is irritable, gives way at times to volcanic
bursts of temper, for which, says Dr. Busch, he is copiously
supplied by the stupidity and malignity of parliamentary
parties and of Court cliques.   Dr. Busch, however, informs
us these outbursts rapidly subside, and are not succeeded by

sulkiness or rancour. On April 1, 1870, says Dr. Busch, I congratulated him on the recurrence of his birthday, and expressed a hope that I should remain with him for a long time to come. He replied : ' I hope so too. But it is not ' always agreeable to be with me; only people should not ' attach too much importance to my irritability.' Dr. Busch says it is a calumny to speak of him as a cynic or a misanthrope, a satirist or a backbiter. ' He only hates and ' despises what is unmanly in men, and he only jeers at ' them when they make themselves ridiculous. It is not his ' fault that this is frequently the case,' and claims for him some allowance on the ground that he has become peculiarly 'susceptible to mistrust and suspicion,' on account of his experience 'that nowhere under the sun are to be ' found more hypocrites, intriguers, and liars; more vanity, ' falsehood, malignity, double-dealing, and envy, than within ' the sphere of diplomacy, and in the higher circles of Court ' life.'

A grateful king and a grateful country have taken care that the Chancellor should be well provided for. He has been created a Prince, and as German Chancellor receives 2,700*l.* per annum. Besides his ancestral estate of Schönhausen he has two others—Varzin, in Nether Pomerania; and the Sachsenwald estate, near Hamburg. Up to 1867 he only owned the Schönhausen estate, of about 2,800 morgen in extent. With the grant of 60,000*l.* made him by the Prussian Diet he bought Varzin, which with some additions comprises 30,000 morgen; and the Emperor, as Sovereign Duke of Lauenberg, gave him the Sachsenwald domain, which produces about 5,000*l.* a year. His favourite place of residence is Varzin. The Chancellor, we are told, is an adept in farming and forestry, and applies to Nature, we are told, the same rule which he has applied with such success in politics—she must, whether she will or no. He takes pride not only in his success as a statesman, diplomatist, and soldier, but as a farmer, forester, and manufacturer; and besides directing the affairs of Prussia and Europe, manages breweries, distilleries, and sawmills, and has some intention of becoming a paper-manufacturer.

We are prevented by our limits from taking notice at any length of the abundant materials contained in Dr. Busch's volumes respecting the Chancellor's theories of constitutional government, if they can be called so. As a constitutional minister he has got no further than Strafford, and he was prepared, if he failed at Sadowa, and did not die on

the field of battle, to undergo Strafford's fate; for both the
military preparations for the war and the war itself with
Austria were made in defiance of all constitutional principles. It is said that the last resistance of the king to
the declaration of war was overcome by a very forcible use
of the scaffold as an argument. The king, while he was still
hesitating, drew Bismarck to the window and showed him
the statue of Frederic the Great, and said, ' That statue will
' be thrown down, and a scaffold erected in its place.' ' If
' such is the situation, sire, would it not be more worthy of
' you and myself to die on the field of battle, sword in hand ? '
However, considering his monarchical views, it must be
allowed that the Chancellor gives himself more trouble in
arguing with his opponents and in the management of
constitutional assemblies than might be expected. His
enormous prestige and his vast intellectual power have succeeded in maintaining the royal power at its present height
in Germany, and in establishing, for the time at least, the
unconstitutional doctrine that the Prime Minister is not the
minister of a parliamentary majority but of the King, and
can set at defiance the usual results of parliamentary defeat.
But it remains to be seen how the external and internal relations of Prussia will hold good in the hands of his successor,
who will find the Chancellor has left him a legacy the administration of which will present difficulties sufficient to
tax the highest powers and virtues of statesmanship.

We cannot conclude this article, which has been written
in no unfriendly spirit to Prince Bismarck, without expressing our regret at the language which he thought proper to
address to the ministers of this country in a recent speech
delivered in the Reichstag, although he has since endeavoured
to qualify the effect of it by the mission of his son to London
and by the friendly assurances of the Emperor, his sovereign.
But if his object had been to inflame the German nation
with jealousy and resentment towards England, he could
scarcely have employed more offensive and insulting expressions. Prince Bismarck's outbursts of temper remind us
of the puerile splenetic explosions of the First Consul.
Like Napoleon, although he has no disinclination to the
use of force, he is at least equally disposed to the use of
cunning. His misunderstanding with England is entirely
due to the fact that he has overreached himself. Instead
of simply and frankly stating what he wanted, he resorted
to equivocations, of which the Prussian agents in London
were made the reluctant instruments. He seems to have

imagined that the colonial extension of the German Empire could only be effected by trickery. The consequence is that at Angra Pequena, at the Cameroons, and in New Guinea, his infant settlements are founded on false premises, for we presume that even Prince Bismarck does not suppose that the Pomeranians or the Rhinelanders will migrate to labour in the tropics. The first use made by the Germans in their newly acquired territories has been to fire upon natives, suspected of British sympathies, and to expel foreigners. Their policy is arbitrary and exclusive. We take the liberty to remind Prince Bismarck that in every British colony under heaven there are swarms of German traders, conducting their affairs and gaining wealth with a degree of freedom they would not enjoy in their own country; and that the largest of all the German colonies is that settled in the heart of London, where the Germans number about 40,000. Does Prince Bismarck imagine that the acquisition of questionable rights on the coast of Africa or New Guinea is at all comparable to the enormous advantages the Germans enjoy under British laws and British colonial rule? We have no inclination to pursue this controversy. It is pitiable to see a man of such commanding gifts, who has even in other fields achieved greatness, descend from his real eminence to petty tricks, to spiteful language, and to narrow prejudices. In our eyes the common interests of Germany and England rest on broader principles; and in the long run they will not be sacrificed to the ill-humour or caprice of a masterful minister. Happily the sentiments of the Court of Berlin, and, we believe, of the best part of the German nation, are of a more sincere and friendly character, and Prince Bismarck himself has been compelled to defer to them. The mission of Count Herbert Bismarck to London was received as an *amende honorable* for the intemperate language of his father, and responded to with courtesy and good humour. There may have been misunderstandings on both sides, but we trust they are now removed, and that no fresh differences will arise to disturb the harmony of two great nations. The opportune visit of the Prince of Wales and his son to Berlin, to congratulate the venerable Emperor of Germany on his eighty-eighth birthday, is a striking and auspicious proof that the intimate alliance of the two Courts has been untouched by the temporary friction of their political servants.

ART. III.—*The Maritime Alps and their Seaboard.* By the Author of ' Vèra,' ' Blue Roses,' &c. London: 1885.

THIS pleasantly written and tastefully illustrated volume addresses itself not to those English sojourners in the Riviera who neither know nor care to know anything of the country in which they seek only rest, health, or pleasure; nor, again, to those who have already made it a subject of historical and archæological research. Between these comes a class, and perhaps the largest class, of English travellers in these favoured regions, who lack time or inclination for extended and careful study, but who would gladly learn something of its past fortunes, of its present condition, and its prospects. For all such the author of ' Vèra ' will be an agreeable and instructive guide, from whose pages they may derive a large amount of valuable and interesting information. She has made the region of the Maritime Alps practically her home for many years; and her accounts of the habits of the people, and their modes of life, are the results of long personal acquaintance with them. Nor has she fixed her attention disproportionately on one part of the country at the expense of others. The reader may accompany her along the whole length of seaboard from the dismantled ports of Fréjus to Mentone and Oneglia, and inland to many a town of historic name, now seldom visited or generally passed by as scarcely worthy of notice. From these chapters he will gather no inconsiderable knowledge of great men and important incidents in the strangely shifting and complicated history of Southern Europe; nor will his enjoyment of them be greatly disturbed if here and there he should notice some defects or mark some palpable mistakes.

The fishermen on the coast stretching from Marseilles eastward are said to have a large number of words in their vocabulary derived from the Greek. This seems to be scarcely proved by the fact that the Provençal mariner calls his nets *bregin,* or the thunder *troun.* La Gaude, we are told, may have obtained its name from a Celtic term, signifying a wood; but the word may also be the result of the process which changed ward into guard, and wise into guise. It is perplexing to hear St. Bernard spoken of as a nephew of Charlemagne. But still more confusing is the habit which may be not unfairly defined as a bondage to the modern map; and, in a country over which the waves of conquest and of other changes have passed in rapid succession, this bondage is the more unfortunate.   It is an anachronism to speak of the ' exploits of the Tyrian Hercules *at Villefranche*; ' and this incongruous practice of mentioning old places by their most modern names is carried out through the long chronological tables interspersed through the volume.   Thus in the second Punic war ' Scipio lands at Villefranche,' and the ' Castrum of St. Vallier ' is built in the second century before the Christian era.   The towns known as Villa Nova become each Villeneuve ; Ventium is Vence in or soon after the days of Julius Cæsar.   Nor is it easy to read without some wonderment the statement that country life was a thing unknown to the Romans.   Horace was not indulging a peculiar or eccentric taste when he spoke of the little farm which never failed to restore him to happiness ; and no poet ever sang of rural life with more enthusiasm and knowledge than the author of the Georgics.

It is enough to say that these chapters are not put forth as the work of an exact philologist or of a critical historian. But the author has dealt conscientiously with her subject ; and this subject is both interesting and important.   Almost the whole of the territory of which she speaks belongs to the French Republic ; and serious questions affecting the welfare of the French nation come up for discussion along the seaboard of the Maritime Alps not less than along the banks of the Seine or the Loire.   For those who care to understand these questions, almost every page of this volume will have its attractions ; and among the most instructive are those which treat of the people, their trades and occupations, their farms, their corn, wines, and oil.

Nature, it might well be thought, has done much for the beautiful region comprised within the great curve which stretches from Genoa to Marseilles.   The impression on the traveller's mind might be that life must be easy in a land where winter is practically unknown, where the heats are tempered by constant currents of air in motion, and where the screen of the Esterel hills serves to shut off the searching Mistral wind which falls like a very scourge on other portions of Provence.   But, although it is a land of many streams and of heavy dews, it is not without periods of drought which becomes sometimes excessive, and of floods which are not unfrequently disastrous.   Against these dangers the agriculture of the country must be guarded, if it is to bring any profit ; and the necessity of these precautions affects everywhere the general character of the landscape. The hedges of England become walls in Provence, and these walls rise one above the other in tiers, which stretch from the base to the summit of a hill or mountain. The amount of material expended on these walls is indeed astonishing, and the care needed to keep them in repair is constant and costly. But what was the cost of their erection in the first instance? A hundred years ago Mirabeau said that, if this soil were valued at the price of the best land in France, its whole rental would not meet the outlay on the walls which hold it up. Time, as the author rightly remarks, is the true explanation of the difficulty.

'These terraces are simply an instance of the truth of the Scottish saying that "many a pickle maks a mickle." Had they all been constructed in the same half-century the rental of the province would indeed have been insufficient to pay for them; but the peasants working at them all day, and often part of the night, through many centuries, have covered Provence with a network of stones. In this way they have preserved to her a soil which is ever ready to run off. Many of the little plots, which really cannot be called fields, rise at an angle of 70°, or even of 75°, and, but for these walls, they might cease to exist after a thunderstorm. As it is, they allow the culture of vines, oats, and plums to creep up the sides of the hills.'

Diminutive though many of these Provençal patches of ground within walls may be, plots of much smaller size may be seen in Capri, where the scantier supply of soil has compelled the people to guard with these stone inclosures bits of land often barely more than two or three feet in length and breadth. The keeping up of these stone dykes, as we should call them in Scotland, is, necessarily, the first care of the farmer or husbandman; but the work of irrigation is only a little less important. A deluge of rain, if it finds any point unguarded, may sweep away his field altogether; but without water his crops may in dry months wholly fail. The indispensable need of watering them entails a constant outlay, for which it seems that the tenant generally receives no compensation; but even under these conditions much is done, and the disadvantages of the tenant do not affect the peasant proprietor. The water is diverted from the streams, as they descend the hillsides, into reservoirs, and distributed along countless little stone channels, and thus the supply can be brought to bear on any given spot. Vegetables are raised in narrow pan-shaped beds, from which the water may be allowed to pass 'by simply pushing 'down the edge of the pan at the side he chooses.'

But the general conditions under which the tenant or the small owner works are, according to the author's descriptions, less favourable than they used to be. The tillage of a country in which the whole annual rainfall is limited to about fifty days out of the three hundred and sixty-five must under any circumstances call for special care; and the reckless destruction of wood and forest has had its usual effect of shortening the rainy and lengthening the dry season. During the latter the only fresh source of moisture is the dew, which throughout this region falls happily in great abundance. But the causes which are supposed to interfere with the prosperity of British farmers seem to press not less hardly on those of Southern France. Mineral oils are leaving the produce of the olives far behind in the race of competition, and the olive-grower finds little consolation in the fact that his trees are still, in their strange loveliness, and their peculiar colouring, the admiration and the despair of painters. Like the olive, the vine has its special enemies in the insect world, while it lies exposed to other enemies in the world of air and cloud. It has to face the perils of the frost which often comes with the red moon, the successor of the Paschal moon; and this frost may at once destroy all the prospect of the vintage. But if this ill fortune be avoided, there are other dangers later on.

'Some afternoon a storm comes beating up against the wind and breaks overhead with flashes and crashes, and such a rattle of hail as makes the heart of the landlord die within him. When the storm has rolled away he goes out to judge of its work. Alas! alas! the path from his vineyard is still running like a river, and a bowing-out wall having fallen into the roadway, he need go no farther to get a sight of the vines. They are all tangled, and ravelled, and drenched, and hashed, and look as if a park of artillery had been driven over them. A week hence they will look even worse, for the scorching and reddening of the leaves will then show how the sudden chill and the evaporation after the touch of the ice have checked the sap and circulation of the plant. In fact, the wine-growers of France have many troubles, and between cold and bad seasons, hailstorms, and phylloxera, their property has of late undergone a deterioration which has reduced many affluent families to the condition of Irish landlords.'

Much has been said and written for many years past on the correctives to the last-named pest furnished by the introduction of American vines or of the ingrafting of American on French vine stocks. We have been told of estates and of whole districts where this method has been adopted, with unfailing success, for ten, fifteen, or twenty years; and the expenditure of that moderate amount of money would insure the extinction of a plague which has reduced hundreds and thousands to want or to poverty. It seems strange, therefore, that a remedy so simple should not have been applied far more largely ; but it is possible that the efficacy of the remedy may have been somewhat exaggerated. The author of the volume before us states with greater caution that the two American vines called in Provence the Riparia and the Jacquet are generally proof against the teeth of the phylloxera ; and by those who examine the roots the reason for this immunity from disease will be easily understood. They will see that from an insect which attacks it at the angle in the fork of the root the French vine has, practically, no chance of escape. The cancer must soon eat into the vital part ; and the poison must be propagated with greater virulence from one plant to another. That the method of ingrafting the American vine would be highly beneficial, wherever it can be adopted, there can be no doubt. The reason why it is not more largely adopted may be found probably in utter want of capital, caused by the ravages and disasters of the phylloxera through a long series of years ; and in the exhaustion of the scanty resources of peasant proprietors.

The decay of the vine-growing and wine-producing industry may be reasonably regretted by all, except by the few who discern in the vine a source of some of the greatest miseries which oppress mankind. In any case the wrath which they feel against the vine should be less severe than their hatred of barley or rice ; and, of all juices which contain alcohol, few can be more harmless than the white and red wines yielded by the vineyards of Provence. Of these wines the latter, we might suppose would, at least in the sunny and dry air of the country, be the more palateable, and therefore the more costly. Whether the white wines are preferable to the red in the matter of taste is a point which we do not presume to decide ; that the white wines are more expensive than the red is one as to which there is no doubt. The author explains the reason in a few lines :—

'The process of making a white wine is always a tedious one, requiring greater care than the preparation of a red wine, and there is the fear that a second fermentation setting in inopportunely may turn the whole cask sour. It requires to be racked and cleared very often, and the waste entailed during the repetition of this process makes the wine dearer. White wine will seldom fetch less than from eighteen to twenty pence a litre, while a very good red wine can be drunk, and is drunk in my house, at sevenpence the litre.'

But in Provence, as in England, there seems to be a strongly rooted conviction that the welfare of a country depends mainly on its grain produce. There is, therefore, a latent anxiety to raise as much corn as possible; but the price at which it can be raised, and the price at which it must be sold, are two entirely distinct questions, and the competition of foreign corn has introduced an element of terrible uncertainty into the answers.

'Wheat,' says our author, 'which it costs forty francs to produce here can be bought on the quay of Marseilles at thirty-five francs, and that after the freight from America, and the duty, and the *octroi de la ville* have all three been paid. This fact is the death-knell of such Provençal farmers whose fields lie in a zone higher than that which can grow oranges, lemons, or flowers for the perfume trade. The taxes are already a fifth of their rental, and the land is no doubt mortgaged for another fifth, so that, considering the rising price of labour, the prospects of the agricultural class may be said to be as gloomy here as they are in Great Britain.' (P. 69.)

There are, however, two classes of persons interested in Provençal agriculture, and thus far we have taken account only of the owner. But the greater part of Provençal soil is not cultivated by the owners, and with it the owners would much rather have nothing to do. These are men of business who have speculated on the necessities of previous owners, and have calculated their own probable profits on the Metayer system. In few words, it may be said that this system works almost wholly to the advantage of the occupant; although, if seasons be fairly good, and the outlay on farm buildings, implements, and repairs be not exceptionally large, the purchaser of an estate may get a not altogether contemptible return for his outlay of capital. Of the occupants or Metayers, not a few are previous owners of property which, while it remained in their own hands, they had worked at a dead loss, but which they now hope to work at a profit. Nor is this hope commonly disappointed. The system, in our author's words, is one 'of the most 'minute and complicated arrangements, all of which are 'palpably favourable to the Metayer.' It is true that on the produce of the olives the Metayer receives only one-third, but he has not to pay for the pruning; and on the cereals he has one-half. All dues are paid by the landlord, and on him fall all costs of renewal, even to the harness and the shoeing of the mule; and if the agreement be what is termed a *chaptel*, or cattle lease, the tenant on its expiration is entitled to one-half the additional value if he can show that in his hands the value of the farm has been, in whatever measure, increased. In spite of these benefits to the man who is occupant without the responsibilities of ownership, there are not wanting in Provence, as elsewhere, preachers who, like Mr. George, insist that the land ought to belong to the man who works it. Our author well says that—

> ' Considering that all the advances and all the taxes are paid by the landlord, the injustice of this proposition is monstrous, and no one ought to be more convinced of its injustice than the Paul, who now lives comfortably as a Metayer on the very spot where his father was ruined as a proprietor. Many good judges are of opinion that Metayage is an obstacle to agricultural progress, and the whole system has been ridiculed by others who forget that here, too, we have a means for the preservation of social order which is worth preserving. When the Paul of whom we have been speaking is a partner with his land-lord, their community of interests is better than either a fixed antagonism under the ordinary system of rents, or than the slow ruin of the fields in the hands of a small and poverty-stricken owner.' (P. 78.)

No hard and fast line, however, can be drawn between those owners who are likely to fail or have failed, and those who are fairly on the way to success. Our author speaks of many of the cultivators round Grasse as being very wealthy, and, from being landowners themselves, having 'none of that ' ill-will towards the upper classes which makes the danger ' to society in countries where the ownership of the soil ' happens to be concentrated in a small number of families.' They have their grievances; and the chief of these are the valuations on which the taxes are levied, and the fees paid on all changes of ownership, whether by inheritance or by purchase, the aggregate of these fees in the whole of France amounting annually to about eight millions sterling.

The mention of Grasse introduces us to another field of industry, to other sources of wealth, and to other topics of interest, which lie beyond the sphere of the laws of mere supply and demand. In spite of narrow and dirty streets, close alleys, and crowded houses, Grasse has many attractions for the visitor who is not bound to spend his time in its gloomier quarters. The situation of the town is picturesque, and the view from the public garden looking over the plain which stretches away to Napoule and Théoule is extensive. In bright sunshine it is in truth magnificent; but it puts on a special beauty after a spell of rain, when the lofty houses rise in clear-cut outlines against the mists as they curl away up the mountain-sides. Grasse is a city which has its wealth of historical recollections. It is also one to which a flower of extreme beauty has brought present prosperity, and seems to insure to it a not less prosperous future. Grasse has grown rich on its orange-blossoms, and therefore it is unnecessary to say that its orange-trees are not raised from any desire of eating or selling their fruit. But the business carried on here is not confined to orange-flowers. The town competes successfully with all other places in the world in the production of 'perfumes, soaps, oils, and *bon-* '*bons*' generally. It has seventy distilleries, which consume vast quantities of jasmine, cassia, tuberose, violets, verbena, and jonquils. The process of manufacture is not altogether agreeable. The jonquils, whose odour is pleasant enough when they are first laid at the factory door, are much changed for the worse after being dipped in a caldron of boiling lard. The remaining processes are carried on by many hands, both of women and men. The extent of the trade is great.

'Germany, Russia, and, above all, America, send immense orders, and the attar of roses now made in Grasse (at twenty francs a drop) will soon compete successfully with the export from the Levant. Essential oil of almonds, and the more deadly extract known as prussic acid, are made here, with orange-water enough to float a frigate. Orange-blossoms constitute the riches of Cannes, Cannet, Grasse, Vallauris, Mougins, Biot, Le Gros, Vence, and St. Paul du Var.'

For the rambler all these places are almost equally attractive. The whole region may fairly be termed enchanting, in all seasons excepting the hottest months of summer. From Grasse alone a multitude of excursions may be made; and it may safely be said that the greatest feast of beauty will fall to the lot of the pedestrian.

'If you choose to go in a southerly direction, you can drive to Mouans, with its modernised castle; or to Sartoux, with its Roman ruins, or to Pégomas, with its anemones; or to Pennafort on the Loup. You can also go eastwards—to Tourrêtes, with its mills; to the gorges of the Loup, to Gourdon on its crag, or to Le Bar, the cradle of the Counts of Grasse. All these expeditions among upturned ledges of limestone, wooded dells, and yawning gorges are enchanting. No winds blow, and the soft air breathes through the pines, while the sunshine glorifies the ruins and the little tortuous streets. What is more, these excursions are fitted for persons of moderate strength and moderate means; but enterprising tourists might by passing westwards do greater deeds than these. They might explore Cabris and the grottoes of St. Césaire, or the sources of the Siagne and the native camps of St. Vallier. There are also the ruins of Calian and of Montaroux, the oak forest of Beauregard, and the bridge and mill of Mons in the gorge of the Siagnole.'

Of all excursions in the neighbourhood of Cannes, one of the easiest and pleasantest is to the two little islands which form in some sort a breakwater for the harbour of that town, and which are interesting to modern visitors in more ways than one. The mere idler may feel his curiosity roused by the sight of the prison in the nearer island, with which are associated the mystery of the Man in the Iron Mask and, more recently, the escape, or, if it be so, the dismissal, of Marshal Bazaine. Neither of these personages belongs to the ranks of great men. The career of the latter must be taken along with the history of the fall of the second French Empire; the story of the former has become more wearisome than attractive from the multitude of guesses which have gathered round it, and from the bulk of the literature in which these guesses have been examined at length, and adopted or rejected. In the chapter devoted to this subject the author upholds the hypothesis of M. Jung against that of M. Topin, who identified the prisoner with Ercole Mathioli, an agent of the Duke of Mantua. It is an easier task to pick holes in the evidence brought together by M. Jung than to substitute for it a theory which shall be in all respects more satisfactory. But we recorded our own opinion on these much controverted subjects some years ago, and we may refer our readers to the 'Edinburgh Review,' vol. cxxxviii. p. 301, where they will find an exhaustive discussion of the question: bearing in mind, however, Lord Beaconsfield's excellent advice to a young man entering society, ' Never ask who wrote Junius, or who was the Man in the ' Iron Mask.'

The real interest of these islands lies in their religious history, and this is a subject which can never be dismissed carelessly or with indifference. The monastic system here established is connected directly with the greatest of the enterprises for the conversion of Northern Europe to Christianity. It contributed powerfully to the growth of religion and intellectual thought in a hard and barbarous age, and its credit lies chiefly in the fact that its influence was exercised in the direction of moderation which may be said not altogether to lack the spirit of true tolerance. But how far this credit belongs to the young Roman Honoratus we can scarcely venture to determine. Nor can we say what may have been precisely the motives which led to the choice of his abode. Our author is, perhaps, influenced by impressions now received on the island when she speaks of Honoratus as feeling the spell of this ' enchanting and enchanted

' spot.' The drawbacks of the island at the beginning of the fifth century are, indeed, duly mentioned; but the language of Hilary's Life of Honoratus, in the Bollandist ' Acts of the ' Saints,' in no way justifies the idea that these drawbacks were compensated by the brightness of sky and sea, or the fertility of the soil. The place was a mere tangled wilderness; and we have the usual tradition of the changes wrought by the new community of rigid anchorites which he gathered round him. The water for which he had sought in vain sprang up at his bidding in a perennial fountain; the venomous snakes disappeared; the desert became a paradise; and in the glowing, if not exaggerated, imagery of M. de Montalembert, Honoratus opened the arms of his love to embrace all who might come to him from every land, and who should here learn to rival or to surpass the austerities of the monks or hermits of the Thebaïd. Our author holds, on the other hand, that severity of discipline was for Honoratus quite a secondary consideration:—

' The two truths grasped most strongly by him were the Fatherhood of God and the brotherhood of men, and his rule was intended to form men in a rude age. He sought to teach them that faith, love, light, order, diligence, and peace are at once the true freedom of the human will and the best consecration of the human spirit.' (P. 149.)

The picture is certainly beautiful, although it may not be altogether clear; nor do we doubt that it is, on the whole, more truthful than the highly-wrought panegyric which, with fatal facility, M. de Montalembert has extracted from the rhetoric of Hilary. That the influence of Western monachism has been on the whole for good may be readily granted; but florid declarations of universal and unfailing love must be taken with large abatements when they come from the lips or the hands of men whose acts seem often to be of a very different complexion. Of Hilary, as the successor of Honoratus in the archiepiscopal see of Arles, we are told only that his administration of the Church was troubled by ' those doctrinal subtleties and definitions ' which it already owed to the Alexandrian schoolmen,' and by the further questions which related to grace and free will. It would have been well, perhaps, had this been all. As to the account given by M. de Montalembert, it is one of those instances of partial indication of the truth which amounts virtually to its suppression. Of the seemingly terrible struggle in which Hilary had become involved, the great historian of the Western monks tells us nothing more than that ' he was for a moment in conflict with Pope St. Leo

' the Great, who deprived him of his metropolitan title by
' way of punishment for certain anti-canonical usurpations.'
This is a very small portion of one side of the story. The
reader will find both sides given at some length by Dean
Milman in his ' History of Latin Christianity.' * It is enough
to say that the two versions exclude each other; but both
assuredly point to a struggle of the greatest moment for the
papacy and for Christendom; and they leave us with the
painful impression that we are dealing with men belonging
to a time the history of which has been deliberately distorted,
misrepresented, and falsified to such a degree that we can
but grope our way to facts like wanderers in dense mist.

The foundation of Honoratus was designed to be one of
those double monasteries in which men and women lived
under vows and rule in adjoining houses. Here the monastery for the women was placed on the neighbouring island,
which bears the name of Margaret, the first abbess, the
sister of Honoratus. The story of this saint, narrated in
the chapter on ' St. Honorat,' runs parallel to that of Scholastica, the sister of the Nursian Benedict. The closeness of
the parallel, and the recurrence of similar tales elsewhere,
suggest inferences affecting more or less the historical value
of such narratives generally. They point unquestionably
to a widely prevalent form of thought, which lighted on its
heroes and heroines wherever it sought to find them; but
they can furnish us with little assurance of their exactness
in the details of biography.

In the chapter on 'Jeanne, Queen of Naples,' we pass
to an atmosphere extremely different from that which surrounded either Honoratus, or Hilary, or Vincent. It is a
narrative of guilt, or imputed guilt, of treacherous bargains
and compacts, of disasters ending with dire catastrophe; and
with it the author has dealt fairly and impartially. There
is little to admire, and certainly nothing to love, in the
Provençal countess and Neapolitan queen, who did more than
anyone else towards establishing the Popes in their vassalage to the French crown at Avignon; but to this day her
memory is not without a certain charm for the people over
whose forefathers she ruled.

' I asked a man once what had been the merits of her person or of
her reign, because, to the best of my recollection, the wars and civil
wars of those years had wrought most cruel evils for her kingdom.
He replied that he did not know, but that when Jeanne was queen

---

* Book II. ch. iv.

" on avait le temps que l'on voulait." I doubt if seed-time and harvest were different then, but it is quite certain that many of the charters and statutes of this great Countess of Provence remained in force for centuries, and that her influence has been an undying one.'

The Knights of the Temple have left behind them traces of their wealth and their power not less durable; but the account here given of their fall betrays too much readiness to admit the worst charges brought against them. The length of the process before Clement is a matter of no importance. The fact that, of two hundred and thirty-two witnesses examined, not six gave testimony in favour of the accused, is one to which not the least weight can be attached. The same fact meets us almost everywhere in the history of the middle ages. It is the great characteristic of almost every trial for witchcraft; and the charges brought against the Templars appealed to precisely the same malignant superstition which never failed to clamour for the blood of wizards or sorcerers. The horrors which attended the suppression of the Order are in strange contrast with the beauty and peacefulness of the scenes in which the lives of those knights were spent who had the good fortune of finding an abode under the shelter of the Maritime Alps. The author speaks of the grange of the Templars of Vence, now called Roquefort and Castelleraz, as an enchanting spot.

' The Loup, forgetting the rapidity of its earlier course, here creeps over sandy shallows. Above a clump of osiers rises a little hamlet. There are red roofs and a white gable, and pools full of dappled shadows; goats browse among the honeysuckles, and the air is perfumed by a dozen scents; for the buds of the cherry and the chestnut trees, and the resinous firs on the Pennafort hill, like the myrtles and the tufted grasses, all give out their breaths—all assure us that Nature is ever hopeful because she is for ever young.'

Nor is this beautiful region poor in associations with eminent men and stirring events of more modern times. The names of Pierre André de Suffren and of Joseph, Count of Grasse-Briançon, are well known in the naval annals of the last century. If their careers were not so successful as those of the British commanders to whom they were opposed, they won the highest respect of their adversaries at once for their skill as leaders, and for their determined and dauntless bravery. The former of these two seamen took his title from the barony of St. Tropèz. He was a man of whom, in spite of his eccentricities and the roughness of his demeanour, his seamen might well be proud. He was a leader formed in a peculiar mould.

'As brave as Nelson, and as rough as Benbow, and so popular with
his sailors that to this day his quaint Provençal humour is remembered,
and his sayings are repeated. A broadside became in his vocabulary
" a basket of Antibes figs; " and, in arranging an attack, he used to tell
his boarding party " to rub these English well with Aix oil." '

More fortunate than his fellow-admiral De Grasse, Suffren
died full of years and honours in the same year in which the
more troubled life of De Grasse came to an end.   The naval
career of the latter was cut short in the great action off
the coast of Dominica, in which Rodney almost destroyed
the whole of the French fleet.   Grasse had fought until men
had failed him for fighting any longer. ' When Lord
' Cranstoun was sent on board with a complimentary mes-
' sage, he found the admiral of the fleet, a tall, pale man,
' standing between the two other men who were left alive on
' the quarter-deck.'   It was a mournful catastrophe for the
French navy; and Grasse in vain attempted to procure a
reversal of the judgement passed upon it by his countrymen.
Neither his bravery nor his ability was called into question,
but they refused to transfer the blame, whatever it might be,
as he wished to transfer it, wholly to his subordinates.

We may part from the author on a spot which is beyond
doubt one of the most beautiful in the whole Provençal
region.   We cannot do better than to cite her description
of the headland of Antibes, with its bold seaward outline,
its woods of pines and holm-oaks, and a shore which rivals
the enchanting bay of Baiæ.

'All these things are delightful, and have but one drawback, namely,
their exposure to all the winds of heaven.   The scenery is extraordinary
at night, when the moon reigns queen of a hushed or heaving sea, and
when from the woods comes the song of the nightingale, or the plaintive
note of the little cue owl, which is as the very voice of solitude.

' The port of Antibes is always full of pictures.   There is the old
town with its two tall *vigies*, its miniature fort, its chapel, and its
cypresses, with the bastions of Guise, of Rosny, and of the Dauphin,
pushed out into the stony fields.   It is from the Place d'Armes that
the best view of the Alps is to be got, when the sky is unclouded, and
cut only by the glaciers of the Gélas range, of the Pic de Mercantour
and of the Pic de Prats.   The coast stretches away towards Bordi-
ghera, all flushed with light.   The delicate tints of the nearer mountains
are set off by the white background of the snowy peaks and by the dark
blue of the sea.   Every glacier from Lescherène to the Col de Tende
seems to assert its cold beauty; the villages beyond the Var look like
castles, and here in the foreground you pace under the boles of the
olives among the rose hedges, the picturesque wells, and all the happy
luxuriant growth of a Provençal spring.'

ART. IV.—*Copy of Correspondence between the Government of India and the Secretary of State in Council respecting the proposed Changes in the Indian Army System, and Copies of Dissents and of Despatches against the Changes proposed or ordered in the Indian Army System.* Ordered by the House of Commons to be printed November 11, 1884.

IN an article on the 'State of the British Army' in our last number, we urged the imperative necessity of a large increase of Her Majesty's military forces, and we endeavoured to point out some of the means by which the army may be raised to its full strength. Recent events, more eloquent than our words, have brought the Government and the House of Commons to adopt these views and to act upon them, not before it was necessary, and we are happy to say that the result is satisfactory. The addition to the strength of the army, including regulars, reserves, and militia, will not be much below the figure at which we put it. We now turn to another branch of the same subject, to which the attempt of Russia to encroach on the frontier of Afghanistan gives a peculiar interest. Whatever may happen elsewhere, it is indispensable that the British forces in the East Indies should be kept up in full strength and efficiency, and the organisation of those forces on the best footing is an interest of primary importance to the whole Empire. We therefore enter with confidence on the bulky volume now before us, and we shall endeavour to lay the most essential parts of it before our readers.

The enquiry into the system under which the Indian army is organised and administered was first instituted in 1879 by Lord Lytton, then Governor-General, primarily with a view to effect a reduction in army expenditure. The Indian Government was at that time under the influence of the financial panic caused by the depreciation of silver, and the burden imposed on the Indian revenues by the operations in Afghanistan, although the great cost of that war was still unforeseen; but the Commission was also instructed to enquire into the whole question of Indian army organisation, and to propose such amendments and changes in it as might serve to bring the system into harmony with the altered conditions of modern India, and to render it thoroughly efficient for military purposes. To mark his sense of the importance of the enquiry, the Governor-General, with the approval of the Secretary of State for India, selected the

Honourable Sir Ashley Eden, then Lieutenant-Governor of
Bengal, the most important and responsible position in India
next to that of the Governor-General himself, to be President of the Commission, of which Major-General Sir Frederick Roberts and several other distinguished officers were
members.   The Commission, although their sittings were a
good deal interrupted by the outbreak of the second Afghan
war, completed their laborious enquiry and made their report in November 1879.   But the consideration of it was
necessarily deferred until the strain of military operations
in the field was temporarily relaxed in the spring of the
following year, and then, when the Government of India
took the report in hand, Lord Lytton's term of office was
drawing to a close, and there was no time available to give
more than a very perfunctory examination to its proposals.
The result was that, instead of the Government of India
sending the report home, with a despatch embodying the
recommendations of the majority of the Council upon the
various proposals of the Commission, the covering despatch
was worded in quite general terms, and was accompanied
by a number of separate minutes by the Governor-General
and Members of his Council, expressing a variety of opinions on almost all the points under discussion.   The Commander-in-Chief, Sir Frederick Haines, who was *ex officio* a
member of the Council, and is evidently a soldier of the
conservative type, objected *in toto* to the proposals made,
being apparently of opinion that the fortuitous combination
of accident and the growth of years which has brought about
the curiously cumbersome state of things now obtaining in
India constitutes a military system incapable of improvement.   General Sir Edwin Johnson, the Military Member of
Council, also gave only a very qualified assent to the proposals in the report, and objected to several of them.   It
was impossible for the India Office to deal with a matter
placed before it in this inconclusive way, and soon after Lord
Ripon had assumed charge of the Government of India, the
report was referred back by Lord Hartington, then Secretary
of State for India, with a demand for the expression of the
detailed opinion of the Government of India on the different
proposals contained in the report.

Accordingly, the greater part of the correspondence now
published is that which has passed between the Government
of Lord Ripon, which practically had to take the matter up
from the beginning, and the Secretary of State for India in
Council.   The Governor-General's Council had in the mean-

time undergone an entire change. Sir Donald Stewart had now entered it, first as Military Member and afterwards as Commander-in-Chief, bringing with him an experience of forty years' service in the Indian army, ending with the command in Afghanistan of one of the largest armies ever assembled in the field in India. The Military Member of the Council was General Wilson, an officer also of great experience with the Native Army, who had served with great distinction in the Mutiny, and came straight from the India Office to take his seat. Colonel Chesney was the newly appointed Military Secretary to Government. The Civil Members of the Council had also all, we believe, been changed. Thus the body on whom fell the task of dealing with the report of the Commission had no share in instituting the original enquiry, and might claim, as they do in these papers, to approach the subject with unbiassed minds. Under these circumstances, the remarkable unanimity of Lord Ripon and his Council in dealing with this matter lends particular weight to their recommendations. And we think no one can rise from the perusal of this bulky volume without recognising that the reform of the Indian army was one of the largest questions with which Lord Ripon as Governor-General had to deal, and that although the issue of the discussion has been so far indecisive, Lord Ripon, by his acceptance of the most important recommendations of the Commission, his hearty advocacy of the reforms put forward by them, and the thorough and complete manner in which his Government worked out a comprehensive scheme of army reorganisation, has unquestionably gone a long way towards carrying out a reform which must sooner or later be adopted, and for which, although the measure has been deferred for the present, he and his military advisers nevertheless deserve a large share of credit.

The ostensible object of the Commission's enquiry was, as we have said, financial, and the Commission claim in their report that the measures they propose would produce a reduction in army expenditure of a million and a quarter sterling. These figures are however open to question; they are challenged by the Secretary of State, and the Government of India in effect admit that the estimate is an over-sanguine one, while they do not accept to the full extent some of the Commission's proposals on which the largest savings would arise, especially the large reduction proposed in the number of regiments. But the Government of Lord Ripon is quite at one with Sir Ashley Eden's Commission in proposing to make a thorough reform of the present system of military administration, which is of even more importance than a reduction of expenditure, and some account of the changes recommended, and the grounds on which they are based, will we believe be found of public interest.

The first thing that will strike the reader of these papers is the extraordinarily cumbersome nature of the Indian military system. Here is an army which musters only about 200,000 men, of whom 60,000 belong to the British army—the whole making a force hardly equal in strength to the army of a second-rate European power—which nevertheless is organised in three, or, including the considerable Punjab Frontier Force, in four separate armies, each furnished with its own complete staff and departments, and each administered by a different and nominally independent civil Government. We say nominally, for the control of the local Governments over their respective armies is indeed little more than nominal, although it is a fertile cause of trouble, expense, and embarrassment. This curious state of things is an inheritance from the original condition under which our territories in India consisted of only three separate provinces, or presidencies as they were called, each under its own Government, and separated from each other by wide territories of Native States, all independent, and many hostile. At that time communication between each presidency and England was more easy and certain than between two presidencies. Regular land communication between the presidencies, until the day of railways, there was none ; there was no practicable road between Calcutta and Bombay or between Calcutta and Madras, and by far the easiest way of going from the east to the west of India was by sea ; in fact, the three presidencies were more isolated from each other than any two European countries. Moreover, each presidency had its own local establishment of European troops. The whole of the artillery serving in India belonged to the East India Company, and were enlisted in separate regiments for service, except in time of war, solely within the territories of their respective presidency. The capital town of each presidency was also the port at which the European troops belonging to it arrived and departed. So long as this state of things lasted, it was both natural and proper that the Government of each presidency should also have the direct administration of its own army, although by law the Governor-General in Council, who had the direct administration of the Bengal army, was

vested with the general control, in military as in all other
matters, over the minor presidencies. This control, however, had reference mainly to the disposal of the troops of
the three armies for military operations. All matters relating to the recruiting, clothing, equipment, and so forth,
of the European force of each presidency were disposed of
by the local Government in direct communication with the
Court of Directors. This state of things, it need hardly be
said, has entirely passed away. The transfer of the Government of India from the Company to the Crown involved the
abolition of the local European forces, which were absorbed
into the British line and the Royal Artillery and Engineers,
while the political and strategical conditions of the country
have undergone a complete change, partly from the fact
that the different presidential establishments have gradually
spread over the whole of India and into contiguity with each
other, still more perhaps from the improved state of communications throughout the country. Railways and the telegraph have now made it more easy to administer the whole
Indian army from one centre than it was formerly to administer any one of the separate presidential armies from
its own local capital. Further, the Indian army has undergone a very large reduction. The Madras army was formerly composed of fifty-two regiments of infantry and eight
of cavalry; it has now been reduced to thirty-two regiments
of infantry and four of cavalry. The Bengal army formerly
comprised seventy-four regular regiments of infantry, besides
a very large number of local regiments and contingents;
there are now only fifty-four regiments of the line, and the
contingents have all been abolished. The Bombay army
has also been largely reduced. And thus it may be said
that the Indian army is now a much more manageable
body than the Bengal army alone used to be in the days of
the Company, while it is actually a smaller one.

Bombay is now the only port for the arrival and departure
of the British troops in relief. The magnificent troopships
belonging to and paid for by the Indian Government, but
manned by the Royal Navy, ply between that port and
Portsmouth, and the complements for the homeward voyages
of these vessels, which carry each about twelve hundred men
besides officers and women and children, are collected from
all parts of India at the depôt of Deolali, situated on the
edge of the tableland which overhangs the port of Bombay.
But the exigencies of the presidential system involve that

the detachments sent from Bengal and Madras, as soon as they arrive within the limits of the Bombay Presidency, should pass from under the control of their own Government and Commander-in-Chief to that of the Bombay authorities. Similarly, when troops arrive from England, they report themselves to the authorities at Bombay, and belong for the time being to the Bombay establishment, under which they remain until the train carries them beyond the limits of the Bombay Presidency. This absurdity appears to be maintained even when the passage is of only a few hours' duration.

But further, the conditions of military operations in India have of late years undergone an entire change. In former times, when a campaign was undertaken conjointly by the armies of more than one presidency, the contingent furnished from each constituted a separate and self-contained force, and usually operated from an entirely independent base. Thus, to go back to the last century, in the campaigns against Mysore in 1792 and 1799, while the main army advanced from Madras, an independent force marched from Bombay, fought its way across India, and did not come under the orders of the Commander-in-Chief until the junction of the two armies was actually accomplished. So also in the great Mahratta war of 1817-18, the operations of the three armies, although tending towards one combination under the general instructions of the Commander-in-Chief, Lord Hastings, who was also Governor-General, were in fact practically quite independent and distinct; and until the termination of the campaign, these three armies were separated from each other by wide extents of country, through which communication was both infrequent and difficult. While this state of things lasted, the maintenance of three separate establishments was expedient and necessary. Again, in later times, geographical and other considerations have sometimes required that for operations beyond India the armies of only one presidency should be employed at a time. Thus, in the China war of 1842, the Indian portion of the force was furnished from the Madras army, which in those days took much more readily to service beyond the sea than the Bengal sepoy. For the Persian expedition of 1856 the troops were naturally supplied entirely from the Bombay Presidency, although as soon as they embarked they came under the direct orders of the Governor-General in Council. In such cases the maintenance of a system of separate military administrations for each presidency did not produce much inconvenience.

In the Burmese war of 1852 the Bengal and Madras armies each furnished a separate division, complete with its own staff, and supplied independently from its own magazines, and they were as much separate and distinct bodies as were the British and Sardinian armies before Sebastopol, the only bond of union being that they were subject to the orders of the General-in-Chief of the expedition. So also in the Abyssinian expedition, when there was a Bombay division, a Bengal division, and a Madras division. On the other hand, the internal wars undertaken in India of recent years have been carried on almost entirely by the Bengal army alone. This bore the entire brunt of the first Afghan war and of the bloody struggles of 1845-46, which ended in the overthrow of the Sikh Government. In the campaign of 1848-49, which was followed by the annexation of the Punjab, the Bengal army was reinforced by a single division from Bombay. The various punitive expeditions which have been carried on in the North-West frontier, since the occupation of that country, have been undertaken by Bengal troops conjointly with the Punjab frontier force, which is in fact a fourth Indian army, or by the latter alone. The chastisement of the wild tribes on the North-East frontier, against which several expeditions have been undertaken during the last twenty years, has fallen entirely to the Bengal army. With the exception of the foreign expeditions referred to, in which the fighting has seldom been of a severe character, Northern India has for nearly half a century been the only school for Indian warfare, and from this, from their geographical position, the Madras and Bombay armies have been practically shut out. It has become apparent that if the military character of the two southern armies is not to degenerate from want of use, some means must be found for employing these troops, in conjunction with those of Bengal, in any future military operations. This has been the policy aimed at of late years by the Indian Government. In the last Afghan war a small number of Madras troops was sent up into the Khyber Pass and mixed with the brigades of the Bengal army, where, although not actually engaged with the enemy, they did good service on the line of communications. On the march of Sir Donald Stewart from Kandahar to Kabul in 1879, the place of the Bengal troops comprising his division was taken at Kandahar by the Bombay army, and the Indian division which was sent to Egypt in 1882 was composed of troops taken from the three presidencies; and this, it may be assumed, will be the policy for the future—to keep the three armies separate in peace time, but to employ all three as much as possible together on active service. For the last two years a regiment of Madras Pioneers has been employed on road-making in the Bolan Pass and on the railway to Quetta, far away from its own presidency; and the expedition sent last autumn into the Zhob Valley to punish the marauders on our frontier was composed of Bengal and Bombay troops in nearly equal parts, together with this regiment of the Madras Pioneers.

Under this altered state of things the continued maintenance of the separate presidential system has become an absurdity. In fact, as the Government of India put it in one of their despatches, the Indian army takes the field with all the inconvenience and complications incidental to military operations undertaken by three allied armies, each with their own independent staff and separate administration, only with this difference, that whereas when allied armies take the field they usually pay each their own expenses, the whole cost here is borne by the Supreme Government, which alone is financially responsible for the cost of the Indian armies. The financial responsibility of the Madras and Bombay Governments over their armies has long ceased to be more than nominal; the form, indeed, is gone through of preparing three separate military estimates for the Bengal, Madras, and Bombay armies, respectively, and keeping up three separate offices of account for dealing with them. But these offices are furnished from one central, or, as it is called in India, imperial department, which is under the direct orders of the Supreme Government, and the staff of which is moved about from one presidency to another; and what is still more to the point, the Madras and Bombay Governments are not called upon to find the money for their armies; the charges for these are not made against the provincial revenues. In the scheme of financial decentralisation, which was inaugurated by Lord Mayo, and has been considerably extended since, all military expenditure is excluded, and is borne solely by the Government of India. And there is a conclusive reason why this should be so. Originally, the Madras and Bombay armies were employed in garrisoning their respective presidencies, but this has long since ceased to be the case. As one province after another has been annexed to the British Empire, or has

been brought under the political control of the British Government, the garrisons of these new territories have been
furnished by one or other of the three armies. The Bengal
army is stationed for the most part in what is popularly
known as the Bengal Presidency, which, however, is a mere
geographical expression, having no legal or actual existence,
comprising the several Governments of Bengal, the North-
West Provinces, Oudh, the Punjab, and Assam, each of
which is administered by its own civil government. Burmah
and the Central Provinces are occupied by Madras troops,
which also furnish the garrison for the important station of
Secunderabad, in the dominions of the Nizam of Hyderabad,
the head British authority at which place, the Resident,
is under the direct orders of the Governor-General. The
Bombay army, besides garrisoning the Bombay Presidency,
also occupies the different Native States to the north of that
presidency, which are divided, politically and for administrative purposes, into two groups, controlled by the agents
to the Governor-General for Central India and Rajputana
respectively. Bombay troops also furnish the greater part
of the garrison of Biluchistan, which territory is administered by a high official subordinate to the Foreign Department of the Government of India.

This statement will serve to explain how entirely the military condition under which the system of presidential armies
was originally created and developed has passed away, and
how utterly unsuited that system is to the existing state of
things. It is not surprising that the Government of India,
adopting the views of Sir Ashley Eden's Commission on this
head, should desire to put an end to all the anomalies and
complications involved in it. The remedy proposed by the
Commission, and supported by the Government of India,
was practically the only one that could arise out of the
enquiry, and it will assuredly commend itself to every reader
of these papers. They propose that the direct administration of all the Indian armies should be vested in the Government of India, although they insist in the strongest way that,
for political reasons, these armies should still be kept separate and distinct. Indeed, they go in this respect beyond
the existing degree of separation, for they recommend the
virtual division of the existing Bengal army into two separate bodies. In their despatch of February 1881, which deals
with the general question of organisation, the Government
of Lord Ripon points out that this army is, so to speak, the
accidental growth of circumstances arising out of the Mutiny

When the Bengal army mutinied in 1857, the small local army which had been raised and was stationed in the recently-conquered Punjab was employed to put it down; and this Punjabi force, largely augmented by newly-raised levies, took a prominent and distinguished share, in conjunction with the British troops, in subduing the rebellion. When peace was restored, a new Bengal army was on foot, larger than that which had been destroyed, and this had to be reduced and reconstituted. This was effected by retaining a few of the old regiments which had remained faithful, by the permanent embodiment of some new levies of Hindustani troops, and by incorporating with these some of the recently-raised Punjabi regiments, the regiments thus retained being numbered anew. This new Bengal army was reconstituted in 1861, on a very reduced scale, from the two elements thus composing it—Hindustani and Punjabi—in nearly equal parts; and the Government of India points out in very forcible terms the political danger of continuing to mix up these two bodies in the bonds of comradeship. Kept separate, the Hindustani and Punjabi regiments might always be reckoned on to act as a counterpoise the one against the other. But all experience shows that the antagonism of race and caste is gradually sapped by the ties of military unity. It was a cardinal principle, which governed the constitution of the old Indian army, to retain a certain proportion of Mussulmans and Hindus in each regiment; this it was hoped would prevent combinations and conspiracies. The Mutiny showed that this precaution was wholly ineffectual. Originally, perhaps, the religious antagonism of the two classes may have been an effective check against combination, but the friction of a century of comradeship had smoothed this away; the Hindu and Mussulman sepoys made common cause against us. And in the same way, if Punjabi and Hindustani are to be mixed together into one heterogeneous mass, the political weapon which was found so efficacious in 1857, and which Lord Lawrence shortly afterwards solemnly warned the Indian Government not to throw away, will assuredly be found wanting should another crisis of the kind arise. The Government of India accordingly propose that the Bengal army, while undergoing for the present no change of name or renumbering of regiments, should be virtually divided into two parts, composed of Hindustanis and Punjabis respectively, the Punjab Frontier Force forming a portion of the latter and passing from the orders of the Provincial Government to that of the military authorities, while however still retaining its separate organisation. These two bodies would garrison in peace time the countries east and west of the Sutlej; and the Indian Government points out that such a division would far more than counterbalance any political danger, fancied or real, to arise from the transfer of the direct administration of the Madras and Bombay armies from the presidential governments to themselves.

It follows as a necessary consequence that the Commander-in-Chief of India would cease to be, as he is now, in immediate command of the Bengal army; on the other hand, the Madras and Bombay armies would come under his orders. The two portions of the Bengal army would be placed each under the command of a Lieutenant-General, while the status of the Commanders-in-Chief of the Madras and Bombay armies would be assimilated to that of the two Lieutenant-Generals in Bengal. This last, it may be observed by the way, is in itself a desirable reform; it was proposed by the Duke of Cambridge so long ago as 1858; and those armies are now so reduced in size that the high-sounding title of Commander-in-Chief is no longer in keeping with the charge. Thus the Indian army would be organised into four separate bodies, each of about the same strength, and commanded by four Lieutenant-Generals, the whole under the general control of the Commander-in-Chief in India, and administered by the Governor-General in Council. That such an arrangement would be symmetrical is its smallest recommendation. The great and paramount advantage claimed for the reform is, that it will bring the military administration of India into harmony with the actual conditions of the present day. The army will then be really under the immediate control of the Government of India, which alone is responsible for providing its cost and for maintaining the peace of the country. The cumbersome and intermediate agency of the local military administrations, which are effective only for delaying business, will be swept away, and the military administration of the country placed upon as simple and economical a basis as the peculiar circumstances of the country admit.

This is the main principle of the reform proposed, to which all the other proposals made, although important, are still subordinate, for until this step is taken, a real reform of the Indian army is impossible. It will be found elaborated in the despatch of the Government of India of February, 1881. The first indication of the attitude taken up by the India Office on the matter is furnished by a despatch of June 1881, in which Lord Hartington puts a number of questions to the Government of India as to how under their scheme the detailed arrangements for the administration of the army would be carried out. In particular, the amount of authority to be vested in the four Lieutenant-Generals; the way in which it is proposed to deal with all the detailed business connected with furlough, pensions, clothing, equipment, and the like, of the armies of Madras and Bombay; the mode of effecting promotion in the various staff and administrative departments; and the arrangements proposed for the conduct of the military works of these presidencies, and for the control of the sea transport arrangements for Madras and Bombay. Lord Hartington concludes by saying,—

' I am not prepared to say that you may not be able to suggest satisfactory arrangements for the transaction of all military business now conducted in Madras and Bombay; but I am doubtful whether on full enquiry you will retain the opinion expressed in the ninth paragraph of your despatch under reply, namely, that the military departments of Madras and Bombay are in truth but little more than transmitting offices for business which might come much more conveniently direct to the Government of India from the Commander-in-Chief. In the proposals to be made, your Excellency will no doubt bear in mind the evils of over-centralisation, or of burdening the military department of the Government of India with a mass of business that it will be unable to grapple with, and I am assured that your Excellency is fully impressed with the necessity that the controlling authorities shall be provided with the means of being at all times accurately informed of the peculiarities, and even the prejudices, of the different armies, and have such knowledge as will enable them to understand and to protect the feelings and just interests, and to foster the separate *esprit de corps*, of those armies.'

This despatch reads as if Lord Hartington, although he had come under the influence of the conservative spirit of his council, still desired to be convinced and supplied with convincing arguments in favour of the change, which would naturally recommend itself to a liberal statesman; these the Government of India had no difficulty in supplying. In their reply of July 29, of the same year, they pointed out, first, as regards the General officers commanding at Madras and Bombay, that although they were to be no longer styled Commanders-in-Chief, their military functions and responsibilities were to remain in all respects unaltered, but that, having no longer a seat in the local council, they would cease to be concerned with the civil administration of their presidency, and they would also cease to correspond direct with the Horse Guards in respect of the British troops under their command. The channel of communication for all British troops in India with the Horse Guards would be the Commander-in-Chief in India, a change of procedure which, it may be observed, was proposed many years ago by the Duke of Cambridge, in evidence given by His Royal Highness before a royal commission. And, having regard to the moderate strength of the establishment of British troops in India, to the improved means of communication, and to the fact that the embarkation and disembarkation of troops, while effected at Bombay, is a business conducted wholly under the immediate administration of army headquarters, the Government of India consider that there should be no sort of difficulty in bringing this business under the direct control of a single authority, through the agency of the General officers concerned, and without the interposition of the civil government of the presidency, and that it would be much more simple and convenient to do so. As regards the native armies of Madras and Bombay, the Lieutenant-Generals commanding would continue to select officers for regimental promotion, and to nominate for staff appointments, and in fact to exercise in this respect precisely the same functions as the local Commanders-in-Chief do at present, the presidential government having, in fact, no sensible degree of responsibility in the matter, even now, subject to the general authority of the Commander-in-Chief in India. The two Lieutenant-Generals commanding the Bengal and Punjab portions of the Bengal army are to be precisely on the same footing as the Lieutenant-Generals commanding in Madras and Bombay. As to the implied doubt whether it would be possible for a centralised military administration to conduct the class of business connected with furlough, pension, clothing, equipment, &c., for all the Indian armies, Lord Ripon and his council point out that, as we have mentioned already, the whole Indian army is now smaller than the Bengal army used to be in former days, and therefore that the amount of business to be transacted is not at all in excess of what it had been possible to transact in the past, while the improved state of communication throughout the country renders the disposal of such business very much more easy than it used to be. They go on to observe,—

' so far from there being any saving in correspondence, by the interposition of the local Government, between the Government of India and the executive departments of the Indian armies, the transaction of business would be much simplified and much more economically conducted if these circuitous channels of communication were removed and the Indian armies administered directly by the Government of India. We cannot insist too strongly on this point; in fact, it may be said without exaggeration that if the Bengal army were at present dealt with through the medium of a local Government, as are the armies of Madras and Bombay, the difficulty of administering the Indian armies would become almost intolerable.'

This hits the nail on the head. If the argument for maintaining the presidential system be worth anything, then undoubtedly it ought to be carried much further; there should be at least a separate army for Bengal Proper, another for the North-West Provinces, and another for the Punjab; to carry out the system completely there should be eight or nine armies in India, one for each of the separate provinces which make up British India, and as many separate military administrations. The Government of India go on to point out—what appears hitherto to have been lost sight of— that 'the amalgamation of Indian army administration ' virtually took place in all essential respects when, some ' years ago, the establishments of army, finance, and account ' underwent amalgamation.' Up to that time, when the Governments of Madras and Bombay had their local departments of finance and account, then no doubt they had a certain amount of administrative independence. But, 'as ' time went on, the anomalous condition under which the ' authority which was financially responsible for all Indian ' army expenditure had only an imperfect control over a ' considerable part of it, became more and more apparent;' and the necessity for bringing the control of military finance under the only authority which supplied the money being at last recognised, the local military and finance departments were fused into one body under the direct orders of the Government of India. That step once taken, the administrative control of the Governments of Madras and Bombay over their armies became henceforth purely formal.

Every one acquainted with the course of public business knows that, where the control over the purse rests, there lies also the only real authority. Every military measure is ultimately a matter of finance; the Governments of Madras and Bombay cannot alter a button on the soldier's coat, or move a corporal's guard, without the sanction of the Supreme Government; 'and when it is remembered that ' the greater part of the Madras army and a large part of ' the Bombay army are serving in territories of which the ' civil administration is directly under the Government of

' India, it may readily be understood that the interpositions
' of those Governments between their troops and the autho-
' rity which really administers the business connected with
' them is not only a mere form, but is the cause of needless
' trouble, embarrassment, and delay to all concerned.'

Nor is there any question of patronage involved. All military patronage rests with the commanders-in-chief of the
different armies, who nominate to all staff appointments, and
actually make all appointments and promotions in native
regiments, the sanction of Government being required only
for the removal of officers from regiments. In the army
departments, which are under the direct control of Government, promotion is practically governed by seniority ; so that
here also there is no room for patronage, which is limited,
therefore, to the first nomination of young officers at the
bottom of the list of the few departments which are still
kept separate by presidencies, almost the only one still on
that footing being the commissariat.

So far, then, from the Governments of Madras and Bombay suffering any loss of dignity by surrendering this last
shred of nominal control over their armies, the result, in
the opinion of Lord Ripon and his council, should be rather
the reverse. They (the presidential governments) would gain
rather than lose 'by the cessation of that interference with
' their military affairs which, although necessary, is no doubt
' vexatious, and which is not extended in the same degree
' to the business of the civil administration. In the latter,
' decentralisation has made great progress, and may go still
' further. But for efficient military administration unity of
' control is essential,' and all that the Government of India
desires is that this should be distinctly recognised and carried
out to its legitimate conclusion. They go on to point out the
absurd anomalies and circumlocution involved in dealing with
military buildings under the present system, especially in the
case of the outlying provinces, such as Burmah, the Central
Provinces, &c., where not only two but three Governments
are mixed up in the business : the Government of India which
gives the orders and finds the money ; the local Government
in whose territories the troops are stationed, and which
carries out the work ; and the Government of Madras or
Bombay, which has really no concern in the matter, but yet
has to be consulted upon every point as a matter of presidential etiquette. Finally, as regards the difficulty suggested
in the matter of sea transport, the Government of India
points out that the Governments of Madras and Bombay

have absolutely nothing to do with the matter even at present, the Indian Marine establishment being already an imperial service. In the case of an expedition being fitted out at Bombay, as, for example, when an Indian division was sent to Egypt in 1882, the whole business is conducted by the Marine Department, an imperial service the head of which, although residing at Bombay, is an officer under the direct orders of the Governor-General in Council, and is just as independent of the local government as is the admiral on the East India station.

After this preliminary discussion between the India Office and the Government at Simla, the latter appears to have submitted a series of despatches dealing in detail with the proposals for carrying out the various measures necessary to give effect to the complete scheme of reorganisation—the reconstitution of the staff, the strength and composition of the army, the ordnance, commissariat, medical, and veterinary establishments, and so forth; and, finally, in a long despatch of October 1881, they sum up the results of their labours, repeating and enforcing the argument on which their recommendations are based. They point out especially that while the reform advocated is imperatively required, the degree of change involved in the status of the native armies, which is admittedly a delicate thing to touch, and about which they evidently anticipate most criticism will be aroused at home,

'will be of a much simpler kind than might at first sight be supposed, the fact being that from a variety of circumstances the Governments of Madras and Bombay have already ceased to have more than a partial control over the armies of those presidencies, and have become, as the Commission observe with perfect truth, but little more than channels for communication between the Government of India and the troops in all matters concerned with military admin stration. . . . Furthermore, the Government of Bengal in course of time has developed into the Government of India; yet while it has long ceased to exercise the direct administration of Bengal or any other province, and its duties are now limited to a general control over all the different provinces of India, it still retains the direct administration of the Bengal army.'

The present condition of that army too is purely accidental. It consists partly of the high caste sepoys of the old Bengal army and partly of the levies, both Hindustani and Punjabi, which were raised in the Mutiny to act against the rebels; and 'that army, as it now stands, is there-' fore a mere fortuitous congeries of regiments, raised in ' haste, brought together in haste, and reduced in haste. . . .

' To speak then of the existing state of things as a carefully
' built up system is to ignore the actual facts of the case.
' The present condition of the Indian army is the result of
' circumstances quite unforeseen by its original founders.'

As to the danger of fusion of the Indian armies if they
were brought under the direct control of one authority, the
Government of India dwells on the extreme importance of
maintaining the separation of the Indian armies in peace
time; this separation, they consider, should be a cardinal
principle to be observed by the Indian Government in the
future, but they contend that the measure which they propose will really be in the direction of safety rather than of
danger. The virtual division of the Bengal army into two
bodies will be a much greater measure in the direction of
decentralisation than what is proposed in regard to the
Madras and Bombay armies can be in the other direction.
They also point out with great force that it has been of late
years the Government of India which, more than any other
authority, has contributed to maintaining the army separate.
The constant effort of the officers commanding regiments in
Bombay has been to recruit for their regiments from the
warlike races of Northern India. In this they have been
supported by their own Government, and it has been only
through the repeated injunctions of the Government of India
that the practice has been put a stop to.

The rest of this long despatch recapitulates the various
detailed recommendations made in the course of the year,
and shows that the reductions proposed by the Government
of India are generally of a less drastic kind than those
recommended by the Army Commission, although very much
in the same direction. Lord Ripon's Government claim for
their proposals a total saving of about 360,000*l.* a year in
direct charges, or, including indirect savings, a financial gain
on the whole of between 500,000*l.* or 600,000*l.* a year, and
conclude by saying that, after giving the subject their fullest
and most anxious consideration during the whole of the year,
they submit the result of their deliberations, ' which have
' been unanimously arrived at by those who are responsible
' for the government of this country, with the hope that it
' will receive the final and unqualified approval of Her
' Majesty's Government, and in the confident assurance that
' our recommendations will commend themselves to all
' persons who examine them in the same spirit of impar-
' tiality and freedom from prejudice as that in which they
' have been made.'

This despatch is dated October 29, 1881. The reply was deferred until July 1883, by which time Lord Kimberley had succeeded Lord Hartington as Secretary of State. This also is a long paper, but a large part of it is devoted to criticism on small points of detail, and picking holes in the figures given in the Governor-General's estimate of the savings claimed for ·his proposals. A long paragraph is devoted to showing that there are doubts on the part of the Indian Council whether ·the one additional Assistant Secretary proposed for the Military Department of the Government of India will suffice to deal with the extra work to be taken over from Madras, Bombay, and the Punjab, while it is observed that if the Madras and Bombay and Punjab Secretariats are to be re- duced, the clerks dispensed with must receive pensions or gratuities. So also, as regards the proposed saving in the medical and veterinary departments, if these savings are ·practicable, why should they not be effected under the present system of presidential armies? Having devoted nearly forty paragraphs to criticisms of this nature, Lord Kimberley goes on to deal with the political and administrative bearings of the question, first observing that, although the Government ·of India are of one opinion as to the necessity of the change, some excellent officers who formerly served in India are opposed to it, so also is the late Governor of Bombay and the late Commander-in-Chief in Madras. To quote the opinion of the local presidential anthorities whose power is to be shorn as an argument against the change is hardly conclu- sive. They are the natural enemies of such reforms.

With regard to the British troops in India, the Govern- ment of India had pointed out not only the administra- tive inconvenience but the extreme absurdity of the exist- ing system, under which the Commander-in-Chief in India · cannot correspond with the local commanders-in-chief, save through the channel of the Government of India on the one hand, and local governments on the other, although the latter have in fact nothing whatever to say to the real administration of those troops in respect of pay, clothing, discipline, or anything else. The reply is that there should be no inconvenience. The control in all these matters rests with the Government of India, and it may be as well ex- ercised through a local government at a distance as direct. As regards the native armies, it is truly observed that any change in their administration is difficult and indeed hazardous. The Government of India had pointed out that, as a matter of fact, the sepoy, in whatever presidency he was serving, saw very little of his Government and knew less about it; that practically the Government was to him an abstraction, just as the old Company was; and that the authorities to whom he undoubtedly looked as representing the Government, in his eye were his commanding officer and his general and commander-in-chief; and that no change was contemplated in this respect. To this it is replied that the native sepoys of the presidencies of Madras and Bombay look up to those Governments as bound in a special degree to support their claims and rights—a sort of general statement which it is impossible to controvert, although it may be observed that it is not at all unusual for a native soldier to petition the Supreme Government in matters of pension, for example, or compulsory retirement, for redress against what he considers the unjust decision of his own government. The Government of India had laid much stress upon the importance of maintaining the complete segregation of the several armies; the Secretary of State replies that he is not satisfied that it will be possible to maintain it as thoroughly under the proposed as under the existing organisation.

In this criticism the important proposal of the Government of India to separate the Hindustani and Punjabi portions of the existing Bengal army as part of the general scheme of reform is altogether ignored. As to the strongly expressed opinion of the Government of India, that the friction caused by the present system of organisation is almost intolerable in time of war, it is replied that, although this system was exposed to the severest strain in the recent campaign in Afghanistan, no complaint reached Her Majesty's Government at the time on the subject. It is, perhaps, hardly necessary to observe that official complaints in a delicate matter of this sort are never made except in the last resort. Until that point is reached, subordinate Governments and all other authorities are deemed as a matter of course to co-operate heartily, just as Cabinets are always declared to be perfectly unanimous until the moment when they break up; but those who were behind the scenes do not need to be told that in this, as in all other wars undertaken by conjoint forces of the Indian armies, the so-called presidential *esprit de corps* takes the form of a feeling of petty jealousy which works nothing but mischief, and which will never be extinguished until all the Indian armies are placed on the same footing and in the same relation of direct subordination to the Supreme Government.

In connexion with this point, it had been pressed strongly by the Government of India that, under the present system, according to which the Bengal army is commanded and administered directly by the Commander-in-Chief in India and the Government of India, the officers of the Madras and Bombay armies are, so to speak, left out in the cold, and that if they were placed in the same relation towards the Government of India as the Bengal army, they would get a fairer share of recognition and larger field for employment. To this it is replied that the Supreme Government living in Northern India would necessarily continue to see much more of the Bengal army than of the a·mies of Madras and Bombay, and that the latter would no longer have the certainty that even the prizes of their own presidencies would be secured and retained to them—a prophecy which it is of course impossible to refute beforehand. And as an advantage of maintaining the presidential system the case of the Mutiny is cited, when Sir John Lawrence, then Governor of the Punjab, raised a large body of troops for service against the mutineers. The despatch concludes by saying that, while the Indian Council are prepared to receive proposals for the reduction of the staff and army departments, the presidential system must remain for the present untouched.

Assuming that the Indian Council have put forth their best arguments against the proposed reform, the Indian Government might confidently rest their case in favour of it upon this reply. They might fairly say that, if nothing better could be brought against their proposals than criticism of the sort here advanced, their case was established in default of any definite rejoinder. And they had no difficulty in replying to what by only a stretch of language can be termed the argumentative portion of this remarkable State paper—redolent as it is of the conservative feeling natural in a body of men who are accustomed to regard the state of things which they left in India, ten or twenty, or even forty years before, as necessarily the only proper and suitable state of things, many of whom too have been accustomed to consider themselves rather as delegates bound to represent what they deem the interests of their respective presidencies, than members of an Imperial Council. The final rejoinder of Lord Ripon's Government will be found in a despatch dated October 1883. Setting out with an expression of their deep regret at the nature of this decision of the Secretary of State in Council, the Government of India deal first with the financial criticism on their proposals, observing upon the objection raised—that the saving to result from their reforms cannot properly be claimed as a set-off against the extra charges created, that the same sort of criticism might be applied to any scheme of administrative reorganisation which might be proposed.

'In proposing' (they say) 'a reform of army organisation to which we attached the highest importance, it appeared to us to be extremely desirable to show how this could be done, not only without any increase of expenditure, but with the result of a saving. In view of the great benefit to be derived by the army from its reorganisation, we should have been prepared to have carried out the reduction of commands and other high appointments very much after the plan proposed by the Commission, believing that the army would have accepted such a reduction as a necessary part of the great scheme of reform. The Commander-in-Chief having to undertake the direct command of all the Indian armies, it was necessary that he should be relieved of the command of the Bengal army. This involved the division of that body into two manageable bodies; hence the appointment was recommended of two lieutenant-generals for Bengal, with the necessary staff.'

A division of the Bengal army also recommended itself from the important political considerations already adverted to. These two Lieutenant-Generals being appointed for Bengal, reduction could be made in the existing staff of districts and divisions; but if the Lieutenant-Generals are not to be appointed, then this part of the saving cannot reasonably be carried out. With regard to some of the criticisms made on detailed items of the new estimates, the Government of India record their opinion that

'so far from the military business of the Government of India being increased by the proposed change, the result will probably be just the other way, from the abolition of the present cumbrous presidential system, which in the case of any military operations places a strain on the military machine quite out of proportion to the extent of the operations, and quite incompatible with a proper military organisation. The fact is, that when any operation, however small, has to be undertaken, in which a share is taken by the three separate armies, each controlled by its own government, each commanded by its own commander-in-chief, each with its own staff—ordnance, clothing and commissariat departments—the burden of working so complicated a machine falls to the Government of India, which has to discharge duties which, under a proper system of organisation, should never go beyond the proper responsible departmental heads. . . . It comes in fact to this, that the Military Department of the Government of India has practically on such occasions to exercise the functions of a chief of the staff, of a commissary-general, and of an inspector-general of ordnance—an arrangement involving an amount of circumlocution quite incompatible with the prompt despatch of business. Such a state of things violates the first principles of vigour and simplicity which should underlie every military system of administration.'

As to the political danger involved with regard to the proposed change in the administration of the native armies, and the solemn caution on this head proceeding from the India Office, the Government of India adds,

' that to speak of the Indian armies as being now separated by nationalities, as if a safe political condition were thereby secured, when Punjabis and Hindustanis have been serving indiscriminately at all the stations between Calcutta and Peshawar—when, in fact, the segregation which obtained before the Mutiny has been abandoned, contrary to the advice of Lord Lawrence and other experienced administrators, whose warning voice has for long been disregarded—it seems to us that the notion of safe political administration being found in the maintenance of this state of things is not justified by the realities of the case. The organisation which we propose will, we are satisfied, be far safer politically than that which obtains at present.'

As to the contention in Lord Kimberley's despatch, that the connexion between the local governments and the local armies tends to create a greater amount of attention to the wants and prejudices of the native soldier than a distant government might be expected to give, thus constituting a source of political safety, the Indian Government reply by pointing out a remarkable fact, that the outbreaks which at different times have occurred in the Indian armies have not been foreseen by the local governments. They quote, for example,

' the Mutiny of Vellore, which was brought about by the injudicious action of the local government, and was entirely unexpected by it; and the still more striking instance of the great mutiny of the Bengal army, which was entirely unforeseen and unexpected both by the Government of India and at Bengal army head-quarters. The conclusion to be drawn from these two notable instances and others which might be cited, is that local knowledge does not always afford that safeguard which might *primâ facie* be expected from it; the real safeguard for maintaining the loyalty and good conduct of the Indian armies is, we believe, to be looked for rather in the maintenance of strict discipline and that segregation of the different races to which we have attached so much importance, combined with a scrupulous regard for the claims and rights, and, we may even say, the prejudices of the sepoy—points as to the importance of which we have reason to believe the Government of India to be as fully alive as any other authorities.'

.As to the citation of the important result which followed from the Civil Government of the Punjab being able to raise a military power of its own during the crisis of 1857, to which reference has been made above, they point out that the great qualities displayed by Sir John Lawrence on that occasion

'were still more markedly manifested in the virtual assumption by him of the command, not only of the troops under his immediate orders, but of the whole forces of the Punjab and of the military resources of that country. Sir John Lawrence practically assumed the military as well as the civil administration of the province. But it was the great qualities of the man and his exceptional experience, much more than his position in command of an independent force, which enabled him to do what he did. Sir Bartle Frere, as Commissioner of Sind, took upon himself the same sort of responsibility in regard to the troops and the military resources of his province, although, in his capacity as Civil Governor of that country, he had no connexion with either the one or the other. And in times of emergency the Civil Government, if in competent hands, will always assume the direction of military affairs, whether or not it has the nominal command of the army, while, if ability and vigour are wanting, the possession of this command will assuredly prove of little value.'

As for the objection that opinions are not unanimous in favour of the new organisation, the Government of India observe, as other reformers before them have had occasion to observe, that ' this must be the condition under which all ' reforms are effected. There are always to be found persons ' who will predict that dangers and inconveniences will arise ' from reforms, and it is impossible to prove beforehand that ' their predictions will not be verified.' But they point out that there is at any rate a remarkable unanimity in favour of the change, and that the existing members of the Government of India came to the enquiry with unbiassed minds, not committed to opinions either way.

This is the pith of the discussion as contained in the bluebook, and we think that there will be no doubt in the mind of any impartial reader on which side lies the weight of the argument. The correspondence presents indeed the extraordinary spectacle of a Liberal Government succeeding to the discussion of a great administrative reform started by their predecessors, blocking its course, and able to find no better argument for such obstructive action than platitudes and petty criticisms, such as those of which we have furnished a few specimens. The truth we take to be that at the time when this discussion was going on, Lord Hartington was unfortunately too fully occupied with the general business of the Government to give the time sufficient to master so novel and extensive a subject; and Lord Kimberley, succeeding him in office when these proposals of the Government of

India had already been many months on the Council table, may have felt himself bound to give a speedy decision, which involved practically adopting the opinions submitted to him by his advisers, and allowing himself to become in a measure the mouthpiece of the conservative sentiments of the India Office.

The reform may be postponed, but it cannot be much longer delayed. The maintenance of the present monstrous organisation of the Indian armies is absolutely indefensible. As was pithily put in a paper, which is not contained in the blue-book, but which we lately read, in order to appreciate fully what the presidential system means, we might suppose the English army to be divided into an English establishment, an Irish establishment, and a Scotch establishment; and further, that these three establishments furnished garrisons, not only for the portions of the United Kingdom to which they belonged, but also for the various foreign stations; that the troops at Gibraltar, for example, were drawn from the Irish establishment, those at Malta from the Scotch establishment, and those at the Cape from the English establishment. If we further assume etiquette to require that the Horse Guards should communicate with the troops at Gibraltar only through the Lord Lieutenant of Ireland, and the troops at Malta through some high civil official in Scotland; if we suppose such an arrangement to have arisen out of a state of things under which there were at one time three separate armies—English, Irish, and Scotch—paid for separately from the revenues of those three kingdoms respectively; and if we suppose this nominal division of the army in three establishments to have been kept up long after the separate local independent governments had been abolished, and that separate estimates were still prepared in respect of the English, Irish, and Scotch establishments, and that the accounts and audit followed the course of the estimates; and if we suppose that on a regiment being moved from Gibraltar to Malta it would also be transferred from the Irish to the Scotch establishment; and if, while all this circumlocution was punctiliously pursued, the whole expense of the three establishments were defrayed by the British Treasury, to which the Audit Department in the three kingdoms was entirely subordinate; that all orders relating to the three establishments emanated in the first instance from the War Office in London, and that the whole proceedings connected with the three establishments were

purely formal and unreal. Make all these suppositions, and
we may form some sort of idea of the present presidential
military system of India. Well may the Government of
India say that such a system cannot be much longer maintained. Meanwhile, until the change is carried out, these
despatches of the Government of India remain on record as
a memorial of the energy and completeness with which Lord
Ripon's Government addressed themselves to the task to
which they succeeded.

It will be of interest to note here that these ideas of the
Government of India first found expression so long ago as
1858, and under the high authority of the late Prince Consort, in a memorandum drawn up on the then pending
measure of the transfer of the Government of India from
the Company to the Crown. The question at issue was not
indeed the precise one now under discussion, but whether
the Indian Council, just created, should retain the same
authority over the Indian army, then still partly European,
which had been possessed by the Company; but the reasoning
in this able state paper is equally conclusive as to the mischievous effect of maintaining the presidential system for the
administration of the Indian army.

'Instead of the proper "chain of responsibility,"' the Prince
Consort writes, 'which is claimed for the system, it would seem more
correct to characterise the system as one of perpetual counteraction
and conflicting authorities. Can anything be more monstrous, for
instance, in a military point of view, than the relative positions of
the Commander-in-Chief for India and the Commanders-in Chief for
Madras and Bombay—that the latter should be perfectly independent
of the former in their respective presidencies as regards the Company's,
or local, forces, but subordinate to him as regards those of her
Majesty? And that the former, in the event of military operations
near the frontiers of the different presidencies, should be absolutely
powerless to combine his operations, as far as the co-operation of local
troops is concerned, beyond the limits of Bengal, without the concurrence, previously obtained, of the Governor in Council and commanders-in-chief of the subordinate presidency? . . . The great
principles on which the efficiency of the military force in any country,
and under any circumstances, must depend, are *simplicity, unity, and
steadiness of system, and unity of command.'* *

We hardly know which is most remarkable—the per-
spicacity with which the Prince points out the blot in the
Indian military system which no one else at the time had
perceived; or that the Indian Government a quarter of a

---

* Sir Theodore Martin's 'Life of Prince Consort,' vol. iv. p. 310.

century afterwards should still be in vain pressing attention to the same point.

We have devoted so much space to what must be regarded as the cardinal principle involved in the proposed reform of the Indian army, that only a brief reference can be made to the other important proposals dealt with in these papers. For example, there is an interesting discussion whether the Commander-in-Chief in India should continue to be a member of the Governor-General's council. The law on this head is permissive only, but it has been the invariable practice to appoint the Commander-in-Chief an extraordinary member. The Commission recommend that the Commander-in-Chief should cease to be a member of council. Lord Lytton, on the other hand, in a minute recorded upon the case, points out the false position which the military member of council, who represents the War Department of the Government of India, holds with regard to the Commander-in-Chief, who is usually an officer of higher rank than himself, and the source of all patronage and preferment in the army. It is true that the military member of council is holding a civil office, and therefore, properly speaking, his rank does not come in question; the office might legally be held by a civilian. But the army cannot be got to take this view. Even at home, where the Secretary of State is a member of the Cabinet, and has the Treasury and Parliament at his back, those who are cognisant of the inner working of our military administration well know that he does not always find it easy to hold his own against the Horse Guards, and no doubt the same difficulty is felt in the military administration in India; and the difficulty must be increased when controller and controlled sit together at the council table, the latter taking precedence. Lord Lytton proposed to get over the difficulty by abolishing the post of military member of council and making the Commander-in-Chief the War Minister, as well as Commander-in-Chief, conducting the executive business of the army, as at present, through the head-quarter staff, and the financial administration of the army through the Military Department, with a strong financial secretary, an arrangement the only objection to which is that it would be perfectly impracticable. Either the financial secretary would be completely subordinate to his official chief, in which case there would be no control over military expenditure except such as might be exercised by the civil department of finance; or it would be necessary to give this financial secretary powers independent of the Commander-in-Chief, which would be merely to reproduce the independent military department over again. Lord Ripon's Government, reviewing in their first despatch on this subject, of February 1881, this recommendation of the Commission, that the Commander-in-Chief should cease to be a member of the Governor-General's council, took a different view. While admitting the degree of inconvenience involved in his exercising double functions, they pointed out the advantage of an arrangement under which he was liable to be called on to submit his proposals for personal discussion with his colleagues, adding —'we believe that the present arrangement tends to pro-'mote harmonious relations between the executive head of ' the army and the Government rather than the reverse, and ' that the advantages outweigh the disadvantages.'

There is no doubt a good deal to be said for the view of the case taken by the Government of India. A Commander-in-Chief detached from the Government, looking at questions from the side of army efficiency only, irrespective of cost, surrounded by an army head-quarter staff proposing all sorts of expensive and impracticable measures, is in a very different position from the same man sitting at the council table and called on to defend his proposals against the criticisms of half-a-dozen colleagues ; and certainly the relations between the Government of India and their most powerful servant have always been somewhat strained whenever the latter has been for long absent from his place in council. But the Government of India appear to have overlooked one consideration of great force. The Commander-in-Chief is for more than half a year in the hills, away from the army ; and the evil is greatly intensified if he is also expected to attend the government in Calcutta for the short cold weather in the discharge of political duties.

We have already mentioned that Sir Ashley Eden's Commission was appointed primarily to bring about a reduction in Indian army expenditure. The Commission put the savings to result from their proposals at a million and a quarter sterling, although on a review of these papers the estimate appears excessive; the saving to result from the amended proposals of the Government of India is set down at the more modest figure of half a million sterling, to which again the Secretary of State takes exception. But the main reason for this great difference is to be found in the more extensive scope of the reductions recommended by the Commission. The costliness of the Indian army is due in great measure to the small size of its regiments. A regiment of native infantry, until the changes recently brought about by this enquiry, mustered only about 700, and a cavalry regiment about 500, of all ranks; and these diminutive cadres are without any reserve or means of augmentation save by the slow process of recruiting. Regiments of this strength, as the Afghan war very plainly showed, are soon brought down under the strain of campaigning to mere handfuls of men, far below the strength of an efficient military unit. The British troops on the Indian establishment are on an even less satisfactory footing. The nominal strength of a European battalion in India is 820 rank and file; but these are seldom all present, and there are no reserves. The statistics of the late war show that the battalions of this nominal strength had often barely half that number really available with the colours. At the present time there are regiments in India which, after deduction for sick and guards, cannot turn out more than 300 bayonets on parade. Such a regiment taking the field, under the stress of campaigning, soon runs down below what is deemed in European armies the proper strength for a single company. Yet for these absurdly small bodies a full establishment of officers is maintained, with two lieutenant-colonels, four majors, adjutant, paymaster, and staff sufficient for a battalion of three or four times the strength.

The British cavalry regiment in India is organised on a still more extravagant footing, having only three squadrons instead of four, as at home, and a smaller number of sabres than even the British peace establishment. On the score both of economy and efficiency the Commission naturally proposed a change in this respect—namely, that the same establishment of British bayonets and sabres should be maintained in a smaller number of regiments. The present establishment of 50 British battalions was to be reduced to 43, the same aggregate force being maintained by increasing the strength of each battalion from 820 to 978 rank and file—a very moderate strength considering that British regiments in India are much scattered in detachments, that the proportion of sick is often large, and that, while they are liable to take the field at a moment's notice, there are no reserves at hand or means of quickly reinforcing them. Similarly, the British cavalry regiments serving in India were to be reduced from nine to six, the number of squadrons per regiment being raised from three to four. The Government of India did not go even so far as this. Under a spirit of compromise, they proposed that only four infantry battalions should be withdrawn, the strength of the 46 to be retained being increased from 820 rank and file each to 920—which, they significantly remark, is 30 less than the strength now fixed for the battalions at home which stand first for foreign service. They also proposed an establishment of eight instead of nine regiments of British cavalry, with an increase to those retained of 65 sabres per regiment, which would give a trifling increase of total strength, but a much more economical and efficient organisation. As regards the artillery, they adopted the proposals of the Commission to reduce the number of batteries from 86 to 77 ; the strength of the garrison battery, which is now very low in India, being considerably increased.

The artillery reduction was accepted by the War Office, but not that of the cavalry and infantry, although it appears to have been strongly pressed upon them by Lord Hartington, then at the India Office. It was not alleged, indeed, that the change proposed was not suitable in itself, or that India does not keep up its European garrison in an administratively inconvenient and highly expensive form. The objection made was, that if a regiment of cavalry and four regiments of infantry were withdrawn from India, the corresponding number of regiments would have to be struck off the British army altogether. Even if this were to be the necessary consequence, the justice might be questioned of requiring India to pay for keeping up a number of skeleton battalions on an altogether inefficient footing in order to suit the convenience of England. But, as a matter of fact, there is no necessity for such a reduction. It is well known to everybody who is conversant with our military administration that the number of battalions on the home establishment is distinctly too small for even the qualified and restricted sphere of operations marked out for them in even ordinary times. The assumption upon which our present military organisation is based is that one battalion of each regiment should always be serving abroad, and one at home ; as a matter of fact, this equilibrium is never maintained. It involves that England shall be in a state of profound peace ; but when is this state ever realised? In the past there has been a succession of petty disturbances in one or other of her distant possessions, and there is no reason to look for greater immunity in the future ; and whenever any small emergency arises, calling for the employment abroad of three or four battalions in excess of the fixed colonial establishment, the equilibrium between home and foreign service is immediately upset, and our very delicate military system breaks down, because both battalions of the regiment are abroad. This is the case with no less than ten regiments at present, and always will be the case to some extent until the home exceeds the foreign establishment. The proposal of the Indian Government, therefore, to dispense with a small number of British regiments entirely harmonised with the actual requirements of home service.

As regards the Native army, the Commission proposed an obvious reform of a similar kind to that proposed for the British troops, a reduction in the number of the attenuated cadres, and an increase to the strength of the remainder. The then existing thirty-five regiments of cavalry and 131 of infantry, composing the three presidential armies and the Punjab Frontier Force, were to be reduced to twenty-five of cavalry and 101 of infantry. The Government of India proposed the more moderate reduction of four regiments of cavalry and eighteen of infantry, bringing down the establishment to thirty-one and 113 regiments respectively, or 144 regiments for the whole Indian army, the strength of each regiment retained being somewhat augmented so as to maintain the total establishment of native troops unaltered. This was agreed to by the India Office, and the measure appears to have been carried out about two years ago. When it is understood that the new cavalry and infantry regiments number only 550 and 832 of all ranks respectively, it must be admitted that the Government of India have not erred on the side of a too drastic measure; but, inasmuch as the abolition of every regiment meant the abolition of a lucrative command and several staff appointments, and that a number of deserving officers were displaced for whom no fresh employment could be found, it will be readily understood that there would be a desire to tread as lightly as possible in the matter. That these reductions, involving so much hardship on individuals, should have been accepted without any sort of remonstrance—indeed, with the tacit approval of the persons whose interests were so materially affected—is a very strong testimony to the propriety of the measure. It might be thought, perhaps that numerous cadres provide a suitable peace organisation. But the retention of very small cadres is justifiable only if the means are available of readily expanding them, and, in view of the actual condition of things in India, the cadres, even as now enlarged, appear quite small enough. A regiment of less than 850 men all told is a very small unit with which to enter on a campaign.

When recruits and the depôt and the sick are deducted, a regiment of even 1,600 strong would not give more than 1,000 in the fighting line; so that the Indian army as now organised might be doubled in war-time without any tactical inconvenience; but, in fact, that army as now constituted does not afford the means for rapid expansion on anything like this scale. During the Afghan war, recruits were obtained with the greatest difficulty, and it is understood that even now, in peace-time, the establishment can only just be kept up to its full numbers. There is, indeed, no reason to suppose that military life is in itself less popular now with the class that furnishes soldiers than it has been for the last hundred years. Thirty or forty years ago the Indian Government could raise as many men as it wanted whenever it desired to do so, and it actually kept up an army nearly three times as strong as the present one. The lack of recruits nowadays appears to be due simply to the increased prosperity of the country, and to the fact that, while wages in all other lines of employment have increased, the soldier's pay has remained practically unaltered. He certainly now obtains some advantages which he did not have before; but his actual pay has not been raised for many years, and this seems sufficiently to account for the difficulty in obtaining recruits. No one, however, who is conversant with the conditions of the case would wish to see a single native soldier retained in peace time beyond the actual exigencies of the service: it is in peace time that mercenary armies become dangerous.

An army which cannot be expanded in war time to the required strength ceases to fulfil the object for which it is maintained, and the remedy for the present state of things would obviously appear to be the formation of a reserve—the great source of strength of all modern armies. This was stated by Lord Lytton's Government, when proposing the appointment of the Commission, to be one of the principal matters which it would have to consider. In their despatch of 1879 the Indian Government observe that—

‘ the Indian army is now the only large army in the world which has no reserves. In other words, India is the only country which, maintaining a large army, pays in peace time for the whole available force which it can put into the field in war. The expense of such a system is patent. Without, therefore, committing ourselves to any premature opinion as to how far a reserve system can or cannot be worked in India, we think that there is at least such *primâ facie* evidence in its favour as to demand the fullest consideration for it; and we would go further and say that, so far as we can at present judge, it is in this direction that there is the best prospect of an important diminution of our military expenditure.'

The Commission accordingly, in that part of their report which treats of this subject, point out that a very large proportion of the native soldiers take their discharge after a few years' service, without waiting for the pension which every man is entitled to earn, and that there is thus always a large number of trained soldiers spread loose over the country, who are bound by no ties to the Government, and whose services might be secured on moderate terms. They go on to elaborate a system which would give a reserve of short-service soldiers of 200 men to every native infantry regiment, or a total strength of less than one-fourth of the active army, or 20,000 men in all, with a second reserve for garrison duty of about twice that number. This very moderate force, they point out, should be easily obtained from the 80,000 men or thereabouts who take their discharge every ten years, and who are at present absorbed in the civil population. So far from such a reserve being a source of danger, they argue that it would rather tend the other way, while at any rate the army cannot be deemed efficient for offensive purposes without some such organisation.

There is perhaps no country in the world in which a reserve system is more adapted to the habits and wants of the military classes. The native soldier in India is usually a petty yeoman, whose family has been accustomed to military service for generations, who has a share in the land of his family or village, but a share too small for his complete support; he is obliged therefore to eke out the means of living derived from it by employment of some sort, and a very moderate addition to his income makes all the difference to him between poverty and comfort. These men can always be found when wanted at their native village, and no people have a keener sense of the obligation involved in a contract of this sort. But the Indian very soon gets tired of service in peace time, especially if it takes him far away from home. One result of our unwise policy of maintaining a single undivided army for the whole of Northern India is that it involves in course of reliefs that the Sikh should be sent down to garrison Fort William, and the Hindustanis of Oudh and Behar up to Peshawar, which means in either case exile in a country and climate very distasteful to each class respectively. This is well understood to be the principal cause of the sepoy's readiness to leave the army, the result being that, although the system is nominally one of long service—every man becoming entitled to pension after fifteen years if invalided, or after thirty-two if in good health--practically it is a short-service system, as the majority of the men stay neither for the one nor the other. We believe that at the present time not far short of one-half of the native soldiers are of less than five years' service. Here then are all the elements for the formation of a reserve; and to those who talk about the political danger of such a measure it seems sufficient to say that the man who has still an engagement with the State, and something to be gained by keeping to it, is more likely to prove loyal in time of trouble than the man who has completely severed his connexion with it. At any rate if the Indian army is to be made a really efficient machine for the duty which is likely to come upon it, some means of rapidly augmenting it on emergency appears to be absolutely necessary.

Another point discussed in these papers is the conversion or amalgamation of the existing single-battalion regiments into regiments consisting of three battalions each. This seems to be recommended by very strong considerations. These single-battalion regiments, although now somewhat stronger than before, are still weak, and, as we have explained, there is no means for their rapid augmentation or replenishment during war. A regiment of multiple battalions, on the other hand, could furnish one or two battalions for active service, and keep them fed by the portion remaining in quarters. It is a strong reason for change that the Indian army is the only one in the world (except, we believe, that of the United States) which is organised by regiments of single battalions, and that the change from such an organisation has at last been deemed necessary for the British army, even at the cost of breaking up the time-honoured traditions attaching to individual regiments. The organisation of the native regiments, recruited as they are for the most part by groups from certain castes or classes, lends itself readily to such an arrangement. The Government of India accordingly recommend that this organisation should be introduced, but for the native element only; they do not attempt to touch the curious system under which each battalion is now officered by an establishment of eight European officers, the posts filled by these eight officers—commandant, second in command, wing commander, &c.—constituting each a specific staff appointment, which is in the gift of the Commander-in-Chief.   Apart from the question of patronage, the arrangement is obviously faulty; it is impossible with such small cadres to obtain a reasonable degree of equality in the rate of promotion throughout the different regiments.   This can be secured only by transferring officers from one regiment to another, which is confessedly a thing to be avoided. But the gravest objection lies in the inordinate amount of patronage it places in the hands of the Commander-in-Chief and his staff.   If we suppose that in the British army, not only the selection of officers for the command of battalions and for adjutancies, but the rank and seniority of each major, captain, and lieutenant in a regiment were arbitrarily fixed by the Horse Guards, without reason recorded and without appeal, we should have some idea of the system under which the Indian army is administered.   However carefully and conscientiously this may be done, it is too great a burden to place on any one man.   The difficulty would be got over by amalgamating the European officers as well as the native troops into groups of three battalions each; this would furnish a body of twenty-four officers, large enough therefore to admit of promotion proceeding on the lines of seniority tempered by selection.   But it is not surprising that the Government of which the Commander-in-Chief is a member should not have proposed a measure which would have relieved him and his successors of this enormous patronage.

The organisation of that curious institution, the Indian Staff Corps, naturally came under consideration as one of the subjects of this enquiry.   It is perhaps necessary to explain that this staff corps has no particular connexion with the staff, but is simply the generic name given to the whole body of officers of the Indian army who, on joining that service from the British army, are thereon posted to one of the three presidential staff corps, and henceforward rise to the ranks of captain, major, and so forth, after fixed periods of service, their advancement in regiments or departments or in civil employ proceeding, however, on lines quite independent of their substantive promotion in the staff corps.   Inasmuch as the three staff corps are governed by exactly the same rules of promotion, there is in fact no necessity for officering the Indian army in these three separate bodies, the only result of the separation being that it contributes to maintain the presidency distinctions, and therefore to foster the baneful presidency jealousies. There is a great deal otherwise to condemn in the staff corps system, but it has the advantage of elasticity, and is therefore in this respect suited to the varying demands of Indian service. Promotion being regulated by length of service, and not in succession to vacancies, the army can be expanded or reduced according to the varying requirements of the time without affecting the interests of individuals already in the service, as would happen with a system of fixed establishments or regimental cadres. The staff corps system has often been condemned, on the ground that it is responsible for the present congested condition of the Indian army, with its great excess of superior officers. This, however, is a mistake. The present extraordinary state of the field officers' lists in India, especially in the Madras army, where there are nearly ten times as many lieutenant-colonels and majors as captains, is due not to the staff corps system, but to the fact that this army has undergone during the last twenty-five years a very large numerical reduction, and that this reduction has been effected by the crude process of allowing the establishment to die out without filling up vacancies by fresh admissions. That army is, therefore, now officered for the most part by old men, who were young men when the number of regiments was largely reduced after the Mutiny, and who have remained ever since in the subordinate positions they held from the outset, at the bottom of the list, but getting substantive promotion under staff corps rules, so that in every Madras regiment there are still majors and lieutenant-colonels performing the duties of subalterns. This is not the fault of the staff corps, but of the short-sighted way adopted in dealing with the reduction. What undoubtedly should have been done when the Madras army was so largely reduced was that which was done when the Royal Navy was reduced in 1871, to pension off a part of the officers in every grade, so as to bring down the establishment at once to the required reduced strength, while still maintaining a due proportion of seniors and juniors. But the India Office would not entertain so comprehensive a measure, although it would have resulted in a large eventual economy, and things have been allowed to drift into their present state; the Madras army is practically composed of field officers; in the other two armies also the number of senior officers is largely in excess of the wants of the service or the sphere of employment for them, and many lieutenant-colonels and majors are still holding quite subordinate appointments and discharging duties which should properly be performed by subalterns.

But this is comparatively a matter of detail. The main and all-important point raised by the Government of India, and on which they have sustained a defeat for the moment, is that the complicated and obsolete presidential system should be swept away, and that the complete and undivided control over the Indian armies should be vested in the authority which is already completely responsible for their financial administration. That this reform, although post-poned for a time, must be carried out before long, is as certain as anything can be which has not yet happened. It is to be regretted that it should not have been accom-plished in a time of profound peace, but deferred until the aspect of affairs on the North-Western frontier calls upon the Indian army for another demonstration of its efficiency and its powers.

ART. V.—*Mémoires et Relations Politiques du Baron de Vitrolles.* Tomes 2, 3. Paris: 1884.

WE make no apology for recurring to this work, and noticing its concluding parts. Last July we reviewed the first volume of the Memoirs of the late M. de Vitrolles, and showed how valuable the book is, as throwing vivid and fresh light on the great events of 1814 in Europe, and not only explaining their secret history, but illustrating the conduct of one of the most active plotters against the throne of Napoleon I., and of his better known but less bold associates. The second and third volumes complete the work, and confirm the forecast we made of them—that they would add much to our knowledge respecting the course of public affairs in France from 1814 to 1830, as it was swayed by influences behind the scenes of the drama. This part of the Memoirs describes the game of intrigue and expedients by which the Comte d'Artois and the Senate contrived out-wardly to compose their differences when the Restoration was first proclaimed; it gives us some instructive details on the government of Louis XVIII. in 1814; and the picture it presents of the conduct and attitude of the king and his court, at the terrible crisis of March 1815, is extremely curious. Historically, however, what is of most value in these volumes is, in our judgement, the account they contain of the events that took place in Paris immediately after Waterloo, and their graphic, minute, and impressive descrip-tion of several passages of grave moment in the Revolution

of July 1830.   These chapters disclose many new facts,
and bring out in clear and striking relief occurrences at the
two periods which hitherto have not been generally known.
As for the personages who were most conspicuous throughout this epoch of mighty changes, if Talleyrand is the most
elaborate and best-drawn figure in the first part of the work,
the portrait of Fouché in this part is singularly life-like, telling, and accurate, and M. de Vitrolles has described, with a
skilful hand, the weak side of the nature of Louis XVIII.,
though, as was to be expected, he is completely blind to
the best features of the king's character.   Like their predecessor, too, these volumes abound in desultory anecdotes
of all kinds ; indeed, the conversations of M. de Vitrolles
with the leaders of the Provisional Government during the
interregnum of 1815, and with Charles X. and his reckless
ministers in the crisis of July 1830, would alone make the
book of sterling value.

As· for the author and his personal history, his conduct during this part of his career is seldom seen in its
brighter aspects, and he sometimes appears a different being
from the single-minded and heroic gentleman who, staking
everything on the hazard of a die, successfully led what
the wisest heads of Europe thought was a forlorn hope, and
showed his faltering master the way to fortune.   M. de
Vitrolles was not in his true element at the council board
of Louis XVIII.; without any of the gifts of a statesman,
irascible, haughty, and full of conceit, he was not liked by
the king or by his colleagues ; and, though he gave valuable
aid to the Bourbon cause when Napoleon fell for the second
time, and retained for a while the royal favour, he soon
ceased to have the slightest influence on the governments
that followed 1815.   Before long, too, he became notorious
as a conspirator against the king and his ministers in their
well-meant efforts to restrain the frenzy and cruelty of the
émigré faction ; and having been summarily dismissed
from his post and charged with a grave political offence, he
was relegated to the obscure position of a mere dependent
on the Comte d'Artois, a disgraced member of an unpa-
triotic cabal.   In short, during this period he was regarded
as a dangerous man, impracticable, and only good for
intrigues ; and when Charles X. ascended the throne, the
king was afraid to make him a minister.   Nevertheless,
discredited as he rightly was, M. de Vitrolles had done
almost priceless services to the Bourbon princes at grave
conjunctures ; and he was soon to show, in the Revolution

of July, that although he did not possess political fore-thought, and his mind was warped by the prejudices of caste, he could give good counsels in the hour of danger, and endeavour, by bold and well-timed conduct, to avert the ruin that menaced the throne. His character, in truth, seemed to change only as it manifested itself on its opposite sides. His statesmanship was a mistake and a failure; but he was a brilliant and capable man of action, and throughout life he remained constant to the lofty principles of honour which formed the moral creed of the old noblesse of France.

The first volume of these Memoirs closed at the entry into Paris of the Comte d'Artois on April 12, 1814. The excited capital had greeted the Prince, but the Senate had avoided the ceremony at Notre Dame, and had refused to acknow-ledge Louis XVIII. without a guarantee of a constitution for France. An arrangement had been hastily made by which the Prince was to be recognised as *de facto* head of a Pro-visional Government, but nothing had been definitely settled. The champions of the old *régime* and the body which, at the existing crisis, comprised the sole representatives of the nation, sate watching each other with jealous suspicion. M. de Vitrolles, flushed with his recent triumphs, at first slighted the demands of the Senate. The difficulty, he urged, would disappear at once if the Provisional Government would but abdicate and surrender its powers to his princely master; but Talleyrand and his troublesome colleagues refused to take a leap in the dark, and meanwhile the State was paralysed. An unexpected personage appeared to act as a mediator at this juncture :—

'One of the bystanders, who, hitherto, had taken no part in the conversation, rose hurriedly from his seat, and addressing me in scarcely civil language, intimated that what I had said was little to the purpose.

'"I presume, then," I replied, "that you have something better to propose?"

'"Certainly," was the answer; "there is but one way to solve the problem; the Senate must, by its own act, make M. le Comte d'Artois lieutenant-general of the realm."

'I then recognised the speaker: it was Fouché. I had known his appearance, but I was not aware that he was in Paris.'

The Royalist agent and the old regicide proceeded to discuss this fresh project. Fouché, already eager to court the Bourbons, made the terms as easy to the Prince as possible; but the Senate, he felt, would not be led to abandon the strong position it held.

' I approached him, and drew him into an embrasure of the window.

' " At all events," I said, " you make an offer. . . . I cannot antici-pate the opinion of Monsieur; but were he to agree to anything resembling your improvised plan, who would guarantee to us the con-sent of the Senate? "

' " I," replied Fouché eagerly; " I will if M. le Comte d'Artois will make a declaration that will satisfy the public mind."

' " What kind of declaration ? " was my answer. Finding some difficulty in explaining, he took a sheet of paper and began to write, in his bad hand, on a marble stand. He read out what he had written, first to me, and then to all those who were present. The composition was as incorrect as the substance was faulty. According to Fouché, the prince was to declare " that he recognised the constitutional decree which had recalled his august brother; and that, being aware of his sentiments and political views, he was not apprehensive of being dis-avowed in swearing in his name to observe the bases of the constitution and to cause them to be observed." The articles of the constitution were then summarily set forth.'

M. de Vitrolles, greatly to his astonishment, found his master not unwilling to treat even on conditions wholly opposed to the high theory of the right of kings. Not improbably, however, the Comte d'Artois either did not fully understand the proposal, or thought it could be evaded with ease, and it was finally agreed not to reject the com-promise, but that M. de Vitrolles should adopt the language of the declaration to be made by the prince as nearly as might be to Bourbon ideas. Fouché seemed willing to accept everything. M. de Vitrolles thus describes their singular interview :—

' I met Fouché near the Tuileries. " I was looking for you," I exclaimed, and then requested him to enter the Pavillon Marsan for a moment, and to hear the reply to his overtures agreed to by Monsieur.

' " It is quite useless," he urged; " I am in a hurry; I am going to the Luxembourg."

' I persisted : I only asked for a moment; it was necessary that he should be made aware of the changes we had made in his paper.

' " It was not correctly composed," I added, " and you know our princes are Frenchmen, and profess to speak their own language properly."

' " You recollect," replied Fouché, " how I dashed it off; there was much noise, many were present. I did not even read over what I had written."

' We arrived at the main door of the Pavillon Marsan.

' " No doubt," was my answer; " so we have corrected the mistakes caused by your precipitate haste; for instance, people do not say, ' We swear to observe bases.' "

' " Of course not," he said.

' I did not like, however, to tell him, one by one, all the changes we had made: I was afraid I should alarm him, and cause him to break off. I thought he would notice them less if I read the whole thing off, and I begged him to step in. I held him, nay, pulled him by the arm. He resisted.

' " You have made corrections; all right," he said. The discussion was a curious one, even for the sentinel who was looking on.

' " Well, we have done more," I remarked ; " we have expunged some things." I began enumerating those of the least importance.

' " That is excellent," continued Fouché, trying at the same time to liberate his arm, " but let me go ; I must go to the Senate ; there is not a moment to lose."

' " Well, but," I said, " we have erased the article about the hereditary quality of the Senate and the arrangements concerning its property and dotations."

' " You have done very well indeed," he cried, at last extricating his arm briskly, and he hurried off, leaving me in a state of astonishment.'

Notwithstanding, however, all this facility, the Senate really yielded nothing; for it asserted in no ambiguous language its right to dispose of the Crown of France, and to confer it only on the condition that Louis XVIII. should accept a charter and give the nation a constitutional *régime*. Talleyrand made the announcement in characteristic fashion :—
' M. de Talleyrand soon came in, careless of success pro-
' vided he got the credit of it. He approached us slowly,
' and, throwing on the table the official despatch, said,
' " There, M. de Vitrolles, there is your affair ! " '

The Comte d'Artois, disabused at last, protested vehemently against this document, and vowed that he would not see ' those insolent lawyers.' His purpose, however, was soon changed. M. de Vitrolles had been informed by Nesselrode that the Czar had resolved to back the Senate ; and the keen-witted Frenchman, one of whose special gifts was to know how to yield when there was no help for it, urged his master, whatever the conditions might be, to accept the Crown in his brother's interest. An interview followed in which Talleyrand reiterated, though in courtly phrase, the terms distinctly laid down by the Senate; the prince gracefully expressed his assent, and after an exchange of effusive compliments, the conference ended in seeming amity. The deputation, however, had scarcely left when the Comte d'Artois significantly remarked :—

' " Well, the die has been cast ; we stand bound by our engagements. These we must frankly accept and carry out honestly whatever the result. Experience will show if the welfare of the State can be assured in this way. If at the end of ten or a dozen years this shall have been proved impossible, we shall have to do what the interests of France demand." '

We pass over the short-lived and provisional rule of the Comte d'Artois during which M. de Vitrolles filled the important but anomalous post of Secretary to the Provisional Government. On April 25, 1814, Louis XVIII. reached the shore of Calais, revisiting France after twenty years of change which had done the work of centuries. Yet even the Great King, at the height of his glory, was never received with a louder acclaim than that which greeted the returning exile; and this, too, in the case of a people which had shed oceans of its best blood to keep his House and himself away from its borders, and which at this moment was widely divided from his antique dynasty in its essential interests. The progress of the king was a scene of triumphs : towns and villages strewed his path with flowers; his presence was hailed by shouting multitudes; and even the late chiefs of the imperial armies, won over by flattery, bribes, and honours, were enthusiastic in words of loyalty. M. de Vitrolles has given us this portrait of Louis :—

'We found the king seated in the middle of the room; his bearing and person had the stamp of supreme rank; a look of youth still lingered on his face; his cheeks were full and lessened the relief of an aquiline nose; his broad forehead was slightly too much thrown backward, but a quick and penetrating glance lit up his countenance; he wore his hair in the fashion of his youth; it was withdrawn from his brow, cut as it were in lengths, powdered, and then tied by a riband at the back of the neck. His dress was a simple blue coat with gilt buttons that bore the fleur-de-lis; epaulettes on which a crown was embroidered, were the only mark of distinction; and he wore the order of the cordon bleu, and the cross of St. Lazare at his button-hole.'

The royal entry into Paris resembled that of the Comte d'Artois, with some shades of difference :—

'The king occupied an open carriage; Madame sat by his side, and the Prince de Condé and Duc de Bourbon were in front. Monsieur and Monseigneur le Duc de Berry rode on horseback beside the royal carriage. It chanced that I was by myself in one of the carriages of the suite of the king. The enthusiasm of the people of all classes and ages was remarkable. I was distracted from the spectacle only when I reflected what must be the thoughts of Madame at this moment. The summit of the Donjon of the Temple was within sight; what terrible memories it might recall to her heart ! At the Tuileries the 10th of August awaited her. I was still under those impressions when the triumphal march of the king, accompanied by ever-increasing crowds and renewed acclamations, was stayed before the image of the statue of Henry IV., which had been raised on a platform on the Pont-Neuf, until a new bronze figure should replace that which the sacrilegious hand of the Revolution had broken. A simple inscription was on the base:—" Ludovico reduci Henricus redivivus." After a brief delay we arrived at Notre Dame, and this time everything was well arranged. The crowds were kept outside, but the interior of the church was quite full, and you could see young men and even women perched on the projecting parts of the high building as high as the dome. Seats had been reserved to the right and left of the nave for the great Bodies of State, for the Municipal Council, the Courts of Justice, the Treasury, the Legislative Body and the Senate — that Senate which still had several regicides of the Convention among its members.'

Before this ceremony, as is well known, the king had stayed a few days at Compiègne, in order partly to receive the homage of public bodies and other dignitaries, and partly to take counsel as to his future policy. M. de Vitrolles contradicts a common tradition that the Czar took on himself to lecture the king on his constitutional duty to France:—

' Very different from what historians of this epoch have invented, the interview of the two sovereigns was simply an exchange of courtesies and compliments. In this kind of thing Louis XVIII. had certainly the advantage; the Emperor of Russia had too much sense of the becoming to appear to give lessons to the old king, and the king in turn was of too flexible and intelligent a nature to set himself in opposition to the Czar.'

Talleyrand had carefully arranged his part before his first meeting with Louis XVIII. :—

' M. de Talleyrand attracted much notice amongst the crowds of courtiers. People were curious to see how he would present himself and be received. It was supposed that he would be engaging, supple, artful, a flatterer; he chose a wholly different part. He was cool, serious, and made no kind of advances; in short, like a man who had no pardon to ask, and who wanted no assistance. He tried to bring his wit and intelligence into accord with the mind of the king, and was facile on every question of the time.'

A day or two was given up to rejoicings before entering on the grave questions of the settlement of France and peace with Europe. M. de Vitrolles does justice to the conciliatory attitude of the two sovereigns who were still the real masters of Paris.

' The allied sovereigns led in Paris the life of mere private gentlemen, with no affectation of power and none of the pomp of royalty. They had refused to occupy the royal palaces, the Tuileries, the Luxembourg, and even the Palais Royal—simple good taste, in marked contrast with the arrogant vanity of Bonaparte, who, in Vienna, in

Berlin, and at Moscow, trampled underfoot the abodes of kings as
though to enhance his exploits. They often walked out without any
distinctive dress, and without an escort, as if to remove from the eyes
of the people of Paris the signs of defeat, and they received their
reward. Popular favour welcomed them in the streets where they
were recognised by shouts and *vivats ;* they were loudly applauded at
the theatres; and when they were expected there songs were sung in
their honour, the exaggerated language of which surprised us.'

During the brief regency of the Comte d'Artois M. de
Vitrolles had contrived to secure a post which, he believed,
would give him immense influence. The Secretary of State
in Napoleon's Council was the interpreter of the Emperor's
commands and his intermediary with the remaining ministers ; and in the case of officials, who were merely clerks to
register the will of a despotic master, the position made
M. de Bassano supreme. M. de Vitrolles had obtained this
important place ; Louis XVIII. had allowed him to keep it,
and—for his estimate of himself was prodigious—he probably aspired to play the part of Maret among the ministers of the king. This ascendency, however, was not
possible in the case of the parliamentary rule which was
to form the new constitution of France; at the instance of
Talleyrand and other councillors, M. de Vitrolles was by
degrees deprived of his more invidious and vexatious functions; and, as the result, there were frequent scenes of
bickering between himself and his colleagues, who regarded
him with suspicious distrust. He continued, however, in the
Royal Council, though as an observer rather than an active
minister; and the account he gives of the conduct of the
king and his government during the months that followed
is full of interest and very suggestive. The views and
thoughts of the *émigré* noble show how little, like all his
class, he understood the signs of the times, and the real
bearing of events before him. What France most required
in 1814 was a large-minded and able ruler, who would accept
frankly the constitutional *régime* on which the nation had set
its heart, and a government which would completely secure
the interests created since 1789, and above all would sternly
restrain the excesses and folly of the extreme Royalists.
Some of these conditions Louis XVIII. fulfilled : he was
not opposed to the control of the Chambers, and did not
dream of dispensing with them; but his exalted notions of
his divine right, and the associations that surrounded his
throne, made him out of accord with the national sympathies;
and he was so irresolute, weak, and timid, that he was in no

sense a capable sovereign.   As for his Government, it was a
mere junta, without unity or essential strength; it had not
the cordial support of the Chambers, or any real hold on
the mass of the people; and if it did not expressly conspire against the settlement and distribution of property
which had been effected by the Revolution, it certainly allowed it to be called in question, and it was weak enough
not to punish the insolence of the nobles and priests who
clamoured against it.   These things, however, could not
occur to the prejudiced mind of M. de Vitrolles; and in his
estimate of Louis XVIII. and his rule, during the first period
of the Restoration, he is wrong alike in his praise and censure.   He extols the absolutist notions of the king, and his
exaggerated conception of French royalty; but, though he
is not blind to the serene insouciance and indifference of
the aged monarch, he blames this chiefly because it encouraged the Chambers to interfere with prerogative.   As
for the government of Louis, it was, no doubt, weak; but
its weakness chiefly consisted in this—that it did not possess
the despotic force of the empire, and that it did not give
full scope to the fierce passions and extravagant hopes of
the Counter-revolution.

M. de Vitrolles, like most of the old French noblesse,
regarded England with special dislike; and the Memoirs
contain a curious passage, in which the author, with characteristic arrogance, lectured Castlereagh on our 'rapacious
'ambition.'   It is remarkable, however, that M. de Vitrolles
was less indignant than most Frenchmen at the settlement
of the Continent at Vienna; the Royalist party was not sorry
if Europe destroyed the abhorred work of the Revolution,
even at the expense of France.   The Memoirs record, at
considerable length, the discussions through which the well-
known Charter of 1814 was arranged and perfected; and
these throw fresh light on the Bourbon councils.   M. de
Vitrolles, who had had a hand in preparing the celebrated
Manifesto of St. Ouen, was much displeased at not being
employed in making the new constitution of France; but
the king, who really wished the Charter to be a comprehensive and liberal measure—it being conceded that it was a
gift of royalty—quickly put aside the offers of a partisan
whose ideas of political reform for France were partly those
of a noble of *ancien régime* and partly those of the imperial
régime.   Louis XVIII. and his cabinet were sincere in desiring that France should be governed by a parliamentary
system like that of England; but their political experience

was so limited, that they failed to perceive the real securities for constitutional liberty. For instance, they had not grasped the principle which has made the House of Commons supreme; and they gravely argued that the ministers of the Crown could retain office and carry out a policy against the expressed will of the popular Chamber. M. de Vitrolles protested against a doctrine which would have reduced the Chamber of Deputies to the level of a Tudor House of Commons; but probably he was chiefly influenced by the traditional jealousy of the old Parlement men towards the Beds of Justice of the ancient monarchy:—

'I said that this principle that ministers could continue to perform their functions in defiance of a distinct majority against them was not admissible; since another principle had been adopted, its consequences must be accepted. No law existed in England to compel ministers to resign when a majority of either House had pronounced against them, but this usage had become established as a necessary consequence of the constitutional system, and it followed from this that a minister could no longer direct the affairs of the nation or sustain the rights of the Crown when he had lost the confidence of the Chamber.'

The enthusiasm which greeted the Bourbon princes had given place to distrust and aversion before the beginning of 1815. No government, perhaps, however able, could have wholly prevented this change of sentiment; in the case of a people proverbially fickle, the hot fit would have led to the cold; and if the Restoration brought peace with it, it involved the loss of national glory and power. But the favouritism and weakness of the king and his Government, and the short-sighted violence of the extreme Royalists, had united the interests and feelings of Frenchmen in hostility to the restored monarchy. The army, wounded where it was most sensitive, was eager to overturn the throne; the middle classes, exposed everywhere to the insolence of a privileged caste, were discontented and in a sullen mood; and the mass of the nation, whose dearest rights depended upon the undisturbed permanence of an order of things on all sides assailed, and not firmly upheld by the Government, was irritated and alarmed in the highest degree. M. de Vitrolles, as we have said, was unconscious of the main causes of this state of affairs, but he has indicated one cause of the general sentiment; and this might, even now, be observed by Frenchmen, though it is not flattering to the national character. France had flung herself at the feet of the Bourbons; she had hailed Louis as her lord and master; nay, she had thought so little of her legitimate rights that, without a murmur, she had allowed the king to set at nought the conditions imposed even by the Senate on the Comte d'Artois, and had accepted her Charter from the royal hands, not as the carrying out of a national compact, but as an extraordinary concession of royal bounty. Had the nation been less unwise and compliant, had it shown more self-respect and firmness, the government would not have dared to connive, as it certainly did, at the reckless language and conduct of its extreme partisans ; the sacerdotal and feudal factions would not have gone the full length of extravagance ; and not improbably a fierce reaction of national opinion would not have occurred. Undoubtedly there is truth in the following remarks :—

'The confidence inspired by this universal and eager loyalty, unchecked as it was by resistance where it might have been expected, was a source of errors and a snare for the Restoration. We accepted these evidences of devotion as though they were wholly sincere ; we believed they were deserved ; we did not foresee a change in a contrary direction. We thought that we were as assured of the good faith of others and of the support of public opinion as we were of our own conscientious desire to do good ; in a word, we did not stand on our guard against what was to come. How could we anticipate a revolution in the minds of men, and the extraordinary changes it brought with it ? If, instead of this chorus of unanimous welcome which flattered and misled us, we had encountered from the first moment the hostile parties, the open opposition that usually attends a transfer of power, the king's government would have been more on its guard.'

France was in this disturbed and critical state when Napoleon embarked on the bold enterprise which crowned the wonders of his eventful career. M. de Vitrolles, who bore the telegraphic message, describes how the king received the intelligence that the exile had landed on the beach of Cannes :—

'His eyes rested on the paper much longer than was necessary to read its contents, he then threw it on the table.

' " You do not know what is in the message ? " he said.

' " No, Sire, I am in complete ignorance."

' " It informs me," he said, in a voice that disclosed no emotion, " that Bonaparte has landed on the coast of Provence." '

The Comte d'Artois at first treated the news as not of particular moment :—

' I went without stopping, and myself opened the door of the closet of Monsieur, when an usher behind me, astonished at my distracted look, said that Monsieur was not at home, he was at vespers.

' " At vespers ! at vespers ! " I said to myself, and began walking alone in the great reception-room of the Pavillon Marsan. " How can a man be at vespers in circumstances like these? James II. lost his kingdom for a mass; will these princes lose theirs for vespers? "

'I waited nearly half an hour in a state of unspeakable impatience. I had brought myself, however, to make an excuse for Monsieur and his vespers, in the belief that probably he was unaware of the tremendous news, for even he had not been excepted from the secresy the king and I had mutually agreed to.

' " Still," I said to myself, " secresy in the case of Monsieur—it is impossible ! "

'I was in this state when the prince returned followed by his brilliant *entourage.*

' " Come in, come in," he said to me, as he opened the door of his closet.

'I followed : as soon as I found myself alone with him, I tried to read in his eyes if he had been informed of the great news, and at first I judged that he had not. I did not say a word.

' " Well," he remarked, " have you brought us any news of our travellers? Have you any letters from Bordeaux? "

'I replied, " No," and then hesitated, feeling a difficulty in speaking about that which filled my thoughts should the king not have told him. On the other hand I could speak of nothing else.

' " Monsieur," at last I said with hesitation, " has not seen the king since mass? "

' " Yes, I have,—by the bye," he suddenly remarked, " what is your opinion about the news of the landing? " '

Even Soult was at first surprised and incredulous, and believed for a time that Italy was the real objective of his old commander. A very able man, but a soldier only, Soult was ignorant of the real state of opinion in France at this crisis, and never understood the astonishing daring and profound insight of Napoleon's genius :—*

'I held the despatch open before the marshal's eyes. . . . The expression of his face was what was to be expected—he was amazed, and even incredulous. . . . He thought it probable that the exile of Elba was seeking to reach Italy through a pass in our mountains . . . that he wished to see what would be the effect of his presence on the theatre of his former victories.'

M. de Vitrolles, quick to recognise facts, endeavoured to rouse the king and his brother out of this dangerous and serene indifference. It was owing to his exertions, so at least he says, that the Comte d'Artois set off for Lyons

---

* In our last article on M. de Vitrolles' work we pointed out that Soult disapproved of Napoleon's strategy in 1814. There is reason to believe that he equally disapproved of the Emperor's plan of campaign in 1815 ; certainly he served as if his heart was not in his work ; he made a singularly inefficient chief of the staff.

to endeavour to arrest the advance of Napoleon, and that Soult despatched Macdonald in the same direction. M. de Vitrolles also contrived that the Duc d'Orléans, suspected by the high Royalist party, should accompany his cousin and leave Paris. He gives us this account of his parting with the Duc; but we have little doubt the sketch is a caricature:—

'The Duc d'Orléans stopped me, and made such low bows that to return them would have been impossible.

'"Monsieur de Vitrolles," he then said, with a trembling voice, "are we to go alone with Monsieur?"

'My face—and I am not in the habit of composing it—no doubt wore an expression of amazement as I made answer.

'"No, Monseigneur; the Minister of War has made a list of the generals who are to lead the troops, and Marshal Macdonald should be even now on his way to take his command under the order of Monsieur."

'At these words the Duc d'Orléans seized my hand and squeezed it.

'"Ah!" he exclaimed, "you restore me to life!"'

M. de Vitrolles, indeed, by his own account, was the only one of the royal advisers who showed decision or had a rational plan. He insisted that the king should disband the army by a vote of the Chambers; that a large royalist force should be formed from volunteers and National Guards, and that funds should be raised for these purposes. It would have been impossible, however, to break up an army, already ripe for universal mutiny, and conscious of its overwhelming strength; as for volunteers and National Guards, they were scarcely forthcoming even in Paris, disgusted with the Bourbon *régime*, though not disposed to welcome Napoleon; and money was certainly not to be had when the throne of Louis XVIII. was tottering. We may dismiss these grandiose fancies, but there was more sense possibly in another project—insisted on by the bold man of action— that the king should raise his standard in the South and West, should summon their loyal people to arms, and should seek assistance from England by sea. The Cabinet, however, was lukewarm or hostile:—

'The opinion of the ministers was that the plan was a fine one, but too vast. Beugnot and Dessolles were the most disposed to support it. The first, indeed, requested those who were listening without answering to pay attention. The Abbé Montesquiou alone opposed my project vehemently. Such a notion, he contended, would ruin the king by giving his conduct a Vendéan complexion; the whole of France would be alienated; the king of La Vendée would not be, and would never become, the king of France.'

The attitude of the king at this crisis seems to have been one of studied inertness. Except to answer the Chambers he did scarcely anything; and he followed his ministers' advice, and his own wishes, in quitting the throne and crossing the frontier. All this was not the contemptible weakness M. de Vitrolles assumes it to have been. Louis XVIII. firmly believed that Europe would be obliged to secure his crown, and had little faith in his own power or in that of his party to maintain his government; and he rightly thought that the Bourbon cause would not be promoted by civil war. Besides, he had resolved to take no course without the support of the great Bodies of the State; this was his notion of constitutional duty; and as the Chambers effected nothing, he waited on them and remained inactive. We can understand why he bore himself thus; yet he shows badly beside his mighty adversary, and he did not display the high qualities of a king. M. de Vitrolles thus glances at his conduct at this time :—

' It was not from the king that great resolutions were to be expected. According to his conception of royalty, they were no affairs of his. . . . During the first days that followed the descent of Napoleon, he reassured himself, believing that the consequences would be averted. But when the enemy had advanced beyond Lyons, he passed two or three days of uneasiness. . . . After this, he had made up his mind and consented to submit to circumstances, whatever they might be, with the most sublime indifference. His serenity was quite of a piece with his royal attitude.'

M. de Vitrolles describes how the king received an account of the critical state of Lyons just before Napoleon's triumphant entry, and when the defection of Labédoyère had revealed the temper of the army in revolt:—

' The king was so corpulent that he filled the width of the camp-bed, and seemed to exceed it ; a white nightcap was on his head, and he looked like a colossal child. He made me sit by his side, and told me to read the letter of his brother. . . . The king listened without apparent emotion, but evidently it was an effort. He desired me to write an answer, but, as well as I recollect, he said nothing of importance.'

While his enemy was advancing with a giant's strides, the king was trifling with phrases in his speech to the Chambers. The following is very characteristic :—

' I was struck with the words, " he is coming to light up among us the horrors of civil war."
' " Horrors," I said aside to Blacas, " do not burn."
' " What do you say ? " remarked the king, interrupting himself.

'A little embarrassed by my criticism, I made no answer. Blacas explained what I had said.

'"He is right," said the king; and he substituted the words " torches of civil war." '

The Cabinet, according to M. de Vitrolles, was nearly as inactive as the king himself. The ministers sought votes from the willing Chambers; but they had no policy or distinct aim, though it should be said that, after the defection of Ney, the cause of the Bourbons was for the moment lost. The Abbé Montesquiou had nothing to propose but resignation in the last resort.

'To-day we have a higher mission to perform. We must abandon personal considerations which might blind us, and acknowledge that all of us, while in office, are of no use as a means to preserve for France her legitimate monarchy; the last and only service we can render to the Crown is to recognize this fact, and to place the interests of the king in hands more capable to maintain them than ours.'

As has often happened in similar crises, especially in France, in this century, men of the highest station proved themselves capable of the most selfish and basest acts. General Maison was a very distinguished soldier, illustrious for his late defence of Flanders. General Dessolles, one of the ablest lieutenants of Moreau, was at this time a minister. Yet each of these worthies, in their master's peril, demanded hard cash as the price of their services. Where now, alas! is the France of Bayard?

'They declared that, in this situation, they would be obliged to have recourse to the munificence of the king. M. de Blacas replied, in the most polite language, that they could not entertain a doubt of the gratitude of the king, who would know how to appreciate their services and loyalty. But he kept within generalities that did not suit them. General Maison broke in with that cynicism that marked his character. "You perceive," he said to General Dessolles, "he pretends not to understand us; we must speak out plainly. You must make up your mind," added he, turning to M. de Blacas, "either not to reckon on our assistance, or to pay each of us 200,000 francs." '

The most characteristic feature of the time, however, was the conduct of the *entourage* of the court, of the 'friends' of the king, and the Comte d'Artois. Exasperated, alarmed, and losing their heads, they scented everywhere treason in the air; charged Baron Louis, a thoroughly upright minister, with applying the revenue in Napoleon's interest; and denounced Masséna, the governor of Provence, who, ever since his campaign in Portugal, had been under the imperial ban, as countenancing his old master's adventure. As for Soult, certainly still faithful, he was not admitted into the king's presence without the permission of the royal favourite ; and M. de Vitrolles declares that M. de Blacas had this extraordinary conversation with him :—

' " What is the use of all your reasoning ? It does not convince me. I must have an explanation with the marshal, and if he does not reply to everything in a satisfactory way, I have his dismissal in my pocket."

' " Bah ! " I exclaimed ; " have you already arranged with the king about it ? "

' " I have his dismissal in my pocket, I tell you. Would you like to see it ? "

' Upon this he drew a tolerably large pistol from his pocket.

' " Ah, ah ! " I said. " Come now, you are joking."

' " Indeed, I am not," he answered, in a half-heroic, half-comical tone.'

The terror of the partisans of the court gave birth, too, to the wildest projects. This crazy suggestion, M. de Vitrolles assures us, was also an emanation from the brain of the most trusted of the advisers of the king :—

' M. de Blacas seriously proposed to the Council that the king should quietly await the arrival of the Emperor ; and, when made aware that Napoleon was a few miles from Paris, that he should enter an open carriage with the first gentleman of the bedchamber, the captain of the bodyguard, and himself, Blacas. The carriage was to be escorted by the Chamber of Peers and the Chamber of Deputies on horseback. All the *cortège* was to advance to meet the Emperor, and to ask him what he was coming for. Perhaps his notion was that Bonaparte, finding an answer difficult, would retreat ! I did not amuse myself by discussing this plan, which had been submitted to the king before it was laid before the ministers. I merely said that one essential feature seemed wanting ; the procession should be preceded by an Archbishop of Paris, carrying the Holy Sacrament, like St. Martin of Tours, going in advance of the King of the Visigoths.'

The events of a period still distant were to show how absurd was the following plan proposed by the shallow and luckless Marmont, and justly ridiculed by our keen-witted author :—

' The marshal presented a memorial to the king, recommending that his Majesty should remain at the Tuileries. He pledged himself to defend the palace for six weeks. To sustain a siege, he did not require more than the king's household troops and a few other regiments. He thought that Bonaparte would be perplexed and troubled in attacking the aged monarch, even in the midst of Paris. I discussed this project with the king, and showed that it was quite irrational. In fact, the Emperor would take up his abode at the Luxembourg ; he would invest the Tuileries, and isolate it from the rest of the city ; he would lay hands on the machinery of administration, and would, without difficulty, cause himself to be obeyed in Paris, and throughout France. Then, when the provisions in the palace should have been exhausted, and the besieged were reduced to extremities, the king would be obliged to capitulate, or rather to surrender at discretion. Everything would pass off with perfect decorum. An aide-de-camp of the Emperor would hand the sovereign, the princes, and all the royal family into the best court carriages, would accompany them in the most polite fashion, and would lead them across the frontier.'

If M. de Vitrolles is to be believed, the marshal, at the last moment, urged the necessity of a *coup d'état*, which would concentrate military power in himself, and make M. de Vitrolles a civilian dictator :—

'It was essential to carry off M. de Blacas that very night. All precautions had been taken, and the affair was easy enough. . . . This obstacle having been removed, the king should be made to see how necessary it was that authority should be centralised in the existing extraordinary state of things, and no one was to mind any objections he might urge as to the means. Next day, the "Moniteur" should publish the appointment of the Baron de Vitrolles as first minister, and the appointments made by him, and Marshal Marmont was to be made commander-in-chief by land and sea, with full control over military affairs.'

The reply of M. de Vitrolles was very much to the point :—

'The troops would not obey you for twenty-four hours, and you would give them a complete excuse to justify their defection. And if you were alive in three or four days—a doubtful contingency—you would see Bonaparte enter Paris, lament the misfortunes of the old king, a victim of an odious act of treason, pretend to be his avenger, and hang the traitors. Neither you nor I would be able to prevent such a consummation.'

Louis XVIII. preserved his demeanour of calm indifference to the last moment, and made his exit from Paris in this fashion :—

'As I was taking my departure at nine o'clock, the king sent for Marshal Marmont in command of the king's household troops; and, maintaining the most profound secret on the journey he was about to make, his Majesty, with great coolness, wrote an order to the marshal, on a little piece of paper, to "transport the king to St. Denis," reserving for the present further directions.'

It is unnecessary to contrast the dull apathy, the distracted councils, and the half-witted projects of the Bourbons and their affrighted courtiers, with the astonishing energy, the decided purpose, and the admirable adaptation of means to ends that characterised the advance of Napoleon. The southern provinces were hostile to him, and it is a

mistake to suppose that the mass of the nation was eager
to welcome him as a deliverer.   But he turned, so to speak,
the obstacle of the south by his wonderful march through
the hills of Dauphiné, and finding France disgusted with
the existing *régime*, he fascinated her, and won the people
over by the splendour of his unparalleled enterprise.   Nor
would he, perhaps, have gained the army, ready as it was
to revolt from the Bourbons, but for his extraordinary
boldness and self-confidence.   History, perhaps, can show
no more striking example of military sympathy with commanding genius.   M. de Vitrolles, of course, was blind to
these truths; he simply ascribes the success of the exile
to treason, defection, and the imbecile weakness of Louis
XVIII. and a worthless Cabinet; and he plainly intimates
that, had he had his own way, Napoleon could never have
reached the Tuileries.   In his sketch of the march from
Cannes to Grenoble, he recounts an anecdote very suggestive
of his exquisite sense of his own importance:—The emperor,
he assures us, on reaching Sisteron, instead of addressing
himself to the urgent task of mastering a pass of extreme
difficulty, when a few hours' delay might have proved fatal,
turned aside to look at the château of the De Vitrolles, and
let fall these significant words, which, we venture to say, he
did not utter:—'There then,' he exclaimed, 'there is the
' château of the celebrated Baron de Vitrolles!'

The fussy meddling of M. de Vitrolles and his avowed
contempt of the court and its conduct were naturally dis-
pleasing to the king and the ministers.   At the moment of
his departure for Lille, Louis XVIII. sent for his officious
counsellor, and commissioned him to promote the royal
interests, by all 'means in his power, in the South and West,
inviting him, in a word, to carry out the policy of which he
had been the passionate advocate.   This was probably a
device to put out of the way a troublesome and not too
discreet a censor; and it was a piece of malice to order
M. de Vitrolles to attempt to work out his own projects,
when obviously the occasion had passed.   The king parted
with him with his usual nonchalance:—

'I found the king calm, and as if he was leading his ordinary life.
He held a little note, like a visiting card, in two fingers.

'"You are to go to Bordeaux and to Toulouse," he said.   "You
will act as may be best for my service.   You will give this letter to my
niece; tell her to defend Bordeaux as long as she can, and as soon as
she cannot, she is to act like myself." . . .

'I expressed my regret that I had no instructions.

'"Mitte sapientem et nihil dicas," was the king's only reply.'

M. de Vitrolles felt it was a mere forlorn hope; but he addressed himself bravely to the task before him. He persuaded Gouvion St. Cyr, near Orleans, to endeavour to defend the course of the Loire; had an interview with Madame at Bordeaux, and fired the hopes of the royalist city; and set off almost alone for Toulouse, where he hoped to combine the southern provinces and make a diversion against Napoleon. He displayed no ordinary resource and energy, seized the revenues and the administrative service, made a vigorous attempt to enrol volunteers, and sent messengers across the Pyrenees to invoke the aid of the Spanish Bourbons. But the Empire had been already restored. The Government in Paris, as has always happened, soon imposed its will on the South as elsewhere, and M. de Vitrolles' efforts were vain and too late.

'It was not the imperial army that attacked us, it was the mail, bringing us the official correspondence from Paris, which informed the prefects, the receivers-general, and the administrative departments, of the names of the new ministers and their superiors. . . . The poison soon began to produce its effects: the Emperor was acknowledged, the tricolour replaced the white flag, and all this was accomplished without a struggle or resistance.'

The few regiments stationed in the south had been quiescent during these eventful days, and, aware that all would be soon over, had generally maintained a peaceable attitude. But at the first orders despatched from Paris they summarily put resistance down. In truth, resistance was not really made, and the lieutenant of the king, as he styled himself, was easily arrested by a few soldiers on a charge of provoking a civil war in France. M. de Vitrolles describes how he was taken prisoner, the prelude of the complete submission of Toulouse:—

'General Laborde (a Peninsular veteran) took a chair by my side, and sate down, his staff remaining standing.
'"You must not be surprised, Monsieur le Baron, that as you have so bravely defended your cause, we shall uphold ours."
'I interrupted him.
'"General, I request that you make no comparisons. An hour ago our duties were the same; we were under the same flag, and I have not changed mine."'

M. de Vitrolles was detained at Vincennes and the Abbaye during the memorable period of the Hundred Days. He was so great a personage, in his own opinion, that he expected the fate of the Duc d'Enghien. But Napoleon, engaged in a contest with Europe, did not think of making such a man a victim. Madame de Vitrolles brought the prisoner the news of Waterloo. How strangely their conversation sounds, as we measure that event with the eye of history :—

'Madame de Vitrolles spoke very fast, and was in the habit of blundering about proper names.

' "Marshal Grichoux," she said, "has had his leg shot off."

' I burst out laughing, and this put her out of patience.

' "Had any man such a disposition as yours ! I bring you the most joyful news—the deliverance of France, your safety, your life—and you fix upon a word that has been mispronounced. You will always be the same ! " '

Through the good offers of Marshal Oudinot, M. de Vitrolles easily obtained his release. By this time Napoleon had fallen; the Chambers, never sincere or loyal, rising wildly against him in the hour of danger; and Fouché had been made the head of a Provisional Government charged with the defence of the national interests. The details contained in this part of the Memoirs are not the least interesting passages of the work, and throw a vivid light on the history of the time. Fouché, playing a game of deceit and intrigue, as had been his habit throughout life, addressed himself to M. de Vitrolles, as he was about to set off from Paris for Ghent, and assured the author that he was, even now, labouring with all his might in the interests of the king :—

' "You will see the king," he remarked, "and you will inform him that we are working for his cause; even if we cannot go straight to him, we shall reach him at last. Just now, we must go through with Napoleon II., and probably, after him, with the Duc d'Orléans; but we shall settle on the king at last."

' I could scarcely believe what I heard.

' "What ! " I exclaimed. "Is that your game? This unhappy Crown of France has not been dragged enough through the mire ! You wish to pass it from one head to another—and what heads ! "

' "I do not say," replied the head of the Provisional Government, "that that is exactly what I wish, but I foresee it will happen. I have already, in a measure, put difficulties in the way of Napoleon II. as a sovereign. Yesterday we were discussing in whose name acts of State were to run. Carnot observed, 'Why, plainly in the name of Napoleon II.' 'Not so,' I retorted; 'they must bear the name of the French people.' The fool assented." '

Always faithful to his ideas of duty, M. de Vitrolles discerned in these overtures an opportunity of serving the king. Fouché readily came to an understanding with him : he was to remain in Paris, and to have full liberty to corre- ̶ ̶ ̶ ̶nd with Louis XVIII., and to do all he could for the royal interest; and as for his safety, he was to run the same risks as the crafty head of the Provisional Government. M. de Vitrolles once more in his proper sphere—that of bold conduct and clever intrigue—proved of real use to the Bourbon cause, and certainly facilitated the march of events which led to the Restoration of 1815. With his wonted perception of present facts, he moderated the ardour of the extreme partisans, who wished to proclaim the king at once and to array numbers of loyal volunteers. Such a premature movement, he rightly judged, had scarcely a solid chance of success, and possibly it would defeat its author's purpose by provoking the wrath of the jealous Chambers. M. de Vitrolles, too, served the Bourbons well by keeping a watchful eye on Fouché, who, according to him, was still scheming for Napoleon II. or the Duc d'Orléans; though he claims too much for himself in this matter; for certainly Fouché gave up this game when made aware of the real objects of the allies after the success of Waterloo. M. de Vitrolles, however, proved most efficient in his efforts to aid his master's cause by seconding, at this critical juncture, the crooked and base, though ingenious, policy of the man whom fortune had for the moment raised to the head of affairs in Paris. Fouché by this time had become convinced that the Restoration could not be avoided; and his conduct was directed to making the way for the return of the Bourbons as smooth as possible, and to placing his own services in so clear a light as to secure the favour of Louis XVIII. Afraid, however, to confront the Chambers—almost to a man opposed to the Bourbons,—or incapable of taking a straightforward course,—he thought that he would best attain his ends not by open negotiation with the allies and the king, but by practising on Davoust, the Minister of War, and the chief of the wrecks of the French armies; and he calculated that, could he gain over the marshal and obtain from him an official statement that Paris could not withstand an attack, and that France must submit to the conqueror's terms, he would not only possess the means of leading the Chambers to accept Louis, but would escape the responsibility in the eyes of France of consenting to an ignominious peace. The first thing, therefore, was to sound Davoust; and Fouché permitted M. de Vitrolles to undertake the delicate mission.

The passages that followed are very curious, and have never been fully revealed before. M. de Vitrolles, through the aid of his friend Oudinot, addressed himself to the Prince of Eckmühl; and, thinking first of his master's interests, urged the Minister of War to declare for the king, and to bring the army over to the royal standard. Davoust, who, as is already known, had for some days been advising Fouché to treat with the Bourbons, sent the following not unbecoming reply:—

'Marshal Oudinot brought me, next day, eight or nine articles, written on a sheet of paper with a margin, from the hand of the Minister of War. He laid down conditions for the recognition of the king. In the first place, a complete amnesty should be given for all the defections of the Hundred Days, all existing rights were to be maintained, and all ranks and pensions of the army were to be preserved. Next, the king should govern in the interests and ideas of the nation, and should forego every kind of preference for the Royalists and the Vendéan party; in a word, nothing was omitted, except the question of the tricolor, of which he did not speak, no doubt because he had forgotten all about it. The last article declared that the marshal asked nothing for himself except a military command, if war with the enemies of France should become necessary.'

An opening with Davoust had thus been effected, though the marshal, when secretly urged by Fouché, had evaded giving the official report which was to justify the schemer's conduct, and sent only an ambiguous reply. M. de Vitrolles, accordingly, had two interviews of a singular kind with the Minister of War :—

' I went under the protection of Marshal Oudinot. I found Davoust stretched on a mattress, and just sufficiently covered to be decent.

' I complained of the inutility of the letter addressed to the Duc d'Otrante. He defended it at first as amply sufficient; but when I proposed that he should employ the language suggested by Fouché, the marshal, turning about on his couch, and making strange movements with his legs and arms, offered all kinds of objections. He declared that he was afraid to compromise himself with the Chambers, and seemed greatly alarmed.

' "Really, gentlemen," I exclaimed, addressing myself to both marshals, " I can scarcely say how you surprise me ; you, who are accustomed boldly to confront the dangers of war, tremble at the pen of a lawyer stuck behind his ear. . . . What could the Chambers do were you to close them to-morrow, and to make the army proclaim the king, with the acclaim of Paris and France ? "'

While Fouché was thus intriguing with Davoust, and the marshal, anxious to restore the king, but suspecting treachery and not knowing whom to trust, was hesitating to take a decided part, M. de Vitrolles found unexpected allies of the Bourbon cause in another quarter. The extreme Jacobin party, kept down by every government of France for years, had raised its head after the defeat of Waterloo ; and, forming its masses into armed bands, had offered to make Napoleon its chief, to put down Fouché and the *régime* of the Chambers, and to inaugurate a crusade against the allies on the pattern of that of 1793. The fallen emperor having rejected these overtures, its leader actually turned to the royalists, and, in their hatred of the existing government, proposed to lend their aid to restore the king if the royal favour were extended to them. M. de Vitrolles plunged into this intrigue also, and had an interview with two or three old Terrorists at the house of a great royalist noble. Merlin de Thionville made a curious speech :—

'Disgusted with the tyranny of the Emperor, they had welcomed the return of the Royal House, as though it was to be the beginning of justice and lawful liberty. They had gone to the king with full hearts; he himself had had interviews with M. de Talleyrand; he had asked and obtained permission to form a body of irregulars, whom he would have employed in the service of the king. . . . And what, after the Restoration, had been the result? They had been thrust aside like scabby sheep; every door had been closed to them; in a word, they had been humiliated in every way. Notwithstanding all this, as they attributed these acts of injustice to M. de Talleyrand alone, they were still ready to attach themselves to the royal cause. In Paris they could dispose of 20,000 fédérés, and of the vast population of the faubourgs; they could direct these in the interests of the king, and could cause the gates of the capital to be opened to him.'

M. de Vitrolles replied in the vaguest terms, and declined to make specific engagements; but at last, vexed at being confounded with Talleyrand in a charge of ingratitude, hinted that a place might be possibly found for a revolutionist in the royal councils to represent and look after Jacobin interests. The answer was significant :—

'Merlin did not speak until after a moment's silence; the muscles of his face grew contracted.

'"Ah! I see how it is. . . . It is Fouché you are thinking of! What, Fouché!"

'He did not venture to accept or to repudiate a guarantee of the kind; but rage could be perceived in his face and his accent.'

Meantime, events were rapidly tending to a crisis in the affairs of France. The allied armies were approaching Paris, and the remains of the imperial forces (including Grouchy's intact divisions) were being collected around the capital. A terrible conflict was still possible, and the soldiery and the people of Paris were in a vindictive and troubled mood, that boded ill for the Provisional Government. The Chambers, too, feeling themselves powerless, were agitated, and with-

out a purpose ; but, with true instinct, they singled out
Fouché as the object of general distrust and suspicion.   The
veteran intriguer was in real danger, and although, according
to M. de Vitrolles, he had obtained the report he had sought
from Davoust as to the impossibility of defending Paris,
he hesitated to disclose it to the angry deputies, lest they
might see in it a clear proof of treason.   In this state of
things he bethought himself of sending M. de Vitrolles to
the allies' camp, with the twofold object of providing means
for his own safety and that of his colleagues, and making the
Restoration certain :—

'An hour after his message I was at the public office of the police.
Fouché was standing, shaving his beard, before a mirror hung to the
window.   I can scarcely express what a disagreeable spectacle was
presented by that weasel-like face, that negligent undress, and the
razor which he moved along his throat.   In spite of myself, I thought
of that instrument which, by his orders, had struck necks very different
from his own.

'He turned round for a moment.

'"We cannot take another step," he said, "unless you can obtain
an assurance that the allied armies will stay hostile operations and their
march on Paris, on the condition, of course, that the authority of the
king is to be recognised.   I have explained the affair to Marshal
Grouchy; he will accompany you to the head-quarters of Blücher
and Wellington; but no one but you can arrange the business." '

Davoust, as general-in-chief of the army, was necessarily
to concur in this overture, but, always careful not to commit
himself, Fouché sent him the vaguest possible message :—

'The letter which ought to have contained the instructions of the
Government to the Minister of War, and to have authorised him to
open a conference with the generals of the allied armies, was a mere
piece of ambiguity.   It was nothing but a set of phrases on the necessity
of averting the dangers that threatened the capital; the thoughts were
concealed, not expressed.   I made serious remarks on the subject to
the Duc d'Otrante ; but he replied, with his customary levity, " Why,
what more should I write?   That is enough, since you will be the
bearer of the letter." '

Characteristically, Fouché thought it advisable to offer a
bribe to the allied generals :—

'Sums of money will be required; these people would have a right
to them if they occupied Paris.   You must give two million francs to
the English, and fifteen hundred thousand francs to the Prussians.'

M. de Vitrolles, as usual with his friend Oudinot, set off
to the headquarters of Davoust.   The rude soldier, who had
always been for plain dealing with the allies and the king,

on reading Fouché's ambiguous letter, instinctively felt that he was being made a dupe, and at first refused to agree to anything. He was beginning, however, to lend an ear to the observations of M. de Vitrolles, when a singular incident suddenly brought the intended negotiations to a close. A deputation—sent by the Chambers to thank the army for its late services—having been admitted into Davoust's presence, the marshal in the course of his reply * incautiously blurted out that M. de Vitrolles was about to proceed to the allies' quarters, and that peace would probably be the consequence. A scene of passionate tumult followed. On hearing the name of one notorious as a royalist of extreme views, the members of the deputation, already haunted by the suspicions, so to speak, filling the air, broke out into indignant protests ; and the lieutenants, aides-de-camp, and staff of Davoust, who crowded the room, were equally vehement. The situation became so menacing that Oudinot and Grouchy quickly disappeared, the latter marshal (who had been profuse in loyal professions) being the first to go, and M. de Vitrolles was left alone to reason with a half-mad assembly. He showed remarkable courage and tact, but was overwhelmed with abuse and threats :—

'A general thrust his fist in my face. " The faults of the Bourbons, sir ! " he exclaimed ; " they have been guilty of much more than faults." . . . A young lieutenant-general, M. Dejean, who owed his promotion to the government of the king, unable to penetrate the group around us, kept screaming out in infuriated language, " We will never submit to the Bourbons ! We had rather all perish than endure such disgrace." '

---

* It is very difficult to pronounce a positive opinion on the conduct of Davoust throughout this brief period. Charras represents him as a corrupt imperialist, half coerced, half cajoled by Fouché into accepting the Bourbons ; conniving at Fouché's intrigues, and finally betraying Paris to the allies. This criticism, however, is wholly unjust. The marshal, as we know from his own correspondence, advised, from the outset, that frank overtures should be made to the Bourbons ; but he had scarcely any part in Fouché's schemes, and evidently stood on his guard against him ; and as for betraying Paris, he declared that he was ready to fight the allies, but very sensibly pointed out that even a victory could not prevent the ultimate triumph of Europe. We very much question M. de Vitrolles' statement that Davoust gave Fouché a formal and personal assurance that Paris could not be defended. A Council of Marshals, including the great names of Masséna and Soult, did ; but not until the last moment, when Blücher's forces had crossed the Seine.

Guilleminot, a well-known Waterloo name, alone in the crowd preserved his senses :—

' The contrast between his demeanour and that of the other madmen caused me to interchange a few words with him ; this was the beginning of his fortune under the Restoration.'

Curiously enough, too, old Marshal Lefebvre, a veteran of 1793-4—who a few days afterwards stood alone in urging his colleagues to defend Paris—seemed to have been playing a double game :—

' On the side of the bystanders he appeared intensely hostile ; but as he turned towards me, he smiled and winked his eyes, as though to express his approval and to encourage me.'

. M. de Vitrolles escaped with difficulty, and repeated what had occurred to Fouché, convinced that his mission had failed for the time.   A characteristic interview followed :—

' Fouché, calm as an old soldier, inured to greater dangers, replied, coolly, " Well, that is excellent ; there you are in the midst of that camp ; you are planted there like a white flag ; what more could you desire ?   You have broken the ice.   That is a great deal."

' " Yes," I replied, " perhaps the ice has been broken, but it was nearly breaking on my head."

' " What matter ? " he said ; " the effect has been produced all the same."

' From what he informed me he had explained everything satisfactorily to the Deputies, who had asked him to account for his conduct.

' " They are such fools ! " he said, more than once.   We then did ample justice to the tact of the commander-in-chief and to the political courage of Marshals Grouchy and Oudinot, who had deserted me.'

Notwithstanding his boast of hoodwinking the Chambers, Fouché, nevertheless, thought it best to remove his royalist agent from the public gaze.   M. de Vitrolles remained a few days in concealment, and took no part in the ignominious scenes which ended in the capitulation of Paris, an unconditional and abject surrender.   When the Bourbon princes re-entered the capital, he was heartily welcomed by the Comte d'Artois ; but the king, who did not like him, was less effusive :—

' The expressions of the king were very gracious ; he said, in concluding, " Happy those who have suffered ; theirs is the kingdom of Heaven ! "

' This, however, was not a promise as regards an earthly kingdom.'

The greeting of Talleyrand was characteristic :—

' " Good morning, M. de Vitrolles," a sweet voice behind me murmured.

'It was M. Talleyrand. He took my hand with every expression of affection, and made use of the most gracious language.

' " It is not your fault that we see you here again; you will then always be prodigal of your life? But this must not be, so at least we think."

'A quarter of an hour afterwards I was talking to Monsieur in the middle of the salon, when M. de Talleyrand, leaving the piece of furniture on which he was leaning, came to me and took me by the hand.

' "Monsieur must know," he said, dwelling on the words, "that I am very fond of M. de Vitrolles, since his late unfortunate adventures." '

One of the first questions for the restored government was the position to be assigned to Fouché. A variety of causes had raised the schemer to an eminence he in no way deserved. He had rendered the allies good service, he had handed over Paris to the king, and he had deceived the Chambers with such success that he appeared to many of the thoughtless royalists the only personage able to control the forces of revolutionary France. M. de Vitrolles, however, tells us that Fouché had in fact little hope of much royal favour :—
' " I hope, at least," he said to me two or three times,
' " that, after what I have done, I may be allowed to remain
' peaceably in my own country." '

Be this as it may, the pretensions of Fouché were supported by the allies and their ministers, and by the great authority of the Duke of Wellington; and M. de Vitrolles thus describes the sentiments of his friends :—

' There was a universal cry to raise Fouché to the office of Minister of Police. He alone, it was said, could preserve the king from the designs of enemies, and fear, too, came to his aid. All, even to the Bailli de Crussol, an old captain of the bodyguard of Monsieur, a man of fixed principles and stiff in his opinions—all preached on the housetops that the safety of the king and the monarchy depended on Fouché.'

The indignation of M. de Vitrolles knew no bounds when he became aware that Fouché was to be made a minister, and that his own opinion had not been even asked. He made an angry protest, answered by Talleyrand in a different fashion from his wonted suavity :—

' Tell M. de Vitrolles that Lord Castlereagh will be here at once, and that I have no time to reply. We are about to sit down to table, and after dinner I shall accompany the Duc d'Otrante to St. Denis, where he will take the oath of office, in the presence of the king.'

M. de Vitrolles had several interviews with the Duke during the first days of the occupation of Paris ; indeed, his name

finds a place in more than one passage of the Supplementary
Despatches of Wellington. According to his own account,
he was the first Frenchman who interfered to prevent the
destruction of the Pont de Jena, threatened by Blücher. He
tells us the story :—

> 'Alexis de Noailles and I went to see the Comte de Goltz, the
> Prussian minister; he was not at home. We then called on the Duke
> of Wellington; we were told that after dining he had gone to the opera.
> M. de Noailles hesitated, and did not like going. I differed from him.
> I caused the door of the opera box to be opened, and there was the
> Duke of Wellington in company with the Comte de Goltz. I asked
> the Comte de Goltz if he was aware of what his officers were about to
> do. . . . The answer of the Comte was in accordance with the rudeness
> of his character and the spirit of revenge which animated the Prussians.
> The Duke of Wellington was more courteous, and said that an under-
> standing should be come to on the subject.'

M. de Vitrolles returned to his old office of Secretary of
State under the restored government. It was a season of
woe and ruin for France; the armies of Europe, spread
over her soil, exacted the vengeance of unchecked conquerors; and it was due only to the jealousies of the allies
that the provinces lost in the great war of 1870 were not
torn from her in 1815. Yet more fatal, perhaps, than
foreign oppression was the vindictive fury of her own
children. The royalist faction, incensed at the thought of
their own sufferings and their country's shame, rushed into
the excesses of the White Terror; and, not to speak of the
savage proscription of Ney and other distinguished names,
the partisans of the Bourbons were guilty of atrocious crimes
in the South and West. M. de Vitrolles, who, if not greatly
belied, encouraged the movement in different ways, passes
lightly over these terrible scenes ; just as true to the
peculiar spirit of his class, he has not a word of regret for
Waterloo, and he scarcely alludes to the second fall of
Napoleon. One of the first results of the extreme violence
of the Counter-revolution was to cause an outcry for the
dismissal of Fouché from the councils of the king ; and
Talleyrand gladly threw over a personage who, after a few
weeks of favour and power, became an object of general contempt and aversion. The crafty minister, M. de Vitrolles
informs us, addressed him thus on this critical subject, and
the following curious conversation took place :—

> ' I was leaving the minister's house one night, at about one o'clock,
> when the master called me back. He was leaning against a piece of
> furniture in his principal reception-room.

' " Do you know, M. de Vitrolles," he said, " that if it be the king's pleasure he can easily send away the Duc d'Otrante ? "

' I tried to discover from his face for what reason he held this language.

' " I tell you, the king can readily dismiss Fouché."

' " No doubt," I replied ; " the king can dismiss Fouché, as he can dismiss you or me. That is so obvious that you must mean something more in what you say."

' " You do not understand me ; I tell you the king can send away Fouché whenever he wishes it."

' " I understand that so well, that, since you will not explain, I will do so. I always opposed the admission of Fouché into the ministry, and I believe that sooner or later he will have to be removed. But three questions must be first settled—when and how is Fouché to be dismissed ? who is to be responsible ? and what will you do with Fouché when you have got rid of him ? "

' " I know nothing about all that," said M. de Talleyrand ; " but I do know that the king may dismiss Fouché if he likes ! " '

Fouché was made to understand what his fate was to be in a singular and very characteristic fashion :—

' Next day the council had risen ; it was at M. de Talleyrand's house. He was half sitting, upon his bureau, between the windows of the room. His lame leg hung down, and the other rested upon the floor. All the ministers had shut up their portfolios, some were seated, others standing about the round table, and I was in a great arm-chair between the door and the mantelpiece.

' " As for me, gentlemen," said M. de Talleyrand, in a voice that made itself heard, " I have the best place in the gift of the king at my disposal."

' " What place ? " said M. Pasquier, turning round.

' Prince Talleyrand then set forth the annoyances and humiliations that awaited the ministers compelled to treat with the allied sovereigns for the ransom of France. What, too, would be for a long time the position of our ambassadors with these Powers ? There was one country, one only, he added, where a minister of the king would possess all the advantages of his rank and enjoy real influence.

' " That minister," he remarked, after a pause, " would be the representative of France at the United States."

' The prince had scarcely uttered these last words when Fouché, who was sitting on the opposite side of the council table, and was furthest off, cast on me a look from his little glittering eyes, measuring me from head to foot, as though to accuse me of the attack that was being made upon him. I confess that on this occasion, and this only, he made me look down. M. de Talleyrand, in order to break the silence which had followed his speech, began to chattter about America.

' " It is such a fine country. Are you acquainted with that country, M. de Vitrolles ? I am ; I have travelled through it, I have lived there ; it is a noble land. It possesses rivers of a size unknown to us ;

for instance, the Potomac—nothing can be finer than the Potomac.
And then such magnificent forests, full of those trees some specimens
of which we have in greenhouses—what are they called ? "

' " Daturas," I observed.

' " Just so, forests of daturas."

' He entangled himself in the Potomac and the daturas, and one
could not understand what he was at. The ministers had soon gone,
one after the other, and I remained alone with the prince.

' " You are a strange personage," I said; " last night you seemed as
if you would not understand me, and now you go forward, though no
preparations are made."

' " Yes," he replied, " that is so; I thought it as well to throw a few
words beforehand as an essay; besides, I am about to wait on the king,
and we shall talk on the subject." '

The consummation was not long retarded :—

' It was I who, when the council broke up, usually gave the king
an account of what had been done. Nevertheless, when M. de Talleyrand attended I naturally yielded this duty to him. That evening
when I entered his closet the king exhibited a delight he could scarcely
restrain.

' " Do you know," he said, " M. de Talleyrand was here this
morning to propose to me that the Duc d'Otrante should be dismissed ? " '

The influences that caused the disgrace of Fouché soon
proved sufficient to overthrow the minister who a few weeks
before had appeared all powerful. The circumstances that
led to the fall of Talleyrand are already sufficiently known
to history;* but M. de Vitrolles adds a few particulars.
Talleyrand, undermined by intrigues at court, had endeavoured to obtain a pledge from the king of sincere support
in his difficult post when he was suddenly dismissed by
Louis XVIII. :—

' M. de Talleyrand, usually so skilful in adroit insinuation, had, no
doubt, thought that, on this occasion, a more peremptory tone ought to
be adopted; the king, who was not accustomed to this, became angry,
and, fixing his eyes on the ceiling, remained silent for an instant.

' " Well," at last he said, very quietly, " I shall, in that case, form
another ministry." '

The old statesman, who, whatever his faults, had admirably served the Bourbon cause, especially at Vienna in 1814,

---

* M. de Vitrolles does not mention that the disgrace of Talleyrand
was, in part, due to the influence of the Emperor Alexander, who had
never forgiven Talleyrand's attitude at the Congress of Vienna; but
there can be little doubt of the fact.

assumed his habitual air of indifference ; but he was justly indignant, and Europe with him :—

'M. de Talleyrand was dumbfounded. He especially feared that it should be supposed that he had fallen into a snare. He concealed under a show of studied insouciance his resentment at having fallen in so sudden, so unexpected, so unintelligible a way. The ministers of the allies and the sovereigns themselves, even those who least liked M. de Talleyrand, were disquieted at his removal. The king seemed like a ship without a rudder, and they tried to find out how we should replace the old diplomatist. Talleyrand spoke lightly, and almost jestingly, of the affront.

' "The king seems to have been only too happy to get rid of us," he said to me, in a mocking tone.'

. The fall at the same time, and through the same means, of the two leading men who, after deserting Napoleon in 1814-15, attained marked eminence in the Bourbon councils, induces us to make a few remarks. Talleyrand and Fouché had some common qualities : both were skilful pilots in troubled waters; both were supple, adroit, and versed in intrigue; both had few scruples and hard consciences; and both concealed ambition and a thirst for power under a calm, easy, and impassive demeanour. Yet the resemblance is superficial only, and it has been chiefly due to accidental circumstances that they have been often compared in history. Though trained to his calling in the worst of schools, Talleyrand was, in no doubtful sense, a statesman ; the ideas of the Revolution and the force of the empire never wholly perverted his fine intellect; and something of the moderation of the great churchmen who, at different times, have been supreme in politics, may be seen in the many attempts he made to restrain Napoleon's unwise ambition, and to uphold the just rights of the vanquished Continent. At Vienna, too, he displayed capacity and intelligence of a high order, and represented France with address and dignity; and, in 1815, he at least endeavoured to check the madness of the extreme Royalists, though his efforts ought to have been more decided. Talleyrand, therefore, many as his faults are, remains a great historical figure; and if time has almost effaced his work, he retains a claim on his country's gratitude, and he stands high among illustrious Frenchmen. Fouché, on the other hand, was a mere schemer, a creature of low intrigue and device, who never rose superior to self-interest; and on the one occasion when he had the chance, he signally proved that in the great game of politics he had little insight or real ability. If he had an idea in 1815, it

was that Europe might be induced to try the experiment of
the Empire again, and to place the crown of Napoleon I.
on the baby head of Napoleon II., as if the lessons of 1814
were nothing, and as if, after Waterloo, and the new arrangement of the map of Europe made at Vienna, any king
but a Bourbon for France was possible. As for his policy
after the Hundred Days, it was a specimen of mean craft
and cowardice ending in utter and disastrous failure. A real
statesman, as Siéyès observed, ought at this crisis either to
have urged the agitated Chambers to support Napoleon, and
to enable him to continue the war, or he ought to have
frankly made overtures to the Bourbons and the allies at
once, and endeavoured to obtain some kind of conditions for
the interests of his defeated country. Fouché never contemplated either course; but, chiefly thinking of his own
objects, and floating weakly on the tide of events, pursued
a game of intrigue and deceit which ended in the Restoration
—indeed the necessity of which he at last recognised, but
which placed France, the Chambers, and his own party at
the mercy of Europe and Louis XVIII., and that, too, after
a display of feebleness and of indecision in camp and in
council humiliating in the highest degree. The result was
that, although the allies, to whom his treachery had proved
useful, and a party among the vehement Royalists, who
looked only to their own triumph, contrived to place Fouché
in high office, and surrounded him with fictitious renown,
his real littleness was soon made evident; he was quickly
forgotten after his fall; and he is now only known as one
of those base natures occasionally raised to undeserved
eminence in the chances of a revolutionary time.

M. de Vitrolles continued to hold office for a time after
the fall of Talleyrand. The services he had lately rendered
had increased his influence in the royal councils; and,
though not liked by the king or the ministers, his position
gave him a good deal of authority. He made himself useful
in many ways to Louis XVIII. as a kind of companion; and
the old king, who was pleased with his wit and intelligence,
employed him in some affairs of importance, without giving
him his full confidence. His position at court appeared so
eminent that Talleyrand, he assures us, gravely asked if he
was not to succeed him as first minister; and Gouvion
St. Cyr, when Minister of War, was so irritated at the way
in which the king made some appointments through him,
that the marshal threatened to resign his office. The Duc
de Richelieu, when in Talleyrand's place, soon found out that

the undefined power and secret influence of M. de Vitrolles were unconstitutional and not to be borne; and Louis XVIII., at his minister's instance, dismissed his faithful emissary at a moment's notice. M. de Vitrolles thus describes how he parted with the king:—

'My only revenge was the extreme embarrassment of his Majesty, and the cowardly weakness he displayed when obliged to tell me what was to happen. He tried every turn of coquettish flattery; never was his look more gracious, or his language more sweet. From these signs I guessed the explanation he had so much difficulty in giving, and I endeavoured to make it easy for him. Instead of expressing surprise, of complaining, of entreating, I remained calm, and received my sentence with a smile on the lip, and with an almost insolent indifference.'

The retirement of M. de Vitrolles from office restored him to what had always been his proper sphere, and his true allegiance. He became one of the small junta of councillors who crowded the closet of the Comte d'Artois, and made the Pavillon Marsan the seat of a vehement Opposition, in the extreme royalist sense, to the Constitutional Government of France. His attitude was caused, in some degree, by personal disappointment and pique, for he cordially disliked MM. Decazes and Villéle, the ministers who followed the Duc de Richelieu; but he honestly thought parliamentary rule incompatible with the Bourbon monarchy, and pregnant with grave and increasing dangers. In 1818 he committed an act which brought him within the reach of the law, and exposed him to the wrath of a government eager to strike down a troublesome enemy. At the instance, he tells us, of a friend, he wrote a memorandum, of which the purport was to prove that France, under her existing rulers, was still in such an alarming state that the throne could not stand without the allied armies; and his friend gave the missive to an aide-de-camp of the Czar, with an assurance that it fell short of the truth. The "Secret Note," as it was called at the time, having gone the round of the continental cabinets, made a great impression in France and Europe; and the government of Louis, naturally incensed at the charge of incapacity alleged against it, denounced the author as chief of a plot to impair or subvert the royal authority. M. de Vitrolles was arrested and charged with a crime not widely removed from high treason; and though the evidence against him was not sufficient, he was loudly condemned in public opinion, was forsaken by most of his royalist friends, and was even abandoned by the Comte d'Artois, who, he informs us, had read and approved his paper. During the next eight years he remained in disgrace, taking little part in the politics of the day; and he was so unpopular and fallen in esteem that Charles X., on ascending the throne, as we have said, was afraid to make him a minister, though he had never ceased to seek, in private, his counsel. In 1827, through the king's favour, M. de Vitrolles emerged from his late obscurity; but he received only the subordinate place of minister at the court of Florence. In this position he was introduced to the discrowned Empress, Marie Louise, and his Memoirs contain details of interest respecting Napoleon's luckless widow. We have only space for the following:—

‘What surprised me most in her conversation was her remarkable forgetfulness of Paris, and of her life and existence in France. She asked me what had become of the Pantheon, and, soon afterwards, what was the metropolitan church of Paris. The family of Napoleon seemed to be unknown personages when one spoke to her about them. Even those who had been attached to her service were so completely forgotten, that she asked questions as to their appearance, their beauty, their intelligence. In a late conversation she said to me, referring to the time she had spent in Paris, "Ah! I have hitherto been very happy here, and the first period of my life seems to me only a troubled dream." ’

The secret influence of M. de Vitrolles in the royal councils increased from this time. By his own account he had much to do with the formation of the Martignac ministry—a final and insincere effort to reconcile the divine right of kings with constitutional and modern France. He was at Florence when the news arrived that Polignac had been appointed minister, and he was clear-sighted enough to perceive that a ministry the leaders of which, as was happily said, chiefly represented Coblentz and Waterloo, was of evil omen to the House of Bourbon. His estimate of the favourite was not high:—

‘M. de Polignac was completely ignorant of the condition and the public opinion of France when he chose to take the helm of affairs with silly foolhardiness. Nobody, too, was more mistaken than he was as to his own character and capacity; this is intelligible, for he imposed on other people. His conversation was easy; and he possessed a kind of grace of manner and an address which led one to believe that he had more intelligence than could be gathered from his words. He understood things readily, but superficially; suavity, politeness, and the habits of society made up the rest of him.’

Having returned to Paris at the end of 1829, M. de

Vitrolles witnessed the great events which terminated in the Revolution of July. The part of his Memoirs which contains these scenes abounds in details of extreme interest, many of which have never been published before. M. de Vitrolles, we doubt not, somewhat exaggerates the influence which, he takes care to tell us, he would have had on the course of affairs had his voice prevailed in the king's councils; but at this juncture he certainly displayed intelligence, zeal, and unselfish loyalty; and, possibly, had Charles X. heeded his advice, he might have retained his crown for a time. After the general election of 1830, following what we may call the Grand Remonstrance addressed by the Chambers to the king, M. de Vitrolles saw that a crisis was near; and, keen as he always was to interpret facts, he implored the ministers not to commit themselves to the extreme measures he believed were imminent:—

'I was convinced that the ministry was about to embark in a dangerous enterprise; public opinion, as it had shown itself during six months, seemed to render success impossible. Under these impressions I addressed several ministers, and spoke to each of them as they were entering the closet of the king; I spoke nearly in the same way to all, and forcibly, and bitterly, to make them understand my meaning.

' "I do not ask your secret," I said, " but I warn you that, at this moment, you do not possess the power to commit an act of insolence. You would find no support, no, not even from the Royalists, whose confidence has been shaken; it would be an insult to the newly-convened Chamber, strong as it is through the late elections. The monarchical majority would turn against you. Beware ! the occasion is more dangerous than you imagine. Do not play with fire over a powder magazine ! " '

This prophetic warning was not well received; and within twenty-four hours the famous Ordinances which wrecked the monarchy were all over Paris. M. de Vitrolles, curiously enough, had met the Duc d'Orléans the evening before, at a dinner-party of the Duc de Bourbon. The Citizen-King of the near future spoke anxiously of the state of affairs, but evidently as yet had not a thought of playing with revolution to win a crown:—

'I have always felt assured that at this moment the prince had neither foreseen nor prepared the events which led him, as if by fate, to power. I was prejudiced against him and disapproved of his hidden and cowardly opposition during the whole period of the Restoration; but I could not perceive in all that he said to me that day an illegitimate thought or hope. Nay, his face did not wear the disagreeable smile which would have flickered across it could he have anticipated the misfortunes of others and the good he could secure for himself from them. He could not see through the clouds, and was alarmed.'

An accident enabled M. de Vitrolles to play a remarkable part in the events that followed. The Ordinances appeared on July 26 ; and, after having dined on that day with the well-known favourite of Louis XVIII., the French Krüdener of the Holy Alliance, M. de Vitrolles went to an evening party at the house of the Duchesse de Vicence, the widow of Napoleon's Foreign Minister, and long an ornament of Parisian salons. He was waited on by a trusted agent of the justly indignant Liberal party, who, imagining, as was generally believed, that his influence with the king was great, informed him that Paris was about to rise, and that the army would not be faithful, but promised that, if concessions were made, the popular movement could be checked, and entreated him to negotiate with General Gérard, the foremost military Opposition chief. The capital had as yet been scarcely disturbed, and M. de Vitrolles declined the interview; but, with a true instinct of impending danger, he did not wholly reject the overture, and assured the agent he would reflect upon it. The aspect of Paris on the next morning, with Revolution already in the streets, and armed mobs beginning the work of Terror, induced him to set off for St. Cloud, where Charles X. had taken up his abode, surrounded by the court, and serenely confident. M. de Vitrolles was graciously received by the king, but was told that Paris would not dare to stir; that the troops would easily quell resistance ; and that the leaders of the Left were under arrest; and, in reply to an earnest request to hear, at least, the proposals of Gérard, the ill-advised monarch stiffly replied, ' No; it does not become me to appear to treat with rebellious subjects. Let them lay down their arms, and they will obtain all that will flow from my bounty. It is contrary to my nature to begin an insincere negotiation.'

M. de Vitrolles left St. Cloud with a heavy heart, and addressed to Polignac a grave warning to pause upon the brink of an abyss. The issue of events was still doubtful ; for, though a large part of the insurgent capital was in the hands of the excited populace, the soldiery were as yet staunch. Marmont, lately placed in command in Paris, held the Tuileries and Louvre in sufficient force ; and the Liberal leaders, not unmindful of the anarchy of 1793–4, were still willing to treat with the king. Their emissary met M. de Vitrolles again on the morning of the fateful 28th ; and a specific compromise was distinctly offered. The conversation deserves quoting, though it is questionable if the agent possessed the plenary powers M. de Vitrolles supposed :—

' " Yes," he said, " there is still time ; let the king consent to sacrifice ministers, objects of universal hatred; let him choose men invested with public confidence, and the people will be disarmed."

' " Well, but," I replied, " who are the personages surrounded with this halo of popular favour ? "

' I was afraid that he would mention dreaded names—Lafayette, Benjamin Constant—but not at all.   He tried to recollect the name of the Duc de Mortemart, but was unsuccessful.

' " The member of the Chamber of Paris, who was ambassador at St. Petersburg."   He recognised the name when I mentioned it.

' " Well, who next ? "

' " Well, General Gérard as Minister of War."

' " What then ? "

' " Why these two, if commissioned to form a ministry, would probably appoint Casimir Périer Minister of Finance or of the Interior."

' " Pray put that in writing.   Have you anything more to ask for ? "

' " No ; these men will do all that is required." '

M. de Vitrolles hastened to St. Cloud again, rightly judging that the proposed terms were worthy, at least, of serious attention.   On reaching the palace he found the ministers, who had been at the Tuileries the day before, in council upon the state of affairs ; and two well-known members of the Chamber of Peers, MM. d'Argout and de Semonville, had recently come, and had offered their aid. M. de Vitrolles made a strong appeal to Polignac to sacrifice himself for the safety of the throne, and to urge the king to form a new ministry ; but he was treated with cool insolence by the Duc d'Angoulême, just made commander-in-chief of the army, who, ignorant of what was going on in Paris, exclaimed that no truce was to be made with rebels. The obstinate folly of the prince almost passes belief :—

' I learned afterwards that Monseigneur the Dauphin, on returning to the council, and on hearing the proposal to change the ministry, declared that there was but one thing to do—namely, to shoot the Baron de Vitrolles ; that negotiations enfeebled councillors and troops.'

The situation was suddenly changed by the unexpected arrival of Marmont.   That luckless general, always disposed to make efforts too great for his force, had attempted to clear the insurgent quarter of the capital by a general movement ; the attack, in part successful, had scattered his troops ; and the Louvre and Tuileries, left ill-defended, had been exposed to the whole weight of the revolt.   A mistaken order to the Swiss Guards gave an opportunity to the swarming assailants; the palace and its precincts were stormed and plundered; and Marmont, who, a few hours before, had boasted that he could defy Paris, was compelled to draw off in hasty retreat. The scenes of 1789 were then renewed; appeals were made by the mob to the troops; and regiment after regiment, baffled and half-starved, and without heart for the Bourbon cause, showed signs of breaking away from their officers. The Revolution had now triumphed; and Marmont having declared that he could fight no longer, Charles X. sullenly yielded to fate. Prince Polignac and his colleagues resigned; a promise was made to recall the Ordinances; and the Duc de Mortemart was named minister, with Gérard as head of the War Office. The king, however, only gave in at the last moment and against his will:—

‘ “Gentlemen,” he exclaimed, “in yielding in this way, perhaps unwisely, to the stress of circumstances, I must tell you I am thoroughly, and at heart, convinced that, considering the line of action we are forced to take, no good can be done either as regards the future of France or the welfare of the Monarchy.” ’

M. de Vitrolles, with MM. d’Argout and de Semonville, was deputed to wait on the Liberal leaders—already installed at the Hôtel de Ville—and to inform them of the promised concessions. The party threaded their way with difficulty through the approaches of the insurgent capital, and found Jacobinism triumphant as they reached the Tuileries:—

‘ We met figures such as are not seen on other occasions: some covered with rags, some scarcely clothed; you saw many in torn shirts and worn-out trousers tied by a cord to the shoulders—some, indeed, without even this kind of braces, hitched up their only garment with one hand, while with the other they brandished sticks or like weapons. Most had their legs naked, or were shod in such a way that sabots would have been deemed a luxury. But these were the least offensive features of this hideous and revolting spectacle. Judge what was the expression of these faces, with every imaginable shade of frenzy or stupidity, of ferocity or cowardice. They were intoxicated with every sort of intoxication. Wine was the least cause; the smell of gunpowder, victory, which for them was only a reaction from terror, shouting, and bloodshed, had set them mad. Such was the aspect of those multitudes.’

M. de Vitrolles and his colleagues found Casimir Périer and other members of the Opposition already forming, at the Hôtel de Ville, a Provisional Government generally obeyed. M. Périer, however, received the envoys of Charles X. with unfeigned courtesy. The whole tenor of events proves that the Liberal chiefs were not disposed to call up anarchy to overturn the throne; but he justly remarked that M. de Vitrolles bore no written assurance from the king that the proposed arrangements would be ever carried out. M de Vitrolles, with characteristic loyalty, offered to become a hostage for his master's faith; and it was agreed, after a brief interview, that the king should give the required credentials, and that the re-establishment of the National Guard — dissolved by Charles X. in a fit of anger—should be another of the conditions of peace. M. Périer parted from M. de Vitrolles with expressions of good will and surprise that so well-known a partisan of royalty should have ventured to show his face in Paris; and he insisted on giving the bold emissary a safe-conduct under an assumed name. M. de Vitrolles was still confident of ultimate success; but the aspect of the Parisian populace, and of the tricolor floating from a thousand housetops, would have undeceived a less sanguine mind. The Revolution, indeed, had, perhaps, by this time gone beyond the control of the Hôtel de Ville. M. de Semonville, a veteran of 1789, had found it convenient to disappear; but M. de Vitrolles, with his remaining colleague, reached St. Cloud early on the morning of the 29th. M. de Vitrolles insisted on awakening the king. Charles X., during these eventful days, had, with real or assumed indifference, pursued the ordinary course of his life; and the loyal councillor spoke out plainly to his irritated and still unconvinced sovereign. The author has left this record of their last interview :—

'The king had never been pressed so severely before; the signs of this were apparent: his face was flushed, and my task was a disagreeable one. His silence was only interrupted by words that implied resistance. "We have not come to this ! that is too much ! " I thought it necessary to strike hard.

' " I am surprised, Sire," I said, " that your Majesty does not see where affairs are now. The question is not of disputing about this or that measure; it is essential that, whatever the means, the royal authority, nay, the title of the king, shall be acknowledged in Paris, and we have not even gained this point. Things have come to such a pass that I should consider it a miracle if M. de Mortemart, now here, and your minister, should within the next three days be able to form a ministry and to countersign an ordinance of the king. Yes, Sire, it would be a miracle ! " '

The king, having at last agreed to everything, it was

arranged that the new minister should proceed to the Hôtel
de Ville, but unaccompanied by M. de Vitrolles, whose
presence was not considered advisable. The occasion, however, had been allowed to pass, and the Provisional Government, possibly yielding to circumstances it could no longer
master, was already treating with the Duc d'Orléans.
M. de Vitrolles had seen his master for the last time; and
in the new world that opened in France he was relegated
to obscurity and soon forgotten. He probably has given too
much prominence to the part he played in the Revolution of
July; and even if Charles X. had assented in the first instance to all that was asked of him, we believe that, after the
events of the 28th, the Revolution could not have been
stayed. M. de Vitrolles, however, at this great crisis gave
real proof of undoubted courage, of fine intelligence, nay, of
true wisdom; and had Polignac minded his first warning,
the monarchy might have been saved for the time. His high
qualities of head and heart must be set off against obvious
faults; and, for the rest, his Memoirs remain a possession
of lasting value for the literature of France.

ART. VI.—1. *India, what can it teach us?* A Course of Lectures, delivered before the University of Cambridge, by
F. MAX MÜLLER, K.M. 8vo. London: 1883.

2. *The Origins of Religion and Language.* Considered in
five Essays by F. C. COOK, M.A., Canon of Exeter. 8vo.
London: 1884.

3. *Religious Thought and Life in India.* By MONIER WIL-
LIAMS, M.A., C.I.E., Boden Professor of Sanskrit in the
University of Oxford. 8vo. London: 1883.

4. *Problèmes et conclusions de l'histoire des religions.* Par
l'Abbé DE BROGLIE, Professeur d'Apologétique à l'Institut
Catholique de Paris. 12mo. Paris: 1885.

IN the varied and great advance made by modern research
there is one feature which most impresses itself on the
mind of the philosophic observer. It is that of the historic
progression in our thinking. We may trace in it the three
ages of man. In the first we have the mere observation of
facts, and as its result a knowledge which is chiefly pheno-
menal. In the second these facts or phenomena are traced
back to their underlying causes, forces, laws, or whatever
else one may choose to call them. The result of this might

be designated as scientific knowledge. But thinking cannot rest satisfied with this, nor stop short at it. There comes yet another stage, when the results of scientific knowledge are placed side by side, and compared, that so the great underlying unity of all within the range of our ken may appear, and its genesis upwards be ascertained. This is philosophical knowledge. And the aim of all systems of philosophy is to discover the formula by which this problem may be solved, to find the key that shall open the door into this, the innermost, sanctuary.

It cannot be our object here to discuss how far this aim has been attained by modern research; whether, indeed, it is wholly attainable, and all things so move along straight lines that, by following them, we can reach one central point of unity. The difficulties of the task are at least sufficiently obvious, as well as the temptations besetting it, arising in part from the dominance of some, it may be brilliant, idea, and, in a subject so engrossing and attractive, even from the power of the imagination. But much, if not everything, has no doubt been attained. This all must admit, that we have reached a stage which is alike in itself full of deepest interest, and also of promise of future results. It is the stage of comparative study. It is not long since such terms and pursuits as comparative physiology, comparative philology, comparative mythology—and why should we not add —comparative theology, were so little known as to make us forgetful of, or ungrateful for, the real advance which they indicate. It cannot be necessary to explain what these terms imply of increased and increasing depth of knowledge, breadth of view, and clearness of perception. Certain it is, that along this path our future enquiries must move, and that in this direction their goal must be sought.

We have been led into these general remarks, no less by the character of the books mentioned at the head of this article, than by the subject of which they treat. Briefly— since a detailed review is not here intended—they occupy each a distinctive standpoint. But they all bear on 'Hin- ' duism,' chiefly in its religious aspect, viewing not only its growth, character, and outcome, and tracing it to its root in Vedism, but seeking to fix its place in the general history of religions by a comparison of its primitive form with that of other religions. And here, at least, two of our authors are at opposite poles. In the language of Canon Cook—though it is perhaps somewhat exaggerated—the difference is ' be- ' tween those, on the one hand, who maintain the doctrine

' of evolution in its broadest sense, especially as applied to
' the history of religion; and those, on the other side, who
' hold fast to the belief that all truths which affect the rela-
' tions between man and God were made known by Divine
' revelation.' Whether or not the antagonism between the
two sides is in reality so sharp—whether, indeed, it is necessary, and an intermediate position between them cannot be
found—will appear in the sequel. There can, however, be
no doubt how Canon Cook views the question, and what
position he takes in regard to it. He writes (and we quote
without at present expressing any opinion) : ' It is main-
' tained by eminent scholars, especially by Professor Max
' Müller, to whom this department of Old Indian literature
' is deeply indebted, that we find in this book [the Rig Veda]
' an independent progressive development of fundamental
' religious principles.' To which statement he adds this as
the question at issue : ' Is it a fact that in its main fea-
' tures the Rig Veda presents a development of religious
' principles? Do we find in it proofs or indications of an
' ascent from the lower to the higher, from naturalism, the
' worship of physical forces or natural phenomena, to the
' recognition of pure, spiritual morality, and to the establish-
' ment of a system in which we find clear indication of prin-
' ciples recognised as fundamental by all monotheists ? ' *

On both these points Canon Cook pronounces a most
decided opinion. In fact his book is an elaborate attempt
to prove the original unity of the whole human race, both as
regards language and especially religion. Originally there
was only one language, of which he sets himself to trace
the indications by an elaborate comparison, as well as to
explain the causes and the origin of what he regards as only
later divergences from a common ancestry. Similarly, there
was originally only one religion : that pure faith which came
to man from heaven, but which in the course of time and
of migrations became first mixed up with the opposite element and then superseded by it—although it is his ' convic-
' tion that the same God who gave the truth to man in the
' beginning, wills that it shall be presented again and again
' in a form accessible to all, surrounded with evidence
' which meets the requisitions of the most cautious judge-
' ment, and appeals with irresistible force to the con-
' science and the heart; and, further, that it is His will to
' give it a complete and permanent victory.' And, especially

---

* Origins of Religion and Language, p. 38.

as regards the religion of India (with which alone we are at present concerned), Canon Cook maintains: ' As for evo-
' lution, if we are to understand that word in the sense
' of progress, advance, continuous movement in an upward
' direction, it is assuredly no characteristic of Indo-Aryan re-
' ligious systems.' He is confident that they were ' at first
' probably an unconscious modification of the true primeval
' monotheism, as revealed to and apprehended by the Hebrew
' seers'—although before the great final separation of the whole Aryan race ' religion must have undergone consider-
' able changes, tending towards polytheism, but with recog-
' nised principles adverse to all forms of superstition ; far
' more vital and grievous was the deterioration afterwards.'
One other extract to mark the fundamental position of our author in contrast to the opposite view of the question :—

'Taking the facts as they stand before us, clear, undisputed, and indisputable, we have proof positive that the two systems [the existence of which Canon Cook traces in Vedism], naturalistic or material on the one hand, and ethical or spiritual on the other, were entirely distinct from the beginning, in every stage of their several development, and in their issue. Neither of them could possibly be developed from the other ; they were based on totally different principles. They had their origin in utterly different wants, desires, fears, or aspirations of our common nature.'

Of these two different systems, existing side by side, our author believes the purer to represent the earlier faith of the Indo-Aryans, the other its later corruption.

We have presented the views of Canon Cook with such detail because there is a unity and grandeur of conception underlying his theory of ancient religions, and, in part, an accordance with certain phenomena, which command atten-tion ; and also because of the respect due to its author. It is easy to caricature the somewhat fanciful, and certainly not convincing, speculations which he hazards as to the causes of the separation of the early races and their sequences; or to point out important gaps in the argument and mistakes in its details. But, however taking or damaging a criticism may be which picks out faults while it ignores excellences, the argument deserves serious consideration; and it would be not only ungenerous but unjust not to acknowledge in this instance the wide erudition and research as well as the earnest purpose of a writer who, in other fields, has so many claims on the reading public. And we say all this the more readily that, as may have been perceived, we cannot admit the cogency of his reasoning. We are not here referring to his ultimate conclusions, the discussion of which might lead into theological questions. But whether or not his case be good, he has not in this book made it out to our satisfaction, although there are not a few important points in it which we shall have to place side by side with the reasoning of Professor Max Müller. As regards the other two works mentioned for review, very few sentences will suffice for the present. To the very able and interesting treatise by the Abbé de Broglie we shall have occasion to refer in the sequel, meantime only expressing regret that controversial matter as between Roman Catholicism and Protestantism should have been introduced into it. Lastly, Professor Monier Williams's 'Religious Thought and Life in India' * exactly fulfils the promise of the title-page. But we are bound to add that it contains not much that is either original or that had not been presented before, while the arrangement and style are deficient in attractiveness, if not occasionally in clearness. Perhaps this could not be helped in a work of the kind, and we can only hope that it will not deter the general reader from access to what would prove to him a storehouse of most interesting information.

Certainly no exception of this kind can be taken to Professor Max Müller's course of lectures, delivered in Cambridge, on 'India, what can it teach us?' Whatever objection may be raised on other grounds, they are brimful not only of information but of interest. The most abstruse discussions, which in other hands would be dull, become sparkling in his setting. There is a vivacity and originality about his mode of presenting things; a capacity of grouping together most varied facts, deducing from them general principles, and founding upon them wide-reaching speculations, which must have held the young Indian civilians of Cambridge charmed, and which will carry the reader through this volume without break or omission, and that whether or not he agree with the inferences or adopt the conclusions. The latter, indeed, are open to many objections. Serious and, as we believe, well-founded exception will be taken not only to the reasoning, but to the speculative views on the origin and developement and the comparative history of religion, more frequently indicated than elaborated, suggested rather than fully set forth and defended.

A more practical question could scarcely be propounded, nor one which, on many grounds, has more present interest

---

* Part I.   Vedism, Brahmanism, and Hindūism.

than this: ' India, what can it teach us?' 'Much, every
' way.' The most superficial observer will admit that we
have a great deal both to unlearn and to learn regarding
India, whether as rulers, administrators, or, in what we
would fain believe to be our mission, as civilisers of the
East. Indeed, according to Professor Max Müller, there
is much more to be done in these respects than any not
thoroughly acquainted with the subject could imagine. And,
considering that the population of India alone amounts to
about 240 millions, the sooner we learn it the better.

The first lecture in Professor Max Müller's course is
devoted to the general consideration of this point, showing
how much, especially as regards thought and the science of
language, is to be learnt from India. By India, he reminds
us, he means not that of to-day, but the India of 'a thou-
' sand, two thousand, it may be three thousand years ago,'
and, as regards social and moral matters, 'the India of the
' village communities,' not that of the towns. The caution
was requisite, considering that on those philosophical and
religious problems to which the larger part of Professor Max
Müller's volume refers, we are directed back to the original
text-book of the Indo-Aryan faith, the Rig Veda, which
dates from fifteen to ten centuries before our present era.
This is to go somewhat far back for our teaching, even if
we were prepared, which we are not, absolutely to accept
the presentation of the general teaching of the Rig Veda,
and of the interrelation of its different parts which is
offered to us. Thus the permanent interest attaching to
it is mainly historical. Bearing this in mind, a somewhat
strange light is cast upon this sentence in the opening
lecture :—

' If I were to ask myself from what literature we, here in Europe,
we who have been nurtured almost exclusively on the thoughts of
Greeks and Romans, and of one Semitic race, the Jewish, may draw
that corrective which is most wanted in order to make our inner life more
perfect, more comprehensive, more universal, in fact more truly human,
a life, not for this life only, but a transfigured and eternal life—again I
should point to India.'

We take leave to express our dissent, in which we feel
assured we shall not be solitary. Even remembering that the
language just quoted refers to the India of two or three thousand years ago—for no one would bid us look for a corrective
to our inner life from *modern* Hinduism—the facts concerning
Vedism presented in this volume do not bear out this promise of a moral and religious ' corrective,' nor, so far as we

can see, are they even set forth with a view to this, since the highest inference aimed at seems to be that the Rig-Veda, in certain parts or in certain aspects of it, comes up to, not that it surpasses, the thoughts of the 'Semitic' race, or is needed as corrective and perfective of them. And here we have the aid of that bizarre party, with which we have otherwise so little sympathy, which is trying to introduce a version, modification, or adaptation of Buddhism, in certain *fade* and satiated circles, where what is odd is hailed as being new by way of covering little knowledge by much talk. For the Buddhism which is so much vaunted, but which in reality is the want of all mental and moral muscle, and which, if consistently carried out, would lead to the extinction of all that is masculine and elevating, is, if anything, a reaction and a protest against that Brahmanism which, in the words of Professor Monier Williams, 'grew [in its turn] out of Vedism.' And if, following the same authority, we regard 'Vedism as the earliest ' form of the religion of the Indian branch of the great ' Aryan family,' and Brahmanism as growing out of Vedism, and, lastly, Hinduism as growing out of Brahmanism, then surely 'the principle of evolution,' against which Canon Cook so earnestly warns us, must at least have stopped at a very early period ' in its steady progress from the lowest to ' the highest stages.' There are, we believe, other modes of accounting for the undoubtedly higher and purer elements in Vedism, and, for that matter, in most if not all religions, than by 'evolution' or developement. There are in the more sober, calm, and thoughtful moods of mankind a consciousness and a feeling of common wants, and, both in its instinctive and in its higher aspirations, common answers to these questions, which, explain their origin as we may, make all men kindred, and which may account for the common elements in all religions. And if we are to study the comparative history of religions, it would seem to us both more needful and more philosophic to trace the points of fundamental difference, and to account for their origin, rather than exclusively emphasise those of similarity. And if we wish to know the absolute value and character of a religion, we must look at these points of divergence from others before forming our comparative estimate.

In truth, preconceived opinions, the power of imagination, and even differences of taste, go, quite unconsciously to ourselves, a great way towards our judgement of similarities. We will not be hypercritical, but the very first lecture in,

Professor Max Müller's volume furnishes an instance of this. He is comparing the well-known story of Solomon's mode of ascertaining which of the two women who contended for the living child was its real mother * with a somewhat similar narrative 'told by the Buddhists' ' in the Kanjur, which is ' the Tibetan translation of the Buddhist Tripi*t*aka.'† To begin with, we ought to keep the following in mind :—

'That at the time of Solomon there was a channel of communication open between India and Syria and Palestine is established beyond doubt, I believe, by certain Sanskrit words which occur in the Bible as names of articles of export from Ophir, articles such as ivory, apes, peacocks, and sandalwood, which, taken together, could not have been exported from any country but India. Nor is there any reason to suppose that the commercial intercourse between India, the Persian Gulf, the Red Sea, and the Mediterranean was ever completely interrupted, even at the time when the Book of Kings is supposed to have been written.'

With this in view we follow Professor Max Müller's comparison of the two stories. 'Not having a legal mind,' he tells us, 'I could never suppress a certain shudder when ' reading the decision of Solomon.' Considering that it was not a 'decision,' but only a truly Oriental device for testing which of the two claimants was the mother of the living child, we confess to have never felt a similar tremor passing through our frame. Be this as it may, the Buddhist version of settling a dispute of the same kind is as follows. After much useless wrangling between the rival claimants, the decision was thus reached: ' " What is the use of examining ' and cross-examining these women ? Let them take the boy ' and settle it among themselves." Thereupon both women ' fell on the child, and when the fight became violent the ' child was hurt and began to cry. Then one of them let ' him go, because she could not bear to hear the child cry.' On which Professor Max Müller continues: ' This seems to ' me, if not the more primitive, yet the more natural form ' of the story, showing a deeper knowledge of human nature ' and more wisdom than even the wisdom of Solomon.' There may be two opinions on this point. Both stories proceed on precisely the same 'knowledge of human nature' in the unerring instincts of a mother's heart. But as the Biblical story is the more dignified, as avoiding a fight of

---

* 1 Kings iii. 25.

† 'Tripi*t*aka' means the three *baskets* or *collections*, and is a collective name for the three classes of Buddhist writings : the Sūtra-pi*t*aka,. the Vinaya-pi*t*aka, and the Abhidarma-pi*t*aka.

the two women around the child in the presence of the king, so it seems to us 'the more natural,' since a mother would scarcely give up her child to a stranger because she heard him cry, and assuredly 'the more primitive,' as, on comparison of the two narratives, the more simple and sure of success.

If we have given so much space to a comparatively trifling detail, it will help to explain what, from the more general standpoint, we must regard as a somewhat exaggerated accentuation of the whole subject by Professor Max Müller. It is probably natural, on the part of one who has devoted a life of severe study, and, what is more, his genius, to Sanskrit and its literature; and it may in this instance be further explained by the wish to turn the minds of the young Indian civilians from the more practical—shall we not say the lower—considerations, which might so easily preoccupy them, by kindling in them a generous enthusiasm, and pointing out to them how much of deepest interest was to be learned in India, where they would find themselves 'every-'where between an immense past and an immense future, 'with opportunities such as the old world could but seldom, if 'ever, offer.' And, in general, it were impossible to inculcate more truly or more forcibly the philosophic study of history, with special reference to that of India, than in such words as these:—

'Why does history form a recognised part of our liberal education? Simply because all of us and every one of us ought to know how we have come to be what we are, so that each generation need not start again from the same point and toil over the same ground, but, profiting by the experience of those who came before, may advance towards higher points and nobler aims. As a child, when growing up, might ask his father or grandfather *who* had built the house they lived in, or who had cleared the field that yielded them their food, we ask the historian whence we came, and how we came into possession of what we call our own.'

Nor yet could any account be more lucid or engaging than that in which Professor Max Müller tells once more how the affinities between Latin and Greek were at last understood by tracing them up to a higher unity in the great Aryan family of languages, in which Sanskrit is seen to be 'the 'eldest sister of them all,' thus opening to our view 'the 'state of civilisation previous to the Aryan separation,' and beyond this, how that Proto-Aryan language itself must have been 'the result of a long, long process of thought,' looking 'like a rock washed down and smoothed for ages by 'the ebb and flow of thought.' It is truly a wondrous *vista*

that of this old-world civilisation when, starting from the
first Sanskrit literary monuments fifteen centuries before our
era, we have to travel upwards to the common source whence
the Teutonic, Italic, Greek, Celtic, Slavonic, Iranic, and
Indic languages equally spring, and even beyond that along
the course by which, in the progress of developement, the
Aryan language became what it was before its separation
into its several branches.   Most surprising—delightfully so,
we should have imagined—must the discovery of all this
have been not more than half a century ago ; bewildering also,
at any rate to the youthful mind, even although we cannot
quite understand, how ' all one's ideas of Adam and Eve,
' and the Paradise, and the tower of Babel, and Shem, Ham,
' and Japhet, with Horace, and Æneas, and Virgil too,
' seemed to be whirling round and round, till at last one
' picked up the fragments and tried to build up a new world,
' and to live with a new historical consciousness,'
    Yet, apart from our personal interest in India, the student
of any other hoary civilisation might plead almost the same
considerations.   Not to speak of Egyptology, where the
oldest and most deeply interesting documents take us back
fifteen hundred years beyond the Rig Veda, to about three
thousand years before our era, there is much more in the
study of the Avesta, the text-book of ancient Parsism, to
engage thinking : questions far deeper are stirred, and solu-
tions hazarded far wider reaching, more original, and to
which we feel more sympathetic.   And, as Spiegel has shown,
the earliest ideas which Parsism embodies must have origi-
nated when Indians and Persians still lived together as one
nation, at a period when the Vedas did not yet exist, and
when the fundamental views of the two nations, though in
form undeveloped, were the same.   Therefore, even on this
as on other grounds, we can only accept with modifications
such a statement as that implied in this question concerning
religion : ' Where can you study its true origin, its natural
' growth, and its inevitable decay, better than in India, the
' home of Brahmanism, the birthplace of Buddhism, and the
' refuge of Zoroastrianism, even now the mother of new
' superstitions—and why not, in the future, the regenerate
' child of the purest faith, if only purified from the dust of
' nineteen centuries ? '
    It would, however, be untrue, as well as unjust, not to
place by the side of the exceptions implied in some of
the previous remarks certain extracts from Professor Max
Müller's preface to the translation of ' The Sacred Books of

' the East,' of which the second large series is now in course
of publication.   He writes :—

' Readers who have been led to believe that the Vedas of the ancient
Brahmans, the Avesta of the Zoroastrians, the Tripi*t*aka of the Buddhists, the Kings of Confucius, or the Koran of Mohammed, are books
full of primeval wisdom and religious enthusiasm, or at least of sound
and simple moral teaching, will be disappointed on consulting these
volumes. . . . It is but natural that those who write on ancient religions, and who have studied them from translations only, not from
original documents, should have had eyes for their bright rather than
their dark sides. . . . Scholars, also, who have devoted their life either
to the editing of the original texts or to the careful interpretation of
some of the sacred books, are more inclined, after they have disinterred
from a heap of rubbish some solitary fragments of pure gold, to exhibit
these treasures only, than to display all the refuse from which they had
to extract them. I do not blame them for this; perhaps I should feel
that I was open to the same blame myself.'

And again :—

' No one who collects and publishes such extracts can resist, no one,
at all events so far as I know, has ever resisted, the temptation of giving
what is beautiful, or it may be what is strange and startling, and
leaving out what is commonplace, tedious, or it may be repulsive. . .
We must face the problem in its completeness, and I confess it has been
for many years a problem to me, ay, to a great extent, is so still, how
the sacred books of the East should, by the side of so much that is
fresh, natural, simple, beautiful, and true, contain so much that is not
only unmeaning, artificial, and silly, but even hideous and repellent.
This is a fact, and must be accounted for in some way or other.'

These sentences contain most necessary cautions for those
on whom, in their partial knowledge of the subject, the one-
sided presentation of beautiful extracts might leave, almost
unconsciously, the impression that there was here something
of quite the same kind—and not merely containing cognate
elements—if not even better, higher, and purer than they
already possessed.   And they also point out the great
problem, how we are to account, not only from the literary
aspect of their juxtaposition in the same sacred books (which
is comparatively easily explained), but, from a wider aspect,
for the coexistence in the same, nay, in all religions of two
so widely differing and antagonistic elements.   This dualism
does exist, and it exists as high up as we can historically
trace these religions.   Whence did it come ; how did it continue ; was one of these elements prior to the other, and if so
which of them ; or did the one evolve from the other, and in
what order ; or is there yet a primal unity behind them
both? On the answer to these questions will depend not

only our views of the origin of these religions, but of the comparative history of religion ; and, indeed, beyond all that is theoretical, much that is most practical. In fact, it will influence our whole thinking on these subjects. But, before addressing ourselves to them, it will be necessary to collect and present some further materials on which to ground our conclusions.

The next three lectures in Professor Max Müller's volume, although devoted to other topics, still advance us in the way of our present enquiry. Lecture II. has some very useful practical remarks on the feelings, or rather prepossessions, with which so many enter on their life in India. For these, indeed 'for some of the greatest misfortunes that have ' happened to India,' the Professor holds Mill's ' History of ' British India ' responsible. There may be exaggerations and optimist views on the other side also. We leave it to those best acquainted with the matter to judge whether or not to admit the plea of this lecture for the ' truthful character ' of the Hindus,' * their sincerity, frankness, and the absence of servility, ' when left to themselves ' in their village life, not in the great towns, and even there before the advent of an English official, which ' is often said to be sufficient to drive ' away those native virtues which distinguish both the private ' life and the public administration of justice and equity in an ' Indian village.' The statement, if not too sweeping, would certainly be humiliating enough. Yet there can be no doubt that the foolish and ignorant prejudices with which young officials often enter on their work, together with the supreme self-consciousness and contempt for other nations to which we Britons are specially prone, as well as the temptations of

---

* But we would take leave to ask whether it was necessary, or even discriminating, in illustrating the beautiful import of the word *sat*— that which is—for the true, to say to a college audience: ' Whosoever ' has once stood alone, surrounded by noisy assertions, and overshadowed ' by the clamour of those who ought to know better, or perhaps who ' did know better—call him Galileo or Darwin, Colenso or Stanley, or ' any other name—he knows what a real delight it is to feel in his ' heart of hearts, this is true—this is, this is *sat*—whatever daily, weekly, ' or quarterly papers, whatever bishops, archbishops, or popes may say ' to the contrary.' Certainly—if it be true. But does the mere presence of opposition prove it such? Or does it follow, because Galileo was so beaten down by ignorant fanaticism, and the reasoning of Darwin for a time opposed by those who, in ignorance of its meaning, dreaded what they regarded as its consequences, that the criticism of Colenso was not exceedingly poor, and the reading of Stanley, in spite of his genius, sometimes discursive, and his conclusions sometimes illogical?

a more or less absolute rule over what is regarded as an inferior race, too often not only produce those evils with which Hindus are afterwards charged, but are the source of endless misunderstandings and incalculable mischief.

In the third lecture we are invited to consider what is called the 'Human Interest of Sanskrit Literature.' In one sense, no doubt, Sanskrit is a dead language, and has been so for more than two thousand years. But it is not only to this day the language of the learned—as Latin was in Europe—while journals and serials continue to be published in it, but even in the villages large crowds gather around the Kâthaka, or Brahman narrator, as during many weeks in succession he recites to his entranced and deeply moved audience the ancient epic poems in the Sanskrit, interpreting them the while in the vernacular. Still further, Sanskrit is really the mother of 'all the living languages of India.' But what constitutes its chief claim is that it gives access to the literature of Vedism and Buddhism. Few, indeed, have any conception how large Sanskrit literature is. Professor Max Müller tells us that a bibliographical survey, made by order of the Indian Government, has brought to light the enormous number of 10,000 separate works. With all deference to the Professor, we are thankful to know that much of this is not likely to see the light. He himself divides Sanskrit literature into two periods: the ancient, anterior to the so-called Turanian invasion (by which between the first century B.C. and the third century A.D. the Northern conquerors possessed themselves of the government of India), and the modern artificial literature which succeeded that period. And of this latter even so ardent an admirer confesses that, despite points of interest 'and occasional beauty,' it is 'curious only, 'and appealing to the interests of the Oriental scholar far 'more than the broad human sympathies of the historian and 'the philosopher.' It is, therefore, only the ancient Sanskrit literature, which discloses to us the Vedic and Buddhistic religions, that can be of general interest. And even here, while fully admitting the immense importance in it of the Vedas, we can scarcely admit, at least without limitation, that they present to us the first intelligible developement of religion and mythology. For behind the Vedas there is another and a fundamental question, to which, as we shall soon see, at least three different answers can be given.

It is time that we addressed ourselves to what gives its real and universal interest to Sanskrit literature: its religious aspect. Fully to appreciate it, we must in some

measure realise the totally different point of view of existence in India—and in the East generally—from that which
obtains in Europe, and especially among ourselves.   Instead of our constant struggle for existence and race for
advancement, chiefly of the practical, if not the material,
kind, we have to deal with the contemplative and meditative
character of the East.   There the outward wants of man
are few and easily supplied; while the grandeur of Nature
and of her phenomena disposes the dreamy spirit to absorp-
tion in that which is without, into whose mysteries the
analysis of practical science has not broken.   And they
lead the soul not only outward but upward, into the mist
peopled with dim forms and sounding with far-off voices;
some of them heard long ago, whether as echoes from
without or as whisperings from within, but in either case
God-sent; others, the outcome of childish or of perverted
imagining.   So we can understand alike the true and the
false in it all.   We can understand it in the East—not
only in India, for we might quote from other Eastern nations
most striking parallels to those adduced by Professor Max
Müller in proof of such disposition.   Favoured by outward
and inward conditions, the mind is wholly absorbed by this
Beyond, which is outside and above all empirical knowledge,
and yet so constantly and everywhere around the soul, filled
with the *sensus numinis,* as to be the ever-present.   Thus to the
Eastern there is religion in everything—not only in worship,
but in thought, science, government, life; and no other
writer has more fully apprehended this element, or shown
deeper sympathy with it, than Professor Max Müller.   In
part this may have led to the expression of views from which
we shall have to dissent.   But, in another direction, what
has been stated will suffice to show the grotesqueness of
any attempts to transplant to the West what is essentially
Eastern.   That which in a child is beautiful, true, and full
of lessons, becomes not only unnatural but repulsive when
grown-up people play at it and pretend to be in earnest.

It is this inner child-life of the human spirit that gives
its interest to the text-book of Vedism, the Rig Veda, but
also marks its essential difference from the Old Testament.
There, indeed, we have also growth and developement, but not
into something essentially different; nor have we, in juxtaposition with that which is pure and elevated about God and
man, the false, silly, and repulsive elements which we shall
find in such abundance in the Rig Veda.   The student
of the history of religion, if he refuse to admit that there

the subjective truth was met by the objective, will have to account for this. From this point of view we venture to think that a comparison in favour of Vedic literature cannot be drawn as ' far more important and far more improving . . . ' than the dates and the deeds of many of the kings of Judah ' and Israel.'

The term *Veda*, which means knowledge, is in Hindu usage specially applied to sacred knowledge or the sacred writings. These embrace four collections,* of which the most important consists of the ancient sacred hymns which the early Indian ancestors brought with them. Of these a selection and recension was afterwards made, which constitutes the first and by far the most interesting of the four collections just mentioned : the Rig Veda, or knowledge (book) of the hymns. The second ' collection' is Sâma Veda, or knowledge of the songs, consisting of 1,800 verses, chiefly derived from the Rig Veda, and strung together without any internal connexion. The third collection, the Jagur Veda, contains the knowledge of the prayers. As the Sâma Veda contained the verses to be recited, the Jagur Veda embodied the formulas and prayers during the regular sacrificial services. It contains also many verses from the Rig, but marks a later date, when the priesthood had already attained supremacy. Considerably later than these three ' collections' is the Atharva or Brahma Veda, the knowledge of magic formulas. The difference from the Rig is very marked. Instead of the sense and love of nature, we find everywhere fear of demons and magic ; the very word *brahman*, which had meant devotion, prayer, has become a formula of incantation by which the priest could obtain everything, and even oblige the gods to obey his behests. Beyond these four collections—the Mantra—it is not necessary for our present purpose to descend in Vedic literature. The date of the Rig Veda may be fixed at from 1500 to 1000 B.C., although there are authorities who place it higher.

The glimpses which, through these thousands of years, we obtain of the Vedic people are most interesting. We see them in their homes and villages, rudely protected against the inroads of wild beasts or the attacks of foes. Their chief means of support are herds and flocks, and, next to this, agriculture, which yields its harvest twice a year.

---

* We are here throughout following the brief but masterly sketch of Professor Kaegi : 'Der Rigveda, die älteste Literatur der Inder.' 2nd edition. 1881.

They are also hunters with bow and arrow, as well as by snares and gins. Their food is chiefly farinaceous or of milk, and, although the use of water is so extolled, their favourite drink is a kind of spirit made of corn or barley, but especially *soma*, the drink of man and of gods, so inspiriting and gladdening as to have itself been raised to the rank of a god. Among the various kinds of handicraft we mark specially that in wood, while the women are busy weaving and sewing or making adornments. Trade is still most primitive, chiefly that of barter; the cow forming the unit or standard by which the relative value of things is estimated. The introduction of money, specially of the Babylonian *mana*,* points to intercourse with the Semitic races of the West. The formation of the marriage-bond and its character are in strict accordance with what we know of the primitive East. Youths and maidens meet on festive or similar occasions. The intending suitor seeks the consent of the father or eldest brother of the maiden through 'the friend of the bridegroom,' who must be the eldest unmarried son of a family, since marriage must proceed in the regular succession of age. He has to purchase his bride by rich gifts to her father, when the marriage is celebrated in the home of the bride, in the presence of the two families and of friends. Probably the maiden had a dowry, and such prospects or that of an inheritance seem to have been as helpful to matrimony as in our days. The wife was subject to her husband, but ruled not only over her household, but also over her brothers- and sisters-, and even her parents-in-law. The relation between man and wife seems to have been the most close and tender, and monogamy was the rule, polygamy the exception. The great desire and prayer was for the birth of a son; the advent of a daughter was certainly not hailed. The exposure of infants and of the aged seems quite exceptional, and the burning of widows is nowhere indicated in the Rig-Veda, although the practice must be traced up to very ancient times. The same simple, primitive character appears in public life. The rule is vested in a king, hereditary or elective; it is not absolute, but controlled by the popular will, expressed in the great assemblies of the tribe or clan. In times of peace the king is 'judge and protector,' to whom presents—not taxes—are given. In war he is leader, and on him devolves the duty of offering the public sacrifices,

---

* Professor Max Müller, however, denies such Babylonian derivation of the *mina*.

either himself or by a priest-poet. And to this the unique position of the Indian priesthood and the origin of 'caste' have been traced, the existence of which in earliest Vedic times has been strenuously denied.

It need scarcely be said that there is also another side to this picture, alike as regards family and public life. There are allusions to lying and cheating, to theft and robbery, not to speak of other vices. The culprit was bound by the toes to a pillar, and, if his guilt was clear, expelled from the community; if doubtful, decision was sought by divination or even by the judgement of God. On the other hand, charity to the poor, benevolence, kindness, and faithfulness to friends are extolled. When the business for which a popular assembly had been called was finished, the more serious would gather for earnest friendly talk, while others would indulge in jest and drinking, most frequently in gambling. Drink and dice, in which all, even personal liberty, was often staked, were the master-passions of the people. But there is a brighter aspect also than drunkenness or gambling from early morn to dewy eve—that, when in the 'spring-time' there was 'pretty ring-time,' and to the sound of the loud cymbals lads and lasses swayed in dance till earth and air resounded with the merriment. We will not further trace this portraiture of primitive society, which recalls what we know of early Semitic times, the very institution of the Levirate marriage having apparently been introduced; and still more what we know of our Teutonic ancestors. It is scarcely necessary to add that science and art were in the most primitive condition among the Vedic people, with one exception only, that of poetry. It is to the deep, all-pervading religious sense combined with this high poetic temperament that we owe the Rig Veda.

The Rig Veda consists of ten books (*maṇḍala*), containing 1,017, or, adding other eleven from another recension, 1,028 hymns. According to Professor Max Müller, they comprise 10,580 verses, about 153,826 words, and in all 'nearly ' 30,000 lines, each line reckoned as 32 syllables.' We mention these particulars not only as indicating the extent of this literature, but to call attention to the mode of its transmission. As writing was not introduced in India before the fourth century B.C., and the close of the Rig Veda dates from about 1000 B.C., it follows that it must have been orally transmitted. Indeed, this is still the case so far as theological students are concerned, who spend eight years in the house of their teachers acquiring from their lips the knowledge of the sacred hymns. This tenacity of memory, of which other Eastern parallels might be mentioned, and the transmission of the *ipsissima verba* of these hymns during three thousand years by memory alone, are exceedingly important factors in the history of tradition, and as regards the verbal trustworthiness of what at first was transmitted from memory and only afterwards written down, deviations in which must be due to other causes than merely their dependence on memory and oral transmission.

Of the ten *Maṇḍalas* of the Rig-Veda, Books II.–VII. contain the oldest hymns, and are the product of one family in which they were preserved as a sacred family heirloom. The hymns of Book IX. are exclusively addressed to *Soma*, the intoxicating drink which was elevated to the character of deity. Such a deification of drunkenness and the consecration to it of one out of ten books of sacred hymnody should be kept in view in our thoughts about Vedism. Lastly, Books I. and X. contain also the products of the latest Vedic period. The language in which these hymns are composed is a very archaic popular dialect, which differs in its grammatical re-lations from the later Sanskrit, a more artificial and ornate mode of speech. It is in this primitive form of it that we obtain ' glimpses of the development and history of language ' and into the workshop of that enormous mental labour by ' which the languages of *our* races have become the most ' highly developed of all.'

It has already been indicated that by far the largest number in the Rig Veda are religious hymns, but few of a secular character having been preserved, chiefly in Book X. But these hymns do not profess to embody a revelation; they are the outpourings of the heart, chiefly in invocation or exaltation of the various deities. Being the work of different poets, separated by long periods of time, we must not expect to find in the Rig Veda any unity of religious conception, or imagine that it represents either modern Hinduism, or, indeed, anything more than, in the words of Professor Max Müller, 'a small and, it may be, a priestly minority of ' the ancient population of India,' bearing still further in mind that the India of the Veda is not the vast country to which we now give that name, but the valley of the Indus and the Punjab. Nor would anyone contend that Vedism represents the absolutely primitive stage in the strict sense, since behind it lies a long developement, mental, moral, religious, and social, of which no historic record exists. But even in this modified view of it, the question is whether we

are to regard the different elements in the Veda as lying
incongruously by the side of each other, being due to different causes, or else as exhibiting to us 'the developement of
'religious views from their first beginnings up to a deeply
'spiritual conception of the Deity and its relation to man.'
For this latter conclusion it would be necessary not only
to trace the principle of developement in Vedism, but so to
group its discordant elements as to find in them a progress
upwards, and lastly to recognise in the latest phase of the
Veda 'a deeply spiritual conception of the Deity.' No one
would think of questioning the facts on which those who
advocate these views base their conclusions; but it is open
to all to controvert the inferences which they draw from
these facts.

Viewing it as a whole, Professor Max Müller declares
himself unable to say whether the religion of the Veda
should be described as monotheistic or polytheistic. Monotheistic it certainly was not, since by the side of a few
hymns 'that assert the unity of the Divine,' 'there are thou-
'sands in which ever so many divine beings are praised and
'prayed to:' three times eleven for sky, earth, and waters—
nay, many more up to 3339. And yet the designation of
polytheism is refused to the Vedic religion on the ground that
that term applies to 'a certain more or less organised system
'of gods, different in power and rank, and all subordinate
'to a supreme god,' whereas in the Veda no one god 'is
'first always, no one is last always. Even gods of a
'decidedly inferior and limited character assume occa-
'sionally in the eyes of a devoted poet a supreme place
'above all other gods.' The question may be raised whether
something similar could not be traced in the earlier stages
of all mythology, especially in the religions of the East,
where the supremacy of a god, in himself inferior to another,
is at times determined by circumstances, national, family,
and even individual relationship of the worshipper. Professor Max Müller has assigned to this the designation of
Kathenotheism (the worship of one god after another) or of
Henotheism (the worship of single gods) to mark this worshipping 'of single gods, each occupying for a time a
'supreme position.'

This is one important element. We mark that the Old Testament not only excludes this as well as all Polytheism,
but that its emphatic assertion of the unity of the living
and true God implies a protest not only against Polytheism,
but against the subtler form of Kathenotheism and Heno-

theism. Other essential differences multiply upon us at
every step in our progress. The religious thinking in the
Veda is that of awakening infancy, when all the phenomena in
nature are personified and deified, not viewed as the manifestations and messengers of the one God. The same dualism
which has previously been referred to appears in the religious
feelings of the worshippers, and by the side of that which is
more pure we find elements of a very different character, and
the supremacy of the latter is shown by the gradual transformation of ancient Vedism into the present religion of
India. Indeed, in the Veda itself, the ancient deities Dyaus
(Zeus), the divine pair, Heaven and Earth, and others, have
already receded and given place to those deifications of
phenomena which, according as one or another more mightily
impressed a tribe, would lead to the prevalence of one god
over another. This so far explains Henotheism as to show
how a poet would address a request to one or another god
to whose sphere he would imagine the subject specially to
belong, and who would in that special instance appear as if
he were not only the supreme but the only god.

Leaving aside the consideration whether the philosopher
or ' inspired poet ' might perceive that these deities were but
names for the one only divine, since ' this was certainly not
' the idea of the Vedic Rishis (poets, seers), still less of the
' people,' we mark that the Vedic gods are arranged into
those of the earth, of the air, and of the heavens. Besides
all the divine powers active upon earth, the gods have especially placed one among men, *Agni*, the god of fire. Born of
the floods of heaven, the clouds, he descended upon earth
in the lightning. Disappearing again, a semi-divine being
had fetched him from his hiding, and brought him to the
clan of the Bhrigus. Since then they can procure him for
themselves, as he is begotten of the rubbing together of two
pieces of wood. In the softer of them he rests as in a
chamber, till wakened at early morn he bursts forth in his
glory. Then as in the sacrifice he is laid to the wood, he
licks it up with greedy tongue, and as the butter of the
offering is poured on him, he rises upwards with sound as a
neighing horse, the while adorning himself with sheen of
varying colours. As bursting forth every morning, he is also
the youngest of the gods. Rolling heavenwards the sacred
cloud, he rises upwards from out his flames, brushes heaven's
arch with his locks, and mingles with the rays of the sun.
Up he bears the hymns and sacrificial gifts of man; down
he brings the gods, whether for our help or to drink of the

soma prepared for them.   Nor did he ever weary of the service but once, when, before continuing it, he required of the god Varuna the best of the sacrifices.   And so he is the chief priest for man.   He also vanquishes darkness and its ghostly terrors, and he chases from their seats hostile clans, burning them up like dry brushwood, while he presides over his own, protects them, gives them all good, and is the loved inmate and friend of their homes.

Among the gods of the air we mark those of the wind and of the storm, and the genii of the three seasons—divine artificers whose deeds the myth recounts with the same poetico-symbolic meaning as in regard to Agni.   *Váta,* the wind, rises at morn to drink *soma,* and then brings up the early glow; the winds of every 'airt' follow as maidens to the feast.   *Rudra* is the god of the sweeping storm—fairer than the fairest, stronger than the strongest, who with arrow and spear smites the wicked, but who favours the just—nay, he is also the healer, as purifying the air from noxious vapours.   His children and companions are the *Marut,* the gods of thunder and stormy weather—' the singers of heaven '—they who also bring *Parǵanya,* the god of rain.   But mightiest far, not only among the gods of the air, but first of all gods, is *Indra.*   There can be no doubt that in the progress, if not in the developement, of Vedism, he came to be regarded as the great national deity, and to him the largest number of hymns is addressed.   First and foremost stands his great contest with the demoniac power, in which all the other gods retreated behind him, and his great conquest of it.   Thus he is the god of battle and of victory, who gives it to them who trust in him and pour forth to him the richest gift of *soma.*   The further developement of this may be easily anticipated.   In the language of Professor Kaegi (whom we have followed in this sketch): Thus he came to be viewed as creator and preserver of the world, as chief of all the generations of gods and men, as the mighty and boundless lord and ruler, as the cruel judge of the ungodly, and the sure defence of the pious.   As we listen to the many-toned song in which his creative power, his absolute greatness, his unlimited might, his resistless sway, his constant presence and rule, are extolled and vindicated against the sins of the wicked or the questions of the doubter, we feel that we are in presence of the real chief of the Indian Olympus.   Here also we come again and again on passages in the hymns which recall the language of the Old Testament.   This not only from fundamental kinship of mind in the nations of the East, but because the

same wants and views are in us all—or, at least, were in all—
and would find similar expression in circumstances of similar
education, surroundings, and even climatic impressions. But
all the more important is it to view the moral relation
between the supreme god of Vedism and Him of the Old
Testament. It cannot be necessary to mark the absolute and
wide contrast between them. One point will suffice to explain our reluctance to institute any comparison. *Indra*, as
Canon Cook reminds us, was drawn to the Aryans by copious.
libations of *soma*, which had thrown him into a state of wild
intoxication, and endued him with tenfold powers. Nay,
the exaltation of *Indra* was due to the power of *soma*. Here
are four lines given by Canon Cook in the German rendering of Grassmann : –

> ' O trinke, trinke, Indra, Held, den Soma :
> Berauschen mögen dich des Rausches Tränke,
> Den Bauch dir füllend mögen sie dich stärken ;
> Der wohlgebraute Füller labte Indra.'

This is from an ancient Rig (ii. 11), but there are others
of a later date, such as the soliloquy of *Indra* drunk with
soma, of which we cannot bring ourselves to reproduce
any part. Surely we look in vain here for an upward ascent
to the more pure and spiritual, nor do we feel specially drawn
to ' the corrective ' which we are invited to apply to our
previous notions and views.

   We are not forgetting that by the side of *Indra*, as the
representative of power, we have other deities which represent a very different religious element. We are here referring to the gods of the heavens. Among them we have
first the two *Açvin*, the heavenly charioteers. As the night
wanes, *Súryá*, the fair daughter of the sun-god, who has
chosen the two divine youths to be her husbands, ascends
with them the marvellous chariot made by the *Ribhu* (the
genii of the seasons). And so they bring the morning-light,
and glide onwards, as winged with the wind, or as the stream
falls from the mountain height, bearing with them healing
to the sick, youth to the aged, light to the blind, and
straightness to the lame. Closely following the two *Açvin,*
appears *Ushas,* Eos, Aurora, decked with manifold adornment
as a dancer. The sisters Aurora and Night, though of different colour, are of one mind, and peacefully follow and
relieve each other, Aurora wakening with light touch all
nature. And as a youth follows the maiden, so follows.
Súrya, of the golden hair, the Sun, on the track of *Ushas.*

We need not explain with what poetic beauty the divine functions of *Sûrya* are traced and described in accordance with what we already know of the general system. Nor can we speak of *Pûshan,* of *Vishnu*—the only one of the Vedic gods preserved in the triad of Hinduism, although he occupies only a subordinate position in the Veda—or of *Savitar.* But beyond and above the *Açvin,* or *Ushas,* or *Sûrya,* are yet another class of celestial gods, the highest of all, the *Áditya.* They are the seven sons of *Aditi,* which is infinity. There are not any hymns addressed to, but we find frequent invocation of Aditi, as the rich dispenser of blessing. Of the *Áditya,* or children of *Aditi,* the chief are— *Varuna, Mitra,* and *Aryaman.* As Dr. Kaegi puts it, one might be tempted to imagine that the Áditya represent ethical conceptions, not phenomena of nature. But it seems more accurate to regard them also as 'spiritually conceived ' personifications of the heavenly light and its manifold ' manifestations.' It is a further progress in this direction to view them as having created the eternal order both of the natural and the spiritual world, and as still ever maintaining it. Even in this modification of our estimate of the *Áditya,* it will be seen that they lead up to a totally different and far higher aspect than that hitherto noticed. First, the eternal light, and with it, order, are viewed as divine; next, the divine is order and light in every sense. It is now not only the heavenly light which is divine, but the divine is the heavenly light, alike in the material and in the mental and moral world. Here Vedism, both in its religious conceptions and in the aspirations of its worshippers, would reach its highest point, and that nearest to the Old and New Testaments. And because this view of the Divine as the creator and preserver of order, as the light that shineth in the moral world, is so far the same as that which, in one aspect of it, underlies the Old Testament, we find so many parallelisms, at least in expression if not in thought, between this class of hymns in the Rig Veda and verses in the Psalms, in the Book of Job, and even in some of the Prophets. For it is the idea of the Divine, as moral order and the light of the world, which underlies all higher faith and worship; all religious striving after righteousness; all aspiration after the higher, as both coming from and leading to the Divine— nay, even all sense of guilt as before this God; and all desire for forgiveness from Him, or entreaty of help for the better life. Equally would it follow from the contemplation of light and order as divine, to which the almost necessary converse would be the Divine as order and light; that sin would be viewed as the contrast of darkness to this light, and, in connexion with the prompting of conscience, as guilt, from which, on the one hand, forgiveness, and, on the other, spiritual help, would be sought by the interpenetration and the healing of that light which was divine. Thus there is a point of connexion between, and transition from, the material to the spiritual, or else from the spiritual to the material—or, as we prefer to say, a rational explanation of the juxtaposition and co-existence of two totally different and opposing elements.

This higher point once reached, all else seems to follow as of necessary sequence. The highest of the Aditya is *Varuna* (*ouranos*), originally the personification of the all-comprehending, all-compassing heaven. It is therefore in him that all which was associated with the Aditya, both as regards the physical and the moral world, appears concentrated and reaches its climax. To emphasise its moral and spiritual aspect, it is from *Varuna* that both forgiveness and help are ever sought. Here, as might be expected, where a similar fundamental tendency in the soul formulates itself in kindred Eastern minds, and, as regards nature, under similar impressions—the language of the Rig, in its comparatively few hymns to *Varuna*, often recalls the Old Testament. It is with *Varuna* also that the belief in individual immortality and the bliss of the soul after death are connected. But here also we observe the same interpenetration and transference of the materialistic into the spiritual. It is not only that *Agni* is invoked in connexion with the dismissal of the soul, that in general all the gods are introduced, and that the soul, in trying to pass the terrible dogs that bar the entrance into bliss, must claim to be a worshipper of *Indra*—whose character and worship the reader will remember—but that all presents the like mixture of the two elements. The soul of the pious, which had originally come from heaven, would go to the place which from of old the pious ancestors had prepared for it. It was *Yama* the divine who had first opened the way to it—*Yama*, also the first man, son of *Vivasvant*—the god of the morning-light and personification of all luminous appearances, the ancestor of the gods. Traversing the air, the soul, led by *Púshan*, crosses the stream, and has to pass the two broad-nosed, four-eyed, spotted dogs—the çarvára, the same as the Greek *Kerberos*—offspring of *Saramá*, the female messenger of *Indra*, whom thus we meet here again. These

guardians of Paradise, with baleful intent and gnashing teeth,
bar access to the wicked, but are conjured by the pious. We
pause again to mark not only the mixture of widely differing elements, already referred to, but how all this has its
equivalent in all other ancient religions. Professor Max
Müller has rightly reminded us of the words of Lessing, that
' without faith in a future life, in future reward and punish-
'ment, no religion can exist.' And such faith in a personal
immortality is found not only in general outline, but even
with many details, in the most ancient Indo-Germanic times;
it equally exists in Vedism, among the Iranians, and the
ancient Greeks, Romans, Germans, and Kelts. It would lead
us too far to give detailed proof of this, or even to indicate
the works in which the students of ancient nationalities and
their faiths have, with unvarying accordance, marked their
discovery of these expectancies. But the student of the
origin of religion cannot fail to perceive the deep importance
of the universal existence of these elements. In details also
there is a curious accordance which, so far as ancient Greek
and Roman notions are concerned, will already have been observed. But the Avesta also often speaks of a ' bridge '—and
in the ancient faith of the Iranians the 'bridge of the
' Assembler ' (*Kinvat*), which leads into Paradise, is likewise
guarded by two dogs against all but the pious.

In that highest heaven of light, in view of the gods
Varuna and Yama, what awaiteth the soul of the pious?
Enjoyment and bliss of every kind; and not only of the
soul, but also of a new body. For, although the Rig Veda
enters not into details of that future bliss, and it is true
that 'ancient Hindu wisdom sought no answer' to the
question, 'What shall be the employment of the blest?' yet,
on the other hand, the delights of earth, and even of sensual enjoyment, were connected with it. Under the leafy
shade of that tree where Yama drinks with the gods, our
first progenitor and father lovingly makes provision for
the great ancestors. More of this kind occurs in the
popular Atharva Veda, and later on, when we are told of
ponds of cream, rivers of honey, streams of milk, shining
cows, which ever offer their milk to the pious without
endangering them by their hoofs, besides similar realistic
presentations of good things to come. But closely connected alike with the thoughts of that happy Beyond and
with the worship of the gods was the *cultus* of the dead
ancestry—both those that were known and those that were
not known—who were invited to share with *Yama* and *Agni*

the sacrificial food prepared, as well as the draughts of *soma*.
Much do we owe to those blessed ancestors who look upon, and
still surround us, mingling with us when we sacrifice, and
bringing us gifts, blessing, and help.   Strength also do they
dispense to us, wealth, and progeny; they fight in our
battles; they reward, whether for good or for evil; 'they
' bear to heaven the morning-red, and guard in a thousand
' ways the sun; they deck, as a dark horse with pearls, the
' sky with stars, and lay darkness into night, and into the
' day the brightness of light.'* We need scarcely remind our
readers that this *cultus* of 'the fathers' (*pitri, pitaras*), born
of belief in immortality, reverence for ancestors, and family
and clan feelings, is also found among the Greeks, and in the
divi Manes and *Lares* of the ancient Romans.   The same
cultus of the departed existed among the Iranians as that
of the righteous spirits, *fravashi*.   From the point of view
of the mixture and interpenetration of the material and
spiritual views of light, this *cultus* of the departed as the
children of light and the bearers or ministers of light is easily
accounted for.   On the other hand, the souls of the impious
are cast into outmost darkness; but the Rig Veda knows
nothing of the later doctrine of the transmigration of souls.
    This account of the Āditya must reduce to much more
moderate proportions any extravagant estimate that may be
formed of even the highest elements in Vedism; and this
more sober view will be strengthened as we recall the position
occupied by two other deities in the Vedic Olympus.   To
each of them were transferred in course of time all the properties and peculiar activities of all the other gods.   To one
of them, *Soma*, repeated reference has already been made.
A whole book of hymns is, as we remember, devoted to him.
Properly speaking, *Soma* was the juice of a plant bearing
the same name, which originally the fair-winged falcon had
brought from the highest heaven, or else from the far-off
mountains, where *Varuna* had placed it.   This is the first
point of connexion between *Varuna* and *Soma*.   This juice,
purified, mixed with milk or the boiling of barley, and left
to ferment for some time, was the intoxicating drink which
formed the delight of gods and of men.   Under its beatific
influence, or rather in its intoxication, man forgot his sorrow,
lost disease and pain, seemed to become rich; while gods
fought and conquered, and *Indra* reigned supreme.   This
Soma was personified as a real deity; he is addressed in

---

* Kaegi, p. 98.

the highest strains, all power is ascribed to him, and all
blessings are sought from him.   It was the same among the
Iranians, where *Haoma* occupies the place of *Soma*.   *Soma* is
loved of all gods, and intoxicates them all.   Each of the
peculiar activities and properties of *Agni*, *Açvin*, *Púshan*,
and even *Indra* is ascribed to him.   But he is not confined
to these spheres, nor does he merely bring outward deliverance or bodily healing, so that the blind see and the lame
walk, and that he besets his worshippers before and behind.
He also bears up the heavens, supports the earth, and
holds all nations in his hand.   But, far beyond this, all that
has been associated with the highest and most spiritual
personifications of the divine, with *Mitra*, *Aryaman*, and
even *Varuna*, is also ascribed to *Soma*.   The commands of
Varuna are his also ; he likewise punishes guilt, and to him
does the sinner address himself for help and even for forgiveness.   This statement may appear so incredible that we
quote (after Kaegi's rendering) at least one passage, for
which no fewer than three references are given : ' This
' *Soma*, drawn into my inside, I invoke as quite near ;
' whatever sin we have committed, may he graciously forgive
' it ! '   To this we may add the following stanza as reminding
us of similar addresses to *Varuna* :—

> ' Be gracious, Soma, King, for our salvation,
>   Be well assured thou, that we are thine.
>   Against us rise both wrath and cunning, Soma :
>   Oh, leave us not in power of the foe.'

It is scarcely necessary to do more than mention, for completeness' sake, besides *Soma*, yet another deity : *Brihaspati*,
or *Brahmanaspati*, ' the lord of prayer '—' a later abstraction,
' alike the creation and the personification ' of the priesthood.

It is time to draw this sketch of Vedism to a conclusion.
Our main object has been to present the simple facts from
which every unprejudiced thinker may draw his own inferences, free from those philosophic theories which have put
upon Vedism a construction most attractive, indeed, from
its ingenuity and its accordance with certain general ideas,
and very seductive, but not borne out by impartial consideration of the whole case ; and in which too often comparisons,
which on a general view appear inapplicable, and are not
unfrequently painful, are—we feel bound to say, sometimes
needlessly—introduced.   But beyond the original Vedism
'at Professor Monier Williams calls ' the second phase

' of the Hindu religion,' Brahmanism, which surely no one would commend to us either for correction or instruction. Most notable among what are described as its four phases is the philosophical, which, indeed, had its germ in Vedism itself. This is the Vedânta, ' the end, the goal, the highest ' object of the Veda.' But a sadder end or more terrible condemnation of its object could not be imagined. In fact, it is not religion at all, nor even a system of philosophy, but, in the words of Professor Monier Williams, ' a form of ' mystical religious speculation.' We should be sorry to refer to it for religious direction or for philosophic teaching, or to recognise in it any of the highest elements for mind or heart. The reader who wishes to have a brief but lucid general view of it must consult Professor Monier Williams's book, which in this, as in its general account of Hindu religions, is very satisfactory. Here it must suffice to say that the Eastern mind is not adapted for rigid philosophical processes, and that dreamy, purely imaginative speculation constantly intrudes itself, ending at best in a misty Pantheism, in which this Self and that Self—the subjective and the objective—are merged in a sort of shadowy nihilism. This, apart from philosophical absurdities—partly the outcome of previous developement—is the last and highest word of philosophical Brahmanism. But this its last word we can study far better in its Western expression. And it cannot be the last word in our thinking of, and aspiring after, the highest and best truth—unless, indeed, the goal of humanity be the pessimism of Schopenhauer.

If at the close of these investigations we place before ourselves the problem of the comparative history and origin of religion, with which we began, we shall find the Abbé de Broglie both an able and a pleasant companion. With peculiarly French lucidity he sets forth the results of thinking, often acute and convincing, and always worthy of consideration, applied to a subject which his entire religious faith makes only the more interesting, and on which he brings to bear a wide course of reading. If we understand the Abbé aright, his language seems at least to point to the conclusion which we have previously expressed: that, in the comparative study of religions, the fundamental differences obtaining among them are really of greater importance than their similarities. Yet the latter also — especially by the side of these differences—raise the most serious questions. The superficial observer may, by exclusively emphasising similarity, reach conclusions pleasing to himself in his capacity of philosopher and critic of religions. But the earnest thinker will also have to apply himself to the problem, and at least seek some solution of the question of the co-existence and juxtaposition of two so very different elements in the most ancient religions. This purer element, whence is it? whither does it lead, and how far in the upward direction? The materials for answering the two last questions have already been furnished, and it must have been perceived that, on the one hand, while there is this co-existence, there is not any evidence of a developement to the purer, but on the contrary a commixture indicative of decline. On the other hand, despite points of actual contact, for which reasons have already been indicated, no comparison can be instituted between Vedism and the pure and high teaching, say, of the Old Testament, if it were only because in Vedism the purer elements are relative, not absolute, and intermixed with those of the opposite character. Assuredly it is not—as the Abbé de Broglie reminds us—by calling upon his god, as does the Aryan poet, ' to inebriate ' himself with Soma; to fill his belly with it, that in his ' drunkenness he might the more strongly strike the dark- ' some serpent,' that the Hebrew seer expects deliverance.

Yet whence comes that common belief in one supreme God, in punishment and reward, help and vengeance, judgement and forgiveness, which, with more or less clearness and consistency, we find in all primitive religions: all of them finding expression not only in beliefs, but in worship and in rites? At least three different answers have been proposed, of which the Abbé Broglie gives both a clear and fair discussion. According to the one system, man slowly developed from the animal, gradually rose from the grossest notions, till, by a series of evolution, he reached up to the highest and noblest. To this theory, which bears the name of ' animism,' the lessons derived from the Veda concerning a high and spiritual divinity present an absolute negative. According to the second system, those higher views are the spontaneous product of two elements, the one subjective, the other objective. As regards the former, man possesses, as distinctive from the lower creation, a sense of the Divine —*sensus numinis*. This is his inherent and inalienable birthright. Looking out with this *sensus numinis* upon the great phenomena of nature which he encounters everywhere—in the East in special grandeur—man arrives at the primitive idea of the Divine: not Monotheism, from which Polytheism could never spring; nor yet Polytheism, since the idea of a

God would necessarily precede that of many gods; but it would be *Henotheism*. This idea, applied to the different phenomena of nature, would lead to Polytheism, and this again would in turn, by reflection, give place to the idea of a divine unity, whether monotheistic or pantheistic. To this view it would suffice to object that all the premisses might be granted, and yet the conclusions denied. Admitting the *sensus numinis* within, and its being called forth by the phenomena without, the result would much more likely be Polytheism. It would not by itself lead up to those purer and spiritual conceptions of the Divine which we find in the Rig Veda; while, lastly, *henotheism*, which is really the name of a complex phenomenon, is by a somewhat strange process made the explanation of the origin of that phenomenon itself. For, as M. de Broglie rightly urges, *henotheism* is really a synthesis of two ideas: that of the Infinite, which implies unity, and that of the multiplicity of gods. Thus it is not a primitive idea, but the juxtaposition of two fundamentally opposite ideas. We will not speak of other difficulties which prove that this view is rather a philosophical speculation than based on facts of history. We are therefore still in presence of a dualism, consisting of the coexistence of not only the monotheistic but the moral and spiritual element by the side of the polytheistic, and the materialistic and naturalistic. The origin of this latter we can understand; for the former M. de Broglie would account by a primitive Monotheism, the result of perhaps not an outward, but an inward, communication to man from his Maker. And here we might possibly see in the purer, moral, and spiritual conceptions of the Divine, a reflection, or, may we not rather say, an idealisation and perfection of the moral elements which man finds within his own inner consciousness.

Beyond this we may not go. But if this in any manner indicates the right path, then India can teach us yet another and a better lesson. It is this, that, as regards all that is highest, India has not anything to teach us that we cannot learn far better in a quite other direction. For, without entering into the labyrinth of theological controversy, could any unprejudiced person in sober earnest propose to compare the jargon of these inebriated divinities either with the sublime imagery and profound moral insight of the Book of Job, or the devout adoration of the Hebrew Psalms?

ART. VII.—1. *Navy Estimates for the year* 1885–86, *with Appendix.* Ordered by the House of Commons to be printed, February 19, 1885.

2. *Return to an Order of the Honourable the House of Lords, dated December 2, 1884, for Tabular Statement of the Ships laid down by the Board of the Admiralty since* 1880, *and Diagram illustrating the Armoured and Unarmoured Tonnage, built in her Majesty's Dockyards and by Contract, and the Total Naval Expenditure from* 1865–66 *to* 1883–84, *inclusive.* March 1885.

3. *Return of the Amount of Shipping—Tons' Weight of Hull—Estimated for, and calculated to have been actually built, from the year* 1865–66 *to the year* 1883–84, *together with an Appendix.* Ordered by the House of Commons to be printed, August 8, 1884.

4. *Report of the Committee appointed to inquire into the Conditions under which Contracts are invited for the Building or Repairing of Ships, including their Engines, for her Majesty's Navy.* Presented to both Houses of Parliament, by command of her Majesty. October 1884.

5. *Memoirs of the Rise and Progress of the Royal Navy.* By CHARLES DERRICK, of the Navy Office. 4to. London: 1806.

DURING the past few months the condition of the navy has been much discussed and commented on, as well out of Parliament as in it, and public attention has been awakened by persistently repeated statements that our navy has fallen far below its necessary strength; that it has, practically speaking, ceased to exist; that not only our national prestige but our national safety is endangered; and that, in fact, we owe our continued existence as a free state to the mercy or goodwill of our more powerful neighbours, who may at any moment yield to the temptation which our weakness offers them. Such statements cannot and ought not to be passed over in silence; for their frequent repetition is calculated to create alarm, if not panic. And they have been repeated very widely indeed, and with an air of authority, not only by numerous powerful though anonymous writers on the daily press, but by men whose name and former position seem to vouch for their knowledge of the facts: by Sir Thomas Symonds, retired Admiral of the Fleet; by Sir Spencer Robinson, ex-Controller of the Navy;

by Sir Edward Reed, ex-Chief-Constructor of the Navy; and they have been accepted by Mr. W. H. Smith, late First Lord of the Admiralty; by Lord Henry Lennox, late Secretary of the Admiralty, and by very many officers of rank and recognised ability. They have therefore a claim to a full and candid examination, and are of a nature to demand it. They may be false or they may be true, but they neither refute nor confirm themselves: if false, the falsehood ought to be exposed, and the public mind set at rest; if true, it is impossible to over-estimate their gravity, or to find language strong enough to condemn the torpor or the parsimony of the Government which has permitted a blight so deadly to fall upon us.

Of all these charges so freely made, the one to which most weight has been popularly attached is that, whilst the strength of a navy can be counted only by the number and force of its heavy ironclads, the capital ships of our navy at the present time are not superior in number and are inferior in force to those of one possible enemy, and are hopelessly inadequate to sustain a conflict against a possible coalition of two or more adversaries. So enunciated, the proposition divides itself into three parts, an assumption and two sequences. But the assumption is by no means axiomatic, though it has been commonly put forward as such; and the proof of the sequences has been based on carefully manipulated statistics, and on unsupported assertions.

Of these last, that which has sunk deepest into the minds of hearers and readers is the statement, repeated in various language, that, during the last 150 years, it has always been a maxim of English state policy that the number of English ships of the line should be double that of French, or equal to that of the combined navies of Europe; and that, as a well-known fact, this proportion has always been approximately maintained. A reference to the pages of Derrick or Beatson or Schomberg * will appear to confirm this statement; for it will show that, on the eve of our greatest wars, the numbers of ships of the line were approximately—

In Year	English	French	Spanish
1756	142	90	50
1778	131	63	62
1793	141	82	77

and these, or something similar, are the numbers which have been commonly quoted, though at least one paper of the

* Naval and Military Memoirs, 1804; Naval Chronology, 1802.

highest repute * has committed itself to the extraordinary statement that 'in 1779 we had 293 ships of the line.' Putting, however, this singular mistake altogether on one side, the numbers as shown above are fairly in agreement with the assertion to which such prominence has lately been given; but what does not appear in this table, what does not appear in Derrick, is the fact that, so far as the English navy was concerned, these numbers are obtained by counting as a ship of the line every ship on the list of the navy, quite regardless of her age or fitness for service, whether still on the stocks, or rotten from hoar antiquity. In so forming a numerical estimate of the capital ships in our navy at the present time, a modern Derrick would include, not only all existing ironclads, even of the most obsolete types—the 'Royal Oak,' 'Zealous,' or 'Royal Sovereign'—but all the old line-of-battle ships which, in different stages of decay and inutility, crowd our harbours; such as the 'Vigo' receiving hulk at Devonport; the 'Pitt' coal depôt at Portsmouth; or the 'Warspite' training-ship in the Thames. A glance through the pages of the Navy List will show that, reckoned in this way, the gross number of our capital ships is extremely great; and as no other country has got anything at all approaching to such a museum of antiquities, it would be no difficult matter to show—on paper—that the English navy is at the present time numerically stronger, far stronger, than the combined navies of the whole world. Now, it was exactly in this way that our numerically large lists of the last or the first half of this century were made up. Of effective ships we never had, at the beginning of a war, any overwhelming preponderance. This statement is so distinctly contrary to the one which has been so often repeated and generally believed, that it is perhaps necessary to examine it in closer detail.

It has been already said that at the outbreak of the war with France in 1756, the number of English ships of the line is given as 142. Of these, in May 1756, ninety-three were in commission, or fitting for service; of the other forty-nine, six only were in commission during the whole period of the war; the rest being hulks, prison ships, church ships, and the like. Of the ninety-three which were commissioned at the beginning of the war, twenty-four were 50-gun ships, which were no longer considered as fit for a place in the line of battle, and several of the rest were in the last stage of

---

* Engineer, October 3, 1884.

decrepitude; so much so, that during the war five were condemned abroad as unfit for the passage home from the East or West Indies, and two others actually fell to pieces by the way, the men being fortunately saved. According to any strict perquisition, such as would be now judged correct, there were not in the English Navy, in May 1756, at the very outside, more than sixty-five effective ships of the line. At the same time the French navy mustered a nominal ninety, of which ten were 50-gun ships. The French 50-gun ships were much more powerful than the English; and of the other eighty, all, or almost all, were in active commission during the war, though some of them were probably crazy enough. Ten, however, is a most liberal deduction on that score; and applying it, as well as the ten 50-gun ships, we have the number of effective French ships of the line as not less than seventy. Spain did not join France till five years later, but she is said to have had in 1756 forty-two new and effective ships of the line ready for sea. These numbers can only be approximate, but they result from an honest attempt to apply a sound and critical canon to the navy lists of 1756. They most probably err by representing the English navy in too favourable a light; and yet they must seem extraordinary. We therefore repeat that, in 1756, on the eve of one of our most glorious wars—one in which we virtually wiped the French from off the sea, towards the end of which our ships lay in Quiberon Bay or Basque Roads as safely and as free from annoyance as in the Sound or at Spithead—the approximate numbers, in respect of line-of-battle ships of the principal navies of Europe, were :—

	English	French	Spanish
Nominal	142	90	50
Real and effective	65	70	42

And, as is very well known, the size of French ships was much greater than that of English ships of the same class, and their armament was much heavier.

But it must be borne in mind that these numbers refer to the beginning of the war. A similar comparison, referring to the end of the war, marks the real difference between the two countries. In England, forty ships, mostly of seventy-four guns, were launched during the war; but some ten of these are included in the former statement as having been launched early in 1756; and twenty-one, taken from the French or Spaniards, were added to the English navy. On the other hand, three were captured by the enemy, and

seventeen were lost; but, with few exceptions, these were small
or much decayed, so that the total loss of effective ships did
certainly not exceed eight. The French, on the other hand,
had lost—wrecked, destroyed, or captured—thirty-eight or
forty, and had not built many; they could not have had
more than thirty-five effective ships of the line remaining at
the peace. The Spaniards, having had a shorter period of
war, had not lost so many, though the capture of Havana
was peculiarly fatal to them. Of what they lost by wreck
we have no account, but thirteen of their ships were captured. In 1763, the numbers of effective ships of the line
in the three navies were something like :—

English	French	Spanish
108	35	25

But this period of extreme success and brilliant achievement was followed by one of extraordinary decadence; so
much so, that during the Spanish armament of 1770,

'much dissatisfaction and no small degree of surprise was occasioned
by reason of the bad condition of a very large proportion of the ships
which were ordered to be fitted for sea, and which were obliged to be
set aside soon after they were taken in hand; and many of the said
ships, which before the armament were ranked among those in good
condition, underwent a considerable repair after the armament was
over, in order to put them into that state. Had a war of any long
continuance taken place at this time the bad condition of the ships
must have proved incalculably injurious to the country. . . . The
store of oak timber in the dockyards, which had been upon the decrease
from about the conclusion of the war, was reduced to a very low ebb
by the end of the year 1770. This, and the state of the ships, as
related above, caused considerable alarm to Government, and probably
became an object of public attention, as a committee of the House of
Commons was appointed in March, 1771, to consider how his Majesty's
yards might be better supplied with timber. The committee made
their report in April or May following . . . [but] it does not appear
that anything material resulted therefrom.' *

It was this want of stores, this depletion of our arsenals,
more even than the want of ships, which told so terribly
against us when war with France again broke out. In June
1778 the number of English ships of the line, exclusive of
50-gun ships, was, according to Derrick, 131; but Beatson,
who gives a nominal list, has only 122, of which twenty-
seven were either wholly worn out or building; and that
ships were not hastily condemned is proved by the fact
that the 'Princess Amelia,' 'Buffalo,' 'Leviathan,' 'Royal

---

* Derrick, pp. 158–9.

'George,' and some others equally rotten, were counted as effective. Four years later, the 'Royal George' had a chance of proving herself fatally so—for the enemy. These figures would seem to put the numerical strength of our navy in 1778 at ninety-five ships of the line; but it is a matter of familiar history that the utmost efforts of the Admiralty could not get to sea more than fifty-three; and that, in the following year, under the threat of invasion and the most severe pressure ever put on the country, the aggregate number of the ships at sea, at home and abroad, amounted to only seventy. But in 1778 the French had sixty-three and the Spaniards sixty-two, or jointly 125 ships of the line, mostly new and efficient; and we know that in July the French had forty-six actually at sea. In July of the following year they had fifty-five; and it was then that the combined fleet of France and Spain, numbering sixty-six ships of the line, invaded the English Channel, and held it for several weeks, in defiance of the English fleet, which, after every exertion, numbered only thirty-eight ships for the defence of the country.

Before 1793 we had in some degree taken to heart the lesson which had been so rudely taught us. We had then, omitting 50-gun ships, not indeed the 141 ships reckoned by Derrick, but 113 actually fit for service; two more were launched early in the year, and, within a few months of the declaration of war, we had eighty-five in commission. Against them, the French had in their harbours something like eighty-four, of which seventy-six were said to be fit for service; and of these the average size and weight of metal were considerably in excess of those of the English ships; so much so, that James, comparing the two navies at the time, tabulates them thus :—

	Ships of the Line	No. of Guns	Aggregate Weight of Broadside in lbs.
English . .	115	8,718	88,957
French . .	76	6,002	73,957

and quotes, though without a reference, Jean Bon Saint-André as having said, 'Avant la prise de Toulon, la France ' était la puissance maritime la plus redoutable de l'Europe.' At this time, Spain had seventy-seven ships of the line, of which fifty-nine were in commission, though sixteen of these must, from their age, have been barely fit for service. Holland had about twenty; Portugal and Naples, ten; the Baltic powers, eighty-two, of which probably not more than fifty could be considered efficient. The true comparison, then, of the navies of Europe, in respect of line-of-battle ships, at the beginning of 1793, is approximately :—

England 115
France 76
Spain 43
Holland . . . . 20 } 199
Portugal and Naples 10
Baltic Powers 50

And after-events showed that a coalition of these several navies, though it never took place, was by no means out of the range of possibility. In the face of such figures, which have been public property for the last seventy years, to repeat the customary story of England's navy being numeri-cally equal to that of all Europe is palpably absurd.

We are not now speaking of the efficiency of the ships' companies, or the relative value of the ships with their men on board, as they were or might have been on the day of battle. It is nevertheless interesting to note that, after a short visit to Cadiz, in June 1793, Nelson wrote: 'They 'have four first-rates in commission . . . very fine ships, 'but shockingly manned. . . . I am certain if our six barges' 'crews, who are picked men, had got on board one of their 'first-rates, they would have taken her. The Dons may 'make fine ships; they cannot, however, make men.' Or, again, that on July 7, 1793, a fleet of twenty-four Spanish ships of the line 'did not, after several hours' trial, form 'anything which could be called a line-of-battle ahead.' * The French were undoubtedly never quite so bad, but they were heavily weighted by the loss of all their officers and the greater number of their trained gunners and disciplined seamen.

After the Peace—it might more properly be called the truce—of Amiens, which did not last long enough to permit the enemy to recruit their exhausted navy, the number of French ships of the line appears to have been but twenty-six, though the list may be swelled to sixty-six by including ships building, and was actually raised to about forty-five within eighteen months. Of English ships, the gross number is given as 177, which is often quoted as a measure of the over-whelming force at our disposal. This is, of course, quite wrong; for, though we had a force both absolutely and relatively very large, the number of effective ships was not more than 111.

It is unnecessary to follow the comparison of the fleets

* Nelson Despatches, vol. i. pp. 300–312.

through the present century of peace; it is enough to have illustrated the method of reduction by its application at three important epochs of our history. But it must be remembered that a similar reduction must be applied to all the numbers which have been of late so freely quoted, although they give no idea whatever of the effective strength of the English navy at the times named, or of the true relation between the fleets of the different countries. It may be difficult, or even impossible, to obtain comparisons rigidly accurate; but to obtain them within a fair approximation is open to anyone who will take the trouble to scrutinise our old Navy Lists. And it is from a consideration of these historical and reduced numbers that we say that the comparisons now given of the English and French fleets, *however they may be taken,* show that, so far as its capital ships are concerned, our navy has never, in time of peace, been relatively stronger than it is at the present day. And it is necessary to emphasize the words, *however they may be taken,* for it is almost impossible to say what these comparisons really are; every self-constituted censor and judge has a standard of his own, and no two agree. In comparing the navies of former days, it has seemed not unfair to take the aggregate number of effective ships of the line, bad and good together, as affording a rough estimate, irrespective of the difference between ships of one hundred guns and ships of sixty; but we are now called on to examine, to exaggerate, and to reckon up every defect or shortcoming or weakness of every English ship; and to count as effective every French ironclad, including many as yet unbuilt, and a number of small protected gunboats. Figures so manipulated have perhaps the appearance of statistics, but in reality have no meaning whatever. According to the comparison made out by the Sea-Lords of the Admiralty, with the best means of knowing the facts, the present relative strength of the English and French navies, as far as ironclads are concerned, may be stated thus:—

	English		French	
	No.	Displacement in tons	No.	Displacement in tons
Modern . .	30	210,430	19	127,828
Quasi-obsolete .	16	115,520	12	53,066
Total . .	46	325,950	31	180,894

This is, however, the comparison made by men, who, whatever their professional attainments and reputation, may be considered as now on their trial at the bar of public opinion. It is well, therefore, to add that it has not been contradicted on any material point, though it has been objected to as incomplete, as not taking into account the ships fitting and building. There is no reason why these should not be counted, provided always it is understood that they are not real and effective ships. Thus amended, the statement will appear :—

	English		French	
	No.	Displacement	No.	Displacement
Ready . .	46	325,950	31	180,894
Fitting . .	7	58,030	7	54,398
Building . .	5	46,200	6	59,093
Coast defence :				
Fitting . .	—	—	1	4,707
Building .	—	—	4	31,090
In all . .	58	430,180	49	330,182

To which may be added, on both sides, some twelve or fifteen vessels, more or less completely obsolete, capable, perhaps, of being utilised on emergency for harbour defence, but not to be properly reckoned as effective ships. The French have also eight armoured gunboats fitting or building; vessels averaging about 1,300 tons' displacement, and carrying one large gun. It may be admitted that, as gunboats, they will be very formidable; but their right to be classed as capital ships does not appear, and at any rate they have not yet a nautical existence. The same may be said of two powerful French ships, 'Brennus' and 'Charles Martel,' which have been commenced only within the last few months; as also, on the other side, of the four first-class ironclads, and of the five so-called 'belted cruisers' which are really ironclads, provided for in the estimates for the current year. Such ships, which can scarcely be ready for sea within the next four years, do not enter into any comparison of the present day; but if it were permissible to reckon them, the English strength would appear in a still more favourable light.

So far, then, as the alleged inferiority of numbers is concerned, the outcry, amounting almost to panic, which has been raised, would seem to spring out of a total misconception of the facts of our past history, and an ignorant belief that numbers, such as those given by Derrick, were rigidly and scientifically accurate. It is only so that we can explain the statements made, from different sides of the House, by Sir Donald Currie and Sir John Hay, to the effect that 'Great Britain should have a naval force sufficient to con- ' tend against any three powers combined together, and ' double the navy of France;' and that 'no Estimates are ' satisfactory which do not enable the Admiralty to com- ' plete, without delay, as an addition to those now building, ' thirty-three completely-armoured ironclads.' * On which Sir Thomas Symonds remarks: 'As an Admiral of the Fleet, ' bound to understand the subject, I am convinced that, ' without such a force, we shall have a naval Sedan, at war ' with France alone;' † and goes on to propose an immediate additional expenditure of 42,500,000*l.* We can only say that, though an Admiral of the Fleet, Sir Thomas Symonds seems *not* to understand the subject.

But quite independent of numbers, a certain class of critics have displayed considerable ingenuity in arguing that we have practically no navy at all. The principle on which such a comparison is made is the carefully selecting, according to the caprice of the tabulator, some quality which ideal ironclads ought to possess; and rejecting, as unworthy of any serious consideration, all those which do not come up to the fancied standard. And this standard is very variable; it has run through many fashions. A few years ago the condition in vogue was extreme size; a ship must be over 10,000 tons. Afterwards, there was a rage for extremely thick armour; nothing less than twenty inches could be accepted. At present, the demand is for side armour, stretching the whole length of the ship; none not so armoured is effective or even seaworthy. As very few of our ships are so armoured, and none of our largest, most recent, and most powerful, it follows that our navy is practically reduced to some half-dozen weakly-armoured and semi-obsolete vessels.

Some of these and other fancies have been specially advocated by Sir Edward Reed, who, at different periods of his unofficial life, has publicly testified his admiration and

---

* Times, December 3, 1884; March 17, 1885.

† Our Great Peril if War overtake us with our Fleet deficient in Number, Structure, and Armament; 2nd edition, 1885.

approval of almost every possible type of ships of war except those which, at the particular time, happen to be accepted by the Admiralty. He has himself the credit of having, whilst Chief Constructor of the Navy, first solved the problem of building armoured ships of moderate size; and the ' Bellerophon,' of 7,550 tons, which he designed more than twenty years ago, though quasi-obsolete, is still a good and effective ship; but now he is unable to find becoming language in which to express his opinion of an Admiralty which has built, or is building, our largest ships with an average displacement of only 9,363 tons, whilst the average displacement of the largest French ships is 10,490. ' English ' ships,' he says, 'have been deliberately made inferior by ' our Admiralty, ship by ship, and squadron by squadron; ' and their marked inferiority is not a very pleasant fact to ' begin with, nor one that gives to the English Admiralty a ' very patriotic air.' * He has attempted to support his position by reference to an unfortunate statement of Mr. Barnaby's in the ' Encyclopædia Britannica,' that 'the ' fairest available approximate measure of the power of the ' ships is their displacement or total weight.' It is unfortunate because it is possible, by separating it from the context, to misunderstand and to misrepresent it. Sir Edward Reed has chosen to avail himself of this possibility: he has misrepresented it, and he has done so deliberately; for the meaning of the passage, as it stands in the article from which he has removed it, is plain and unmistakable; and Mr. Barnaby has often and publicly avowed his preference for ships of comparatively moderate dimensions, both as costing less and as more efficient weapons of war.† In this view he has been supported by the general consensus of naval opinion, and the Admiralty has made no secret of its determination to keep down the size of even the largest ironclads below 10,000 tons as an extreme limit. To detect this, now, did certainly not call for a large amount of critical acumen; but to condemn it, in the language which Sir Edward Reed has used, did indeed require a very full measure of effrontery and virulence.

Nor is he better pleased with the construction of our recent ships than with the size. The problem which the design of an ironclad sets before the naval architect is, to a given tonnage, to apply the permitted weight of armour

* Times, February 19.
† Brassey's ' British Navy,' vol. iii. p. 14.

in the most effective way. The Constructors of the Admiralty have solved this by massing the great bulk of the weight for the defence of a central citadel, within which are sheltered the engines, boilers, and magazines, the rest of the ship being protected by a comparatively light armoured deck, and by cellular subdivision. Sir Edward Reed does not approve of this solution of the problem, and he has written to the 'Times' to say so. According to him—

'Our ships have been reduced in size, stripped of armour, and made individually and collectively unspeakably inferior to the French, and no compensation whatever, by an increase in the thickness of their armour, has been provided. It seems incredible, but so it is, and we have to face the miserable truth. It would have seemed dreadful even to know that there were to be found within the limits of Great Britain any set of men capable of entertaining the thought of stripping all of her Majesty's principal ships, one after the other as they were laid down, of two-thirds of their protecting armour . . . but what are we to think or say when men capable of this appalling conduct have been constituting for years past the Board of the British Admiralty, have been all that time controlling the destinies of the Navy, and through the Navy the destinies of the country, and are at this moment pursuing, as far as they dare, this inexplicable and infatuated course?' *

All which, and a great deal more, is merely Sir Edward Reed's very disagreeable way of saying that just at present his views on certain points of naval construction differ from those of Mr. Barnaby. But, as Mr. Barnaby has a far greater experience of the construction of first-class ironclads than Sir Edward Reed, and has had under him a large and carefully-trained staff of competent assistants—including Mr. White, now Chief Constructor for Sir William Armstrong's Company, and Mr. Barnes, of whom Sir Edward Reed, when writing for critical and appreciative members of his own profession, has almost at the same time recorded his opinion that he 'has distinguished himself more than any other ' Englishman by the novel application of graphic and other ' eminently practical processes to the production of simple ' and trustworthy methods of calculating stability,' †—a general public, without entering into the abstruse and technical question of curves of stability, may reasonably believe that the Admiralty have been guided by sound judgement and discretion. Sir Edward Reed has now announced his intention of bringing the matter before the House of Commons. He has given notice of a motion which amounts

---

* Times, February 19.
† The Stability of Ships. By Sir Edward J. Reed (1885). P. xvi.

to a sweeping condemnation of the Admiralty policy; though how this purely technical question is to be discussed by the Members of the House of Commons is not quite clear. It is, however, worthy of remark that Sir Edward Reed has always avoided the discussion of it before a competent tribunal. He refused to attend before the 'Inflexible' Committee. A few months ago, addressing a naval and professional audience at the United Service Institution, he declined to discuss it; and in his recent work on 'Stability of Ships' he has not ventured on one word in illustration of his views on this most important subject. But in the columns of a newspaper, or before an audience ignorant of his technicalities, he has accustomed himself to an unrestrained indulgence in flowers of rhetoric, in flights of imagination, and, we are compelled to add, in disingenuous presentation of facts and in illegitimate distortion of evidence. It is painful to have to say this, but it is necessary to point out that, in writing to the 'Times' the gross and vehement letter to which we have already referred, he did not scruple, by the omission of some words and the alteration or insertion of others, to give a widely different colour to a remark made by Admiral Wilson, the present superintendent of the dockyard at Devonport. The charge is so grave that it is incumbent on us to substantiate it by repeating the passage, marking in italics the words which Sir Edward Reed omitted, and by brackets the words which he inserted.

'I do not like these soft ends at all; they may *not* [all] be breached, and *have* a *big* hole knocked into *their deck* [you] big enough to drive a coach and four through; *but* [even] if one or two shots *penetrate* [get in], *and* water gets in, the ship *will get* [gets] down by the nose, she won't steer, she cannot steam, [and] she is thrown out altogether, *and you* [. You] lose confidence in *the* [your] ship. [And] What is the result? You are at a [great] disadvantage, and you are [soon] knocked into a cocked hat.' *

Lord Henry Lennox, who boasts himself as Sir Edward Reed's pupil, has imitated and improved on the tactics of his master, in a letter to the 'Morning Post' (March 11), in which he says:—

'It is very certain that our present system of armouring the central portions only of our ships is wrong; a fact which, in reality, was proved years ago in the case of the "Inflexible"—the committee which investigated her design having, in so many words, reported that

---

* Journal of the Royal United Service Institution, vol. xxviii. p. 1039. Times, Feb. 19, 1885.

in the very probable event of water gaining access to her unarmoured ends, she would become next to a helpless log at the mercy of the enemy. . . . It is impossible to understand the policy which has permitted so many ironclads to be built on the same principle as the "Inflexible" (with unarmoured ends), in the face of the adverse opinions formed on her by so many reliable naval officers and experts.'

As matter of fact, with which Lord Henry Lennox is or ought to be familiar, the 'Inflexible' Committee said nothing whatever about 'water gaining access to her unarmoured ' ends,' the probability of which was never for a moment in doubt, and about which their opinion was not asked.   What they did report was that—

'The committee are of opinion that the complete penetration and waterlogging of the unprotected ends of the ship . . . is not likely to happen very early in an engagement; further, that it is in a very high degree improbable, even in an engagement protracted to any extent which can be reasonably anticipated. Nor do they think it possible, except in the event of her being attacked by enemies of such preponderating force as to render her entering into any engagement in the highest degree imprudent. . . . It cannot be said that the armoured citadel is invulnerable, or that the unarmoured ends are indestructible, although the character of the risks they run is different. But, in our opinion, the unprotected ends are as well able as the armoured citadel to bear the part assigned to them in encountering the various risks of naval warfare, and, therefore, we consider that a just balance has been maintained in the design, so that out of a given set of conditions a good result has been obtained.'

When it is remembered that the members of this Committee were Admiral Sir James Hope, Dr. Woolley, Mr. George Rendel, and Mr. Froude, and that their report was based on an enormous mass of professional evidence, it will be seen that Lord Henry Lennox's statement as to the adverse opinions of naval officers and experts compares very exactly with his former statement as to the tenor of the report itself.   But after all, to the lay public, the merit or demerit of our large ironclads can only be a question of authority, and we are disposed to place confidence in the carefully considered and deliberately formed judgement of the Admiralty Staff of Constructors, whose ability even Sir Edward Reed cannot dispute, and whose experience his own cannot approach, rather than in the frenzied denunciations of any self-constituted critic, who is but partially instructed and wholly irresponsible.

The fact, then, is that, so far as a comparison with other navies is possible, our fleet is not in the dangerously reduced condition which has been alleged. There is, however, one point on which, more perhaps than on any other, the efficiency of a ship of war depends, but as regards which comparison is not possible. We know absolutely nothing concerning the state of the boilers of the ships of any other navy, and we have experienced so many startling and disagreeable surprises as to those of our own ships that we have learned that nothing on this head can be taken for granted. The assumption which underlies all controversial estimates of the strength of other navies is that their boilers are all sound, and that some of ours are not. But we know, to our cost, that boilers have a lamentable tendency not only to wear out by use, but to decay, from many, and often inexplicable, causes. The assumption is, therefore, inadmissible; and of evidence there is absolutely none. It would be more legitimate to suppose that at any given time the proportion of weakly boilers was the same in our own and foreign navies, though even that is perhaps undervaluing the skill and experience of our boiler-makers and of our engineers. It is, indeed, quite possible that the Admiralty have some intelligence on this point; but if so, it is necessarily secret and confidential, and is most probably not altogether trustworthy. Their only true resource is to provide that, so far as it is practicable, the boilers under their own control are thoroughly efficient; and, amidst the many charges of neglect and apathy which have been recently scattered broadcast against them, none on this score has as yet been included.

But, whatever the number, the size, and the force of our large ironclads, it may be doubted, and has been doubted, whether these will in the future play any such part as the old line-of-battle ships have done in the past; whether, in fact, it is on these that, as has been so generally taken for granted, he strength of a navy depends. It appears every day more and more probable that the action of torpedoes, as yet but dimly understood, may render the operations of a large fleet impossible or useless; and that, under suitable protection, sea-mines or torpedoes may seal up a port and effectually prevent all ingress or egress. The use of these weapons is only in its infancy, but already foreign nations, more especially Russia and Germany, are constructing torpedo-boats in large numbers. These would, it must be conceded, form a powerful adjunct to a fleet, but they are principally intended for home defence; for war in the open sea, vessels of a larger class are in favour, and our own torpedo officers especially commend the 'Polyphemus,' which Captain Gallwey, in a lecture at the United Service Institution a few weeks ago, described as—

'one of the most formidable engines of naval warfare yet built, and a type of ship which, unless some better protection than we have at present can be found for the bottom of an ironclad, may necessitate the abandonment of monster ironclads in modern fleets.' 'With what weapon,' he asked, 'is the ironclad going to vanquish the numerous torpedo rams that are being built in every country, and of which class the "Polyphemus" is the most formidable? All experience shows that the heavy guns of an ironclad cannot be depended on to hit, much less to stop, a vessel moving at high speed and showing only four feet of surface above water. She is proof against machine-guns, and being smaller, handier, and faster than most ironclads, should have the best chance with her ram, more especially as it is provided with a weapon that can be discharged with the greatest certainty to a distance of 300 yards. . . . . If a submarine ship armed with locomotive torpedoes is ever built, then we shall have the most formidable antagonist for large ironclads which it is possible to imagine; and the nearer the special torpedo-ship can resemble the submarine boat the more formidable does she become.'

The 'Polyphemus' has the further recommendation of costing only one-sixth of the price of a first-class ironclad, and of requiring but one-fourth of the number of men; she is, however, described as a most uncomfortable ship to live in or to cruise in; and the Admiralty, in determining to repeat the experiment, have decided on making the new torpedo ram, now provided for in the estimates, 600 tons larger. She will also have a slightly higher speed, but in all essentials, as 'a 'weapon of naval warfare,' she will, it is understood, be the same as the 'Polyphemus.'

Of a very different type, the 'Scout,' denominated a 'torpedo-cruiser,' which is building on the Clyde by Messrs. J. and G. Thomson, is to be completed this year. The 'Fear-'less,' a sister ship, building at Barrow-in-Furness, is also well advanced; and the Admiralty so far favour the type that another is ordered to be built at Devonport, and six more are offered for contract. The 'Scout,' which may be taken as a representative of the class, is of nearly 1,500 tons' displacement; her engines are to have an indicated horse-power of 3,200, and it is estimated that she will have a speed of 16·5 knots. Her armament is to consist of four 5-inch guns, six Nordenfeldts, and ten torpedo-tubes. She will doubtless be a very formidable vessel, but naval opinion inclines to the belief that she is too large and too costly, and would prefer something of one-third the size, or even smaller. How far this idea may be correct, it is impossible to say;

but it is certain that a considerable number of naval officers, and especially among the more scientific members of the profession, suspect that the days of monster ironclads are numbered, and that the methods of naval warfare, even in the immediate future, will attain some new and terrible developement, which will set at naught the traditions of the past, or the preparations of the present; and we conceive that, in view of this possible, or indeed probable, reconstruction of the navy, within a very few years, it would be a mark of fatuous imbecility to strain—as we have been urged to strain—our resources, and to add enormously to our estimates, in order to increase the number of ironclads of any existing type. We have shown that, so far as our old history is any guide, our navy in this respect compares favourably with that of any other country. There is no probable coalition which could overwhelm us by mere numbers; and, on the other hand, we know that combined fleets of different nations have always been at a disadvantage, which at the present time would be intensified. We have therefore no hesitation in saying that the outcry of urgency which has been raised is entirely uncalled for, is mischievous and dangerous. Panic and wild expenditure are fatal to the permanent efficiency of the navy, and few things could be more injurious than that we should be weighted with a large number of ships, unnecessary now, and likely to become obsolete almost before they are launched. The increase which the Admiralty, yielding to some extent to popular clamour, has now asked the House of Commons to provide for, is not sufficient to bring this evil on us; and the laying down of four ironclads instead of two is but a forestalment of the necessary work of providing against deterioration and decay. To have gone further in that direction would, we think, have been an error and a misapplication of money which might be spent to better advantage.

For when we turn away from the exaggerations which have been published as to our pressing need of large ironclads, our attention is arrested by the evidence of the fact that the stress of any future naval war will fall first on our commerce; and the question which necessarily suggests itself is, Are we in a position to give adequate protection to that commerce? The question is a very wide one, and one which, in the total absence of experience, it is difficult to answer. Our past history here lends but a faint glimmering light, for the circumstances of the day are curiously different from anything hitherto known. In former times, England was a corn-growing, cattle-growing, agricultural country: we could feed ourselves; we had no provision fleets to protect at the hazard of our lives or of our national existence; we had few isolated dependencies, and no coaling stations; our commerce was indeed considerable, but the great prizes of war were offered by Spain. Treasure-ships, such as the 'Covadonga' or the 'Hermione,' were the counterparts of our Australian ships with their freights of gold, or our Cape ships with their cargoes of diamonds. The essential difference is that these belong to us, those belonged to the enemy. The capture of those laid the foundation of princely fortunes; the capture of these would cause wailing and wringing of hands from Lombard Street to Charing Cross. But more than ever were the galleons to Spain are our provision ships to us; they are a necessity of life itself. The loss of gold and diamonds would be disaster; the loss of cotton and other staples of commerce would be ruination; the loss of corn and beef and mutton would be death. These are the dangers to which we shall be exposed if a war break out and find us unprepared. There is nothing in our past history or present condition to waken any serious apprehension as to the future, so far as the clash of contending fleets is concerned. But in former days, we had the sea alive with our cruisers—king's ships or privateers; and wealthy settlements or rich trade belonged in great measure to the enemy. This is changed. The settlements and the trade are now ours. It is more than ever necessary for us to be sure that the swarms of sea-hornets are ours also.

In considering our stock of these, it must be borne in mind that to be efficient they must be superior to the ships against which they will have to act, not only in number and in armament, but in speed. A merchant-ship overtaken is virtually captured, and the first requisite of a ship intended to cruise against merchant-ships is speed sufficient to enable her to catch them. A cruiser-destroyer must have still greater speed, or she will be useless. And cruiser-destroyers alone will serve our turn; nothing else can ward off the danger of fast cruisers taking up positions on the great ocean 'crossings.' To drive them away would be useless; they would merely seek other hunting-grounds. To adopt the miserable subterfuge of transferring our ships to neutral flags would be equally useless, if—as is announced from Germany and France—provisions are henceforth to be considered contraband of war.

Now, though we have a very respectable number of so-called cruisers, we have not many of great speed. Most of them, including the whole of the C class, good ships in many respects, have a nominal speed of only thirteen knots, which, in time of emergency, would be probably found to be much less; whilst the so-called gun-boats or gun-vessels—vessels of about 500 tons displacement—can, under favourable circumstances, steam six knots, and with a moderate breeze on the bow can do nothing but drift to leeward. The duties of peace-time they manage to perform, though not brilliantly; but for any conceivable operation of modern war they are utterly and absolutely useless. Of really fast ships, the ' Iris ' and ' Mercury ' are the only two which claim a speed of more than eighteen knots; the 'Leander' and her three sisters, now nearly ready, are estimated at seventeen knots, so also is the still more powerful ' Mersey,' the first of the ' river-class,' which is to be completed this year, and so are the despatch-boats ' Alacrity ' and ' Surprise.' The ' Inconstant ' and ' Shah,' now getting old, have a nominal speed of sixteen knots; and the ' Scout,' to be completed this year, is estimated to have the same. Thus, taking the most favourable account of our fast cruisers by including all that are ordered to be ready, we have twelve of sixteen knots and upwards, and four more of above fifteen knots. Any drawbacks from these rates presumably apply equally to the ships of other countries, and thus do not affect the comparison.

As yet the French have but two so-called cruisers, the 'Duquesne' and 'Tourville,' with a speed of more than sixteen knots, but they have ten ranging from fifteen to sixteen. So far the comparison does not seem very unfavourable to us: but a remarkable feature in the present French programme is the large number of small but fast cruisers which are being built, many of which are nearly ready. Four of these, suggestively named after birds of prey, have a displacement of 1,268 tons, with an estimated speed of seventeen knots; and eight others, ' torpedo-cruisers,' with an estimated speed of seventeen knots, have a displacement of only 280 tons. These, it is said, will be ready this year. They are probably intended primarily as satellites of the main fleet; but, if used as independent cruisers, they may well prove exceedingly dangerous—difficult to catch, by reason · of their speed; awkward to approach, by reason of their torpedoes. The only efficient answer to such boats will be vessels of eighteen or nineteen knots, with an armament heavy enough to sink them. It is such vessels that we ought to have, but as yet have not.

Sir William Armstrong's firm has lately turned out of hand such a one, whose design and performance have at once awakened attention and made the name of 'Esmeralda' typical.

The 'Esmeralda' is of 3,000 tons' displacement, can steam for 8,000 miles at eight knots, and has an actual mean maximum speed of 18·3 knots. She has an armament of two 25-ton guns, with a penetrative force equivalent to twenty-one inches of iron; she carries besides, six 4-ton guns, two of the new rapid-firing 6-pounders, and some Nordenfeldts; she has also a 1-inch protective steel deck, and is minutely subdivided. It is fairly claimed for her that she can fight or run away from anything that floats on the ocean; and though Mr. White, speaking in the name of Sir William Armstrong, has expressly said that they do not consider the 'Esmeralda' as 'the typical protected ship,' there can be but few to dissent from the opinion that she might very well be the typical cruiser-catcher or destroyer; for the vessels to which Mr. White's firm give the preference as 'protected ships,' 'auxiliaries to the battle-ship of the 'future,' though 'stronger in protection, larger in coal 'supply, more powerful in guns and in fighting efficiency,' 'are also larger and more costly.' So far from the ideal cruiser being larger or more costly than the 'Esmeralda,' our preference would be distinctly for one smaller and cheaper : the extremely powerful armament is not needed by all cruiser-catchers; and we should hail a proposal to build a large number of 18-knot vessels of the 'Esmeralda' type, but of one-third the displacement, which might serve as auxiliaries to the ships of the 'Leander' or 'Mersey' class, or the new belted cruisers, in the design of which strength rather than extreme speed appears to have been aimed at. But supported by such ships, vessels of 1,200 or 1,000 tons, or even less, if only fast enough, would be most efficient; and their cost being small, their number might be large. The question, as it would come before Parliament, is, of course, primarily one of expense; and it is on this account, rather than from any economic aversion to see the number of our capital ships increased, that we cannot but regret the determination of the Admiralty to build four instead of two ironclads. For the cost of these two additional, eight or nine 'Esmeraldas,' or two dozen small auxiliaries, might have been obtained, and would, we think, have better answered the needs of the navy. The eight new 'Scouts,' building or to be built, are undoubtedly something towards our want; but they are only 16-knot vessels: with less than 18 knots we cannot be fully content.

And it is not only in the number of fast cruisers that our navy does not seem quite abreast of the possible exigencies of modern warfare. Our supply of torpedo-boats is extremely small, relatively to the work for which they would be required in time of war. It may be that we have of them a sufficiency for the alleged primary duty of attending on the main fleet; but far beyond that is the much more important duty of protecting our ports, our colonies, and our coaling stations. It has been computed that for this defence alone, less than 300 would be too few. This may well be an exaggeration: but what is—it is to be feared—no exaggeration, is the statement everywhere made, and which all evidence seems to confirm, that very many of our mercantile harbours, and more especially of the coaling stations, are at the mercy of any enemy who should choose to dash in and destroy them. We are told that the defence of these is to be provided for by the War Office, that is, by forts and guns and mines. Forts and guns and mines are excellent things in their way, but forts take long in building and are very costly; the heavy guns have no existence; under the present wretched departmental organisation they do not seem likely soon to have an existence; and without the support of guns, mines are worthless. Nor, indeed—though it is a hundred years ago—can we quite forget that when Paul Jones made an attempt to burn the shipping in Whitehaven, in which he failed only through the treachery and imbecility of his own men, the fort, to which the safety of the town had been entrusted, was in ruins; the guns were honeycombed and utterly useless; and the few old pensioners, who formed the garrison, were asleep.

But apart from the tendency of forts to crumble to ruin, and of old pensioners to go to bed and sleep, the conviction of every naval officer is that the most effective, the most certain and the cheapest defence of a harbour is with a cluster of torpedo-boats. In certain special positions, mines, if supported by guns on shore, are convenient and cheap. But electrical mines cannot be laid out any distance to seaward; so that they do not necessarily prevent the enemy from making what may be a dangerous approach; whilst mechanical mines close the harbour to friend as well as foe, and render egress, as well as ingress, impossible. On the other hand, torpedo-boats can be managed perfectly well by naval volunteers with some little training; these are men for the most part accustomed to boats, and about the torpedo itself there is no difficulty. But, to quote the words of Captain Gallwey, whose familiarity with the subject is equalled by few, 'the efficiency of a torpedo-boat mainly depends on the 'amount of practice and experience the crew have had in 'her. A nation with no boats to practise with in time of 'peace will find but little value in the few she may hurriedly 'get together in time of war.' Even the mere sitting or standing in boats of this character requires practice; and when one, from slow speed, suddenly starts forward at a speed of twenty-four knots, a raw hand is not altogether unlikely to tumble overboard. The Admiralty now propose to build thirty first-class torpedo-boats in the next three years; it is difficult not to think that it would be sounder policy and surer economy to build four times that number within the next eighteen months; for if our naval volunteers are to be trained to the use of these boats, the sooner they begin the better; and in any case, it would seem desirable, even at the cost of 1,440,000*l.*, to put an end to these frequent scares, and to satisfy the public mind as to the safety of our harbours and shores.

At the worst, however, torpedo-boats do not take long to build, and within a few months could be supplied, in almost any numbers, by several private firms. It is not then the want of torpedo-boats which has given rise to the present feeling of alarm, amounting almost to panic. Neither is it the want of fast cruisers and faster cruiser-catchers, though that might be a legitimate cause of anxiety. Neither is it the want of the heaviest new guns, though that, indeed, is most serious, and is likely to continue so until Parliament puts an end to the deplorable system which it ordered, or sanctioned, thirty years ago, and by which all control over the manufacture or purchase of guns for the naval service is taken out of the hands of the Admiralty. The alarm has really sprung from ignorance and misrepresentation: ignorance of the facts of our navy as it has been, misrepresentation of the state of our navy as it is. That much of this misrepresentation has been made in perfect good faith, there is no reason to doubt; that some at least of it has been made to serve some hidden party or personal end, there is also no reason to doubt. But panic is the child of darkness and ignorance; with light and knowledge comes a return of steadfast courage and sober judgement.

Art. VIII.—*George Eliot's Life as related in her Letters and Journals,* arranged and edited by her husband J. W. Cross. 3 vols. 8vo.   Edinburgh: 1885.

Few books in recent literature have called forth a greater or more general interest than the life of George Eliot. There has been something unusual in every way in the fame and in the position of this great writer—a something almost unparalleled in the history of literature, a charm, an enthusiasm, a sudden and universal subjugation of the public mind, which it is difficult to account for.   Scott is the only parallel we can think of; but he was to a great extent first in the field, bringing with him a new and unaccustomed delight and opening up a dazzling world of romance and wonder; while the age of George Eliot was one in which the art of fiction was already represented by competitors as important, with a stronger hold upon the usual materials of success than she had.   Dickens had the force of animal spirits, exuberant fun, frolic, and youth to give impulse to his genius; while Thackeray had a hard uphill struggle before his fine humour, his delicate insight, and the tenderness of his noble perceptions overcame those susceptibilities which satire always calls to arms, or got recognition as anything superior to a clever cynic taking the worst view of humanity. George Eliot began her work in the less expansive period of middle life, without any overwhelming impulse, such as breaks all boundaries between a great writer and his predestined audience, and carries home to the hearts of the readers an individual message burning with earnestness and power.   She had no aid of romantic interest in her subject, and even her style, though full of power and humour, had not that charm which at once captivates the ear.   The subjects she chose, the people whom she pictured, were all of the region of commonplace.   The sad fortunes of the Rev. Amos Barton, over which we have all had our hearts wrung, and out of which there has entered into that most real yet immaterial world, in which dwell so many of our dearest friends, the lovely figure of Milly, is not a story at all, and possesses not one adventitious attraction.   And yet it penetrated in a moment into the very heart of the English-speaking world, and threw open all doors to the new power which had arisen among us.

Nor was the effect produced upon the public mind by the personality of this great writer much less than that effected by her genius. It was not long before it became known that this purest preacher of domestic love, of fidelity, and self-sacrifice, had, in her own person, defied the laws and modest traditions that guard domestic life, and had taken a step which in all other cases deprives a woman of the fellowship and sympathy of other women, and of the respect of men. But the rule which holds universally from the duchess to the dressmaker, and which even the least straitlaced of moralists would think it dangerous to loosen, was abrogated for her, and the world agreed to consider that permissible or even justifiable in her special case which neither in that of the dressmaker nor the duchess there would be any question of tolerating. To attain this position is a triumph such as scarcely any woman before her has known. Men have got themselves pardoned for all breaches of the law, but women much more rarely. To attain it required more than great literary gifts, more even than genius: a great personal influence, an individual charm or power quite beyond the sway of ordinary laws, seems necessary to account for it. Yet personally the mistress of this great influence was something like a recluse, appearing never in public, and in private only under such restrictions as made the approach to her court a privilege. Perhaps this retirement had something to do with the effect produced. A kind of awe was thus made to mingle with the general admiration. When the first burst of applause was over, and it began to be possible to hint a criticism, even the most daring skirmishers of literature, those bold sappers to whom nothing is sacred, held their breath as they threw a furtive arrow into that sacred enclosure. They fired and ran away, terrified to be identified, knowing the penalty of discovery. A hedge of spears, but more effectual still an atmosphere in which opposition could not breathe, surrounded the oracle. That wide and voiceless public which speaks by purchase, and records its opinion on the publishers' account-books (dear public, precious, irresponsible, whose utterance is as the verdict of the gods!) silently recorded, in its own effectual inarticulate way, its approval even of the less worthy productions of the idol; and society held her peculiar views as to its most fundamental institution and its most sacred beliefs to be palliated—in her case and for her alone.

All this implied something more than a mere literary power even of the greatest order; it supposed a great person. So did the veneration of all who surrounded her, of all who had her confidence, the awe and profound respect with which echoes of what went on in her presence were heard outside; and when the time came to reveal this mysterious life the interest was universal, the expectation almost breathless. Before the volumes were cool from the press, the literary expositors of the day—the newspapers, and such magazines as were lucky enough to be in time—flung themselves upon them. At this present date we have no longer the strain of that excitement. The picture has now got into perspective, and judgement has had time to form itself. But after the first fervour a sudden pause fell upon the crowd of eager critics; something like a gasp of that unlooked-for disappointment which feels like a personal mortification came from their startled bosoms. The faithful, indeed, gave forth their trumpet-note, all the louder for the sudden check, yet underneath a fine attention could descry the vibration of doubt. A general sense of the inadequate, of promises unfulfilled and expectations deceived, came like a blight across that eagerness which filled all readers, and the high anticipations of most. The literary world seldom comes to a crisis which can be called picturesque, but this was one.

For there can be little doubt, and we are now in a position to say it calmly, that this book is a great disappointment. Its purpose, the very reason of its being, the excuse for it, was, that it was needed to explain and account for a very extraordinary career, an influence very nearly unprecedented. Except George Sand, an entirely different person, and one who, to do her justice, was never uninteresting, however much we might disapprove of her, no woman of her generation has taken so large a place in the opinion of the world; certainly no one at all in England has filled anything like a similar position. Mrs. Browning, if as great in her way, makes no personal stand, but is a poet, a beautiful voice, and no more. But George Eliot's place is different from hers. She did not refuse, nay, she claimed, the position of a great moral teacher. In her later life she put on something more than the professor's gown, something like the camel's hair of the prophet. And from the beginning she secured for herself a quite exceptional personal as well as literary eminence. Of this singular influence we had the just expectation of finding the secret and explanation in the record of her life.

But we are obliged to confess that we have not done so, nor, so far as we can hear, has any one else done so. The George Eliot who wrote ' Adam Bede ' is a more completely veiled prophet than ever. Now that we have heard everything that her biographer has to tell us about her, we know

as little as ever how it was that suddenly out of the plain
of middle life she stood up all at once and made herself an
authority and a power—as little, nay much less, for all our
previous conceptions are confused and confounded. The
picture which Mr. Cross has set before us, in so far as it can
be called a picture at all, is like one of the portraits which
before the age of photography used to hang in the best
parlours of the Gleggs and Tullivers whom she knew so well,
gazing blankly at their originals with a ludicrous likeness
which made the incapacity of flat paint and canvas to represent anything that had breath all the more distinct and unmistakeable. In some cases we are glad to have even such
portraits when no others are to be had; even the black
silhouettes of our grandfathers and grandmothers are not
without interest. But these images are scarcely the sort of
exposition which we should care to place before strangers in
order to depict those whom we respect most. The biography
of George Eliot as here given is a gigantic silhouette, showing how her figure rose against a dull background. Background and figure are alike dull. To a distant spectator, to
one who knew George Eliot only by her books, the possibility of attaching that adjective to her name would have
seemed not only impossible but profane. But Mr. Cross,
who ought to know better, and she herself, who ought, one
supposes, to have known best of all, have here put it down
for us in black and white with a fulness and repetition which
it is impossible to oppose. Let no one say henceforth that
out of his own lips a man or a woman can be best judged.
This is the second instance within a very short space of time
that it is not so. We are in an age when every belief is
tampered with and our dearest associations are turned up-
side down. Carlyle has been made out of his own mouth to
prove himself a snarling Diogenes, a compound of spite,
falsehood, and meanness; and George Eliot by the same fine
process has been made to prove herself a dull woman. We
take leave to say that we do not believe her, any more than
we believed him: and can only hope that the biographers of
the future may be arrested in this strange new art of transformation.

It is unnecessary to say that Mr. Cross is absolutely
without evil intention in his work. He has used the materials in his hands, which were evidently most abundant, with
no sort of desire to harm or injure his subject. Much the
reverse: he has sought to exalt her in every way, to prove her
superiority, to mark with almost a solemnity of emphasis

her elevation over the heads of ordinary men and women. His devotion is conspicuous in every line; he has spared no trouble to fulfil what he evidently believed to be the proper aim of such a task as his, to make it appear that in every line and feature of her character, both mental and moral, the lady whom he has the honour to call his wife was perfect, without even an irregularity of outline or temporary lapse from the high places of sentiment. This was the old rule of biography, and one for which there is a great deal to be said. It is better than systematic detraction: it is better than the tearing out of all dust-heaps and collections of broken crockery and rusty iron in the hope of finding something derogatory. The man who left out the wart on the great Protector's face would have done less harm to posterity than he who painted it in such relief as to overshadow both features and textures of the natural countenance. But yet, when all is said, it has to be acknowledged that it is not an interesting method or a true one. A photograph may be less pleasing than the original, but it is more real than a painted portrait. Mr. Cross sets up, or endeavours to set up, before us a large image without a broken line or indiscreet wrinkle, like that colossal ' Bavaria ' which overshadows Munich, and which (oddly enough) George Eliot took the trouble to examine, admire, and describe. When we venture, after our excitement, expectation, and interest, to acknowledge our real impression of this book, the result is very much the same. George Eliot under this treatment is like the ' Bavaria.' The figure is large and imposing, but it is lifeless. If we seek in her expressions, in her personal utterances, for sympathy and human fellowship, we find it not. It seems as if this woman had no such disturbances in her life as ordinary people have. She had none of the doubts and vacillations, none of the struggles of more common human creatures; even when she did wrong she did it with a high hand, declaring her *faux pas* to be superior virtue. She stepped from evangelical faith to philosophical atheism as you would step from one street to another without turning a hair. All this is astounding and confusing. Is it possible that she was so entirely beyond the agitations of nature, she to whom human nature as a subject of analysis had so few secrets? Did she never doubt whether she was wholly right, or fear that she might be wholly wrong? Did she never falter when she turned from all she had been taught to love and reverence in one case, and from all the traditions of the strait respectability in which she had been bred in another? To those who are disposed to ask such questions, this book has no reply to give. The image here presented to us is that of an excellent woman, very serious, highly intellectual, a little prosy, a little sentimental, living among books and exalted subjects of thought, but without a laugh in her, or a weakness, or a movement of temper, or an impulse of folly. Had we known nothing else about her, one would have thought her a most proper correct unimpeachable person, a model of all the virtues, with a certain solemnity of diction and sense of responsibility for all she said, like one who is aware that for every word she must enter into judgement—a woman oppressed by a sense of duty, and by the necessity of setting an example, putting down the right sort of thing in her diaries, and writing her letters with a determination not to be trivial or descend from the altitude of thought which was expected from her. Is this the woman who wrote 'Adam Bede'? or is it the frightened retirement of a man not strong enough to trust to his own judgement from all the risks of frankness and plain speaking?

The early life of George Eliot, or of Marian Evans, as it is more natural now to call her, is already well known, and by a very different method from that which discloses the actual circumstances of her existence in the present book. No one can have forgotten the wonderful pictures, so large, so noble, so small and sordid, so warm with humour and passion, so extraordinarily representative of the least attractive phase of English life, against which the fine figure of Maggie Tulliver rises before us, a being entirely distinct from her surroundings, and yet, perhaps, scarcely possible to realise without those surroundings. In any other *milieu*, either higher or lower, the visionary sensitive girl, full of contradictory impulses, with her unity and simplicity of soul, her capacity for great emotion, her constitution 'as if she had been con-' 'structed of musical strings,' might have had some chance of being comprehended. It requires the atmosphere of the Gleggs and Pullets to explain how entirely such a nature was astray in that English middle-class life of which we have never before had so uncompromising a picture. Other writers have touched its peculiarities more gently, have given us indeed to see some beauty and much ordinary human feeling dominating the peculiarities of the class. But no one else has come within a hundred miles of this vivid representation, so remorseless, so living, lit with endless gleams of comicality, yet of its very nature tragic. It is perhaps too much to take it for an actual picture of the scenes which surrounded the child of genius; but yet there are many circumstances so like it in her own experience as to make it very probable that much was taken direct from nature. Mrs. Evans had three married sisters, as Mrs. Tulliver had; and Marian, like Maggie, had one brother. There seems little doubt that she took in with dreamy childish ears unconsciously, little knowing that it was to float forth again in after days and be considered the ripest fruit of observation, those talks in the mill-parlour, in the sitting-room where her active mother managed her housekeeping and discoursed about her linen. The aunts have no place in the biography, and Mr. Evans of Griff is a far more dignified figure than poor passionate Tulliver at the mill. Indeed, there is very naturally a certain gloss of superiority given to all the dim and half-seen persons of the history when we hear of them by their real names, from which the fictitious story is quite free—a little weakness so very comprehensible that it would be both cruel and unnecessary to blame it. ' My father did ' not raise himself from being an artisan to being a farmer; ' he raised himself from being an artisan to be a man whose ' extensive knowledge in very varied practical departments ' made his services valued through several counties. . . . ' He was held by those competent to judge as *unique* among ' land-agents for his manifold knowledge and experience, ' which enabled him to save the special fees usually paid by ' landowners for special opinions on the different questions ' incident to the proprietorship of land.' This is the account which his daughter herself gives of him (to Mr. Bray, oddly enough, who must have known perfectly well all about him) in after years. And it is not at all necessary to identify with any individual character in fiction a real name from whose personality a few suggestions may have been taken.

There is very little about the father in this book. He was Adam Bede, he was Caleb Garth, and yet he was neither, but a man who possessed his daughter's confidence to a very limited degree, and by times so strongly differed with her, that a question arose at one time whether they should not separate altogether. The brother is still more completely absent from the record. It cannot be doubted that the childish relations between the adoring little sister and the boyish idol whom she followed about in his holiday time and was faithful to through all the stages of her youth, must have a certain truth to fact as well as to nature. But the biographer omits all record of anything which could in the

most distant manner correspond with the persistent and
rigid incomprehension of Tom Tulliver, or with the incidents
that broke the bond between them. There might, indeed,
have been no incidents at all in the early years of this wonderful young woman who grew up like Maggie Tulliver
among people unacquainted with the very species to which
she belonged, for anything the record tells us. Perhaps it
was not to be expected that anyone in Mr. Cross's position
should have raked up the ashes of the past in search of some
lingering warmth which should betray the Philip Wakem
or Stephen Guest of that distant period; but it is extremely
comical to find ourselves thrown instead, as the only chronicle remaining of that visionary fervid existence which has
found a reflection in the passionate and suffering young life
of Maggie Tulliver, upon a couple of prim correspondents, as
unlike the intensely feeling and vividly living creature with
whose sensations George Eliot unquestionably associated her
own, as it is possible to imagine.

The first of these correspondents was a Miss Lewis, a
governess in a school in which Marian Evans received part
of her education, 'an ardent Evangelical Churchwoman,'
with whom she formed an admiring friendship, and whose
exalted views of piety she shared. The atmosphere of the
school was eminently calculated to produce and foster such
views. It was ruled by dissenting ladies on the strictest
Evangelical principles, and Marian Evans took at once a
'leading position' in it; not only writing incomparable
themes which the teacher did not criticise and correct along
with the others, but 'reserved for her private perusal and
'enjoyment'—(a very enlightened schoolmistress this, and
evidently never met with by the unappreciated Maggie)—
but also 'became a leader of prayer-meetings among the
'girls.' It was from the ladies who kept this school that
she afterwards received an introduction and recommendation
to new friends in Coventry, as a person 'sure to get up
'something very soon in the way of clothing club or other
'charitable undertaking.' This might have come out of the
'Mill on the Floss,' but not as applied to Maggie. It is one
of the few gleams of humour in the book; but, alas! it is
not at all intended as humorous, either by the Miss Frank-
lins who gave it, or by the biographer who records it, or
apparently, funniest of all, by the girl to whom it was
given. The account of the school, indeed, carries our profane
thoughts back with an irresistible impulse to a certain
famous academy for young ladies in Chiswick Mall. 'Miss

' Rebecca Franklin was a lady of considerable intellectual
' power, and remarkable for her elegance in writing and con-
' versation, as well as for her beautiful caligraphy.' Does
our memory deceive us, or is not something of the same high
character on record in respect to the elder Miss Pinkerton,
who surely was a Rebecca too ?

The letters to Miss Lewis quoted extend from the year
1838 till 1841—that is, from Miss Evans' nineteenth year,
exactly the period at which the climax of Maggie Tulliver's
existence arrived, to her twenty-second, when she changed
her religious views and naturally withdrew from the correspondence, or so at least we may suppose. These letters
have very little that is characteristic in them. They are
the letters of a young Puritan writing within conventional
lines, very hard and fast, but without any of that fervour of
personal conviction which gives life to so many effusions
of the kind. Perhaps Marian's religiousness was the result
of the atmosphere in which she found herself, and of that
longing for something higher and greater than anything in
her dull existence which made Maggie Tulliver fling herself with such devotion into the more poetical aspirations
towards perfection of Thomas à Kempis. The impression
of orthodoxy and correctness which, oddly enough, it seems
the intention of the book to create in us, becomes prim and
prudish in this first chapter. Miss Evans, at nineteen, tells
her correspondent that ' for my part, when I hear of the
' marrying and giving in marriage that is constantly being
' transacted, I can only sigh for those who are multiplying
' earthly ties which, though powerful enough to detach their
' hearts and thoughts from heaven, are so brittle as to be
' liable to be snapped asunder at every breeze.' From all
such temptations she thinks it necessary to detach herself,
feeling, with Dr. Johnson, ' total abstinence much easier
' than temperance.' She thinks novel reading undesirable,
but limits her verdict against it in a style and with exceptions which are so curious that we must quote the passage :—

' I would put out of the question standard works whose contents are
matters of constant reference, and the names of whose heroes and heroines
briefly, and therefore conveniently, describe characters and ideas. Such
were " Don Quixote," Butler's " Hudibras," " Robinson Crusoe," " Gil
" Blas," Byron's poetical romances, Southey's ditto, &c. Such too are
Walter Scott's novels and poems. Such allusions as " He is a perfect
" Dominie Sampson ;" " he is as industrious in finding out antiquities,
" and about as successful as Jonathan Oldbuck," are likely to become
so common in books and conversation, that, always providing our
leisure is not circumscribed by duty within narrow bounds, we should,

I think, qualify ourselves to understand. ·Shakespeare has a higher claim than this upon our attention; but we have need of as much power of distillation as the bee to suck nothing but honey from his pages.'

It is extremely curious to know that these utilitarian views of literature and disparaging conceptions of ' earthly ' ties ' were being uttered at the age when Maggie Tulliver was just about going down the Floss on that dismal voyage with her lover which led to so much misery. How life must have expanded, sweetened, filled itself with a savour and a glory unknown of at the time when she looked back upon her youth! Or is it possible that the romance was over and buried, and that all these admirable sentiments were the result of the dimness that had come over the world, and the despondency of the after life out of which enchantment had gone? The dates give great probability to this suggestion. We must add that there is scarcely one of the young judgements pronounced in these letters which is not afterwards contradicted expressly in the after record. She asks her friend ' to love for her sake ' certain lines in Young's ' Infidel Reclaimed,' beginning ' Oh! vain, vain, vain, all ' else eternity,' which she would quote were it not that Miss Lewis dislikes quotations—Young, as the reader may remember, being in mature years the subject of an unnecessarily severe criticism, reprinted in the last volume of George Eliot's collected works. She records her ' high ' enjoyment of Hannah More's letters,' and conviction that ' the contemplation of so blessed a character as hers is very ' salutary;' though ' I am glad you detest Hannah More,' she says a few years later. And what is still more extraordinary, she raises the objections common to the highest evangelical Puritanism of the period on the subject of music, à propos of an oratorio which she had heard in Coventry. ' I have no soul for music,' she says, evidently belying herself in the most extraordinary way in the fervour of her scrupulousness. ' I am a tasteless person : but it would not cost ' me any regrets if the only music heard in our land was that ' of strict worship ; nor can I think a pleasure that involves ' the devotion of all the time and powers of an immortal ' being to the acquirement of an expertness in so useless (at ' least in ninety-nine cases out of a hundred) an accomplish- ' ment can be quite pure and elevating in its tendency.'

The maze of fictitious sentiments and phantasmal beliefs among which the young woman must have been wandering when she made this utterance takes something of the wonder

from the revolution which follows. That she was sincere
enough in the expression of opinions which the curious
docility and *leadableness* of her mind had made her believe
were her own, there can be no doubt. But this echo of the
voices that had been about her all her life is curiously
unreal from her lips. Not very long after the denuncia-
·tion of this ' useless accomplishment ' she was so overwhelmed by her own emotions during the performance of
another oratorio that her hysterical sobbing disturbed the
persons near her.

In 1841 Miss Evans, carrying with her in all humility
and gravity that characteristic recommendation that she
was ' sure to get up something very soon in the way of
' clothing club,' went to Coventry. We must give here, in
distinction to all the heavy and formal proprieties of the
letters already quoted, one scrap in which for the first time
we see the handwriting that is to be.

'Is not this a true autumn day? Just the still melancholy that I
love that makes life and nature harmonise. The birds are consulting
about their migrations, the trees are putting on the hectic or the pallid
hues of decay, and begin to strew the ground, that one's very footsteps
may not disturb the repose of earth and air while they give us a scent
that is a perfect anodyne to the restless spirit. Delicious autumn ! my
very soul is wedded to it; and if I were a bird, I would fly about the
world seeking the successive autumns.'

She wrote this on the eve of ' effecting a breach in the
' thick wall of indifference behind which the denizens of
' Coventry seem inclined to intrench themselves ' by making
acquaintance with a group of her neighbours in that town.
This was a step which had very grave results. She was at
this period twenty-two. Her father had given up residence
in the country, the house in which her childhood had been
spent having been transferred to her brother who had recently married : and the father and daughter were alone in
their new quarters. Notwithstanding the many eulogiums
pronounced upon him, it is possible that Mr. Robert Evans
was not very enlivening company for his young intellectual
ambitious daughter longing for books and congenial souls;
and she soon found herself on the edge of one of those
' thoughtful ' and superior little coteries which are nowhere
so characteristic as in the midst of the active practical life
of a provincial town, where an inspiring sense of being
better than their neighbours, and indeed evidently the salt
of the earth and *élite* of society, is so forced upon the select
group that it cannot, if it would, resist the delightful con-

viction. Mrs. Pears, the next-door neighbour of the Evanses, to whom apparently had been sent the certificate about the clothing club, was the sister of Mr. Bray, the author of the ' Philosophy of Necessity,' and his wife sprang from a highly intellectual family of Hennells, one of whom, the brother, had written an ' Inquiry into Christianity' which, in the opinion of this highly cultured group, disposed of that worn-out religion quite conclusively. Miss Marian Evans, fresh from the monotony of the country, where there were few, very few, with whom she could talk about books, and where the poet Young, and such blessed characters as Hannah More and Mr. Wilberforce, still held the day, came suddenly into the midst of these intellectually fine people. Mr. Bray and Mrs. Bray and Miss Sara Hennell, not to speak of the brother who had written the ' Inquiry,' were philosophical unbelievers on the platform of phrenology, whose talk was of nothing but books and bumps. It is no fault of ours if we feel inclined to believe that had Miss Evans happened to light upon a party of clever Jesuits, or of enthusiastic and entertaining High-Churchmen, her mind, to which Puritanism was a sort of masquerade costume, perfectly sincere but quite superficial and inappropriate, would have in all likelihood turned to the side of her new friends as infallibly as it now turned to the interesting atheists in whose company she felt for the first time the joys of intellectual intercourse. Nothing can be more worthy of respect and sympathy, of awe and painful interest in some cases, than the conversion of a soul from the tenets in which it has been trained, and which have hitherto been the inspiration of its life, to opinions absolutely opposite to those which it has once reverenced— especially if this conversion carries with it the instant loss at once of the stimulants and the consolations which have previously been all in all to its experience. No reader, even one most deeply convinced that unbelief is guilt, could read the heartrending verses in which Leopardi records his acceptance of the gloomy creed of the atheist without a pang of profoundest sympathy. But whether from indifference on the part of the biographer, or from absence of materials, or from reluctance to enter into details which might be disagreeable to the existing members of the family, it is certain that this great revolution occurs without a single trace that it cost her anything, or was not adopted in *gaieté de cœur* as the easiest of transformations.

The first intimation of a possibility of change is conveyed in a letter to Miss Lewis, whom she informs suddenly that

' my whole soul has been engrossed in the most interesting
' of all inquiries _for the last few days_, and to what result
' my thoughts may lead I know not—possibly to one that
' may startle you.'　What was the immediate cause of
these inquiries, how they were conducted, what effect they
had upon her being, are matters left out as if of no particular interest.　We are led to believe that the reading of
Mr. Hennell's ' Inquiry' was the instrument, and Mr. Bray
claims to have been the guide of the neophyte.　Few people
now-a-days, however, know anything about Mr. Hennell's
' Inquiry,' nor how far the power of its arguments is compatible with such a result.　But in any case the result was
accomplished, and the rapid action of these obscure agencies,
the easy acquiescence of the intellectual girl, the conversion
which comes about without any trouble as the most simple
thing in the world, and the separation from all the traditions of her youthful piety and the deepest sympathies of
her natural friends which follows, without calling from her
lips a word of regret, are most remarkable.　It seems incredible that so much could have happened with so little
notice.　The indifference and the calm are disrespectful to
the greatness of the event.

The only person at all excited by this revolution seems to
have been the father, who naturally did not like it, being old-
fashioned and a good churchman.　When his daughter, ' in
' the enthusiasm of the first great change,' concluded, not
without justice, we think, that to continue to go to church
might place her in an equivocal position, and gave up that
practice, Mr. Evans was very wroth, and declared his intention to break up his house and remove from Coventry
altogether, leaving the young sectary to provide for herself.
The mediation of friends, however, and specially, it would
seem, of her brother, prevented this extreme measure, and
after a visit paid to Griff, where Mr. Isaac Evans lived,
Marian returned home and settled down again, going to
church as before.　It is curious to find her justification of
this conformity some time later treated not as a matter
of her own experience, but as the discussion of an abstract
principle.　The sophistry of the reasoning is clearly quite
unconscious, and the writer seems carried away by a sort of
magnanimity of idea, as of one on a higher platform condescending, by grace of a common sentiment, to those below
her in every other point.　Perhaps a faint disappointment
breathes in the preliminary statement that the emancipated
mind, in the glory of its newly attained freedom, believes at

first that it will soon have 'something positive which will
' more than compensate us for what we have renounced,' and
in that hope is ready to thrust all external compliances out of
its way.

'But a year or two of reflection and the experience of our own miserable weakness, which will ill afford to part even with the crutch of
superstition, must, I think, effect a change. Speculative truth begins to
appear but a shadow of individual minds. Agreement between intel-
lects seems unattainable, and we turn to the truth of feeling as the
only universal bond of union. We find that the intellectual errors
which we once fancied were a mere incrustation, have grown into the
living body, and that we cannot, in the majority of cases, wrench them
away without destroying vitality. We begin to find that with individuals, as with nations, the only safe revolution is one arising out of
the wants which their own progress has generated. It is the quackery
of infidelity to suppose that it has a nostrum for all mankind, and to
say to all and singular, "Swallow my opinions, and you shall be
" whole." If we are then debarred by such considerations from trying
to reorganise opinions, are we to remain aloof from our fellow-crea-
tures on occasions when we may fully sympathise with the feelings
exercised, although our own have been melted into another mould?
Ought we not on every opportunity to seek to have our feelings in
harmony, though not in union, with those who are often richer in the
fruits of faith, though not in reason, than ourselves? The results of
nonconformity in a family are just an epitome of what happens on a
larger scale in the world. An influential member chooses to omit an
observance which in the minds of all the rest is associated with what
is highest and most venerable. He cannot make his reasons intelligible,
and so his conduct is regarded as a relaxation of the hold that moral
ties had on him previously. The rest are infected with the disease
they imagine in him. All the screws by which order is maintained
are loosened, and in more than one case a person's happiness may be
ruined by the confusion of ideas which took the form of principles.'

It seems scarcely necessary to point out the curious confusion of ideas which lies under this piece of special pleading,
which would be entirely applicable to the case she suggests
of nonconformity, of those divergencies in Christian doctrine
which have torn the churches asunder. That a man who
held special views of his own on minor points should, on this
principle, find it possible and even desirable to make no
breach, but to maintain the truth of feeling, whatever might
be the difference of doctrine with those who held, like himself, the central and all-important tenets of religion, we can
well believe. Even to do this requires a special balance of
mind and temper attained by but few, as experience proves,
and to many, perhaps to the majority of ordinary intelligences,
there will always be a possibility of dishonesty, a suggestion

of hypocrisy in it; and it must be fully proved that no personal advantage is involved before the ordinary critic will
altogether acquit the man who thus, for harmony's sake,
consents to keep *in petto* his distinctive opinions.   But when
the question is whether a man who believes in no God shall
continue to present himself among those who come together
expressly to worship a God, its aspect is entirely altered.
An English officer is bound to be respectful of the religious
feelings of the worshippers of Siva and Vishnu, but he would
not be justified in making offerings at their altars, much less
would it be a lofty evidence of elevated conceptions were he
to do so; though even in this case the analogy is not complete: for the believer in God may see with sympathy a dim
traditionary worship in which the true and only Deity may
still reveal Himself to humble worshippers who have been
taught to know the Supreme under the many titles of Brahma.
But between those to whom God is, and those to whom He is
not, there is a wider gulf, and no emotional pleasure in the
union of human spirits, or in the feelings of reverence or
brotherhood excited among them, can make prayer and praise
anything but a pitiable comedy to those to whom heaven
holds no Godhead, and earth no hope save in the present life.
It is curious, however, to see how a great intelligence could
content itself in the comfort to be derived from this theory,
and the practical use made of it afterwards in her greatest
imaginations.

With this change Miss Lewis and the Evangelical correspondence naturally died into distance, and her new friends
and new subjects engrossed her life.   The letters to Miss
Hennell and the Brays, which now come in, are not, however, more interesting or lifelike.   They are very fine, high-
flown, and superlative, but keep us in ignorance as profound
of the natural woman as if she spoke to us with the trumpet
and through the mask of a Greek actor.   Take the following
sentence, for instance, in answer to the common argument
that human dissatisfaction with all its possessions is a proof
of a future life: ' The non-satisfaction of the affections and
' the intellect being inseparable from the unspeakable ad-
' vantage of such a race as that of man in connexion with its
' corporal condition and terrene destiny forms not at present
' an argument with me for the realisation of particular
' desires.'   We need not attempt to make many quotations from correspondence conducted in this strain.   Her
new friends, however, introduced her to others of their way
of thinking, and the translation of Strauss's ' Leben Jesu '.

fell, through their means, into her hands—a piece of work which was her first literary performance. Strauss does not seem to have produced much enthusiasm in her mind, and she felt the oppression of the continuous labour; while the extraordinary muddle in her brain, if we may venture to use such a word, of the sentiment of faith and the reality of unbelief is apparent from an incident related by Mrs. Bray in a letter to her sister: 'Miss Evans is Strauss-sick. It makes ' her ill dissecting the beautiful story of the Crucifixion, and ' only the Christ image and picture make her endure it.' The crucifix has carried consolation to many simple souls, but how it should comfort a writer in the act of making out the sufferings commemorated by it to be without any special significance, or to represent anything more than the fate of an unsuccessful teacher, is a mystery which we do not pretend to solve. And that it should be the supposed stern followers of truth—truth at any price—who comfort themselves by such sentimental pretences, is more extraordinary than words can say.

There is a certain pathos, however, in the curt and inexpressive story. Here was a large soul straying vaguely about in a world not realised, with a feeble tether of half-fictitious traditionary beliefs conventionally held, with no individual interests of its own, awaiting what tenant fate might bring to the vacant place, what guide might come out of the unseen. When this celestial wanderer stumbled into the rich ribbon-weaver's garden, into the midst of the clever folk with their books, might there not have been a sighing among the spheres, a regret that breathed through earth and heaven? She neither knew what was in her, nor did they. They pitied her, ' poor thing, with her pale sickly ' face and dreadful headaches;' while she, 'ivy-like as I am ' by nature,' clung to her new instructors, the only representatives to her of a world wider than that of her rustic kindred, or where anything was thought of beyond the material occupations of life.

This propinquity settled the colour of her future career. She never, so far as appears, came into familiar contact with any other class, but was handed on within the boundaries of the sect from one to another, and had no possibility afforded to her of reconsidering the conclusions arrived at so easily, with so little apparent strain or suffering. In all this there is no question of George Eliot, the as yet undeveloped greatness, but of a young woman to all appearance very apt to take the colour of those whom she cared for, extremely sensitive to impression, eager for the excitements and satisfactions of intellectual life, and altogether dazzled and transported by the atmosphere in which she now found herself, and the delight of intimacy with a group of people, each of whom had written, or was about to write, a book on the highest subjects—'Inquiry into Christianity,' 'Philosophy of Necessity,' and so forth. No doubt the foolish Christians were made but little account of in that intellectual circle. 'These dear orthodox people talk so simply 'sometimes that one cannot help fancying them satirists of 'their own doctrines and fears,' Miss Evans writes to Miss Hennell; and they prattle of 'our blessed St. Francis' (Newman), and are glad in each other's enjoyment of the 'Nemesis 'of Faith,' while at the same time mixing up their philosophy with easy quotations from the Bible and a great many pseudo-Christian phrases, which startle us by their juxtaposition with much that is very frankly anti-Christian. 'Paint soap-bubbles,' Marian says to Sara; 'paint the 'crucifixion in a bubble, after Turner, and then the resur-'rection.' These are the pleasantries of the correspondence, and they are not in very good taste. But we cannot find a word to show that it was a pain to the girl who but a short time before had been writing to her evangelical friend about 'fellowship in the sufferings of our Saviour,' to give up her faith. The question of going or not going to church made a little storm for the moment, but the change from belief in Jesus Christ to belief in Messrs. Hennell and Bray produced no convulsion nor any sign of trouble. In this lame and impotent evasion of human history, surely the biographer must be to blame.

She had not, however, it would seem, the least inclination to proselytise, and snubbed severely a certain young lady of the neighbourhood who carried her budding difficulties to the translator of Strauss, doubtless feeling the force of the tide which bore the best society around her into unbelief. When the girl, who was to some extent her pupil, prattled of her religious difficulties, Miss Evans steadily turned 'my 'attention from theoretical questions to a confession of my 'own want of thoroughness in mathematics, which I pre-'tended to teach,' with a 'request that I would specially 'give attention to this study and get my conscience clear 'about it, and that I would not come to her again till my 'views of religion were also clear'—a delightful piece of humorous realism, which refreshes amid all the verbiage, and shows a light of steady human understanding burning.

all the while behind these fine abstractions. It is to this same young lady that she gives, a little afterwards, a very curious piece of advice, in which there is a possible reflex of past suffering, as well as a somewhat stern adaptation of her new views. 'Never,' she says, 'go to old people as ' oracles on matters which date any later than their thirty-' fifth year.' 'However just old people may be in their ' principles of judgement, they are often wrong in their ap-' plications of them from an imperfect or unjust conception ' of the matter to be judged. Love and cherish and venerate ' the old, but never imagine that a worn-out, dried-up organi-' sation can be so rich in inspiration as one which is full ' fraught with life and energy.' This is a startling deliver-ance, and though it is an entirely logical deduction from the belief that humanity is altogether mortal, and has no continuity beyond the grave, it is yet very unusual to state such an opinion. Leopardi (if the reader will permit a second comparison), after he adopted the tenets which crushed his soul, bursts into impassioned and despairing celebrations of youth as the only thing on earth that is worth having. Miss Evans does not do this, but in the calm of an age much short of thirty-five she is able to think with composure of the natural decay which ought to begin after men have turned the corner and passed the *mezzo di cammin.* What so natural as that body and soul should begin to decline together after that climax—that the worn-out organisation should have nothing further to give forth, and that the counsels of thirty-five should be infinitely more to the purpose than those of fifty, not to say threescore and ten? If this were really so, it might not be pleasant to many of us, and yet it would bring the human problem much nearer solution. But it must be a confusing thought for those who acknowledge no hereafter that human experience contradicts this assumption, and that the maturing and growth of the soul (so foolish and unnecessary if it is about to die) as the body decays is one of those universal certain-ties against which there is no argument. Yet why should the mind grow while the man fades? Miss Evans's view is much more logical, though there never was a case which contradicted it more completely than her own.

Life went on thus with little external movement in it until her father died. He was a man who had been greatly respected and beloved in his time, and his daughter was his devoted nurse and affectionate companion: but the years which ought to be the most beautiful of life had passed

while she performed by his side the natural duties of the
last remaining daughter, and her flight out into the world
after his death has a certain eagerness of youth in it, very
fresh and simple considering her philosophical and other
attainments, and the ripe age of thirty to which she had
arrived.   The engraving from the portrait made of her at
Geneva, though poor in point of art, presents us on the
whole with an agreeable idea of the young woman setting
forth for the first time upon independent life.   There is
something sweet, deprecating, prepossessing in the eyes, and
a sort of subdued smile in the countenance which seems to
look out with a hope of pleasing, a desire to make friends,
upon a world of which she was not afraid.   And there is
nothing in Mr. Cross's three volumes so spontaneous and
lifelike as the letters from Geneva.   Here we have for the
first time a glimpse of her, apart from the everlasting think-
ings which make her letters to the Bray family and the other
intellectualities of Coventry read like so many little essays.
Here, in a strange place and new atmosphere, she has life
itself and other living creatures to think of, and the change
is extremely agreeable.   She went to nothing more dignified
than a *pension* on the banks of the lake of Geneva, but it
was full of new people and new ways, and took her out of
herself. 'Madame says things so true that they are insuffer-
'able,' she says with almost the first gleam of humour that
has appeared.   There are French people, German people,
one or two English, all new, amusing her in spite of herself,
and with an evident readiness to perceive that the young
English lady in her mourning was very well worth talking
to, and not at all an ordinary person. 'Every one is kind
'to me and seems to like me,' she says very prettily and
simply, and as a matter of fact all the inhabitants of the
pension, who are many, seem to have been captivated by her.
The pleasant breath of reality blows through these pages with
quite a new effect.   The little group detaches itself delicately
from the background, all kind, even affectionate, and each
with a pleasant individuality.   The hand is not the hand of
George Eliot, but it is that of a natural young woman, for the
first time feeling herself an object of interest to all about
her, and for one happy moment neither teaching nor being
taught.   After a time, either on the ground of economy, or
because her friends were leaving, or for some other reason,
she removed into Geneva, where she was fortunate enough
to get herself established in the house of an artist with
whom and his wife she formed once more a warm and last-

ing friendship.   She was not rich; but ' I hope I shall have
' enough for daily bread,' she says : and there is every reason
to suppose that she was happy and at her ease among the
kind foreign people who gave her spirit the impulse of
novelty as well as the delightful sensation of being admired
and highly thought of.   After a while the anxious friends
at Coventry seem to have thought that she was enjoying
herself too much, and she makes a little protest.   'I want
' encouraging rather than warning and checking,' she says;
' if human beings would but believe it, they do me most
' good by saying to me the kindest things truth will permit.'
This was what everybody seems to have done in this brief
episode; and what was certainly much better for her style
at least, she was kept free of philosophisings, and cheerfully
occupied with the routine of external life.

Coming back to England was not pleasant.   ' Oh the
' dismal weather, and the dismal country, and the dismal
' people !' she exclaims, writing from her brother's house at
Griff, the home of her own youth, in a way not complimentary to her kindred.   They did not probably understand
that need for having the kindest things possible said to her,
which indeed is often not the way of relations.   And under
the renewed impulse of the philosophical trio at Coventry, she
fell headlong into intellectualism once more.   Events, however, which were to withdraw her into a larger circle, were
now beginning to shape themselves, and in the autumn of
1851 Miss Evans went to London permanently as assistant
editor of the ' Westminster Review,' taking thus at once a
position in the literary world.   Mr. Chapman, the editor of
that periodical, kept, it would appear, a sort of *pension* at his
house in the Strand, where she took up her abode.   This
household, of which from time to time various distinguished
persons formed part, and where many of the best known
writers of the day were frequent visitors, would have been
well worthy of a little elucidation had Mr. Cross been able
to supply it; but he has not thought it necessary to do so.
Frederica Bremer was one of the guests when Miss Evans
joined the circle, but the Swedish novelist did not attract
her.

The names that appear in her letters afford an amusing jumble of the well-known and the obscure—Carlyle,
Herbert Spencer, Mazzini, Harriet Martineau, Lewes, &c.,
mingling with various others evidently quite as well known
to Miss Evans and her friends, the authors of obscure works
in opposition to Christianity, classed generally by Mr. Cross

as ' representing the most fearless and advanced thought of
' the day.'

Among these by far the most important, from our present
point of view, was George Henry Lewes, with whose appearance on the stage all the other surroundings sink into insignificance. ' Mr. Lewes had already secured to himself a
' wide reputation in the literary world by his " Biographical
' " History of Philosophy," his two novels, and his volu-
' minous contributions to the periodical literature of the
' day.' Perhaps this is an over-statement of Mr. Lewes's claims,
for his novels had fallen dead from the press, and his ' His-
' tory of Philosophy ' has never been of particular importance
in literature. But he was a man well known to all the
members of his craft; he had been a theatrical critic; he
was an admirable mimic ; and he had passed through all the
lowest scenes of London life. At this period of his career
he was neither prosperous nor happy, and his story, very
well known in the section of the world to which he belonged, was one which called forth sentiments not entirely
of pity. It has been said that there was no Divorce Court
in those days, and that this was the reason why he could not
free himself from a bond which had become impossible. But
as a matter of fact it was well known that he was in no
position to claim that freedom. Miss Evans must have been
aware of what had happened or was happening in his history.
Without any external attractions—' a sort of miniature Mira-
' beau in appearance,' she describes him after their first meeting—he had the happy gift of making himself interesting and
attracting sympathy ; and apart from moral questions there
could scarcely have been a more pitiable position than that
into which he found himself thrown in the middle of his
life—in indifferent health and circumstances, and with dependents hanging upon him, who could not be otherwise
than a painful burden. That a woman should pity a man
in such a strait, that she should feel the wrong done to him
to be more bitter than the wrong he had done, taking his
part in the unlovely story, was very natural. And Miss Evans
had long put aside the principles of Christianity. The fact
that no religious sanction could be given to the union of a
woman with a man whose wife, however unworthy, was still
living, would not in any way affect her mind. She would
feel that by the laws of nature the previous marriage was
dissolved by the one cause which in all time has been considered reason enough for its dissolution. We do not justify,
but we may attempt to account for, the resolution to which

she came.   Lewes was no doubt to her a man by natural
law and right divorced, to whom a woman ready to accept
the inevitable penalties might join herself without sense of
wrong.

It was not to be expected that Mr. Cross should enter
into any explanations on this subject, neither perhaps could
the progress of events be traced by any other hand.   But
Miss Evans was a high-minded woman with whom no
thought or inclination that was less than pure had ever been
connected.   It is impossible but that she must have thought
over and somehow justified to herself the tremendous step
she took.   That she did it in the way indicated above we
have very little doubt, any more than we have any doubt that
she was, even from her own point of view, entirely wrong.
For the more the bonds of religion are slackened the more
absolutely necessary it is, as in other matters she would have
been the first to acknowledge, to redouble the force of law
upon which all human order must rest; and were the license
which she took to herself general, the great institution upon
which morality rests as between man and woman, must
utterly fall to nought, and disorders of the vilest description ensue.   Such an argument might have been supposed
to have special force with such a woman.   But she was
alone, her life going on under conditions which could not
have been satisfactory, in the comfortless publicity of a
boarding-house, with no prospect of any better fate than
that of a literary hack among other literary hacks, without
home or family support.   The sort of acquittal which society
afterwards gave her, as if the mere possession of great genius
made that justifiable which nothing else could excuse, is a
thing with which we have no sympathy.   What is wrong in
any woman is more, not less, wrong in a woman gifted
beyond her neighbours.   At the same time we would not
refuse to acknowledge the excuses that soften her great
mistake in life.   No one, we think, qualified to judge will
believe that impure motives or overmastering passion were
the cause of it.   As a question of mere natural right and
wrong she would feel herself justified, the forfeiture of all
claims upon the part of the erring wife being indubitable;
and as for society, it is evident that either she believed
that she cared nothing about its judgement, or was really
prepared to accept its penalties.   That she was altogether
wrong in her decision as a question of morals, no one
will venture to contest; and few, we think, will consider
the high-handed way in which she treats the subject in

the statement she makes as consistent either with good taste or good feeling. But a woman who is in the wrong may perhaps be pardoned for a more than usually hot determination to declare herself in the right. This is how she states her case to Mrs. Bray, who had apparently at the first hearing been startled, if no more :—

' If there is any one action or relation of my life which is and always has been profoundly serious, it is my relation to Mr. Lewes. . . . Light and easily broken ties are what I neither desire theoretically nor could live for practically. Women who are satisfied with such ties do *not* act as I have done. That any unworldly, unsuperstitious person, who is sufficiently acquainted with the realities of life, can pronounce my relation to Mr. Lewes immoral, I can only understand by remembering how subtle and complex are the influences that mould opinion. But I *do* remember this, and I indulge in no arrogant or uncharitable thoughts about those who condemn us, even though we might have expected a somewhat different verdict. From the majority of persons, of course, we never looked for anything but condemnation.'

This fine assumption of a superior position, and abstinence from arrogance and uncharitableness, has a tragic humour about it which George Eliot, had the case not been her own, would have been the first to seize. For surely it required no analysis of the influences that mould opinion to show that on the broadest principles a breach of the law upon which society is founded must be condemned; and that only a very subtle and complex action of the mind upon the individual elements in this particular case could secure indulgence at all for that breach. The whole matter affords as curious an instance of the force of unconscious sophistry in dealing with one's own individual case as is on record. We could imagine such a woman speaking in a very different tone; we could, were it not an overboldness, put words into her mouth such as might have brought from human eyes that tear which it is the part of the recording angel to shed. She might have lifted her eyes upon the world and said, ' The man is miserable, and I can help him. He has no wife, for she has forfeited all claim to be so considered. According to natural laws, were we together in the desert, in the old-world dispensations, in the life which we call primitive and savage, but which is free from the conventional and the religious, the dogmas which to me are worse than useless, our union would be unforbidden. By society and a Christian community it will, I know, be condemned and forbidden. In ordinary cases I acknowledge the justice of such prohibitions, but not in my own. I do not blame my judges. I accept the penalty. That which I have in view is a higher good, in my opinion, than the approbation of the world, and in what I do I have my own approbation, the approval of my conscience.' We venture respectfully to submit that such a plea might have been received at least with respect, whereas the real statement can only awake surprise, indignation, and derision—the latter in the largest proportion of readers. George Eliot had far too profound a sense of what is and is not permitted by art, ever to place any imaginary woman in a similar position; and in the only case which, in all her productions, at all approaches her own, the decision of Maggie Tulliver is never doubtful for a moment. It is unnecessarily stern, since perhaps it would have been actually better for everybody had she consented to marry Stephen Guest; but all her instincts, as well as her judgement, rise against it. Here the sanctity of a tie as yet unformed is more to the high-minded girl than all the plead_ings of her lover and all the rebellion of her own young heart and passion. No one has ever made a stronger protest than this in favour of fidelity and duty. In all poetry and romance it has always been held that wherever love enters, lesser potencies must give way. George Eliot, so far as we can remember, alone bids love go by and permit the ac_complishment of engagements which are sanctioned only by honour and duty. Yet in her own case she believes that only worldly and superstitious persons can fail to understand her. The contrast is very wonderful, and proves for the hundredth time, were it at all necessary to prove it, that the circumstances in which we are least capable of judging are our own circumstances, and that, in respect to these, the wiles of a casuistry more than Jesuitical are always at the actor's command.

How far she did pay the penalty in the beginning of her career as Mrs. Lewes—which name, with a sort of con_ventionality which is a little surprising, she at once assumed, resenting any mistaken idea that there could be doubt about it—we are not informed. Acting on the same principle which has left us unaware of any human crisis or movement of feel_ing in her youthful life, Mr. Cross has left out every refer_ence to any disagreeables that might have existed in her new life. Perhaps there were no such disagreeables; but had there been, we should have felt more sympathy for her. Her friends in Coventry, however, stood by her without apparent faltering, and very soon other names came in; while, in the meantime, she had all the solace of that life *à deux* which was her ideal of the perfect life, and read, wrote, and walked in the society of the man she had chosen with a thorough satisfaction, about which there could be no doubt or question. Unlawful though it might be, the union was perfectly successful. The wife (if we may use these words) made the husband not only a happy but a respectable man (he might not have relished the adjective, but it is true), and the husband not only converted a dissatisfied and uncheerful life into one of endless content, but also developed out of the clever and accomplished woman who had become his companion a dormant genius, scarcely suspected, and unsurpassed in her generation. If ever the end can justify the means, it may be allowed to have done so in the present case. It is a test to which it is hard to put our conscientious judgement, yet it has to be faced. If the result is to be accepted as a conclusive justification, these two people did well to defy the laws that bind ordinary mortals. And yet they did not do well.

In the beginning of their union they lived very quietly and in somewhat obscure places, always together, with only one sitting-room to work in, with the scratching of each other's pens in their ears—she writing articles for the ' West- ' minster ' or the ' Leader,' he finishing his life of Goethe. A kind of comfortable middle-class veil of retirement and warmth and commonplace falls around them. In the evenings one reads aloud with many a pause for comment and comparison of opinions. Sometimes they have a little walk, coming in again with pleasure to the fireside, to the suspended book. There is a whiff as of tea in the air, and all is blameless, virtuous, *bourgeois*. Such perfect domesticity, such superiority to all outside attractions, never was. To Lewes, who had been something of a Bohemian, addicted to the keener delights of London, to the carelessness of loose society, one can imagine it must have been a novelty not without its drawbacks, this unbroken round of conjugal happiness; if she had sacrificed something, he too must have sacrificed a little. But the charm of perpetual intercourse with a mind so rich seems to have made up for anything, and by-and-by an entirely new excitement sprang up, which changed the current and prospects of their lives.

Up to this time only the foreign ladies in the *pension* at Geneva, only the Swiss artist and his wife, who saw her in her simplicity, a mere human creature unmarred by too much intellectualism, had found out what was in her. To all the others she was a very clever woman with a more than

feminine capacity for philosophy and big words. There are
no letters from the Brays to let us know what they thought
of her, but probably they were a little patronising towards
a girl whom they had themselves found and drawn out of
the ordinary level. But now she was subjected to the closer
observation kindled by affection, of a man who knew what
genius was when he saw it, and who began, as these long
talks went on, to perceive that he had got even more than
he was aware of in this woman who had picked him up in
his low estate. They were poor, and had to work at their
articles both of them 'for needfu' cash.' No doubt it was
in the midst of some story of her youth, at which she had
made him laugh or cry, that he suddenly said one day 'You
' must try and write a story.' The idea had lingered in her
own mind as ' a vague dream' for years, and she had written
an introductory chapter describing a Staffordshire village
and the life of the neighbouring farmhouses. One morning,
in the doze which precedes awakening and in which so many
of our dreams take form, ' I imagined myself writing a
' story of which the title was " The Sad Fortunes of the
' " Rev. Amos Barton." ' Lewes thought it was a capital
title, and encouraged her to try what would come of it.
It is evident that they had many talks and consultations
on the subject, in which the absence of any certainty either
on one side or another as to what the result would be is
very curious, seeing that she was thirty-seven at the time
and had been doing literary work for years. ' George
' used to say " It may be a failure—it may be that you are
' " unable to write fiction. Or perhaps it may be just good
' " enough to warrant your trying again." Again : " You
' may write a *chef-d'œuvre* at once—there's no telling."
The result of all these talks, however, and of the revelation
in her dream of poor Amos Barton's name, was that she began
the story. The subsequent events had better be told in her
own words :—

' About a week afterwards, when I read him the first part of " Amos,"
he had no longer any doubt about my ability to carry out my plan.
The scene at Cross Farm, he said, satisfied him that I had the very
element he had been doubtful about—it was clear I could write good
dialogue. There still remained the question whether I could command any pathos : that was to be decided by the mode in which I
treated Milly's death. One evening G. went to town, on purpose to
leave me a quiet evening for writing it. I wrote the chapter from the
news brought by the shepherd to Mrs. Haskit to the moment when
Amos is dragged from the bedside, and I read it to G. when he came

home. We both cried over it, and then he came up to me and kissed
me, saying, "I think your pathos is better than your fun." '

Nothing can be more interesting and pretty than this narrative of the beginning of work so great and so unlike the
work of a beginner.   The simplicity almost childlike with
which the mature woman who has been all unconscious of
her power for so long, brings her manuscript to the absolute
judge who holds her fortune in his hands, with faith and
dependence as complete as if she had been sixteen, produces
the most curious effect upon us.   It is all as sincere and
genuine as the story of a child.   Would she have thrown her
work aside with the same docility had he condemned it?
She was neither weak nor to all appearance unduly yielding
in other matters, but could defend herself stoutly and give
judgement sternly when need was.   Would she have carried
her genius like an unlighted lamp to the grave with her
had not her little Sultan struck the spark that was to throw
its light over half a world?   The native impulse has burst
forth in many ways, but perhaps never before with so little
personal consciousness, so unspontaneous, a thing brought
out from unknown treasures by the docile spirit to please
her master.   With what excitement the keen and sharp-
witted critic must have listened while this wonderful Ariel
did his bidding, producing before him riches which he had
not dreamed of, things immeasurably above his own power,
yet in absolute subjection to his judgement! a little Pros-
pero, sharp, shaggy, clear-sighted, knowing what it meant
though it seems she did not, while that delicate spirit performed the impossible task he had set her, with the ease and
simplicity of nature.   No wonder he cried: for not only
must any man who was not inhuman have been touched beyond measure by the sight of this slave of genius, but so far
as concerned external matters all their troubles were over
and their fortune made.

It was no small addition to the good fortune of George
Eliot (as we may now call her) that the publisher to whom
Lewes introduced her first work was John Blackwood.   The
insight, the quick understanding, the excellent judgement
represented by that name are known to many, yet not perhaps to so many as the place he held deserved.   For it is
not too much to say of John Blackwood, though he never
wrote a line, that he was a power in literature.   Trusting
to no opinion but his own, with no middleman between him
and the literary workers to whom he was able to open the
gates of access to the public, his excellent judgement had

the additional advantage of being unprofessional, not that of a competitor and fellow-craftsman, but of a man of the world, living in the atmosphere of the reader rather than of the writer.   His instinct was almost infallible as to what would and would not stand the ordeal of public discussion.   His quiet 'That will do' was more satisfactory to those who were acquainted with the man than many a gush of praise, and at the same time his eye was keen and quick to see the weak point of either a story or an argument. Few better or bolder critics ever existed.   His pithy letters and terse indications of what dissatisfied him were not to be lightly disregarded, and he was always liberal, nay generous, in recognition, not only of that which pleased the general audience, but of that which he felt to be good and worthy.   His, with the exception of a few of the first acknowledgements of George Eliot's merits, are the only letters not her own which are included in this record.   The first which he wrote after reading 'Amos Barton' is highly characteristic in its guarded expressions and instinctive criticism :—

'I am happy to say that I think your friend's reminiscences of clerical life will do.   If there is any more of the series written, I should like to see it, as, until I saw more, I could not make any decided proposition for the publication of the tales, in whole or in part, in the magazine.   This first specimen, "Amos Barton," is unquestionably very pleasant reading.   Perhaps the author falls into the error of trying too much to explain the characters of his actors by description instead of allowing them to evolve in the action of the story; but the descriptions are very humorous and good.   The death of Milly is powerfully done, and affected me much.   I am not sure whether he does not spoil it a little by specifying so minutely the different children and their names.   The wind-up is perhaps the lamest part of the story; and there too the defect, I think, is caused by the specifications as to the fortunes of parties of whom the reader has no previous knowledge. . . . I dare say I shall have a more decided opinion as to the merits of the story when I have looked at it again and thought it over, but in the meantime I am sure that there is a happy turn of expression throughout, also much humour and pathos.'

To the worshippers of George Eliot this calm approbation may seem almost profane, and it discouraged her, as Lewes writes, in her shrinking susceptibility to criticism.   It must be remembered, however, that the stranger whose modest little manuscript came to hand among a dozen others had no aureole of coming glory to indicate that here was a new star about to rise upon the horizon.   Blackwood's second

letter, however, was warmer than the first, and he accepted
'Amos Barton' unconditionally for the magazine.

We need not enter into the somewhat elaborate mystifica-
tion of the incognito. Nor is it necessary to add any criticism
of the book which, when published complete, took the public
by storm, and produced from all quarters letters of applause
and thanks. One or two things, however, will strike the
reader on comparing this first work with the story of its
production. The timidity or rather docility of the new
author, young in everything but years, and so entirely dependent upon the approbation of her companion, making his
fiat the 'to be or not to be' of her genius, is most curiously
unlike the mature and easy force of the style, the command
of all her materials, and the freedom and power with which
this shy and susceptible feminine soul sets forth some of the
darkest and least attractive features of rural life. The scene
at the workhouse—so hideous, so humorous, so real—seems
almost absurdly incompatible with the charming story of
that first essay at fiction, the pretty uncertainty of the
writer, the experimental character of the whole. We cannot
for a moment suppose that the little domestic romance is
insincere, but yet there is perhaps nothing in fiction more
unlike such an entrance into the world. Had it been Miss
Austen's dainty steps that were thus encouraged to cross
the threshold of literature, we might have acknowledged
the fitness of it. But that keen and clear-eyed little cynic
would have put Mr. Lewes in a book and laughed at him to
his face. That it should be George Eliot, with her voice and
touch of power, her large freedom of speech, her emancipation from all bondage of the pretty and proper, who was
the heroine of this little conjugal drama, is in the highest
degree bewildering. It may also be remarked that, whereas
in the course of so many letters and journals, we have as
yet come upon only one characteristically humorous remark
(faithfully quoted above), there are a dozen such in the first
few pages of the first story. The excellent farmhouse, 'in
' which the mice are sleek and the mistress sickly,' where
the doctor enjoys himself; the description of Mrs. Haskit as
' a thin woman with a chronic liver complaint which would
' have secured her Mr. Pilgrim's entire regard and unre-
' served good word, even if he had not been in awe of her
' tongue, which was as sharp as his own lancet;' and of the
knitting which is the constant accompaniment of her conversation, 'so that in her utmost enjoyment of spoiling a
' friend's self-satisfaction, she was never known to spoil a

' stocking; ' of Mrs. Patten, to whom ' quiescence in an easy
' chair under the sense of compound interest perpetually
' accumulating has long seemed an ample function; ' and
of Mr. Haskit, ' whose advice about crops is always worth
' listening to, and who is too well off to want to borrow money.'
All these keen touches of humoristic description occur within
the space of two small pages, and the whole story bristles
with them, with an irresistible glow of suppressed laughter
and whimsical insight.   Where did she bottle up all this
drollery for so many years?   The deadly seriousness, the
philosophical essays, the perpetual mind-improving and self-
culture of all her earlier life, did it never blow aside for a
moment and show the warmer life behind? or was it a revelation to Lewes as well as to the world that the translator
of Strauss and Spinoza had the freest, strongest, most penetrating comic faculty of her generation, with the exception
only of the two great humorists who were her contemporaries yet predecessors?

' Adam Bede ' followed in the course of the next year. Mr.
Blackwood, with a caution in respect to his beloved magazine
which is delightfully characteristic, though he approved the
earlier chapters highly, yet hesitated to conclude upon its
publication in ' Blackwood,' ' wanting to know the rest of
' the story before deciding.' ' I wrote in reply refusing to
' tell him the story,' says the proud and sensitive writer.
The idea of serial publication was therefore happily put
aside, and the book was not given to the public until it was
complete. This was in the beginning of 1859. The success
of the ' Scenes of Clerical Life ' had prepared the way for the
greater and more complete work, and it was received with
enthusiasm. Not only was every journal eloquent in its
favour, but letters poured in from all sides to the author,
under the disguise of her *nom de plume*, in several of which
her secret was so far penetrated that she was recognised as
a woman. We are still at a loss to know on what grounds
this discovery was founded; for to ourselves George Eliot's
books remain (with the exception, perhaps, of the ' Mill on
' the Floss ') less definable in point of sex than the books of
any other woman who has ever written. A certain size, if
we may use the word, and freedom in the style, an absence
of that timidity, often varied by temerity, which, however
disguised, is rarely absent from the style of women, seems to
us to obliterate the distinctions of sex; and her scientific
illustrations and indications of a scholarship more easy and
assured than a woman's ordinary furtive classical allusions,

no doubt added greatly to this effect. But yet there were some who could see through a millstone, and made the discovery. The history of her first great book is again given at length, and shows both the strength and weakness of a mind which was so little that of a critic, and which combined womanly prejudices so ineradicable with so much of the unscrupulousness of a masculine intelligence.

'The germ of " Adam Bede," she tells us, was an anecdote told me by my Methodist aunt Samuel, an anecdote from her own experience. We were sitting together one afternoon during her visit to me at Griff, probably in 1839 or 1840, when it occurred to her to tell me how she had visited a condemned criminal, a very ignorant girl, who had murdered her child and refused to confess ; how she had stayed with her, praying, through the night ; and how the poor creature, at last, broke out into tears, and confessed her crime. My aunt afterwards went with her in the cart to the place of execution ; and she described to me the great respect with which this ministry of hers was regarded by the official people about the gaol. The story, told by my aunt with great feeling, affected me deeply, and I never lost the impression of that afternoon and our talk together ; but I believe I never mentioned it through all the intervening years, till something prompted me to tell it to George, in December 1856, when I had begun to write the " Scenes of Clerical Life." He remarked that the scene in the prison would make a fine element in a story, and I afterwards began to blend this and some other recollections of my aunt in one story with some portions of my father's early life and character. The problem of construction that remained was to make the unhappy girl one of the chief *dramatis personæ* and connect her with the hero.'

It is evident in all that follows that, to the author, the central and most important figure in the book is Dinah Morris, and that here, as elsewhere, George Eliot has all a girl's love for her ideal, and places her pride and joy in the glorification of the white-angelic heroine in whom goodness itself is to be held up to the adoration of the world. The wonderful study of Hetty, made with so much boldness ; the extraordinary creation of that trifling and shallow nature, in whose anguish, helplessness, and despair one of the most penetrating notes of tragedy has been sounded, though the artist must have expended so much creative force in the work, obtains from the woman scarcely any notice at all : ' Hetty—i.e. the girl who commits child-murder '—she says, with an almost inconceivable indifference, as if this part of her story was a mere expedient of construction, and had no interest for herself. In such a feeling she would carry with her the great bulk of the simple-minded public, which loves to see virtue glorified, and to bow before a heroine who is perfect, yet human. But it is strange to find her in her own person so little conscious of excellence in art, even her own, and so artlessly devoted to moral excellence and the ideal. When the book was published, and the reviews came (already carefully filtered through the ever-watchful, ever-anxious husband, lest something should jar upon her sensitive spirit), the fact that in the 'Saturday,' though it was laudatory, 'Dinah is not mentioned!' is recorded with bitter amusement. With 'Adam Bede' began that high sense of her position as a moral teacher which increased with the years. All is serious, almost solemn, in her own high approbation of the completed work. 'I love it very much, and ' am deeply thankful to have written it,' she says, with a consciousness of excellence which is really impressive. Perhaps, only the conviction that she was thus actually becoming a great influence in the world could take from such consciousness the edge of self-admiration which always moves the spectator to profanity.

It was not till some time after this that the friends in Coventry, with whom her correspondence had always continued, were told who George Eliot was. She had taken them very seriously to task some time before for the mild suggestion that she might possibly be writing a novel, informing them that if she did anything of the kind, and concealed it, they might be sure she had excellent reasons for so doing; which seems a high tone to take with friends so intimate. They had not divined her, but were disposed to believe in Liggins; a double offence. The feelings which she expresses after her now-assured success have much *naïveté* and simplicity in them, when they descend from the higher level. 'Few authors, I suppose, who have had a real ' success, have known less of the flush and sensations of ' triumph which are talked of as the accompaniments of ' success,' she says; and she expresses great alarm at the possibilities of interruption, with what seems a reflection of some girlish dream of the consequences of fame—the rush of all the world to applaud and admire. 'If people were to ' buzz round me with their remarks and compliments, I ' should lose the peace of mind and truthfulness of produc-' tion without which no good, healthy books can be written.' . . . 'As soon as the Liggins falsehood is annihilated, of ' course there will be twenty new ones in its place; and one ' of the first will be that I was not the sole author,' she adds on another occasion; a most strange subject of alarm, and one entirely without justification, for there was but one

Liggins, and he a poor wretch very easily disposed of; and everybody knew that Lewes, her only probable assistant, could not have written a chapter of 'Adam Bede' to save his life.

The 'Mill on the Floss' followed in the next year; a book of which strangely enough she writes to Mr. Blackwood that 'the characters are on a lower level generally and the en-'vironment less romantic' than 'Adam Bede.' If there is one of her books more than another upon which the truest partisans of George Eliot would take their stand, it is, we think, this book, which, with all the tremendous prose of the circle of relations—the Gleggs, the Pullets, and the rest—is nevertheless, with the exception of 'Romola,' the most poetical of her productions; the character of Maggie, all through, having the unity and depth—along with a spontaneousness and simplicity not attained in any other of her ideal figures —of a great poetical creation. To show, however, how curiously public opinion is balanced, the facts of George Eliot's history, which had by this time percolated through society, so influenced the duller sorts that this superlative tale of duty, with its central incident of a self-sacrifice above all the ordinary requirements even of the noble mind, was discovered to be improper, and Maggie Tulliver met in the book with the fate which her author determined she should meet with in St. Ogg's. This is, however, a fact that perhaps only lingers in the memories of contemporaries, as there is nothing said about it in the biography, and there was no falling off in external success. 'Silas Marner' followed very shortly, her work in these brilliant years being continuous; the stream of inspiration running strong.

With this story her first period of authorship came to an end. We may say, as if she had been a painter, that these works were in her first manner. She had now come to an end of that reservoir of first impressions and original conceptions which had been accumulating in the long slow years of her imaginative and ambitious youth. From henceforward the strain is changed. A different region of life and different developments attract her. She is a conscious priestess elevated high upon a tribune, to which the eyes of the world are reverently turned; and the problems of a more advanced civilisation, or of a more conventional life, the life of the people among whom she has now come to live, in place of the surroundings of her youth, call for her attention. Everything is changed: the features of the landscape, the atmosphere, the thoughts that come naturally to the lips of the characters in the drama. It is difficult to express how great the difference is when, instead of being seen from among the farmyard ricks, the landscape is looked at across the velvet glades of a park. The very perspective alters, the sense of differing magnitudes. The peasant class, with all its natural preoccupations, the respectable farmers, the rural artisans, limited by the country doctor and clergyman, the highest eminences known, were all familiar to her mind ' as ' household words,' and drawn with the utmost force of an art which was nature. Her ladies and gentlemen, notwithstanding the pleasant picture of Mr. Irwine and his beautiful old mother, had not been very successful. Even the fine people at St. Ogg's are touched with a hesitating hand, and Captain Wybrow and his betrothed are very nearly vulgar, the lady especially. But the time for that limitation was over, and, herself living in a different world, she began to feel it expedient to follow the necessities and more intricate problems of a different sphere.

We cannot, however, leave this noble group of books without some reference to the continual use of religious subjects and characters in them. We ourselves remember the shock, almost a pang, with which a young reader was slowly and with difficulty brought to understand that the author of ' Adam Bede ' and of ' Janet's Repentance ' was not herself, in the most formal meaning of the word, a Christian. To be compelled to allow that the great author whose conception of religious faith was so elevated, whose acquaintance with all the phraseology of religious life, the fervour of prayer to God, and the impassioned pleading of the ambassador of Christ with man, so large and complete— was treating as mere mental phenomena, curious and memorable, yet entirely unreal, the exalted piety and profound belief of Mr. Tryan and of Dinah Morris, gave the keenest moral wound to this unsophisticated observer. What! follow a good man through the almost ecstacy of his ending life, and believe that the eyes, which like Stephen saw the Son of Man in the skies, in reality saw nothing but a collection of vapours, a devout imagination ! What! pray with Dinah in the prison, yet know the prayer was all delusion, that there was no God to hear, and no heavenly pity to forgive ! The youth rose stumbling, trembling, his eyes full of tears from the death-bed, from the prison-floor, with a hot indignation in his heart which even mature reason has not altogether cooled. We do not venture to determine how far the writer was to be blamed for such a use of the

elements of life so well known to her, but this natural and
unconscious criticism is worth recording.   The artless reader
was wounded to the quick; he felt himself cheated of his
tears, of the emotion in his inexperienced heart; he felt
himself insulted even in his faith.   Perhaps it was not
reasonable, but it was very natural.   And we ask ourselves
whether that supreme truth to which George Eliot appealed
on all occasions consists with such treatment, or whether
there lay in her heart a force of deeper conviction still, which,
when her garland and her singing robes were on, brought
back the belief which her lips disavowed and her reason
rejected.   If this hypothesis cannot hold, we ask, does
absolute sincerity and truth of soul consist with the expedient of securing our admiration and sympathy by such means?
Art for art may be a sound principle; it may justify, though
we do not think it does, a manifestation of all the sores and
loathsome diseases to which flesh is liable: but does it warrant the exhibition as the highest good of what is untrue?
It may be said that Dinah Morris and Mr. Tryan were true
to nature, and that their faith and emotions were absolutely
sincere.   But their author held their faith to be delusive,
and their emotions mere phenomena, like headache or gout.
Is it right, then, to clothe an ideal in stolen garments and
move us to the depths by exhibitions of false sentiment?
Morality in art is a very difficult question, and there are
many artists who are entirely indifferent to it: but George
Eliot was not so.   She was nothing if not a truth-seeker, a
teacher of the highest morality.   Was she justified in thus
procuring a high light for her picture by false means?   We
cannot think so, though we are not aware that her use of
these means to produce emotion has ever been questioned.

   It was befitting, in her transition from one manner to
another, that the great intermediate work, which now calls
our attention, should belong to neither.   'Romola' stands
by itself, one of the noblest attempts that have ever been
made to embody for us the life of a past age, and one of
the very few that have been successful.   It was the result
of the subtle and strong enchantment which the great city
of Dante and Savonarola exercises upon many souls, and was
a very sudden and complete step out of the lowly midland
scenes—the lanes and meadows of the English landscape.
She gives us no account of how the work presented itself first
to her imagination, but only occasional references to it, from
which we learn that its composition was accompanied by

much discouragement and oppression. Not much wonder, for she had to undertake a laborious research through many books, and to read through piles of ancient literature before she could set such a picture even upon her canvas—a very different process from that easy use of her own materials and resources which had been heretofore possible. Mr. Cross tells us that she complained of having ' worked under ' a leaden weight all the time. The writing of " Romola " ' ploughed into her more than any of her other books. . . . In ' her own words, " I began it a young woman, I finished it an ' " old woman." ' She was over forty, an age neither old nor young—but age is always relative; and it is very comprehensible that the unaccustomed labour, often no doubt distasteful enough, should have told heavily upon her strength. Even her partial failure in respect to Savonarola, her treatment of whom is a conspicuous example how far the intellectual understanding of spiritual phenomena can go, must have tried her mind and spirits deeply, since she could scarcely have failed to perceive that, notwithstanding all her labour and all her genius, the *fin mot* of that great enigma had escaped her. She says nothing, however, of Savonarola, nor of the amazing and merciless conception of Tito, which is the strongest feature in the book. Once more the girlish ideal, the too-perfect and sternly-spotless heroine is her first thought.

This work brought her increase of fame and a large sum of money, though, beguiled by the blandishments of Mr. George Smith, she had left her original and faithful publisher and given ' Romola ' to the ' Cornhill.' It was the only one of her longer books which was published in a magazine, and there were a few indications at first, in consequence of the very perfection of all those details that make it so striking a picture of mediæval life, of languor in the public interest. But this was soon overcome, and most likely was never known to the too easily affected author.

It was after ' Romola '—in itself poem enough to have satisfied the highest ambition—that the idea of writing a poetical work first seized upon George Eliot's imagination. The idea came to her, she tells us in a very elaborate statement and explanation, at Venice, suggested, oddly enough, by a small and, among his great Venetian works, insignificant, picture of Titian, an Annunciation which hangs in the great stair of the Scuola di San Rocco. She must, of course, have seen a hundred Annunciations elsewhere more remarkable than this little picture; but, in the caprice of human affairs, it caught her eye and imagination.

'This small picture of Titian's, pointed out to me for the first time, brought a new train of thought. It occurred to me that here was a great dramatic motive of the same class as those used by the Greek dramatist, yet specifically differing from them. A young maiden, believing herself to be on the eve of the great event of her life—marriage—about to share in the ordinary lot of womanhood, full of young hope, has suddenly announced to her that she is chosen to fulfil a great destiny, entailing a terribly different experience from that of ordinary womanhood. She is chosen, not by a momentary arbitrariness, but as a result of foregoing hereditary conditions; she obeys: "Behold "the handmaid of the Lord." Here, I thought, is a subject grander than that of Iphigenia, and it has never been used. I came home with this in my mind, meaning to give the motive a clothing in some suitable set of historical and local conditions. My reflections brought me nothing that would serve me except that moment in Spanish history when the struggle with the Moors was attaining its climax, and when there was the gipsy race ever present under such conditions as would enable me to get my heroine and the hereditary claim on her among the gipsies. I require the operation of race to give the need for renouncing the expectation of marriage.'

This seems a strange magnificence of motive to account for the 'Spanish Gipsy.' Out of pure love and enthusiasm for the author, the world made a great and conscientious effort to put this poem in the highest place—an effort which is a much greater proof of her personal influence than if it had been a good poem, but which is now allowed, even by the most enthusiastic, to have been a failure. As is so often the case with the least successful works of a writer, perhaps on the principle that the deformed child has always the mother's kindest word, she herself gives a great deal of space and explanation to her poem, analysing it minutely, and evidently expecting to give by it a sort of climax to her fame. She even asks, with a little unnecessary *jactance*, 'Don't you imagine how the people who consider writing 'simply as a money-getting profession will despise me for 'choosing a work by which I could only get hundreds 'when for a novel I could get thousands?' which is a little below the level of the occasion as the motive was above it. The poem was successful enough in the commonplace pecuniary way, the number sold being 'unusually large, even for 'what is called a successful poem,' and afforded the writer at least that satisfaction.

The two last books have no description attached to them, nor much light thrown upon their production. They are both, as has been said, of another sphere from that of the earlier works, and both were laboriously written with the interruption of much ill-health and a discouraging sense of weakness.   In the meantime, life went on without any events to record except the conception of a new book, or its appearance: doubts as to the effect it might produce, re-assurances on all hands of its excellence, and a final grateful sense that it was, as the others had been, enthusiastically received by the public.   In this there is not much incident to lighten the record; and the chronicles of thought, observation, and reading, the journals of travel, and communications to friends, though all very excellent in their way, afford little break to the monotony.   One day and one year pass as another.   Intellectual interests never flag, but as for other interests there are none, and life languishes in the well-understood and much-occupied routine.   Sometimes George Eliot, from her secluded throne, bends with gracious courtesy to comfort a fine lady who has lost her faith in God, by ex-plaining that this is not at all necessary to a healthy affec-tion for man; sometimes she pauses to utter a kind word on behalf of the charitable occupations of her friends, or in com-mendation of their children; but in everything she is philo-sophical, disposed towards the abstract, little apt to touch the affairs of life such as are brought under her notice with a light hand.   The intense seriousness of her life, the pre-dominance of thought, the absence of any relief save that given by accounts and calculations of the success and profits of her productions, grow greater as we go on.   Even in the thought there is little novelty, but a perpetual revolution round the same subjects, which do not seem to expand, and which in their supposed freedom and breadth have a strange narrowness, and look as much like the perambulations of a soul with a tether, as if Calvinism or Lutheranism or any other ism was the centre of the little round.

The reader will find but little light thrown upon the authoress in these volumes, but he will make acquaint-ance with a woman of a remarkable character, with a mix-ture of strength and weakness for which it is not at all likely he will be prepared.   The strongest of all female writers, he will find in her what is almost the conventional type of a woman—a creature all conjugal love and depend-ence, to whom something to lean upon is a necessity, who is sure of nothing until her god has vouched for it, not even of her own powers.   Moved to make in her life two very great and momentous decisions, involving in one case all that is dearest to the spirit, and in the other everything that is most important in the life of a woman, she takes these steps with an ease which confounds the spectator, making far less fuss about them than many people make of periodical transition from the blue room to the brown; but, lest we should think her nature was apathetic, shrinks and trembles before the touch of a critic, and has to be enclosed in a sort of moral cotton-wool and watched over by the most unwearying of sentinels to keep from her all inharmonious sounds. It may be, it is true, the fault of her biographer that she seems to take the great crises of her life so calmly; but some sign of the convulsion of nature, of the swing of the tremendous balance, must have been visible had these decisions been to her what it appears on the surface they must have been. We would say that a great self-confidence lay at the bottom of this calm, if we were not called on to remark how little confidence she had in herself in respect to her work. Perhaps the secret which underlies the paradox may be found in the fact that, with the immediate backing up of someone who thought her always right, she was impervious to all other influences. Protected by the sympathy of the Brays, her break with all that was most sacred in her previous life could be accomplished with serene satisfaction; and, under the protecting ægis of Lewes, her great practical defiance of the world appeared to her the act of a heroine. So long as those about her said 'the kindest ' things,' and supported her by their approval, her soul floated in a sea of content, and she was capable of doing everything they wished or recommended. This type of feminine character is one which has been much applauded in its day; it is perhaps that which, at the bottom of our hearts, most of us like best. The ivy which clings round the sheltering oak was a favourite image in the day when Miss Evans was at school, and no doubt was often recommended to her attention. But it is not the type of character with which we connect the possession of powerful genius, nor should we have expected to find it in George Eliot.

The history of her later years contains little to dwell on. The reverential circle that gathered round her in her own house, agape for every precious word that might fall from her mouth; the carefully-regulated atmosphere into which nothing from the outer world, save the most delicate incense with just the flavour that suited her, was allowed to enter; the ever-watchful guardian who preserved her from any unnecessary contact, are curious accessories little habitual to

the possessors of literary genius.   What a different picture
is that of Scott, working his noble faculties to exhaustion in
the tragic fight against failure and dishonour; and how few
whose names we could place beside that of George Eliot have
had a better fate !   Had her life been less sheltered and
sweetened, she would have ·left us a more interesting biography, which is all that we can say.   For though ' Middle-
march ' and ' Deronda ' are more artificial and not so perfect
as their predecessors, it would be hard to find another hand
which could have executed even these less excellent works ;
and it cannot be said that the adoration and the seclusion
injured her books.   But they very much injure the interest
of her appearance as an individual.   In the curious dim
artificial scene our sympathy drifts to the less noble, not
imposing figure by her side, who gave up his own objects
and life to become her custodian, her man of business, the
sentinel of her peace.   When her prop failed her, she fell
into utter wretchedness and helplessness, and found no
better thing to do than to take hold of another who continued the same worship, at the risk of mingling a dash
of unspeakable bathos with the conclusion of her life.   This
last postscriptal chapter might have been omitted with
advantage, considering the nature of so much that had gone
before.

We have now had considerable experience of the in-
expediency, the disadvantage of hurried biographies.   This
book will be less prejudicial, however, than others which we
might indicate, because of the absence of all personal comment and gossip, because even of its reticence.   No one will
be wounded, none injured, by a record in which nothing is
said to the detriment of any human being.   As it has no
very strong claim, in the force of the portraiture presented
to us, upon our interest, it will probably fade away like an
old photograph, leaving to the world a much stronger and
nobler image, the picture of the girl who was Maggie Tulliver,
who was Dorothea, the visionary, whose soul was athirst for
everything that was lovely and of good report, for all the
glories and mysteries of life.   With these and a host of
other characters to speak for her, George Eliot needs no
other expositor; the smaller voices, even when, by some
mystery of nature, they are joined and echoed by her own,
must fall before them and die away.

ART. IX.—*Lettres de la Marquise de Coigny et de quelques autres personnes appartenant à la Société Française de la fin du dix-huitième siècle.* (Privately printed.) Paris: 1884.

WE are indebted to a distinguished foreign bibliophile and collector of autographs for this curious volume—a posthumous memorial of one of the brilliant women of the last century. It consists of one-and-twenty letters addressed by Madame de Coigny to her friend and admirer, M. de Lauzun, Duc de Biron (whom we do not venture to call her lover), and of a few other letters of the same period, though of a more miscellaneous character. From these slender materials the editor has found means to compose a striking picture of a French society in the first eventful years of the Revolution, and to rescue from oblivion lives which are almost forgotten by or unknown to the present generation. A limited edition of this collection has been printed with the utmost typographical elegance for private distribution, not for the public; but we gladly avail ourselves of the editor's permission to lay some account of it before our readers. Without the introduction and the notes, executed with great care and research, the allusions with which these letters abound would be scarcely intelligible; and, although we have detected here and there a slip of the pen, or of memory,* they may be said to offer an animated picture of the society of the French emigration, and of London, nearly a hundred years ago.

Madame de Coigny had a tongue as sharp as her pen. Her keen wit, and what she herself terms her '*insolence*,' made her a legion of enemies, especially amongst her own class of society—the 'racaille aristocratique' of the emigration. She chose to distinguish herself by an early and passionate adoption of revolutionary principles, by a fierce and bitter hatred of the Royal Family and especially of Marie-Antoinette, who it seems had affronted her, and by an ardent friendship for Lauzun, the most dissolute man in France, and the only French officer of ducal rank who took the command of a revolutionary army, and expiated his apostasy on the scaffold. The Paris insurrection of June 22, 1791, and an adventure which Madame de Coigny met with

---

* Thus, strangely enough, the Prince of Wales, afterwards George IV., is described as 'Frederic-Augustus;' and the name of Lady Elizabeth Foster is spelt 'Forster.'

in the streets, warned her that Paris was no longer a safe residence even for a great lady of revolutionary opinions. She accordingly repaired to London, where she was cordially received into the society of the Prince of Wales and Mrs. Fitzherbert. She lived chiefly with that section of society which sympathised with the cause of liberty in France; but the progress and violence of the Revolution compelled her to remain in exile for about ten years, and it is from London that her letters to Lauzun are addressed. This circumstance led her to contract very intimate relations with this country. Her only son acquired by marriage large estates in Ayrshire, and she is still represented amongst us by her two grand-daughters, the Countess of Stair and Countess of Manvers.

Louise-Marthe de Conflans was nobly born in 1760. Her father, son of Louis de Conflans, Marquis d'Armentière and Marshal of France, married Jeanne-Antoinette Portail, the issue of an ancient Parliamentary family; on the one side ran the blood of a gallant race, on the other the culture of the *noblesse de robe*. She was a tall handsome girl with a high temper, and an intelligence which her mother is said to have cultivated. Those who like to take the trouble to read the memoirs of Madame de Genlis can judge of the nature of such an education for themselves, and it consisted no doubt of some acquaintance with musical instruments, and with passages from Racine and Corneille, along with the manufacture of those little *vers de société* in which it is so difficult for sober English folk to find either rhyme or reason. Of Louise's father Madame de Genlis says that he and his friends, De Coigny and FitzJames, were among the most reckless men of the court, and that their habits were not precisely domestic is plain from the fact that the fathers of the bride and bridegroom on the eve of Louise's wedding confessed to one another that they had never yet supped at home, and felt embarrassed on having to meet their wives. Under such auspices the young lady was married in 1775, that is to say, when she was fifteen years of age, to the son of the Duc de Coigny, a descendant of that Maréchal de Coigny who, in the reign of Louis XIV., got into dis-favour for want of zeal in following the household of the king, of which he formed a part, to the seat of war.* These

---

* The Coigny family was not ancient or illustrious. Saint-Simon says of the first of them, amusingly enough, ' Coigny était fils d'un de ' ces petits juges de Basse-Normandie, qui s'appelait Guillot, et qui, fils ' d'un mauant, avait pris une de ces petites charges pour se délivrer de

young people had no acquaintance with each other, and no wish to come together. It cannot be said that their marriage was a happy one, though the first troubles seem to have arisen from a jealousy between the relations, soon to become much more bitter in the breast of the high-spirited Louise. She was presented at court on a Sunday in June, 1780. Already well known by reputation for her beauty and her wit, she instantly became what our grandfathers would have called a *toast*, went to Marly, formed the acquaintance of Lauzun, and made a display, under the eyes of the young queen, of the haughty and indomitable temper of a *Frondeuse*. When a man and a woman, destined to have an important influence on each other's life, meet for the first time, their biographer may well pause. But this was no common meeting.

The French aristocracy of the last half of the eighteenth century was held to be a model of grace and elegance, and in its ranks there was no other man to compare with Armand-Louis de Gontaut, known in all the courts and *boudoirs* of Europe as the Duc de Lauzun, and to be afterwards known in the camp by his title of Duc de Biron.* He was thirty-four years of age, as handsome as he was chivalrous, and known to be a lady-killer, and an unfaithful husband to Amélie de Boufflers, whose society he left to follow frailer beauties into England and even into Poland. More than this, Lauzun was one of the friends of La Fayette, one of the French nobles who thought a republic attractive, who had gone with his leader to America, but who had returned to France to promulgate the new ideas, and to foment in the anterooms of Versailles a spirit of dissatisfaction and intrigue.

The Marquise de Coigny adopted his views: first, because he made love to her; and secondly, because she wished to

---

' la taille après s'être fort enrichi. L'épée avait achevé de le décrasser.' He married a woman with money, took the name of Franquetot, and might have died a marshal but for his refusal of a command. His son, however, did get the *bâton de maréchal*.

* Madame de Coigny's friend was the grand-nephew of the well-known Duc de Lauzun, who inspired La Grande Mademoiselle with so desperate and hapless a passion. He died in 1723 at the age of ninety, and as he left no children his vast fortune eventually descended to the hero of this correspondence, who was born in 1747. In thirty years the younger Lauzun had contrived to dissipate this large inheritance, and he surrendered his estates to the Princesse de Guéménée for an annuity of 80,000 francs a year.

lead a *fronde* against the queen and against the family. of her husband. That family was represented at Versailles by the Chevalier de Coigny, better known as *Mimi*, a man of extreme fashion and of more affectation, and by his elder brother the Duc de Coigny. What caused his daughter-in-law's antagonism to this individual, who was her father-in-law, is unexplained, though our editor is of opinion that it may have been first suggested to her by her own mother. Madame de Genlis, not apt to speak well of anyone, describes .this duke as being so amiable that he was generally liked and esteemed, and at court he was so great a favourite that his daughter-in-law did her best to throw an odious colour on his relations with the queen. Society soon drew off into two camps. France was suffering from want; Necker's administration was unsteady; and on the eve of the great Revolution womanish spite and ambition did their best to hasten the catastrophe.

Madame de Coigny's arrival in London coincided curiously with the business of the party in England, and the mission of both Talleyrand and Lauzun to the Court of St. James's. Louise's friendship with the latter had already lasted for ten years. She was a woman who had made and cared to make many conquests; but warm as was her regard for Lauzun, she never accepted him as a lover. 'To take a 'lover would be to abdicate' was her own motto; and the best proof of the nature of her regard for Lauzun is to be found in her indifference to his *amourettes*, even when they extended to her pretty niece Aimée de Coigny, the lady who inspired André Chenier with the charming verses addressed to 'La Jeune Captive.' But it is time to let Madame de Coigny's letters speak for themselves.

They defy translation. It is impossible to render, in any language but the original, the mixture of false sentiment and genuine sympathy—the bitterness and the gaiety—the levity with which the most serious things could be spoken, and the audacity with which the coarsest things could be touched—the vulgar passions of a *poissarde* marked by the arrogance of a Marquise. But, as a specimen of the time and of the woman, we will venture on a long extract.

'Londres, 1 Août 1791.

'Votre lettre a pris le chemin de Londres tout aussi directement qu'elle a trouvé le chemin de mon cœur. Elle m'est arrivée avec toute la promptitude, non pas d'une réponse, mais d'une repartie. Je vous en remercie comme du plus grand plaisir que je puisse éprouver ici. Si vous saviez combien ma vie y est désintéressée, vous jugeriez aussi le charme que votre souvenir peut apporter dans ma journée.   C'est du bonheur tout pur pour mon esprit et pour mon cœur, et l'un et l'autre en jouissent bien peu depuis longtemps.   Le prince de Tarente, qui ne parle pas plus à l'une qu'à l'autre, m'excède de son *désœuvrement* : ne prétendant plus à me faire vivre d'amour, je crois qu'il veut me faire mourir d'ennui, et je suis effrayée de la prodigieuse facilité qu'il y trouve.

'Madame de Piennes, qui est revenue tout exprès pour le seconder dans cette louable entreprise, le fait valoir à mes dépens d'une manière tout à fait onéreuse pour mon amour-propre.   Elle prétend que je suis l'objet de son voyage, et que Lady Argill n'en est que le prétexte. Elle raconte, ou plutôt improvise, sans cesse mille bêtises, que j'aurais honte de retenir.   Enfin elle me devient si insupportable qu'elle finira par me chasser d'Angleterre si elle y reste.   Vous pensez bien que je n'en partirai que pour retourner en France.   Tant de choses m'y appellent qu'il est juste qu'il y en ait une qui m'amène.

' Mais dites-moi donc, avant de m'y laisser entraîner, où en est la maison du roi ?   On affirme ici que Sa Majesté n'attend que sa composition pour faire la *fugue* qu'il a essayée jusqu'à présent infructueusement.*   Ne prenez pas ce bruit pour une imposture ; j'ose vous assurer qu'il arrive de très bonne part, et qu'il m'a été confirmé par une naïve indiscrétion du Prince L—— plus probante que vous ne pensez.   J'ajouterai que les choix des différents officiers de cette maison peuvent bien servir de témoignage à ces soupçons.   En vérité, ils seraient dictés par le cabinet de Coblentz qu'ils ne seraient pas différents.

' Je ne crois pas, quoi que vous en disiez, que le nouveau parjure de Louis XVI lui enlevât un de ses partisans.   Ils se vantent d'avoir abjuré la religion du serment depuis que nous en avons pris la mode, et manquer à leur foi me paraît la vertu comme le principe de leurs espérances.   Adieu ! donnez-moi celle de vous revoir, dussiez-vous même la tromper.   J'aime l'illusion ; la réalité m'y attache chaque jour davantage.   Le duc de Queensberry est amoureux de Madame de Gand ; elle s'en divertit. . . .

                                                              '1 Sept. 1791.

' Voici cette grande affaire dont j'ai promis de vous parler. Ecoutez-la avec attention, et promettez-moi de la servir avec intérêt.   Vous saurez que les ministres de l'Empereur, de l'Espagne, &c., voient ici les duchesses de Gloucester et de Cumberland,† que la dernière est aussi bien née que la moitié des princesses d'Allemagne que les princes

---

* The allusion is to the flight to Varennes.

† The Duchess of Gloucester was the illegitimate daughter of Sir Edmund Walpole, married *en premières noces* to the Earl of Waldegrave.   The Duchess of Cumberland was Lady Anne Luttrell, daughter of the Earl of Carhampton, and widow of Christopher Norton, Esq., so that neither of these ladies had any pretensions to rank with the princesses of Germany or of any other country by their birth. This was the reason that the Queen of France had ordered the French Ambassador not to pay them any attention.

épousent, et qu'en Angleterre elle a une maison et une considération personnelle qui la font également estimer et aimer. " *Qu'est-ce que tout cela me fait ?* " dites-vous. Je vous entends d'ici, et aussi je vais vous y répondre : *Cela fait* que vous devez tâcher de persuader au ministre des affaires étrangères (Montmorin) que la France, étant une puissance plus libre, ne doit pas pour cela être plus fière, et qu'il est convenable que son représentant soit ici pour les frères du roi ce que sont ceux de tous les autres souverains. Je suis d'autant plus attachée au succès de cette petite négociation, qu'il vous fera fort aimer dans ce pays et impatientera excessivement la reine dans le nôtre. C'est elle qui de sa suprême autorité a fait dire à M. de la Luzerne, il y a deux ans, qu'il eût *à ne pas visiter ces deux femmes* ; sa morgue allemande ne soutient pas l'idée de sanctionner un mariage qui n'est pas dans les règles de tous les chapitres, et puis elle ne pardonne pas à la duchesse de Cumberland surtout d'avoir témoigné une propension remarquable pour la Révolution. C'est au point, à ce que me disait sa sœur hier, qu'elle a fait écrire aux Français à Aix-la-Chapelle d'éviter de lui faire la moindre politesse, sa démocratie reconnue la rendant indigne de leurs hommages. Vraiment cette Marie-Antoinette est trop insolente et trop vindicative pour ne pas prendre plaisir à la remettre à sa place, en l'ôtant de celle du roi, qu'elle voudrait usurper. C'est un vrai service à rendre à la France que de vous demander, comme bon patriote, de ne pas vous y refuser. . . . Je voudrais bien que la poste aujourd'hui ne tournât pas à mon plus grand regret, et que, comme la dernière fois, elle n'arrivât pas sans m'apporter des lettres de vous. Je ne puis m'accoutumer à passer sans bonheur le seul jour que je ne vois pas venir sans intérêt. . . . Est-il vrai qu'une campagne de Flandre va s'y trouver ? que vous êtes parti au moment où cette lettre arrivera ? Madame de Fitzherbert n'est pas encore en ville, ce qui fait que je n'ai pu risquer les tentatives dont vous me chargiez pour son prince. *About* le vôtre (Orléans), que devient ce dernier ? Quelles manières a-t-il prises dans la société ? Je la trouve si anglaise que je pense qu'elle pourrait lui convenir assez. . . . Nous disons ici que jamais Paris n'a été plus brillant en étrangers, et plus rassurant par sa tranquillité. Dieu l'y maintienne, voilà le vœu de mon cœur, encore plus que son espoir ! Où en sont les intentions hostiles des princes ? Est-ce pour leur faire rebrousser chemin qu'on vous mit sur le leur ? Adieu ! Mandez-moi tout de suite ce que vous devenez, pour que je sache aussi ce que je fais. Je ne veux pas revenir à Paris avant vous: c'est décidé dans ma tête *de par mon cœur.* Mon *Pierrot* n'est pas arrivé, ce qui m'attriste beaucoup ; parce que mes succès tiennent plus à mon *élégance* qu'à mon *excellence*.'

We think these passages very curious. Politics, feminine spite, Court intrigues, friendship, gossip, and questions of dress, all jumbled up together in short trenchant paragraphs; discontent and restlessness colouring every page, and prudence only dictating those reserves which propriety is not always able to enforce. The writer, who frequented the society of Mrs. Fitzherbert and of Lady Jersey, while she aspersed the fair fame of her own Queen, seems to have endured, even in London, the pangs of rivalry. Madame de Piennes, afterwards Duchesse d'Aumont, was a perpetual annoyance to her, both by her influence directed against the party of the Duke of Orleans, and by her acknowledged place in English society. Not only was the fair Marquise de Coigny disappointed of the *pierrot* (the postilion's jacket) she hoped to wear, but her husband began to withhold the means of supplying the *élégance* in which she trusted.

'Vraiment, entre les nouvelles des gazettes, les conseils de l'amitié, les avis de parents, les lésineries du ménage, je ne sais quel parti prendre, ni quoi devenir. Rester ici serait commode, mais comment le pouvoir, avec aucun moyen d'y vivre ? Retourner à Paris serait sage, mais comment l'oser, avec tant de raisons d'y trembler ? D'honneur, d'honneur je ne sais que faire, et je crois que, ni plus ni moins que le Roi, je vais jouer mon avenir à tête ou couronne : peut-être le hasard me conduira-t-il mieux que la prudence. En attendant, celle-ci inspirant à M. de C——* la plus rigoureuse économie, je languis ici dans la plus cruelle détresse : condamnée à vivre d'emprunts et à mendier l'obligeance de chacun, je ne vois de ressources, pour acquitter leurs secours, que celle de mettre en gage mes diamants. Vraiment, c'est sévère à penser, quand on se sent destinée à avoir si prochainement cent mille écus de rente, et qu'on se trouve à côté d'une Madame de Piennes qui n'en aura jamais deux, et qui vit le plus honorablement possible. En attendant, que, pour ne pas être arrêtée ici, je prenne le parti de la fuite, dans deux jours je vais m'établir pour quinze jours chez Lady John Russell. J'y verrai le prince de Galles, et j'espère le ramener un peu sur le compte de votre prince d'Orléans. Imaginez qu'il a fait ôter son portrait de sa chambre, il y a trois jours. J'en suis indignée contre lui d'autant plus que c'est aux conseils d'une autre [Madame de Piennes] que je m'en prends. Quels sont ceux qui ont dicté au Roi sa démarche sur les émigrés ? En vérité, si elle est telle qu'on me l'a dite, je crois que c'est mon bon ange, ou plutôt celui de la France. Mandez-moi, je vous en prie, ce que vous en pensez, non pas dans la bonté de votre cœur, mais dans sa sincérité. . . . Je ne veux pas finir l'année [1791] sans vous dire combien je regrette de la commencer sans vous. . . . Vous me plaisiez, vous m'intéressiez, et vous m'amusiez tant, même avec ceux qui m'ennuyaient et m'impatientaient le plus. Ah ! comment la peur a-t-elle pu l'emporter en mon âme sur tant d'impressions douces et sensibles ! Comment l'idée d'un danger possible . . . m'a-t-elle fait renoncer à tant de biens certains ! Plus j'y pense, et moins je me l'excuse et me l'explique à moi-même. Je crois sincèrement que la fatalité s'en est mêlée, et m'a fait une prudence de circonstance, comme une destinée d'occasion. . . . Adieu ! Je monte en voiture, pour aller chez Lady John Russell ; car la fille de Lady Jersey est tout-à-fait bien, et moi tout-à-fait

---

* Her husband.

ennuyée de la monotonie de la vie à Londres. J'ai besoin de mouve-
ment et de distractions.'

A great surprise was in store for the Marquise. She hears
a rumour that Lauzun and Talleyrand were to leave Paris on
a secret mission to London. Their ostensible, though non-
official, business was to propose to the Cabinet of St. James
a national alliance. They were in reality agents of the
Revolutionary party, and as such they actually landed in
England in January 1792. If the joy of the Marquise was
great, it was destined to be short-lived; for Lauzun was, on
February 6, arrested by a horse-dealer for debt, and kept in
a sponging-house, from which his colleague, the wary Bishop
of Autun, used no great diligence to get him released. This
was a discouraging incident. Lauzun's affairs had long
been embarrassed, and his wife had once already pawned
her diamonds for his sake, but this time it was for Madame
de Coigny to come forward. She offers to see Talleyrand
for him, but adds that she has no great confidence in that
Bishop : 'J'espère seulement qu'il ne se laissera pas influencer
' par sa tête. Je la crois bien mauvaise en fait d'intentions
' et de conduite.' The Duke of Orleans is to be appealed to,
but then the question is on what terms.

'Très certainement si M. le duc d'Orléans vous prêtait aujourd'hui
de l'argent pour vous tirer de l'embarras, vous ne le recevriez pas
comme un présent. . . . M. de Coigny tient de si mauvais propos en
fait d'argent, que je crois que je partirai aussitôt que vous serez *out*,
mais je ne veux pas absolument rentrer en France avant que vous
soyez sorti.'

She appealed to the Prince of Wales for Lauzun, and writes
that since he sees less of the Piennes that prince is better
disposed towards the Duke of Orleans. She offers a loan of
600 louis, and blames Lauzun for not having applied to her
for her diamonds; but the Piennes are more to be disliked
than ever, for they go back to France every now and then
to draw their revenues and pensions. Could Lauzun not
manage to prevent them receiving their money?

When Lauzun is again free and in Paris, the Marquise is
still full of troubles. Their letters are opened and read; her
husband, who belonged to the friends of the Queen, had not
only read one, but had published it in one of the newspapers.
The revolutionary party, even, is not blameless as regards
tampering with her correspondence. But she must make
the best of it; so she continues to live at 41 Hertford Street,
Mayfair, sups with Mr. Sheridan, whom she takes to be

really 'l'homme de feu de Prométhée,' and who tells her that Tom Paine's book is admirable; and she then goes to stay with 'une Lady Melbourne, ci-devant maîtresse du ' prince, à présent du duc de Bedford; mais toujours tant ' tenu tant payé.' * Clearly the friends of this vivacious *émigrée* had good cause to dread both her tongue and her pen.

By midsummer, Lauzun had passed, or was on the point of passing, from the Army of the North to the Army of the Rhine, his nomination to the command of the latter dating July 1792. The Commissaries of the National Assembly, while approving this choice, took an unfavourable view of the state of the troops : 'We cannot but be aware that the ' army of General Biron is mined in all directions by the ' most dangerous intrigues. General Biron alone holds it ' together by the ascendant which his frankness, his courage, ' and his boundless devotion to the cause which he has em- ' braced, and in which he has constantly progressed without ' deviating for a single instant.' One asks oneself how the gay and gallant Lauzun liked this curt designation of 'General Biron.' Perhaps it amused him, as it did Beaumarchais when he described to his wife a social gathering with all the new fashions : 'What is to become of us? My ' dear, we are losing all our dignities, and are reduced to our ' simple surnames, without either coats-of-arms or liveries. ' Good heavens, what a fall! I dined the day before yester- ' day at Madame de la Reynière's, and we called her, under ' her very nose, Madame Grimod; Messeigneurs the Bishops ' of Rodez and Agen got nothing more from us than "Mon- ' sieur; " and we all looked like people come out from a ball ' at the opera when they unmask.'

Events were soon to show that the changes to be effected in the political and social life of France were to be no comedies fitted for Beaumarchais' talent, but the most terrible of tragedies. The 10th of August 1792 had passed, and even on the flippant temper of Madame de Coigny it had made a most painful impression. Paris, in addition to its own proletariat, was invaded by the bands of scoundrels known as Marseillais; the *Suisses* who defended the King and the Tuileries were massacred; and thousands of persons had lost their lives in the sanguinary excesses to which the Duke of Orleans lent his sympathy and, report said, even

---

* This expression conveyed a malicious allusion to Marie-Antoinette, who was said to have used those words in speaking of the conduct of some of the ladies of her own court.

his presence. Did some prescience stir in her at last? Was she aware that, having so busily sown the wind, it remained for her and hers to reap the whirlwind?

One letter of this collection is a wail, worthy of Cassandra :—

'Eh bien [Juillet 18, 1792], où en sont les affaires publiques? Tournent-elles toujours aussi honteusement que prochainement à une chute absolue ? Je vous avoue que je le crois bien autant que je le crains. La conduite lâche et féroce de l'armée ne promet que des revers et des crimes. . . . *Pourvu encore qu'ils vous épargnent dans leurs implacables soupçons ?* Ah ! mon Dieu, que je voudrais vous voir sorti patriotiquement et honorablement de ce dédale de périls et de perfidies ! Ah ! je vous assure que la chose publique m'importe peu en comparaison de cet intérêt particulier, et que le " *Salvum fac regem* " *et legem* " est bien négligé dans mes prières.'

Here speaks the woman. Madame de Coigny had enjoyed playing the part of a Duchesse de Longueville in what she had taken to be a new Fronde. Philippe d'Orléans and Lauzun were to be the Condé and Conti of the piece. And even if a barricade or two were thrown up in the streets of Paris—why, that had been done in 1648, and Anne of Austria had then had to endure annoyances which it would be delightful now to inflict on this new '*Autrichienne.*' But our Marquise, though she had studied both the old piece and her own *rôle*, miscalculated the size of the modern theatre and the temper of the modern audience. Other actors were binding on their sandals, and from the unmasked chorus rose the cry in hoarse unison, '*à bas les aristos ! à la lanterne ! à la lanterne !*'

Her nerve suddenly failed her, less for herself or for her class (certainly not for her husband's family) than for the soldier she had loved so closely.

'17 Août 1792.

'Mon intérêt à vous est l'âme de mon existence ; ainsi, ne me sachez pas plus gré de vous aimer que de vivre. Mais prenez pitié de mes inquiétudes, auxquelles ce tendre sentiment me laisse en proie. J'ai vraiment l'âme glacée d'effroi et l'esprit frappé de terreur des événements que je viens d'apprendre. Vous pensez bien que c'est surtout pour leurs conséquences relatives qu'ils m'occupent et me tourmentent à cet excès. Sauf les massacres publics et particuliers, qui font toujours horreur à penser comme à voir, la conséquence directe de la déchéance me trouverait très philosophe, et je ne croirais pas le royaume perdu parce qu'un roi qu'on soupçonne de conspirer contre lui n'est plus chargé du soin de le défendre. Mais ce qui me trouble, me désole, me terrifie, au-delà même de l'exagération, c'est l'effet que produira sur l'armée ce grand événement. Je crains que sa confiance en son vieux chef ne la conduise directement à la trahison, et que vous ne deveniez une malheureuse victime de tant de lâches et abominables perfidies. De grâce, prenez pitié de mon bonheur, *et aux dépens même de votre honneur sauvez-vous des dangers*, non pas que vous courez, mais qui vous courent, pour ainsi dire. Par tous les courriers adressez-moi un " je vous aime, et je me porte bien." Mon cœur ne forme pas d'autres vœux. . . . Il arrive, au moment où j'en suis là de ma lettre, un courrier de la maison Thélusson qui annonce que la Normandie s'est déclarée contre les mesures prises par l'Assemblée, et que les troupes sont prêtes à marcher sur Paris. Cette nouvelle est certaine et bien effrayante. Mon Dieu ! voici donc la guerre civile et la guerre étrangère établies à la fois dans ce malheureux pays. O Liberté, quel mal tu nous causes pour les biens que tu nous as promis !'

With this cry ends the correspondence of the Marquise de Coigny with the soldier so soon to forfeit his life. The particulars of his fate have never been known as they now are through the papers which our editor has acquired, and which he prints as an appendix to his volume. Space forbids us to give them *in extenso*, but a sketch of their contents may interest our readers.

Narbonne, the Minister of War, of whose sentiments towards the handsome favourite of fortune the Marquise was so suspicious, was the first, in March 1792, to announce to him the military promotion in store for him.

' Certainly,' writes the Minister, 'you must have a legion. You know that this is one of the finest corps anyone can have under his command; and you will, I hope, forgive me for insisting on your acceptance of it. As for the place of residence, Marshal de Rochambeau gives you the choice between Valenciennes and Douai. I, if you would prefer it, propose to you neither the one place nor the other, but to take the command of the troops raised on the borders of Piedmont.'

Lauzun, when named maréchal-de-camp, went to replace General d'Hasville at Valenciennes, and prepared for a move on Mons. But Dumouriez misled him as to the strength of the Austrian army which he was to encounter; and the letters that during the month of April reached him from head-quarters are certainly strangely suggestive of the '*per-fidies*' on which the Marquise insists so bitterly in her letters to her friend. His old comrade La Fayette, taking alarm about him, wrote:—

' I see with sorrow that M. de Biron has been forced to fall back, and that M. de Dillon has been repulsed. . . . I regret that the Government should not have left us time to assemble our armies before it declared this war; and I am as much surprised as you are at the promptitude with which this campaign has been arranged.'

Lauzun, in his retreat from Mons, was nearly the victim

of an insurrection on the part of his own troops, who, in their turn, accused him of having betrayed them. He addressed to the Chevalier de Grave, the new Minister of War, the following report:—

'Valenciennes, this 2 May, the 4th year of Liberty.

'Monsieur,—I have the honour to report to you that, in consesequence of the King's orders transmitted by you to me, I occupied with my division, on April 28, the camp of Quiévrechain, near Quiévrain. . . . I marched upon Mons with three columns; that on the right passing through Quiévrechain was to join me near Orun, and that of the left, going by way of Crépin, was also to unite with me at Orun. . . . The advanced guard of hussars was fired upon and charged by uhlans and Tyrolese chasseurs. . . . I dispersed the uhlans by some shots from my guns, and continued my march. . . . I could clearly see that the heights before Mons were occupied by a considerable body of troops, and that of Berteaumont, by which I should have to attack Mons, was entrenched and provided with batteries. This position being one of great advantage, and very easy for fresh troops to hold against tired regiments, and not finding in men exhausted with heat all the strength needed for such an attack, I thought it as well to allow them to rest, and to wait for some more positive tidings from Mons, which I had a right to hope for. The enemy, estimated by me as outnumbering us, made movements symptomatic of turning my right flank. I made it my business to reinforce it by posting detachments in an advantageous manner. I took up a position, and M. Berthier, Adjutant-General, thought, as I did, that the Austrians were unassailable; but he also thought, as I did, that I might, without danger, await the tidings of the French corps marching on Tournay. . . . I was informed by Marshal Rochambeau of the defeat of this corps, and I intended to retreat at once. But this design I was not able to execute, the troops being exhausted by fatigue and want. It had been found impossible to prevent the soldiers, when harassed by the heat, from throwing away their bread. The troop horses, like those of the artillery, had no forage. I had not been joined by the field hospital, as I intended; and I foresaw the incalculable dangers of a retreat by night to be attempted by weary troops before an enemy who was fresh. I determined then to give some hours of repose to mine, and to try to get food for men and horses. Towards ten at night I saw the 5th and 6th Dragoons first get into their saddles, though I had not given the order, and then form on the camp in order of battle, and then in column. I arrived in hot haste to ask what might be the meaning of such an eccentric movement; but this column, which I had sought to stop, set off at a trot, crying, " We are " betrayed ! " I rode more than a league with them before I could get myself obeyed. At last I succeeded, and formed them up again in a plain between Boussu and Orun. . . . The stragglers went as far as Valenciennes, crying always that they had been betrayed, and that I had deserted before Mons. I have not been able to penetrate the criminal mystery of this alarm. . . . I shall have the honour to give

you further details about my losses, which I do not yet thoroughly
know. . . . I could have wished to make my report to you more
circumstantial, but I am exhausted with fatigue and distress, and I am
not capable of more. MM. de Chartres * and de Montpensier marched
with me as volunteers, and, as such, encountered for the first time many
shots, all in the quietest and most brilliant way.'

Marshal Rochambeau had more than once pressed Lauzun
to take the command in chief of the Army of the North.
But nothing could vanquish Lauzun's irrevocable determination to refuse it. He had no reproaches to make to himself,
but the attitude of its troops had become so menacing for
him that, to escape from the undisciplined bands which
shouted ' *Treason!*' he returned to Paris to ask leave to serve
with another army. This is the moment when Madame de
Coigny's last letters were written to him.

The Commissaries Carnot, Coustard, Prieur, and Riller,
were ready to attest that the unsuccessful general was a
good and steady republican, but he had, unfortunately, no
opportunities of distinguishing himself when placed at the
head of the Army of the Rhine, a body intended rather for
observation and defence than for aggressive warfare. But
so insecure was his popularity that it was felt to be inex-
pedient for him to receive letters from a lady in emigration,
and the correspondence with the Marquise was suspended
before he left this position to replace Anselme, and to achieve
the submission of the county of Nice. Dumouriez had never
been favourable to him, and the Jacobins of 1793, whether
to ruin him or to test him, presently arranged another
appointment for him. He was sent to La Vendée, and fought
against Frenchmen at Saumur and at Parthenay. On July
10, 1793, he went alone to Paris to tender his resignation,
and to reply to the many accusations made against him.

The feelings of the Marquise may be imagined when she
heard that he had been arrested and transferred from
Ste. Pélagie to the prison of the Abbaye.

Jean Bon St.-André, in the name of the Committee of
Public Safety, had already (14th July) demanded the recall
of ' General Biron,' but had not formulated any accusation
against him.

' We cannot hide from ourselves that there is *no positive* accusation
against this officer, but he *is* reproached with not having displayed all

---

* Afterwards Louis Philippe, Duke of Orleans and King of the
French. He had joined the army with his brother, the Duc de Mont-
pensier, who died during the Revolution, and is buried in Westminster
Abbey.

the needful energy in the operations entrusted to him, and yet no war could have made more continual demands for it. The Commissaries of the Convention make unanimous reports on this head, all reproaching Biron with slow operations, likely to endanger the interests of the Republic.   Gasparin, while on his commission with the army, has already apprised the General that his frequent ailments, his gout, and his worn-out constitution, render him very unfit for the important functions which the Republic has entrusted to him.   There is a sure and unalterable principle from which those who hold the reins of government ought never to depart, and *that is the adequacy of men to places*. Since the General admits himself to be inadequate for the place assigned to him, and finds it beyond his strength, your Committee proposes to you to decree that the Minister of War shall recall General Biron.'

The broken health of the once active and valiant Lauzun was no fiction invented by his enemies. Confined in the Abbaye, he was a cripple from rheumatic gout; and if he received any letters then from the despairing Marquise, he can only have replied to them by telling her that he was tormented by pain, and preparing to close on the scaffold a life from which all the splendours and all the illusions had fled.   To the Convention he simply intimated a hope that his trial might be speedy, as his health was broken.   It was first proposed that he should be kept in his own house, but a voice from the *Montagne* drowned the pleadings of his friend Lecomte-Puyraseau, and he was ordered to be kept in prison till his case came up for judgement.   This was on September 4, 1793, and another month was to elapse before the tidings how his friend and leader Egalité had lost his head on the scaffold on October 6, 1793, reached the cells of the Abbaye.

False to every noble sentiment and to every tender tie, the Duke of Orleans none the less met death with the courage and breeding of his race. For the hour he became again a prince of the blood. To show his contempt for the tribunal which arraigned him, he read a newspaper during his interrogatory; and when he was asked if he had anything to say, he replied, 'Merely that I had as soon die to-day as to-'morrow; you can think over it.' The Duke's head fell that day. Now Lauzun's turn had come, and now the old *savoir-vivre*, the heroism, and the unconscious grace of *la grande tradition*, woke in the breast of the broken-down *roué*, who testified to his judges his impatience alike of their low birth and their crass ignorance of military matters. 'You are 'insolent,' they replied. 'And you are utterers of senseless 'chatter (*verbiageurs*)' was the retort, as if Lauzun had been on his way to some alcove and not to the guillotine. 'Well, 'yes, I am to be guillotined; that is all you have to say

' to me, and I have nothing to say to you. I have laid an
' account of my conduct before the Committee of Public
' Safety, which was wont to approve of it. To-day it has
' changed its way of thinking, and bids you execute me. Do
' as you are bid, and do not put off the time.' Sentence was
pronounced, and Lauzun, during his last night on earth, may
possibly have asked himself how it was that the government of France had drifted away, not only from the King he
had served so ill, but from all the *élite* of the nobility, clergy,
and *tiers état* who in 1788–9 first tried to secure purer laws
with the suppression of privileges, and the relief of an indi-
gent and overtaxed peasantry. The men who then deliberated, administered, and commanded, who knew something
of the practical life of diplomacy, justice, and finance, were
all discredited and in danger, and a new governing class had
come to sweep away the culture of centuries. Everyone knows
the story of Lauzun's breakfast, of his plate of oysters, and of
his politeness to his executioners. This is not a legend. But
uncertainty gathers over what has been called Lauzun's confession. He is reported to have asked pardon for his past
life ' from God and the King,' while admitting that his
treachery to his sovereign and his order had brought on him
a well-deserved doom. Mallet-du-Pan gives the first half of
this sentence as a fact, other authors add the remaining
phrase; but our editor denies that the condemned man
made any such speech or part of such a speech, and relies
for his authority on the ' Galerie des Contemporains ' (Frankfort, 1817–1818). We are inclined to think that the duke
did not make it, less from the *légèreté* of his character than
from his absolute contempt for the bystanders. The public
might see a Lauzun eat his oysters, they might even see him
guillotined, since that was the turn affairs had taken, but
with his private thoughts and feelings they and their equals
had nothing whatever to do.

If the publication before us were a novel, it would contain
at this place the fitting expressions of grief from those most
concerned with the execution of this celebrated lady-killer:
of the Marquise de Coigny, of her niece Aimée de Coigny, to
whom Lauzun had once made ardent love, and of his deserted wife, Amélie de Boufflers. But this is not a novel.
An accident only gave into our editor's hands some letters
written by them to Lauzun, but all of a date previous to his
great reverse of fortune. All the three women survived him.
His duchess was at one time reported to have been executed,
but the researches of our editor go to prove that though
long in prison she was able, after the events of the 9th

Thermidor, to escape with her life, and to live in Paris in great poverty into what may be called old age. Madame de Genlis, who always liked her, records her death at the age of seventy-six.

The Marquise de Coigny was prudent enough to remain in emigration. It has always been a question whether she was originally led away by the democratic illusions of Lauzun, or whether her friend and admirer was originally diverted from his allegiance to the court by her imperious wish to lead a party against Marie-Antoinette, and to revenge what she chose to call the wrongs of the Cardinal de Rohan in the affair of the diamond necklace. If she ever dreamed of the supremacy of her party, we have seen how agonising must have been her waking from such a dream to the realities of mob law and of the Terror. She followed, however, with pleasure the career of the First Consul, and hailed with rapture the beginning of the Empire in France. This young dictator had nothing in common, she thought, with the ' Capets et Capètes,' nor yet with the strange demigods of the Jacobin Walhalla. The new ruler appeared to her imagination clothed in the brightest hues. Napoleon, who feared and hated clever women, did not respond to her enthusiasm. He did not banish her as he did Madame de Staël, but when he met her in society he was wont to enquire satirically after the health of her tongue! But the Marquise, who had always an answer ready for him, was not to be discouraged, and she chose among his staff a husband for her only daughter Fanny, to whom she was passionately attached. In General Sebastiani she discerned all the qualities she sought in a son-in-law, and her gentle Fanny left France with her husband on a diplomatic mission to Constantinople. It would be to trespass on private feelings if we were to continue this narrative, after the early death of Madame Sebastiani, to the soldierly career of her brother, the late Duc de Coigny, and to the education of her only child in the Hôtel Sebastiani by a gifted aunt of Félix Mendelssohn. That child was the future Duchesse de Praslin. It would seem as if a curse hung over the dearest objects of Madame de Coigny's affections, and the last we have heard of her is that she was seen by one of her English friends, much advanced in years, boiling her coffee over a small fire in a shabby apartment of the Faubourg St. Germain. But these details lie beyond the sphere of this review, for our attention is chiefly due to the incidents in the later career of Lauzun and to the life in London of the witty but unhappy *émigrée*, Louise de Conflans, Marquise de Coigny.

ART. X.—1. *Hansard's Parliamentary Debates.* 1831, 1832.

2. *Hansard's Parliamentary Debates.* 1866, 1867.

3. *Hansard's Parliamentary Debates.* 1884.

4. *Molesworth's History of England,* 1830–1874. 3 vols. 8vo. London: 1879.

5. *History of the Radical Party in Parliament.* By WILLIAM HARRIS. London: 1885.

'ENGLAND will never be undone but by a Parliament.' The saying, if something musty with age, has truth to recommend it; and it certainly is no less true than it was in former days, when considered with reference to modern England and reformed parliaments. If it is Parliament alone that can make or mar the future of the country, it is important that we should weigh accurately the effect of the changes that legislation and the progress of events have made and are making in the circumstances and position of this the great fundamental political institution of the nation. The almost superstitious belief once held that the greatness and prosperity of the nation were due to its government by the Sovereign, the Lords Spiritual and Temporal, and Commons in Parliament assembled, and that under no other constitution could any people be expected to flourish, may have lost ground; yet to British subjects, whether at home or in the colonies, as to American citizens (together no small portion of the progressive peoples of the earth), government through an executive, more or less chosen and more or less checked and controlled by two legislative chambers, still seems the only 'natural' constitution for a free people. *They*, at all events, have experience of no other; and Englishmen will almost cease to be Englishmen when they prefer to English habits and English precedents schemes of government, maybe perfect in theory but certainly untried in practice, recommended for their adoption either by platform spouters or constitution-mongering De Siéyès. Such as are the main characteristics of the nation, such in the future will be more than ever the main characteristics of its Parliament; where the one House, as it becomes more truly representative of the whole people, is steadily absorbing a larger share of the legislative authority of the old estates of the realm and of the executive authority of the Ministers of the Crown. On the whole the authority and the character of Parliament 'have grown with our growth ' and strengthened with our strength,' and assuredly this high reputation will 'diminish only with our diminution, and ' decay only with our decay.'

How many of the throng of Liberal members who on December 6 last crowded round Mr. Gladstone as he stood behind Speaker Peel at the bar of the House of Lords called to mind the scene of June 7 fifty-two years before, when Lord Althorp and Lord John Russell followed Speaker Manners Sutton to the bar of the old House to hear the royal assent given to the great Reform Act of 1832! The two Houses of that day have themselves long since perished; and the slow lapse of more than half a century has proved as fatal to the actors in the great drama upon which the curtain was then dropping as was the conflagration of 1835 to the historical stage on which they played their parts. How like, after all, are the new Houses to the old! True, that on looking at the well-known picture of the House of Lords on the famous June 7 certain differences in ornamentation and of detail strike the eyes of such of us as are very familiar with the appearance of the present Chamber. The Whig lords and the one bishop, sole occupants of the Chamber, are seated under those classical 'tapestries of the House of the Lords' upon which we see depicted the naval victories of Queen Elizabeth. The tapestries and the Lords belong of course to the past, and of the members of the House of Commons standing at the bar the present Lord Grey is probably the sole survivor. Upon the hereditary House it is time alone that has worked its inevitable changes; the Restorer's hand has not yet touched either to adorn or disfigure that quaint bit of early architecture in the massive and often repaired pile of the British Constitution. With the Commons it has been very different; but, once more, as our glance falls upon the pre-Reform M.P.'s at the bar—Lord John Russell, Lord Howick, Lord Althorp, and Lord Fitzwilliam, Francis Jeffrey, Sir Francis Burdett, Mr. O'Connell, and Mr. Sheil—we find, though two Reform Acts have been passed, far more of resemblance than of difference between the present and the past, and we doubt not that even one more Reform Act, larger than any of its predecessors, will operate usefully and powerfully and yet leave the constitution of the House of Commons in its main features such as it has always been.

Since the royal assent was given to the Act of 1832 twelve parliaments have come into existence. In nine of these the House of Commons was elected upon the basis of representation established by that Act; in the remaining three upon the wider basis adopted in 1867. The twelfth of these has now accomplished its main work, it has reached its last session; and in a few months more the nation, through the intervention of a much wider electorate, will be invited to elect a new House of Commons. The time appears, therefore, appropriate for taking a short survey of the effects produced by parliamentary reform, a survey for which the light cast by a dozen parliaments affords sufficiently ample means.

Parliamentary reformers, whether they have in view the reform of the one or the other branch of the legislature, have always to bear in mind the two great ends to be attained. The Chamber should be composed of the individuals in themselves best qualified to judge of, and to take part in, the political business of the country; secondly, it should be composed in such a way as to merit, or rather as actually to receive, the public confidence. A House of Lords composed of four hundred wise men, with nothing but their wisdom to recommend them, would have no authority whatever. A House of Commons, it may well be, composed of members nominated by town councils, quarter-sessions, and lord-lieutenants, would contain 652 members fully equal or superior to the present; but it would not enjoy the public sympathy or respect. The position of the House of Lords is thought unsatisfactory at the present time not because it does not contain members of equal political qualifications, to say the least, with those of the House of Commons, but because as a whole it is not *en rapport* with the general feeling of the country. Those who most dread the effects of democratic reform upon the House of Commons admit that it will be more than ever in sympathy with the constituencies, but urge that but one class of opinion will be represented, that eminence will find no place in the new Chamber, that local vestrymen will take the place of statesmen, and in fact that it will become the desert imagined by Mr. Lowe, 'where every ' anthill is a mountain and every thistle a forest-tree.'

It need scarcely be said that the *personnel* of Parliament is of the utmost importance. In spite of Mr. Lowe, and of more democratic philosophers, who have feared the dull uniformity of democracy, it would be easy to prove that the House of Commons contains a far greater *variety* of distinction than in pre-Reform periods. Probably no Tory is so foolish as to wish members to be confined solely to the social class of the community that would find admission into an exclusive West End Club. In the present House there are eminent members of almost every class in the community— the landed gentry, the professional classes, the commercial

classes, shipowners, bankers, brewers, farmers, and two excellent representatives of the working men. Upon *any* subject a member can find an authority in some brother member;
and setting aside Ireland, a country which cannot be quoted
as a satisfactory example of parliamentary government, and
speaking very generally, we should say that the House of
Commons is composed of the right sort of men to make it
fairly representative of the nation. Are the motives that
now actuate members very different from those that actuated
them in less democratic days? are the objects of reformers
to-day very different from their objects fifty-three years ago?
In the recent Reform struggle many no doubt honestly
believed that the Radical measures of Mr. Gladstone's
Cabinet would have shocked the timid nerves of the fine
old Constitutional Whigs of 1832. It appears to us, on the
contrary, that the recent Reform contest has shown more
clearly than ever that the Liberals of 1884 are the true
heirs of the Whigs of 1832.

The spirit in which Mr. Gladstone has approached and
successfully dealt with Reform is precisely the same as that
which actuated Lord Grey and Lord John Russell. From
Conservatives and half-hearted Liberals praises are now
common enough and loud enough of the patriotism and
statesmanship of those active Liberals who in their day were
the terror and the object of obloquy of the whole Tory party.
To those, however, who take the trouble to read the debates
of 1831 and 1832, of 1866 and 1867, and of 1884, the extraordinary resemblance between the advocacy of reform by
reformers in the three periods is as remarkable as is the
resemblance of the arguments against it.

Long before the Reform Bill, in 1792, the well-known
association of the Friends of the People, which counted
amongst its members Mr. Grey and the Lord John Russell
of that day, had described its object to be to 'reform the
'Constitution because they wished to preserve it.' * The
last words spoken by Lord Grey on the Reform Bill, in the
House of Lords in 1832, were an expression of the hope
'that those who augured unfavourably of the Bill would
'live to see all their unfavourable forebodings falsified, and
'that, after the angry feelings of the day had passed away,
'the measure would be found to be, in the best sense, con-
'servative of the Constitution.' The whole tone of Mr.

---

* Letter to Society for Constitutional Reform from Friends of People,
signed John Russell, from Freemasons' Tavern.

Gladstone, during the last year's contest, has been that of one who was anxious so to reform within the lines of the Constitution as to give fresh strength and durability to those institutions under which the nation has long grown and prospered.

In those days, as in these days, there were Whig reformers and Radical reformers; but if we are to judge the real motives of the Government at either day by the utterances of policy made by its most responsible members, we shall find but little difference between the two policies. Then, as now, the Opposition maintained that the country did not really care for reform; that the reforms contemplated led directly to anarchy and revolution; that reformers were actuated solely by personal and party objects, and that all patriotic men should unite in the resistance which would alone save the Constitution.

The debates in 1866, 1867, and 1884 are but a renewal of the discussions on the great Reform Bill. Many will remember the eloquent appeal of Mr. Lowe in May, 1867, to the 'gentlemen of England : '—

'I am not the least surprised,' said Mr. Lowe, 'that the fertile genius I see opposite me [Mr. Disraeli] has hit upon this scheme; there is nothing new in it; it has ever been part of the tactics of an oligarchy to ally itself to the lower sections of a democracy. It was so in the course of the French Revolution, and it is recorded over and over again in the annals of other countries. I say I am not the least surprised at this; but what I am surprised at is that you, the gentlemen of England—you, with all you have at stake; you, with your ancestry behind you and your posterity before you; with your great estates, with your titles, with your honour, with your state of every kind, with the amount of imperial prosperity and happiness, of dignity and honour, which you have enjoyed for the last 200 years, such as never before fell to the lot of any class in the world—that you will fling all this away, without, as far as I can see, the shadow of an equivalent of any kind. Do you look for an equivalent in any personal good? Your interests are directly opposed to the course you are pursuing. Is it for the good of your country? Have you so totally unlearnt the simplest lessons as to believe that it is by going into the depths of poverty and ignorance that we are to find the wisdom to manage the delicate affairs of this great empire? I believe you have, and by so doing you have branded yourself with a stigma that your party can never escape from.'

To such appeals and to such reasoning no better answer can be found than that given in 1831 by Lord John Russell to those arguments, born of selfishness and fear, upon which the Tory party was then relying; and these extracts from two speeches may well serve to point the difference that has always existed, and will always exist, between the standpoints of the two great parties in the State :—

'It may be said, too,' said Lord John Russell, introducing the Reform Bill, March 1, 1831, 'that one great and injurious effect of the measure I propose will be to destroy the power and privileges of the aristocracy. This I deny. I utterly deny that this plan can have any such effect. Wherever the aristocracy reside, receiving large incomes, performing political duties, relieving the poor by charity, and evincing private worth and public virtue, it is not in human nature that they should not possess a great influence upon public opinion, and have an equal weight in electing persons to serve their country in Parliament. Though such persons may not have the direct nomination of members under the bill, I contend they will have as much influence as they ought to have. But if by aristocracy those persons are meant who do not live among the people, who know nothing of the people, and who care nothing for them, who seek honours without merit, places without duty, and pensions without service, for such an aristocracy I have no sympathy; and I think the sooner its influence is carried away, with the corruption on which it has thriven, the better for the country in which it has repressed so long every wholesome and invigorating influence. Language has been heard on this subject which I hope will not be heard in future. A call has been made upon the aristocracy; all who are connected with it have been summoned to make a stand against the people. . . . I appeal, sir, in my turn, to the aristocracy. The gentlemen of England have never been found wanting in any great crisis. When the country was engaged in war against the national enemy, when the honour and security of the country were assailed, they were ever foremost. When burdens were to be borne, they were ever ready to take their share as any other class of the community. I ask them now, when a great sacrifice is to be made, to show their generosity, to convince the people of their public spirit, and to identify themselves for the future with the people. Upon the gentlemen of England then I call. I ask them to come forward, and by their conduct on this occasion to give security to the throne, stability to Parliament and the constitution, and strength and peace to the country.'

If, however, there was much of the same foolish talk in 1885 among anti-reformers that was common among them in 1832, it must be admitted that on the earlier occasion far wilder fears were genuinely entertained of the impending danger of democracy. It is lamentable to find such complete misunderstanding of his own countrymen, and of the circumstances of the time, as is shown by the Duke of Wellington a fortnight after the passing of the great Reform Bill :—

'The government of England is destroyed,' he writes. 'A Parliament will be returned by means of which no set of men whatever will be able to conduct the administration of affairs and to protect the lives and properties of the King's subjects. I hear the worst accounts of the elections; indeed, I don't believe that gentlemen will be prevailed upon to offer themselves as candidates.' *

Again on July 11 following :—

'The whole question of the British monarchy now depends on the discipline and efficiency of the British army. . . . We may rely on it that from henceforth we shall never be able to carry on a government without the assistance and support of a military body.' †

And, indeed, during the crisis, his language had been even more extravagant, for he had declared that if the Bill should pass, 'the race of English gentlemen would not last long 'afterwards.' ‡   Yet, after a few weeks' experience of the first reformed Parliament, Sir Robert Peel, the leader of the Tory party, writes to Mr. Croker that the House is a good one to speak to, too impulsive, perhaps, to possess steadiness, for 'the force of party connections, by which alone a govern-'ment can hope to pursue a consistent course, is quite 'paralysed. . . .   The Reform Bill had only worked so far 'because the Conservatives had been too honest to unite ' with the Radicals.'

The weakening of party in the House of Commons is not one of the faults which experience teaches us to attribute to a lowering of the franchise. In pre-reform times the members of the two branches of the legislature had probably nearly as many of the failings of humanity as their successors.   The obstruction and the scenes which have discredited the present House of Commons had their proto- types in the doings of earlier days.   The braying, the cock- crowing, and the bleating which, in the good old days of Sir Robert Peel and Lord Althorp, on several occasions enlivened the House of Commons, have given place to out- bursts which, if not less annoying, are at all events not more unseemly.   In 1829 some Tory peer, in mockery of the tergiversation of his friends, had so little respect for the dignity of the House of Lords as to turn out *a live rat* into the midst of the assembled senators.   We can hardly, there- fore, accept without demur the sweeping assertions of the decadence in manner and dignity of the modern legislator from the lofty standard of the past.

The general public probably hardly realises the exact cha-

---

* Duke of Wellington to Duke of Buckingham, June 23, 1832.
† Duke of Wellington to Lord Howe, July 11, 1832.
‡ To Lord Wharncliffe, November 29, 1831.

racter that obstruction in the present House of Commons has assumed. It is not so much that what may be called the great full-dress debates are longer now than in former Parliaments of the present century. The complaint of excessive talk, probably always true, is not new. Sir Robert Inglis, in opposing the introduction of the first Reform Bill, in March 1831, said that 'formerly very few members, per-'haps forty, were wont to address the House; that now the 'speaking members had become not less than four hundred; 'and of the representatives of the sister country probably 'not four were silent.' And this, of the pre-reform period, and before the passions excited by the Reform Bill had unloosed the tongues of the most silent members! The debate on the motion for leave to introduce the Reform Bill in 1831 lasted seven nights. The Committee on the second Bill lasted almost continuously from the middle of July 1831 to the middle of September; and on the third Bill from the middle of September 1832 to the middle of March. The debate on the second reading of the Reform Bill of 1866 lasted eight nights. The debate on Sir Robert Peel's free-trade policy in 1846 lasted for twelve nights. Probably the longest debate of the present Parliament was that on the second reading of the Irish Land Act 1881, which lasted for nine nights; and the nights, curtailed at the beginning by questions, and at the end by the determination of members not to speak after an hour at which the morning papers can do justice to their eloquence, are shorter than they used to be. It is natural that when an important debate is carried on day after day an impatient press should cry out against the waste of public time in the useless flood of talk. But the serious obstruction, the obstruction of modern growth, is generally practised on less important occasions—in the small hours of the morning, for instance, when the House is 'in Supply.' The rambling and interminable debates that in recent years have taken place at the opening of the Parliamentary session on the address to the Queen's Speech have very seriously shortened the business time at the disposal of the House of Commons. The practice of putting questions to Ministers on every conceivable subject of imperial or local interest, in its present developement, is also new, and consumes an hour, an hour and a half, sometimes even two hours of the afternoon, before the business of the day can be reached. On an average fifty questions, printed on the notice paper, with the supplementary questions to which the replies to the former give rise, take an hour to answer;

and now-a-days fifty questions is by no means an unusual number. In very many respects improved rules of procedure would do much to restore a business character to the House, but care must be taken to distinguish between faults capable of remedy and those incidental to the Parliamentary system. No House of Commons will ever exist, in this world, in which neither bores nor factious members are to be found. The ministerial newspapers often on party grounds decry the 'obstructive tactics' of a few Tory members whose indiscreet zeal has led them into factious courses; but we do not know that that wretched and reckless factious spirit, which is always ready to injure the Government at the cost of injuring the country, animates a Tory opposition more strongly than a Liberal opposition. With neither party is such a spirit prevalent, each of them being in the main composed of persons feeling some sense of individual responsibility. But along with each main body of regular troops there is associated a small force of irregulars, the Bashi-Bazouks of politics, whose allegiance to their chiefs is of the slightest, whose feeling of responsibility is nil—

> Whose gain and glory and delight,
> To sleep the day, maraud the night,

make still more weary the hard labours of Ministers of the Crown, and incalculably increase the difficulties of the performance by Parliament of its proper functions. The organised obstruction practised by some twenty-five Irish members is largely carried out by wasting time over matters of very slight importance. Their object is avowedly to clog the wheels of the Parliamentary machine. Hence their debating is frequently and transparently not *bonâ fide*. It is bad enough that bores and egotists should waste time which might be usefully employed; but it is intolerable that it should be wasted of set and deliberate purpose by those whose chief object it is to discredit Parliament and delay business. When discussion ceases to be *bonâ fide*, it should be put down, and no great improvement in the conduct of business in the House of Commons can take place till this is recognised.

But, in spite of many failings, we do not believe that the character of Parliament is deteriorating, and we feel sure that the Parliamentary history of England from 1832 to 1885 compares favourably with any equal period of that history, whether we consider the statesmen who have been its ornaments or the rank and file of their supporters. As a whole, the House of Commons of this period, in patriotism and in wisdom, and in purity from personal and selfish interests, has no cause to blush at any comparison with its predecessors.

Perhaps, however, it is fair to remember that whilst, on the one hand, time has proved the fears of the opponents of democratic reform to have been groundless, so, on the other hand, many of the sanguine expectations of reformers have been doomed to disappointment. That, under more democratic institutions in the past, the nation would have avoided the mistakes and escaped the disasters recorded on too many pages of its history; that these mistakes were due to the government of the day being in the hands of an ignorant or selfish class, while greater wisdom and truer patriotism existed in some lower stratum of society without influence on public affairs, are naturally favourite topics with those orators of the platform whose object it is to please the multitude by flattery, rather than to guide them to a true understanding of the lessons of history. No doubt it is true that class selfishness was encouraged by the exclusive character of the political institutions of the past. No doubt, also, now-a-days politics being considered the business of the whole nation, and being moreover conducted under the full blaze of publicity, there is much greater security that national ends are not sacrificed to personal or class interests. But when we are told that with the new democracy wise government at home and peace with our neighbours abroad will be assured; that former maladministration and wars have been due solely to monarchical or aristocratic rule; that now ' the people ' rule the millennium is at hand,—we fear that enthusiasts are but worshipping 'a fond thing vainly ' imagined,' and we ask what is this people whose strangely tardy discovery is to bring such manifold blessings upon a hitherto afflicted land. ' L'Etat c'est moi!' was the remark of the French monarch. Perhaps in answer to our question ' What is the people?' the British householder will reply, ' Sir, it is I!' Well, but we have made acquaintance with the British householder before. He is not new to the political stage, and his voice was heard long before his vote was counted. For the last eighteen years he has had everything his own way in large towns, in very many small towns, and in several rural districts in different parts of the country. He is a sound-hearted, healthy-minded individual enough, sharing and helping to form that general national sentiment called ' public opinion;' but neither possessing nor claiming immunity from all the infirmities of judgement and temper,

and not pretending to that infallibility in matters political
in some quarters so foolishly attributed to him.

Is it *his* rule that is to be always wise and always peaceful ? It has been said that the rule of the aristocracy ended
in 1832 ; that of the middle classes in 1867 ; and that the rule
of the working-classes, commencing partially in the latter
year, has obtained its full developement by the Act of 1884.
We doubt whether there has ever been a strictly class government in this country. At all events, for a very long period
there has been a national public opinion, to which each
person competent to form an opinion has contributed ; and
it is because Parliament has on the whole truthfully reflected
this opinion and given expression to the feelings of the day,
and not merely to those of the limited class possessing the
electoral franchise at the time, that parliamentary institutions have worked successfully. It would be difficult to
point to any period of strong national emotion at which
Parliament, even in unreformed days, did not beat in sympathy with the heart of the people. We have seen it stated,
in strange forgetfulness of history, that the war of Great
Britain with its American colonies was attributable to the
unrepresentative character of the House of Commons during
last century. Modern historians declare, and contemporary
writings prove, that the overwhelming weight of the public
opinion of the country was with the Government and the
King in favour of reducing the colonies to submission by
force of arms ; and Whigs at the time sadly confessed in
private to one another, that 'not only were they patriots out
' of place, but patriots also out of the opinion of the public.'*
The Government of Lord North had become unpopular for
many reasons long before its fall in 1782 ; and ' if it had had
' more lives than a cat . . . they must have all dropped had
' it not been . . . the wish of Great Britain to recover
' America. The Government aimed at least at this object,
' which the Opposition rejected.'† Two or three years later,
William Pitt was able to establish his authority by relying,
against the will of Parliament, not merely on royal support,
but also and chiefly on the fact that the *country* was with
him ; and when the appeal to it was made, the Parliament
at once gave ready expression to public opinion. The House

* Sir Geo. Savile to Lord Buckingham, January, 1777.
† Sir Gilbert Elliot to Hugh Elliot, April, 1782. 'Life and Letters
of Sir G. Elliot,' vol. i. See also Mr. Lecky's 'History of England,'
vol. iv.

of Commons of 1831 was elected upon the old exclusive franchise, the merest mockery of representation, but it reflected the overwhelming feeling of the nation in favour of reform, and had probably a more thoroughly reforming character than any subsequent House though elected on a popular franchise. Never since the Reform Act of 1832 have the Tories been driven completely from the English counties. When the nation is really moved by a strong feeling, that feeling, though perhaps stronger in one class than in another, is felt through them all. As regards questions of peace and war, he would be a very rash man who would calculate implicitly on the peaceful nature of the British democracy. In 1854 it was the nation that forced, rather than the Government that led, Great Britain into the Russian war; and even Mr. Bright, full of faith as he is in popular institutions, honestly tells the people that popular government at home and abroad provides but slight security for rigid orthodoxy on the two main articles of the ' Old Radical ' creed, and for steady adherence to the two great aims of his political life—namely, peace and free trade.

Important and far-reaching as were the changes effected by the Reform Acts of 1832 and 1867, they constituted no breach in the continuity of our history. Political development continued, progress was steady, and immense reforms, vigorously contested by Tories and Conservatives at the time, have almost invariably, after party passions have passed away, received the best of all testimony to their merits in the approval of their former opponents or their political heirs. It has not been found necessary or desirable in any case to undo the work which has been done. Reforms and changes have not been pushed beyond the requirements of the time; and consequently each reform, instead of being followed by reaction, has in due time been succeeded by another step in advance. So with the Reform Acts of 1884–1885. The nation will recognise itself as the same notwithstanding its new suit of clothes; and the House of Commons of 1886 will not be utterly different from previous assemblies in composition, in conduct, or in aspiration.

It is not on matters of absorbing general interest that the coming democracy may be expected to show itself at issue with public opinion, such as we have hitherto known it. Government resting directly on a wider basis will undoubtedly be stronger than heretofore. No change is more remarkable than the increased respect for law and order contemporaneous with the democratising of our institutions. That the laws are such as *we* have made them, or such as *we* maintain them, and therefore must be obeyed, is the general feeling. Political rioting seems to have entirely disappeared from among us. Even the breaking of windows, once regarded as the natural expression of popular dislike, is almost unknown, and orderly 'demonstration' has become the approved method of testifying to political feeling.

Mr. Harris has pointed out in his recently published 'History of the Radical Party in Parliament' that Lord Palmerston's Government of 1859 was the first into which Radicals were admitted as Cabinet Ministers, not so much with the object of satisfying personal claims as with the view of influencing the general policy of the administration. Yet the last government of Lord Palmerston is regarded by most Liberals as the strongest example to be found of unprogressive Whiggism. The change that has come over the attitude and conduct of the Radical party contemporaneous with the democratising of our institutions is a remarkable one, and worthy of more careful attention than is given to it by Mr. Harris. Immediately after the first Reform Act there took place, as had been anticipated, a very large addition to the Radical party in the House of Commons. These men held political opinions more 'advanced' than those held by the Cabinet of the day; and they were always ready to urge forward their reforms, however hopeless the chance of acceptance, as a protest against the political lukewarmness of their allies. In 1835, during the second Parliament after the Reform Act, every metropolitan member of Parliament was a Radical. Fifty years later we find, with an immensely extended electorate, out of twenty-four seats (including the two seats for Middlesex), the Conservatives holding ten; whilst it would be a misdescription to reckon the whole of the fourteen Liberals as belonging to the Radical party. It is quite true that advanced Liberals or Radicals have penetrated into Whig Cabinets, and that a more Radical spirit than heretofore 'permeates' the whole party; but it seems sometimes to be forgotten that the process of permeation is reciprocal in its character. When hot water is poured upon cold, the effect of heating the latter is balanced by that of cooling the former. The Radical is permeated no less than the Whig, as we believe to the great advantage of them both. What has happened to the historic 'party below the gangway'? Political

' opportunism' and close intimacy with Liberal officialism
have shorn it of its strength.   In 1837 the Radical party

' included such men as Grote, and Molesworth, and Roebuck ; and
Col. Thompson, and Joseph Hume, and William Ewart ; and Charles
Buller, and Ward, and Villiers, and Bulwer, and Strutt : such a
phalanx of strength as these men, with their philosophy, their science,
their reading, their experience—the acuteness of some, the doggedness
of others, the seriousness of most, the mirth of a few—might have
become if they could have become a phalanx at all.   But nothing was
more remarkable about these men than their individuality.' *

Long afterwards Mr. Bright and his friends below the gangway exercised much Parliamentary influence.   At a still more
recent time Mr. Fawcett, at the head of a small band of
thoughtful Liberals, commanded universal respect. Sir Wilfrid
Lawson and Mr. Labouchere and Mr. Jesse Collings may
have each his own individuality ; but whether it is, as Miss
Martineau might say, that ' the mirth of a few ' has overcome ' the seriousness of most,' it is certain that neither
Parliament nor public have as yet paid any very great attention to their teaching.   In Mr. Morley and Mr. Courtney
we have ' individuality ' enough, and all the personal qualifications which would enable them to play the part of the
independent Liberals of old days.   If they do not do so, it is
some evidence that a change has come over what used to be
the independent Radical party, and that the time for wield-
ing power from below the gangway has passed away.

But what views, what political opinions, will the new democracy embrace ?   On great national questions it will be a
national rather than a class policy which will prevail.   It is
from Liberal statesmen, or from the Liberal party, whose
concern is chiefly with the future, that answers to these
questions must be sought.

Of all Liberal statesmen, Mr. Trevelyan has been the most
faithful to the cause of the rural householders, and to the
belief in the good results which their enfranchisement will
bring about :—

' If,' says Mr. Trevelyan, ' I had to define in one sentence what it is
that the Liberal party will do in the future, I should say it will do
that which the Liberal party has wished to do in the past.   A change
has come over not our intentions and our creed, but over the strength
which will enable us to act up to that creed, and to carry those intentions into effect.'

He proceeds to mention the subject of local government with

---

* Miss Martineau's ' England.'

control over local taxation and expenditure in the counties and in London; the insistence by the State that public funds shall be administered for the benefit of the public, it being

'a broad principle of the Liberal party that all public funds and endowments are in their essence public property, subject to public enquiry; and if they are unjustly, injuriously, wastefully applied, a proper field for public interference.' . . .

On the other hand,

'Private property is the right of the individual who possesses it, and if it becomes necessary for the public advantage to interfere with his holding of it or enjoying it, the public is bound to give him fair compensation. It is on the security of this doctrine that the landlord holds his land, the fundholder his stocks, the shipowner his fleet, the manufacturer his mill and plant, the working-man the house which he has acquired through his building society.'

This private right, he goes on to explain, is subject to what lawyers know as the doctrine *sic utere tuo ut alienum non lædas,* and he therefore approves legislation which would prevent the manufacturer using his rights to the injury of the health of his operatives, the shipowner from employing his so as to imperil and perhaps destroy the lives of his sailors; the landlord from keeping his buildings in a condition to endanger the health of their occupants. He would facilitate the hiring of allotments by agricultural labourers; he would diminish (apparently) that share of the national burdens which falls upon the agricultural interest; he would ' use every means in the power of the State—erring, if it ' is to err at all, on the side of precaution—to keep our ' islands free from the scourge of cattle disease.' He would make land as easily transferable as gas shares. All these, he declares, have been the creed of the Liberal party; and now, thanks to the new Reform Act, momentum sufficient to give effect to them has been found.[*]

Mr. Trevelyan says with truth that these objects and principles of the Liberal party are not new. The wide distinction he draws between public endowments and private property is hardly an extension of the principles laid down by Hallam (assuredly no Radical) in his second chapter of the ' History of England ' in reference to the possessions of the State Church; but whilst Mr. Trevelyan looks to increased strength, rather than new aims, as the probable characteristic of the Liberal party under the new dispensation,

---

[*] See Mr. Trevelyan's speech at Manchester, Feb. 10, 1885.

it must be admitted that speeches have been made by one Cabinet minister directly or indirectly advocating doctrines not only never yet professed by leading Liberals, but positively opposed to the views they have long entertained and often publicly expressed.

The speeches of Mr. Chamberlain, as a member of the Cabinet, have a representative as well as an individual political character. It is to the speeches of Cabinet ministers that the public look for explanations and announcements of the Cabinet policy. The public, not being admitted into Cabinet councils, has nothing else to guide it as to what are the views of the Prime Minister and his colleagues than the statements of Cabinet ministers. When, therefore, the President of the Board of Trade expressed his approval of a land system for England based upon the three F's; when he declared that the taxation at present raised upon tea, coffee, and sugar should instead be raised by means of a graduated income-tax; when he advocated the turning into salaried officials all members of Parliament; and, lastly, when, founding himself on the ' origin of things,' he declared that the title to property was so bad that a ransom should be paid to those, who would otherwise soon make short work of it, for the security which it enjoyed, it is not surprising that many Liberals, by no means weak-kneed, received a shock to their confidence, and began to fear lest clever electioneering was taking the place of patriotic policy in the counsels of leading statesmen.* These crude opinions of Mr. Chamberlain were

---

* 'I am not afraid of the three F's in England, Scotland, or Ireland.'—Speech at Ipswich, January 14, 1885.

'Now, if Parliament would only support the Chancellor of the Exchequer, if they would give him leave to equalise the duties payable on land and on personal property when those pass on death and by inheritance, and if in addition they would consent to impose a higher tax upon incomes exceeding a certain amount, I believe my friend Mr. Childers would be bound at once to remedy this injustice, and to give you a free breakfast-table to-morrow, and to enable you perhaps, in addition, to double and treble the currants and the raisins that you put in your Christmas pudding.'—Speech at Birmingham, January 29, 1885.

'If you go back to the origin of things, you will find that when our social arrangements first began to shape themselves every man was born into the world with natural rights, with a right to a share in the great inheritance of the community, with a right to a part of the land of his birth. But all these rights have passed away. The common rights of ownership have disappeared. Some of them have been sold; some of them have been given away by those who had no right to

thrown out, as if it were quite unnecessary to meet the reasoning which had always been directed against them. Why, for instance, the work done by members of Parliament should be paid by the taxpayer, while so much voluntary work of other kinds done in the public service should remain unremunerated, was not explained. Members of school boards, of sanitary boards, town councillors, justices of the peace, vestrymen, all voluntarily give their services for the benefit of the public. Is the State no longer to be permitted to appeal to the desire to serve it, as a sufficient motive for undertaking public duty? Is it desirable to increase the very large personal interest which already operates on the independent judgement of members of Parliament? Would the payment of members tend to produce an improved *personnel* in the House of Commons, or to render more patriotic the behaviour of members and candidates? As regards a graduated income-tax, surely some reference might have been made to Mr. Mill, or some explanation offered of its having found no place in Gladstonian finance.

On the land question, Mr. Chamberlain was, if possible, still more opposed to the views of Liberal reformers, unless indeed that name is to be monopolised by the unpractical and ignorant dreamers who have lately been attracting much more attention than they deserve.

Let us consider for one instant Mr. Chamberlain's airy reference to the introduction of the so-called three F system into Great Britain. Mr. Goschen had of course no difficulty in pointing out, in his speech at Edinburgh, that where farming is a trade conducted on business principles, two of

---

dispose of them; some of them have been lost through apathy or ignorance, some have been stolen by fraud, and some have been acquired by violence. Private ownership has taken the place of these communal rights, and this system has become so interwoven with our habits and usages, it has been so sanctioned by law and protected by custom, that it might be very difficult and perhaps impossible to reverse it; but then, I ask, what ransom will property pay for the immunity which it enjoys? What substitute will it find for the natural rights which have ceased to be recognised? Society is banded together in order to protect itself against the instincts of men who would make very short work of private ownership if they were left alone. That is all very well, but I maintain that society owes to these men something more than mere toleration in return for the restrictions which it places on their liberty of action. I think in the future we shall hear a great deal about the obligations of property, and we shall not hear quite so much about its rights.'—Speech at Birmingham, January 5, 1885.

these F's, viz. fair rents and free sale, are mutually destructive. Fair rent, meaning a rent fixed by a court, if lower than the market rate, enables the tenant to sell to an incomer at an enhanced value. The intending farmer will not, therefore, be able to obtain land simply by paying the rent that the court has determined to be a fair one, but he will have to pay in addition the interest on the capital sum representing the tenant's goodwill, which, of course, will be large in proportion as the rent is small. The introduction of the three F system into Ireland three years ago could only be justified on the ground that business relations did not in that country prevail in the hiring and occupying of land. At the time, ordinary social relations had broken down, and, classes being almost at war, the State had to be called in to make terms between them. A *modus vivendi*, as Lord Hartington said, had to be found, rather than a model land system set up; and there have been many signs since then that no permanent settlement of the Irish land difficulties has been found in the Irish Land Act of 1881. Such a system would be neither durable, nor even endurable, in a country where farming is a trade, into which intelligent and prudent men enter as they do into other businesses, with a certain amount of capital at their disposal. That the State should attempt to fix the rate at which men should be allowed to invest their capital in the farming business alone of all trades, is not a proposition likely to obtain public favour. But putting aside the evident difficulties and absurdities of such a scheme, what good would the three F system have been able to do in mitigating the distress under which for several years the agricultural interest has been suffering? Where things are improving, and the land-market rising, it is evident that a rent previously fixed, and a right of free sale, are highly beneficial to the existing tenant. But that is exactly the reverse of the present state of affairs. Where land is falling in value, where competition for farms is diminishing or is at an end, free sale is a useless and valueless right. Had rents been fixed six or seven years ago for a fifteen years' term, what possible advantage could the tenant have got by the right of free sale? Who at present would pay the Scotch tenant under a nineteen years' lease, made a few years ago, to stand in his shoes? The effect of the system would have been to throw upon the tenant a loss of capital (due to the depreciation of land) which now falls on the landlord. This was proved to be the case under the free-sale system of the Ulster custom; for 'when the great depreciation of land

' took place in 1848, the state of parts of the counties of
' Armagh and Monaghan was nearly as bad as in the King's
' County or Tipperary.   To those who wanted to part with
' their farms the tenant-right was valueless, as there were no
' purchasers.   The tenants were unable to sell what they had
' bought at a very high price.' *

Free trade in land has long been the ideal at which
Liberals have aimed, and to which Mr. Bright and other
reformers still declare their adherence; and to this the
Rent Court and State regulation system, it need hardly be
said, are fundamentally opposed.

It is astonishing to observe the hazy condition of mind of
many speakers and writers upon the land question, and the
inappropriateness of the means they advocate to bring about
the end they desire.   The same people who wish to increase
the owning of land by small farmers are found strongly
urging the necessity of increasing its burdens!   Mr. Frederic
Harrison says: ' One of the first things which will occur to
' the new rural voters is the ridiculous minimum to which the
' land-tax is reduced.   It is a farce; not one-tenth of what
' is usual in the nations of Europe. . . .   I am quite pre-
' pared to see it raised till it ultimately brings us some ten
' or twenty millions instead of one million.' †   Is it conceivable that a writer of the eminence of Mr. Frederic Harrison supposes the land-tax to represent the taxation which
falls upon the land?   Do not landowners and farmers pay
income-tax on the profits derived from their land?   Are
there not local burdens which fall solely upon the land?
And is it fair, considering that the land in Great Britain is
more heavily charged for public purposes (taking imperial
and local taxation together) than in any country in Europe,
to represent that in this country alone the burdens upon it
are ' a farce'?   We have no space here to deal with the
subject of peasant proprietary.   We hope sincerely that the
policy of making land ' as transferable as gas shares ' will
greatly multiply the number of cultivating owners; but it
must be remembered that the chief reason why men do not
buy or do not retain small farms is, that it pays them better
to do something else with their money.   The flocking of
the population from the rural districts into the towns is
due to the superior advantages, pecuniary and otherwise,

' * 'Tenure of Land in Ireland.'   By the Right Hon. F. M. Longfield.
Cobden Club Essays.
 † Fortnightly Review, February, 1885.

to be found in the towns, and it is a mistake to suppose that this change of population is due solely to the departure of the agricultural labourer. The village carpenter, the village tailor, the small shopman, who formerly added to the number of the rural population, now find it answer better to remove to some thriving neighbouring town. We may sentimentally regret the changes which the circumstances of the time are producing, but our lamentations are not much wiser than those feelings which in former days led to the machine-breaking riotings of ignorant labourers, who were unable to see that even themselves in the long run would benefit by that which tended to more efficient and more economical production.

In the past, it has been by the Liberal party that the doctrines of political economy have been most strenuously upheld; and adherence to principle was occasionally maintained only at the expense of passing popularity. The Poor Law legislation of 1834, though of the most beneficial character, brought down upon its Whig supporters much popular odium. If, as seems probable, what is known as 'social 'legislation' is to play a larger part in the future than it has ever done in the past, the greater the necessity for making sure that the action of the State rests upon a sound basis of principle. The main positions of the political economists have been regarded as truths, any departure from which would inevitably entail, sooner or later, much trouble to the State. The doctrine of *laissez-faire*, at one time much favoured by large numbers of Liberals, has apparently had its day; and it would not be surprising if an enlarged electorate, conscious of its own immense power, and containing a large proportion of electors new to the exercise of political privileges, conceived an exaggerated idea of the possibility of curing most of the ills that mankind is heir to by the sovereign remedy of an Act of Parliament. There is danger, however, that something may be lost to the public in the diminished self-reliance of the individual, a necessary result of the practice of subjecting everything to the control of Government inspectors. Where the State undertakes the protection of individuals, they trust to the State rather than to themselves; and it is often extremely doubtful whether they would not, in the long run, have succeeded better by declining Government assistance and by relying solely on themselves. Sir Thomas Farrer, the experienced Permanent Secretary of the Board of Trade, tells us that 'he had tried ' very hard to ascertain the results of the laws which for

' half his life he had been helping to administer, and that
' he is quite unable to say with any degree of accuracy what
' amount of evil had been prevented by them. Still more
' difficult would it be to say whether, with the evil, any
' and what good had been prevented.' * In these circumstances much caution should be used before the State takes
any new steps towards universal superintendence. The onus
of proving any State interference to be generally beneficial
lies upon those who are anxious to bring it about. *Primâ
facie,* the rule of individual freedom of action should prevail, since most men can do far better for themselves, in
driving bargains, for instance, than the State can do for
them.

'Treat grown men or women as incapable of judging and acting for
themselves, and you go far to make them so. Our daily life is beginning
already to be hedged round by inspections, regulations, and prohibitions. The coming democracy has much of promise in it, but one of
its failings is impatience. It cannot bear to see an evil slowly cure
itself, which can, as it imagines, be cured at once by the use of its own
overwhelming force. It is passionately benevolent, and passionately
fond of power. To preserve individual liberty in trade, as in other
matters, from the impatient action of philanthropy, will probably be
one of the great difficulties of the future.' †

Mr. Goschen very recently, at the Eighty Club, pointed out
the same danger, and, through that medium, has warned
the public against the danger of accepting legislation with
its eyes shut merely because the object aimed at is a good
one. Care must be taken that the means provided will
really secure that object, and free criticism of proposals must
not be stinted from the fear that the critics will be taunted
with heartless indifference to public evils which are crying
for redress.

It is curious to observe that whilst in most departments of
life the State is inclined to assume an aggressive attitude,
and to take under its control what was formerly left entirely
outside its jurisdiction; whilst now-a-days the landowner and
the shipowner, the manufacturer, the farmer, and the mine-
owner find their several businesses the subject of anxious
watchfulness on the part of the statute law, there is a
tendency of an exactly contrary character as to all that
touches the religious life of the nation. Formerly the
religion and form of worship of every citizen were the object

---

* Sir Thomas Farrer's ' State in relation to Trade,' p. 163. English
Citizen Series.

† Ibid. p. 165.

of much solicitude to all politicians. Now the tendency is towards an absolute withdrawal of State interference from the free action of citizens or combinations of citizens in everything affecting religion. In this respect, at all events, the general feeling of the day is in favour of letting people do as they like, and make such arrangements as they please, the State of course throwing its protection over the property of individuals, to whatever societies they may belong. Even at a time when the State seems likely to relieve the parent of the burden of educating his child by throwing that burden upon the shoulders of the tax- or rate-payer, it is felt that the State is going too far in providing out of equally public endowments for the spiritual teaching of the people. If the position of the parish priest and the parish minister regulated by Act of Parliament, and maintained out of public endowments, excites the hostile criticism of religious voluntaries, who think that in the present day the spiritual safety of the people, long defended by the regular army of the Church, may now be entrusted to the zeal and devotion of the -volunteers, it must be remembered that a new parish authority is rising up, paid out of public funds, whose duties are closely regulated by Act of Parliament, in the person of the parish schoolmaster.

Recently there has been much speculation as to what subjects would mainly occupy the attention of the future electorate; and naturally the special advocates of special views see in the coming changes the near realisation of their hopes. Mr. Henry Richard, we doubt not, thinks that democracy is peace, and we trust his anticipations may prove to have been better warranted than those of the late Emperor Napoleon, when he said the same thing of the Empire. The voluntaries in matters of religion look forward to speedy disestablishment, and the commencement of a new reign of religious equality. Some urge forward a revolutionary treatment of the land question, in language sometimes violent and always vague, as the first object of the next Liberal majority, hoping no doubt that, with such a matter before Parliament, no breach would be effected between British and Irish Radicals, whilst Whigs and moderate reformers would be driven from the field or into coalition with the Conservative party. For our part we are inclined to think that Ireland once more will claim the main attention of the coming Parliament, to the exclusion unfortunately of much else. How is the government of Ireland to be carried on? How (a closely allied question) is the work of the British

House of Commons to be carried on? The clouds which
have darkened the whole existence of the present Parliament are not dispersed, but still hang threatening the horizon
of the future. Mr. Trevelyan's saying that 'strength' will
be the characteristic of the new electorate is worth remembering, for it is strong treatment that will be required. One
thing is certain, that the time will soon have arrived when
the nation must decide whether its refusal to break up the
Empire is to be punished by the destruction of the character
and much of the usefulness of the House of Commons. To
give an independent legislature to Ireland, it can hardly
be doubted, would be a step leading very rapidly indeed
to civil war, and the subsequent temporary ruling of that
country by military force. Home Rule, then, being inadmissible, is the present condition of the House of Commons to continue—a condition caused almost solely by the
misconduct of Irish members? Is it to be permitted that
practices avowedly indulged in by a few members for the
purpose of preventing the working of the parliamentary
machine should be continued? The present Speaker, while
scrupulously fair to all sections and members of the House
of Commons, has shown himself on several occasions determined to uphold the authority of 'the Chair.' In a new
Parliament, we feel confident, a much more rigorous treatment of parliamentary misconduct will prevail; and order
will be maintained and business accomplished, not so much
by the addition of fresh rules to the Standing Orders, which,
after all, a combination of members can always in practice
evade, as by giving increased authority to 'the Chair.' The
Speaker is the representative of the House of Commons, with
general authority to preserve order and assist the conduct
of business, rather than a mere judge bound down by statute
law which it is his whole function to interpret. Speaker
Peel on his assumption of his office expressed in· exceptionally eloquent language the high ideal he had formed of the
duties of his great position. The new House, we hope, will
trust the Speaker, knowing that at its own will his authority must cease, and knowing also that in his firmness and
judgement is the only hope of maintaining the freedom of
Parliament at present endangered by a band of avowed
enemies. Maybe in another year some dozen or twenty or
thirty of these enemies of Parliament may find themselves
relieved for a session or for a Parliament, by a vote of the
House of Commons, from further attendance. What then?
If the alternative to this is civil war in Ireland, or the

reduction of Parliament to a condition of helpless feebleness, the former will certainly be preferred. Irishmen must be made to know that they are to be governed upon the same principle as other British subjects; they have the same privileges, they must be subject to the same obligations, and if they choose not to respect the Parliamentary law and custom binding on all members alike, they must take the consequences.

Mr. Parnell has shown his great ability in nothing more than in the selection of his lieutenants, in this far excelling O'Connell, whose 'tail' is well remembered by the older members of the present Parliament. Between the days of O'Connell and Parnell there existed nothing which could be called, in the sense now attached to the phrase, an 'Irish 'party.' Mr. Parnell's rule over his followers is absolute, and his ascendency is such that his own immediate presence in the House is by no means always required. He can trust Mr. Healy and Mr. Sexton, Mr. Justin M'Carthy, and the rest to carry on the war in his absence, and to do the commonplace obstructive everyday fighting, whilst when he appears it is always in the character of the general who directs operations and encourages the troops.

The extreme Irish party has never been able, and probably never will be able, to act in any permanent alliance with the advanced Radical party out of Ireland. Here and there a few English Radicals may give a vote in the same lobby as Mr. Parnell; but their real objects and their methods of procedure are so different, that the cause of advanced Radicalism in England would suffer rather than gain by any *rapprochement* with the Parnellite band.

We believe, indeed, that the mere dread of some future alliance between advanced Liberals and the so-called Irish party hinders seriously the growth of public confidence in the coming Liberal leaders.

There can be no doubt that lately one effect of the apparent recklessness of language of a few Liberal politicians and political writers has been greatly to strengthen in the public estimation the position held by independent moderate statesmen of the stamp of Mr. Goschen and Mr. Forster in the one House, the Duke of Argyll and Lord Lansdowne in the other. The speeches of the former, delivered a short time ago in Edinburgh, as a possible candidate for one of the divisions of that city, excited universal attention and very general approval. On domestic politics he showed himself a thorough reformer of a practical kind.

Indeed, as regards one of the main subjects to which it is universally agreed the new Parliament must turn its attention, that of local government, Mr. Goschen has for many years been regarded as the great authority of the day; and it would be lamentable if, in framing and passing through Parliament for this purpose some great measure of constructive reform, the country was to lose the benefit of his powerful assistance. At the present time, such is the weakness of the hold on the public mind of the opposition leaders, there is little to induce moderate or timid Liberals (of whom there must always be a very considerable number) to make common cause with the Conservatives. If many reprobate the language of Mr. Chamberlain, the same persons fail to get consolation from the contemplation of the politics of a party of which Lord Randolph Churchill is an eminent leader. Mr. Goschen would find it difficult to act with Mr. Chamberlain; *à fortiori* would he find it impossible to combine with Lord Randolph, or with those Conservatives who for party ends are ready to tamper with the principles of free trade. Of Mr. Broadhurst's truly eccentric Leaseholders Bill Lord Randolph was one of the strongest supporters; and, indeed, there may some day be found to be more possibility of concerted action between the leaders of the Tory democratic and the ultra-Radical parties than the interchange of amenities between eminent candidates for Birmingham in view of an expected election would have led a superficial observer to suspect. If the supposed calculation of the Tory wirepullers is correct—namely, that whilst, under the New Reform Act, the Liberals will gain largely in the counties, the Conservatives will gain largely in the towns—the change will undoubtedly affect the character of the two parties if it does not greatly alter their balance. A new dividing line between parties may, before many years are over, make an end of the political combinations to which at present we are accustomed; and the early departure from the House of Commons of its three most trusted statesmen adds to the probability that a time of political transition is at hand, whilst it renders even more vain than usual the endeavour to pry into the secrets of the future.

For the moment, and we trust it is but for the moment, the public interest in domestic politics has been diverted to the critical position of our foreign affairs. The Afghan boundary question and the conduct of Russia have called forth a unanimous feeling on the part of the public to resist by force, if necessary, further Russian aggression on the frontiers of India. But with respect to Egypt and the Soudan it is very different. If everyone knows what to do with Russia, no one knows what to do with North-east Africa. The line which the Government had marked out for itself upon the defeat of Hicks Pasha seemed the true one. Egypt could not govern the Soudan, even if she would, without our assistance; and it was no part of our interest or our duty to reconquer for Egypt or for ourselves the wild Arab tribes of a boundless and desert region.

To administer and protect Egypt, and to leave the Soudan alone, has turned out to be a policy to which the Government did not—perhaps could not—adhere. The mission of General Gordon to Khartoum, and the military expedition of a year ago to Suakim, were unfortunate departures from the policy previously laid down, entered upon, no doubt, under the influence of humanitarian feelings, and with the full approval of the public, but nevertheless both of them steps which the light of subsequent events shows to have been mistaken, and without good results even in the humanitarian objects it was hoped to accomplish. The failure to relieve General Gordon, owing to the treachery of his garrison at the very moment when the relief expedition was but a few hours from the gates of Khartoum, gave a shock to the public feeling which was reflected in the small majority in the House of Commons by which the Government was enabled to defeat a direct vote of censure. The expedition, admirably fitted out and commanded, did its work so as to call forth the praises of Europe. It was within an ace of achieving success. Arriving, after hard marching and severe fighting, on the Nile, only one hundred miles from Khartoum, with Gordon's steamers waiting for them, and with a note from Gordon himself to say that he could hold out for years, no wonder that our troops thought the work was accomplished, and the fruits of victory their own. The public at home shared the same belief, and the nearness of success served to embitter the sense of disappointment and grief with which the news of the treachery in Khartoum and the death of its defender were received. Mr. Goschen and Mr. Forster took a step of very doubtful wisdom in joining the Opposition on the vote of censure, especially as the Opposition leaders had no definite line of policy to suggest, and as it was far from clear that a change of government would produce the slightest change in our Egyptian policy. Really there are but two practicable policies: one, to retreat from the Soudan, taking only such measures as may be necessary for the defence of Egypt; the other, an advance upon Khartoum to overthrow the Mahdi, a policy which must entail an indefinitely long stay in the Soudan and the expenditure of much life and money. The vast majority of Liberals undoubtedly would prefer the former, while Lord Salisbury has expressed his approval of the latter. The Government have not yet declared definitely for one or the other, and are consequently liable to be harassed in any action they may take by attacks from the regular Opposition, from a considerable section of steady Liberals below the gangway, and from that extreme and unpractical party who would at once, apparently with no regard to consequences, abandon both the Soudan and Egypt to their fate.

Probably it is to domestic rather than to foreign politics that the attention of the coming electorate will eventually be turned, and at all events it is with reference to domestic questions that party lines will be drawn. As regards any great struggle in which the nation may be engaged, no doubt the whole public interest would be concentrated upon that struggle rather than upon home questions; but in these days great wars waged by this country must be essentially national wars, favoured not only by the party in power, but supported also in great measure by the party in opposition. Mr. Goschen has pointed out the enormous ' reserve ' of power ' which is to be found in the fact that in very critical periods the nation acts as one man. And the hour in which

> ' None are for a party,
> But all are for the State,'

if a brief one, will be long enough to prove the irresistible strength of a united nation. The rule of public opinion, to which so much reference has been made, would now render it impossible for any Parliamentary Opposition to display the same sympathy with the enemies of the country as was shown by Opposition members in the days of the American and Napoleonic wars.

Whilst we close these pages, the question of peace or war with a great European power is quivering in the balance, and it may well be that England finds herself once more on the verge of a conflict of no common magnitude. The Government has shown by its recent measures that it is resolved and prepared to defend the threatened territories of Afghanistan, which are the bulwark of India, with all the military and naval powers of the Empire; and no mistake could be more fatal than to suppose that because Great Britain is desirous of peace, she is unprepared for war. This is no contest, as the organs and agents of Russia represent, for a few square miles of barren territory inhabited by a roving population; the question involves the good faith of England, the security of India, and the ascendency of Great Britain over Southern Asia. Voltaire exclaimed, at the outbreak of the Seven Years War, that France and England were about to shed their blood for a few acres of snow in Canada; but the result of the struggle decided the controversy whether the French or the English races were to be the masters of North America. Between Russia and England a similar question has arisen in Asia; and although we have never been disposed to regard the advance of Russia with excessive apprehension, she must be told, and she is told, that when she touches the frontier line of British ascendency, her further progress will be stayed. That might have been done by a treaty of delimitation, honestly entered into and faithfully observed; but Russia equivocated and evaded the arrangements made for that purpose, and the inevitable result is the effective defence of the territory in dispute. We entertain no doubt of the resolution of the Government, or of the result. This question must be settled once for all, and it is manifestly the interest of England that it should be settled now. The mind of the country is united on this point, with a few dissentients of questionable honesty and patriotism; and, what is of scarcely less importance, the native princes of India, the great feudatories of the Empire, are animated by the same conviction, that the defence of Southern India against a northern invasion is the common paramount interest of them all. We trust that the Cabinet of St. Petersburg may still have the wisdom and the power to withdraw pretensions which may lead to the most disastrous consequences to Russia; but as far as this country is concerned, it was never better able to maintain the integrity of the Empire, and the more so as we have just terminated the momentous question of the extension and reconstitution of the electorate of the United Kingdom.

If the new democracy, to which next autumn is to give Parliamentary representation, brings with it new strength to government, that alone will compensate for many a disadvantage. The doubts and the fears that are so often expressed by Conservatives at the evident onward march of democracy are the same doubts and fears which have been heard before, and which every forward step in the history of this country has shown to be groundless. For the benefits which Liberals anticipate, on the other hand, from a Reformed Parliament, they have not merely the inward faith resulting from their own more sanguine temperaments, but also the confidence arising from the precedents of the past and the unbroken stream of English history.

Note on the 'Secret Papers of the Second Empire.'

WE have received from Messrs. Baring the following letter, which explains the misstatement it is intended to correct:—

'*To the Editor of the* EDINBURGH REVIEW, *London.*

'8 Bishopsgate Within,
London: March 16, 1885.

'Dear Sir,—Our attention has been called to the following paragraph in an article on the "Secret Papers of the Second Empire" in the January number of the "Edinburgh Review:" -

'"In 1866 the Emperor appears to have had nearly a million sterling in "money and securities deposited with Messrs. Baring. This, however, was the "nominal value of the securities, which was contested by M. Piétri. At page "152 we find Messrs. Baring's list of the investments."

'We think it our duty to bring to your notice the fact that this statement is entirely erroneous. In 1866 we had neither money nor securities belonging to the Emperor of the French, and the only financial transactions between us were some small payments made by us for purchases here, amounting in all during the year to about 5,000*l.*, for which we reimbursed ourselves by direct drafts on the French Treasury. Neither then, nor at any other time during his reign, did the Emperor remit to us any large amount either of money or securities. The list said to have been made by us is entirely imaginary.

'We beg to remain, dear Sir,
'Your very obedient servants,
'BARING BROS. & Co.'

As far as the main fact of the alleged deposit of investments to a large amount by the late Emperor in the hands of Messrs. Baring, this explicit declaration is conclusive, and it is satisfactory that the truth should be made known. But we are at a loss to explain or understand the detailed statement of these alleged investments which was published by the Commission appointed by the French Republican Government to examine the papers found in the Tuileries on September 4. The Commission not only published this statement as an authentic record, but they added that the estimated value of the securities had been disputed by M. Piétri.

We merely borrowed from their Report a document which appeared to have the same claims to belief as the other papers contained in it. But as the fact is now positively denied and has some historical interest, we should be glad to know on what evidence the members of the Commission based their assertion. They laid claim in their Report to strict accuracy and veracity, and the papers they printed were said to be deposited in the national archives. Where, then, is the list of deposited securities which Messrs. Baring declare to be entirely imaginary?

No. CCCXXXI. will be published in July.

INDEX.

—•—

A

amount of work for three judges, 93—the question of a 'travelling court,' 96—reservation of certain cases to Parliament, 97—the one great danger of the tribunal, 98—selection of the judges, 103.

R

Reform, Parliamentary, the two great ends of, 572—circumstances of resemblance in past and present reforms, 573—the Duke of Wellington's groundless dread of reform, 575—influence of popular feeling on the action of Parliament, 580—the Radical party, 582—Mr. Chamberlain's speeches, 585—the three F system, 586—social legislation, 589—attitude of the State towards religious questions, 590—government of Ireland, 591.

Rothan, G., his 'Souvenirs Diplomatiques' reviewed, 332.

S

Scotland, historical investigation of the ownership of land in, 307—the feudal system, 308—examples of land charters, 309—personal eminence of the grantees, 312—early systems of agricultural occupation of the land, 313—the lease system, 315—legislation connected with land tenures, 319—introduction of the system into the Highlands, 322—relations of leaseholders and subtenants, 326.

Skene, W. F., his 'Celtic Scotland' reviewed, 299.

Soudan question in Parliament, 595.

Spenser, Edmund, a philosophic poet, 142—a prophecy of the social equality imposture, 144—anticipation of the woman's-right craze, 147—philosophy of human life in three aspects, 149—the 'two cantos of Mutabilitie,' 160—points of resemblance and contrast between Spenser and Lucretius, 170.

V

Vitrolles, Baron de, review of the concluding volumes of memoirs of, 423—result of the negotiations for the Bourbon restoration, 425—return of Napoleon, 433—De Vitrolles imprisoned, 441—Fouché's intrigues with Davoust in the Bourbon interest, 443—dismissal of Fouché, 450—fall of Talleyrand, 452—De Vitrolles' 'Secret Note,' 455—the Revolution of July, 457.

W

Williams, Monier, his 'Religious Thought and Life in India' reviewed, 462.

Westropp, Hodder M., his 'Promenade Lectures on the Archæology of Rome' reviewed, 38.

Y

Yarrell, W., his 'History of British Birds' reviewed, 213.

END OF VOL. CLXI.

Spottiswoode & Co., Printers, New-street Square, London.

Lightning Source UK Ltd.
Milton Keynes UK
UKHW012211070119
334855UK00010BA/1801/P